Endangered

Mitch Tobin

Biodiversity on the Brink

FULCRUM
GOLDEN, COLORADO

Library of Congress Cataloging-in-Publication Data

Tobin, Mitch.
  Endangered : biodiversity on the brink / Mitch Tobin.
  p. cm.
  Includes bibliographical references and index.
  ISBN 978-1-55591-721-0 (hardcover)
  1. Endangered species. 2. Wildlife recovery. 3. Biodiversity. I. Title.
QH75.T63 2010
333.95'22--dc22
                                  2010001296

Printed on recycled paper in the United States by Malloy, Inc.
0 9 8 7 6 5 4 3 2 1

Design: Jack Lenzo
Cover image: © Ferenc Cegledi/Shutterstock
Map: Gray Mouse Graphics

Fulcrum Publishing
4690 Table Mountain Drive, Suite 100
Golden, CO 80403
800-992-2908 • 303-277-1623
www.fulcrumbooks.com

In memory of my mother,
Phyllis Tobin

Nothing is more priceless and more worthy of preservation than the rich array of animal life with which our country has been blessed. It is a many-faceted treasure, of value to scholars, scientists, and nature lovers alike and it forms a vital part of the heritage we all share as Americans.

—President Richard Nixon,
upon signing the Endangered Species Act,
December 28, 1973

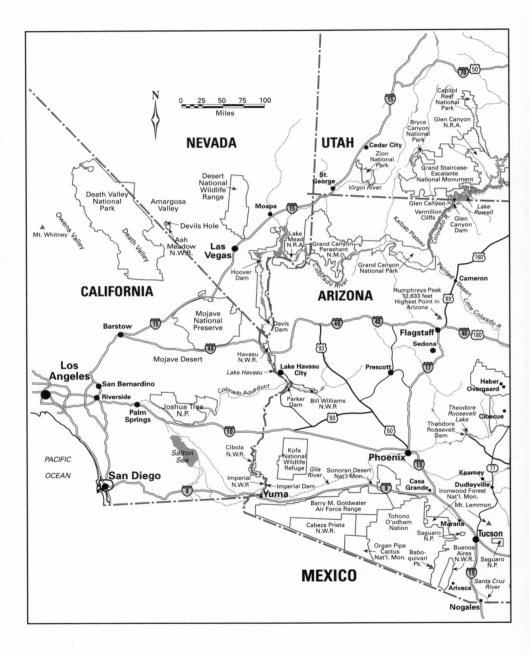

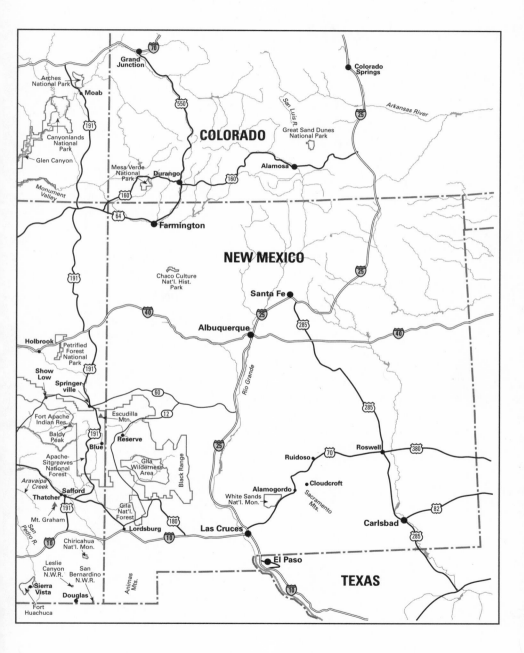

Contents

Introduction

Species have always come and gone. More than 99 percent that have inhabited the earth have disappeared forever, so extinction is nothing new. But what's happening today is different. Scientists believe the current rate of extinction may be 1,000 times faster than the pace that prevailed before humans entered the scene. The estimates are necessarily fuzzy because biologists still know precious little about the plants and animals around us, let alone the efficacy of our assault upon them. Researchers have identified nearly 1.8 million species, but less than one-tenth of those are well understood, and the total number of species may be in the tens of millions, most of them insects. The cruel irony is that we have entered a golden age of species discovery, with science and technology able to unveil thousands of new microbes, plants, and animals every year. On average, we name about two new species every hour—and drive another three extinct.

A dire situation threatens to get much worse. Climate change, which is already transforming the planet, could trigger the greatest spasm of extinction since the demise of the dinosaurs 65.5 million years ago, when an asteroid struck near the Yucatán Peninsula and three-quarters of the planet's species died out. There is little doubt that we are in the early days of the earth's sixth great extinction event, with some scientists predicting that one-third or more of all species will be gone by the end of the 21st century if emissions of heat-trapping greenhouse gases continue to increase. Even under optimistic projections, rising levels of carbon dioxide will continue to acidify the oceans and harm the base of the marine food chain, while higher water temperatures will wipe out the coral reefs that harbor tremendous biodiversity. With enough warming, the Arctic ice that polar bears depend on will melt and rising seas will swallow up the homes of coastal and island species. Around the world, more-extreme storms, floods, droughts, and wildfires could create deadly synergies with the other traditional threats—habitat loss, invasive species, pollution, hunting—that have already pushed so many plants and animals to the brink.

Loss of species is just one consequence of climate change, and in comparison to the other problems, it may seem like a minor concern. Some public health experts estimate that global warming is already claiming hundreds of thousands of human lives a year, nearly all in the developing world, and they believe climate change will kill even more people in the decades to come due to resurgent pandemics, catastrophic storms, water shortages, agricultural collapses, broken economies, and civil strife. Given all of the other mortal dangers and pressing needs, why should we use scarce resources to save rare species?

Scientists and others have come up with plenty of reasons why it's worthwhile to protect all plants and animals, even if it eliminates jobs or consumes tax dollars that might be spent on other problems, including global warming. I lump the reasons into a group of *E*s:

- *Ecology*. The vanishing of a species can have radiating effects on the web of life. Kill off a keystone species like the wolf and you affect the elk the wolf preys on, the plants the elk eat, the bugs that consume the plants, and so on.
- *Education*. Extinction is tantamount to burning the last copy of a book that holds answers to questions we haven't even asked yet.
- *Economics*. A species may be an important pollinator of cash crops or hold the cure to disease.
- *Esthetics*. We marvel at nature's complexity and feel good inside to know there are grizzlies lumbering across some far-flung wilderness, even if we never see them with our own eyes.

In all these ways, saving biodiversity is in our self-interest. We rely on other species for food, clothing, shelter, medicine, clean air, drinking water, and a variety of other so-called ecosystem services, which researchers valued at $33 trillion per year back in 1997—nearly double the world's combined gross national product at the time. Just think, for example, of how much it would cost for humans to pollinate all of the world's crops.

Any given endangered species may not appear to advance any of the *E*s: Its loss wouldn't immediately topple an ecological house of cards. It seems to hold no valuable scientific secrets. It has no obvious monetary or medicinal value. The problem is that we're often unaware of a species' value until it's gone. Aldo Leopold, the environmental philosopher, father of US wildlife management, and onetime Forest Service ranger in Arizona, put it best:

The last word in ignorance is the man who says of an animal or plant: "What good is it?" If the land mechanism as a whole is good, then every part is good, whether we understand it or not. If the biota, in the course of aeons, has built something we like but do not understand, then who but a fool would discard seemingly useless parts? To keep every cog and wheel is the first precaution of intelligent tinkering.

Ultimately, the fate of our endangered species comes down to another E, Ethics. Is it immoral for humans to wipe out a plant or animal that has evolved over thousands or millions of years, even if it's a bug that eats cricket feces in a deep, dark cave?

For some, the ethical imperative is found in the biblical account of Noah's ark, a tale of rescuing species from an acute case of climate change: 40 days and 40 nights of rain. The story, which has variants in religions and cultures around the globe, may have roots in reality and a connection to global warming. About 8,450 years ago, as the earth was pulling out of the last ice age, a superlake in central Canada rapidly drained into the Hudson Bay after the frozen dams holding back its waters collapsed. Lake Agassiz held nearly eight times the volume in all of the Great Lakes combined, and its contents surged into the Atlantic at a rate of up to 2 billion gallons per second. The sudden freshwater pulse lifted sea levels by more than four feet, inundating coastal settlements worldwide. In Turkey, the rising waters breached a ridge that had kept the Mediterranean Sea at bay and preserved today's Black Sea as a freshwater lake. The incoming salt water spilled over the Bosporus ridge with the power of 200 Niagara Falls, flooded some of the world's oldest agriculture, and displaced as many as 145,000 people. The greatest flood ever to strike our civilization, preserved in fossils and sediments, was also recorded by prehistoric cultures. Many scholars now believe this deluge inspired the story of Noah's ark.

Besides the biblical example and the Es described above, Americans have another important reason to protect imperiled species: it's the law. With the stroke of a pen in the waning days of 1973, President Richard Nixon signed the Endangered Species Act and created our most powerful and polarizing environmental statute. In essence, the ESA codified God's command to Noah and legislated its moral: we depend on other species for our survival and we have a duty to prevent their premature extinction. Because the ESA compels the government to protect and recover species, no matter the cost or inconvenience, some legal experts have described it as the world's toughest environmental law. Plenty of other policies give environmentalists some sway, but no other piece of legislation has the sweep or swagger of the ESA, nicknamed the Pit Bull of Environmental Law by a former World Wildlife Fund leader serving in the Clinton administration.

For nearly four decades, the ESA has shaped our nation's entire approach to managing natural resources and become an arena in which core conflicts play out: How should we balance the needs of humans and nature? How should we govern our common resources, such as the oceans, public lands, and the sky above? Which level of government—federal, state, or local—should take the lead?

Because these tensions run so deep and the ESA has such sharp teeth, it's no wonder that the law has triggered bitter fights and generated political positions that are diametrically opposed. To those out on the Right, the ESA is a costly, unfair, inflexible, Draconian tool for promoting the agenda of anticapitalist Chicken Littles who want everyone to stop hunting, eating beef, and riding ATVs. To those out on the Left, the ESA is the last chance for thwarting an ecological apocalypse sanctioned by corrupt, conservative politicians and perpetrated by bovine ranchers, blade-and-grade builders, slash-and-burn loggers, scrape-and-rape miners, and don't-tread-on-me property-rights zealots. This age-old battle is bound to become even more pitched in the days ahead as climate change pushes more species toward oblivion and our expanding population steps up the competition for land and water.

To get beyond the heated rhetoric and shed light on our biodiversity policies, this book examines the ESA through the eyes of a dozen or so species from the American Southwest, our hottest, driest, fastest-growing region. Can one part of the nation and a fraction of its more than 1,300 listed species teach us what the ESA has accomplished, where it has failed, and how we can do better? I think it can. Too often, partisans have focused on broad generalizations about the ESA, then cherry-picked individual recovery efforts from around the country to bolster their predetermined point of view. Instead, I think we need to go deep into one part of the country to get beyond the oversimplifications and understand the complexities that surround our endangered species.

The Southwest may seem like an unlikely setting for this exploration. If you've only visited Las Vegas or the Grand Canyon, it's easy to underestimate the region's biodiversity. Movies, car commercials, and cartoons pitting a mischievous roadrunner against a wily coyote portray the ecology in the arid West as rather dull. To the casual observer on an interstate road trip, much of the region is a monotony of empty basins, denuded mountains, and stark chasms where the geology, rather than the biology, seems most interesting. In reality, the Southwest is one of the continent's hot spots for species richness—and endangerment. Acre for acre, rain forests around the equator have the most species by far. But many deserts and arid shrublands are among the most biologically diverse ecosystems on Earth. In the Southwest—which I define as Arizona and New Mexico plus adjoining portions of California, Nevada, Utah, Colorado, and Texas—the roller-coaster topography and feast-or-famine weather create a unique montage of habitats. In Southern California, only 85 miles lie between Mt. Whitney and Death Valley, the highest and lowest points in the lower 48. In Arizona, weather stations less than 200 miles apart at times record the nation's highest and lowest temperatures in a single day.

The area around Tucson, my home for nearly a decade, exemplifies the tremendous biodiversity in the Southwest; for many years, this landscape has also been ground zero for conflicts over the ESA. The Tucson metropolitan area, which grew from about 10,000 to almost a million residents over the course of the 20th century, is nearly surrounded by "sky islands": imposing, isolated mountain ranges that jut up from seas of desert and are crowned with lush forests. Ascend one of these sky islands and you pass through a layer cake of life zones as cacti give way to grasslands, oak woodlands, ponderosa pines, then spruce-fir forests filled with moss and mushrooms (fig. 1). It's equivalent to the progression of plant communities that you'd experience on a 1,200-mile journey from Mexico to Canada.

This elevated archipelago of sky islands is also an ecological crossroads. Two of North America's four major deserts, the Sonoran and Chihuahuan, meld here, as do the Rocky Mountains, Mexico's Sierra Madre, and the Great Plains. Alpine species infiltrate from the north; tropical plants and animals come up from the south (fig. 2). The result is a harsh yet fragile land with wolves and jaguars, ferns and prickly pears. Eons of evolution have imbued plants and animals with specialized strategies for surviving an exceptionally demanding environment. Tally up all the known species in Arizona and New Mexico and these two states rank third and fourth among all 50, even though neither has any coastal or marine habitat.

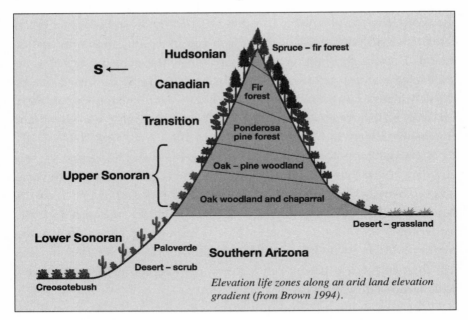

Figure 1: Life zones on a typical southern Arizona mountain.
Source: US Climate Change Science Program Synthesis and Assessment Product 4.3, based on Brown, D. E., ed. *Biotic Communities of the American Southwest United States and Mexico.* Salt Lake City: Univ. of Utah Press, 1994.

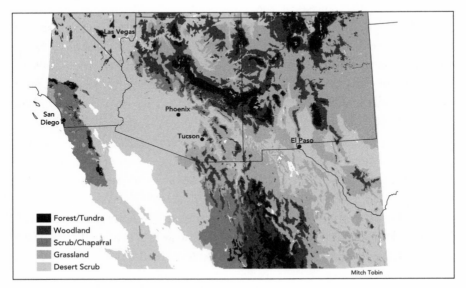

Figure 2: Biotic communities of the Southwest.
Source: Simplified version of David E. Brown and Charles H. Lowe's classic map using GIS layer from The Nature Conservancy. Brown and Lowe's 1980 color map shows 28 types of terrestrial communities. (Brown, D. E., and C. H. Lowe. "Biotic Communities of the Southwest." Forest Service General Technical Report RM-78. 1980.)

Over the past century, a single species, *Homo sapiens*, has caused the greatest ecological upheaval in the Southwest since the last ice age retreated. Lured by cloudless skies, cheap real estate, and the lore of the Wild West, tens of millions of people have flooded into the region. From 2000 to 2009, Nevada, Arizona, and Utah grew faster than all other states. In an otherwise unforgiving land, where the mercury may top 100 degrees for 100 straight rainless days, concrete rivers pump water uphill to irrigate golf courses and subdivisions named for displaced animals.

Tucson has been center stage in America's biodiversity battles, partly due to its natural surroundings and Arizona's meteoric growth. Just as important is the city's tradition as a hotbed for environmentalism. The cow town turned boomtown, once home base for writer Edward Abbey and the eco-saboteurs of Earth First!, became the headquarters for a new breed of hard-line activists in the 1990s. Trading civil disobedience for civil lawsuits, the Center for Biological Diversity forced the federal government to protect about one-quarter of the nation's endangered species, including corals, polar bears, and other creatures that aren't too fond of deserts.

The Southwest may not encompass every threat or issue related to endangered species, but its biodiversity, breakneck growth, and long history of ESA conflict make it the ideal setting for assessing the law's performance—and for learning how to build a better legislative ark. Already an epicenter of endangerment, the region is warming faster than other parts of the country and is in the bull's-eye for projections of even hotter, drier weather. The Southwest, full of species living near their physiological limits for temperature and water, may be at the leading edge of a wave of extinctions in the 21st century. In this one corner of the country, a close look at our attempts to recover a select number of plants and animals tells us most everything we need to know about the ESA: its successes, its shortcomings, and the urgent need for supplementary policies. To grasp why the Southwest's species and ecosystems are so endangered is to understand the many ways our nation has mismanaged its natural resources and forced the ESA to shoulder too heavy a burden as it backfills the many holes in our other environmental laws.

Besides focusing on the Southwest, this book also views endangered species through another lens: its author's eyes. I've tangled with the ESA since 1995, when I arrived in Tucson and started working as a door-to-door canvasser for the Arizona League of Conservation Voters, a ragtag group of University of Arizona students and others led by a jaundiced ex-biologist who was somehow cynical and inspiring at the same time. Under the afternoon sun, we'd walk from house to house with an earnest prepackaged plea for donations to support a modest lobbying effort directed at the state legislature in Phoenix. It didn't take me long to realize that the ESA isn't just about saving rare plants and animals; it's also the biggest hammer in environmentalists' toolbox and a fulcrum for leveraging change when all else fails. When I headed to graduate school to become a political scientist, I learned how science is politicized—in all quarters—and why there's invariably a wide gap between what the ESA says and what the law actually does. But it wasn't until I became a journalist and I set out to actually find the species causing all the fuss that I could paint a fuller portrait of the ESA, its defenders, and its detractors. When I could see the birds, bats, fish, and frogs eye to eye, I felt farthest from the tired talking points I was transcribing on deadline and closest to the truth.

My exploration has led me to a sobering conclusion: if the world's species are to survive the coming floods, which will be accompanied by deeper droughts, bigger wildfires, and smaller habitats, they'll need a fleet of arks piloted by a navy full of Noahs. The arks will include our national parks, wildlife refuges, and wilderness areas, plus connected areas that enjoy lesser protection. They will take the form of doomsday vaults where seeds, plants, animals, and other natural materials are kept in cold storage for repopulation after a climate catastrophe or other disaster. The word *ark* also describes the vessel that held the tablets inscribed with the Ten Commandments. Whether or not you believe the Israelites carried such an ark while wandering through the desert, preserving the planet's biodiversity will depend on our own species living by a similar set of "thou shalls" and "thou shall nots" that regulate our use of natural resources, put some places off-limits, and protect the most vulnerable members of ecological communities. Without smarter, stronger policies that extend far beyond the ESA, we'll never be able to protect the wildlife and wild places that sustain us all.

1
Saving 134

I walk inside the Phoenix Zoo's animal clinic and blinding sunshine turns to cool fluorescent light. When the heavy metal door slams behind me, it shuts out the Wurlitzer organ music coming from a nearby carousel. The smell of cotton candy is replaced by the odor of a hospital and the stench of a pet store.

I'm led into the operating room, where I find veterinarian Dean Rice giving mouth-to-mouth resuscitation to a California condor. Rice puts his lips on a plastic tube protruding from the beak and tries to breathe life into bird 134. When Rice blows, he turns beet red, but the jet black condor is motionless. The bird's eyes are rolled up inside his head.

A surgical light bounces off the perspiration beading on Rice's balding head. He puts on a stethoscope and bends over to check 134's pulse. The bird's wingspan is more than nine feet and its body is bigger than any Thanksgiving turkey I've ever seen. It takes three of Rice's assistants to prop up 134 on the surgical table. While Rice searches for a heartbeat, one of his assistants holds 134's featherless head up high, revealing a gooseflesh neck arrayed with a rainbow of pinks, yellows, oranges, and purples. Then Rice resumes mouth-to-mouth.

A few hours earlier, a FedEx truck delivered 80 cubic centimeters of condor blood from the San Diego Zoo's Wild Animal Park, where 134 hatched a decade ago. Brought into this world with the help of humans, 134 is once again in an emergency room of sorts, this time receiving a blood transfusion to save him from lead poisoning, the number one killer of condors. Somewhere near the Grand Canyon, 134 swallowed bullet fragments as he ripped decaying flesh from a dead animal, almost certainly a deer, elk, or coyote shot by a hunter on the forested North Rim. When a lead rifle bullet hits its quarry, the projectile typically explodes into scores of tiny pieces that contain enough poison to kill North America's largest bird.

As I snap photos of Rice doing mouth-to-mouth and scribble illegible notes in my reporter's pad, I'm reminded of another self-imposed assignment in an emergency room. I was the city hall reporter for the *Tucson Citizen* and desperate to break out of the rut of interminable public hearings animated with backslapping politicos, so I shadowed the crew of a city fire engine that had become one of the nation's busiest. There was some news value in the profile—Tucson's unrelenting growth was stressing its emergency medical system—but mostly I was trying to live out my childhood dream of being a firefighter. Back on Long Island, where I'd grown up, Jewish boys are supposed to become doctors, not paramedics.

Predictably, the shift I was observing was exceptionally quiet—the curse of the ride-along, I called it. But around 10 PM, long after the photographer had bailed, a piercing tone sounded in the station and the call came in over the loudspeaker: pedestrian hit outside Lim Bong's Liquor. In a blur, they pushed me into the cab of Engine 8 and we were weaving through traffic on a divided highway at double the speed limit, blowing through stoplights with air horn blasts that pierced my ears and tickled my diaphragm. Arriving at the scene, the first thing I noticed was the compound fracture to the femur of an emaciated, gray-bearded homeless man. A paramedic said he couldn't find a pulse. In what seemed like seconds, the firefighters had a cervical collar strapped around the man's neck, an IV tube in his arm, and off we went to University Medical Center. On the operating table, the homeless man was completely naked, the contours of his ribs visible beneath his bruised, ghostly white torso. My eyes were repeatedly drawn to the black holes of his dilated pupils. The firefighters told me it was time to leave. "This guy is CTD," one said. I asked for a translation. "Circling the drain," another firefighter replied before we climbed back in the truck for a much slower—and dead silent—ride back to Station 8.

Back in the firehouse, there was the same gallows humor I knew from newsrooms. It's an essential defense mechanism if you make your living off others' misfortune, like a condor does. For an environmental journalist, the death force that drives so much of our news coverage—"if it bleeds, it leads"—doesn't compare to what occupies a police reporter or combat correspondent. But it's there. A 300-year-old pine tree turns into a torch as a wildfire roars through. A dehydrated pronghorn lies down one last time beside a creosote bush that holds neither nutrition nor water. A condor starves as fragments of a lead bullet dissolve in its gut. As I'm watching Rice try to revive 134, I'm staring squarely at the ESA's reason for being: death, and not just the loss of a bird here and a fish there, but the permanent destruction of an entire species that somehow figured out how to make a living in a brutish world.

Starting with bacteria in the primordial soup, life on Earth unfolded over 3.8 billion years and branched out into millions of different species like the canopy of an ever-expanding tree. Plate tectonics, asteroid impacts, and natural fluctuations in the climate, some of them quite abrupt, sheared off large sections of this tree of life. Yet the boughs that remained radiated outward like leafy stems seeking sunlight as the survivors filled empty niches, developed specialized survival strategies, and evolved into entirely new species. Now, in a tick of the geologic clock, humans are pruning the tree of life like careless gardeners who could care less about the health of the plant.

For nearly four decades, the ESA has sought to curb such unwise meddling, and the law is now akin to our emergency room for nature. In most cases, the ESA's administration never involves actual clinics and surgeries, as it does with the California condor. But our nation's biodiversity policy does share much in common with our practice of emergency medicine. Anyone who has been unfortunate enough to land in an ER knows it's not how you want to deliver healthcare to society at large. In ERs for both people and nature, overwhelmed personnel perform triage and force patients to endure long waits even if they are seriously injured. The services delivered are often astronomically expensive; in many cases, they would have been unnecessary had the patient received preventive care. If more people had health insurance, or if fewer homeless people were wandering the streets, our ERs would still be critical, but also a lot less crowded. Likewise, if we did a better job managing our land, water, and other natural resources, the ER that is the ESA would still be absolutely essential, but not nearly as busy.

Our nation's biodiversity policy is actually worse than our unenviable healthcare system: with endangered species, we put the bulk of the conservation burden on the ER and do little beyond its confines until the patient arrives there in critical condition. When a species is finally protected by the ESA, it's already in miserable shape. One study found that at the time of federal listing, a median of about 120 individual plants and 1,000 individual animals were left. For the biologists and land managers who care for endangered species, the threats are as grave and intractable as the ones facing the trauma surgeons in Tucson when the dying homeless man arrived. While I watched him expire, I didn't blame the firefighters, nurses, or doctors for failing to save him. And I wouldn't blame Dean Rice and the other vets if they couldn't revive condor 134. Assigned a nearly impossible task, these emergency workers do the best they can with the resources at hand.

It's also unfair to automatically blame the ESA if a species isn't recovering, especially when hardly any of the plants and animals shielded by the law have gone extinct. Since 1973, only eight of the nation's more than 1,300 listed species have vanished, a "success" rate of more than 99 percent. Without the ESA, scientists believe that hundreds of other species would have disappeared forever or been so decimated they would have been impossible to recover. But if the ESA is succeeding at preventing extinction, it is falling far short of its ultimate goal: recovery of species so they no longer need our help. Just 21 endangered species have recuperated sufficiently to the point where they could be delisted and discharged from nature's ER. So about 98 percent of the nation's endangered species, including the California condor, lie in between these extremes: saved from extinction but still not nursed back to health. Only 8 percent of listed species are improving, while one-third are stable and one-third are declining. The status of the other quarter is unknown, largely because of a lack of funding for monitoring.

No matter how hard we try, some species will forever be on life support because they are so rare, isolated, or vulnerable to change. A tiny pupfish found in a single desert spring will always be at risk of extinction. With other plants and animals, however, the lack of progress is simply due to insufficient spending. The Interior Department's annual expenditure on its endangered species program, roughly $150 million, is less than the military spends on a single F-22 fighter plane, just 0.005 percent of the federal budget, and only 50 cents per American per year. But money hasn't always been the issue, especially with charismatic species that the public finds fascinating, endearing, or otherwise appealing. With the California condor, more than $40 million has been spent on a species with about 300 remaining individuals. Compare the expenditures made on behalf of condor 134 with the resources devoted to the homeless guy hit outside Lim Bong's Liquor, and the bird might come out ahead. More often, the fundamental problem confronting endangered species is a lack of habitat and a shortage of political will to address the root causes of their endangerment. We let economics trump ecology, give lobbyists more say than biologists, and simply refuse to change policies and practices that push plants and animals toward the abyss.

It was miraculous that 134—and his fellow condors—had made it this far. Thousands of years before Leif Erikkson and Christopher Columbus landed in North America, the California condor population was already in decline. We know that condors once soared across a large share of the continent because their fossilized remains have been found as far east as Florida and as far north as New York. In the Pleistocene Epoch, which began about 2 million years ago and ended as the ice age glaciers receded around 12,000 years ago, North American condors were at their height and could feast on a smorgasbord of behemoths that are no longer with us. Saber-toothed cats with half-foot-long fangs, carnivorous bears that were 10 feet tall, and wolves double the size of their modern-day descendents chased down sloths standing six feet tall, mastodons weighing six tons, and herds of camels indigenous to the New World. If you made your living off carrion, it was like an all-you-can-eat buffet. But by the end of the last ice age, not long after humans first entered the Western Hemisphere via the Bering Land Bridge, all of these creatures—the Pleistocene megafauna—had vanished forever. As the condor's food sources declined, so did its numbers and geographic range, leading some scientists to label the surviving birds "ice age relics."

The changing climate surely had some role in diminishing the wildlife that the condor depended on because new weather patterns rearranged the mosaic of vegetation cloaking the landscape. There is also strong evidence that overhunting by the first North American peoples played a decisive role in the extinction of many animals. This "blitzkrieg hypothesis," first proposed in 1967 by University of Arizona paleoecologist Paul Martin, is chilling: bands of Stone Age hunters armed with little more than spears, arrows, and human cunning eliminated most of the hemisphere's largest land animals. Martin and others argued it was no coincidence that most of the Pleistocene megafauna had made it through the rise and fall of previous ice ages, only to disappear in the most recent flipping of the climate when humans arrived. The people who colonized the New World moved from northwest to southeast in North America, as did the string of extinctions. Martin and colleagues calculated that if a band of 100 Paleo-Indians on the eastern Canadian plains moved south 20 miles every year, killed a dozen animals per person, and doubled their population every two decades, it would only take three centuries for the first North Americans to kill more than 90 million 1,000-pound animals and reach modern-day Mexico.

Other continents provided support for the blitzkrieg hypothesis. About 50,000 years ago, there were more than 150 genera of animals larger than 100 pounds; by 10,000 years ago, at least 97 were gone. On Australia, a similar and earlier extinction event had claimed nearly 90 percent of the megafauna. This lent credence to the theory that large animals living outside Africa and Eurasia were doomed since they lacked the skills and instincts needed to flee human predators, while Old World species had been coexisting with people for millennia. In North America, it was the large animals endemic to the New World—musk ox, 300-pound beavers, and the mighty glyptodont, a relative of the armadillo as big as a Volkswagen Beetle—that suffered the worst fate. Other prey species that migrated with humans across the Bering Land Bridge, such as the moose, fared better.

Besides hunting the Pleistocene megafauna, the first humans in the New World altered habitat for countless species. They set fires to clear vegetation for crops and steer game toward their stomachs. They modi-fied the flows of streams for irrigation. Yet in much of North America, the effects were relatively minor. It was not until the past century or two that the impacts expanded exponentially, heralding the onset of a new age: the Anthropocene Epoch, in which the human species is modify-ing all of creation. There is no consensus on when this new epoch began. Many scholars argue it was at the onset of the Industrial Revolution, some say it began thousands of years ago, and others dismiss the notion entirely. But scientists do agree we are now in the midst of the most profound transformation of the natural world since the waning days of the last ice age, when condors were picking apart the remains of the last woolly mammoths.

Besides reducing the condor's food supply, the first North Ameri-cans posed a direct threat to the birds. Indigenous people honored both California and Andean condors by sacrificing them in funeral rites and stealing eggs from their nests, foreshadowing the thefts that early orni-thologists would later commit to enrich museum collections. By the 1800s, Anglo settlers would only find condors in a narrow band along the Pacific Coast, from British Columbia to Baja California. The birds may have held on in coastal areas because they could consume beached whales and seals as an alternative to the declining herds of deer, elk, and bison.

By the mid-19th century, the remnant population of condors was also in trouble. The 1848 discovery of gold in the foothills of California's Sierra Nevada spurred a mass migration to condor country. Prospectors soon discovered that the birds' strong, hollow quills made perfect con-tainers for gold dust. More than a century before Rachel Carson's *Silent Spring* and the first Earth Day, settlers in awe of the condors' dimen-sions brandished guns, not binoculars, upon seeing the birds. In ensuing decades, condors also suffered collateral damage when they ate carcasses that ranchers and predator-control agents had laced with strychnine, arsenic, and other poisons in a quest to kill wolves, bears, coyotes, and mountain lions. By the mid-20th century, the world's California condor population had been reduced to only a few dozen in a 5-million-acre wishbone-shaped area northwest of Los Angeles—a range that a single condor could cover in a day or two.

Other US species suffered an equal or greater level of deliberate persecution and indirect harm in the 19th and early 20th centuries. At least 100 US species, including the Maryland darter, Carolina parakeet,

Florida mountainsnail, Louisiana vole, Las Vegas leopard frog, and Tennessee riffleshell, are gone for good, while another 439 species have been missing for so long that they are possibly extinct. California condors hung on, barely, but the birds are equipped with the worst possible reproductive strategy to rebound from the onslaught. The birds, which can live more than 40 years, take at least 6 years to sexually mature, then lay a single egg and lavish attention on the new hatchling. Turkeys and quail may pump out a dozen eggs in a year; a pair of condors, which sometimes mate for life, usually produce only one chick every other year. The condor's glacial reproductive rate was recognized early on by scientists concerned about hunting and egg collecting. "Almost any other bird might hold its own in the struggle for existence against these forces, but the condor is too slow in recuperating its numbers," pioneering researcher William Finley wrote in 1908. "Unless the needed protection is given, this bird will undoubtedly follow the Great Auk," a large, flightless seabird of the North Atlantic coast that was hunted to extinction in the mid-19th century.

Condor advocates agreed that the bird faced a grim prognosis, but starting in the 1940s they split into two camps. Some said the bird was too fragile to be captured for research and pushed for creation of sanctuaries in Southern California, where the condors' nests and food supply would be secure. Others thought habitat loss was just one piece in a much bigger puzzle and argued for more intensive studies to determine why the birds were dying. According to these biologists, it wouldn't be possible to save the condors without first attaching radio transmitters to the birds and monitoring them intensively in the field. As the species continued to decline, many scientists went a step further and pushed for a captive breeding program that could bolster the wild population.

The hands-on versus hands-off debate would rage for decades and become a key policy dilemma in the recovery efforts for a host of other endangered species. To this day, biologists, environmentalists, and government officials routinely clash over the ethics and effectiveness of intervening in the natural world. Do our actions invariably injure animals, spoil nature, ignore the root causes of species' endangerment, and remove the "wild" from both wildlife and wilderness? Or do we have enough skill to manipulate species and enough ecological wisdom to modify their habitats by introducing nonnative species, building artificial water holes, cutting down trees, or killing weeds? The California condor's plight exposed a fundamental rift in the environmental community that climate change has only widened: one side thinks our knowledge of nature is too poor and the risk of unintended consequences is too great to justify aggressive measures; the other sees captive breeding, even assisted migration, as the only hope for saving species in a world indelibly stained by humans. Many environmentalists and scientists are torn between the two philosophies.

The hands-off view held sway among many environmentalists in the 1970s and 1980s as the condor's numbers continued to plummet. Several groups that now hail the condor's rebound as an ESA success story even tried to block the captive breeding program. David Brower, the Sierra Club leader and founder of Friends of the Earth, opposed the capture plan. Other activists were worried that the breeding program in zoos would undermine their efforts to stop sprawl in Southern California that was imperiling so many other species. Some said condors should be given "death with dignity" and referred to the captive birds as "feathered pigs." Two early missteps did provide ammunition to critics of the hands-on approach. In 1980, a chick died due to capture-related stress. A year later, researchers test-fired a net on a dry hillside near Los Angeles and sparked a wildfire that nearly destroyed high-priced homes.

The dispute came to a head in early 1985. In a matter of months, the wild population's reproductive potential was destroyed after four of the remaining five pairs lost one or both birds, leaving just one pair intact. Lead poisoning was the culprit in at least one of the deaths. The US Fish and Wildlife Service proposed capturing the entire wild population, but the plan prompted lawsuits from the National Audubon Society and members of the Chumash tribe along the California coast. The litigation failed, so on Easter Sunday 1987, the last wild condor was captured, marking the first time since the Pleistocene that the species no longer flew above North America. The last 27 condors on Earth were now in zoos, which tightened security for fear of sabotage by extremists. The San Diego Zoo strung concertina wire around its condor facilities. In Los Angeles, one zoo official slept on a roof near the breeding compound with a rifle by his side, listening as protestors scaled nearby trees and howled like wolves.

Despite the initial objections by some environmentalists, the federal government continued one of the most elaborate and expensive efforts ever attempted to rescue a species. To accelerate the condor's reproductive rate, biologists tricked the birds with "double clutching" by removing the first egg laid to encourage a second attempt. By 1992, breeding in zoos had created a large enough captive population to allow biologists to release the birds in Southern California; in 1996, the program expanded to the Grand Canyon region, where condors had last been reported in the 1920s.

––––––––––

For many years, condor 134 had exemplified the success of the recovery program. Ten years before his blood transfusion at the Phoenix Zoo, 134 was developing in an egg inside an incubator at the San Diego Zoo's Wild Animal Park. Twice a day, zookeepers wearing surgical gloves turned the half-pound aqua-colored egg and held it up to a bright light to check on the progress of the embryo within. On April 2, 1996, 134 pecked away at the shell and hatched. Technicians then used hand puppets resembling condors to feed minced mice to 134 and make sure the impressionable chick didn't become attached to the humans he was totally dependent upon. Two years later, 134 was set free on a precipice north of the Grand Canyon. As he soared thousands of feet above northern Arizona and southern Utah, 134 quickly learned to survive on his own by scavenging the remains of big game. Unlike many of the younger birds, 134 didn't depend on the subsidy livestock carcasses doled out near the release site by the Peregrine Fund, the nonprofit group that manages the birds on a daily basis.

I once witnessed this subsidy feeding as the Peregrine Fund readied four captive-bred birds for release atop the Vermilion Cliffs, a 3,000-foot escarpment just south of the Arizona-Utah border. On a slab of sandstone colored like a faded penny and partially shaded by a piñon-juniper woodland, a team of biologists used a giant net to snag the juvenile condors that were being housed in a large outdoor cage known as a flight pen. Then it took three or four people to hold down each condor as one of the team members punched a hole in its wing and attached a two-ounce radio-transmitter that would allow scientists to track the bird's movements. "Their neck muscles are unbelievably powerful. They can hit you so fast, it's like a snake," biologist Sophie Osborn told me, her gloved hand clasping a beak so sharp it could pierce the hide of a horse. Osborn showed me how a condor's tongue and the roof of its mouth are serrated, adaptations that allow it to rasp tissue off bone and grasp slippery innards. The condor's feet, however, are like a turkey's. Because the birds only eat dead animals, they don't need the piercing talons of a raptor, which must first kill its prey. Instead, their feet were made for walking, and for providing leverage while the birds tear meat off a carcass. As Osborn and her colleagues fitted the birds with radio transmitters, a half-dozen wild condors clustered on a nearby rock outcropping and ripped apart a stillborn dairy calf that some unlucky biologist had hauled there in a backpack. From several hundred feet away I could hear the whooshing of the birds' massive wings. They formed a gory tableau, with the calf's ribs exposed and rivulets of its blood running down a boulder stained white by bird droppings.

Condor 134 didn't need handouts and instead found food on his own. "He was a perfect example of the fact that they don't need us all that much," Peregrine Fund biologist Thom Lord told me. Even so, 134 still wasn't truly wild. Because of the lead poisoning threat, the Peregrine Fund's biologists were forced to repeatedly capture 134 and all the other condors for blood tests. Such monitoring was especially critical in the months following the fall hunt, when scores of carcasses and gut piles lay out in the field, riddled with lead fragments that could poison condors and other scavengers. Big game hunting posed such a dire threat to condors that biologists were now calling it the lead season.

In December 2005, when Lord and his colleagues tried to snag 134, the bird was characteristically savvy and refused to be caught. Shortly after the failed capture, 134 disappeared in the Grand Canyon. On the frozen North Rim, Lord and others with the Peregrine Fund held up their antennas to track the bird, but they heard no beeps coming from the transmitter attached to 134's wing. A few days without a signal from a condor would be no cause for alarm, since the canyon's legendary topography might be temporarily blocking the radio signal. But after more than two weeks of scanning the airwaves and peering into the canyon with binoculars, the biologists had neither seen nor heard any sign of 134.

The disappearance of 134 was especially distressing because he had paired up with 210, a female condor that was once notorious for hanging around the developed part of the South Rim. That naive curiosity, a possible by-product of captive breeding, put 210 at greater risk of human hazards, but biologists succeeded in their hazing and turned her into a model condor. Now it looked like 210 and 134 would be mating, maybe even producing a chick, something that had happened only a handful of times since condors were reintroduced. The rebound in the condor's free-flying population wasn't due to birds breeding in the wild; the numbers were going up thanks to the continual release of zoo-reared birds since 1992. It wasn't until 2001 that a chick hatched outside a zoo, and only in 2003 did a wild-hatched chick fledge and leave its nest. Birds 134 and 210 may not have needed humans' help, but the condor population still did.

Although biologists couldn't snag 134, they did capture his potential mate. When they drew blood from 210, the results came back positive for lead poisoning. Because 134 and 210 spent so much time together, it was very likely that both birds had eaten from the same carcass and that both had ingested the lead. With 210 in captivity, biologists could administer painful injections of calcium disodium versenate, a chemical that binds to lead in the blood and ferries it out of the body (this same chelation therapy is used on children who've eaten lead-based paint). Out in the wild somewhere, 134 was grappling with the illness on his own. Every day that 134 remained missing only increased the odds that he would become another victim of lead poisoning and illustrate the condor program's failings, not its progress.

In a stroke of incredible luck, a supporter of the Peregrine Fund happened to be floating down the Colorado River on a rafting trip when she saw a condor on the beach. The woman could read the condor's numerical tag, and she noticed 134 was acting strangely. Rather than hitching a ride on the thermal air currents rising from the sunbaked earth, then gliding above the Grand Canyon at speeds up to 55 mph, 134 was stumbling around the shoreline like a drunken sailor. When the woman was back in civilization, she relayed what she had seen to the Peregrine Fund. "Had we not gotten word from the river trip," Lord said, "the bird would have disappeared and we would have never known where to look."

Desperate to find 134, Lord took to the skies above the Grand Canyon in a single-engine Cessna fitted with antennas on each of its wings. By crisscrossing the airspace near the last sighting and consulting a satellite-guided GPS unit, Lord could pinpoint 134's location in the bottom of the canyon, about 30 miles northwest of the South Rim visitor center. From thousands of feet above, it was impossible to see 134, let alone check on his condition. Lord did know 134 was still alive, since the bird's radio transmitter wasn't emitting the quickened beeping of the mortality mode, triggered when the device is motionless for more than a day. But because 134 had barely moved since the last sighting, Lord also knew the bird was in deep trouble. Hoping to get a visual on 134, the Peregrine Fund told one of its veteran crewmembers, Eddie Feltes, to load up his backpack, hike into the Kanab Creek Wilderness on the North Rim, and scan for 134 in the river corridor below. Feltes's antenna picked up 134's signal, but the cliffs, mesas, and spires of the Grand Canyon blocked his view, so he hiked out the next day and drove all the way around to the South Rim, a journey of more than 200 miles. Once again, he couldn't get a view of the bird.

Time was running out, so Lord decided the only option was to backpack to the bottom of the Grand Canyon and find 134. "You can't imagine a worse place to have to bring a bird out of," said Lord, who also rappelled down cliffs in the canyon to retrieve eggs that condors abandoned. On the morning of February 16, 2006, Lord left the North Rim and began to walk alone down Bill Hall Trail. By day's end, after traversing innumerable switchbacks covered with loose rock, he'd hiked around 12 miles, lost about 5,000 feet in elevation, passed through more than a billion years of geology, and arrived at the Colorado River. Lord camped close to where Deer Creek enters the river after it carves narrow slot canyons in the orange sandstone and plummets 100 feet into a turquoise pool, an enchanting site many canyon rafters describe as a highlight of their trip.

The next morning, Lord found 134. "He was tucked up under a rock and I could see some tail feathers. It looked to me as if he was dead," Lord said. "I went to go pull it out, and then he turned around and looked at me." Condor 134, impossible to capture just a month before, was now partially paralyzed and didn't even try to escape. "This bird," Lord said, "was about as sick as they can get before they die."

It wasn't feasible for Lord, 28 years old and in excellent shape, to hike out with 134 on his back. Condors weigh about 20 pounds, and Lord would need a crate weighing nearly as much. The stress of the journey would probably kill 134, if not his savior. The only real option for rescuing 134—or any seriously injured person stuck in the bottom of the Grand Canyon—was a helicopter ride out. "It seems like a lot to do for an individual bird," Lord said, "but if you imagine how many resources have been invested in each of these birds, they're all certainly worth that, if not more...each one is a pretty significant portion of the total population, so we basically do whatever is in our power to save each individual."

With 134 fading, Lord couldn't waste any time, so he hoofed it out of the canyon the same day. That evening, Lord's boss, Chris Parish, called the National Park Service and secured one of its helicopters for the next morning. Lord and Parish slept for a few hours and then made the long drive to the South Rim. The helicopter took off from the park's landing pad and touched down on the beach where 134 was stranded. Spooked by the commotion, 134 tried to run away, but he could barely flap his wings. Lord and Parish netted 134, gave the bird a shot of fluids and calcium disodium versenate, packed him into a kennel, loaded it into the helicopter, and flew out of the canyon.

After landing at the South Rim helipad, Lord put 134 into the back of his truck and drove the bird 80 miles to Flagstaff to meet a twin-engine Cessna owned by the Arizona Game and Fish Department. Several of the seats were removed from the plane in order to fit the crate and two human passengers: Lord and Kathy Sullivan, the state's condor coordinator. The bird looked lethargic to Sullivan, but what struck her the most was the condor's noxious odor. "When they're in that phase of lead toxicity, basically they suffer a whole paralysis of their digestive tract. It had this mass of food inside that had just stopped moving," Sullivan told me. "Condors smell pretty bad anyway, and it was magnified big-time because the bird had food rotting inside of it." A half hour later, the Cessna touched down at Deer Valley Airport, just north of Phoenix. From there, 134 was driven to the Phoenix Zoo's tiny animal hospital, arriving about three hours after he was netted in the bottom of the Grand Canyon.

Plenty of other condors had perished from lead poisoning before being rescued. Since 1992, more than two dozen condor deaths have been attributed to lead, making it the number one source of mortality in the population. Nontoxic ammo, which performs just as well as lead and is only slightly more expensive, has been slow to catch on among hunters, so the condor population lives under the constant threat of catastrophe. Because the birds feed communally, a single lead-laden carcass could poison a significant fraction of the world's free-flying population. The known death toll from lead also understates the problem, because biologists can't always determine why a condor died. More than a dozen dead birds have never been recovered from the field. And other condors that succumbed to predators or power lines may have met an untimely end because sublethal doses of lead impaired their eyesight, flying skills, or mental abilities.

Condor 134 couldn't even stand up on his own when he arrived in Phoenix. Hatched in one zoo, he was on the verge of leaving this world in another. Although 134 still tipped the scale at 16.8 pounds, he had lost 10 to 20 percent of his body weight in a matter of weeks. Unable to swallow any food, 134 was starving to death. Blood tests revealed a lead level of 440 micrograms per deciliter. It was the most severe case of lead poisoning veterinarian Kathy Orr had ever seen in a condor since she began treating the birds in 1996. And it was quite possible that 134's lead level had come down since ingesting the bullet fragments as his body slowly tried to rid itself of the poison.

No one knows how much lead it takes to kill condors, but scientists believe levels above 60 micrograms per deciliter can cause mental and health problems, while concentrations above 100 can be toxic. By comparison, a lead reading of 10 is considered elevated in children, and even that level may be too high. Other scavengers and birds of prey also ingest bullet shards. Biologists have documented deaths from lead poisoning in at least 59 avian species. But condors appear to be especially vulnerable since they only eat carrion. Compared to owls and hawks, condors also cough up pellets of indigestible material far less often, and some scientists have speculated that the birds may intentionally swallow the lead particles, mistaking them for calcium-rich bone.

Chelation therapy is effective at removing lead from a condor's blood, provided that a piece of ammunition isn't trapped inside the bird and continually leaching its poison. Luckily, 134 didn't appear to have any lead in his crop, the pouchlike organ below the throat where the bird can store several pounds of food and partially digest the material before it reaches the stomach. Although 134's crop was clear, his digestive system was still paralyzed, so Orr and her colleagues surgically inserted a plastic feeding tube to supply liquid nourishment to the stomach. To help 134 flush any remaining lead from his digestive tract, zoo staff administered Metamucil, the same constipation-relieving product used by humans.

Despite all the interventions, 134 was still in trouble. Tests revealed he was becoming increasingly anemic. If the slide in his blood proteins weren't reversed, he'd soon be dead. The only solution, Orr decided, was to conduct a transfusion. With about 300 condors left in the world, their blood wasn't exactly easy to find. Fortunately, the vets at the San Diego Zoo's Wild Animal Park, where 134 hatched, agreed to send over some blood from one of their captive birds. Once the FedEx package arrived, Orr, Rice, and their colleagues knocked out 134 with gaseous anesthesia and switched out his blood. After Rice performed mouth to mouth and the vets were convinced that 134 was breathing on his own, they removed the plastic tube from his beak. It would be weeks until they

knew whether the infusion of fresh blood would unlock the bird's digestive tract and save his life.

As 134 was carried back to his cage to recover, Orr took me to her
office down the hall. She was wearing a Phoenix Zoo baseball cap, and
her gray ponytail poked out the back. It had been a busy few weeks, and
134's transfusion had left Orr a bit flustered. "The lead," she said, "is
what's going to kill the program."

Not long before 134 arrived at the zoo, Orr had been treating two
other condors for lead poisoning. One of them, bird 149, was among the
first six condors reintroduced to Arizona, in 1996. She went on to produce, rear, and fledge a chick in the Vermilion Cliffs—all major mile-
stones. But after 149 swallowed a piece of bullet, she was captured and
transported to the Phoenix Zoo with a lead level of 350. Surgeries and
chelation therapy worked well enough that Orr and her colleagues could
send 149 and a male bird, 304, back up to northern Arizona for further
recuperation before they were rereleased into the wild.

Orr summed up the lead problem by showing me two X-ray images.
The first one depicted the area around the spine of a deer that was shot
with a .270 Winchester rifle. Dozens of brilliant white specks were
sprinkled among the beige-colored vertebrae and surrounding black
tissue: what some biologists call a snowstorm. Lead jumps out on X-rays
because it's impenetrable (this is why your dentist shields your body with
a leaden apron while radiographing your teeth). Sometimes a hunter's
lead bullet passes cleanly through its quarry and comes out the other
side, but even then some fragments are left behind in the carcass; more
often, the ammunition shatters upon impact. Hunters will pack out the
valuable meat, but lead is often left behind in the offal, gutted carcasses,
or when wounded animals die in the field without being recovered. "If
the birds eat carcasses," Orr said, "they can't avoid the lead." In one study,
researchers examined the remains of deer killed with lead bullets and
found an average of 160 fragments, some as far as six inches from the
wound channel and some so small they were invisible to the naked eye.
The bits of lead are so tiny that the condor's potent stomach acids may
completely dissolve the fragments, leaving behind no direct evidence of
the poisoning.

The second X-ray Orr showed me was of 134's digestive tract. At
first, I couldn't see the bright signature of lead. Orr then used a pen
to point out a spot smaller than a grain of rice. "You've got this big,

magnificent bird, 1 of 273 in the whole world, and this little piece is all it takes," she said. "Politically, they're being really careful to not offend the hunters. They're just trying to talk them into switching over to non-lead ammo. But I'm getting to the point where I feel like it's taking too long—we've just got to get rid of it. You can't keep putting in this much time, money, and effort. This one bird—if it makes it—will have required a helicopter ride, a drive to Flagstaff, an airplane ride, another car ride, then all this intensive care, including having blood FedEx-ed from San Diego. You can't manage a wild population that way forever."

A few weeks after I visited Orr, the two other condors she had treated just before 134 arrived took a turn for the worse while in the Peregrine Fund's holding facility near the Vermilion Cliffs. The birds had been feeding on their own, but biologists noticed their crops growing larger, suggesting that the birds' digestive systems were once again becoming paralyzed. One died the day he returned to Phoenix; less than a week later, the other was dead.

Soon after those condors were lost, another bird suffering from lead poisoning, 122, arrived at the Phoenix Zoo and was placed in a cage beside 134. When 122 was captured for treatment, he and his mate were taking turns sitting on an egg in a huge cave in the Battleship, a butte in the Grand Canyon visible from the South Rim. A pair of condors will typically share the incubation duties equally, so without the help of the father, the egg was doomed. The Peregrine Fund put out food near the nest so 122's mate wouldn't have to fly very far to eat, but she eventually abandoned the nest and left the developing embryo for dead.

The solution seemed simple: get rid of lead ammo. The only question was how to do it. All the biologists I spoke to agreed that if the lead poisoning weren't addressed, the condor would never truly recover and would forever need constant human supervision. In a 2000 article in *Conservation Biology*, some of the leading condor experts laid out the unforgiving math: because of the condor's achingly slow reproduction, if the population's annual death rate stayed above 10 percent per year, the species would never thrive without humans continually releasing new birds into the wild. "We'll be dealing with a California condor program that's a little bit like any downtown lake stocked with trout," Vicky Meretsky, one of the coauthors, told me. "You stock it, fish 'em out, and stock it again."

Coauthor Noel Snyder, head of the condor recovery program for many years, told me that lead poisoning was the main reason Fish and Wildlife decided to capture the last wild birds in the mid-1980s. "This is not a new problem," said Snyder, author of the definitive textbook on the species, *The California Condor: A Saga of Natural History and Conservation*, with his wife, Helen. "We've gotten rid of lead in gasoline, we've gotten rid of lead in paint, we don't have lead in pipes, and it's all for the same reason: lead is a really toxic material. Why should we accept it for bullets?"

While 134 was dying in the Phoenix Zoo, the National Rifle Association and other elements of the gun lobby were busy blocking efforts to ban lead bullets in California's condor country. They argued that the added regulation would cause an undue burden on hunters, and they claimed not enough science proved the link between lead bullets and dead birds. They said the same thing 30 years before, when the federal government began to phase out lead shotgun shells in waterfowl hunting. By the mid-20th century, biologists had known for decades that ducks and other aquatic birds were dying by the millions after they swallowed the lead pellets that were strewn about wetlands. One 1959 study estimated that lead poisoning was killing 2 to 3 percent of North America's waterfowl every year. Confronted with overwhelming evidence of lead shot's toxicity, the federal government started to clamp down on lead-based shotgun shells in the 1970s; by 1991, there was a nationwide ban. Just in the Mississippi Flyway, that move saved the lives of more than 1 million ducks a year.

By the time 134 arrived at the Phoenix Zoo, the NRA looked silly disputing the connection between lead ammo and dead condors. After all, Orr, Rice, and other vets kept plucking the metal fragments out of the birds' digestive tracts. In Arizona, pieces of lead ammo had been found in 16 birds. There was no doubt about the cause of the problem, but devising a solution would be tricky. With millions of lead bullets sitting in hunters' closets and gun safes, how could the government ever enforce the prohibition? A sizable fraction of game was already poached by hunters without a legal license, and in California, hunters left behind the remains of more than 36,000 deer, coyotes, and wild pigs in condor country every year, plus an untold number of smaller animals. Even some of the staff at the Peregrine Fund told me they had reservations about banning lead bullets, fearing that it would prompt a lethal backlash against the birds. Perhaps it would be better to use a carrot and offer hunters free nontoxic ammo rather than wield a regulatory stick and alienate the very people whose behavior would help decide the condor's fate. Which side was right?

Driving back home from the Phoenix Zoo on I-10, I had 90 minutes to think about that question and others. The next day would be my last day at the *Arizona Daily Star*, the newspaper where I'd spent the past five years covering the environment, plus the occasional homicide and rubber-chicken banquet. As a journalist, I had always bent over backward to remain neutral about everything I wrote. With a few stories, I went so far as to print out drafts, draw a plus or minus next to each paragraph, then tally the results to see whether the piece was properly "balanced." (I'd still get complaints from readers who thought it was unfair that the other side was quoted first.) What often resulted from my obsession with impartiality was metronomic he-said-she-said journalism that ticktocked between the partisan poles in a political debate.

By now, I knew the truth wasn't so black and white. I was finding the ESA's performance and its politics filled with paradoxes that defied the stereotypes. I met meat-eating environmentalists who wore Stetsons and fought to preserve grazing in the desert as a bulwark against the subdivision of rangeland. I dined with wine-drinking ranchers who belonged to environmental groups and went out of their way to improve habitat for critters. Two of the leading advocates for jaguars were hunters who would tree mountain lions with hound dogs, then shoot the cats at close range. Scientists were telling me we had to cut down more trees to save the forest. Atop one Arizona mountain, an endangered owl occasionally ate an endangered squirrel. Down in the valleys, endangered flycatchers were nesting in nonnative tamarisk. And out in the nation's busiest bombing range, I found some of the most pristine habitat left in the Sonoran Desert.

For all the challenges of reporting on the nation's most controversial environmental law, it was also easy in one key respect: I never had to decide who was right or how the problems should be solved. There were good reasons for journalists to remain agnostic and report without fear or favor. But driving home from the Phoenix Zoo after seeing 134, the role of neutral observer no longer felt so comfortable. With global warming under way and an epic drought gripping the West, it was time to get the lead out.

Eleven years before, on another clear evening in spring, I was driving down the same stretch of I-10 on my first visit to Tucson. A college buddy and I had flown into Phoenix to begin a two-week road trip in search of someplace fun to live out West for a few years after graduation. Arizona immediately seemed magical. The mountains glowed orange at sunset. It was March and I was wearing shorts. A few hours later, I was freezing my tail off outside a bar in Tempe, chatting up bleach-blonde sorority girls from Arizona State University who looked—and sounded—nothing like the women I had met at Yale. Two months later, I moved out to Tucson, and in the years since I had spent much of my time thinking and writing about an environment around me that seemed to be changing by the day. By the time I entered the clinic at the Phoenix Zoo and met 134, I had crisscrossed the Southwest, tracking down endangered species, and I had seen many of the region's biological gems. But most every place I looked, there were only harsh reminders of just how badly humans had upset the natural order, and confirmations of Aldo Leopold's conclusion: "One of the penalties of an ecological education is that one lives alone in a world of wounds."

2
A Fierce Green Fire

Harmony with land is like harmony with a friend; you cannot cherish his right hand and chop off his left. That is to say, you cannot love game and hate predators; you cannot conserve the waters and waste the ranges; you cannot build the forest and mine the farm. The land is one organism.

—Aldo Leopold

The day after I visited 134 at the Phoenix Zoo, I left the *Arizona Daily Star* to begin a journalism fellowship that would allow me to take a deeper look at the ESA. When I searched for the legal, political, and philosophical roots of the law, I often found myself back in the Southwest. Other regions and their species had played a significant role in inspiring the ESA and our interest in protecting biodiversity, but few if any were as influential. Well into the 20th century, the Southwest remained one of the least developed corners of the country, so the landscape reminded Americans of what had been lost elsewhere. But after the postwar boom, the region's own scars—rivers sucked dry, canyons turned into reservoirs, basins filled with lights—were impossible to hide. Many of the environmental movement's watershed battles were fought in the Southwest, especially over dams along the Colorado River. Many of the people who advocated for the ESA were born or lived in the region and had watched the land evolve before their eyes.

Aldo Leopold, whose innovative ideas about wildlife biology and environmental ethics would underpin the ESA, continually returned to the Southwest, in his writings if not in person. When he first entered the Arizona Territory, in July 1909, Leopold was 22 years old and had just graduated from the new forestry school at Yale. At the start of the summer monsoon, he arrived by train in Holbrook, a frontier town beside the Little Colorado River that was flanked by the cinder cones and pastel mesas of the Painted Desert. Leopold, who would later become the father of the US wilderness system, was beginning his career as a foot soldier in the federal government's quest to tame the West.

Leopold's grandfather, a German immigrant, had settled in Burlington, Iowa, along the Mississippi River, in 1850. In the ensuing decades, the Leopold family watched as forests headed downstream as lumber, and as the seemingly limitless herds of bison in the tallgrass prairies became piles of bleached bones. Young Aldo, a precocious student, became an amateur naturalist and enjoyed sketching birds in the wilds around his home on a bluff overlooking the Mississippi. His father, owner of a successful desk factory, taught him how to hunt and appreciate the frontier that was fast disappearing around them.

While Leopold attended boarding school near Princeton, New Jersey, President Theodore Roosevelt started laying the cornerstones of US environmental policy. In 1903, he signed an executive order to create the first federal preserve for wildlife on Pelican Island, five acres of crucial habitat for birds on Florida's east coast. Roosevelt, an avid hunter, would go on to create another 52 preserves, America's first arks for wildlife and the nucleus of today's 95-million-acre National Wildlife Refuge System. Roosevelt went even further in 1905 by pushing for creation of the US Forest Service to manage the vast acreage that had recently been federalized; he appointed his friend Gifford Pinchot to lead the agency.

Consistent with the Progressive Era approach to government, Pinchot sought to use science and a quasi-military bureaucracy to efficiently exploit the nation's timber, forage, and wildlife. The key was to leave behind enough trees, grass, and game to allow those resources to replenish themselves. In a sense, the nation could live off the interest without depleting the principal. Pinchot's utilitarian outlook—"the greatest good for the greatest number, for the longest run"—was what Leopold learned in the Yale forestry school that Pinchot's family endowed in 1900, and it was the philosophy Leopold would put into practice as a Forest Service ranger.

Leopold's first posting was to the one-year-old Apache National Forest, about 150 miles northeast of the farming settlement in Maricopa County that would later become known as Phoenix. When Leopold got off the train in the mile-high town of Holbrook, the Forest Service's office in Springerville was still a long way off. Today, the trip from Holbrook to Springerville takes less than 90 minutes on a smooth ribbon of blacktop highway. A century ago, Leopold spent two days aboard a stagecoach, bouncing like so much cargo as the horses pulled the wagon past the stony logs of the Petrified Forest and over hills clad with shrub forests of piñon and juniper.

The Apache National Forest remained one of the least explored sections of the Southwest. Yet it really wasn't a virgin wilderness. In the 16th century, Spanish explorer Francisco Vásquez de Coronado had introduced livestock to the region when he passed through in a fruitless search for the golden Seven Cities of Cibola. Missionaries followed and imported other nonnative animals, along with new weapons and foreign germs that would devastate the indigenous people. Toward the end of the 19th century, the Apache raids that thwarted settlement petered out, prompting farmers and ranchers from Texas and Mexico to make a mad dash for the unclaimed lands in the Arizona and New Mexico territories. The settlers brought along great herds of cattle, goats, and sheep. In 1870, there were an estimated 5,000 cows in Arizona; by 1890, there were around 1 million. The hordes of livestock spread across the entire West, which became home to 26 million cows and 20 million sheep by 1900. There was virtually no government oversight of grazing practices, so the range was grossly overstocked. When severe drought struck, cows dropped dead and ranches went belly-up.

Even with the influx of man and beast, the Apache National Forest remained one of the wildest swaths of the Southwest when the federal government expropriated the area from its namesake tribe in 1886. Gray wolves, grizzly bears, and even an occasional jaguar still roamed its woods, part of the world's largest contiguous expanse of ponderosa pines. When Leopold arrived in 1909, not a single road had been staked through the heart of the national forest, which boasted a stunning variety of vegetation due to its elevation range of 8,000 feet. To the south of Springerville loomed 10,912-foot Escudilla Mountain and 11,403-foot Mt. Baldy, long-dormant volcanic domes whose barren, windswept peaks resembled the Canadian tundra and were buried in snow in winter. These mountains, the second and third tallest in Arizona, were encircled by hundreds of square miles of subalpine forests filled with spruce, fir, and shimmering aspens. Farther south, as the elevation decreased, the woods were drier and dominated by three-foot-wide ponderosas, which smelled of vanilla and butterscotch. The pines had been scarred at their base by mild ground fires that periodically cleared the underbrush and allowed the trees to be spaced far enough apart that a stagecoach could ride between them. About 40 miles south of Springerville, the terrain suddenly plunged thousands of feet, the local expression of the Mogollon Rim, which extends from near Sedona through west-central New Mexico to form a sharp boundary between the Colorado Plateau to the north and the Sonoran Desert to the south. Below the scarp of the Mogollon Rim, it was 20 or 30 degrees hotter: naked desert with cacti and scant water.

In his later writings, Leopold would become an eloquent spokesman for wilderness and preservation, but he began his career by assessing how much timber the Apache National Forest could provide for the burgeoning copper mines around Clifton and Morenci. For weeks at a time, Leopold and other Forest Service employees scouted the Apache by foot and horseback, taking stock of a largely unknown entity. Biographer Curt Meine notes that Leopold's correspondence "waxed enthusiastic about moving the timber." "I am lucky to be here in advance of the big works," Leopold wrote while reconnoitering the forest.

One day in the fall of 1909, as Leopold and his party were eating lunch on some rimrock, they noticed something fording the turbulent river below. It looked like a doe, but when the animal reached the other bank and shook out its tail, Leopold knew it was a wolf. A half-dozen pups emerged from the willows along the river and began cavorting beneath Leopold's perch. Instinctively, the men brandished their rifles and began pumping lead into the pack. Back then, wolves were viewed as varmints and pests, such a menace to livestock and game populations that the government put bounties on the predators' heads. Out of ammunition, Leopold descended to the river. One of the pups was dragging a wounded leg as it tried to escape; its mother was down on the ground, mortally wounded and unable to flee. "We reached the old wolf in time to watch a fierce green fire dying in her eyes," Leopold would later write. "I realized then, and have known ever since, that there was something new to me in those eyes—something known only to her and to the mountain."

In the years that followed Leopold's slaughter of the pack, other rangers, as well as ranchers, trappers, and predator-control agents, killed thousands of wolves in the Southwest. It was a systematic extermination repeated across the continent as settlers and their livestock displaced coyotes, bears, lions, and jaguars. Wolves were shot on sight, as Leopold had demonstrated, and hunters in Arizona could receive a bounty of $50 as late as 1960, plus some cash for the pelt. Predator-control agents fooled wolves into poisoning themselves by lacing livestock carcasses with poison. M-44s, buried like land mines, would fire lethal doses of sodium cyanide into the mouths of any animal that tugged at the bait. In spring, when blind, deaf, and utterly helpless wolf pups were born, hunters would engage in "denning." They would either bury the litters alive or dig them out and finish off the young with bullets and so-called numbing clubs.

Leopold's encounter with the wolf pack in 1909 left a deep impression on his 22-year-old mind, but it would take him another two decades to renounce predator control. Initially, Leopold supported the federal government's campaign as he rose through the ranks to become supervisor of the Carson National Forest and a researcher at the Forest Service's laboratory in Madison, Wisconsin. As late as 1921, he was still advocating total elimination of top-level carnivores in the Southwest. "It's going to take patience and money to catch the last wolf and mountain lion in New Mexico," he wrote. "But the last one must be caught before the job can be called fully successful."

By the end of the 1920s, however, Leopold had done a 180-degree turn and was arguing that "no predatory species should be exterminated over a large area." Nowhere else was the price of predator control more apparent to Leopold than on Arizona's Kaibab Plateau, the forested expanse on the Grand Canyon's North Rim that became a prime foraging ground for reintroduced California condors, including bird 134. After settlers wiped out the natural enemies of the Kaibab's deer, the herd's population exploded. The irruption, as Leopold called it, wreaked havoc on the plateau's vegetation and thousands of deer died of starvation, though some revisionist studies would question the connection between predator control and the health of the Kaibab ecosystem. Elsewhere in the Southwest, as civilization's imprint expanded, Leopold saw an increasing need for the total protection of some public lands. In 1924, he convinced the Forest Service to designate its first wilderness area in the headwaters of the Gila River in southwestern New Mexico, not too far from where he'd shot the wolf pack in 1909.

Leopold's instrumental role in creating federal wilderness areas allied him with Sierra Club founder John Muir's preservationist approach, but his early ideas about wildlife management put him closer to the conservation ethic espoused by Pinchot. Leopold's writings, including his seminal 1933 textbook, *Game Management*, reveal a search for rational regulation that would allow people to use, but not abuse, natural resources. In essence, Leopold wanted to take the systematic approach to forestry that he learned at Yale and employed as a Forest Service ranger—exploit the resource wisely but spare enough trees to support future harvests—and apply it to the allocation of hunting permits. Whether the commodity was elk, wood, or grass, Leopold and a growing cadre of land managers were grappling with one of the fundamental questions in environmental policy: how do you control a shared resource so that it can sustainably yield lumber, meat, or other material? Left to their own devices, individual hunters, loggers, and ranchers would have an incentive to harvest as much as they could because any trees, game, or forage left behind would be used up by their competitor or neighbor. This overexploitation of a shared resource, known as the "tragedy of the commons," is what drives many of our environmental problems, including overfishing, depleted rivers, and plunging water tables. Besides being plundered, the commons can also be polluted in the absence of regulation, with global warming serving as the best—and most troubling—example.

The notion that the oceans could run out of fish or that humans could alter the earth's climate would have seemed chimerical in Leopold's day. But in an era when the word *biodiversity* still hadn't been coined, Leopold was already beginning to formulate the scientific and ethical basis of the ESA. One of his most important contributions was to broaden the field of wildlife management beyond ducks and deer to include nongame species that wouldn't end up on the dinner table. Leopold also became one of the first and foremost advocates for rescuing specific species from extinction. "Few would question the assertion that to perpetuate the grizzly as part of our national fauna is a prime duty of the conservation movement," he wrote in an influential 1937 article in *American Forests* titled "Threatened Species." In that piece, Leopold called on the nation to identify imperiled animals—condors, grizzlies, ivory-billed woodpeckers, and sandhill cranes were some of his candidates—and use the list to guide research, habitat purchases, and other conservation measures. Leopold argued that if a species was common in some parts of the country, it could still deserve protection at the edge of its geographic range, where the animal was rare or had evolved into a slightly different form. "That there are grizzlies in Alaska," Leopold wrote, "is no excuse for letting the species disappear from New Mexico." The wolves of the American Southwest and northern Mexico offered Leopold a prime example of how animals evolve into distinct subspecies as they adapt to varying conditions. The desert wolf, as Leopold called the animals that lived south of the Mogollon Rim, had become the smallest variety of *Canis lupus*. Weighing no more than 75 pounds, the lobos native to Arizona, New Mexico, and the Sierra Madre were about the size of a German shepherd and could weigh less than half as much as a timber wolf in Alaska. This latitudinal variation in size—the farther north you go, the larger the animal—is common among mammals and largely due to their warm-blooded nature: smaller animals have more trouble staying warm because their bodies have a higher surface-to-volume ratio and lose heat more readily through their skin.

The desert wolf, like its relatives in the frozen north, hunted cooperatively to bring down an adult elk or cow that weighed more than the entire wolf pack put together. Because most chases were unsuccessful, the wolves could go for days, even weeks, without a substantial meal, leaving them so gaunt they looked like scraggly coyotes. This binge lifestyle favored wolves with stomachs that could expand easily, so natural selection caused the animals to develop highly elastic pouches that could pack in 20 pounds of meat in a single sitting. The desert wolf came to be known as *Canis lupus baileyi*. It was named for biologist Vernon Bailey, an early leader of the nation's predator-control program who proudly reported in 1908 that hunters had killed 127 wolves in Arizona and 232 in New Mexico. By 1925, the Mexican subspecies had been virtually eliminated from the United States. Two other subspecies, the Southern Rocky Mountain and Mogollon Rim varieties, were driven extinct.

Wolves were also persecuted south of the border, but the terrain in the Sierra Madre was even more inaccessible, so the lobos hung on and would repeatedly seek to reoccupy their historic territory in the United States. From the Great Depression to the mid-20th century, predator-control agents acted like the Border Patrol and stopped the wolves from coming north. In the rolling high-desert grasslands of southeastern Arizona and southwestern New Mexico, hunters learned to place their steel-jawed traps along the wolf runs that snaked through the hills and offered prime spots for interdiction. Decades later, illegal immigrants would use those same trails while trekking north from Mexico.

Shortly before Leopold's death in 1948, as the last of the Southwest's grizzlies were killed along the New Mexico–Colorado border, he delivered an extended mea culpa for shooting that mother wolf in the Apache National Forest nearly 40 years before. "I was young then, and full of trigger-itch," he wrote in "Thinking Like a Mountain," an essay centered on Escudilla Mountain. "I thought that because fewer wolves meant more deer, that no wolves would mean hunters' paradise. But after seeing the green fire die, I sensed that neither the wolf nor the mountain agreed with such a view." Rather than regard the wolf as a pest, Leopold had come to see it as a vital regulatory tool in the ecosystem, a thread in the tapestry of life that could unravel the entire fabric if pulled. "Since then I have lived to see state after state extirpate its wolves. I have watched the face of many a newly wolfless mountain, and seen the south-facing slopes wrinkle with a maze of new deer trails," he wrote. "I have seen every edible bush and seedling browsed, first to anaemic desuetude, and then to death." Wolves not only kept deer herds in check; to Leopold, they also embodied the wildness and wilderness that was shrinking as the country grew. A forest where a wolf's doleful bawl echoed in the canyons was a qualitatively different—and decidedly superior—place than a landscape purged of the predator. "Every living thing (and perhaps many a dead one as well) pays heed to that call," Leopold wrote. "To the deer it is a reminder of the way of all flesh, to the pine a forecast of midnight scuffles and of blood on the snow, to the coyote the promise of gleanings to come, to the cowman a threat of red ink at the bank, to the hunter a challenge of fang against bullet." Long before the federal government would obligate itself to recover endangered animals and protect the ecosystems they rely on, Leopold had made the essential link: not only is a species in trouble without its habitat, the wild and open spaces that nurture us are at risk of ruin once a species like the wolf is heard no more.

When Leopold died in 1948, the ESA was a quarter century away from becoming law and the federal government was still solidifying its constitutional authority to regulate plants and animals, which had traditionally been managed, protected, exploited, or ignored by the states. To this day, if you want to go hunting or fishing, you get a license from a state game and fish department, not the US Fish and Wildlife Service or federal land agencies. Yet over the course of the 20th century, as the ecological costs to American prosperity became self-evident, a series of federal laws and supportive court rulings gradually eroded states' hegemony in regulating wildlife. Just as the Great Depression spurred FDR to dramatically expand the federal government's power over banking, labor, and other aspects of the economy, mounting threats to the nation's flora and fauna inspired the federal government to gradually enlarge its authority over wildlife and wilderness.

The accumulation of power in Washington did not go unchallenged. Judicial conservatives who favored states' rights and Americans suspicious of big government fought almost every attempt to create and expand federal regulations, especially in the West. Some of these critics still question the very constitutionality of the ESA and other environmental laws, seeing them as anathema to the rights of private landowners. Their legal challenges would actually help define the overall shape of federalism in the 20th century.

For most of American history, what little wildlife regulation existed was a matter for the statehouse to decide. There's no mention of wildlife in the US Constitution, and the Tenth Amendment says that any powers not expressly delegated to Congress are reserved for the states. If there was any doubt about the balance of power, the Supreme Court seemed to settle the issue in 1896 when it decided a landmark case, *Geer v. Connecticut*. Geer had been convicted under a Connecticut state law for possessing game birds with the intent to ship them out of state, even though the birds had been legally hunted in Connecticut. Geer argued the state's prosecution was an infringement of the US Constitution's commerce clause, which gives the federal government the exclusive right to regulate economic activity among the states. The Supreme Court disagreed. Writing for the majority, Justice Edward White said Connecticut's actions were justified because the state held wildlife "as a trust for the benefit of the people." This fiduciary responsibility had been established as far back as the Roman Empire and was also enshrined in feudal Europe.

Geer v. Connecticut would turn out to be the low point of federal influence over wildlife; in ensuing decades, Congress and the high court would chip away at the principle of state ownership and legitimize increasing federal power over species, regardless of whether they occupied federal, state, tribal, or even private land. Four years after the *Geer v. Connecticut* decision, the federal government took its first bold step into the arena of wildlife law. In 1900, just before Theodore Roosevelt asserted broad executive power in the environmental arena, Congress passed the Lacey Act, which prohibited the interstate transport of wild animals and birds killed in violation of state law.

A major impetus for the Lacey Act was the recent disappearance of the passenger pigeon, a species that once numbered in the billions and constituted one-quarter to two-fifths of the total bird population in the United States. The pigeons, relatives of mourning doves, used to darken the skies. After witnessing the display, John James Audubon wrote that "the light of noonday was obscured as by an eclipse." He likened the sound of the birds flying over to a "hard gale at sea." By the 1890s, the passenger pigeon was nearly gone due to overhunting and habitat loss. At one Michigan site, 50,000 birds were killed every day for five months straight. Responding to the plight of the passenger pigeon and other birds, the Lacey Act gave the secretary of agriculture authority to adopt measures for the "preservation, distribution, introduction, and restoration of game birds and other wild birds." It would be too little, too late for the passenger pigeon. Once America's most numerous bird, the species finally went extinct in 1914, when the last known passenger pigeon, Martha (named for George Washington's wife), died in captivity at the Cincinnati Zoo.

Avian species were also the focus of another early piece of federal wildlife legislation, the Migratory Bird Treaty Act of 1918, and a key legal challenge to the rise of federal power. Two years after the treaty act's passage, Missouri officials tried to stop a US game warden, Ray Holland, from enforcing the act's provisions in the state. With the *Geer v. Connecticut* precedent in mind, Missouri argued that the Migratory Bird Treaty Act was an unconstitutional infringement on its powers. The federal government, however, contended that its authority derived from the Constitution's supremacy clause, which holds that treaties and federal statutes are the "supreme law of the land." When the case reached the Supreme Court, the justices sided with the feds. Writing for the majority in *Missouri v. Holland*, Justice Oliver Wendell Holmes Jr. said that Missouri's claims of state ownership caused it to "lean upon a slender reed." "But for the treaty and the statute there soon might be no birds for any powers to deal with," Holmes wrote. "We see nothing in the Constitution that compels the Government to sit by while a food supply is cut off and the protectors of our forests and our crops are destroyed." Even in 1920, at least some scholars understood that human prosperity was necessarily bound to the fate of other species.

In ensuing decades, birds would continue to drive much of the federal government's involvement in wildlife regulation. In 1934, the federal government began printing stamps with images of ducks as a way to license waterfowl hunters and generate funds for wetland protection. In 1940, Congress passed legislation to protect the national symbol, the bald eagle. In the 1950s, many Americans were captivated by government efforts to recover the whooping crane, which had dwindled to 18 birds in 1938, four fewer than the condor's nadir.

Public consciousness of wildlife conservation was slowly taking root in America, but the environmental movement would remain in its infancy until the federal government began proposing major dams in the West. Nowhere else was the price of this policy more striking than on the Colorado River, the waterway that drains much of the intermountain West. In the 1950s, the Bureau of Reclamation tried to plug one of the Colorado's tributaries, the Green River. Doing so would submerge half of Dinosaur National Monument, an impressive, though seldom-visited canyon in northwestern Colorado. David Brower, the Sierra Club's executive director, was outraged at the prospect of the federal government flooding one of its own national monuments and led the fight against the project. The bureau also wanted to put a dam on the main stem of the Colorado River in northern Arizona, just south of the Utah state line. Erecting a dam in Glen Canyon would inundate a stunning landscape that had been proposed for national park status by Harold Ickes, FDR's interior secretary; it also would dramatically alter the ecology of the Grand Canyon downstream. But for most Americans in the 1950s, the canyonlands of the Four Corners region were a blind spot. By the end of World War II, only about 100 people had floated through Glen Canyon. In 1956, Brower and the Sierra Club board accepted a horse trade: Dinosaur National Monument would be spared and Glen Canyon would be drowned. Brower didn't realize what he was sacrificing and would carry regrets to his grave. "Glen Canyon died, and I was partly responsible for its needless death," he wrote in *The Place No One Knew*, a Sierra Club book published in 1963 as the canyon began to fill. Brower wasn't the only leader who regretted accepting Glen Canyon Dam. Republican icon Barry Goldwater, a US senator from Arizona when the project was approved, would later call his support of the dam "the one vote I wish I could take back."

For generations of southwestern environmentalists, Glen Canyon Dam became a sort of original sin: it flooded an Edenic landscape upstream and upended the hydrology of the Grand Canyon downstream to support development they viewed as unnatural, unsustainable, and immoral (even if they had emigrated to the region from elsewhere). Edward Abbey, a Pennsylvania native whose books railed against the human intrusion into the Southwest and attracted millions more people to the region, liked to call Lake Powell "Lake Foul." For take-no-prisoners environmentalists, the dam symbolized the perils of political compromise and the high costs of working within the system. When it came time for the radical group Earth First! to stage its first major protest, the eco-insurgents went public at Glen Canyon Dam. Egged on by Abbey, whose novel *The Monkey Wrench Gang* glorified a band of saboteurs plotting to blow up Glen Canyon Dam with a houseboat packed with explosives, the Earth First! activists unfurled a 300-foot piece of black plastic down the dam's ivory face. The zigzagging banner made it look as if they'd cracked their concrete demon.

The destruction wrought by Glen Canyon Dam inspired other environmentalists as well. Determined not to make the same mistake twice, the Sierra Club and its allies tried to block two other dams proposed for the Grand Canyon in the 1960s. Lawsuits weren't an option since many of the pillars of federal environmental law were years away from being erected, so the nascent movement turned to the force that would become its other staple: the media. When dam backers argued that a reservoir in the Grand Canyon would allow boaters to admire the chasm's rainbow geology up close, environmentalists shot back with a full-page newspaper advertisement that likened the proposal to flooding the Sistine Chapel in order to get a better view of Michelangelo's paintings on the ceiling. The resulting public outrage nixed the proposal.

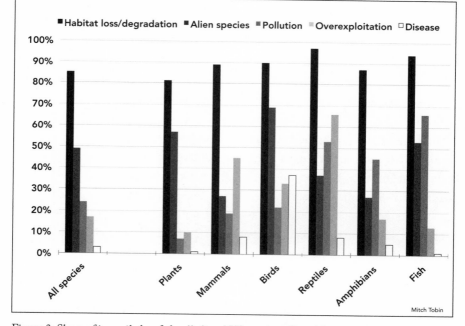

Figure 3: Share of imperiled or federally listed US species affected by major threats.
Source: Wilcove, David S., et al., "Quantifying Threats to Imperiled Species in the United States: Assessing the Relative Importance of Habitat Destruction, Alien Species, Pollution, Overexploitation, and Disease." *Bioscience* 48 (1998): 607–615.

The federal government's interest in the environment was steadily expanding, as Leopold hoped it would. But it wasn't until the late 1960s that the nation began to purposely protect all manner of species, not just game populations and charismatic birds. By the time Congress waded into the biodiversity arena, threats to native plants and animals had grown more stubborn and complex (fig. 3). The deliberate hunting that had doomed the passenger pigeon and nearly driven the California condor and Mexican gray wolf extinct was now joined by habitat loss, invasive species, and toxic chemicals like the pesticide DDT, a problem highlighted by Rachel Carson in her 1962 best seller, *Silent Spring*.

Another key player in launching the nation's biodiversity policy grew up in the high country of eastern Arizona, close to where Leopold began his forest career. Stewart Udall, a descendent of Mormon pioneers, represented Arizona in the House from 1955 to 1961, then served as interior secretary under presidents Kennedy and Johnson from 1961 to 1969. (The Udalls have since become a political dynasty in the West: Stewart's brother Mo was an Arizona congressman for three decades and ran for president in 1976; his son Tom is a New Mexico senator; and his nephew Mark is a Colorado senator.) In 1964, Stewart Udall helped convince Congress to pass the Wilderness Act, four decades after Leopold had persuaded the Forest Service to set aside its first wilderness area in New Mexico's Gila National Forest.

Legislation like the Wilderness Act, new national parks, and other federal actions that safeguarded habitat benefitted innumerable species, but they did not directly confront the growing threat of extinction. Wilderness areas were often in the most rugged, high-elevation sections of national forests, where building roads was a challenge and timber resources were meager or nonexistent. This "rock-and-ice" bias wound up protecting gorgeous peaks and alpine meadows covered in snow much of the year—not necessarily jewels of biodiversity. Similarly, national parks were often set aside based on aesthetics, not ecology.

To shield endangered wildlife, Congress enacted two laws, in 1966 and 1969. Neither had any punch. Both acts avoided regulating government projects or private economic activity; the laws also completely ignored plants and insects. The 1966 act authorized the interior secretary to buy important habitat and urged some federal agencies to avoid harming endangered species to the extent it was "practicable." This wording meant species conservation was a matter of convenience, not a federal mandate. Udall's office published a list of 36 birds, 22 fish, 14 mammals, and 6 reptiles and amphibians that were "threatened with extinction." The 1966 act, however, didn't make it illegal to injure, kill, or traffic in those animals.

The 1969 law expanded habitat acquisition and prohibited the importation of imperiled wildlife from around the world. But federal agencies still had no duty to protect declining species, let alone recover them. The weak language in the act led President Richard Nixon to say in 1972 that existing legislation "simply does not provide the kind of management tools needed to act early enough to save a vanishing species." As a Republican, Nixon would seem an unlikely advocate for environmental legislation, but support for those measures offered Nixon a chance to burnish his credentials among voters outside his conservative base. Within a few years of the first Earth Day in 1970, the federal government had adopted a wave of green legislation that remains unsurpassed in American or world history: the ESA, Clean Air Act, Safe Drinking Water Act, Occupational Safety and Health Act, National Environmental Policy Act, Marine Mammal Protection Act, Federal Insecticide, Fungicide and Rodenticide Act, and an early version of the Clean Water Act.

Congress passed the ESA in December 1973 with a near unanimity that is shocking given today's polarization over the law. In hindsight, it appears that many legislators didn't know what they were getting into and simply saw the ESA as a feel-good measure that would please some constituents and impose few costs on society. "Commercial interests did not testify in either House or Senate hearings," social scientist Steven Yaffee noted in his 1982 book, *Prohibitive Policy*. "In fact there was very little opposition to the major concepts of the bills because they did not threaten any readily identifiable interests." Only four votes were cast against the final bill in the House of Representatives. Zero were in the Senate, where the ESA earned support from future critics, including Alaska's Ted Stevens and North Carolina's Jesse Helms. The press and the country at large barely noticed the ESA's passage. In *The New York Times*, the ESA's adoption was given the same prominence as a new law providing nursing homes with mortgage insurance and fire safety equipment. The *Los Angeles Times* gave the ESA's approval one sentence.

The ESA was subsequently changed by three sets of amendments— some of them curtailing the law's reach, others making it more flexible— but most of the act's essential provisions were enacted on the first run, in 1973. Congress declared that various species had already gone extinct because of untempered development and predicted that more species would join them unless the nation took action. In the purpose section of the ESA, Congress stated its desire to conserve "the ecosystems upon which endangered species and threatened species depend," an intention that would later be ignored by critics who claimed the law was somehow supposed to focus on critters without also addressing threats to their habitat. The architecture of the statute was simple enough: identify troubled species and their habitat, forbid the government and private sector from pushing those species closer to extinction, devise a plan for recovering their numbers, and only allow species to be harmed or killed under special circumstances.

The ESA amounted to a huge leap forward in biodiversity protection because it widened the government's focus from fish and wildlife to include plants, insects, and other less charismatic species. It was finally illegal to "take" an endangered species; that is, to "harass, harm, pursue, hunt, shoot, wound, kill, trap, capture, or collect, or to attempt to engage in any such conduct."(*Take* is unrelated to *takings*, another term common in environmental debates that refers to the government's Fifth Amendment power to expropriate private property without the owner's consent if it provides "just compensation.") In contrast to earlier legislation—and in line with Leopold's thinking—the ESA also expanded the government's authority to include species that were at risk of disappearing from large portions of their historic range, not just those facing worldwide extinction.

The ESA now runs about 22,000 words, a quarter the size of the Clean Water Act and one-seventh as long as the Clean Air Act, but the law's power and controversy center on a handful of words and phrases like *take*. Section 3, which methodically lays out the definitions of terms used in the act, is perhaps the most important passage and remains the source of much legal wrangling—and billable hours. After all, biologists usually don't have a bright-line rule for determining when a plant or animal becomes endangered, and nature rarely separates out species with the black-and-white precision lawyers might prefer. The ESA says a species is endangered if it is "in danger of extinction throughout all or a significant portion of its range," though it does exclude insect pests that "would present an overwhelming and overriding risk to man." Threatened species are those that are likely to become endangered "within the foreseeable future." The distinction is a fine one because threatened species typically receive the same protections as those that are endangered, leading many policymakers and land managers to speak of "T and E species" in one breath or use the term *endangered species* to cover all plants and animals protected by the act. The ESA defines *species* broadly to include subspecies, which make up one-fifth of listed plants and animals, plus special populations of animals that are isolated or unique, known as "distinct population segments," which make up 6 percent of the list. This expansive definition of *species* is critical: it forces the government to restore gray wolves in Arizona, even though there is an abundance of similar animals in Alaska. Biologists generally prefer this approach because it protects the unique evolution that occurs in isolated populations, a process that can give rise to entirely new subspecies or species, as Leopold noted with the desert wolf. Distinct populations are also a major driver of the genetic diversity that has allowed species to survive past episodes of climate change.

Passage of the ESA suggested that Americans wanted to atone for past sins and recover species they had nearly driven extinct. Many had followed the U-turn in Leopold's thinking about the wolf. The nation would go on to lap up Kevin Costner's *Dances with Wolves*, purchase maudlin nature films set to New Age music, and, at the extreme, paint romanticized portraits of the wolf as a cute doglike friend to us all. The pendulum has probably swung too far in the other direction, for many people today ignore some inconvenient facts about wolves: they have, on very rare occasions, attacked people, killed livestock for no apparent reason, and devoured their own young. Still, in the space of a few decades, the American public recognized it was losing irreplaceable parts of its national heritage and it began embracing elements of creation—predators, deserts, wildfires—that had long been demonized. California condors, once shot for fun and despised for their association with dead animals, were now featured on television shows and magazine covers.

With the condor, the wolf, and most other endangered species, our attitudes did not change until we had pushed scores of animals to the brink—and sometimes right over the edge—by hunting them, poisoning their food, and destroying their homes. By the time the ESA became law in 1973, there were only 60 California condors left in the wild. Three years before the law's passage, the last known Mexican gray wolf north of the border was shot near Alpine, Texas. A wolf also may have been killed in 1976 near Aravaipa Canyon, a riparian oasis north of Tucson.

Perhaps that lobo had come up from Mexico and sought refuge where he knew he could find water year-round. Either way, when the ESA became law, the United States had succeeded in its quest to remove an emblem of the frontier that Leopold had helped settle, then tried to save. Long ago, the wolf was probably the most widespread mammal in North America, numbering in the hundreds of thousands and found everywhere except the rain forests and most arid deserts that could not support its natural prey: deer, elk, bison, moose, and other ungulates. Now wolves were essentially gone from the lower 48, except for the handful of animals that ranged into northern Minnesota and those that lived on Isle Royale National Park in Lake Superior. To recover the wolf and other species, the government would need to go to extraordinary lengths. When those efforts came up short, it would often say more about the efficiency of our past attacks on wildlife than the effectiveness of legislation belatedly created to undo our mistakes.

———————

Without realizing it, many members of Congress had voted for a law with very strict rules for protecting and recovering imperiled species. But it would take a dam and a tiny fish in another biodiversity hot spot, southern Appalachia, to determine whether the ESA was really the 700-pound gorilla of environmental law, or merely a paper tiger.

The conflict was born on August 12, 1973, about four months before the ESA's passage, when University of Tennessee zoologist David Etnier discovered a three-inch fish he didn't recognize while snorkeling in the Little Tennessee River. A few miles downstream, a 3,228-foot-long earthen embankment called Tellico Dam had been under construction for the past six years and was nearly complete. A bystander noticed Etnier emerging from the river. "Wha'cha got?" he asked. "Mister," Etnier replied, "this is the fish that will stop Tellico Dam."

Etnier and his students determined the fish was an undiscovered species that might soon be extinct. When the floodgates closed on the Tennessee Valley Authority's Tellico Dam, the upstream riverbed would be buried by silt and the only known population of snail darters would be destroyed. Dam opponents took advantage of a key provision in the ESA that allows anyone to petition the government to protect a species, then used another important lever in the law, a citizen enforcement provision, to file suit to stop Tellico's completion. After opponents' successful appeal at the circuit court level, the Supreme Court agreed to hear the case, *TVA v. Hill*, in 1978. At the time, Tellico Dam was 90 percent complete and the federal government had spent more than $100 million on the project.

The Carter administration was divided on the case. One of its departments, Fish and Wildlife, wanted to kill a major project sponsored by another federal agency, the TVA. In an unusual move, Attorney General Griffin Bell argued on behalf of the TVA. During his oral argument before the Supreme Court, Bell produced a vial containing a dead snail darter. He had the justices pass it among themselves so they could inspect what all the fuss was about. It was absurd, Bell said, to let such an insignificant creature stop such a massive public works project. That was the emotional argument. On legal grounds, the TVA believed Tellico Dam should be grandfathered in because the construction was half done when the ESA became law in 1973. The TVA also said Congress's continued funding for the project after the ESA's passage constituted an implied repeal of the act, at least as it applied to Tellico Dam. Speaking on behalf of the snail darter was University of Tennessee law professor Zygmunt Plater. The appellant, Hiram Hill Jr., was a student of Plater's and one of the people who petitioned Fish and Wildlife to list the snail darter.

On June 15, 1978, the Supreme Court returned its verdict and enshrined the ESA as one of the nation's most powerful laws. Chief Justice Warren Burger, writing for the 6–3 majority, acknowledged that it "may seem curious to some that the survival of a relatively small number of three-inch fish among all the countless millions of species extant would require the permanent halting of a virtually completed dam for which Congress has expended more than $100 million." But the ESA's wording "admits of no exception," Burger wrote, and an examination of the act's language, structure, and legislative history "indicates beyond doubt that Congress intended endangered species to be afforded the highest of priorities." The congressional debate in 1973 was "replete with expressions of concern over the risk that might lie in the loss of any endangered species," Burger wrote, citing an assistant interior secretary's congressional testimony on the South's mollusks, which include the snails that snail darters eat:

> It is often asked of me, "What is the importance of the mollusks for example in Alabama." I do not know, and I do not know whether any of us will ever have the insight to know exactly why these mollusks

evolved over millions of years or what their importance is in the total ecosystem. However, I have great trouble being a party to their destruction without ever having gained such knowledge.

Congress "viewed the value of endangered species as 'incalculable,'" Burger wrote. "The plain intent of Congress in enacting this statute was to halt and reverse the trend toward species extinction, whatever the cost."

For the dissenting justices, Lewis Powell Jr., Harry Blackmun, and William Rehnquist, assigning infinite value to endangered species was preposterous and a threat to the nation's prosperity. "This decision casts a long shadow over the operation of even the most important projects, serving vital needs of society and national defense," Powell wrote. "I cannot believe that Congress would have gone this far to imperil every federal project, however important, on behalf of any living species however unimportant, without a clear declaration of that intention." Justice Powell invited Congress to amend the ESA, predicting that few of its members would ever defend legislation that "requires a waste of at least $53 million."

The lawmakers took Powell's advice to heart. Shortly after the Supreme Court decision, Congress expressed buyers' remorse by amending the ESA, just five years after it had created the law. The amendments, the first in a series of legislative and administrative changes to the ESA over the next three decades, weakened the government's obligation to protect species, let economics help decide which habitats to protect, and created a major loophole: a cabinet-level seven-member committee that could exempt projects from complying with the ESA. Because this group could, in essence, bless extinction, it became known as the God Squad. To everyone's surprise, when the God Squad convened for the first time to evaluate the dam versus darter debate, the panel voted unanimously against the TVA, citing Tellico's lousy cost-benefit ratio. "Here is a project that is 95 percent complete," said God Squad member Charles Schultze, chairman of the Council of Economic Advisers, "and if one takes just the cost of finishing it against the benefits, and does it properly, it doesn't pay, which says something about the original design."

After the God Squad failed to approve Tellico Dam, Congress sought to complete the project by legislative fiat. The House snuck a provision into a spending bill that exempted the dam from the ESA and all other federal laws (a young Democratic Congressman from Tennessee named

Al Gore supported the move). The Senate eventually passed the spending bill with the ESA rider, 48–44, so the legislation headed to the desk of President Jimmy Carter. Many expected a veto from the Democratic president, but Carter, in need of congressional support for the Panama Canal Treaty, chose to sign the bill in September 1979. Three months later, Tellico Dam was complete and the snail darter's habitat began to disappear under 80 feet of water.

The Supreme Court may have upheld the ESA's power in *TVA v. Hill*, but the congressional end run around the ruling provided an early and enduring lesson about the nation's biodiversity policy: in high-stakes conflicts between humans and endangered species, people would always hold the trump card. While Leopold and his disciples had revolutionized how we think about nature and cultivated the environmental consciousness that engendered the ESA, the more progressive outlook and the pioneering legislation would continue to be constrained by political realities. Plenty of Americans still didn't give a hoot about biodiversity and enforcement of the ESA was often lax, particularly if protection of a species conflicted with human needs or desires.

The snail darter controversy was the perfect embodiment of a David versus Goliath battle between a diminutive species and an expensive construction project, but it wouldn't be the last. As the fight over Tellico Dam faded in the early 1980s, another conflict was heating up atop southern Arizona's tallest peak, Mt. Graham, where the needs of a squirrel were beginning to clash with an unlikely adversary: astronomers.

3
Scopes versus Squirrels

The Endangered Species Act, which protects isolated populations even of unthreatened species, often attracts intense opposition from those whose economic interests are imperiled, as in the cases of the snail darter and the spotted owl. To invoke this helpful act in frivolous causes is to invite its demise.

—Editorial in *The New York Times*, May 29, 1990

Imagine that the earth's 4.5-billion-year existence took place in a single year. In this highly compressed version of history, the end of the last ice age, about 12,000 years ago, would occur one minute before midnight on December 31. At this moment in our very recent past, when condors were feasting on the carcasses of North American elephants and ice still covered much of Canada, the topography of southeastern Arizona had the same contours it has today. A dozen or so isolated mountain ranges jutted into the sky and were surrounded by broad valleys. These flatlands, now home to cacti and creosote, held shallow lakes lined with spruce, fir, pine, and aspen.

The squirrels that lived in these ice age forests had barely changed in appearance for several million years, leading modern biologists to call them living fossils, a moniker also applied to the California condor. One type of tree squirrel with a hint of red in its coat scampered around the forest floor, perpetually searching for food to support its hyperactive metabolism and a heart beating hundreds of times per minute. The eight-ounce squirrel scurried into the branches above to rip the scales off the cones of the coniferous trees, spinning them like cobs of corn in order to devour the calorie-rich seeds within.

As the planet warmed up, the vegetation in southeastern Arizona migrated both poleward and skyward, just like the glaciers and ice sheets. Spruce and fir trees that were once able to survive in valleys only found a suitable combination of temperature and rainfall at the very top of the tallest mountains. As the vegetation shifted, so did the squirrels. Once able to roam across much of the region, the red squirrels in Arizona and New Mexico found themselves stranded atop a handful of ranges like shipwrecked sailors. Unable to cross the intervening desert seas, the squirrels reproduced and evolved in isolation on these forested sky islands, their appearance and DNA drifting away from the form and genetic makeup of squirrels that lived nearby. Thousands of years later, the divergence in the beaks of finches living on another set of islands, the Galápagos, would help Charles Darwin and others develop the theory of natural selection that guides modern biology.

The only sky island in southeastern Arizona with any red squirrels left is the Pinaleño Mountains, which reach 10,720-feet atop Mt. Graham. Situated about 75 miles northeast of Tucson and shooting up nearly 7,000 feet from the desert in the space of a few miles, Mt. Graham is a paragon of biodiversity. This one mountain, about 10 miles wide and 25 miles long, is home to some 900 types of plants, several found nowhere else, and it is thought to have a richer collection of species than any similarly sized range in North America.

Biologists aren't the only scientists who prize Mt. Graham. It is equally important to astronomers because it is one of the better places on the planet to position a telescope. The rarefied air above Mt. Graham's summit is relatively free of dust, clouds, and water vapor, affording astronomers a sparkling view of the heavens. Similar conditions are found elsewhere on mountaintops in the Southwest, Hawaii, and northern Chile's Atacama Desert, but many prospective sites are either too snowy, spoiled by light pollution, too far from civilization, not open to development, or so high that astronomers would need to wear oxygen masks.

In the early 1980s, a consortium of astronomers led by the University of Arizona's Steward Observatory and the Smithsonian Institution began to zero in on Mt. Graham as they searched for a location to build the first in a new class of telescopes, instruments able to peer so deep into the universe and so far back in time that scientists could nearly see the Big Bang. It looked like Mt. Graham fit the bill. The mountain, part of the Coronado National Forest and surrounded by vacant public land, was still topped by dark skies and it only took three hours to drive from the UA campus to the summit on an existing road that was paved almost the whole way. Other sky islands in southeastern Arizona, most managed by the Forest Service under the multiple-use doctrine, already had their own observatories, so UA officials felt they had precedent on their side in selecting Mt. Graham as the home for the new telescope complex. The $200 million project promised to solidify the school's position as a global leader in astronomy, bolster Tucson's bid to become "Optics Valley," and help scientists better understand the birth of galaxies, stars, planets, even life itself. The centerpiece would be the Large Binocular Telescope, or LBT. More powerful than the orbiting Hubble Space Telescope, the LBT would be equipped with a pair of 27.6-foot-wide mirrors fashioned in a lab beneath the bleachers of UA's football stadium. The mirrors would be buffed so precisely by a computer-guided disc that if the surface were as wide as the United States, the biggest imperfection would be less than an inch tall.

UA astronomers began to lay the groundwork for the LBT by performing optical tests on Mt. Graham. At the same time, state and federal biologists were conducting wildlife surveys atop the range, in part to determine if any species deserved to be listed under the ESA. The results of these two inquiries put the telescopes and the squirrels on a collision course and drove a wedge between most of the school's astronomers and nearly all of the region's environmentalists, two groups that put faith in science, believed in conserving dark skies, and tended to be liberal in their politics. In 1982, Fish and Wildlife ruled that the red squirrel, thought to have gone extinct in the 1960s, might deserve federal listing, pending further studies. Two years later, UA submitted a proposal to the Forest Service to build up to 18 instruments atop Mt. Graham. By 1985, biologists estimated there were only around 300 red squirrels left on Mt. Graham, leading the Arizona Game and Fish Department to recommend that the federal government declare the squirrels as endangered. After lengthy delays, and under the threat of litigation, Fish and Wildlife finally listed the squirrel in June 1987.

As soon as the squirrel gained federal protection, the telescopes faced scrutiny under the ESA. When Congress passed the law in 1973, it said that any project connected to the federal government must be reviewed for its impact on endangered species. Federal agencies are generally forbidden from taking actions that are "likely to jeopardize the continued existence" of a listed species or that cause the "destruction or adverse modification" of a species' "critical habitat," which the ESA defines as areas essential for a plant or animal's conservation. Virtually anything done on federal land, which constitutes nearly a third of the nation and the majority of some western states, must therefore pass through the ESA's filter. Since UA was seeking to build telescopes in the Coronado National Forest, the Forest Service would have to consult with Fish and Wildlife to determine the project's impact on the red squirrel.

ESA consultations extend far beyond national forests and other federal lands. Projects that have the barest of connections to the US government—a so-called federal nexus—are also evaluated for their effects on endangered species, even if they're on nonfederal land and even if they're carried out by a state government or private party. A developer who intends to build a shopping mall on a piece of private land may still have to tangle with the ESA if the work involves any federal funding, loans, or permits. Such connections to the federal government are surprisingly common and sometimes counterintuitive: until recently, filling in a sandy wash in the Arizona desert that only flows with water a few times a year required a Clean Water Act permit from the US Army Corps of Engineers and therefore generated the federal nexus.

"Consultation" may sound innocuous, but it can significantly modify a project, or block it outright, although in practice neither outcome is likely. It gives managers and biologists in the civil service the rather exceptional power to require multimillion-dollar changes, and subjects those decisions to intense political pressure. Developers and landowners tend to hate the process because even a positive outcome may entail costly delays. Since 1973, hundreds of thousands of projects have triggered consultations, but studies have found that more than 95 percent are resolved informally and virtually none stop a project in its tracks. Politicians and journalists, of course, focus almost exclusively on the tiny fraction of consultations that produce dramatic story lines, such as the snail darter versus Tellico Dam and the squirrels versus the scopes.

By the time Fish and Wildlife began its Mt. Graham consultation, UA had already scaled back its proposal to seven telescopes atop the range's two tallest peaks: Emerald and High. Even this more modest proposal troubled Fish and Wildlife's biologists because the squirrel had such little spruce-fir habitat to begin with, maybe 2,000 acres. Fish and Wildlife concluded that the tree-cutting needed to clear the telescope sites and the increased, year-round human activity atop Mt. Graham would jeopardize the squirrel's continued existence. As required by the ESA, Fish and Wildlife issued a draft biological opinion in August 1987. It offered the Forest Service and UA two "reasonable and prudent alternatives": move the project off the mountain entirely or restrict it to a relatively degraded portion of High Peak, leaving the more pristine Emerald Peak untouched.

Fish and Wildlife's alternatives didn't sound reasonable or prudent to UA officials, so they lobbied the regional directors of Fish and Wildlife and the Forest Service to come up with something better. It worked. In June 1988, Fish and Wildlife biologist Leslie Fitzpatrick was ordered by her supervisors to create a third alternative: allow three telescopes to be built on 8.6 acres of Emerald Peak, a site that Fitzpatrick and other government biologists had said couldn't withstand *any* new development. Their draft biological opinion had concluded the squirrel was in such jeopardy that "the loss of even a few acres could be critical to the survival and recovery of this species." Although the footprint of the three telescopes was only 8.6 acres, biologists estimated that a total of 47 acres of squirrel habitat would be rendered unsuitable by the logging since the forest adjoining the clearing would become too dry and open. The third alternative did offer some concessions to environmentalists (and the squirrels). UA was required to fund an extensive monitoring program. The Forest Service would bar the public from the upper reaches of Mt. Graham and reforest a road leading up to High Peak, though return of mature spruce and fir trees could take centuries.

After the biological opinion was rewritten to satisfy UA's demands, environmentalists cried foul. It appeared that Fish and Wildlife had violated the ESA, and a congressional inquiry ensued. When investigators with the nonpartisan Government Accounting Office (now Government Accountability Office) looked into the allegations of political interference, they found solid proof it had occurred. Fitzpatrick told the GAO that her supervisor gave her an ultimatum: if the biological opinion didn't include a third alternative that allowed for telescopes on Emerald Peak, the document would be prepared by another office. "In a biologically based biological opinion," Fitzpatrick would later tell Congress, "the Emerald Peak alternative would not have appeared."

The science seemed stacked against the scopes. But Fish and Wildlife Regional Director Michael Spear admitted to the GAO that he had considered nonbiological factors, including the need to make an expeditious decision, pressure from UA officials, his belief the school would probably win in court, and his favorable view of the telescopes' scientific value. Spear's own interpretation of the ESA was that officials must try "to devise compromises that accommodate both needed projects and endangered species." As a political matter, that may have been true, but on legal grounds Spear was subverting the ESA.

By the time the GAO's report appeared, in June 1990, construction on Emerald Peak looked like a fait accompli. Two years before, UA officials decided that Congress should write the project into law rather than have it dissected by more biological studies. To convince lawmakers to go along with the plan, UA paid more than $1 million to the swank DC lobbying firm of Patton, Boggs and Blow. Then Arizona lawmakers tacked a special provision sanctioning the Mt. Graham project onto a land-exchange bill known as the Arizona-Idaho Conservation Act. The Mt. Graham rider passed a week after it was introduced, on the last day of the 100th Congress, without any public hearings.

UA won a legislative victory by colluding with top officials in Congress, the Forest Service, and Fish and Wildlife. But the strong-arm tactics enraged many on campus, and the school's seeming disregard for the rule of law hardened opponents' resolve to stop the project by any means necessary. Just a few weeks before the rider passed, in 1988, Tucsonan Dave Foreman, a founder of Earth First!, vowed that like-minded activists would destroy the telescopes. "There are people who are prepared to make them put the scopes up there several times—which means a telescope doesn't see the stars very well if its mirror is broken," he told Jim Erickson of the *Arizona Daily Star.* "It's certainly not something I would do myself, but anybody with any sense has to realize that's something that will happen." Foreman's threat was taken seriously because he had recently written a manual on sabotage titled *Ecodefense: A Field Guide to Monkeywrenching.* The 185-page illustrated manual, a sort of do-it-yourself companion to Edward Abbey's *Monkey Wrench Gang,* teaches readers how to make stink bombs, destroy billboards, and spike trees with metal that could ruin saws and potentially injure lumberjacks. The book also advised embedding trees with ceramic rods to avoid metal detectors, though the practice of tree-spiking was renounced in 1990 by Earth First! leaders protesting logging of redwood forests in Northern California.

Earth First! may not have spiked trees on Mt. Graham, but they and other antiscope activists tried just about everything else to impede the construction and make UA astronomers' lives miserable. They mailed a dead squirrel (though not an endangered one) to the director of the Steward Observatory. They plastered the campus with No Scopes bumper stickers. They stormed the UA administration building and fought with police clad in riot gear. They locked themselves to cattle guards in the road that corkscrews up Mt. Graham. They camped out in trees slated for cutting. They put an abrasive compound inside the motors of a snowblower and front-end loader. And they robbed $20,000 worth of electronic equipment from the mountain. The Tucson Police Department tried to infiltrate Earth First! with an agent provocateur, but the instigator blew his own cover during a 1992 Columbus Day protest on campus. After the portly policeman-*cum*-protestor and his ostensible allies charged into the offices of the Steward Observatory, the cop-in-disguise accidentally dropped his pistol on the floor. Realizing his cover was blown, the mole flashed his badge and slunk out of the building. When it came time for the UA to truck a $1 million mirror from the campus to Mt. Graham for installation in a smaller telescope, the highway patrol had to provide an armed escort and close the overpasses on I-10 so saboteurs couldn't use them as platforms for launching attacks. During a subsequent Earth First! rally on the mountain, the state Department of Public Safety deployed a phalanx of 96 officers wearing helmets and shields to defend the two telescopes that had already been built.

Environmental activists also united with Native Americans who opposed the project. Some Apache Indians said Mt. Graham was sacred to them and described the telescopes as blasphemous. Franklin Stanley, a spiritual leader of the San Carlos Apaches, equated the mountain with an altar and said UA's project was akin to "taking an arm and a leg off" his tribe. The Apaches' complaints opened up new avenues for litigation and added an air of cultural imperialism to UA's plans, but according to some experts, the claims of the indigenous activists were disingenuous. Charles Polzen, curator of ethnohistory at the Arizona State Museum in Tucson, argued that "the mountain itself was subject to only the most casual and ephemeral use by the tribe." "The reality," Polzen wrote, "is that no Apache bothered to take up this cause until non-Indians coaxed certain long-term political dissidents to block construction of the telescope."

The civil disobedience by Earth First! made for engaging political theater and exciting newspaper copy. But it probably backfired by making the public even less sympathetic toward the ESA and activists' goals atop Mt. Graham. As the controversy was raging, a 1987 poll of Tucson-area registered voters found that 62 percent supported construction of the telescopes, but a majority didn't want to see any logging or a ski resort atop Mt. Graham. Nine years later, when the LBT's construction was stalled by litigation, another survey found that about three-quarters of Tucsonans favored completion of the project.

The Mt. Graham fight drew attention from national media, and the coverage that followed sometimes played into the hands of ESA detractors at a time when the act was under assault. In February 1990, when the northern spotted owl was proposed for listing and preemptive logging restrictions were already roiling the Pacific Northwest, the first President Bush's interior secretary, Manuel Lujan Jr., responded to the Mt. Graham controversy by asking, "Do we have to save every subspecies?" "The red squirrel is the best example," Lujan told a *Denver Post* reporter. "Nobody's told me the difference between a red squirrel, a black one or a brown one." Describing the ESA as "too tough," Lujan sought to include more economic considerations in endangered-species policy making and encouraged Congress to weaken the law. Lujan's skeptical view of subspecies protection threatened to sharply curtail the ESA's reach because one-quarter of the plants and animals protected by the law aren't full-fledged species.

To telescope opponents, the battle on Mt. Graham exemplified how political appointees were doing the bidding of moneyed interests. But to ESA critics and many opinion leaders, the fight illustrated how endangered species were being used as surrogates to carry out a left-wing agenda. Following Lujan's broadside against the ESA, the liberal editorial page of *The New York Times* said environmentalists opposing the Mt. Graham telescopes were on the "wrong side of a silly debate" and jeopardizing the ESA itself by focusing on a population that wasn't a distinct species. "There is an unattractive absolutism in the environmentalists' arguments," *The Times* said. Six days earlier, the conservative *Wall Street Journal* had cited activists' "holy war on Arizona's Mt. Graham" as an example of the ESA's excesses. "The law shouldn't make absolute protection a form of worship if the same animals are found elsewhere, have many subspecies or can be relocated," *The Journal* said.

Telescope opponents were right that bureaucrats had gone against biologists in approving the construction on Emerald Peak, and they were justifiably outraged that Congress had circumvented the ESA. But as the critics' rhetoric grew more strident, the practical needs of the squirrel were sometimes subsumed to a messianic campaign against the telescopes and their sponsors. "It's not biology," one UA graduate student and squirrel expert said about her fellow telescope opponents when interviewed by *The New York Times* in 1990. "It's esthetics. They're tired of all these white things on the tops of mountains. Pretty much the only legal way they've got to save an area from development is to find an endangered species and it looks like they've got one."

The struggle atop Mt. Graham would influence a generation of conservationists in the Southwest. Many future leaders of environmental groups in the region cut their eyeteeth defending the red squirrel, sometimes while allied with Earth First! The controversy also taught practitioners of conservation biology, an emerging field described as a "crisis discipline" by one its founders, Michael Soulé, that ignoring the political environment could render their science academic. Writing in the journal *Conservation Biology* in 1994, Peter Warshall, the UA scientist in charge of the Mt. Graham environmental impact statement, argued that "good conservation biologists must be part lawyer, part teacher, and part biogladiator as well as scientist." To be a biogladiator, however, scientists would have to risk their credibility and open themselves up to prickly questions: Was their work really objective, or instead carried out with an agenda that obscured the truth? Even without committing fraud, were biologists abiding by the scientific method if they had a stake in the outcome, financial or otherwise? Could you study an esoteric creature for years and not become an advocate for its protection, especially when federal listing would boost funding opportunities?

UA astronomers weren't the only scientists who felt that Mt. Graham's squirrels could do fine with telescopes in their midst. At least a few biologists thought the plan Congress mandated provided a net benefit for Mt. Graham's red squirrels. One of those scientists was Conrad Istock, chairman of UA's Department of Ecology and Evolutionary Biology. To Istock, who received a death threat in the mail in return for supporting the telescope project, the squirrel certainly exemplified the ecological costs of human development. Inherently at risk due to its isolation on a single mountain, the subspecies had also suffered from decades of logging, grazing, camping, snowmobiling, road construction, cabin building, Christmas tree cutting, and even legal hunting until 1986. Still, Istock argued, for a species that had already survived the destruction of some 12,000 acres of its habitat, the loss of a few more acres to the telescopes was a minor insult, especially since the project was predicated on a number of conservation measures. There would never again be timber sales on the mountain. The Forest Service would cancel plans to build recreational sites and communications towers. And the public would be kept out of a 1,700-acre squirrel refuge around Mt. Graham's summit. The upshot, according to Istock, was that Mt. Graham had "greater protection, and a more concerted effort at ecosystem restoration, than any of the other Southwestern mountain islands."

Mt. Graham's red squirrels would need all the help they could get, because their home was starting to change in subtle yet significant ways that had nothing to do with the telescopes. In the early 1990s, a cascade of insect infestations began to ravage the forests around the telescope site, setting them up for a potentially catastrophic wildfire. An inferno could fulfill the prophecy emblazoned on a popular Earth First! bumper sticker: Nature bats last. Given the history of sabotage on the mountain, an activist might even load up the bases for Mother Nature by setting fire to the forest. Whether ignited by lightning or an extremist, a wildfire would not only threaten UA's $200 million telescopes; it would also jeopardize the remaining red squirrels atop Mt. Graham.

4
Take Me to the River

Hush little baby, don't you cry
When we get to Tucson, you'll see why
We left the snowstorms, and the thunder and rain
For the desert sun, we're gonna be born again

—"Thumbelina," The Pretenders

The first time I saw Mt. Graham was through the windshield of my white Toyota Camry station wagon. It was Memorial Day 1995, and I was heading west toward Tucson and a new life. I didn't know Graham's name. I didn't realize there was a lush spruce-fir forest at its top. And

I didn't have the slightest inkling about the tortuous politics that had swirled around the summit in the preceding decade. But I did know that mountain was one of the more imposing pieces of topography I had ever seen. As I sped toward Tucson on I-10, accompanied by all the possessions I could cram in the car for my cross-country journey from Long Island, I vowed to reach the apex of that anonymous mountain some day.

It was a cloudless morning and the blazing sun in my rearview mirror made the sky islands before me look tack sharp, as if I'd put in stronger contact lenses. Seeing the greenery atop the mountains lifted my spirits, which had been in decline since I left Abilene, Texas, the morning before. West of the 100th meridian, the world appeared increasingly brown, dry—and dead. The view of El Paso from the interstate was less than inspirational and left me wondering whether I was making a big mistake by moving to the Southwest.

I spent my final night on the road in a Motel 6 situated amid alkali flats in Lordsburg, New Mexico, a windswept pit stop with three exits: East Motel Drive, Main Street, and West Motel Drive. The roar of the big rigs, the yelping of their air brakes, and the high beams scanning my room like searchlights made for a fitful night of sleep, even though I was fried after more than 600 miles of monotonous interstate driving. When I stepped outside in the morning, ready to make the final push for Tucson, I was stunned by the heat. It was the coolest part of the day, and not even summer yet. Driving by Mt. Graham, the stereo and air conditioner on full blast, I put my hand to the closed window and found it hot to the touch.

The heat made the desert seem intimidating and uninhabitable, but there was also something attracting me to that stark landscape. From my vantage in the valley bottoms, it looked like the desert winds had sandblasted the vegetation right off the mountains, except for their tallest reaches. The exposed geology offered a window into essential forces—air, water, fire—that shaped the earth in deep time. It felt like appropriate scenery for self-examination, a setting that would inspire me to look inside, clear back the underbrush of my upbringing, and reveal the core within.

By the time I reached Tucson, after four days of driving alone, my mind was mush from self-analysis and repeat plays of all my cassettes, especially *Nirvana Unplugged*, its stripped-down acoustic versions of the grunge rock a hollow echo of the days behind me. I took the exit for Speedway Boulevard, which I remembered from my visit to Tucson the month before. I had been scouting for a fun place to live out West with

Tim, a buddy from Yale who came from a big Mormon family in Utah but was guided more by LSD than the LDS Church. Tim had bailed on the plan to move out West, so I was going solo, and Tucson now looked a lot less appealing as I projected my anxiety onto a pedestrian procession of billboards, strip malls, convenience stores, and fast food joints that was downright hostile to pedestrians. I checked into a motel and my room was like a sauna when I walked in, so I set out on foot to explore Tucson. My East Coast mind told me you could walk around a city, surely one with a fraction of New York's population. But after 10 minutes I still hadn't reached the next major street on my map and I was dying of thirst. I retreated to the motel in disgust. My internal compass—and my expectations about Tucson—needed recalibration.

To get the lay of the land, I drove downtown. It was midafternoon on Memorial Day, so I didn't expect to find much going on there. But I was shocked by just how little life was stirring. Aside from the homeless, there was hardly anyone on the streets. Stores on the main drag were vacant, though there was no shortage of tattoo parlors and taco trucks. I kept driving and ascended A Mountain, a cone-shaped jumble of mahogany boulders that rises just west of downtown. From the top, where University of Arizona students paint a huge *A* on the rocks, I got a commanding overview of Tucson. Now I could see why a metropolitan area with 750,000 people had such a lonely downtown. The development had lurched outward, not upward, following the same growth pattern that shaped Houston, Phoenix, Las Vegas, and other Sun Belt cities. Right before me, there were a handful of minor skyscrapers, and behind them a football stadium and some decent-sized red brick buildings on the UA campus. Beyond that, however, hardly any buildings were taller than a few stories. The thin layer of suburban sprawl extended outward for 10 miles from A Mountain, petered out as the landscape rose on the edges of the valley, and halted at the base of two 9,000-foot mountain ranges that overshadowed the city and were joined at the hip: the Santa Catalinas to the north and the Rincons to the east.

Below me, at the base of A Mountain, there was something resembling a river. But it didn't contain a drop of water. The winding channel, lined with cement, was filled with sand, scraggly bushes, and a few overturned shopping carts. Along the banks were a bunch of vacant lots littered with mounds of dirt and broken bottles glinting in the sun. Here was the Santa Cruz River—or what remained of its course, now emptied of water. I had pictured Tucson as an oasis, but after driving 3,000 miles, it felt like I'd been chasing a mirage.

What Tucson did to the Santa Cruz and the surrounding desert was repeated across the West as cities boomed and car-based development spread out from urban centers, many of which became black holes. Other rivers and streams in the Southwest also died due to the influx of new residents, and the loss of these habitats did as much as anything to threaten the region's biological diversity. About half of the 73 Arizona species that are listed under the ESA or are candidates for listing depend on riparian or aquatic habitat. The harm to fish and frogs is only the most obvious impact. In deserts, habitat that is dense and lush is as rare as running water and vital for most terrestrial species' diet, reproduction, and other essential behaviors. Riparian habitat covers less than 1 percent of the Southwest, but it supports more breeding bird species than all of the West's other habitats combined. Even outside arid and semiarid regions, freshwater habitat is rich with life: nearly one-third of all vertebrate species are confined to these areas. To the detriment of wildlife around the globe, these natural meccas for biodiversity have always been the real estate most prized by humans. The competition for water has, by and large, ended with humans on top and native species left high and dry. Riparian areas are now considered the most altered habitat type on the planet. In North America, at least 61 freshwater fish are presumed extinct, and nearly 40 percent of the rest are considered imperiled. By the time the ESA was enacted, most of the Southwest's riparian habitat had been damaged or destroyed due to dams, ditches, wells, chain saws, bulldozers, cattle, and cement. Cottonwood-willow forests, home to the greatest number of bird species in North America outside tropical rain forests, became the continent's rarest type of woodland.

The first Anglos to lay eyes on the Santa Cruz saw water in the river and were probably in a party led by Eusebio Francisco Kino, a Jesuit priest, cartographer, and astronomer. Born in Italy in 1645, Father Kino set sail for the New World in January 1681; he spent the next decade exploring and mapping unknown reaches of Spain's empire as he traveled by horseback across thousands of square miles of *La Pimeria Alta*, the high country of the Pima Indians.

Riding north in 1690 in what would become the Mexican state of Sonora, Kino met up with the Santa Cruz. The river was more of a stream and had already traveled about 30 miles from its spring-fed source in a broad, grassy valley just north of the future border. Shallow and marshy, the Santa Cruz would only occasionally swell with runoff after monsoon cloudbursts or winter rains dumped water on the impermeable desert surrounding the river. As the Santa Cruz made a giant U-turn below the border and headed north, it would sometimes disappear entirely into the desert sands, only to reappear downstream where the underlying geology forced its waters to the surface. Even where the flow remained subterranean, the Santa Cruz supported a strip of dense riparian forest. The trees survived by tapping the aquifer below, a massive reservoir of groundwater that had accumulated during the Pleistocene ice ages.

As Kino followed the Santa Cruz north, he established a string of missions along the river, including Tumacácori and San Xavier del Bac in modern-day Arizona. In 1692, he rode into a Pima settlement about 60 miles north of the border that was clustered around A Mountain, minus the *A* and the road to the top. The Pimas called their village Chuk Shon, meaning "water at the foot of the black mountain." On a map, Kino labeled the village San Cosme y Damián de Tucson, and the last part stuck.

The Santa Cruz was Chuk Shon's lifeblood. Though fickle in its flow, the river delivered enough water to the base of the black mountain to irrigate fields planted with maize, beans, melons, tobacco, and cotton. The Santa Cruz was reliable enough to continuously support people for at least 3,000 years before Kino arrived, making Tucson one of America's oldest settlements. From 900 to 1300, the Pima's ancestors, the Hohokam, thrived along the Santa Cruz and numbered in the thousands. One hundred miles to the northwest, in a valley where the Salt, Verde, and Gila rivers converged—today's Phoenix—Hohokam villagers irrigated 200,000 acres with 185 miles of canals, some of them 10-feet deep, 30-feet wide, and lined with adobe to reduce water lost to seepage.

By 1500, the Hohokam were all but extinct, the latest victims in a series of societal collapses in the Southwest that included the disappearance of New Mexico's Mimbres culture and the abandonment of Colorado's Mesa Verde site. In the Pima language, *Hohokam* means "that which has vanished," "those who came before," or perhaps most fittingly, "all used up." The reasons for the fall of these cultures are still debated by scholars, but much of the evidence points to a changing climate and environmental degradation, including soil erosion, deforestation, increasing salinity of cropland due to irrigation, and two megadroughts in the 13th and 15th centuries. Long after the Hohokam's fall, the Santa Cruz Valley remained sparsely populated. When Kino arrived in Chuk Shon in 1692, there were no more than a few hundred souls at the base of A Mountain.

Setting out from Chuk Shon, Kino followed the Santa Cruz northwest. Beside the nearby Gila River, he discovered the great ruins at Casa Grande, abandoned by the Hohokam around 1450. Kino would go on to explore and map much of the region, pioneering an important trail westward to California, along the future border and through the hottest, driest section of the Sonoran Desert. The route became known as El Camino del Diablo, "the Devil's Highway." It wasn't any picnic traveling north or east from Tucson. In the high country of the Mogollon Rim and White Mountains, where Leopold would later work as a Forest Service ranger, nomadic bands of Apache warriors repelled settlement for nearly two centuries. In 1849, when gold seekers passed through Tucson on their way to California via El Camino del Diablo, they only found a few hundred inhabitants eking out a living beside the Santa Cruz. "To our regret," a correspondent from New Orleans's *Daily Picayune* wrote, "we found the town old, dilapidated, and the poorest of the poor. There was no such thing as a store in the whole rancho."

Everything changed when a Southern Pacific locomotive arrived in Tucson on March 20, 1880. Once isolated, the town was now linked to both coasts. Silver and copper mines around Bisbee, Tombstone, and Morenci attracted thousands to southern Arizona and turned Tucson into an economic hub. Near downtown, crops lined the Santa Cruz, and much of the riparian forest along the river was cut down for fuel and lumber, yet the river's flow was still voluminous enough to power gristmills and fill artificial lakes stocked with trout.

When the surface flows of the Santa Cruz were exhausted from growing crops and supplying drinking water, settlers used windmills to run pumps and intercept groundwater before it reached the river. Toward the end of the 19th century, steam-powered pumps fueled by the mesquite forests along the Santa Cruz allowed Tucsonans to reach even farther into the earth. With the advent of the internal combustion engine, electricity, and turbine pumps, the wells became ever more powerful. By the middle of the 20th century, a single well could extract more than 1,000 gallons per minute from a depth of several thousand feet.

To understand the hydrological consequences of this groundwater pumping, it helps to imagine the Santa Cruz River Valley as if it were a colossal bowl. The jagged mountaintops surrounding Tucson are like the rim of the bowl, and the city sits atop what's inside: thousands of feet worth of sand, dirt, pebbles, and rocks that washed down from the surrounding peaks—what geologists call alluvium. For eons, raindrops and snowflakes falling atop the Rincons, Santa Catalinas, and nearby Santa Ritas trickled down into the Tucson basin, though much of the water was lost along the way to evaporation or sucked up by plants. The water that reached the valley accumulated in the alluvium, quite slowly during the desert climate that has prevailed for the past 8,000 years and far more rapidly during the preceding ice ages, when piñon-juniper forests covered Tucson and nearby peaks were snowcapped much of the year. The runoff cascading down from the mountains and precipitation falling into the valley itself percolated toward the bottom of the bowl, where a layer of impermeable bedrock blocked its flow. Drip by drip, millennium by millennium, the pool of water at the bottom of the bowl filled the alluvial layers of sand and dirt. On the surface, in a few low-lying sections, the water reached daylight: the places we now know as the Santa Cruz River and its tributaries.

Despite the proliferation of high-powered wells, Tucson's aquifer wasn't immediately at risk of drying up. In an average year, runoff and snowmelt added nearly 50 billion gallons to the aquifer; by one estimate there were 23 trillion gallons of groundwater left beneath the Tucson basin at the start of the 20th century. Because early Tucsonans' wells withdrew so little, the supply of groundwater below them actually grew a bit each year, like interest in a savings account. It didn't take long, however, for Tucson to start tapping into its hydrologic nest egg. By 1940, perhaps even earlier, Tucsonans were pumping more from the earth than nature returned each year. Below the desert, the water table started to sink as ever more straws sucked on the ice age aquifer. Eventually, it fell below the roots of the cottonwood-willow forest. Just a dozen-foot drop in the aquifer could prove fatal. Even the mesquites, which could send taproots more than 75 feet into the earth, died of thirst. By the end of the 1950s, a decade marked by severe drought, the Santa Cruz River near Tucson was practically dead.

Like other western cities, Tucson's population exploded in the postwar era. In the quarter century after World War II, Pima County grew from about 100,000 to 400,000 residents. Year after year, bulldozers bladed the thin layer of desert scrub and spread suburbia across the

Tucson basin with the same ruthless, mechanical efficiency as the wells that were draining the city's aquifer. By the 1970s, the city, farms, mines, and other well owners were pumping more than 150 billion gallons each year, exceeding the natural recharge by a factor of three. Tucson became the largest US city entirely dependent on groundwater. In his prescient 1977 book on overpumping, *Killing the Hidden Waters*, former *Tucson Citizen* reporter Charles Bowden explained the perils of "mining" groundwater. "Sinking water tables, like sinking bank accounts, deliver but one conclusion," he wrote. Nevertheless, Tucson Water, the city-owned utility, continued to pump the aquifer so intensively that it plunged by more than 200 feet. So much water was siphoned out of the earth that the ground began to sink and crack the foundations of homes in midtown. As city-owned wells searched deeper for more groundwater to support Tucson's growth, they began to suck up trichloroethylene, a toxic solvent that aerospace firms had blithely dumped on the desert for decades, sickening hundreds in Tucson's poor, mostly Hispanic south side. Not only was the city bleeding its native groundwater supplies, it was poisoning itself in the process.

There was nothing illegal about what Tucson Water, Pima County's cotton farmers, or the open-pit copper mines were doing to the local aquifer, the Santa Cruz River, and the many species that depended on the aquatic and riparian habitat. In fact, anyone with a well had a vested interest in extracting as much as possible, because the state's water laws were rooted in 19th-century ignorance of hydrology. Despite the clear connection between groundwater and rivers, Arizona remained one of many western states with separate, and conflicting, legal doctrines to govern well pumping and the use of surface flows. As the West was settled, surface water was usually divvied up according to the legal principle of prior appropriation, which gave priority to the most longstanding users of a stream or river. The prior appropriation doctrine, encapsulated by the phrase "first in time, first in right," typically had a use-it-or-lose-it corollary: if landowners didn't withdraw water from a stream or river, they risked forgoing their water rights and watching their neighbors take what could have been theirs. Predictably, settlers often pulled as much as they could out of rivers, with terrible consequences for the West's water and wildlife.

In some parts of the country, the doctrine of prior appropriation also governed the use of groundwater. More often, landowners were free to extract as much water as they could, provided they didn't cause obvious harm to their neighbors' wells and their consumption of water was "reasonable." The upshot of this system was yet another tragedy of the commons: since anyone with a deep enough well could tap the aquifer, no one had an incentive to conserve their water use, just as the earliest ranchers had no interest in grazing cattle lightly on the public domain and leaving grass behind for their neighbors' cows to eat.

As Tucson sucked the Santa Cruz dry, animals dependent on the river's flow or its riparian habitat were forced to adapt, move, or perish. Yellow-billed cuckoos, relatives of the iconic roadrunner, found some suitable habitat downstream of the border town of Nogales, where treated sewage released into the river channel kept the cottonwoods and willows alive. But some species simply needed more water to make it.

One bird, the southwestern willow flycatcher, faced especially daunting odds because it was utterly dependent on the streamside thickets for nesting, what biologists call a riparian obligate. The small olive-gray birds were only part-time visitors to Tucson. They migrated north every spring from the tropics of Latin America to lay eggs along the Santa Cruz and similar watercourses, where humid, shady forests afforded the birds and their chicks an ample supply of insects to eat ("mosquito king" is the translation of the bird's genus, *Empidonax*). Snagging all those bugs allowed the flycatchers to fatten up before beginning their long journey south each fall, accompanied by their offspring.

By the late 20th century, the flycatchers could still migrate each spring to the Southwest and spread out across a 1,000-mile-long range from the Southern California coast to the West Texas desert. Within that expansive territory, however, the bird's presence was always as spotty as the region's streamside vegetation. As human society displaced and damaged the riparian forests, a naturally rare habitat became an endangered one, leaving species like the flycatcher in jeopardy of disappearing themselves.

The southwestern willow flycatcher would seem to be the canary in the coal mine, its decline a harbinger of a societal collapse along the Santa Cruz River that could have echoed the Hohokam's fall in the 15th century. But unlike their forerunners, Tucsonans in the 20th century were able to transcend the limits of their local water supply by tapping, and harming, another river hundreds of miles away.

From the earliest days of the territory, Arizona's leaders knew their state's future would hinge on exploiting the Colorado River, which runs along the western border with California. After decades of political machinations and an 11-year legal fight that wound up before the Supreme Court, President Lyndon Johnson signed legislation to build the $4 billion Central Arizona Project, the 336-mile canal that would use 14 pumping stations to raise the Colorado's waters more than a half mile in elevation from Lake Havasu to Phoenix and Tucson. The CAP would become the state's largest user of electricity and run on power generated by a coal-fired plant near Glen Canyon Dam that uses 9 billion gallons of water a year and contributes to haze in the Grand Canyon.

Many environmentalists opposed the CAP since it would grease the wheels of growth, but the majority of Arizonans and the state's political establishment treated the project like a birthright. As the aqueduct began its journey from the shores of the Colorado, across Arizona's unpopulated western deserts and toward Phoenix and Tucson, the state's leaders hailed the dawn of a new, more prosperous era. But just as the vision was within reach, it nearly vanished. The Carter administration threatened to kill the project unless Arizona passed comprehensive legislation to stop overpumping groundwater. If Carter scotched the CAP canal, Arizona's major population centers would be totally dependent on their local water supply: for Tucson, the Santa Cruz and its groundwater aquifer; for Phoenix, the Salt-Verde-Gila river system. Arizona would give up a renewable, if not generous, supply from the Colorado River, and whatever water Arizona left in the river, Southern California would surely scoop up to support its own rapid growth. Without a way to transport Arizona's share of the Colorado to its two biggest cities, the state's economy would be land rich and water poor. And it would be open season on any drop of water in a river or underground aquifer near Tucson or Phoenix. What little riparian habitat was left for species like the southwestern willow flycatcher would be even more endangered.

As political legend has it, Bruce Babbitt, the new Democratic governor and future interior secretary, herded the state's "water buffalos" into his office, told the officials to hammer out a deal, and locked the door. In reality, more than two years of marathon negotiations produced the 1980 Groundwater Management Act, one of the West's most progressive water policies, at least in principle. It forbids new irrigated farms in many parts of Arizona and seeks to shift Phoenix, Tucson, and other areas from finite aquifers to renewable supplies, namely the Colorado River. The act also sets a lofty—but unenforceable—target for sustainability: by 2025,

Phoenix and Tucson should achieve "safe yield," at which point their local water budgets would be balanced and the volume of groundwater pumped each year would equal the amount that naturally seeped into the earth.

Arizona's 1980 groundwater act convinced the Carter administration not to kill CAP, so the canal advanced to Phoenix, arriving there in 1985. It wasn't until 1991 that the aqueduct reached the outskirts of Tucson. On the northwest side of town, custom-made excavating machines cut a trench parallel to I-10 and the Santa Cruz so that the Colorado could flow through the artificial river in the opposite direction that the Santa Cruz once traveled. Engineers then routed the CAP canal to the west and tunneled it under the highway and river so that water originating as snow in Colorado's Rockies and Wyoming's Wind River Range could flow beneath the ghost of the Santa Cruz. Day and night, crews carved the channel and poured concrete, steering the aqueduct west of the Tucson Mountains. After 336 miles, the aqueduct ended unceremoniously in a retaining basin near the Santa Cruz River, a short walk from where Father Kino established the mission at San Xavier del Bac.

In 1992, three centuries after Kino arrived at Chuk Shon, the city of Tucson took its first gulp of CAP water, and gagged. Poor planning, aging pipes, and faulty treatment methods made the river water corrosive. Water mains ruptured and indoor plumbing burst, leaving thousands of Tucsonans with homes and appliances damaged by brown, smelly, foul-tasting water. CAP was stigmatized and Tucson Water shut off the spigot. Utility officials got canned and local politicians cast around for blame.

As I arrived in Tucson in 1995, an outraged local car dealer was busy bankrolling a ballot measure that would ban delivery of Colorado River water, squaring off against a rival car dealer who favored the project. Once again, CAP became the focal point for attitudes toward growth. To many business leaders and working-class Tucsonans, CAP was a lifeline that would allow their city to flourish. Even people with serious reservations about development didn't necessarily oppose CAP; some saw it as a battle already lost and preferred to see Tucson use a renewable supply like the Colorado to support the inevitable arrival of newcomers. For others, however, CAP was a Faustian bargain, an enabler of sprawl that would spoil the city's charm and cause it to keep spreading outward into some of the most biologically diverse habitat in the nation.

Most Tucsonans simply associated CAP with lousy tasting water, so when the ballots were counted, 57 percent of voters said no to delivering

Colorado River water to their homes and business. After decades of legislative maneuvering, epic court cases, and $4 billion spent on the CAP
canal, Tucson had killed the Santa Cruz River, contributed to the Colorado River's demise, and was once again entirely dependent on a groundwater supply that was shrinking with each passing year.

5
A Movement

Weather-wise, the end of May is a bad season to arrive in Tucson, but it's a great time to find a place to live. School is out, snowbirds have reversed their migration, and anyone who can afford to escape the city seeks out cooler climes. When I arrived in 1995, it was the pre-Craigslist era, so I scoured the classifieds of the *Tucson Weekly*, the local alternative rag, and I found plenty of inexpensive options. The listing that jumped out came from a self-described environmentalist who was offering a room in her adobe near Saguaro National Park. It was in the days before cell phones were widely used, so I called the landlady on the pay phone at my motel and she gave me directions to the place, out in the foothills of the Tucson Mountains.

The pavement yielded to a dusty washboard road, and I arrived at a round house set amid several acres of cactus forest. There were solar panels for hot water on the roof. When the landlady opened the door, she reminded me of Joni Mitchell, only with a tan. Joni looked about 40 and struck me as intense, intelligent, but a bit prickly. She was divorced, getting her doctorate in philosophy, writing her dissertation on the ethics of biodiversity protection, and looking for someone to help pay the mortgage. Two dogs and a bunch of cats followed us around on a tour of the chicken coop out back and a cloth tepee tucked behind some mesquites. The ground rules were reasonable and the rent was $250, so I moved in the next day. I was thrilled, but when I called my parents, they weren't so jazzed. "Is her name Mrs. Robinson?" my mom asked.

My relationship with Joni was strictly platonic (we actually did talk about Plato), and she took it upon herself to educate me about the desert and green living. I had to buy recycled toilet paper at the Food Conspiracy Co-op, compost my garbage, and keep my showers supershort. The weather was infernal, but I was in heaven during my first days in the round adobe. I explored a labyrinth of trails on my mountain bike, setting off after soaking my jersey in water to keep cool. I saw my first rattlesnake, followed a mule deer over hill and dale, discovered two desert tortoises humping behind a bush, and stared down a pack of javelinas, boarlike, musky smelling creatures with a taste for the spiny pads of prickly pears. I woke up to a chorus of birdsong, found a scorpion in my room, and spent balmy evenings sitting on the porch, one hand holding a cold beer bottle, the other patting the head of an Anatolian shepherd.

I looked in the local papers for jobs, but there were slim pickings. Call centers were a big driver of the local economy, so there was plenty of work in telemarketing. After a few weeks trying that, I worked as a shadow shopper and would pose as a new-car buyer, walk into a dealership, and keep score as an eager salesman tried to talk me into a new set of wheels. I didn't make it to the end of the week. So when I called about a door-to-door canvasser job at the Arizona League of Conservation Voters, I wasn't expecting it to be the start of a career.

Like its national counterpart, the AZLCV created scorecards of politicians' voting records and tried to block a continual onslaught of hostile bills in the Arizona legislature. The Arizona chapter had been founded a few years before by Bob Beatson, a biologist who had done the fieldwork for his master's degree at the Buenos Aires National Wildlife

Refuge. The high-desert grassland near Tucson had been converted from a working ranch to a cow-free preserve in 1985, when the government purchased the property to recover endangered masked bobwhite quail. Bob had wavy gray hair and a beer belly. He was eating a burrito at his desk when I walked in.

The canvassing job was the type of position in which the employer, not the applicant, had to do the convincing, and Bob was a good salesman. There was certainly no shortage of work to do. In the mid-1990s, the Arizona legislature seemed as conservative as any statehouse in the Deep South, especially when it came to the environment. Arizona's political landscape was dominated by Republicans from the Phoenix area, which accounted for nearly two-thirds of the state's population. Decades ago, mavericks like Barry Goldwater had injected a libertarian streak into the GOP's DNA, and much of the lawmaking since then in environmental and other spheres gravitated toward angry, often symbolic expressions of states' rights. In 1987, a year after the federal holiday for Martin Luther King Jr.'s birthday went into effect, Republican governor and millionaire car dealer Evan Mecham rescinded the celebration within days of taking office.

The statehouse hadn't changed much by the time I arrived in Tucson. In 1995, the legislature passed a law that would allow Arizona businesses to produce Freon, thereby ignoring both the Montreal Protocol and a corresponding act of Congress meant to protect the ozone layer and prevent even more Arizonans from developing skin cancer. "Just because the federal government passes a law," Governor Fife Symington III said as he signed the pro-Freon bill, "doesn't mean we always have to live with it." On this lopsided political playing field, the AZLCV and its allies were always on defense and hardly ever had a chance to develop their own affirmative proposals. To stem the tide of bad bills, the group relied on old school grassroots lobbying: as a critical vote neared, calls would go out urging members to phone or fax their state legislators.

To have any sway in the policy-making process, the AZLCV needed to sign up more members willing to pressure their lawmakers. Direct mail and the telemarketing that was so prominent in Tucson's economy would cost too much and yield too little in return. So around 3 PM each day, we headed out to a chosen neighborhood by piling into the back of Jennifer, a 30-year-old Ford pickup with bald tires and loose brakes. We carried clipboards and wore buttons on our T-shirts to distinguish us from the Mormons and Jehovah's Witnesses. To prime the pump, I fastened bogus checks to my clipboard and scribbled fictitious names, addresses, and donations on the sign-up lists, all to give the illusion that plenty of folks down the block had already donated that day. Bob taught us how to smoke out people in the first 30 seconds and then bail if it seemed hopeless. There was no point debating policy with someone for five minutes if they weren't going to write you a check. During the "ask," we were supposed to stare the prospect straight in the eye, smile, and say nothing, not a peep, while she squirmed and wrestled with her cognitive dissonance. People always made the same excuses—it was amazing how many had just run out of checks that day—and nine out of ten times I walked away from the door empty-handed. Dogs would bark like crazy when I knocked or rang the bell; a few chased me down the block as soon as I stepped in the yard. Frat boys offered me bong hits before I could smoke *them* out. An out-of-work miner shoved me off his front porch and threatened to get his gun. In the tony Catalina Foothills, a perky house-wife came to the door in a bathrobe, just out of the shower, and offered me a seat, some ice tea, and an opportunity to "hang out"—an invitation I declined and rued from that day forward. At the end of the night, we handed in our donations, and every two weeks I got about 40 percent back in a handwritten paycheck. The rest of the revenue would pay for Bob's meager salary, the office rent, and other overhead. Depending on the kindness of strangers was a dubious business model, and I only made a couple hundred bucks a week.

Before all of the canvassers went home, we would gather around a huge legislative map of Tucson and use fluorescent highlighters to mark off the streets we had hit that day. Bob liked to spend time before that map tracing its political topography and outlining pockets of support in unlikely quarters. It's easy, Bob would say, to get the liberals to sign up—the professors in the Sam Hughes neighborhood, the students living around UA—but those districts were already represented by legislators sympathetic to the cause. Those weren't the swing votes you need to beat back a bad bill. To win, you needed to sign up new members in neighbor-hoods where calling someone an environmentalist might be an insult.

My fellow canvassers were an eclectic bunch. One guy looked like Wavy Gravy and wore a Montreal Canadiens hockey jersey, even in sum-mer. There was a whip-smart bearded guy from New York who learned the tricks of the trade while working for Ralph Nader's Public Interest Research Group; he was headed to Lewis and Clark, one of the nation's top law schools for environmental attorneys. Another fellow was just as eloquent and passionate; he would later serve 182 days in a federal penitentiary next to Mt. Graham after he walked onto Georgia's Fort Benning to protest the training of death squads at the School of the Americas. The turnover among canvassers was incredibly high, especially among the glassy-eyed hippies who would sometimes drift in. After a day or two of knocking on doors, they realized they could make just as much money hitting up tourists for spare change on Fourth Avenue.

To Bob, dreadlocks and tie-dye shirts were liabilities for a canvasser, and in those first few weeks as a card-carrying environmentalist, I was exposed to the movement's awkward relationship with its true believers. The folks out on the left end of the political spectrum might have the purest convictions, the most dedication, maybe even the strongest arguments, but they weren't necessarily an asset when you were hitting up people for money. Conservation-minded hunters who might support your agenda would avoid any outfit with New Agers and animal rights activists. Country-club Republicans who wanted to protect the same places you did would blanch at the first whiff of patchouli. This is why Bob told us to steer the conversation away from the Mt. Graham controversy, which came up frequently at the door since it was in the news so often. "Are you those wackos fighting the telescopes?" was a common refrain. I'm not sure what Bob felt personally about the scopes versus squirrels controversy, but he was certain that to grow the AZLCV and its influence he needed to distance his group from the hard-core activists who were monkey wrenching atop the mountain and getting arrested on campus. He told us to use some innocuous statement about balancing interests and then move on to another topic.

Bob was perpetually stressed out. He spent a lot of time fetching coffee from the café on the corner and smoking cigarettes out on the front steps. He worried aloud about making payroll and only drew enough of a salary to afford a tiny apartment. Despite being so jaded about Arizona politics, he cared about the cause and took time to educate the staff about the issues. A few weeks into the job, he handed me two books: *A Sand County Almanac* (I didn't know Aldo from Adam) and *Cadillac Desert*, Marc Reisner's masterpiece on water in the West.

Bob also took us on field trips to teach us about the desert we were supposed to be saving. He had big ideas about using the AZLCV to spin off a service organization that funded and carried out habitat restoration.

Once he took us in Jennifer the truck to the back side of Aravaipa Canyon, a steep-walled riparian corridor that flowed with runoff from Mt. Graham's southern slopes. I'd never seen a stream run with water in southern Arizona, and I was surprised to learn from Bob that there were native fish in the creek, many of them endangered. The trip was devoted to "tammy-whacking": cutting down exotic tamarisk shrubs that were drinking precious groundwater and setting up the riparian corridor for a destructive burn. On a field trip to the Buenos Aires National Wildlife Refuge, we planted seeds and built erosion-control barriers to help the grasslands recover from decades of overgrazing. After a long day's work, we had only covered an acre or two in a refuge spread out over nearly 200 square miles. Like the door-to-door canvassing, the fieldwork left me wondering whether I was making any difference at all or merely engaging in some symbolic gesture.

At the doorstep, it helped a canvasser's cause to offer something tangible to prospective members, so every quarter the AZLCV would put out a slapdash newsletter. Bob, always scrambling for content, gave me $50 in gas money and sent me out to western Arizona to write about the four national wildlife refuges along the lower Colorado River.

Thinking a wildlife refuge would be like a national park, I departed with high expectations. Instead, I arrived at a shrunken, straightened river surrounded by farmland and slept in my car next to an irrigation ditch. The trip improved over the next few days as the managers of the Havasu, Imperial, Cibola, and Bill Williams River national wildlife refuges showed me around by boat, took me on hikes to see petroglyphs, explained the area's importance along the Pacific Flyway for migratory birds, and let me handle some bizarre razor-backed fish that looked like something from the age of dinosaurs. They explained how the river ecosystem had been totally transformed by dams, diversions, tamarisk, nonnative predators, and drunken Jet Skiers. Foursquare against these forces, the refuge managers were struggling to prevent simple vandalism of their equipment and were too cash strapped to hire more than a token law enforcement presence to stop the weekend tourists from trashing the place, or killing one another. These refuges and the others in the network that Teddy Roosevelt created in 1903 were as valuable as any federal lands for protecting biodiversity, but they usually lacked the esthetic wonders of a national park or monument. As a result, the managers told me, the refuges were the backwaters of public lands, lacking a solid constituency to support them. It also didn't help to be assigned as daunting a task as recovering species at the threshold of extinction after a century or more of human impacts. Along the lower Colorado, the federal government had established many of the refuges as a halfhearted apology for the damming—and damning—of the river.

The more I learned about the plants and animals around me, the more they seemed at risk. In Tucson, habitat loss wasn't some abstract notion; you could watch it unfold around town every day. On mountain bike rides I would dead-end at construction sites where the excavators had scraped the desert clean, sometimes spinning around a sole saguaro propped up with some two-by-fours and left behind as a stark reminder of what had been destroyed. Joni told me about big plans to develop other parts of the neighborhood, to cover the hillsides I was now hiking and biking with frame-and-stucco homes. I had fallen hard for the Sonoran Desert, only to realize the object of my affection was leaving, never once making the connection between my own contribution to Tucson's growth and the changes I was witnessing.

I felt compelled to physically protect the resources and applied to be a seasonal ranger with the park service, then started to volunteer at Saguaro National Park in a bid to be like Leopold or Abbey. The rangers at Saguaro National Park gave me a uniform and a walkie-talkie, told me to hike the trails in search of tourists in distress, and let me take first aid and search-and-rescue classes for free. I needed all the help I could get. My dad had never taught me how to camp or hunt. Our bonding in the outdoors was limited to December afternoons shivering in Giants Stadium in a sea of red plastic chairs, staring through binoculars at a field of Astroturf. During one of the trainings at Saguaro National Park, I nearly stepped on a rattlesnake and turned the exercise into a real emergency. On one of my first patrols, I brushed up against a jumping cholla cactus, then got the barbs stuck in my hand while trying to yank them out of my ass.

While I was canvassing for the AZLCV, we discovered there was a rival operation in town. An upstart group, the Southwest Center for Biological Diversity, had recently moved its headquarters to Tucson and was starting to knock on doors in the same neighborhoods we were hitting. If our canvassers arrived after the Center did, sympathetic people would tell us they gave last week. One afternoon, we actually crossed paths with the Center's canvassers and, like two territorial animals, negotiated some division of turf. Bob dismissed the competition, even though at that moment the Center was making a lasting imprint on the nation's endangered species policies and the Southwest.

The group, which eventually dropped the "Southwest" from its name, traced its origins to 1989, when two Earth First! activists, Kierán Suckling and Peter Galvin, met in New Mexico and worked for their nemesis, the US Forest Service. Their job was to survey for Mexican spotted owls, close relatives of the birds in the Pacific Northwest that the federal government would soon list under the ESA. Suckling, the son of a civil engineer who designed industrial infrastructure around the globe, had moved about as a kid. After earning a philosophy degree from the College of the Holy Cross and canvassing for the Public Interest Research Group in Massachusetts, he headed west to Montana, got involved with Earth First!, and hopped around the country on graduate fellowships in linguistics, mathematics, and philosophy. In the summer of 1989, Suckling wound up in northern New Mexico, where he met Galvin, a recent graduate of Prescott College who had studied biology and spotted owls. Galvin had survived a bout with cancer as a teenager and, like Suckling, committed himself to fighting the environmental destruction around him. Suckling and another surveyor, Todd Schulke, bought 40 acres and lived along the San Francisco River in southwestern New Mexico. Galvin bought another 40 aces nearby. The Gila National Forest surrounded them and offered plenty of inspiration for action: three-foot-wide ponderosa stumps in the woods and cattle grazing the saplings of cottonwood and willow in unfenced, eroded streambeds. Their cabins and tepees lacked power and plumbing, but the fax machine ran on solar. To do research, Suckling would hitchhike to Albuquerque, study in the university library by day, and sleep in the bushes at night.

The Forest Service was already concerned about the spotted owls—hence the surveys they were paying Suckling, Galvin, and Schulke to carry out—but the agency was still intent on logging the old-growth forests where the three hooters were documenting the birds. The trio connected with Robin Silver, a wildlife photographer from Phoenix who was documenting the spotted owl and the Mt. Graham red squirrel for the Arizona Game and Fish Department on breaks from his demanding day job as an emergency room physician. Like other biodiversity activists, the four men faced a basic choice between two styles of advocacy, both of which had serious drawbacks. "One path, represented by the national organizations, provided political access but was hindered by compromise and constraint," sociologist Douglas Bevington wrote in his 2009 book, *The Rebirth of Environmentalism*. "The second path, embodied by Earth First!, offered an unconstrained approach to biodiversity advocacy, but it was not particularly influential." The Center and like-minded groups chose a third path and became "the unsung heroes of American environmentalism during the past twenty years," Bevington wrote. Like Earth First!, the Center refused to let ecological concerns be compromised by the political calculations that inhibited mainstream environmental groups. But unlike the monkey wrenching eco-saboteurs, the Center could wield influence over millions of acres by using the courts to aggressively enforce environmental laws. The ESA offered an especially powerful lever because it allowed any citizen to petition the federal government to protect species.

The process for listing a species is perhaps the most important, and politicized, section of the ESA because no federal protections are extended to plants or animals that don't pass the test. Fish and Wildlife was supposed to ignore economic impacts and decide "solely on the best scientific and commercial data available." The agency had a vested interest in adding new species to the endangered list—after all, bureaucracies generally try to enlarge their budgets and power—but Fish and Wildlife and its counterpart for oceanic species, the National Marine Fisheries Service, were subject to other powerful forces that could discourage listings, even if they were biological no-brainers. One of the first scholarly works on the ESA, published in 1982, concluded that politics, mainly in the form of congressional intervention, frequently tainted listing decisions and either prevented or constrained the mapping of "critical habitat" where protections were enhanced.

Even species that federal biologists decided were at risk of extinction were not given a berth aboard the ark. A gaping loophole in the ESA allowed the government to declare a species' listing as biologically "warranted but precluded" by budget constraints. Fish and Wildlife is only supposed to use this exception if "expeditious progress is being made to add qualified species" to the endangered club. In reality, the exception has become an all-too-convenient way for the government to abdicate its responsibilities under the ESA. About 250 species remain in this regulatory purgatory; at least 24 species have blinked out while in the listing pipeline.

For the Center's founders, there was no shortage of species in the Southwest that might deserve federal protection. The Mexican spotted owls they were hooting for were only the most obvious candidate. Like its relatives in the Pacific Northwest, the Mexican subspecies of spotted owls prefer forests with closed canopies, a diversity of ages among the trees, lots of standing dead snags, and plenty of downed logs: hallmarks of woods that haven't been visited by loggers. In both the Southwest and Pacific Northwest, destruction of such old-growth forests faced few obstacles in the postwar era as the Forest Service made logging its highest priority and approved major timber sales to meet aggressive targets.

Just as destructive was the agency's policy of suppressing wildfires, which Aldo Leopold and other Forest Service rangers pursued with as much vigor as predator control. Trying to prevent fires in the Southwest and other regions with dry forests was like fighting against gravity. Scars on tree rings dating back centuries showed that flames naturally visited the ponderosa pines once or twice *every decade*. Sparked by lightning or Native Americans, these fires usually crept along the ground. Mature pines may have had their thick bark scorched, but the flames generally didn't climb into the forest canopy and kill the big trees. The fires did, however, clean out the saplings, brush, and debris on the forest floor, preventing that fuel from accumulating.

Initially, foresters did not understand the harm of fire suppression and the Forest Service sought to put out every fire by 10 AM the day after the blaze was spotted. In 1920, Leopold railed against the "light-burning propagandists" who wanted to set deliberate fires to burn up fuel, arguing that "this theory would not only fail to prevent serious fires but would ultimately destroy the productiveness of the forests on which western industries depend for their supply of timber."

Wildland firefighting, once a haphazard vocation that employed drunks lured from saloons with the promise of a hot meal, evolved into a serious profession that drew lessons and technology from the military and national laboratories. As fire suppression grew more effective with the addition of bulldozers, helicopters, slurry bombers, and parachuting smoke jumpers, the fuel accumulated even faster. The once spacious forests became "dog hair" thickets that were as dense as a canine's coat. An acre that once had a couple dozen trees now had many hundreds. Young trees competed with the older ones for water and nutrients in the soil, leaving the entire forest weaker and less able to ward off disease and insects. When fire arrived in such overgrown woods, it found plenty of kindling on the ground and could use the smaller trees like ladders to ascend into the canopy. On a hot, dry, and windy day, flames could skip from treetop to treetop in an unstoppable crown fire that incinerated every plant cell around. The heat could be so intense that the charred earth became "hydrophobic" and shed rainfall like a parking lot, causing deadly flooding and scouring fragile riparian areas downstream. Soil that took eons to accumulate could be washed away by a single postfire thunderstorm and end up clogging vital aquatic habitat.

Decades of excluding fire and the removal of the biggest, most fire-resistant trees—a process known as high-grading—left the pine belt that arcs across east-central Arizona and west-central New Mexico in miserable shape. Only about 2,000 Mexican spotted owls were left in the United States, with an unknown number living south of the border. No one was sure how many owls were around in presettlement days. Presumably there were many more, because lumberjacks had been chopping down the forests for more than a century. One study found that 10 percent of the owl's habitat in the Southwest—400,000 acres—had been lost just in the 1980s, about four-fifths due to logging and most of the rest due to increasingly severe wildfires. There was also a logging–fire connection. Roads built to harvest timber stands gave the public, a key ignition source, access to previously inaccessible backcountry, while clear-cuts created ideal growing conditions for thickets of small trees that could serve as kindling.

Four days before Christmas in 1989, Silver submitted a four-page petition to the US Fish and Wildlife Service requesting ESA protection for the Mexican spotted owl. Three years and three months later, the federal government listed the bird as a threatened species. Fish and Wildlife concluded that the status quo management of southwestern forests put the Mexican spotted owl at risk of extinction. Three-fifths of the bird's remaining habitat was available for timber harvest, and the other two-fifths consisted of scattered patches that might be too small to support viable populations of owls.

Simply banning loggers from the woods would not be enough to ensure the owl's survival, because the region's forests were so out of whack due to fire suppression. But to have any hope of recovering the bird, the Forest Service would have to start by cutting back on logging, even stopping it altogether. Responding to litigation from the Center, in August

1995 a federal judge halted all timber sales on national forests in Arizona
and New Mexico until the Forest Service revised its guidelines to better
protect the owls. During the 16-month injunction, which was partially
lifted after a few months, the same jobs versus owls debate that played out
in the Pacific Northwest also riled the Southwest. Unemployed loggers
and others descended on the State Capitol in Phoenix, snarling traffic
with their pickups and tractor-trailers. The spotted owl's reputation was
further bruised by what seemed like a callous federal response. People
couldn't take Christmas trees out of national forests, even if there were
no owls around. Impoverished Native Americans couldn't collect firewood in northern New Mexico's Carson National Forest, even though
a $1.5 million survey had turned up no owls there, only potential habi-
tat. The Center's founders received death threats, had their tires slashed,
and found excrement dumped on Suckling's car. After the *Albuquerque
Journal* did a profile of the group, the front-page photo of Suckling and
Galvin showed up on a bulletin board in the Catron County courthouse
with a bull's eye added to the image.

 In the Southwest and Pacific Northwest, the sound bites surrounding spotted owls were similar. The underlying economies were not. In
Washington, Oregon, and Northern California, where moisture pouring off the Pacific supported enormous trees, the timber industry was a
major employer. In the Southwest, where meager rainfall suppressed the
growth rate of timber and most of the easily accessible trees had already
been sawed down, the logging business was a minor player by the 1990s.
The lumberjack was still the mascot of Northern Arizona University in
Flagstaff and small lumber mills were still a big deal in a few rural out-
posts, but the harvest from national forests in Arizona and New Mexico
amounted to less than 1 percent of the national total. Employment in the
region's timber industry peaked in the late 1970s at 4,300 and declined
to about half that by the late 1980s. Years before the 1993 listing of the
Mexican spotted owl, global competition and the unsustainable harvests
of the past had left southwestern logging companies staggering, though
still in the fight (figs. 4 and 5). The owl delivered the uppercut that sent
the industry to the mat. The amount of timber harvested from national
forests in the Southwest fell 90 percent. More than a dozen mills in Arizona and New Mexico went out of business. "We've basically crushed the
timber industry," Suckling boasted in a long profile in *The New Yorker*
that described him as a "trickster, philosopher, publicity hound, master

strategist, and unapologetic pain in the ass." The profile of the Center, one of many that appeared, called it "the most important radical environmental group in the country."

The spotted owl was just the start. Across the region, dozens of species were in decline and candidates for listing. Nationwide, there were hundreds, maybe thousands of species that warranted protection. The beauty of the Center's approach was that it could partially pay for itself. If Fish and Wildlife did not respond to a petition by the deadline in the statute, the Center could win the case in court easily and recoup its legal costs from the government.

The Center, recognizing the importance of riparian habitat, sought ESA protection for the southwestern willow flycatcher and a raft of other species dependent on the region's dwindling streams and rivers. The flycatcher's 1995 listing carried far-reaching consequences because the bird's range extended from the California coast to Texas and the species was dependent on the very water sources the Southwest's human residents were fighting over. The setting was ripe for another David versus Goliath battle, this one centered on Arizona's Roosevelt Dam.

Built with irregular blocks hewn from the surrounding cliffs by Italian stonemasons, Roosevelt Dam, 50 miles east-northeast of Phoenix, was the federal government's first big reclamation project in the West. The dam began to plug the Salt River in 1911 and converted its mineral-laden waters from an erratic, sometimes wrathful force in the Phoenix Valley into a steady and dependable water source upon which to found a metropolis. As Roosevelt Lake filled, creating the largest reservoir in the world at the time, the rising waters claimed some 20,000 acres of habitat along the Salt River and Tonto Creek, a major tributary. In the early 1990s, changing safety standards forced the federal government to raise Roosevelt Dam's height by 77 feet. The taller dam would boost the reservoir's capacity by 20 percent, enough to serve 1 million Phoenicians. But as the reservoir expanded, it would also inundate hundreds of acres of habitat for the flycatcher. To protect the endangered species, the Fish and Wildlife Service could require the Salt River Project to spill water from Roosevelt Dam and keep the lake level below the bird's habitat, crimping Phoenix's water supply and forcing the utility to find a substitute at ratepayers' expense. In the end, a deal known as a habitat conservation plan was worked out that allowed the dam project to go forward, but by getting the flycatcher listed, the Center forced the Salt River Project and

Figure 4: Timber sold and harvested from national forests.
Source: US Forest Service.

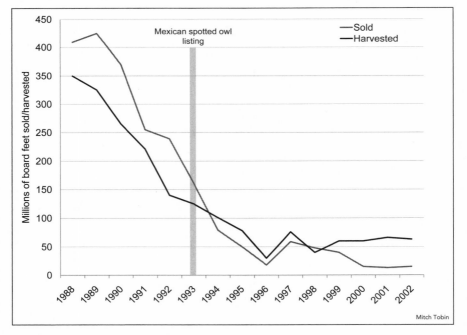

Figure 5: Timber sold and harvested from southwestern national forests.
Source: US Fish and Wildlife Service Draft Environmental Assessment of Critical Habitat
Designation for the Mexican Spotted Owl.

the federal government to spend millions of dollars on monitoring, land purchases, and the management of replacement habitat.

The Center also made waves in Tucson, where it relocated in 1995 after bouncing around New Mexico, by securing ESA protection for the cactus ferruginous pygmy owl. The tiny but truculent raptor was fairly numerous in Mexico and south Texas, but rare in southern Arizona. Conveniently, one of the pygmy owl's redoubts was the northwest side of Tucson, the fastest-growing part of town. Fish and Wildlife officials held up developments until owl surveys were completed and caused some landowners to set aside big chunks of their property. The conflict came to a head when environmentalists sued to block construction of a new, badly needed high school planned in the middle of the owl's critical habitat. Nobody had ever managed to stop Tucson from spreading out across the desert at will. Now a few three-ounce owls were keeping the bulldozers at bay. Despite their diminutive size, the owls were fearsome predators, able to pounce from their perch and sink their talons into lizards, rodents, and other birds that outweighed them, a mismatch akin to the Center's own struggle against entrenched interests from Tucson to Washington, DC. The high school was eventually built, but the conflict helped convince local officials to take a hard look at how they would manage growth in one of the nation's most biologically diverse counties.

Even as the Center's influence expanded, it remained true to its crunchy roots, according to the journalists who profiled the group. Staff lived and worked in a communelike setting and still took part in traditional demonstrations. The Center's staffers were making $400 a month, Suckling just $1,000. A couple thousand members gave small donations. All the while, lobbyists on K Street and attorneys for developers, builders, ranchers, loggers, and other property owners were beginning to grapple with a spate of new restrictions connected to the Center's petitions and lawsuits. Despite having hardly any money, the group's founders were able to build a stable of pro bono attorneys who could press their case in court. "We had studied all of these species, studied the law, and we could go to the lawyer and say if you take this case, we'll give you all the support you need. We'll basically be your science paralegals, so this is going to be relatively easy for you," Suckling explained. "Once we did it a few times, the lawyers realized that (a) If I help these guys, I won't be on my own; and (b) I'm probably going to win and get my legal fees back." In addition to the listings, the Center and others initiated a fresh wave of litigation that forced the federal government to map critical habitat for species already protected by the ESA, increasing the government's regulatory power even further. Prior to 1990, only two species were listed in response to lawsuits, but from 1990 to 1995, 243 plants and animals won protection after judges ordered Fish and Wildlife to take action.

Unlike Earth First!, which emphasized civil disobedience, the Center was using the legal system to hold agencies accountable. At the same time, the group was animated by Earth First!'s noncompromise ethos and unconventional communications strategy. "At the end of the day, fundamentally Earth First! was a media project. That was their essence. These were the people who would go out, do outlandish things, and draw all the TV cameras and newspapers into the woods, where they wouldn't have gone before," Suckling said. "There's a reason we came out of that movement instead of working for The Wilderness Society or getting a master's degree in conservation management." In the courts and in the press, the Center was effectively combating federal foot-dragging, but the unrelenting approach attracted some scorn from other environmental groups who saw Republicans in Congress starting to use the Center's persistent litigation as a grounds for weakening the ESA itself.

6
Political Science

I didn't see much of a future with the Arizona League of Conservation Voters, or as a seasonal park ranger, so I followed my default plan of going to graduate school and left town. I had been in Tucson for only 364 days, but my outlook had pivoted away from the East Coast and my parents, and toward the West and my own path.

Eight years before, I had entered Yale a teenage Republican, fascinated by free-market economist Milton Friedman, interested in investment banking, and fond of wearing yellow power ties, even bow ties, like Michael J. Fox on *Family Ties* or a young Tucker Carlson. I might have stayed on that track had I gone to school somewhere else or been assigned different roommates. But Yale broadened my horizons and the demographics of my freshman suite—a Jew from Long Island, an African

American from Brooklyn, an Irish-Catholic from Boston, a prep school graduate from the DC suburbs, and an Asian American from Silicon Valley—looked like one of those politically correct Benetton ads. In New Haven, which had been ravaged by the exodus of manufacturing jobs and the recent arrival of crack cocaine, I found myself tucked away in Gothic architecture, complete with turrets and moats, and I developed an acute case of white guilt. In Arizona, Joni, canvassing, a romance, and the desert had pulled me out of my shell, exposed vulnerabilities, and opened up new possibilities for work and life, but I wasn't quite ready to abandon my course or turn down free rides at good schools.

In the fall of 1996, I entered a PhD program in political science at the University of California at Berkeley. Smug and self-righteous, I arrived at Cal a vegetarian and a technophobe, convinced that the American political system was on the verge of embracing third parties and root changes. Eight years after voting for George Herbert Walker Bush, I cast my ballot for Ralph Nader, despite my professors' dismissive attitude toward the Green Party and their ridicule of Nader in particular.

I became a research assistant to Nelson Polsby, an expert on Congress, the presidency, and American politics. Polsby was intimidating, both physically and intellectually. "A mountain of a man, he looked like an American footballer gone to seed," the *Times of London* once wrote of him. Had I worked for other professors, I would have shuttled back and forth to the library, conducted literature reviews, or written code in statistical software. With Polsby, the job entailed sitting in his office, listening to him hold forth on politics, and serving as a sparring partner. Polsby knocked me out with ease.

My other teachers also thought I had drunk too much green Kool-Aid in Tucson, and they were determined to set me straight. I may have thought environmentalists' motives were pure, but to political scientists they were just another power-hungry interest group clamoring for their share of the pie and just as likely as loggers or land developers to use propaganda and misinformation to further their cause. Lobbyists for the Sierra Club and National Cattlemen's Beef Association weren't as different from each other as I thought. I came to Cal believing that the Forest Service was a shill for the timber industry and easily swayed by pressure from astronomers, ranchers, and other interests. But political scientists who actually studied such things painted a more subtle portrait of the agency and the political ecosystem in which it lived, especially in modern times. All of the federal bureaucracies, including the Fish and Wildlife Service, which had primary authority in administering the ESA, served a complex set of clients, constituents, and congressional committees, with the agency "captured" to varying degrees by the competitors. A highly decentralized organization like the Forest Service also struggled to ensure that orders issued from the generals in Washington, DC, filtered through the hierarchical triangle, all the way down to rangers like Aldo Leopold, who were stationed in the boonies and subject to intense local lobbying that could fragment the agency. Political scientist Herbert Kaufman's classic 1960 study, *The Forest Ranger*, argued that these "centrifugal forces" posed a challenge akin to the army's and were why the Forest Service, in a bid to build discipline and allegiance, adopted a quasi-military style and forced some of its employees to wear uniforms with badges.

In retrospect, I learned a lot at Berkeley about how politicians, bureaucracies, and voters behave, but at the time, the coursework seemed as dry as the desert. Like the other social sciences, political science had become dominated by the modeling and quantitative analysis of economics. The focus was on a single species, *Homo economicus*, the theoretically rational, self-interested individual who made choices to maximize his "utility function" and could be reduced to a series of mathematical expressions. I grew weary from all of the statistics, the econometrics, the clinical, academic writing that forced me to use words like *endogenous* and *heteroskadicticity*. It was all Greek to me, and frequently expressed in Greek symbols. I found myself writing too many formulas, not enough sentences. The superspecialization in academia made me feel like I was painting myself into a corner. Instead of plodding through Herbert Simon's *Administrative Behavior: A Study of Decision-Making Processes in Administrative Organizations*—even the title made my eyelids droop—I read Jack London's *White Fang*, John Muir's *My First Summer in the Sierras*, and Jon Krakauer's *Into the Wild*. By the end of my first semester, I was ready to leave the program, and clueless about what to do instead.

To some political scientists, the ESA's power and durability are curious. The listing and protection of endangered species can impose real, immediate, and concentrated costs on taxpayers, industries, and campaign contributors, but such actions confer vague, distant, and diffuse benefits for creatures that can't vote, lobby, protest, or maybe even move.

"Endangered species do not now possess the attractive features to make them prime candidates for sustained political attention," political scientist Richard Tobin (no relation) noted in his 1990 book, *The Expendable Future*. The general public doesn't share the same interest in biodiversity that motivates scientists and environmental activists. The public's understanding of ecological threats tends to be clouded by scientific uncertainty, while regulatory impacts, such as the closing of a timber mill or the denial of a building permit, are easily identified and quantified. Politicians are asked to defend hardships now for the sake of species recovery efforts that may reach fruition decades after they've left office, if ever.

Endangered species also don't impact human health and welfare in the obvious way that smokestacks and sewage discharges do. They're not connected to disasters like Three Mile Island and the *Exxon Valdez* that have spurred political action. "Air and water quality programs attempt to reduce or eliminate what are familiar and proximate problems," Tobin wrote. "In comparison, the goal of preservation programs is to prevent a speculative and poorly understood evil. This difference becomes important because many people do not appreciate the absence of evils that fail to occur." Even today, environmental issues rank at the bottom of Americans' concerns, according to public opinion surveys. Among environmental problems, concern about the loss of species comes in way behind air quality, global warming, water pollution, and garbage.

Perhaps the biggest political challenge facing the ESA is the nature of its beneficiaries. The public is clearly enamored with wolves, manatees, and polar bears, the sort of charismatic megafauna that many legislators were thinking of when they voted for the ESA in 1973. But look through the list of our more than 1,300 listed species and you'll find louseworts, mold beetles, rice rats, wolf spiders, water snakes, and other creatures whose names sound creepy enough to inspire eradication campaigns, not recovery plans. Allergy sufferers may be troubled to learn the federal government is committed to protecting the Virginia sneezeweed.

Does a species' image and popularity affect our commitment to recovering its numbers and protecting its habitat? You'd expect it would, given that the World Wildlife Fund is symbolized by a panda, not a pseudoscorpion, and Defenders of Wildlife puts a wolf, not a wood rat, on its logo. An imperfect proxy for the political will to preserve specific plants and animals is how many tax dollars we spend on each species, something the Fish and Wildlife Service has tracked since 1989. These reports are not a comprehensive accounting of the ESA's financial impact. The agency makes no effort to tally spending by local governments and private groups that help endangered species, nor does it capture the extra financial burdens shouldered directly by businesses and individuals. Adding up all of these expenditures for more than 1,300 species is next to impossible, and no economist has ever been so bold (or foolish) to estimate the overall financial impact of the ESA. The closest attempt was a study that found no significant relationship between the number of listed species in a state and its economic performance.

Despite the limitations, the spending data do tell us something important because there is evidence that greater funding for a plant or animal makes it more likely the species will recover. When researchers looked at how much was spent on 243 endangered species and compared that to the total amount of money biologists asked for in recovery plans, they found that plants and animals that were shortchanged were less likely to be stable or improving than those that received the requested funding. The trend was especially true for plants and animals imperiled by development and industry rather than more complex biological threats such as invasive species, perhaps because the government is better able to control human activities. With funding for the 243 species at less than 20 percent of what was needed for recovery, the researchers concluded that "we are practicing something far worse than triage. Our current scenario is akin to starving hospitalized patients."

Not every patient walking into the emergency room is treated equally. The spending data reveal that the government devotes large sums of money to protect a small number of species and very few resources to protect and recover the rest. The most obvious trend that jumps out of the data is the significance of salmon and steelhead. The six protected species accounted for 41 percent of expenditures from 2001 through 2004, but salmon's prominence is a bit deceptive (fig. 6). Much of the cost comes from lost power revenues at hydroelectric dams in the Pacific Northwest that must spill water, rather than run it through turbines, to avoid grinding up fish. Were the steelhead and salmon not federally protected, the dams could make more money. However, such foregone revenues are usually not calculated for other species and they are unlike typical expenditures in recovery efforts, such as buying land or conducting surveys.

Figure 7, which excludes salmon and steelhead, shows that the top species for spending tend to be animals the public admires: sea lions, bears,

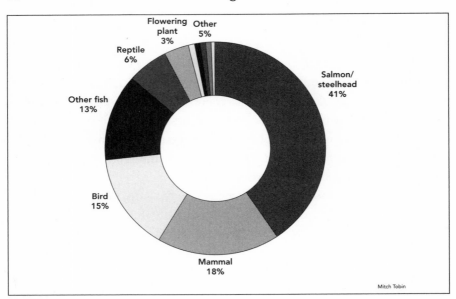

Figure 6: Distribution of spending by order of species, FY 2001 through FY 2004.
Other = 240 species of insects, clams, amphibians, crustaceans, snails, arachnids, ferns,
lichens, and conifers/cycads.
Note: Figures add to more than 100 percent due to rounding.
Source: US Fish and Wildlife Service.

Rank	Species	Spending
1	Steller sea-lion *(Eumetopias jubatus)*	$200,523,877
2	Bull trout *(Salvelinus confluentus)*	$117,082,818
3	Bald eagle *(Haliaeetus leucocephalus)*	$85,672,436
4	Louisiana black bear *(Ursus americanus luteolus)*	$79,984,675
5	Red-cockaded woodpecker *(Picoides borealis)*	$53,184,402
6	Desert tortoise *(Gopherus agassizii)*	$46,153,248
7	West Indian manatee *(Trichechus manatus)*	$42,141,962
8	Right whale *(Balaena glacialis)*	$38,618,422
9	Southwestern willow flycatcher *(Empidonax traillii extimus)*	$38,585,361
10	Razorback sucker *(Xyrauchen texanus)*	$33,744,745
11	Rio Grande silvery minnow *(Hybognathus amarus)*	$33,666,962
12	Green sea turtle *(Chelonia mydas)*	$31,864,539
13	Pallid sturgeon *(Scaphirhynchus albus)*	$29,759,975
14	Colorado pikeminnow *(Ptychocheilus lucius)*	$29,349,943
15	Loggerhead sea turtle *(Caretta caretta)*	$25,756,084
16	Grizzly bear *(Ursus arctos horribilis)*	$23,905,501
17	Gray wolf *(Canis lupus)*	$23,611,446
18	Indiana bat *(Myotis sodalis)*	$22,299,318
19	Black-capped vireo *(Vireo atricapilla)*	$22,099,000
20	Golden-cheeked warbler *(Dendroica chrysoparia)*	$21,526,130
21	Florida panther *(Puma concolor coryi)*	$21,440,440
22	Mexican spotted owl *(Strix occidentalis lucida)*	$21,087,647
23	Northern spotted owl *(Strix occidentalis caurina)*	$20,899,742
24	Humpback chub *(Gila cypha)*	$20,288,906
25	Marbled murrelet *(Brachyramphus marmoratus marmoratus)*	$20,207,549

Figure 7: Top species for state and federal spending, FY 2001 through FY 2004.
Note: Salmon and steelhead excluded.
Source: US Fish and Wildlife Service.

woodpeckers, and whales. If you're a species that's cute, charismatic, or otherwise endearing to humans, odds are you'll get more money spent on your behalf. This holds true in the Southwest, where the bald eagle, desert tortoise, Mexican gray wolf, California condor, and Sonoran pronghorn receive far more money than the Zuni fleabane, Navajo sedge, and other plants.

Figure 8, which divides the species by their scientific order, shows that fish, birds, mammals, and amphibians (mainly frogs and toads) have the most money spent per species. At the bottom are plants, lichen, and arachnids. Because of the inevitable limits of funding, there are clear advantages in focusing the public's attention on beloved flagship species and protecting the habitat of wide-ranging umbrella species that can shield the plants and animals in their ecosystem that do not have an interest group in their corner. Safeguard an area for grizzlies, and you'll also help the rats and flies that share the same habitat.

Even if you ignore the steelhead and salmon, a handful of animals still attract the lion's share of money. Nineteen types of fish, mammals, birds, and reptiles accounted for half the spending; about 10 percent of species consumed 90 percent. The huge sums allocated to a small number of species distort the averages, the same way that mansions inflate average housing prices, so it makes more sense to look at the median, or middle value, of the distribution. For all species, median spending was $20,895 per year, with a range from $1,655 for ferns to $25.8 million for salmon and steelhead.

The plant kingdom, which accounts for three of every five listed species, gets less than 4 percent of the money. About half of the plants received less than $10,000 per year, and one-sixth got less than $1,000 annually. The lack of funds dedicated to plant conservation appears consistent with God's command to Noah. The Bible tells us that the ark was to be filled with "every creeping thing of the earth," which presumably includes insects, but there is no mention of God asking Noah to save any vegetation. Apparently the plants regenerated on their own, because Noah knew the flood had abated when the dove returned with an olive branch.

While plants may not be sexy, they're the foundation for animal life and the type of species most likely to yield valuable chemicals and medicines. The anticancer drug Taxol, which has generated more than $1 billion in annual sales for Bristol-Myers Squibb is an extract of the Pacific yew, once considered a trash tree that was burned in piles in the Pacific Northwest. The rosy periwinkle, a plant from the island of Madagascar,

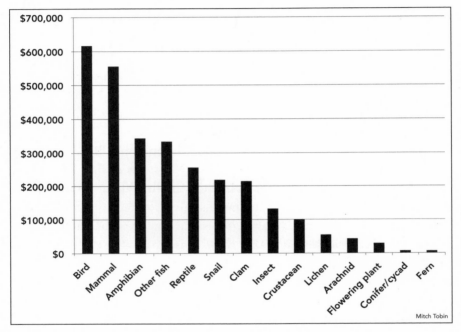

Figure 8: Median government spending per species, FY 2001 through FY 2004.
Note: Salmon and steelhead excluded.
Source: US Fish and Wildlife Service.

is the basis for two cancer-fighting drugs: vinblastine, which has dramatically boosted survival rates for childhood leukemia, and vincristine, which is used to treat Hodgkin's disease. Both medicines now generate more than $100 million in revenue for Eli Lilly each year. One study found that between 1959 and 1980, a quarter of all US prescriptions contained extracts or active compounds from plants.

The fact that most plants receive scant funding doesn't necessarily mean they're going unprotected. For a small, isolated population, all that may be required is a fence. Consider the Cochise pincushion cactus, a two-inch-wide plant that's limited in the United States to a few limestone hills on a single ranch in the Malpai region of southeastern Arizona. In some years, not a single cent has been devoted to the plant because the feds don't do much more than conduct an occasional survey. The cacti are found on a ranch managed by the Magoffin family, who voluntarily shifted their fencing so their cows wouldn't trample the cacti. Otherwise, the plants are a nonissue for them.

Not all species are lightning rods, and simply listing a plant delivers a number of immediate benefits: the federal protection raises its profile, attracts research dollars, and forces officials to consider its fate when approving projects with any connection to federal funding or permits. Plants, however, receive far less legal protection than animals under the ESA. While it's illegal to "take" a listed animal, private landowners who find endangered plants on their property can legally squash, bury, burn, unearth, or otherwise destroy them, though they might run afoul of their state's native plant law.

The patterns in species-by-species spending are consistent with other research on how the public and government values endangered plants and animals. Simply getting aboard the ark is often the biggest hurdle for a species, and that decision may hinge on a creature's charisma or a congressman's clout, not the threat of extinction. When J. R. DeShazo, a University of California at Los Angeles economist, and Jody Freeman, a Harvard law professor, looked at the world through the eyes of a declining species, they concluded:

> The best-case scenario for your survival and recovery would be that your geographic range falls within states with exclusively Democratic representation; that your elected members of Congress—especially your senators—sit on committees with oversight and appropriations authority over the implementation of the ESA; and that you are a

mammal (or at least not a mollusk, arachnid, or reptile). As it turns out, who you are matters, but who you know—who represents you on committees—might matter more.

The public's attitudes also count. One poll found that 92 percent of Americans were willing to protect bald eagles and 78 percent favored protecting trout, even if it meant higher costs for an energy project, but fewer than half would make that sacrifice for eastern indigo snakes, furbish louseworts, or Kauai wolf spiders. A 1993 survey by University of Chicago public policy professor Don Coursey asked people to rate the importance of 247 endangered species. The top 20 were all mammals, relatively large birds, or turtles, while the bottom 20 were mostly rodents, snakes, insects, or snails. While some respondents favored saving all species, many excluded creatures they didn't like, leading Coursey to conclude that the nation focuses on saving a subset of endangered species, a "Beauty Pageant" or "Noah's Ark Minus Undesirables" in his terms. Another study found that charismatic species tend to have the most advocates working on their behalf. Borrowing from the literature of political science, Brian Czech classified mammals, birds, and fish as "advantaged" groups that have both political power and a positive image. Reptiles, amphibians, and bugs were labeled "deviants" since they lacked power and status. Plants, which have a positive image but little clout, were called "dependents," akin to disabled veterans and the frail elderly.

As both Coursey and Czech point out, even the most deviant species may play a pivotal role in an ecosystem, and Congress didn't mean for the ESA to protect only attractive creatures. Basic biology and legal precedent suggest the ESA should protect *all* imperiled species. In the real world, however, the government will never have enough money—or political capital—to protect every last plant and animal. "Practical reality resembles that of Noah managing an ark on a budget constraint," Coursey wrote. "This budget constraint may exclude some animals from the ark. It may also result in unequal berthing accommodations on the ark."

Even Noah's vessel was only so big, so just how many species should the government list? There are about 200,000 named species in the United States, perhaps half the total number that inhabit the country. With some types of animals, such as birds and mammals, scientists have identified nearly all species; with others, such as insects, only a fraction have been classified. Over the past 20 years, The Nature Conservancy and state wildlife officials have assessed the conservation status of about 20,000 species from the 14 best-known plant and animal groups, including all vertebrates and vascular plants. They concluded that about 3,300 are possibly extinct, critically imperiled, or imperiled (fig. 9). Throw in the next category, vulnerable, and the list of possible endangered species doubles to 6,630. Comparing these rankings to the federal government's list of threatened and endangered species confirms that the administration of the ESA has been biased toward higher-order life-forms. For example, an even greater percentage of mammals are federally protected than The Nature Conservancy considers imperiled or worse; by contrast, just a tiny fraction of imperiled crayfishes and conifers have been listed under the ESA.

The ESA's cost to taxpayers and its regulatory impacts are what the public and politicians hear about most. Far less attention is paid to the social and economic benefits that such protections can deliver. Seemingly unimportant insects can pollinate cash crops. Rural communities can reap millions of dollars from tourists who come to see endangered species. At Yellowstone National Park, for example, researchers surveyed 1,943 visitors and concluded that nearly 4 percent of the park's 2.8 million annual visitors wouldn't have come were it not for the reintroduced wolves. Those wolf lovers directly spent $35.5 million a year in Wyoming, Idaho, and Montana; once those dollars were circulated in the regional economy, the net impact was $70 million. Dozens of other surveys have found that taxpayers are willing to fork over money to save streams, open space, and other natural features. One never knows if these people would actually write a check to support these areas or if they're just saying nice things to surveyors, but the basic point remains: the public, and the politicians they elect, put at least some value, financial and otherwise, on saving wildlife and protecting their habitat.

————

The academic track in political science was leading me toward a future of constructing models and formulas to explain the species-by-species spending patterns, with an animal's charisma, economic impact, congressional district, and other factors able to explain the statistically significant differences. But it was the personalities of the players rather than the p-values of multivariate regressions that was attracting me most to the policy world. The founding fathers had aspired to create "a government of laws and not of men," but in reality, a handful of men (and women) who

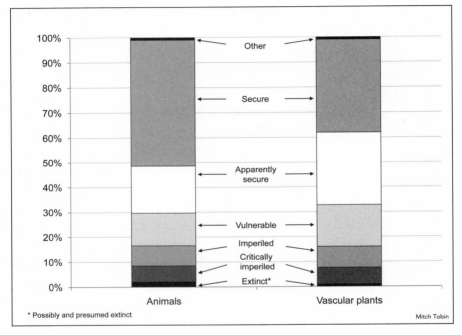

Figure 9: Conservation status of US plants and animals.
Source: Based on data in Stein, Bruce A., Lynn S. Kutner, and Jonathan S. Adams. *Precious Heritage: The Status of Biodiversity in the United States*. Oxford: Oxford University Press, 2000.

interpreted and implemented laws like the ESA were deciding whether it failed or succeeded. While I was at Berkeley in the mid-1990s, two sons of ranching families, Bruce Babbitt, the interior secretary and former Arizona governor, and Richard Pombo, a recently elected congressman from California, were fighting over the very survival of the act.

Babbitt, a descendent of a northern Arizona pioneer family that settled in the territory in 1886, graduated from Flagstaff High School, became class president at Notre Dame, and earned a law degree at Harvard. At 36, the Democrat was elected attorney general of a deep-red state in the post-Watergate election of 1974. Four years later, the death of Governor Wesley Bolin vaulted Babbitt to the governorship, which he occupied for nearly nine years until stepping down in 1987 to run for president. When asked on the campaign trail what book influenced him most, Babbitt told *The Wall Street Journal* it was Leopold's *A Sand County Almanac*, saying the book "awakened in me a sense of ethic about the land." Babbitt never gained much traction with voters, despite being a darling of the media. After withdrawing from the race, he practiced law and became president of the League of Conservation Voters until 1992, when President Clinton tapped him to become interior secretary.

Babbitt seemed perfectly suited for the position. Hailing from the West, of course, was practically a prerequisite for the job: 12 of the last 13 interior secretaries had been from states along or west of the 100th meridian. But Babbitt's hometown was just the top of his killer resume. He came from a ranching family that ran cattle on public lands, operated trading posts on Indian reservations, and managed concessions in national parks. Before attending Harvard Law School, he earned a master's degree in geophysics as a Marshall scholar at the University of Newcastle in England. As Arizona's attorney general and governor, he oversaw large bureaucracies while locking horns with a Republican legislature. He also possessed a love of the land, born of a youth on the Colorado Plateau floating rivers, fighting wildfires, and hiking to archaeological ruins with his dad. Serving as interior secretary was a dream come true for Babbitt, though he nearly left the job for an even more prestigious post shortly after being appointed: Clinton twice considered naming him to the Supreme Court.

Although interior secretary is on a decidedly lower plane than Supreme Court justice, the job allowed Babbitt to wield considerable power over a vast swath of the West. The Interior Department is perhaps best known for overseeing the National Park Service, which manages 85 million acres in units ranging from one-building historic sites to wilderness areas the size of small countries. But the department's reach extends much farther, with about one-fifth of the nation under its jurisdiction. The Bureau of Land Management controls 258 million acres, mostly rangeland in the West, the Fish and Wildlife Service owns 96 million acres of national wildlife refuges, and the Bureau of Indian Affairs manages 66 million acres with connections to 562 tribes (fig. 10). (The US Forest Service, which resides in the Department of Agriculture, wasn't part of Babbitt's portfolio, but he became the Clinton administration's main advocate for reforming that agency's fire policy.) For someone intent on improving the management of the nation's natural resources, interior secretary was the plum job, and Babbitt came into office with strong opinions about its agencies' performance. In assessing the Bureau of Land Management, derided by greens as the Bureau of Livestock and Mining for its history of kowtowing to those interests, Babbitt described the agency as "tainted by politics and incompetence in upper management and heavily influenced by mining and livestock constituencies." He had judged the Bureau of Reclamation's practices as "the most environmentally destructive of all the public land agencies," adding that "it seems to know the subsidized price of everything and the long-term value of nothing." Serving as interior secretary also put Babbitt at the center of a fundamental paradox in the American experiment: a nation with nearly one-third of its land owned by the government is also dedicated to capitalism, free enterprise, and private property.

The prospects for Babbitt to work with Congress were crushed in 1994, when Republicans took control of the House of Representatives. Leading the charge against Babbitt and his allies was Richard Pombo, an upstart legislator from California's Central Valley whose signature issue was rewriting or scrapping environmental laws, especially the ESA.

Like Babbitt, Pombo's roots were in ranching. He grew up in Tracy, about 50 miles east of San Francisco, and his family's real estate business played a leading role in transforming a working-class farm town with a Heinz ketchup factory into a sprawling bedroom community of the Bay Area. One of Tracy's main streets was named for Pombo's grandfather, a Portuguese immigrant, and on the outskirts of town, red-and-white Pombo Real Estate signs advertised farms and rangeland ready for conversion to tract-home subdivisions and big-box retail stores. After high school, Pombo studied agriculture and business at Cal Poly Pomona, then returned to the family ranch before earning a degree to help run the cattle, dairy, and trucking business. He married his girlfriend from the eighth grade and they had three children, Richie, Rena, and Rachel, all named so their initials matched the family's cattle brand. Pombo's parents had done the same, naming his four brothers Ralph Jr., Rodger, Raymond, and Randall.

What lit a fire in Pombo's belly was a dispute with the East Bay Regional Park District over a proposed hiking and biking trail. In 1990, he was elected to the Tracy City Council; two years later, at the age of 31, voters sent him to Congress. In a legislature with a surfeit of lawyers and other professionals with advanced degrees from prestigious schools, Pombo stood out, and not just because of his education. Decked out in a white cowboy hat and ostrich-skin boots, Pombo cast himself as a salt-of-the-earth rancher who had come to Washington to defend the rights of rural residents who were fed up with the feds telling them what they could do on their property or public lands. Pombo was easily reelected in the 1994 midterm elections and signed onto Newt Gingrich's Contract with America. "Today, the government rarely sends soldiers armed with rifles to seize property," Pombo wrote in *This Land Is Our Land*, his 1996 jeremiad against environmental laws and activists. "It sends bureaucrats armed with regulations and environmental impact statements. But the result is the same." For Pombo, the ESA was the most egregious example of federal excess. "Property owners and their families have had their lives and livelihoods ruined by endangered flies, beetles, rats, and shellfish," he wrote. "*Your* property rights—guaranteed to you by the Fifth Amendment to the U.S. Constitution—are under assault by government regulators and environmental zealots who believe that mankind brings only harm to his environment."

Babbitt and Pombo, united by their ranching heritage, clashed over the ESA and virtually every environmental issue that passed through the Interior Department or the House Resources Committee that Pombo served on. Congress went so far as to impose a one-year moratorium on new ESA listings in April 1995. In response, Babbitt sought to bypass the hostile legislature, as he had done in Arizona as governor. Wilderness designations and other land conservation bills were going nowhere in the GOP Congress, so Babbitt turned to the significant powers vested in the executive branch. Depending on who was in the White House, that authority could be used to help or harm wildlife and ecosystems.

One of the available tools for conserving habitat was the little-known Antiquities Act, signed by President Theodore Roosevelt in 1906. Roosevelt held an especially muscular view of the executive branch's

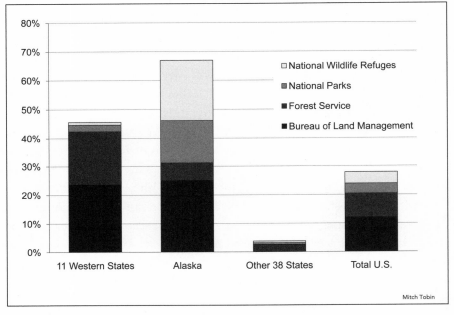

Figure 10: Federal lands in the West, Alaska, and rest of the United States.
Source: Based on data in Wilkinson, Charles F. *Crossing the Next Meridian*. Washington, DC: Island Press, 1992.

environmental prerogatives, and he had put the philosophy into practice in 1903 by creating the nation's first national wildlife refuge. For many years, ornithologists had been seeking protection for Florida's Pelican Island, and when they pleaded their case to Roosevelt, he posed a question to a government lawyer: "Is there any law that will prevent me from declaring Pelican Island a Federal Bird Reservation?" No, the lawyer responded, there was none since the island was federal property. "Very well," Roosevelt replied, "then I so declare it."

The Antiquities Act codified this desire to lock up federal lands by allowing Roosevelt and his successors to set aside "objects of historic or scientific interest." Such monuments were supposed to encompass the "smallest area compatible with the proper care and management of the objects to be protected," and the archaeologist behind the idea was apparently thinking about defending small digs from robbers. But Roosevelt and the presidents who followed took a rather broad view of what "smallest area" meant. Nothing less than the Grand Canyon was one of Roosevelt's first designations. Although the act didn't allow the president to create national parks, more than two dozen areas protected by the statute were eventually upgraded to that level, including the Grand Canyon, Death Valley, Zion, Bryce Canyon, and many others beyond the Southwest. Roosevelt used the Antiquities Act to create 18 national monuments, and by the time Clinton entered the White House in 1992, every president except Reagan and Bush had invoked the law to protect federal land.

The 105th national monument was born on September 18, 1996. Clinton sat at a desk on the Grand Canyon's South Rim, the brush behind him cleared away to improve the visuals, and created the 1.7-million-acre Grand Staircase-Escalante National Monument. The only hitch: the Grand Staircase of the Escalante was in another state, 70 miles north. In Kanab, Utah, schoolchildren released black balloons to symbolize the community's opposition to the largest national monument ever created in the lower 48. The designation effectively killed plans for a coal mine that would have brought hundreds of well-paying jobs to a county where the federal government already owned 95 percent of the land. Utah Senator Orrin Hatch, who said he learned of the monument's creation in *The Washington Post*, called it the "mother of all land grabs." "Isn't it interesting that adherence to an open, public process, where policy decisions are made in the light of day, has always been advocated by environmental groups?" he wrote. "But now, when it serves their own purposes, these groups remain silent and refrain from crying foul to a deal crafted behind closed doors." To many political observers, the Grand Staircase declaration, coming a few months before election day, was designed to shore up Clinton's green credentials, and stop environmentalists in swing states from voting for Ralph Nader.

The 1996 declaration turned Babbitt into a persona non grata in red-state America, as did his unsuccessful attempts to raise federal grazing fees to better reflect their market value and collect royalties from mining companies extracting billions of dollars of metal from federal land. "I could find my way across the West," Babbitt once remarked, "by the fires of my being burned in effigy." Babbitt also drew flak from his left flank. Creating new national monuments, taking sledgehammers to outmoded dams, and making the Bureau of Land Management more environmentally friendly endeared Babbitt to many environmentalists, but his attempts to reform the ESA incurred the wrath of activists who were loathe to dull the edges of the sharpest instrument in their toolbox. Babbitt would later call his dealings with environmentalists a love-hate relationship. "The environmentalists' job is to move the goalpost," he said. "Whenever you get near them [the goalposts], they celebrate briefly, and then they say you haven't done enough. It's part of the job."

With the ESA, Babbitt felt the scoreboard for recovering species would look better if the federal government did less to alienate the landowners whose behavior would make or break recovery efforts. Adding some flexibility to the ESA would also relieve the mounting pressure from critics bent on emasculating the law. Babbitt knew that any attempt to alter the statute in the Republican Congress would open up the ESA to attacks by Pombo and others who wanted to gut its protections. His response was to modify how the federal government administered the ESA through a series of regulatory changes and initiatives that the executive branch could pursue without legislative approval.

Section 10 of the ESA already gave Fish and Wildlife some wiggle room in an otherwise rigid law by allowing for exceptions to the strict prohibitions against killing listed species and destroying their habitat. Habitat conservation plans, or HCPs, allowed some harm to species and their habitat in exchange for protections elsewhere, but the tool had hardly been used since being created in 1982. Another approach that Babbitt championed was the safe harbor agreement. If a landowner wanted to improve habitat for a listed species, the government would offer technical help and promise that it wouldn't impose new land- or water-use restrictions. Likewise, candidate conservation agreements provided an incentive for property owners to improve habitat for species that weren't yet federally protected. If the animal did get listed, the landowner wouldn't have to do anything beyond the conservation measures outlined in their agreement. Babbitt's promotion of these section 10 tools was a turning point in the ESA's administration, a second generation of policies that sought to reconcile economics with ecology and avoid political train wrecks, as Babbitt liked to call conflicts pitting humans against critters. The new approach, however, also came along with a weakening of the ESA's regulatory punch. Many career biologists at Fish and Wildlife felt betrayed, though some would look back wistfully at the Clinton administration after George W. Bush was elected.

Babbitt and his allies spent much of their political capital fighting the Republican Congress, but the ESA also forced them to square off with state officials who felt the federal government was infringing on their traditional right to manage wildlife. The tension over federalism was especially high when it came time to reintroduce wolves to the lower 48. In 1995, Babbitt helped carry crates with the first 14 wolves released into the Yellowstone ecosystem. That program in the Northern Rockies remains the nation's best-known effort to recover the species. With much less fanfare, the federal government was also pursuing a similar effort in the Southwest, to restore the Mexican subspecies of gray wolf. The two reintroduction programs differed in ways other than their varying public profiles. In the Northern Rockies, the government could import wild wolves from Canada and release them into a national park where there was no livestock grazing. But by the time the federal government got around to recovering wolves in the Southwest, there were no free-ranging Mexican gray wolves left to transplant, so the government had to resort to a captive breeding program similar to the one used for California condors. The Mexican gray wolves would also be released into a region where more benign weather allowed for year-round grazing and where cattle often gave birth in the unguarded hinterlands, providing wolves with inviting opportunities to prey on newborns. Beef would always be a menu option for the Southwest's lobos, and conflict with ranchers would be unavoidable.

Just getting the Mexican wolf reintroduction off the ground was a major challenge because so few of the animals were left. After the subspecies was listed as endangered in 1976, Fish and Wildlife sent one of the nation's top wolf trappers, Roy McBride, to the Mexican states of Durango and Chihuahua to find some of the last living examples of *Canis lupus baileyi.* McBride estimated in 1980 that there were fewer than 50 breeding pairs left in Mexico, and he reported to Fish and Wildlife that the subspecies "faces imminent extinction." Since then, McBride has not heard of a credible report that the wolves remain in Mexico, and most biologists now believe the species no longer persists south of the border.

The five wolves that McBride caught in Mexico in the late 1970s were sent to the Arizona-Sonora Desert Museum outside Tucson and served as one of three lineages for the captive breeding effort. All of the Mexican gray wolves in the wild today are derived from just seven founding animals: three from McBride, two from the Aragon Zoo in Mexico City, and two from another lineage emanating from wild wolves captured in 1959 and 1961. It was a small genetic base upon which to rebuild an entire subspecies. As with so many endangered species, the government waited until the very last moment to take action. Fortunately, canines are prolific breeders—think of the overcrowding in your local animal shelter—and they are far easier to recover than condors, which may only produce one chick every other year. By contrast, wolf bitches start breeding when they are two or three years old, then whelp litters of four to eight pups every spring.

Breeding new wolves was not a problem, but finding a state to welcome them was. Texas passed a law forbidding wolf reintroduction, and the governors of Arizona and New Mexico vowed to block the project. Jeff Groscost, an Arizona state representative who would eventually become the state's Speaker of the House, proposed a $500 bounty for each dead lobo turned into the Game and Fish Department. To conservative politicians and many of the folks who'd be living cheek-by-jowl with the wolves, Babbitt and his Beltway bureaucrats were conspiring with environmentalists to upend a solid century of tradition in the backwoods that viewed wolves as varmints deserving of extermination. Nevertheless, the resentment toward wolves in those quarters was overshadowed by strong support in the Southwest's urban centers, home to the vast majority of the region's population. One poll prior to reintroduction found that 79 percent of New Mexico residents favored the project; an equal percentage of ranchers opposed the program.

After nearly two decades of public hearings, litigation, and protests, Fish and Wildlife was finally ready to release 11 Mexican gray wolves into Arizona's Blue Range, the area Aldo Leopold described as "the cream of the Southwest" and not far from where the 22-year-old forest ranger killed the mother wolf in 1909. On the eve of the first release in 1998, Babbitt cited Leopold's "Thinking Like a Mountain" essay. "Once

more, a fierce green fire will glow. Nature will be enriched. The mountains will be glad," Babbitt wrote. The stakes, he said, were even higher
in the Southwest than in Yellowstone, because wolves in the Northern
Rockies had a sanctuary in Canada. For the Mexican wolf, neither a safe
haven nor a viable population existed south of the border. "Our choice is
simple," Babbitt wrote. "Restore *El Lobo* in *el norte*, meaning Arizona,
New Mexico and Texas, or maintain it, on life support, in zoos."

Activists were elated when the wolves were set free in the Blue Range;
before long, they were in mourning. By the end of 1998, 5 of the first 11
wolves released into Arizona had been shot dead, the others temporarily rounded up for fear they would also be killed, either intentionally or
accidentally, and so they could be paired with new mates. Because hunters might be mistaking the smallest subspecies of gray wolf for a coyote,
biologists began to spray the rereleased wolves with splotches of orange-red
paint before they were rereleased. Babbitt and other federal officials also
maintained that at least some of the killings were intentional attempts to
sabotage the program. Residents in the recovery zone only heightened sus-
picions when they were interviewed by the crush of media that came to
cover the story. Rancher Rose Coleman-Autrey told the *Arizona Daily Star*
that the shootings were likely to continue. "There's enough people who don't
want the program who will see to it that it doesn't materialize," she said.

Despite the spate of shootings, Babbitt vowed that the wolves were
here to stay. Fish and Wildlife then proceeded to heighten tensions by
sending out an outrageous questionnaire to New Mexico hunters who
had been in the vicinity of one of the shootings. The focus on hunters
was reasonable because two wolves had been shot on the opening day of
hunting season, but the tactless tactic backfired. Hunters who received
the survey were told to write in pen and correct no mistakes while filling
out the eight-page form, which included the following questions: *Do you
know who shot the wolf? Did you shoot the wolf? If you were asked to pay for
the wolf, how much would you pay? Did you feel afraid while completing this
form? Should we believe your answers to the questions? If your answer to the
last question was yes, give us one reason why. What would you say if it was
later determined that the answers on this form are not the truth?* The New
Mexico Cattle Growers' Association called the questionnaire "Gestapo
tactics by an out-of-control federal agency." Babbitt apologized and under
pressure from three New Mexico congressmen, Fish and Wildlife killed
the query. The federal government's ham-handed approach was making

an inherently divisive project even more polarizing.

Even if the wolves could evade the bullets of ranchers, hunters, and whoever else might be shooting them, their recovery would be hampered by self-defeating policies that the federal government accepted to get the program going. Wolves introduced to the high country straddling the Arizona–New Mexico border were classified as an "experimental" population, deprived of full ESA protection, and would be incarcerated for life or issued a death sentence if they killed one too many cows. Federal predator-control agents would trap the animals, lure them in with bait and shoot them, or, with particularly recalcitrant wolves, take to the air to gun down the offenders. More than two decades after the Mexican gray wolf was listed as endangered, the government was sanctioning the very same hunting practices that caused the lobos to disappear from the United States in the first place.

Another political constraint cut against millions of years of evolution. Instinctively, wolves will travel hundreds of miles in search of food or a mate, but federal policy labeled them as fugitives if they exited a recovery zone whose boundaries were defined more by politicians than scientists. Wolves were never so good at reading signs that mark the limits of national forests and Indian reservations, so the animals frequently violated the boundary rule and triggered trapping efforts that could be extremely stressful, even lethal, for the animals. The Mexican gray wolf—charismatic to most, evil to others—now stood alone as the only endangered species in the nation that was routinely rounded up because it was reoccupying its historic habitat.

From the outside looking in, the difficulties of the Mexican gray wolf recovery effort seemed like a paradox. Healthy majorities of Arizona and New Mexico residents wanted to see the lobos returned to the wild, the ESA compelled such a reintroduction, a Democrat was in control of the White House, and the Southwest's livestock industry generated a fraction of the region's wealth. But to a political scientist, the situation made perfect sense: Critics in the ranching community and elsewhere were well connected. Fish and Wildlife's authority was countered by a Republican Congress. And federal officials had acceded to the demands of state officials to get at least a few paws on the ground. The product was a classic political compromise in which no one was quite satisfied: ranchers felt the program had been rammed down their throats, environmentalists felt the federal government had caved in to a vocal minority, and the wolves found themselves running for cover as poachers and predator-control agents continued to shoot them on sight.

7

Cub

Graduate school was making me miserable. Even Polsby noticed. "You sure don't look happy here," he said. I decided to at least get my master's degree and go through with the second year. Professors and my parents urged me to go to law school, but what I really wanted to do was write stories and witness the world up close, in real time. Unfortunately, I knew next to nothing about journalism. My reporting experience was limited to a few pieces in my high school newspaper, works that included insightful riffs like "with ten players on a side, it is evident lacrosse is a team game."

To get a job as a real reporter, I'd have to gather writing samples that were a little more impressive, so I started to work at *The Daily Californian*, Berkeley's student newspaper. My first stories were short, formulaic, and not about to land me a job at *The New York Times*. But I loved the work. Being a reporter gave me license to quote tarot readers on Telegraph

Avenue rather than just cite peer-reviewed journal articles. And seeing my name in print, even if it was buried at the bottom of page 13, was intoxicating and addictive.

As soon as I produced enough writing samples, I applied for reporter jobs in the Bay Area and got a call back from the *Napa Valley Register*, the daily in the wine country.

The pay was lousy, $18,000 a year in one of the nation's most expensive counties, but coming out of graduate school it amounted to a raise. My official beat was the Napa County Board of Supervisors, though at a small paper you wind up covering just about everything. As fate would have it, an endangered species was the subject of my second story. A local veterinarian was treating a starving northern spotted owl for a bone infection and sent a press release to the newsroom, where my editor immediately saw the potential for a centerpiece photo surrounded by some throwaway copy. It was an early lesson about environmental journalism: a pretty picture of a critter or some bucolic landscape sold papers, regardless of the words, analysis, and weighty issues that surrounded the image.

I couldn't have asked for a better place to be a cub reporter. I chased fire engines to car wrecks. They sent me to Washington, DC, to shadow Congressman Mike Thompson, a Napa native, during his first days in office. The air force let me tag along on a flight to Alaska to fetch sick personnel, including a suicidal patient who was sedated and wrapped in a straitjacket so he wouldn't open the hatch in the cargo plane and take us down with him. But for all the fun assignments, there was a ceiling at a small-town paper, an expectation of gavel-to-gavel coverage of soporific civic meetings, and a seemingly endless stream of the small-bore controversies that make up the inventory of retail politics: stoplights, junkyards, sewer rates. Even with a raise, I was barely breaking even, so I sent out my resume and clips to a bunch of bigger newspapers in the West. A few weeks later, I got a call from Joe Garcia, an editor at the *Tucson Citizen*. He was looking for someone to cover city hall.

I had been away from Tucson only three and a half years, but the place was already different. Some of my favorite biking trails in the Tucson Mountains were gone, converted to tract-home subdivisions. The arterial streets seemed more clogged with traffic.

Within days of starting the new job, I had regrets. Covering the Tucson City Council wasn't much different than writing about the Napa County Board of Supervisors. The politicians were always posturing, and the political process moved in slow motion, with discussions tabled, proposals shelved, and task forces charged with more study.

They say writing laws is like making sausages, and watching business owners go through the grinder started making me more sympathetic to their complaints. There was a big fight over a plan to redevelop the El Con shopping center in the middle of town by attracting Target, Home Depot, and other big-box retailers. It seemed like an antidote to sprawl: revitalize the city center, reduce vehicle travel, and release some of the pressure to blade desert habitat that was vital to endangered species and other wildlife. Yet the neighbors, many of them self-proclaimed environmentalists, were fighting it tooth and nail, even though most had moved next to the mall decades after it was constructed. Similarly, there were people complaining about noise from Davis-Monthan Air Force Base, which had been in operation longer than many of the critics had been alive. What did they expect when they bought a house next to an air force base? I entered journalism wondering whether I could be unbiased in my coverage of environmental issues; after a few years in the business, I was jaded about activists and the movement.

The battle over Tucson's share of the Colorado River, which had serious implications for the region's riparian habitat and species, compounded my cynicism. In 1995, the city had stopped drawing water from the Central Arizona Project canal after a corrosive, foul-smelling liquid came out of residents' taps, but now a Republican candidate for mayor and much of Tucson's business community were pushing for a new approach. The imported river water would be poured into basins west of the city, allowed to percolate into the aquifer, pumped out by wells, and delivered to homes. If the initiative passed, Tucson Water could turn off wells that were continuing to deplete the fossil aquifer and harm streamside habitat. The Democratic candidate and many environmentalists were against the ballot measure. The earlier fiasco with CAP certainly justified skepticism of Tucson Water, but what seemed to drive many people's opposition was the hope that turning off the CAP spigot would stop Tucson from growing so fast. I thought it a false hope that would make things even worse. Thousands of people would still move to Tucson every year, and without CAP, the valley's groundwater basin would be in even more jeopardy. Pressure would also mount to develop areas beyond the Tucson basin, overpump those aquifers, and destroy even more sensitive habitat.

Most voters felt the same. They overwhelmingly approved the new plan for CAP and elected the first Republican mayor in a dozen years. Tucson Water learned from its mistakes, delivered CAP water without a problem, turned off dozens of wells, and allowed the aquifer beneath the city to rise for the first time in generations. I don't think my coverage reflected my personal opinion on the issue, and I was scrupulous about "shooting down the middle," as reporters like to say, but that fight and others were leading me to equate environmentalism with obstructionism. The next election, this one for president in November 2000, soured me even more on greens. I thought enough had voted for Ralph Nader, as I had four years before, to hand the election to George W. Bush.

Immediately upon taking office, the Bush administration swerved the nation's environmental policy sharply to the right and pursued a much different approach to endangered species. Bruce Babbitt's replacement was Gale Norton, Colorado's attorney general and the first woman to lead Interior. A native of Wichita, Kansas, Norton was a protégé of James Watt, Ronald Reagan's interior secretary and a backer of the Sagebrush Rebellion, which sought to put federal lands under state control. From 1979 to 1983, Norton worked for the Mountain States Legal Foundation, a conservative Denver-based group founded by Watt and bankrolled by the Coors family. Watt, who resigned in 1983 after an off-color remark at a breakfast with lobbyists, helped Norton get a job in Washington, eventually as a solicitor in Interior, where she worked on endangered species and national parks issues. In 2001, environmentalists made a failed bid to block Norton's appointment to interior secretary, deriding her as "James Watt in a skirt" and highlighting a paper trail with considerable hostility toward some of the laws she would be enforcing, including one brief that argued the ESA was unconstitutional.

Once in office, Norton, like Babbitt, used the power vested in her position to mold ESA policy. The department refused to list species as threatened or endangered unless compelled by a court order, and it continued to relegate at-risk species to candidate status, where they received no ESA protections. The administration tried, unsuccessfully, to get Congress to pass a rider that would limit environmentalists' ability to force listings through petitions and court orders—the Center for Biological Diversity's bread and butter. Fish and Wildlife also lopped off millions of acres of critical habitat, where species were afforded greater protections. It requested a fraction of the money needed to list species and map their habitat, continuing the policy of the Clinton administration and effectively forcing hundreds of plants and animals to wait in a nearly stationary line to board the ark. Beyond the public's view, in e-mail messages and conference calls, political appointees in the Interior Department started putting pressure on civil servants and agency biologists in the field, demanding that they elevate other priorities ahead of species recovery. I listened to the complaints but initially discounted them because many of the same activists had clashed with Babbitt, a Democrat and environmentalist. I figured the Bush administration couldn't be as extreme as the enviros claimed and it was just another case of crying wolf. I was wrong.

It was early in the Bush administration that I started to write about the Buenos Aires National Wildlife Refuge and the group of ranchers, scientists, environmentalists, and government officials who were trying to shape its future. My former boss at the Arizona League of Conservation Voters, Bob Beatson, had done his fieldwork on the refuge and brought us out to the Buenos Aires a couple of times, first on a service project to reduce soil erosion, then on a 50-mile bike ride to raise money for the restoration work. We started pedaling in the tiny border town of Sasabe and headed north through the full length of the Altar Valley to Three Points, an unincorporated settlement with a sole convenience store and a tendency to wind up as the dateline in police blotter stories chronicling meth labs and domestic violence. The 118,000-acre Buenos Aires refuge lies in the southern part of the Altar Valley, and as the valley slopes gently downhill from the border to Three Points, the vegetation changes from grasslands with lots of mesquites to rocky, sandy desert with saguaros, ironwoods, and paloverde trees. Heading north through the Altar Valley, the mountains to the right are nothing spectacular, but to the left there is a striking, jagged range, the Baboquivaris. The namesake peak, a stark granite dome, looked to Edward Abbey like a "big aching tooth." The Tohono O'odham believe it is the navel of the earth, a conduit through which they emerged after the world flooded.

What got me interested in the Buenos Aires as a reporter were its failings. In 1985, Congress established the refuge to recover the endangered masked bobwhite quail, and in the years since, federal biologists had released more than 25,000 of the birds. Within a year of being set free, 95 percent of the quail were dead, most picked off by predators. To neighboring ranchers, the effort was little more than an expensive feeding program for hawks and coyotes. In 1996, a short-lived group called the Society for Environmental Truth produced a study with the Southern Arizona Cattlemen's Protective Association that compared the program's success rate with its steep cost. By these groups' reckoning, the government had already spent nearly $37 million on land purchases, interest, and day-to-day operations during the refuge's first decade of existence, while also depriving the local economy of $32 million by putting the Buenos Aires Ranch out of business. This economic impact may have been inflated, because it included the squishy category of opportunity costs: the potential benefits locals would have enjoyed had the government not bought the ranch. Still, when the study's authors simply looked at the published cost of running the refuge and reintroducing the quail, then divided that sum by a generous estimate of 300 surviving birds, they concluded that the government had spent $31,080 per quail, or $4,440 per ounce of bird—more than 11 times the value of gold at the time. *NBC Nightly News* picked up on the critique and skewered the quail recovery effort in its "Fleecing of America" series.

The quail's reintroduction to the Buenos Aires may have been destined to fail. Even in historic times, the area protected by the refuge was marginal habitat for the species since it lies at the very northern fringe of its range. Early settlers did record masked bobwhites in the Altar Valley and the Santa Cruz Valley just to the east—some even described them as common in southern Arizona—but the bird apparently wasn't found more than 30 or 40 miles into the United States. Although scientists can't be sure where the quail were centuries ago, many believe that when the weather was favorable, the quail did fine in the Altar Valley. At other times, during drought and cold spells, for instance, the quail probably struggled to survive or disappeared altogether from the valley, their fingerlike range in the United States retracting into Mexico like a tortoise withdrawing into the security of its shell.

The quail's ebb and flow in the borderlands was upended in the late 19th century, when thousands of cows and sheep invaded the bird's habitat. In the decades following the Civil War, new railroad lines, permissive federal legislation, and ample capital from the Northeast and Britain pushed settlers and their livestock farther west. After a devastating dry spell from 1891 to 1893, Herbert Brown, owner of the *Arizona Citizen* newspaper and an amateur naturalist, described the fallout:

From 50 to 90 percent of every herd lay dead on the ranges. The hot sun, dry winds, and famished brutes were fatal as fire to nearly all forms of vegetable life. Even the cactus, although girded by its millions of spines, was broken and eaten by cattle in their mad frenzy for food. This destruction of desert herbage drove out or killed off many forms of animal life hitherto common to the great plains and mesa land of the Territory. Cattle climbed to the tops of the highest mountains and denuded them of every living thing within reach.

Five years before, Brown had named and scientifically described the masked bobwhite quail. Transplanted easterners like Brown were enamored of the bird since its appearance and mating call of *bob-white* reminded them of the northern bobwhite quail that were commonly hunted back home. Recalling his first encounter with the masked bobwhite in 1881, Brown wrote, "Just that simple call made many a hardy man heart-sick and homesick." Brown advocated for quail conservation, but two decades after identifying the species he would lament, "There are none left to protect." With the Altar Valley stripped bare of its grasses from overgrazing, drought, and subsequent soil erosion, the quail were doomed. By 1900, the bird had been extirpated from the United States, and it quickly became a symbol of the ecological havoc caused by the cattle boom that went bust.

The quail hung on in the Mexican state of Sonora, where grazing had done less damage, so biologists held out hope that birds from Mexico could be relocated to the United States. Between 1937 and 1950, there were at least nine attempts at reintroduction in Arizona and New Mexico. All failed. By the middle of the 20th century, many ornithologists feared the masked bobwhite was gone for good. After he visited the bird's habitat in Sonora in 1949 and 1950, biologist J. Stokely Ligon reported that "ranch men who had formerly known of the presence of the birds advised that they seemed to have vanished overnight." No one recorded the masked bobwhite in Mexico from 1950 until 1964, when the species was accidentally rediscovered. That same year, the masked bobwhite ended up on the cover of *The Birds of Arizona*, which described the quail as "Arizona's passenger pigeon" and "Arizona's most famous bird." "From time immemorial it had thrived in the prosperous grasslands of the border," the book said, "but it died almost instantly at the demise of its home with the coming of the great herds and their owners. Let those who really wish to conserve our wild heritage ponder well the lesson!"

The masked bobwhite was an easy choice for the inaugural class of endangered species that was announced in 1967. From 1970 to the end of 1973, when the ESA became law, biologists tried 15 reintroductions. In many cases, the birds were gone within two months of being released. State and federal officials attempted another two dozen reintroductions over the next decade, many in the Altar Valley. In the late 1970s, the birds seemed to take root on the Buenos Aires Ranch, with a peak of 74 calling males observed in 1979. Five years later, after intensive grazing resumed in the area and summer rains came up short, the masked bobwhite population was down to nine. Nevertheless, the quail's rise and fall on the Buenos Aires Ranch suggested to some that reintroduction in the valley was feasible—and that cattle grazing was incompatible with the bird's recovery.

To create a cow-free zone for the quail, federal officials sought to use the authority of the ESA to purchase the Buenos Aires Ranch, which was then controlled by Mexican billionaire Pablo Brener. Not all biologists were convinced that the quail could make it on the Buenos Aires Ranch or in the Altar Valley. At one 1984 hearing, University of Arizona ornithologist Stephen Russell, a leading expert on the region's birds, said the proposed refuge's location on the fringe of the quail's historic range would leave the masked bobwhite vulnerable to weather extremes and other threats. "I don't think a self-sustaining masked bobwhite population can be maintained on the Buenos Aires Ranch without drastic management activities," he said. Still, the bird's past victimization by cattle laid out an easy and morally fulfilling path: boot the cows and the birds will come back. In his book about the Altar Valley, *Ranching, Endangered Species, and Urbanization in the Southwest,* University of California at Berkeley professor Nathan Sayre wrote that "the ambiguity of the scientific research—the fact that no one really knew what the bobwhite's prospects were on the Buenos Aires—was elided, erased by the symbolically powerful and politically palatable notion that the bobwhite would survive 'naturally' if the 'unnatural' element—cattle—was removed." Despite the misgivings, the deal for the Buenos Aires ranch was sealed in February 1985 thanks to the backing of Arizona congressman Morris Udall. To this day, the Buenos Aires is by far the largest of the 57 national wildlife refuges that have been explicitly established to help one or more endangered species.

Most of the Altar Valley's ranchers fiercely opposed the refuge's creation and objected to its no-grazing policy. With only about 14 percent of surrounding Pima County and 18 percent of Arizona in private hands, the federal government was rarely welcomed as a new neighbor. Resentment toward the refuge and its mission also reflected the strained relationships between local ranchers and the manager of the Buenos Aires, Wayne Shifflett. At the helm from the refuge's inception, Shifflett had started working for Fish and Wildlife in 1966, seven years before the ESA became law. He served at a number of refuges around the country, trying to recover endangered species ranging from Houston toads to Mississippi sandhill cranes. Shifflett wore glasses, had a moustache, and carried a trace of accent from his native Virginia. He hardly seemed intimidating when I first met him, but when it came to managing the Buenos Aires, Shifflett was never shy. Others would describe him as almost imperious, with one ex-employee telling me the refuge was "Wayne's World." Under his guidance, the Fish and Wildlife Service gradually acquired more property in the area, along a creek running through the nearby town of Arivaca and in a canyon in the Baboquivaris. All of the purchases were scenic, ecologically valuable parcels, but they had nothing to do with the quail's recovery, which was failing to gain any traction. It struck some in the Altar Valley as a case of "mission creep" and the refuge overstepping its bounds.

Chief among Shifflett's critics were Jim and Sue Chilton, owners of an Arivaca ranch that bordered the Buenos Aires. Interviewing ranchers had always been difficult for me because most were too busy to take a reporter's call and few trusted the media. The Chiltons, however, seemed eager to talk and could be quite eloquent in their critique of the refuge and their defense of the ranching tradition. Jim would go on to testify twice before Congress about his dealings with the ESA. His roots in Arizona dated to 1888, when his ancestors settled in the territory along the Blue River, where Aldo Leopold was a forest ranger. Eleven years later, other family members settled along the Salt River in the frontier town of Livingston, before it was inundated by Roosevelt Lake. Jim's early career focused on politics and economics rather than cows and calves. After earning his bachelor's degree in economics and master's degrees in economics and political science at Arizona State University, he worked as an analyst for the Salt River Project. He then served as an aide to Carl Hayden, a Democrat who was Arizona's first congressman and a US senator for seven terms. In California, Jim jumped from politics to the banking industry, holding positions at Bank of America and Shearson American Express. Starting in 1983, his own firm began to finance billions of dollars' worth of schools, fire stations, housing projects, and healthcare facilities. The lucrative work allowed Jim, his dad, and his brother to buy several ranches southwest of Tucson. As is common in the region, the ranches contained a mix of private, state, and federal property, about 2,000 acres deeded to the family, the rest mostly Forest Service and state land. Nearly half the acreage the Chiltons leased was within the 21,500-acre Montana Allotment, which runs along the US-Mexico border for five miles and abuts the Buenos Aires for 16 miles. Jim and Sue spent $750,000 in 1991 for the right to graze about 500 head on the allotment, they employed several full-time cowboys, and they produced enough cows each year to make a half-million hamburgers.

Local ranchers were unlikely to embrace anyone in charge of the refuge, but Shifflett's ambitions and strong personality seemed to heighten the tensions. Other residents of the Altar Valley feared they would get burned by his aggressive prescribed-fire policy. One rancher told me that Shifflett literally wouldn't mend fences bordering her property. Shifflett didn't think much of the complaints, viewing the hostility as the inevitable by-product of the refuge's controversial genesis, its no-grazing policy, and his commitment to recovering the quail. "Somebody has to be a scapegoat for the government when they come in and do something, so they all hated me," he said. "They were always trying to put cows back on that refuge, and I told them there was no way cows would ever come back. As far as I was concerned, they never belonged there."

Kicking cows off the Buenos Aires Ranch was relatively easy, a matter of federal fiat. Restoring conditions for the masked bobwhite quail often seemed like an exercise in futility. To the untrained eye, the Buenos Aires appeared vibrant, with tall grasses swaying in the breeze and an abundance of hawks perched in the plentiful mesquite trees. But the landscape was full of unnatural elements. The valley was now dominated by Lehmann lovegrass, a species from southern Africa that was introduced to southern Arizona in the 1930s to control soil erosion on lands denuded by overgrazing. The lovegrass, which easily outcompeted the native vegetation, may have hurt the quail's chances by creating a monoculture that crowded out the plants the bird liked to eat. The proliferation of mesquites, a consequence of fire suppression and grazing, was thought to harm the quail in two ways. First, the trees stole water, nutrients, and sunlight from the plants the quail relied on for food and cover. Just 25 trees per acre could cut grass production in half, according to research done in the 1940s at the nearby Santa Rita Experimental Range. Second, the trees provided perches for raptors that preyed on the quail. Taken together, the lovegrass and mesquites further compromised masked bobwhite habitat that was marginal to begin with.

Initially, refuge officials hoped that replicating the natural fire cycle with prescribed burns would knock back the mesquites, restore the native vegetation, and improve conditions for the quail. For many years, firefighters torched one-fifth of the refuge annually. The prescribed burns would leave behind a stark, charcoal landscape that looked radically different, but the fires only killed the top of the mesquites, allowing them to resprout from their roots. In some cases, the lovegrass proliferated in the wake of burns since it had evolved in a fire-prone ecosystem in Africa. The fires could also burn the quail they were meant to aid and torch the endangered Pima pineapple cactus. When University of Arizona researchers examined 37 monitoring plots on the refuge in 2000, they concluded that the exclusion of cows and the intentional fires had done virtually nothing to restore native plants. "The take-home message," said Guy McPherson, coauthor of the study, "is that the management techniques people have attempted don't appear to be working." That was no surprise to the Chiltons, who thought the refuge had been established under false pretenses. Sue told me the chances of eliminating Lehmann lovegrass were "as good as getting you, me, and everyone else who's not a Native American to go back to Europe." If anything, the refuge should allow cows back onto the range to eat the Lehmann lovegrass, the Chiltons and other ranchers argued. Even some biologists thought grazing, if timed right, might do some good.

Shifflett wasn't about to let cows graze the Buenos Aires. He and other backers of the refuge, including my old boss Bob Beatson, disputed the UA study and argued that more time was needed for the land to heal. Describing the results as skewed by a small sample size, Shifflett told me the improvement in the refuge's vegetation was "so dramatic you'd have to be brain-dead not to see the difference." "It took 100 years to screw the area up," he said, "so you can't expect it to come back overnight." Beatson told me the Altar Valley was a "moonscape" when he first visited in 1977. "When it rained, everything that even resembled topsoil was gone," he said. "To me, the message is once you drive something almost to extinction, you pay hell getting it back." Above all, Shifflett and Beatson said, creation of the refuge had prevented the southern part of the Altar Valley from being sold and subdivided. Even if things weren't going so well with the quail recovery, the refuge's raison d'être, the Buenos Aires was still protecting habitat for other listed species, including the jaguar, Pima pineapple cactus, Chiricahua leopard frog, and Kearney's blue star, plus scores of other plants and animals that weren't federally protected.

I went looking for the masked bobwhite just after sunrise on a sultry August day. As we set out, refuge biologist Dan Cohan cautioned the photographer and me not to get our hopes up. At the time, less than 100 quail were thought to live on the 118,000-acre refuge, and the birds were incredibly secretive. "You practically have to step on them before you can see them because they're buried in the grass," Cohan said. The quail nestle themselves in the thick cover as a defense mechanism. Hiding is preferable to fleeing because the quail fly with the same grace and speed as a chicken. Because the quail rarely show themselves, surveyors must rely on the bird's call rather than actual sightings to come up with population estimates. This extrapolation leaves those figures open to plenty of interpretation.

It takes a special combination of temperature and humidity during the summer monsoon for the male birds to produce their namesake breeding call, *bob-white*. On this morning, with the earthy smell of yesterday's thunderstorms still in the air, the mix was just right. A half hour into our hike, Cohan cocked his ear and motioned us to follow him. For the next 45 minutes, we chased the sound *bob-white*, wading through knee-high grass coated with dew and crossing a spiderweb of dry washes lined by crumbly banks. Then, in a moment that repeats only a few times per year, Cohan spotted a masked bobwhite 200 feet away, walking on the ground, its brown-orange coat blending in well with the surrounding dirt. Another quail flapped awkwardly to perch on a gnarly mesquite branch. "No bands!" Cohan whispered while looking through binoculars. Birds without bands on their legs were born in the wild, so this observation offered proof that at least some of the quail had successfully reproduced on the refuge. Our view only lasted a minute before the birds ducked into the cover again and disappeared.

Based on our location, Cohan concluded that the birds were likely the offspring of two dozen quail that were trapped in northern Mexico, then released on the Buenos Aires in 1999. Those wild-born quail were faring better than the captive-bred birds, perhaps because the pen-raised quail had lost survival instincts over many generations of breeding in cages. US biologists occasionally plucked some quail from northern Mexico and transplanted them to Arizona, but large-scale relocations were not an option. The masked bobwhite population in Mexico was nearly gone, with most of the birds found on a large ranch with active cattle grazing. Taking too many birds out of Mexico and dumping them into habitat that many biologists considered inferior could put the entire species in even more jeopardy.

As Cohan and I walked across the desert, we repeatedly passed footprints, empty plastic water jugs, and tuna cans with Spanish labels, the latter two examples of the more than 500 tons of trash migrants were dumping on the refuge each year. Over in Mexico, access to the border was easy, and the rugged mountains flanking the Altar Valley funneled the human traffic right through the refuge. At peak times, more than 1,000 migrants were crossing the preserve each day. Tourists who walked into the Buenos Aires visitor center to inquire about camping overnight were gently guided toward other destinations. Cohan said he saw illegal immigrants virtually every day. Two weeks before we met, one migrant showed up on Cohan's doorstep nearly dead from heat exhaustion. Curious about the impact of the border traffic, Cohan compared aerial photographs of the refuge from 1986 and 2001. In 1986, he could barely find any trails. Fifteen years later, he counted 1,315 miles' worth of paths.

After seeing the quail in the field, I toured the refuge's breeding facilities. Initially, the government propagated the birds at the Patuxent Wildlife Research Center in Maryland. The chicks were packed in crates and refuge officials picked them up at the baggage claim at Tucson International Airport. In 1996, the breeding operation was moved to the refuge. The process borrows heavily from commercial poultry production and relies on the same pens, brooders, incubators, and egg handlers that pump out chickens. Heat, light, and humidity are carefully calibrated to induce breeding. The quail are partially debeaked so they don't become cannibalistic. To calm the birds, refuge workers keep the radio on. Heavy metal music works best, according to one caretaker.

On the surface, the quail program resembles the captive breeding of California condors, but the two birds' reproductive strategies couldn't be more different. Masked bobwhite quail rarely live more than a few years and produce an average of 11 chicks annually. Even in prime habitat, 70 to 80 percent of the birds will die each year because just about every terrestrial and avian predator in the species' range will gobble the eggs, chicks, and adults. So the mortality rate of 95 percent on the Buenos Aires wasn't as bad as it sounded. Condors, by contrast, have a reproductive style closer to humans'. They live past 40, take at least six years to mature sexually, and may produce just one egg every other year. While veterinarians treat each condor egg as if it were a diamond-studded Fabergé, quail curators handle hundreds to thousands of eggs each year and don't shed a tear when one cracks. In the breeding facility, I saw a couple of broken eggs just lying at the bottom of a cage.

Condors' snail-like reproductive rate poses huge obstacles to bolstering that species' captive population, let alone boosting its numbers in the wild. With the quail, it's relatively easy to churn out new chicks, but biologists have an abysmal record in recovering gallinaceous birds, a group that also includes pheasants, turkeys, partridges, and grouse. Steve Dobrott, a refuge biologist from 1985 to 1992, told me there had never been a successful reintroduction of such captive-bred birds. "When you take birds from the wild and put them in a pen environment," he said, "they select for surviving in that environment. In other words, the birds that can adapt to captivity do so, and those that can't die. You lose the 'wildness' this way, and you can't bring it back."

The masked bobwhite quail seemed to fit neatly into the template shared by so many other plants and animals protected by the ESA. Like the California condor, Mexican gray wolf, Mt. Graham red squirrel, and scores of other endangered species, the recovery was predicated on a brush with extinction that left precious few animals to work with and a scarcity of habitat where they might recover.

———————

For ranchers in and around the Altar Valley, the ESA was not only the impetus for a wildlife refuge that many considered an unwelcome neighbor; the law and its protected species were also a direct threat to their way of life. In 1997, the Center for Biological Diversity and a like-minded group, Forest Guardians, challenged more than 100 Forest Service grazing leases in Arizona and New Mexico, charging that federal officials hadn't properly gauged the impact of ranching on various listed species. As a result of the lawsuit, the Forest Service adopted protections for riparian habitat and limited the number of cows allowed on Forest Service leases, including the Chiltons' Montana Allotment. Jim and Sue became outspoken critics of the ESA, and when it came time for Republican governor Jane Hull to make an appointment to the Arizona Game and Fish Commission in 2001, she chose Sue. The Center, the Sierra Club, and other environmental groups tried to block Sue's nomination to the panel, which plays a vital role in many efforts to recover endangered species in addition to fulfilling its traditional role of governing hunting and fishing.

The fight over Sue's appointment played out in the press, and the Chiltons took some lumps from the *Arizona Daily Star*, the *Tucson Citizen*'s rival and the dominant paper in town. The *Star*, nicknamed the *Red Star* by Republicans for its Left-leaning editorial board, had published a "Think About It" piece on its opinion page that was supposed to explain a controversy and ask readers to respond with their two cents. "Tucson environmentalists are troubled by the track record of Arizona's newest Game and Fish commissioner," the story began. "Chilton, a cattle rancher from Arivaca, was appointed by Gov. Jane Hull despite a flood of opposition from activists who fear she will water down efforts to curb overgrazing, a top cause of desert habitat damage." The *Star* quoted two opponents of Sue's nomination, a local activist who had worked for years to end the federal government's predator-control program and a biologist with the Center, but none of Sue's supporters. The environmentalists who were trying to block Sue's nomination had seized on a letter that the Chiltons wrote to Game and Fish that disputed an agency biologist's recommendation that the Forest Service place a limit of 252 head of cattle on the Montana Allotment, a 50 percent reduction. Perhaps the Chiltons' criticism was overwrought, for they argued that the biologist "systematically promoted the antiranching agenda." But given the economic impact of the proposed reduction and the results of the Chiltons' own monitoring studies, they felt both entitled and obligated to challenge the biologist's claim. The *Star* noted none of this as it recounted the incident, writing instead that "as a commissioner, Chilton will have a blatant conflict of interest in such disputes, critics say." (You can get away writing almost anything in a newspaper just by attributing it to some anonymous critics.) By the time the "Think About It" piece appeared, Sue had already been confirmed by the Arizona Senate. Nevertheless, the *Star* quoted the single senator, a Tucson Democrat, who had opposed Sue's nomination in the committee, giving not a word to any of the senators who had backed her.

To the *Star*'s credit, a mixture of endorsements and condemnations from readers ran in the paper a week after the "Think About It" piece appeared. Still, the slanted solicitation prompted the *Star*'s reader advocate to weigh in the following weekend. In her column, Maria Parham said the paper had "made an illogical leap from Sue Chilton grazes cattle to grazing causes species endangerment to Sue Chilton is an endangerment to the Game and Fish Commission." "She earns the description of 'unseemly' because members of certain groups don't want her in the job. Those groups are called the environmentalists, which has come to mean the good guys," Parham wrote. "She has an alleged conflict of interest and track record that troubles because she is a rancher's wife. Rather than watch groups opposed to cattle ranching take away their livelihood, the Chiltons have fought back. That seems to make them the bad guys."

Shortly after the dustup surrounding the "Think About It" piece, the *Star*'s environmental reporter was reassigned, the paper's science writer jumped to the now-extinct *Rocky Mountain News* in Denver, and I switched from the *Tucson Citizen* to the *Star* to cover the environment and parts of the science beat. It was an early sign of the "doing more with less" philosophy that would lead the *Star* and other papers to shrink their newsrooms as the Internet continued to steal readers and revenues.

I started the job with many people looking over my shoulder. The *Star*'s new publisher had issued an edict against using the word *sprawl* to describe growth in Tucson because the term was too loaded. One of my first stories, about a power plant proposed for construction near one of Bruce Babbitt's new national monuments, got sent back to me for a rewrite because an editor thought it relied too heavily on environmentalists. I was finding it tough to distance myself from the advocacy groups because they were often doing my job for me, serving as watchdogs, poring over government documents, developing sources inside agencies, and filing more Freedom of Information Act requests than most journalists in the state. Being the environment reporter without sounding like an environmentalist was proving to be an awkward dance.

8
Ghost of the Desert

The only thing on the planet that can run faster than a pronghorn is a cheetah. If you put the two animals at the starting gate and fired a gun, the cheetah would sprint to an early lead. After 20 seconds, the cat would be winded. That's when the pronghorn would cruise by at 45 mph, and keep going at the same pace for a half hour. A pronghorn could easily defeat the fastest thoroughbred, and knock off a marathon in 40 minutes. Capable of exceeding 60 mph in bursts, pronghorn have been known to pace pickup trucks, then speed up and dart across dirt roads in front of the vehicles, just like the Roadrunner cartoon character or teenagers racing a train.

Curious about the animal's speed, researchers once put pronghorn on a treadmill with an 11 percent incline and logged results that were off the charts. Writing in the journal *Nature*, the scientists concluded that pronghorn can use oxygen three times faster than other mammals their size. Their two-inch-wide windpipes, twice as large as humans', are attached to voluminous lungs. Their blood is chock-full of hemoglobin, the protein that carries oxygen. Their muscle cells are rich in mitochondria, the mini–power plants that convert food to energy. Their padded hoofs act like shock absorbers and allow the animals to cover up to 20 feet per stride. Lead author Stan Lindstedt, a physiologist at Northern Arizona University, describes the pronghorn as "probably the world's greatest endurance athletes." "When these animals are a few weeks old, they can outrun any of us," he says. "We're interested in these extreme examples because we think we can find out something about *all* muscles."

The Sonoran pronghorn's speed, skittishness, and tan coat, which blends into the surroundings, have earned the animal a nickname: *el fantasma del desierto*, the ghost of the desert. Clear physiological traits explain the pronghorn's ability to run like the wind and disappear into the horizon, but its fantastic speed and endurance doesn't seem to make sense ecologically. The animal is indigenous to North America, far from the cheetahs of Africa, and none of its predators—coyotes, bobcats, mountain lions—have any chance of catching it. But what appears excessive today was an absolute necessity just a few ticks back in the pronghorn's 20-million-year evolutionary history. During the last ice age, a pronghorn perished if it could not escape from the American cheetah, saber-toothed cats, dire wolves, and other Pleistocene predators. The prairies, grasslands, and open desert offered few hiding spots. In response, the pronghorn developed eyes nearly the size of an elephant's and as powerful as binoculars so it could spot danger from afar then bolt from threats that have since gone extinct. The ghosts of those predators are still chasing *el fantasma del desierto* and are why the pronghorn remains so fast. That evolutionary pressure also explains why the pronghorn is such a poor jumper. Unlike a deer, which must bound through dense forests to escape attacks, a pronghorn never needed to vault over sizable obstacles since there were few in the valleys where it roamed—until humans began erecting fences, largely to manage livestock.

Dozens of types of pronghorn emerged and vanished over the eons. The only member of the family Antilocapridae that made it through all the evolutionary dead ends and bottlenecks is the species that now inhabits the West. Prior to Anglo settlement, the various subspecies of pronghorn probably numbered in the tens of millions and rivaled the bison herds. By the dawn of the 20th century, the pronghorn population was in the tens of thousands due to unregulated hunting, habitat loss, and a variety of barriers that blocked their movements. Then, in one of the great success stories of American conservation, the pronghorn rebounded. With crucial support from hunters who hoped to someday bag a pronghorn, state game departments captured and transplanted the animals across the region. Several subspecies of pronghorn are now populous enough that they are legally hunted from Montana to Arizona.

Sonoran pronghorn, the smallest and palest of the five remaining types, were never as numerous as their relatives to the north and have been federally protected since 1967, when the first list of endangered species was published. Unless you're a biologist who specializes in ungulates, you'd have trouble distinguishing among the subspecies of pronghorn, yet each is slightly different and shaped by the unique demands of habitats that run the gamut. In spring, snowdrifts and subzero temperatures may challenge pronghorn in Wyoming or Montana; at that same moment, the Sonoran subspecies may be crossing scorching valleys braided by dry washes and nearly devoid of freestanding water. In the desert, the animals get hydration from the plants and cactus fruit they eat and can go for many weeks without taking a single sip.

The Sonoran pronghorn feels right at home in a forbidding land where hundreds of humans have paid for their ignorance or desperation with their lives. El Camino del Diablo crosses through their range. Pioneered by Father Kino, the Devil's Highway offered a shortcut between northern Mexico and the Spanish missions in California. Quicker and more secure, El Camino wasn't exactly safer, because there was no water along a 130-mile stretch, aside from some tiny depressions that might hold a recent rain. High temperatures in summer were almost always in the triple digits and could exceed 120 degrees. "Imagination cannot picture a more dreary, sterile country," wrote one military officer in 1855. "All traces of the road," another one wrote, "are sometimes erased by the high winds sweeping the unstable soil before them, but death has strewn a continuous line of bleached bones and withered carcasses of horses and cattle as monuments to mark the way." El Camino remained a merciless route, and its claim on death experienced a resurgence starting in the late 1990s, after the Border Patrol stepped up enforcement in border cities and smugglers shifted the traffic in drugs and people to Arizona's western deserts. In one incident in May 2001, 115-degree heat claimed the lives of 14 illegal border crossers who were abandoned by their guide in the middle of Sonoran pronghorn habitat.

Despite the adverse conditions along El Camino and elsewhere,

Sonoran pronghorn were spotted in every valley from the Colorado River to near Tucson when surveyors traveled along the border in the 1890s. In historic times, the subspecies roamed some 35,000 square miles in southern Arizona and northwestern Mexico, the population waxing and waning with the availability of forage. In wet years, there was more to eat, so fawns, typically born as twins, stood a better shot of surviving their first summer in the infernal desert. In drought, the vegetation vanished and surface water became even scarcer. Pronghorn does might be so stressed they couldn't afford to give birth, and whatever offspring did drop to the ground were likely to perish before the arrival of monsoon rains in July. Tough times were simply beats in the natural rhythm. Were Sonoran pronghorn unable to cope with these dry spells, the subspecies would have died out long ago in a region where the start of the next drought is always around the corner. To make it through the lean years, the pronghorn relied on their mobility: even in a bad drought there would still be some spots where isolated storms had turned the desert floor green. The nomadic pronghorn, capable of ranging over 1,000 square miles in a year, could also find asylum at the Gila, Colorado, and Sonoyta rivers.

Today's Sonoran pronghorn navigate a far different world. They are hemmed in to less than 10 percent of their historic range due to seemingly minor obstacles. Reliant on their speed for survival, pronghorn won't jump a simple barbed-wire fence, an impediment any deer could leap over without pause. Because pronghorn are such bad jumpers, they face nearly insurmountable barriers in all directions, though they can sometimes scoot under or between strands of barbed wire. To the north of their current range, fences along I-8, the Union Pacific rail line, and the Wellton-Mohawk irrigation canal stand between the pronghorn and the Gila River. Even if the animals could get past those impediments, they'd find a river sucked nearly dry by farms and Phoenix. To the west, sand dunes and barren plains provide a natural barrier, as does development along the depleted Colorado River. To the south, in the Mexican state of Sonora, the Rio Sonoyta has been dewatered by farmers' diversions and water wells. South of the border, summer forage is generally more abundant because of moisture rolling in from the Gulf of California. Several hundred Sonoran pronghorn live in that habitat and are the only other members of the subspecies aside from the US animals. But the populations, separated by less than 100 miles, cannot interact without the help of humans. Even where there isn't a fence, the pronghorn are still extremely hesitant to cross the border in many places because a busy Mexican high-way runs right along the boundary. Nervous by nature, pronghorn rarely approach highways, let alone cross them. As a result, thousands of square miles of additional habitat are inaccessible to them. To the east of the pronghorn's current range is the Tohono O'odham reservation, an area the size of Connecticut with about 11,000 residents. Standing in the prong-horn's way is Arizona 85, a two-lane blacktop highway that Tucsonans and Phoenicians use while driving to the beach resort of Rocky Point, close to where the Mexican population of pronghorn lives.

In this constricted environment, the US population of Sonoran pronghorn probably remained in the hundreds during the second half of the 20th century. In the early 1990s, when rigorous surveys began, biolo-gists counted about 250 animals in Arizona. The pronghorn could still roam about 1.6 million acres, virtually all of it unpopulated and unde-veloped federal property managed by the Bureau of Land Management, Cabeza Prieta National Wildlife Refuge, Organ Pipe Cactus National Monument, and the Barry M. Goldwater bombing range. Yet even this huge swath of Sonoran Desert, the size of Delaware, could not provide enough food and water to the pronghorn when the rain stopped in 2002.

The past decade had included many dry years, so the pronghorn's US population had already dwindled to about 140. As month after month passed without a drop falling from the sky, the population began to crater. For Arizona, Utah, and Colorado, the first half of 2002 was the dri-est in at least 108 years. The Colorado River's inflow to Lake Powell was one-quarter the long-term average and the second lowest level ever measured. On the eastern side of the pronghorn's range, the National Weather Service rain gauge in Ajo records nine inches in an average year. From August 2001 to September 2002, three-quarters of an inch fell there. Even hardy desert plants like creosote and prickly pear suc-cumbed. Adult pronghorn, not just fawns, dropped like flies, either due to thirst or starvation, or because those stressors made them more vulner-able to predation. For three decades there had been no confirmed records of pronghorn crossing Arizona 85, the highway to Rocky Point. In the depths of the drought, two desperate pronghorn gave it a shot. One per-ished shortly after making it to the east side of the highway; the other one crossed back to the west side of the road and died there. "You had highly motivated, highly desperate animals doing things out of charac-ter," John Morgart, head of the Sonoran pronghorn recovery team, told

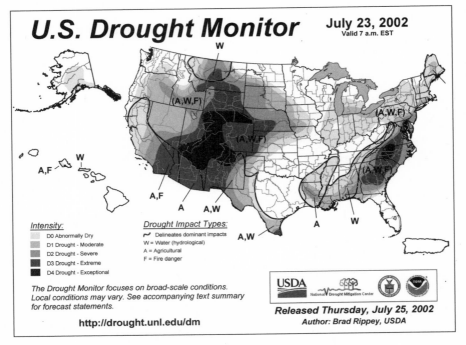

Figure 11: US Drought Monitor, July 23, 2002.

me. "It was do something creative or die, and most of 'em died." Across the pronghorn's range, biologists homed in on the beeping of radio collars only to find them looped around the exposed vertebrae of skeletons. An aerial survey concluded that about 21 animals were left in the United States, down 85 percent in 15 months. The subspecies' prognosis, grim for decades, was starting to look terminal. Morgart and other biologists thought the entire US population could blink out in a matter of weeks.

Years before the pronghorn population crashed, state and federal biologists felt that emergency interventions would be needed to keep the animals alive during a severe drought like the one in 2002. But those plans to provide water and food for the animals ran into stiff opposition from environmentalists and set up a conflict between two key laws: the ESA and the Wilderness Act. In 1999, the government proposed manipulating up to 2,500 acres of habitat, where workers would burn off creosote that could provide cover to predators. Crews would also sink some wells, irrigate small patches of desert so forage would sprout, and construct water holes that could offer desperate pronghorn a drink. Green groups balked at this hands-on management, as had some of their colleagues in the 1980s when federal officials proposed recapturing all the remaining California condors for breeding in zoos. The Friends of Cabeza Prieta derided the project as "farming for pronghorn" and suggested the government alter two acres, not 2,500. Lawyers from The Wilderness Society, cofounded by Aldo Leopold in 1935, tried to block the plan, saying it would "set a dangerous precedent of using habitat manipulation practices to create artificial habitat to aid in the recovery of listed species." The group wanted at least a year of experiments with a miniscule plot, plus a full-blown environmental impact statement that could take years to complete. The 2,500 acres proposed for manipulation would amount to just 0.16 percent of the pronghorn's US range, but the group cited a botanist's claims that "this project will cause irreparable harm to an extensive region of fairly pristine desert" and "these desert feedlots will have little botanical chance of success." Defenders of Wildlife, which had repeatedly sued a dozen agencies over the pronghorn in the 1990s, favored a more hands-on approach, but its "more cautious and methodical strategy" would first grow forage on a tiny plot outside pronghorn habitat to see if the plants would take hold. It was more important, the group said, to get the remaining cows off federal land in the area and to suspend all bombing activities on a large chunk of the Goldwater range for five months, even though there was little evidence that pronghorn were being harmed by the military operations. In response to the criticism, the government dramatically scaled back the habitat improvement plan to just four six-acre irrigation plots, plus a couple of water holes on the Goldwater range and Cabeza Prieta refuge. In the spring of 2000, when it became clear that the watered-down plan wouldn't get through archaeological clearances in time for the summer, The Wilderness Society and Defenders of Wildlife applauded the delay.

Talk of water holes tapped into a sharp division among wildlife advocates. Across the arid West, thousands of man-made water holes, known as guzzlers, had already been constructed with hopes of aiding other ungulates, especially mule deer and bighorn sheep. Often built or funded by sporting groups, the guzzlers were meant to inflate game populations for hunters. Some wildlife biologists supported such projects because they offered substitutes for natural water sources that had been depleted or made inaccessible. Many environmental activists, however, viewed the approach as unwise meddling with nature that was apt to harm the target species by spreading disease and giving predators a convenient spot to ambush prey.

As the Sonoran pronghorn were spiraling down the drain, five environmental groups were simultaneously trying to stop state and federal officials from improving 16 guzzlers to benefit bighorn sheep in nearby Sonoran Desert National Monument. Bill Horn, an attorney for sporting groups, told me hunters across the nation were livid about the litigation. "We hear all these environmental groups bleating and carping," he said, "but we don't see them putting a single damn dime into wildlife conservation." In the age of Teddy Roosevelt, hunters and environmentalists were one and the same. But at the end of the 20th century, two groups with a shared love of open space and a devotion to wildlife were often at odds, divided by the ethics of shooting animals and a clash of cultures pitting bike racks against gun racks. As environmental and sporting groups were battling over the guzzlers at Sonoran Desert National Monument, they could have been uniting to fight a far greater threat to the preserve: sprawl spilling over from Phoenix that would scare off the bighorn sheep and sever the corridors they used between mountain ranges.

The science behind guzzlers is as murky as the stale water they hold. Leopold, both a lifelong hunter and an idol of environmentalists, wrote in his pioneering 1933 text, *Game Management*, that offering food and water to wildlife "is necessarily an empirical art, in which predictions are never wholly safe, classifications of phenomenon are more or less arbitrary, and we know what much oftener than we know why." No one denies that pronghorn and bighorn sheep sometimes drink from the water holes, as do birds, bats, foxes, and mountain lions. But just because tracks in the sand or photographs from automatic cameras reveal that animals are using guzzlers doesn't mean they depend on them for their survival. Many scientists think guzzlers have minimal value until there's a drought, when they can play a vital role in sustaining populations. The water holes also achieve nonbiological goals. Bill Broyles, a Tucson naturalist and author who helped lead the fight against the guzzlers at Sonoran Desert National Monument, wrote that water holes offer "social and psychological secondary benefits" to hunting groups, which use the projects to raise money, generate publicity, bond the organization, and feel righteous. "The image is one of heroism and compassion: Who could resist providing water to thirsty animals?" he wrote.

The challenges from environmentalists made state and federal agencies hesitant about taking bold measures to help the pronghorn. As we drove through Cabeza Prieta on bone-jarring dirt roads, Morgart, the recovery team's leader, said there was "a real cautious approach because of all the litigation and posturing." To Morgart, a PhD biologist who would later head the Mexican gray wolf reintroduction effort, the take-it-slow approach to the habitat work was emblematic of years of bureaucratic fiddling that favored pushing paper to agency lawyers over proactive conservation to aid pronghorn. "I got here four years ago, and in the first couple of years I virtually never got out in the field," said Morgart. "We have limited budgets and person power, but our time was all wrapped up defending ourselves against spurious claims by providing literature reviews, providing information to the lawyers, building administrative records, responding to FOIA (Freedom of Information Act) requests." Morgart said the original plan, which called for planting large tracts of nonnative plants, may not have been appropriate, but the emergency measures that were finally approved did help some pronghorn make it through the 2002 drought. Because of the wilderness regulations, biologists were forced to carry water on their backs to three 30-gallon tubs in the backcountry. "Although small, these waters helped keep pronghorn hydrated and likely kept some from dying," Arizona Game and Fish biologist John Hervert told me. What ultimately saved the US pronghorn was the arrival of late summer rains that happened to fall close to the remaining animals. "Two or three more weeks of the drought," Morgart said, "and we wouldn't be talking about an extant population of Sonoran pronghorn in the US."

Despite the initial skepticism, some environmentalists who questioned the habitat manipulation eventually gave it qualified support because the situation became so bleak. After the brush with catastrophe in 2002, state and federal officials began irrigating small forage plots and building guzzlers capable of holding several thousand gallons of rainwater. "These enhancements should act as a safety net, preventing mass die-offs from occurring during prolonged drought," Hervert said. "Interventions are critical if we are to save this animal."

After the pronghorn population plummeted in 2002, federal officials also finally made some land-use decisions that were overdue, such as removing cattle from pronghorn habitat that many scientists felt was too dry to support livestock. The pronghorn's recovery plan said that "livestock grazing has the potential to alter pronghorn habitat more than any other anthropogenic activity." Cattle could steal forage from the bellies of pronghorn, while barbed-wire fences meant to restrict cows could prevent pronghorn from reaching food and water. In a 2001 biological opinion, Fish and Wildlife said grazing on nearly 214,000 acres in the pronghorn's range "has resulted in a significant level of habitat degradation that will require many years to fully recover."

The last of the permit holders in the Sonoran pronghorn's range was Jeff Cameron, a rancher from Ajo whose grandfather passed through the area in a covered wagon on his way to the California goldfields, then moved back to the Arizona Territory in the 1880s. Nearly a century later, protections for the pronghorn led Fish and Wildlife to kick Cameron's cows off the Cabeza Prieta refuge, but his livestock were still allowed to graze on nearby Bureau of Land Management property. Defenders of Wildlife sued several times, and the agency finally booted Cameron's cows off the 67,234-acre Bureau of Land Management allotment named for his family. "It's a son of a gun when something's been in the family so long and to have this happen," Cameron told me. A few years before his cattle were removed, Cameron had spent $75,000 to drill new wells and make other improvements. After going four years without any income, Cameron got the government to reimburse him the $75,000, but he was never compensated for the loss of his permit, which he estimated was worth $200,000. "I didn't want to go to the expense with a lawyer and fight it," he said. "I just retired and that's it." Don Charpio of the Bureau of Land Management told me he empathized with Cameron's plight, but said the pronghorn had to come first. "There are no rights here. It's a privilege to graze," Charpio said. "It's a discretionary action to graze cattle. It's not discretionary to respond to an endangered species in jeopardy."

––––––––––

A rancher in his 60s was no match for the ESA. Neither was the nation's busiest bombing range, even with one war under way and another about to begin. When the US pronghorn population crashed in 2002, nearly half the remaining habitat was inside the 1.7-million-acre Barry M. Goldwater Range. Named for the hawkish Arizona senator and 1964 presidential candidate, the range started training pilots in 1941, when air power was emerging as the key to US military dominance. Virtually all of the F-16 and A-10 pilots who fly in Iraq and Afghanistan sharpened their skills above the range. "There are lots of folks who talk about this range being a national treasure," Col. Jim Uken, the range's top air force official, told me on a daylong tour. "We take those fledgling fighter pilots and turn them into mission-ready air crews." In winter, pilots come down from frozen bases up north in snowbird operations. Britain, Israel, even US Navy ships docked off the California coast send warplanes to Goldwater to practice dogfights in the skies and strafe targets on the desert floor. With 350 sunny days a year, weather rarely cancels any of the 63,000 annual sorties, and in the vast expanse between I-8 and Mexico, there are hardly any residents to complain about overflights or sonic booms. The range contributes $3.2 billion to Arizona's economy every year; without it, the last round of military base closures probably would have claimed Luke, Davis-Monthan, or the Marine Corps Air Station in Yuma, battering the economies that surround the installations.

After more than 65 years of bombing, you'd expect Goldwater to be a pockmarked moonscape. But when I took an aerial tour with Uken, I saw virtually no damage in the sere valleys and khaki-colored mountains. Our tiny Cessna bucked on the thermals rising from the desert, and I turned various shades of green as we banked left and right on our way to view targets on the ground. Tucked away in one valley, there is an ersatz enemy airport. Fake tank columns are made from surplus military equipment or plywood painted olive. Three small hills are the only places on the entire range where live bombs and missiles are directed, and those really do look like the surface of the moon. In all, military studies estimate 84 percent of the range is "virtually pristine," since the target practice is so concentrated and 98 percent of the ordnance dropped is inert and doesn't explode. Unlike the rest of southern Arizona, the Goldwater range has been spared from grazing, mining, farming, and home building since at least World War II. Consequently, Goldwater's 15 mountain ranges and intervening valleys provide habitat for 610 species. All of the animals and plant communities thought to have existed on the Goldwater range in 1941, when military use began, still exist on the range today.

After the aerial tour, Uken took me up into a control tower to watch some of the strafing runs and bombing practice. A-10s, the slow-moving, straight-winged Warthogs whose withering fire destroyed Saddam Hussein's retreating tank columns in the first Iraq war, pivoted in the sky, maneuvered as if they were preparing to land, then fired the seven-barrel cannons mounted in their noses. The 30-millimeter rounds generated a sonic boom when launched and made it sound as if God were opening a giant zipper in the sky as they streaked toward their target: a parachute hoisted above the desert. Next, an F-16 fighter appeared as a black speck in the cloudless sky. Screaming above the desert at nearly 600 mph, almost twice the speed of the Warthog, the plane was suddenly overhead and dropping a 25-pound cast-iron projectile that replicates the ballistics of real ordnance. Before the fake bomb landed, the jet jerked upward and soared into the heavens, its afterburners crackling like a rocket. Cameras positioned at different vantage points recorded the puff of smoke rising from the bomb's impact. The video was playing in a nearby air-conditioned building where technician Steven Strombis used a joystick to pinpoint the shot on his computer screen. He then sent the scores back to Luke Air Force Base, where they'd be waiting for the pilots when they landed. "Being a fighter pilot is a perishable skill," Strombis said, "and you have to keep honing it."

There's never been a documented case of a pronghorn being killed or injured by military operations on the Goldwater range. Still, biologists and advocacy groups were concerned in the mid-1990s when they started noticing pronghorn hanging around one of the hills where live ordnance was delivered. Some scientists believed that craters on the bombing range were actually attracting pronghorn because the depressions sometimes hold rainfall. The falling bombs and projectiles can also break up ground so impervious it's called desert pavement, and this disturbance can promote the growth of weeds and forbs that pronghorn eat. The military was slow in addressing environmentalists' complaints, so Defenders of

Wildlife sued the air force. A 1997 settlement led to the creation of a monitoring program that sends spotters to hilltops at dawn.

I joined two of those biologists one August morning. The day before, it hit 114 degrees in nearby Gila Bend, where the wind felt like it was blowing out of a hair dryer. The temperature had dropped 40 degrees overnight as the desert radiated heat to the vacuous sky, but it was still quite breezy as Erik Stenehjem and J. T. Hesse climbed a rocky hill to reach the observation post. An orange sun peeked over the horizon and gradually illuminated hundreds of square miles of beige basins studded with saguaro cacti and the occasional mock tank column. Stenehjem peered through a spotting scope and scanned the valleys below for the white rumps of the Sonoran pronghorn. "When the sun hits them they give off this nice glow," Stenehjem said. "We're looking for white asses."

At Luke Air Force Base outside Phoenix and at Davis-Monthan Air Force Base in Tucson, F-16 and A-10 pilots were preparing to take off for Goldwater. If Stenehjem or the biologists on other hilltops saw any pronghorn, they would pinpoint the location on a map, then draw two concentric rings around the spot. Within 3 kilometers of the sighting (1.8 miles), there would be no target practice of any kind, and within 5 kilometers (3 miles) there would no delivery of explosive ordnance. On this morning, Stenehjem saw no pronghorn, but from 2000 through 2002, pronghorn sightings forced the range to cancel 7 percent of the live ordnance sorties and redirect another 26 percent to other targets.

Pundits, politicians, and Pentagon brass seized on the situation at Goldwater as they sought to give the military exemptions from the ESA and other environmental laws. "I want to preserve the Sonoran pronghorn as much as other living Americans," Arizona senator John McCain said in a congressional hearing that was transcribed at length on *The Wall Street Journal* editorial page. "But I'm also interested in winning conflicts and not sacrificing needlessly young Americans' lives." McCain repeatedly claimed that 40 percent of Goldwater's missions were cancelled because of pronghorn. This assertion, echoed in the *Journal's* accompanying editorial, was a wild exaggeration. So was conservative columnist Michelle Malkin's piece, in which she wrote that eco-extremists had forced Goldwater officials "to become traffic cops for endangered lizards and Sonoran pronghorn antelope" (though commonly called antelope, pronghorn are unrelated to that African species). "Instead of concentrating on bombing sorties," Malkin fumed, "our fighting men and women spend their time herding animals in the desert."

When I spoke to Goldwater officials, who neither herd pronghorn nor direct the lizard traffic, they sang a much different tune than their ostensible defenders. "Anytime you end up going to a backup target, it's not what we'd consider optimal training," Colonel Uken told me. Even so, he described the pronghorn closures as "part of the cost of doing business," while one of his deputies told me, "We realize that's the price of dropping bombs in endangered species' habitat."

Peer-reviewed research revealed that some environmentalists' rhetoric was as hyperbolic as McCain's and Malkin's. One press release declared, "Air Force Driving Pronghorn to Extinction," but the science said otherwise. When University of Arizona biologists observed how pronghorn reacted to noise on the range, they concluded that the animals prefer quieter areas. In three years, however, researchers recorded only six cases in which the noise caused pronghorn to move more than 33 feet. One of those six times was when a wounded F-16 jet spiraled into the desert. "Aircraft noise levels were much lower than people thought, and the disturbance from military activity was less than people thought," said biologist Paul Krausman, an expert on large desert mammals who led the studies. The monitoring program for pronghorn has cost federal taxpayers more than $350,000 a year, and the military has devoted millions more to support recovery efforts, including water holes and forage plots. But the animals weren't exactly compromising national security.

Across the nation, the military routinely tussles with the ESA because the 30 million acres managed by the Defense Department include habitat for 420 threatened and endangered species, nearly a third of the total. Listed species do modify training, but they don't give a leg up to terrorists, nor do other environmental laws. While Congress was debating exemptions for the military, Christine Todd Whitman, the Bush administration's first chief of the Environmental Protection Agency, told a Senate committee, "I don't believe that there is a training mission anywhere in the country that is being held up or not taking place because of environmental protection regulation." Whitman, a former Republican governor of New Jersey who was frequently at odds with the Bush White House, resigned three months later and became a vocal critic of the administration.

The military, a seemingly inappropriate caretaker for endangered species, actually does a great deal for biodiversity across the nation, simply by keeping people off its property. Near Denver, the Rocky Mountain Arsenal, a factory for chemical weapons, became a national wildlife refuge, leading some to dub it "the world's most ironic nature park." The military has no doubt caused staggering environmental damage where it operates—in war and peace—but when ordered to change its management practices, it tends to snap to attention and get the job done. Even Sierra Club founder John Muir proposed using soldiers to protect the nation's forests and extolled the military for enforcing laws in Yosemite National Park. "The sheep having been rigidly excluded, a luxurient cover has sprung up on the desolate forest floor, fires have been choked before they could do any damage, and hopeful bloom and beauty have taken the place of ashes and dust," Muir wrote in 1895. "One soldier in the woods, armed with authority and a gun, would be more effective in forest preservation than millions of forbidding notices."

Water holes and irrigated forage on the Goldwater range and Cabeza Prieta refuge helped keep the remaining pronghorn alive. But a population of a few dozen animals was dangerously low. The US pronghorn could soon descend into disastrous inbreeding, if they hadn't already. In biology, there's a 50/500 rule of thumb: at least 50 animals are needed to keep an isolated population viable in the short-term, and more than 500 are required to maintain the population's genetic diversity over the long haul, though more recent research suggests a target of at least 5,000 individuals may be more appropriate.

Desperate to bolster the US herd, state and federal biologists decided to capture some of the Sonoran pronghorn in Mexico, breed them in captivity in Arizona, then release them into the wild. No one had ever tried this with Sonoran pronghorn, though Mexican researchers had successfully transplanted peninsular pronghorn, a closely related and also imperiled subspecies that lives in Baja California. Getting approval for the translocation from south of the border proved to be a herculean task. "It took seven signatures from seven different agencies, not one of which spoke English," said Jim deVos, chief of research for the Arizona Game and Fish Department, "and until I've had three margaritas, my Spanish isn't very good." The Sonoran pronghorn in Mexico, split among three subpopulations, were numerous enough to absorb the loss of a few animals, but not much more. With land use south of the border facing far less scrutiny than in the United States, Rocky Point's population soaring, and vacationing Arizonans treating the desert surrounding the resort town like a motorized playground, few biologists felt the animals had a secure future in Mexico. "When you go to Rocky Point, you pretty much go there to have a good time," deVos said, "so the number of ATVs, sand-rails, and four-wheelers that are invading the heart of Sonoran pronghorn habitat is phenomenal."

US environmentalists didn't object to the translocation, so biologists took to the air in helicopters and fired nets to snag the Mexican pronghorn about 30 miles east of Rocky Point's multiplying condos and rickety dive bars. The blindfolded pronghorn were given chilled intravenous fluids and a mild antianxiety drug, then placed in dark crates to calm them. But the pronghorns' survival instinct, which was urging them to flee, turned deadly. Made hyperactive, the animals apparently overheated and produced too much lactic acid for their kidneys to handle, a condition known as capture myopathy. All five of the captured pronghorn died, including one that suffered a broken neck.

The next day, biologists and veterinarians changed the protocol. They knocked out the animals with anesthesia, didn't bother with the crates, and quickly ferried two pronghorn to Cabeza Prieta in the back of a helicopter. Both of those females survived and were placed in a one-square-mile enclosure protected from predators by a 7,000-volt electric fence, assisted by an irrigation system, and monitored daily by humans on a nearby hill. Additional pronghorn from Mexico and Arizona, including some males, were added to the enclosure, and the population in the pen began to slowly increase. But it would still be a few years until the animals were old enough to be set free in the wilderness. Or what was left of it.

Writers like Edward Abbey had once marveled at the aloneness of Arizona's western deserts, with some calling it "the big empty." Now more than 1,000 illegal entrants a day were crossing through pronghorn habitat. Thirsty border crossers drained artificial waters built for wildlife, and motion-activated cameras filmed humans and pronghorn drinking from the same guzzlers. Some of the water holes were tampered with so often that officials opted to put faucets on the tanks so the migrants wouldn't totally destroy them. With near-total impunity, vehicles were driving across the border and blazing hundreds of miles of new roads through thin-skinned desert. "Once that road is there, it'll be there for 50, 60, or 70 years," Vergial Harp, the Cabeza Prieta's outdoor recreation planner, told me during a ride along on El Camino del Diablo. Between us in the front seat, a brace held up a semiautomatic rifle similar to an M-16. We couldn't see them, but Harp said dozens of cars, SUVs, and trucks were marooned in the surrounding desert. Many would remain there. Dragging the vehicles away could cause more damage, and plucking them out with a helicopter would cost thousands of dollars per hour. "The problems are escalating faster than we can come up with solutions," Harp said. "Is this just going to become a sacrifice area?"

The damage and disturbances in the backcountry not only impacted pronghorn, which were displaced from cooler, shady spots and forced to expend precious energy running away when startled by humans. Covering 860,010 acres, Cabeza Prieta is also home to 20 species of snakes, 6 of them rattlers, 42 types of mammals, and 212 bird species, from hummingbirds to golden eagles. The vast majority of the refuge and neighboring Organ Pipe Cactus National Monument was designated as federal wilderness, but the militarization of the border and the mass migration across southern Arizona were making a mockery of that protective status.

All along the border, what little resources were available to the keepers of national parks, national forests, wildlife refuges, and other public lands were quickly exhausted by the nonstop stream of illegal crossers. The seven national wildlife refuges on the border had six law enforcement officers to patrol 1.1 million acres. Organ Pipe didn't even have rangers on duty 24 hours a day. The Border Patrol became the de facto law enforcement, and public lands managers viewed the agents' presence as a mixed blessing. "We don't like having them out there, and they cause some damage," Roger Di Rosa, Cabeza Prieta's manager, told me, "but without them things would be much worse." Border Patrol officials felt they were caught in their own catch-22. Critics may have faulted the agency for allowing too much environmental damage by not stopping people right at the border, but in many places, including 18 miles in Organ Pipe and Cabeza Prieta, the Border Patrol couldn't get anywhere near the border because environmental regulations forbade new roads. Smugglers, of course, knew the constraints on their pursuers and used them to their advantage.

Because pronghorn are so sensitive to encounters with people, anyone driving a vehicle in their vicinity was supposed to give the animals a berth of one kilometer. On foot, people were not allowed to approach closer than a half kilometer. But with so much traffic in the backcountry, such encounters were increasingly common. "They don't like to be around people," Hervert said. "Whether you're a migrant looking for work walking through the desert, or if you're a felon carrying a load of dope and a machine gun, or if you're the Border Patrol looking for these people, or, for that matter, if you're a recreationist looking at wildflowers, it doesn't matter to a pronghorn—they'll run away." When range conditions are poor and the pronghorn are stressed, "just a five-minute harassment could be the difference between life and death," Hervert said.

The impact of aerial activity was a bit more complicated. Pronghorn didn't seem to mind jet fighters zooming over the Goldwater range and Cabeza Prieta refuge. But the animals were stressed by helicopters, many of them operated by Homeland Security on patrols and search-and-rescue missions. "My assumption is that a plane flying overhead doesn't compute to a pronghorn and they don't see it as a threat," Hervert said, "but helicopters they do see as a threat because that's what we use to capture them." The most extensive field study of how pronghorn react physiologically to aircraft noise found that a subspecies in Utah quickly habituated to sonic booms and wasn't much bothered by subsonic flyovers. But when a Huey helicopter hovered nearby, the animals' heart rates tripled and remained elevated for several minutes.

Military operations on the Goldwater range had been a focal point for many pronghorn advocates in the 1990s; a decade later, it was a minor issue compared to the effects of illegal immigration. A broad-based task force created by Senator McCain concluded that Goldwater's compliance with the ESA had marginal impact on its training capacity; at the same time, there was "a net benefit to endangered species from the presence of the Goldwater Range." In presenting the report to Congress, the air force official who chaired the committee said that "border and associated law enforcement issues have a greater impact on both operational training and the endangered species than either of them have on each other." The Border Patrol was making nearly 10,000 apprehensions each year on the Goldwater range, and sightings of border crossers were canceling bombing missions far more frequently than any pronghorn.

Organ Pipe, named for a columnar cacti whose range barely extends into Arizona, was especially hard hit by the border crisis because its entire 30-mile southern boundary abuts Mexico. Nearby, migrants gathered in the town of Sonoyta before attempting the crossing. For two years in a row, the lawlessness at Organ Pipe earned it the label of "most dangerous national park" from a rangers' advocacy group. In 2001 alone, Organ Pipe authorities found 150 abandoned vehicles on their property, engaged in 30 high-speed pursuits, seized six tons of marijuana, and figured at least 21 border crossers died in the park or shortly after crossing through it. Officials estimated that

300,000 illegal visitors were passing through the park each year, 100 times the number who obtained backcountry permits. "Just by walking they're creating a spiderweb of trails, and there's trash all along those trails," superintendent Kathy Billings told me on one tour of the 330,000-acre national monument. The park service was forced to close nearly all of the main loop road due to the illegal traffic, and Dripping Springs, a rare water source in the area, was now contaminated by *E. coli* bacteria, presumably from the waste of border crossers. "You walk through some of the passes," Billings said, "and the smell overwhelms you." Peter Rowlands, the monument's chief of natural and cultural resources, likened the border to a sieve. "We come up with a measure, they come up with a countermeasure," he said. "It's like predator-prey interactions." Within Organ Pipe, a Border Patrol checkpoint on Arizona 85 led many smugglers to leave the highway a few miles south of the roadblock and drive cross-country, right through nesting habitat for a pygmy owl, the little bird that was curbing development around Tucson. "That owl has not returned; it's gone," Rowlands said. "There's a good chance it is the result of these incursions."

Just south of that pygmy owl nesting area, a flimsy barbed-wired fence at the border was all that confronted two members of a drug cartel fleeing a quadruple homicide in Rocky Point on August 9, 2002. When their carjacked SUV entered the park, Border Patrol agents and Organ Pipe law enforcement ranger Kris Eggle responded to the scene. Eggle, 28, was the valedictorian of Cadillac High School in Michigan and had graduated at the top of his class at the academy. Days before, he had tracked three drug smugglers for seven miles in the backcountry and seized a quarter ton of marijuana. On this day, a helicopter also supported Eggle as he walked through the creosote flats, armed with a pistol and shotgun, until one of the suspects fired his AK-47. The bullet ricocheted off a radio on Eggle's hip and entered his abdomen under his bulletproof vest, killing him. The shooter fled south and was slain by a hail of bullets fired by Mexican officers standing on their side of the border.

Eggle's murder prompted a doubling of the law enforcement rangers at Organ Pipe and spurred the National Park Service to approve an $18-million low-slung vehicle barrier along the border, a measure the agency had rejected for years because of cost concerns. Typically, the barrier is a horizontal rail situated three feet above the ground and welded to vertical rails that are anchored in five-foot-deep holes filled with concrete. In extremely rugged areas, helicopters dropped a string of Normandy barriers similar to what US troops encountered on the French beaches on D-Day. Both designs earned praise from biologists, land managers, and environmentalists because they wouldn't impede wildlife, as a fence or wall would. Where applied, the vehicle barriers did stem the so-called drive-throughs that could scar the desert for decades, but creative smugglers were using ramps to drive over the obstacles.

The barriers also weren't doing anything to stop people from crossing the border by foot. To insulate pronghorn and their fawns during the hottest, driest season, federal officials barred visitors from more than 1 million acres in Cabeza Prieta and Organ Pipe from March 15 to July 15, but that didn't apply to either illegal immigrants or the Border Patrol. The ESA was mighty enough to put huge expanses of public lands off-limits to the public. The law could also cancel training missions for warplanes at the nation's most important bombing range. On the very same land, however, the ESA was helpless to control the flow of border crossers or the pursuing law enforcement officers.

The changes in the borderlands stunned Jim Malusa, a US Geological Survey researcher who spent more than 100 nights backpacking across Cabeza Prieta to complete a detailed portrait of the vegetation available to pronghorn. He pulled up the maps on his screen when I went to see him on the University of Arizona campus. Seemingly uniform terrain in a satellite photo was actually a complex, multicolored mosaic of different habitats, some of which offered a refuge for both border crossers and wildlife. "Back in 1990, I walked across the entire refuge. I spent six days and saw not a person, not a light, nothing. Now there's tracks everywhere, the Border Patrol pursuing people, choppers. It's turned into a very busy place," Malusa said. "I can't imagine a more unfortunate coincidence than these two things happening: the drought and the flood of job seekers."

Even a seemingly innocent encounter with a pronghorn could pose a mortal threat to the animal if it were already exhausted, starving, and dehydrated. Wired to flee from speedy predators in the Pleistocene, a startled pronghorn's escape could be its last run. "To kill a pronghorn, you don't have to run over it or a coyote doesn't have to eat it," Malusa said. "All they have to do is frighten it; they live that close to the edge of survival with their water balance. These things are sitting under a tree and they've got to not move for the next week, particularly any time the sun is out. If anything scares them—an animal, a vehicle, or a person— they get up, run 100 yards, and that could be the end of them."

9

Blame Game

Men argue; nature acts.

—Voltaire

The drought that was killing Sonoran pronghorn in Arizona's lowland deserts did not spare the state's high-country forests, where Mexican spotted owls and other species were struggling in habitat compromised by past abuses. The 2001–2002 winter supplied nearly no snowpack to the mountains, so even the trees that were not dead or dying from a beetle outbreak were exceptionally flammable. In some areas, the woods had been accumulating kindling on the forest floor since World War I; now the downed logs held less moisture than kiln-dried lumber at Home Depot.

If you cut through the biggest ponderosa pines and inspected their rings, each marking a new year, a clear pattern would emerge: around the turn of the century, periodic fire scars become far less frequent or disappear altogether due to overgrazing and the government's policy of putting out fires. The rings also vary in width according to the tree's annual growth, which is mostly a function of the amount of moisture available to the plant. The same pattern of wet and dry years that you would find at the center of a young tree would show up in the outer rings of an older tree nearby. Synchronizing the rings from many trees allows scientists to string together climate histories dating back thousands of years. When dendrochronologists measured the very thin line marking 2002, they concluded it was one of the driest years since the 15th century.

The drought, preceded by a century of misguided fire suppression, would have been more than enough to make 2002 a busy fire season. But along the US-Mexico border, the threat was compounded by illegal immigrants and drug smugglers who built campfires, then walked off without extinguishing the flames. As with the Sonoran pronghorn, an already bad situation due to the weather was being made worse by the unsolved border problem. In late February, migrants were suspected of causing a 4,471-acre fire in the grasslands of southeastern Arizona. Ten days later, a 2,000-acre blaze erupted high in the Huachuca Mountains along a popular smuggling route. At this time of year, the sky islands were supposed to be crowned with snow, not on fire, so the Forest Service scrambled to find enough resources to fight the blaze. Some of the crews who responded camped out on the fire line, and one night they discovered more than 100 illegal border crossers walking through their bivouac. Law enforcement officials could almost never identify individual suspects in the border fires, but when investigators went out and traced wildfires back to their point of origin, they wound up hiking on routes rarely used by legal visitors and found campfires littered with food containers, juice cans, and water bottles with labeling from Mexico. Over the next few months, illegal border crossers would cause at least seven other major wildfires in southern Arizona, charring 68,413 acres and sticking taxpayers with $5.1 million in firefighting costs.

It was the beginning of an unprecedented western wildfire season that would change federal forest policy for years to come and pose a direct threat to innumerable species that had evolved with frequent low-intensity blazes but were totally unprepared for the modern-day infernos. By excluding fire, humans had already diminished the biological diversity in stands of ponderosa pine, creating dense thickets that shaded and crowded out a normally rich array of grasses, wildflowers, and other plants on the forest floor. When these overstocked woods finally did burn, the ecological losses were even more severe. Vast areas could be sterilized by the ferocious heat, then raked by catastrophic soil erosion when monsoon rains finally extinguished the flames.

With fires breaking out so early in the 2002 season and land managers making doomsday predictions, a bunch of us at the paper set out to get certified, or red-carded, as wildland firefighters with the Forest Service. The *Arizona Daily Star* bought us the green-and-yellow Nomex uniforms, gloves, goggles, hard hats, and eight-inch-high black leather boots that would allow us to walk over hot coals. A couple of days in the classroom served as Wildfires 101. Fire, we learned, rested on a three-legged stool: fuel, heat, and oxygen. Our job was to knock out one or more of the legs, either by digging a fire line (cutting off the fuel), dumping water on the flames (eliminating the heat), or smothering the fire with dirt (depleting the oxygen). Wildland firefighting focused on clearing the fuel and encompassed everything from sweeping pine needles away from houses to using bulldozers to blaze impromptu fire roads. Another trio of factors determined a wildfire's behavior. There was the weather: the temperature, humidity, and wind at that moment, plus the climatic conditions over the preceding months and years. There was the topography: the presence of drafty canyons, south-facing slopes exposed to the desiccating sun, or other features that would encourage burning. And once again there was the fuel: the type of vegetation, its volume, its moisture content, and its continuity on the landscape. You couldn't do much about the weather or the topography. Treating the fuel was the only way to make wildfires more manageable and decrease the risk to both human communities and forest habitat.

As part of our final exam, we practiced deploying our fire shelters, which look like silver pup tents when unfolded and have earned the nickname Shake and Bakes due to their limited effectiveness in firestorms. The instructors also took us out in a field to practice digging a fuel break, the grunt work of wildland firefighting. After a minute, I was panting; after five, I felt a heart attack coming on. And this was on pretty level ground, not the 45-degree hillsides in the sky islands around us, one of which was on fire as we practiced. About 25 miles to the northwest, we could see smoke coming from the Santa Catalinas as the Bullock Fire gathered steam at the base of the range that serves as Tucson's backdrop.

As soon as the class ended, I started covering the Bullock Fire, which grew to 30,563 acres and would have entered the town of Summerhaven were it not for favorable winds and a massive suppression campaign. Then it was one fire after another, a blur of long days, tight deadlines, and good times with my colleagues, especially photographer David Sanders. He had peach fuzz for hair and a Jewish schnoz like mine that was frequently pressed against the LCD on the back of his camera. His disposition was like Tucson's climate: perpetually sunny. Sanders became buddies with a crew from the Northwest Fire Rescue District, in the Tucson suburbs, and they let us tag along on their assignments. The Forest Service wasn't keen on having journalists embed with fire crews, even if we were red-carded and had the equipment, but there were ways around that. At road-blocks, sheriff's deputies would see our yellow Nomex shirts through the windshield and just wave us through.

A few weeks after the Bullock Fire, the Northwest crew was assigned to the Walker Fire, another borderlands blaze blamed on illegal crossers that was burning near the Chiltons' Montana Allotment. Sanders and I met at the fire camp before sunrise and then spent the next 10 hours helping the firefighters clear brush along a dirt road leading to the bor-der. The idea was to thin the area, then set it on fire to consume the fuel before the Walker Fire arrived, using the road as a backstop. It was the middle of June, nearly 100 degrees, and a swig of warm Gatorade was like nectar. For the firefighters, the backbreaking work was a welcome departure from their regular jobs, which offered few glimpses of fire and mostly dealt with car crashes, heart attacks, and other medical calls. For some, the work paid less than $10 an hour, but it involved plenty of over-time and could generate thousands of extra dollars for a firefighter whose starting salary might only be $30,000. "Paid camping with a big camp-fire" is how several described the assignment, which was also earning me plenty of overtime. "See that smoke column over there?" firefighter Scott Gillis told me. "That's a big dollar sign."

At sundown, we reached the Mexican border—remnants of a barbed-wire fence—then headed back to our starting point to ignite the intentional burn. Using devices similar to road flares and metal canis-ters dripping gasoline and diesel, the firefighters walked beside the road and left a burning mosaic of flames behind them that eventually merged into one. In stands of brittle vegetation, flames leapt 25 feet high, gen-erated minitornados called fire whirls, and spewed hundreds of embers into the star-filled sky. The successful burnout operation cast an orange glow on the firefighters' soot-covered faces, some of which were smiling.

"Burning is like the dessert," firefighter Steve Encinas explained. "It's every little boy's dream," his partner, Dominic Cuffel, said. "There's a fine line between a firefighter and a pyromaniac."

A few days later and nearly 200 miles north, an unemployed Apache firefighter went to the outskirts of his hometown, Cibecue, and set fire to some dried grass near the old rodeo grounds. Leonard Gregg, 29 at the time, wanted to make $8 an hour while fighting his creation. The flames quickly spread to both sides of a V-shaped canyon in a remote section of east-central Arizona. On average, wildland firefighters contain more than 95 percent of blazes in the initial attack, but the 5 percent that do escape are responsible for more than 95 percent of the acreage burned. Gregg's fire was an example of the latter. Backed by the wind, the flames proceeded north and upstream, using the drainage as if it were a chimney. Just 90 minutes after it started, the Rodeo Fire, named for the landmark near its origin, was 100 acres in size, generating 150-foot flames, and spitting out burning embers a quarter mile ahead of its rapidly advancing front.

Weather, topography, and fuels were conspiring to create a perfect firestorm. Gregg started the Rodeo Fire on a windy day during the hottest, driest time of the year, three days before the summer solstice. Phoenix, 100 miles to the southwest, hit 108 degrees that afternoon; even the nearby mountain town of Show Low, a popular summer retreat for Arizonans, reached 90 degrees. Show Low, named for a card game between two settlers, was now in the crosshairs because it was situated atop the Mogollon Rim, the escarpment that arcs across central Arizona and separates the cacti of the Sonoran Desert from the forests and woodlands of the Colorado Plateau. Gregg's fire could capitalize on that geographic feature because it began near the base of the Mogollon Rim and fire aches to travel uphill. As the Rodeo Fire ascended toward Show Low and other towns along the rim, preheating the slopes above, it entered overgrown forests that contained millions of dead or drought-stressed trees and dozens of nesting areas for Mexican spotted owls. At that moment, 13 other big fires were burning across the West, putting a severe strain on firefighting resources. Stephen Pyne, the eminent fire historian at Arizona State University, likened the situation to drawing a royal flush.

On Day 2, the Rodeo Fire was a monster making its own weather. Overnight the blaze had gained strength when it should have subsided.

As the wind kicked up in the late morning, the flames grew to 400 feet and started spot fires 1.5 miles downwind. The smoke column would soar tens of thousands of feet into the atmosphere, form an ice cap, then collapse onto itself. Like a bellows, the downdrafts would fan the flames with winds in excess of 50 mph, and then the process would repeat. George Leech, a fire manager on the Apache reservation, had been in the business for nearly four decades, but he'd never seen anything like it. From a helicopter, he estimated the flames extended nearly 1,000 feet. "Within a period of about seven hours," he told me, "that fire went from about 600 or 700 acres to just under 50,000 acres."

While the Rodeo Fire was exploding, I was on top of Mt. Graham, 100 miles to the southeast. Several of the sky islands had caught fire in recent weeks, so I was writing a story about the threat of a wildfire destroying the $200 million telescope complex and the endangered squirrels that had nearly blocked construction of the observatory. Next year, the first of two 27.6-foot-wide mirrors for the $120 million Large Binocular Telescope would arrive from the University of Arizona's mirror lab, housed beneath the east bleachers of the football stadium. But the telescope's future was overshadowed by the scientific findings coming from another lab, beneath the west bleachers, where tree-ring researchers concluded that Mt. Graham was long overdue for a major wildfire. The spruce-fir forest surrounding the observatory, mostly dead from insect outbreaks and desiccated by drought, looked to me like it was ready to burn. As University of Arizona officials showed me around the half-built rotating box that would one day shield the Large Binocular Telescope, someone noticed a smoke column rising to the northwest. Soon it resembled the mushroom cloud of a nuclear explosion. I hurried back to Tucson and took off for Show Low the next morning.

On Day 3, there was a stiff breeze coming out of the south, and even from the outskirts of Tucson, 125 miles away, I could see the Rodeo Fire's brilliant white plume against the deep blue horizon. Two hours later, as I drove the switchbacks in the Salt River Canyon, waves of vehicles passed me going the other direction. Pickups were packed with furniture and appliances. Cars had luggage lashed to their roofs. It looked like a caravan of refugees escaping a war zone, or the Okies fleeing the Dust Bowl. On the uphill stretches of highway, I would catch up to fire trucks and pass them; I quit counting the engines after I hit two dozen.

Shortly before I began the drive, a Phoenix woman who had been lost on Apache land for two nights got desperate. Valinda Jo Elliott had driven onto the reservation with her employer to service vending machines. Their car ran out of gas, and without food or water, the two separated to search for help. When Elliott saw a television news helicopter on its way to film the Rodeo Fire, she used her lighter to set a signal fire in dried grass and brush. The helicopter plucked her out of the wilderness about 15 miles from where the Rodeo Fire started. A spotter named the blaze that Elliott left behind for nearby Chediski Peak. By the afternoon, the Chediski Fire was more than 2,000 acres. In their radio traffic, some firefighters likened the pair of smoke columns rising from the Rodeo and Chediski fires to the burning of the Twin Towers just nine months before.

On Day 4, I took off from Show Low's tiny municipal airport with photographer A. E. Araiza to get an overview. From a distance, the Rodeo and Chediski fires looked like volcanoes erupting, their plumes tilted by the strong winds. Heading toward the flames, the pilot told me to keep an eye out for other planes, right before we entered a dense cloud of smoke that infiltrated the cabin. After flying blind for some very long moments, the skies cleared enough to reveal a world on fire. Mile after mile, the wrinkled topography was a patchwork of forests ablaze, glowing hot spots, smoldering hillsides, unburned islands, and blackened watersheds that reminded me of the scoured terrain around Mt. St. Helens. Even this fire would do some good for forest species where it didn't burn too hot, but it seemed like hell was breaking through the earth. Above the fire, the airspace was crowded and the airwaves crackled with the clipped conversation of pilots trying to steer clear of one another. Twin-engine prop planes guided lumbering tankers to the fire's edge so they could lay down a belt of slurry—a cocktail of dye, water, and chemical fire inhibitors colored like tomato juice. Elsewhere, a massive Skycrane helicopter, its dangling hose resembling a mosquito's proboscis, sucked up 1,000 gallons from a pond or from orange plastic tanks nicknamed pumpkins. When the Skycrane dumped its payload, it looked like an eyedropper trying to extinguish a bonfire.

The suppression campaign, growing by the day, was taking place in the middle of habitat for Mexican spotted owls and other endangered species. But the ESA was not stopping firefighters from chopping down trees or preventing bulldozers from scraping firebreaks around houses. Fish and Wildlife officials briefed firefighters about habitat that was especially valuable, but contrary to the claims of some Republican lawmakers, firefighter safety and protection of property took priority.

On Day 5, the Rodeo and Chediski fires began to merge. They now spread across 160,000 acres and had jointly become the largest wildfire in Arizona's recorded history. In Colorado, the Hayman Fire—started by a Forest Service employee torching a letter from her estranged husband—was on its way to a record-setting 138,000 acres. In a few weeks, lightning would spark the 500,000-acre Biscuit Fire in Oregon, that state's largest wildfire in modern times.

At about 7 PM, as I was furiously pecking at my laptop on deadline, the managers of our motel began knocking on doors and telling everyone to evacuate. The exodus was prompted when flames crossed a predetermined trigger point in Hop Canyon. The year before, the Bureau of Indian Affairs had planned to clear fuel in the canyon with a prescribed burn, but Show Low residents killed the project because of concerns about smoke. There was plenty of smoke now. The filthy, billowing clouds filtered the setting sun so that the sharply defined disc glowed mustard, mandarin, and blood red in a preternatural kaleidoscope. The Navajo County sheriff declared a state of martial law, and National Guard troops in fatigues patrolled the streets in Humvees. Homeowners raced to turn on sprinklers and hose down their roofs.

By Day 6, at least 30,000 people, maybe even 45,000, had evacuated Show Low and other communities along the Mogollon Rim. That night, Sanders and I went out with the Northwest crew. Our tour guide was Dave La Tour, head of a 39-person task force charged with defending homes in the community of Linden. As we left Show Low High School in a convoy with a dozen fire engines, the falling ash in the headlights looked like snow flurries. A few miles down the road, the entire procession stopped to let a porcupine creep across the road. Coyotes howled at a nearly full moon tinted orange by the omnipresent smoke, which seeped into the vehicle and reduced the driver's visibility to a few hundred feet. Slowly, we navigated winding dirt roads, passing by houses still unscathed but tucked into a tinderbox that was ready to ignite as soon as a burning ember found its way there. "This is a structure-protection nightmare," La Tour said, pointing to the many log cabins with branches hanging over their wood shingle roofs.

On a street named Dreamy Avenue, we found dozens of homes reduced to their foundations and chimneys. At one smoldering house, a melted white plastic fence drooped on the ground like something from a Salvador Dali painting. At another, aluminum siding had liquefied into a silvery stream, then solidified after the fire subsided. Like most wildfires, this one was laying down at night due to higher humidity, lower temperatures, and calmer winds. Still, dangers were lurking everywhere. There were downed power lines that we could only assume were de-energized. Propane tanks hissed, venting their excess pressure. We came to a tiny log cabin with a ground fire creeping toward it. La Tour ordered the crew, Sanders, and me to grab some hand tools. For the next 45 minutes we dug and scratched a narrow firebreak around the house's perimeter, close enough to the flames that the heat stung my cheeks.

The cabin was spared, but it was the exception. At daybreak, the world looked monochromatic, with gray ash covering charcoal hills and the obliterated neighborhood conjuring black-and-white footage of Dresden, Tokyo, and other cities firebombed in World War II. By the time our overnight shift was over, we counted 94 houses destroyed. Back at fire camp, I could think of nothing other than sleep and staggered to the darkened high school gymnasium, where dozens of firefighters were flat out on the basketball court, creating a symphony of snoring. I unrolled my Therm-a-Rest pad and started sawing logs.

In all, the nearly 470,000-acre Rodeo-Chediski Fire would level 465 homes and force insurers to pay $120 million in claims, making it Arizona's second most expensive natural disaster after the floods of 1983. At its widest, the fire stretched 40 miles east-to-west and 25 miles north-to-south. At least 2,000 homes were saved thanks to the $43 million suppression effort, which included 6,600 firefighters and other personnel, 245 fire engines, 95 water tenders, 89 bulldozers, 26 helicopters, and 13 heavy air tankers. But what really put the fire out was the arrival of monsoon moisture.

Leonard Gregg pleaded guilty to setting the Rodeo Fire, and a judge sentenced him to 10 years in prison. He was also ordered to pay $28 million in restitution, at a pace of $100 a month. Federal prosecutors declined to charge Valinda Jo Elliott, saying she started the Chediski Fire out of necessity and without criminal intent. When US Attorney Paul Charlton made that announcement in Heber, which suffered especially heavy losses, a local resident hurled a burned log onto the gymnasium floor and was taken away in handcuffs.

Besides the lost homes and scarred forests, another unfortunate legacy of the Rodeo-Chediski Fire was the belief that environmentalists suing on behalf of owls and other species were responsible for the damage. A few weeks after the fire subsided, a poll conducted by a Phoenix TV station and the Arizona State University journalism school found that 61 percent of registered voters in Arizona agreed that "environmentalists are largely to blame for the recent forest fires because they have brought lawsuits which prevent the Forest Service from thinning and properly managing the forest." Even 57 percent of Democrats and 38 percent of self-identified liberals went along with that statement. Never mind that the state was in the midst of record drought, or that two people had deliberately started fires at the worst possible time and place, or that residents on the Mogollon Rim had opposed prescribed burns before the fire, or that the Forest Service itself had primed the area for a catastrophe with a century of mistaken policy. It was all the tree huggers' fault.

I had done my part to stoke the embers. On the evening Show Low evacuated, I couldn't get a cell phone signal and I had to call my editor, so I drove to a convenience store to use the pay phone. There I found Tracy Packer crying. She'd just heard from relatives that flames had reached her home in nearby Overgaard. "I think we should sue the environmentalists," she told me. "They're the cause of this for not letting the Forest Service manage the forest." Packer's reflexive response, which the *Star* ran on the front page the next day, was heard over and over that summer as the West burned. When houses went up in flames, angry homeowners blamed activists for blocking timber sales and forest thinning projects meant to reduce the fuel loads. In the Southwest, most of the appeals cited the Mexican spotted owl, the northern goshawk (which the Center for Biological Diversity had failed to get listed), or both. As Rodeo-Chediski was burning, Republican politicians added rhetorical fuel to the fire. Arizona senator Jon Kyl lashed out at "radical environmentalists," saying, "They would rather the forests burn than to see sensible forest management." Arizona governor Jane Hull complained that "the obstructionism of some environmental extremists is putting homes, businesses, wildlife habitat, water and air quality all at great risk by preventing the protection of our forests."

Who was right? I found firefighters to be some of the most credible sources in a hyperpoliticized debate because they lived (and breathed) forest fires. When I asked Dan Oltrogge, one of the generals in the federal government's army of firefighters, he told me, "Special interest groups could be a convenient target, but I believe it's not that simple."

"It's not one initiative or one appeal that has predisposed the landscape to these large, unwanted wildfires," said Oltrogge, a commander of one of the elite management teams brought in to control the biggest and most dangerous wildfires. Like other firefighters, Oltrogge thought it was crucial to thin forests and light more prescribed burns. Yet there was no guarantee those treated areas would stop a fire, or even make it easier to control. "The conditions may set themselves up with weather, fuels, and topography so that you could have done an outstanding job of thinning and the fire will still carry through that area with enthusiasm," he said.

The Republican politicians and the residents along the Mogollon Rim were right about one thing: a lawsuit from the Center had blocked a 7,000-acre thinning project that was subsequently overrun by the Rodeo-Chediski Fire. The Baca Ecosystem Management Plan, approved by the Forest Service in 1999 after several years of study, called for cutting tens of thousands of small trees, clearing fuel with prescribed burns, and logging 31 million board feet of timber. The Center sued in 2000 to stop the Baca project because lumberjacks would be chopping trees wider than 16 inches. To critics, the lawsuit was symptomatic of environmentalists' overzealous litigation and the "analysis paralysis" plaguing the Forest Service. An agency report, "The Process Predicament," estimated Forest Service workers spent 40 percent of their time on planning. Because of excessive study and bureaucracy, Forest Service officials often found themselves in a "costly procedural quagmire, where a single project can take years to move forward and where planning costs alone can exceed $1 million," the report said. "Even non-controversial projects often proceed at a snail's pace."

Whatever the merits of the proposed Baca project, it would have made virtually no difference in the fate of the Rodeo-Chediski Fire. To begin with, it accounted for less than 2 percent of the acreage burned and was located on the very northwestern edge of the fire. The proposed tree-cutting—call it thinning or logging—was nowhere near the houses leveled by the flames. By the time the fire reached the proposed Baca project site and the Sitgreaves National Forest, it had been gaining momentum for three days while burning on the Fort Apache Reservation, where environmentalists had little say in forest practices. On the other side of the Baca site, the community of Forest Lakes never burned. Firefighters defending that community were aided by 306 acres of thinning completed prior to the fire, which the Center had agreed to.

Contrary to the rhetoric, the Rodeo-Chediski Fire didn't burn through forests left unmanaged because of litigious environmentalists. The federal government had been suppressing fires there for decades, and when the flames arrived at the Sitgreaves National Forest, they certainly didn't enter a pristine wilderness set aside for backpackers and spotted owls. The Sitgreaves had produced more timber than any other national forest in the region, and it was still feeling the effects of a century's worth of logging that had only recently stopped. Intensive logging can actually exacerbate a future fire's intensity by removing the biggest, most fire-resistant pines and encouraging the sprouting of dense stands of slender trees that are more apt to burn. Not a single acre within the 470,000-acre fire's perimeter was a roadless or wilderness area, where logging, thinning, or other human activity would have been restricted. But within the burned area there were at least 2,145 miles of roads; in one section, the fire jumped over 25 roads before reaching its final perimeter, according to an analysis of aerial and satellite photos.

The imagery from space combined with on-the-ground surveys of the postfire landscape also demonstrated that the hands-off approach could be just as problematic as logging. In areas that had been thinned or burned intentionally, scientists found that the Rodeo-Chediski Fire's damage wasn't as severe, even during the exceptionally hot, dry, and windy period when it was raging. Jim Anderson, a planner with the Apache-Sitgreaves National Forest, argued that the mechanical thinning and prescribed fires were the "deciding factor whether the fire would roll into Show Low" because they calmed the flames and allowed crews to directly attack the blaze; his assessment was backed up by the officials brought in to fight the fire.

After the Rodeo-Chediski Fire, politicians and media accounts invariably described burned portions of the Baca site and other areas as destroyed. In reality, the postfire landscape was a patchwork of burn severity, with some places unlikely to recover for centuries and others better off after a relatively mild fire cleared excess fuel. Wildfires almost always burn in such a mosaic, and while the Rodeo-Chediski Fire was unnaturally large and intense, 47 percent of the terrain inside its perimeter either didn't burn at all or was only lightly scorched (fig. 12). Years later, an Arizona Game and Fish Department biologist would tell me the fire had done more good than harm, at least above the Mogollon Rim, where the burning wasn't as extreme. It had opened up the forest, added nutrients to the soil, and promoted the growth of forage for elk and deer.

The bumper crops of grass and forbs that can sprout after a fire also translate into booming populations of mice, voles, and wood rats: the spotted owl's prey. Owl experts rank the threat of catastrophic wildfire on a par with logging, but the birds can also respond positively to fires. "It's perhaps not as negative an outcome as common sense would suggest," said Joe Ganey, a Forest Service expert on the owl. It all depends on the intensity of the flames. If a fire gets up into the forest canopy, it can kill chicks left behind and render habitat unsuitable for decades or longer. The Rodeo-Chediski Fire swept through 55 nesting and roosting sites for Mexican spotted owls, about 5 percent of the known total. By looking at maps, scientists concluded that about half the acreage in the 55 sites suffered moderate or severe damage, but many years after the Rodeo-Chediski Fire scientists still hadn't studied its effects on the owl. "We have zero funding to get that information," Shaula Hedwall, a Fish and Wildlife biologist, told me. The ignorance about the bird extended well beyond the perimeter of the Rodeo-Chediski Fire because there was also no money to conduct surveys that would estimate the owl's overall population. "We truly don't know how the bird's population is doing right now. Is it declining? Is it stable?" Hedwall said. "The scary thing is that we know more about the owl than a lot of other species that are listed, but there are still these big nagging questions."

While the Center for Biological Diversity's opposition to the Baca project did not significantly alter the Rodeo-Chediski Fire's course, it did highlight that environmentalists were routinely challenging, delaying, and halting thinning projects. For some activists, stopping *all* logging on national forests remained an article of faith. In 2001, Tom Knudson, a two-time winner of the Pulitzer Prize at *The Sacramento Bee*, concluded that environmentalists were "misusing forest science" to block fuels reduction projects. "In the battle over the majestic conifer forests that blanket much of the West," Knudson wrote, "advocacy is often shoving science aside—and forests, wildlife and human communities are suffering the consequences." Similarly, a 2003 investigation by Mark Flatten of the *East Valley Tribune* in Mesa concluded that over the past decade "almost every major forest-thinning project in Arizona has been blocked by a near-constant chain of lawsuits brought by environmental groups." If you thought all of those projects entailed vital fuels reduction meant to save

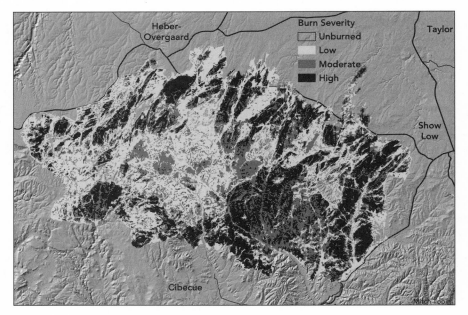

Figure 12: Patchwork of burn severity from Rodeo-Chediski Fire.
Source: Rodeo-Chediski Burned Area Emergency Rehabilitation Team.

homes and wildlife habitat from incineration, the appeals and lawsuits were practically criminal. If, however, you saw many of these plans as destructive timber sales that were gussied up to look like fuels reduction projects, such challenges were noble efforts to stop loggers from pillaging our natural heritage.

Although endangered species were often wrapped up in the thinning controversy and the source of delays, the fights generally revolved around the application of another landmark law, the National Environmental Policy Act. Enacted in 1969, NEPA (pronounced "NEE-pah" by wonks) forces federal agencies like the Forest Service to assess the environmental consequences of their actions. The studies don't only look at critters, pollution, and the like; they also account for socioeconomics, archaeological resources, even traffic. The thick, mind-numbing documents that emerge from the NEPA process can be appealed, and not just by environmentalists.

When the Government Accountability Office, Congress's nonpartisan watchdog, finally did a thorough study of the thinning debate, it found that 58 percent of the decisions that could be challenged were appealed, appearing to vindicate Republicans. But the same study also found that nearly three-quarters of the appealed projects went ahead without any changes at all and only 3 percent of the projects went to court (the Forest Service lost about half the time). Green groups had filed most of the appeals, and those challenges surely had some chilling effect on Forest Service officials. But the GAO also found the appellants included the Capitol Trail Vehicle Association, Minnesota Forest Industries, Inc., and Montanans for Property Rights. In a broader study of all 3,736 appeals the Forest Service received from 1997 to 2002, researchers at Northern Arizona University also found that plenty of businesses, individuals, tribes, and other interests challenged agency decisions. "Although the perception has been that environmental groups are the primary appellants using project appeals to delay Forest Service projects, the data paint a far more complex picture," the researchers wrote in the *Journal of Forestry*.

Out of all that complexity, some clear trends are obvious. For starters, many private landowners don't bother to thin trees on their own property or take commonsense measures like clearing pine needles from around their homes. As a general rule, proposals to remove little trees on adjoining public lands go unchallenged. But support quickly drops if chain saws will be buzzing far from communities and slicing into bigger trees. There is considerable debate about where to draw the line, because there is a spectrum of scientific opinion on which trees should be cut, in part because conditions vary so widely from state to state, even watershed to watershed.

Money is a major reason why commercial-scale logging is included in many thinning projects and why more fuels reduction doesn't take place on national forests. Cutting down thousands of trees is labor intensive, time consuming, and expensive: $500 an acre and up in many parts of the West. Multiply that figure by the government's estimate that 190 million acres of federal land are at high risk of fire, and you've got a nearly $100 billion tab. And that's just the first installment, because the fuel keeps growing back and must be treated over and over. Financially, the big problem is that the little trees targeted in thinning projects typically produce zero revenue because they are too small for making lumber. After the skinny trees are cut, they're usually dumped in piles and burned when weather conditions are favorable. By selling the larger trees to timber companies, the government can recoup at least some of its costs.

What about prescribed burning? By itself, setting intentional fires is far cheaper than thinning, and in grasslands such work may only cost a couple bucks an acre. Reintroducing fire to forests, either manually or by letting wildfires burn, is really the only way to get large-scale results. But in overgrown forests, crews typically must first remove smaller trees and low-hanging limbs to prevent an intentional fire from becoming an accidental inferno. The threat of such a disaster continues to make many people and politicians suspicious of the approach. In April 2000, for example, a prescribed burn near Los Alamos, New Mexico, took off with the wind, burned 43,000 acres, and destroyed more than 220 structures. Public opposition to smoke poses another major obstacle because many people don't realize that putting up with bad air for a short period is needed to prevent conflagrations that will create much worse pollution, torch valuable habitat, and damage critical watersheds.

The controversy over thinning and burning had been brewing for some time and the big fires of 2002—Rodeo-Chediski in Arizona, Hayman in Colorado, and Biscuit in Oregon—elevated the issue to the top of policymakers' agenda. The Bush administration, led by a man who cleared brush in West Texas during vacations, took up the fight and proposed its Healthy Forests plan while the president visited the Biscuit Fire. The initiative sought to dramatically increase both the removal of small trees near homes and the logging of larger trees in the backcountry by making it harder for activists and others to challenge such projects. Many environmentalists pilloried the plan, describing its title as Orwellian Bush-speak similar to the administration's Clear Skies initiative for air pollution. But foresters, firefighters, and even a few conservation groups saw merit in the proposal, especially the promise of an infusion of federal funds for fuels reduction. It was a lack of money, not an excess of lawsuits, that was holding up many thinning projects, including plenty that environmentalists supported.

Arizona's Coronado National Forest was a perfect illustration. When the National Fire Plan was updated in 2000, it estimated the forest needed about $1.5 million for fuels reduction annually. In reality, the Coronado got about half that. After the close call in 2002 with the Bullock Fire, Summerhaven residents pleaded with federal officials to thin a quarter-mile-wide belt around the town, a strategy supported by local environmentalists. "It is only a matter of time," the residents said in a petition, "before a forest fire once again threatens our community's safety, wipes out more of the forest and damages the vital watershed for the mountain and desert below." But even after the Bullock Fire's glancing blow, federal funding for fuels reduction in the Santa Catalina Ranger District *fell* the next year, from $234,000 to $171,000.

Forest service crews had only cleared 70 acres around Summerhaven by June 17, 2003, when a fire lookout atop Mt. Lemmon spotted a wisp of blue-gray smoke two miles from the village. An hour later, a circling pilot reported that flames were leaping into the treetops. It was 106 degrees down in Tucson, and the fire quickly established itself downhill from Summerhaven, the wind at its back. On Day 3, stoked by 60 mph winds, the Aspen Fire swept through the town and destroyed 314 of 467 homes there. Tucsonans' hearts sunk as they watched the dirty plume rise above the Santa Catalinas.

Even some buildings in Summerhaven that were fireproofed went up in flames, so the village's demise also pointed to another variable missing in the calculus of blame: people who built wooden cabins in flammable, overgrown forests. The problem was even more severe outside the Southwest. In the 1990s, 61 percent of the more than 1 million homes built in California, Oregon, and Washington were situated in the fire-prone wildland-urban interface, while in California alone, about 40 percent of the state's 12 million homes faced a high to extreme threat of wildfires.

A few weeks after monsoon rains extinguished the Aspen Fire, *Air Force One* landed in Tucson and *Marine One* whisked President Bush to the top of the Santa Catalinas. Bush's bully pulpit was erected before Summerhaven's charred slopes and singed pine trees to promote the Healthy Forests bill. The 84,750-acre Aspen Fire, which burned most of the mountain that was spared by the Bullock Fire, offered a great visual backdrop for selling the legislation, but the wrong backstory. Nonetheless, Bush's speech focused on appeals and lawsuits, not the lack of funding for forest thinning and prescribed burns. "All too often," he told the crowd and 16 TV cameras, "the litigation process delays forest projects for years and years, and that's a reality. Our forests remain unprotected, our communities are vulnerable."

Despite protests from many leading environmentalists, the Healthy Forests Restoration Act easily passed in the Congress and became law in December 2003, helped in part by the devastating Southern California wildfires that killed two dozen people two months earlier. Some environmental groups, including The Nature Conservancy, backed the bill, which also received an important push from California senator Dianne Feinstein, a Democrat whose rating from the League of Conservation Voters had averaged 90 out of 100 since 1999. Feinstein and other Democrats added provisions to protect old-growth forests and focus more of the thinning around homes, but many environmentalists still ridiculed the bill as the "No Tree Left Behind Act."

The fight over thinning appeals and litigation got all of the media attention, and the Healthy Forests Restoration Act did change how the government evaluates such projects for their impacts on endangered species. It exempted more proposals, expedited the process, and forced officials to balance the positive effects of fuels reduction against short-term harm to wildlife. But the Healthy Forests law also included many noncontroversial provisions to promote community wildfire plans, combat insect outbreaks, and find new uses for the runty trees clogging the West's forests. Most important, the bill authorized a near-doubling of the budget for thinning. At least in the Southwest, the Healthy Forests act didn't lead to major increases in commercial logging because the economics were unfavorable and few mills were still in existence. The big timber plant on the Mogollon Rim was now producing the recycled newsprint used to make the *Arizona Daily Star* and other papers. But the law definitely made it harder for environmentalists to block logging on federal land. In the months following passage of the Healthy Forests Restoration Act, the government won 17 straight court cases favoring tree cutting over environmentalists' challenges.

For all the contention surrounding wildfires, thinning, and Mexican spotted owls, you'd think someone would have studied how the three interact. In reality, hardly anything was known about how various approaches to fuels reduction affected the owl or the forest ecosystem. Pat "Ranger" Ward, a biologist with the Forest Service, hoped to change that. He and Joe Ganey, another Forest Service owl expert, designed a nine-year, $4 million study in south-central New Mexico's Sacramento Mountains. Crews would thin 1,200-acre plots in the Lincoln National Forest according to three different prescriptions. Researchers would monitor the owls, their prey, and the forest environment in the treatment areas, then compare the results to control plots. Ward told me the Forest Service was initially supportive and spent $1.5 million in the first two years, but then funding for the study was slashed and the Forest Service let go of Ward.

When I met Ward for dinner at a Chili's in his hometown of Alamogordo, he began skewering his former employer and the Bush administration before our first beers arrived. "They're using the fire threat as a smokescreen to take out the big trees," he said. "The Forest Service is still in the same old trap that environmental groups warned about." In the 1990s, Ward had surveyed all 11 national forests in the Southwest for spotted owls. He said there were still a lot of unanswered questions about owls, fires, and forest thinning, but it was clear that logging the few remaining big trees was not the answer. "Everyone who works with fire prevention knows that's the last thing you want to do," he said.

The next morning, before heading up into the Sacramento Mountains, we had a hearty breakfast in Alamogordo at the Waffle and Pancake Shoppe, which offered spotted owl omelets. "Tastes just like chicken (recommended by the Sierra Club)," the menu said. Logging now barely registers in Alamogordo's economy, which is largely driven by tourists heading to White Sands National Monument and operations at Holloman Air Force Base, home to bat-winged stealth bombers featured on a slew of billboards in town.

Leaving Alamogordo, it took Ward and me less than a half hour of driving up a steep, winding highway to rise nearly a mile in elevation from the yuccas at the base of the Sacramentos to the pines around

Cloudcroft, a resort town similar to Summerhaven that was also threatened by wildfires. Ward explained how owl conservation is centered on PACs. Not political action committees funded by loggers or tree huggers, but 600-acre protected activity centers where the birds spend most of their time. Spotted owls, which have an average life span of eight years, usually exhibit fidelity to their PACs and their mates. There are about 1,000 spotted owl PACs, nearly all in Arizona or New Mexico; one-fifth are in the Sacramento Mountains and two nearby ranges. Commercial logging isn't allowed in a PAC, but these areas only make up about 3 percent of the region's national forests. Owl-related concerns have also stopped logging on steep slopes, where there hasn't been tree-cutting for 30 years. This puts another 30 percent of the Southwest's national forests off-limits to timber companies, though the Forest Service wouldn't allow logging in many of those areas anyway because of the threat of soil erosion. To reduce wildfire risks, the Forest Service can thin trees in a portion of a PAC, provided that biologists monitor the owls and crews do not disturb the inner 100 acres, where the birds nest and roost.

After Ward's lesson on PACs, we headed out to visit one, but not before picking up some unsuspecting mice that we would use as owl bait. We parked beside the highway, picked our way through the dense forest, and saw the stumps of some giant trees that were logged decades ago. "It's hard to find a tree over 36 inches nowadays," Ward said. "Before there were easily trees over 60 inches." Nearly all the easily accessible timber in the Sacramento Mountains was cut between 1900 and 1940, and much of the early harvest was used in the valleys below as railroad ties. A half mile in from the highway, we came to some big firs that loggers had spared, what Ward called a freckle on an otherwise homogenous landscape of skinny to medium-sized trees. From bottom to top, this freckle was more complex than the thickets we had just passed through. There was a layer of plants on the ground, then low-slung shrubs, then midsized maples and oaks, and finally big firs filled with mistletoe brooms that spotted owls sometimes use as platforms for their nests. The closed canopies of old-growth forests are thought to provide cover from avian predators, and their shade creates a cooler microclimate for the birds, which have trouble regulating their own temperature.

"Hoo hoo-hoo hooo!" Ward shouted, startling me. Then he produced the female's single-note call, which sounded like a cross between a whistle and a farmer shouting for pigs. Within a minute, a female spotted owl called back, sounding just like Ward. "I've been doing this since 1981," Ward explained. With binoculars, he spotted a pair of owls sitting on a branch about 30 feet above the ground. I was impressed by their size, about 18 inches head to toe, and their seeming indifference to our presence. The birds were motionless, except for occasionally rotating their heads nearly 360 degrees. Biologists will lure owls closer with mice so they can read bands on their legs and identify the bird. When Ward placed the rodent on a branch, the owls took note but didn't budge.

At the second PAC we visited, the national forest was living up to its motto, land of many uses. We saw cows, ATVs, hikers, mountain bikers, and a turkey hunter with only his face poking out of camouflage. National forests in the Southwest and elsewhere are now dominated by recreation, not logging, and the spotted owl does nothing to impede those visitors.

For 30 minutes, Ward called for the birds, but there was no response. Finally, near the bed of an abandoned narrow-gauge railroad that once transported timber out of the mountains, a male owl called back. It took us another 20 minutes to find the bird and its mate. The male was skittish, but the female took a liking to us, especially after we started feeding her. On the ground before me, I let loose a white mouse with beady red eyes. After some hesitation, the owl swooped down and snagged the mouse, far faster than I could click the shutter on my camera. Her flight was graceful and absolutely silent. Biologists believe that special serrated structures on owls' wings force air underneath in a way that lets the birds approach their targets in stealth, just like the bombers at Holloman Air Force Base, down in Alamogordo. We fed the female three more mice, and she either returned to her perch to rip the rodents apart or cached them in the top of a snag. By now, it was dark and the owl's eyes glowed purple and ruby red when I used my camera's flash. Without the aid of headlamps, Ward and I slowly descended the steep hillside and made our way through the kindling and ladder fuels. If a fire arrived here when it was hot, dry, and windy, the place would be nuked.

The acrimony surrounding the Healthy Forests initiative actually belied a philosophical agreement among many scientists, agency officials, timber interests, and environmentalists: in at least some types of forests, fuels reduction was urgently needed to restore the ecosystem's health. A few months after the Rodeo-Chediski Fire and the attendant blame game, researchers from academia and the government, plus two founders of the Center for Biological Diversity, coauthored a peer-reviewed paper that laid out 16 principles for restoring the Southwest's pine forests by thinning stands and reintroducing fire without causing even more damage by logging the biggest trees. "A consensus has emerged that it is urgent to restore more natural conditions to these forests," the authors wrote in 2002. "Some stands need substantial structural manipulation (thinning) before fire can safely be reintroduced. In other areas, such as large wilderness and roadless areas, fire alone may suffice as the main tool of restoration." The paper applied to ponderosa pines in the Southwest, where stand-replacing crown fires are unnatural, not to places like Yellowstone, where such blazes are normal and the lodgepole pines need extreme heat to open their cones and spread their seeds. Exporting the prescription from the Southwest to other regions could be bad medicine. But timber interests and others were doing exactly that by advocating for massive thinning and logging of lodgepole, spruce, and fir in the Northern Rockies. "There's no ecological justification for that, although there might be an economic one," said tree-ring researcher Tom Swetnam, a coauthor of the 2002 paper. While the Southwest model wasn't appropriate for denser forests that burned catastrophically every few centuries under natural conditions, its applicability also wasn't limited to just Arizona and New Mexico. "If you look at the history," Swetnam said, "there was a dry, frequent fire regime on the east side of the Cascades in Oregon and Washington, a good part of the Sierras, most the dry forests of the Great Basin, and in some dry, lower elevation area in Montana and Colorado."

Throughout the nation, innovative solutions to the wildfire threat that imperils so many species will be hard to achieve without government and private sector research into potential uses of the excess fuel. Studies at the Forest Service's Forest Products Laboratory in Madison, Wisconsin, where Aldo Leopold was stationed for a few years after leaving the Southwest, could prove as important to forest health as fieldwork in the woods. The Healthy Forests Restoration Act devoted $10 million in new annual funding for research on new products and biomass energy, which is a start. Bureaucratic changes are also needed to give entrepreneurs some assurances that the supply of wood won't suddenly vanish. "One of the reasons people won't invest in infrastructure," former Forest Service chief Dale Bosworth told me, "is that they don't trust we're an organization that will, in the long term, produce small-diameter trees."

To address that problem, the Healthy Forests law let the government enter into longer contracts for forest thinning and allowed contractors to keep the wood as partial payment.

The largest of these so-called stewardship contracts was issued to a partnership of firms in the Show Low area two years after the town was nearly overrun by the Rodeo-Chediski Fire. The 10-year deal calls for paying the contractors $60 million to thin small trees on about 150,000 acres. The companies use the wood to make molding, laminated beams, and pellets that can fuel wood-burning stoves, industrial heaters, and a biomass power plant. In this case, the private sector can thin the forest for $400 an acre, several hundred dollars less than what it would cost if the Forest Service did the work. Environmentalists generally didn't object to the deal since it was aimed at the forest around homes and targeted trees less than 16 inches wide. The project appears to offer communities along the Mogollon Rim a path toward profiting from the forests around them, reducing the wildfire risk, and ensuring the survival of old-growth species like the Mexican spotted owl and northern goshawk.

Thanks in part to the Healthy Forests Restoration Act, cities, towns, and neighborhoods across the country are working to reduce wildfire hazards near homes. On the local level, some of the accomplishments have been impressive, but they have to be scaled up dramatically, especially with the risk of extreme wildfires rising along with the temperature. Rather than think in terms of 10,000-acre projects here or there, planners need to pursue a landscape-level approach that covers 1 million acres or more. With that goal in mind, a diverse set of interests started coming together after the Rodeo-Chediski Fire. Over a period of three years, a 21-person panel that included environmentalists, foresters, biologists, and timber company officials analyzed 2.4 million acres of ponderosa pine forest on the Mogollon Rim and found some common ground: thinning was appropriate on 41 percent of the land and inappropriate on 26 percent due to presence of Mexican spotted owls, erosion risks, steep terrain, and other issues. There were differing views on the remaining 33 percent, though most members favored some mechanical thinning there.

The meeting of the minds led to a watershed agreement to thin nearly 1 million acres along the Mogollon Rim. It will be the largest such project ever attempted and increase fuels reduction in northern Arizona by 30,000 acres a year, nearly double the current rate. A Flagstaff-based company will make a building material similar to plywood, using only trees less than 16 inches wide. Much of the thinning along the Mogollon Rim will focus on vulnerable communities and small-diameter trees, but crews will also work in the backcountry and cut a select number of larger trees to prevent the forest from becoming too uniform.

The agreement signed by the Center for Biological Diversity, Grand Canyon Trust, and Arizona Forest Restoration Products essentially marked the first time that environmentalists and logging interests were on the same page for managing the region's forests. Besides reducing the fire threat, the work was projected to generate 600 jobs and $200 million for the local economy. The federal government might still need to spend $300 million over the next 10 years on thinning, but without private sector involvement, the tab might be $1 billion. Either way, spending money to reduce wildfire risks could avoid the need for expensive suppression campaigns. The Rodeo-Chediski Fire cost $43 million to contain and still did $120 million in damages. "This agreement is unprecedented in the history of Southwestern national forests, and it represents a turning point from the century past to the century ahead," wrote Ethan Aumack of the Grand Canyon Trust and Molly Pitts of the Northern Arizona Wood Products Association. "As Arizona faces continuing drought and the prospect of climate change, forest restoration can no longer be seen as some distant future priority to be tackled when budgets permit. It is needed desperately, and it is needed now."

10

Friends of the Frogs

As the 2002 drought was decimating Sonoran pronghorn and spawning monster wildfires, water holes across the Southwest were drying up. One of the shrinking ponds, near the Buenos Aires National Wildlife Refuge, held a critical population of Chiricahua leopard frogs, a species about to be listed as threatened under the ESA. The water hole, situated in a seldom-visited canyon in the Baboquivari Mountains, was surrounded by mesquites, live oaks, deer grass, and monkey flowers. The spotted leopard frogs swam through the murky, algae-filled pond, spent part of their lives perched on the muddy shoreline, and emitted a call while they were mating that sounded like a snore.

For two Tucson herpetologists, Cecil Schwalbe and Phil Rosen, the shriveling of the water hole was of great concern because it held the westernmost population of the species. The pond appeared to be one of the last hopes for leopard frogs to naturally recolonize their historic habitat on the Buenos Aires, where the only known population had blinked out the previous year. Wayne Shifflett, manager of the Buenos Aires, had tried to prevent that water hole from drying up. He directed fire crews to haul water over 11 miles of mountainous terrain to periodically replenish the pond. But it was just a stopgap measure, not a sustainable conservation strategy. "We just couldn't haul in enough water," Shifflett said.

Saving the frogs in the Baboquivaris meant rescuing them from the ill-fated pond. Schwalbe and Rosen, both of whom had done research for years in the Altar Valley, asked the Arizona Game and Fish Department for permission to move the frogs onto the Buenos Aires. The government had already spent $100,000 to set up a captive breeding program at the refuge and eliminate nonnative fish and bullfrogs from otherwise suitable habitat in anticipation of reintroducing the leopard frogs. But Game and Fish denied the request, siding with area ranchers who feared that frogs released onto the refuge would also colonize their water holes and cause regulatory problems that would limit existing livestock operations, and the development potential of their land. Chiricahua leopard frogs frequently occupied the same cattle tanks that livestock used, and they were one of the species the Center for Biological Diversity cited in its appeal of the Chiltons' grazing permit for the Montana Allotment. Some residents of the Altar Valley had expressed interest in conserving the frog through an ESA tool known as a safe harbor that would forestall added regulation if landowners restored or re-created habitat for the species, but the agreement hadn't been finalized. Ranchers Jim and Sue Chilton, who questioned whether many of the Southwest's endangered species deserved federal protection, didn't deny that the leopard frog was imperiled. They were even interested in restoring the creature on their own private land—provided that it wouldn't affect their ranching operation. "But I got to realizing," Jim told me, "that if I had leopard frogs on my private property and they hopped over to my grazing permit, the Forest Service could shut me down and say I've got to get rid of my cattle."

Game and Fish, overseen by a five-person appointed commission that Sue chaired, wouldn't allow Schwalbe and Shifflett to relocate the frogs to the Buenos Aires, but the agency did permit Schwalbe to move the frogs to his backyard pond in Tucson. Two weeks before the frog was listed under the ESA, Schwalbe's field crew captured 7 adults and 13 tadpoles, dropped them into plastic containers, and drove them to his house. The frogs were eager to breed, and Schwalbe's pond soon held about 1,000 tadpoles.

The sheer number of tadpoles belied their precarious position. When Chiricahua leopard frogs are held in captivity, they often become cannibalistic. Unless the tadpoles were moved, the adults would eat the tiny froglets that developed. Shifflett tried to get approval to relocate the tadpoles to the refuge, but Game and Fish again denied his request. Although the species was now federally listed and Shifflett managed a federal refuge, Game and Fish had for years asserted its right to manage endangered wildlife within its borders, invoking the principle of American jurisprudence that makes states the owners of wildlife.

Without Game and Fish's blessing, Shifflett went ahead with the original reestablishment plan and transported 400 tadpoles from Schwalbe's backyard to three ponds on the Buenos Aires. Shifflett felt he had a duty to save the frogs and the authority to take action. "I'd never yet heard that I needed to have permission from a state agency to move an endangered species," Shifflett said. "That's the reason I thought, *Screw you. The supremacy of the Endangered Species Act has precedence over state law.*"

Shifflett's resume included plenty of experience handling endangered species. During his 38-year career with Fish and Wildlife, he'd helped move everything from Andean condors to Attwater's prairie chickens. As manager of the Buenos Aires refuge, he'd overseen transplants of masked bobwhite quail, razorback suckers, Gila chub, and Gila topminnow. In a file cabinet somewhere, Shifflett possessed an endangered species permit from Fish and Wildlife's regional office, though it didn't specifically mention the leopard frog since it had just been listed. For Shifflett, the paperwork seemed trivial compared to the conservation value of the threatened frogs. "Those animals they took back to Cecil's were the last vanguard of the gene pool in that valley, and if I didn't save them they'd be gone from science forever," Shifflett said. "This is what my career has been all about: trying to save something from going extinct. This was an easy decision for me." After Shifflett moved the tadpoles to the refuge in the spring of 2003, they took hold in the ponds, metamorphosed into frogs, and spread to a water hole that had been restored for their eventual reintroduction. The leopard frog was back on the Buenos Aires.

In December, two federal law enforcement agents came to the refuge to ask Shifflett about the tadpoles. They grilled him about the episode and told him he was facing federal felony charges for violating the ESA, the National Wildlife Refuge System Administration Act, and the Lacey Act. Then Shifflett got a call from his supervisor in Albuquerque. Fish and Wildlife was removing Shifflett from his post as refuge manager and placing him on paid administrative leave. Shifflett's supervisor advised him to get a lawyer.

––––––––––

An amphibian orgy is how I got to know Schwalbe, who was also interrogated by federal agents about the leopard frogs. We'd met once before, and he suggested I accompany him on some fieldwork out at the Buenos Aires. Schwalbe had white hair, an infectious enthusiasm, and a steady supply of nonnative bullfrogs in his freezer so he could make "froganoff" for faculty potlucks. He was a fun guy to hang out with, a well-respected scientist, and a disciple of Charles Lowe Jr., the leading Southwest naturalist in the mid-20th century who had discovered 20 new species and subspecies and coauthored the definitive map of the region's diverse vegetation with David Brown.

At the Buenos Aires, Schwalbe and Rosen, another student of Lowe's, were trying to develop methods for studying desert-breeding toads and spadefoots. These amphibians weren't endangered, but gauging the status of their populations is a major challenge. Unlike Chiricahua leopard frogs, which are active nearly year-round, the toads and spadefoots spend 10 or 11 months each year in underground burrows. There they wait in a torpor until monsoon thunderstorms entice the animals to surface and engage in torrid summer love affairs in the ponds and puddles created by the downpours. The sound or vibration of monsoon storms, not the moisture, apparently triggers these amphibians to emerge from the ground. With all the subtlety of courtship at a fraternity keg party, the toads and spadefoots race against the clock to find a partner, create tadpoles, and pass their genes on to the next generation before the water hole dries up and their tadpoles' survival above ground is doomed.

Like the amphibians' life cycle, this research was totally weather dependent. For a couple of weeks, Schwalbe put me on standby. In Tucson, he watched Doppler radar on the Web and waited like an expectant father until a good-sized storm dumped enough rain to lure the toads and spadefoots to the surface. I got the call late one afternoon and raced down to the refuge, where many of the dry washes crossing the high-way were running with muddy water. We trudged around the ephemeral ponds with nets, capturing as many toads and spadefoots as we could in 25 minutes. The male amphibians proclaimed their procreation with mating calls that were so frantic and deafening that we all had to wear earplugs. "They've been underground since last August, just waiting for this moment," Schwalbe shouted. "This is their wedding night!" Light-ning flickered on the horizon, illuminating the puffy cumulonimbus clouds from within and exposing the bald knob of Baboquivari Peak, sacred mountain for the Tohono O'odham. In their rainmaking songs, the O'odham incorporate the spadefoot's mating call, which a guidebook describes as "a plaintive cry, declining in pitch like the anxious bleat of a sheep." At one pond's edge, Rosen held a contraption that was recording noise levels of 90 decibels—comparable to a lawn mower—with peaks above 100 decibels. By calling, the males were hoping to attract females. I asked Schwalbe what causes a female to choose one male over another. "I've been marveling at that question my whole life," he said. "Why does Lyle Lovett get the chicks? Surely love must be blind in that case as well!"

When a pair of toads or spadefoots finds each other, the male mounts the female and holds on with his swollen thumbs. This mating position, known as amplexus, can last for hours, even a day. Eventually, the female goes underwater to lay hundreds to thousands of eggs. The attached male hangs on, then deposits his sperm in a process similar to the external fer-tilization that fish use to reproduce. For one species of spadefoot, it can take just 24 hours for the eggs to hatch and only a week for the tadpole to metamorphose, a speedy maturation that is motivated by water's fleeting presence in the desert.

Because the habitat of amphibians in the Southwest is so capricious, biol-ogists wouldn't necessarily be worried if Chiricahua leopard frogs were missing from a specific pond where they were seen in the past. But when researchers conducted intensive searches across the species' range in the 1980s and 1990s, the vast majority of historic sites turned up empty. In Arizona, one survey found the frogs at only 2 of 36 sites where they had been spotted in the 1960s and 1970s. In New Mexico, another study recorded the frogs in just 6 of the 33 water holes where they had been

seen in the preceding 11 years. In presettlement days, Chiricahua leopard frogs lived in hundreds of streams, springs, pools, beaver ponds, and
marshy *ciénegas*. But by the end of the 20th century, the frogs had been
extirpated from more than three-quarters of their known locations in the
United States. Scientists couldn't even find the species in its namesake
mountain range. Something had gone terribly wrong.

Coast to coast, scientists found similar declines among the dozen
types of leopard frogs in the United States. The losses were especially
heavy in the Southwest, which boasts the greatest diversity of leopard
frogs in the nation, despite its aridity. The Chiricahua species is one of
the most endangered leopard frogs in the nation. A related species, the
Vegas Valley leopard frog, is already extinct, while another resident of
the Las Vegas area, the relict leopard frog, is barely hanging on. Also in
danger are many of the other 15 North American frogs that belong to the
same genus, *Rana*. The Tarahumara frog, named for the indigenous people of Mexico's Copper Canyon, disappeared from Arizona in the early
1980s due to disease and perhaps pollution. Another imperiled member
of the *Rana* genus, the California red-legged frog, was the subject of
Mark Twain's famous story "The Celebrated Jumping Frog of Calaveras
County." When Twain published the piece in 1865, the species was common enough that it was harvested for food in the Central Valley and
San Francisco Bay Area. But as the population of the red-legged frogs
dwindled, nonnative bullfrogs were introduced around 1896 to satisfy
the demand for frog legs, and these rapacious predators caused further
declines in the native species. In 1996, the frog immortalized by Twain
was judged at risk of extinction and listed as threatened under the ESA.

The vanishing of a wide variety of frog species in the United States
was part of a global phenomenon known as the amphibian extinction
crisis. Starting in the 1970s, biologists began to notice that frogs and
other amphibians were in trouble on all six continents on which they
live, even in seemingly pristine habitat. A 2000 study analyzed data from
936 populations in 37 countries and concluded that the total number of
amphibians had fallen about 2 percent per year since the 1960s. Another
report, published in *Science*, found that nearly one-third of the world's
amphibians were threatened with extinction, compared to 23 percent
of mammals and 12 percent of birds. Along with primates (aside from
humans), amphibians are now considered the most endangered organ-
isms on Earth. At least 122 amphibians may have already gone extinct, a

rate that may be higher than at any time during the 350 million years that amphibians have been hopping and crawling around the planet.

The steep decline of many frog species has been both alarming and potentially instructive because the animals are thought to be highly sensitive to environmental changes. As amphibians, they are exposed to both air and water pollution. Their moist, permeable skin is well suited for hosting parasites and absorbing toxins. And their complex life cycle leads them to feed up and down the food chain, consuming algae and plants as tadpoles, then insects and other small animals as adults. "We ourselves could not have devised a better early-warning device for general environmental deterioration than a frog," wrote E. O. Wilson, the Harvard zoologist and Pulitzer Prize–winning author. A more recent study, however, cast doubt on whether amphibians are truly like canaries in a coal mine. Based on nearly 24,000 toxicity studies of 73 chemicals, the researchers concluded that amphibians aren't especially vulnerable to contaminants and "might more aptly be described as 'miners in a coal mine.'" Nevertheless, the disappearance of amphibians like the leopard frog is especially worrisome to medical researchers. The skin of amphibians is home to more than 400 chemical compounds, known as alkaloids, that scientists have isolated and tested for a variety of applications, including more than 200 antimicrobial agents. Extracts from the Ecuadorian poison frog are the basis for painkillers that are 200 times more potent than morphine but do not build up tolerance in patients.

The demise of Chiricahua leopard frogs could be blamed on any number of factors. In some cases, the frog's watery habitat had been destroyed by dams, diversions, development, and nearby groundwater pumping. Also gone were nearly all of the beavers that once plugged rivers and created pools hospitable to the frogs. Even in locations where there was still enough water, the leopard frogs were being ravaged by voracious, nonnative predators and a fungus that was killing amphibians across the planet.

Bullfrogs are among the most menacing threats to Chiricahua leopard frogs. Native to the eastern United States, the largest of North America's frogs swallows all manner of aquatic life, plus small birds, bats, and tarantulas. Scientists who cut open bullfrogs' digestive tracts sometimes find that other frogs make up half their diet by weight. One of Schwalbe's graduate students, Dennis Suhre, recorded bullfrogs hopping seven miles between water holes in Arizona.

"Almost at every turn, the bullfrog seems to have an advantage," Schwalbe told me one afternoon in a musty lab on the UA campus. "They're just adapted to be a great colonizer." With us was Rosen, who wrote many of the key studies on Chiricahua leopard frogs. We sat at an old lab table surrounded by bubbling tanks and not much light, a dimension apart from the young women in bikinis sunbathing outside. Rosen told me the conventional wisdom was that humans had wiped out the Southwest's wetlands and surface water, but at least in southern Arizona, people also created plenty of new aquatic habitat as they plugged washes and dug water holes, often to support livestock operations. The only catch: both the natural and man-made waters were now filled with bullfrogs, crayfish, bass, and other invasive species that would prevent the natives from taking hold. "Habitat loss is, in some ways, a red herring," Rosen said. "There's water, water everywhere, but not a drop to live in." One of Rosen's papers identified 13 nonnative predators in Chiricahua leopard frog habitat. Other scientific studies have established an unmistakable trend: water holes infested with exotics, especially bullfrogs, almost never contain Chiricahua leopard frogs, while the ponds with the leopard frogs have very few or none of the nonnatives.

Leopard frog tadpoles don't develop as quickly as those produced by toads and spadefoots, so to reproduce, the animals need something more durable than a monsoon puddle. The problem is that bullfrogs and other nonnatives tend to dominate the deep, secure perennial waters because those habitats resemble bullfrogs' natural homes back East. This has squeezed the leopard frogs into a narrow, unnatural niche, where the water supply is especially unreliable. Close to two-thirds of the remaining Chiricahua leopard frogs depend on artificial waters created for livestock. Often called tanks, these ponds typically aren't made from metal and are instead created by excavating holes or erecting small earthen dams across drainages that are dry most of the year. There's no shortage of these water holes in the Southwest, and there's no reason why they can't be made more hospitable for leopard frogs. "Ranching is not the intractable problem it's held up to be," Rosen said. "There are issues with it, but there are suitable ways out." Bullfrogs and other exotics could be controlled by giving their natural predators a leg up, or by taking advantage of the desert's natural drought-and-flood cycle. While native aquatic species have always had to cope with water sources that become smaller and warmer during dry spells, such conditions can prove deadly for nonnatives that hail from wetter climes. Once bullfrogs are removed from a stock pond, they can be stopped from reinvading by erecting short fences around the site. It's also relatively easy to breed and transplant leopard frogs, as Schwalbe and Shifflett showed. "The angst comes in," Rosen said, "because we know we need to do this quickly because of the disease."

The disease is chytridiomycosis, a fungal infection that kills and sickens frogs, perhaps by impeding their ability to move water, oxygen, or vital chemicals through their skin. The chytrid fungus was identified as a menace to frogs in 1998, when scientists discovered it was responsible for catastrophic frog mortality in Panama and Australia. At the time, Rosen and others were also finding the fungus in Arizona, and the disease has devastated populations with hundreds of Chiricahua leopard frogs. Biologists have only recently recognized the role of chytridiomycosis, but tests of museum samples have revealed that the fungus was present in the Southwest at least since 1972. The fungus doesn't produce airborne spores, so humans are apparently to blame for its intercontinental spread. Some biologists believe the plague originated in African clawed frogs that were exported for human pregnancy testing starting in the 1930s (the species ovulates after being injected with the urine of pregnant women). More than 200 amphibian species are now affected by the chytrid fungus, and researchers have found evidence suggesting that pollution, climate change, and the commercial trade of wildlife are helping spread the disease. To control the damage, scientists treat captive populations of frogs with a broad-spectrum fungicide, but there's no effective method for cleansing natural habitat.

Even though many leopard frogs survive the infection, biologists believe the chytrid fungus is an additional stressor that exacerbates other problems. "My fear," Rosen said, "is that the Chiricahua leopard frog will have been made so rare and so scattered by nonnative species that it won't have the opportunity to reach that plateau of adaptation, where the disease will become less virulent and it can live with it and survive." This was why preserving different populations of leopard frogs, including the one in the Altar Valley that Shifflett saved, was so important: one cluster of frogs might develop a resistance to the chytrid fungus that could help rescue the entire species.

The chytrid fungus and nonnative predators are formidable hazards that could, by themselves, wipe out Chiricahua leopard frog populations. These threats, however, are merely at the top of a long list of human-caused dangers. Like other amphibians around the globe, the frogs readily absorb chemicals from the air and water around them. In 2002, University of California at Berkeley scientists reported in the journal *Nature* that leopard frogs from the Midwest had become hermaphrodites after being exposed to extremely low concentrations of atrazine, the nation's second most widely used herbicide. About one-third of the frogs developed deformed testicles that produced eggs as well as sperm after their tanks were contaminated with atrazine levels 30 times lower than the federal drinking water standard. In the wilds of the Southwest, biologists have found that arsenic in runoff from mines and cadmium emissions from copper smelters can be toxic to leopard frogs. Wildfires have always been part of the leopard frog's ecosystem, but because of fire suppression, today's unnaturally intense blazes lead to increased soil erosion and runoff that can fill water holes with sediment. Efforts to stop those fires might also harm the frogs. While the Forest Service no longer uses sodium ferrocyanide in the flame retardant dumped by slurry bombers, some scientists believe that the ammonia-based liquid that tankers do drop—several thousand gallons at a time—is polluting aquatic habitat. Even if a water hole is free of toxins and nonnative predators, frogs may not be in the clear. Massive frog die-offs in ostensibly healthy high-altitude habitat have led some researchers to conclude that ozone depletion high in the atmosphere has caused more intense UV-B rays to reach the ground and damage frogs' eggs, although with many species this is no longer considered a primary threat. All of these dangers do not exist in isolation and may become even more menacing when they interact. Heavy metals released by mines, for instance, may compromise the frogs' immune systems and make them more susceptible to the chytrid fungus.

Although the Chiricahua leopard frog was clearly in jeopardy, the federal government was sluggish in its response. Two federal scientists raised a red flag in a 1989 study, and two years later the frog was labeled as a candidate for listing under the ESA. But the species was still in legal limbo in 1996, receiving no federal protections, when scientists issued two more warnings of their impending doom. One report for the Arizona Game and Fish Department declared, "This species will go extinct in southern Arizona, and probably elsewhere, unless appropriate action is taken." Another study for the US Fish and Wildlife Service said the frog would be gone from 90 to 100 percent of its range in New Mexico "unless these unexplainable trends are quickly reversed." After a 1999 lawsuit from the Center for Biological Diversity, Fish and Wildlife listed the Chiricahua leopard frog as threatened in 2002.

Conserving and recovering the Chiricahua leopard frog would require a delicate touch. The tadpole imbroglio at the Buenos Aires refuge showed that many ranchers viewed the frog and its advocates as a threat to their vocation. Cognizant of the tension, Fish and Wildlife created a special rule when it granted federal protection to the frog: if the species were harmed or killed on nonfederal lands while livestock were using a water hole or while ranchers were maintaining it, these actions would be exempt from prosecution. The provision was important because nearly two-thirds of the frog's remaining populations were dependent on ranchers' stock tanks, though many of those were on federal grazing allotments. "There is a high probability," the species' recovery team concluded, "that the Chiricahua leopard frog would be extirpated from many more areas if ranchers had not built and maintained stock tanks for livestock production." The frogs can definitely coexist with cattle, but grazing is also potentially harmful. Cows may spread disease, foul water with their feces, destroy the banks of ponds, and accelerate soil erosion that clogs water holes with silt. Cow hooves may also squash frog eggs, tadpoles, and adults. Even so, research in Arizona found that leopard frogs fared better in stock tanks than in natural water holes, perhaps because bullfrogs and other exotics were less common.

The potential conflict between cattle grazing and species conservation led most ranchers to oppose the listing of the Chiricahua leopard frog. Many barred biologists from surveying their private land. An even worse outcome was possible: ranchers might purposely eliminate the frogs or infest potential habitat with bullfrogs or sunfish to forestall government interference with their business. The threat is encapsulated in an adage that has become a mantra of rural landowners and inside-the-Beltway critics of the ESA: "Shoot, shovel, and shut up." People who put these words into action show how the ESA can create a perverse set of incentives. Expunge your land of rare species or their habitat, and you'll keep the federal government off your back. Improve your land for wildlife, attract endangered species, and your good deed is rewarded with strict federal oversight of your property. The National Association of Home Builders summed it up in a 1996 publication that offered "practical tips for developers":

Unfortunately, the highest level of assurance that a property owner will not face an ESA issue is to maintain the property in a condition such that protected species cannot occupy the property...The scorched earth management practice is highly controversial, and its legality may vary depending upon the state or local governing laws. But developers should be aware of it as a means employed in several areas of the country to avoid ESA conflicts.

The threat of preemptive habitat destruction is no small challenge for the ESA because about two-thirds of US land is in private hands. Half of listed species have at least 80 percent of their habitat on private property, and less than 10 percent of listed species depend exclusively on public lands. In Hawaii and Texas, which rank first and fifth in the nation in endangered species, the federal government only owns 16 percent and 1 percent of the land, respectively. Our national parks remain vital for many listed species, but they often protect freaks of nature like geysers and geologic formations, not necessarily focal points for biodiversity. Our wilderness areas safeguard scenic wonders and important habitat, but they typically lie at higher elevations, where the prevalence of rock, ice, and poor soils may limit the number of species (the lack of timber, forage, and arable land is why many of these areas were set aside in the first place). By comparison, the bottomlands along rivers and streams, where people have always lived, are often the most critical for endangered species. Three-quarters of a century ago, Aldo Leopold recognized that ordinary citizens and their property would be essential for protecting US wildlife. "Conservation," Leopold wrote in 1934, "will ultimately boil down to rewarding the private landowner who conserves the public interest."

The "shoot, shovel, and shut up" adage, rooted in anecdotal accounts, is supported by some social science research. One study found that the pygmy owl's listing and critical habitat map accelerated development in Tucson by about a year. In another analysis, economists Dean Lueck and Jeffrey Michael looked at patterns of timber harvest in North Carolina and found that the closer a forest plot was to a red-cockaded woodpecker colony, the more likely the trees were to be harvested. Southern pines that were near existing colonies also tended to be cut when the trees were younger. The birds prefer nesting in older trees that have been softened by a fungal infection and are therefore easier to drill into, so landowners apparently figured they could avoid ESA restrictions by chopping down the trees before they became suitable habitat. "Such preemptive activity would be a completely legal land-use decision spurred by the potential for costly regulations," Lueck and Michael wrote in the *Journal of Law and Economics*.

In another study, one that relied on questionnaires rather than raw data on habitat modification, University of Michigan scientists concluded that the 1998 listing of the Preble's meadow jumping mouse prompted a backlash against the species in Colorado and Wyoming. The researchers sent a survey to affected landowners and found that for every acre of private land that was managed to help the mouse, there was an acre denuded or otherwise altered to drive away the mouse. More than half of the respondents said they had not or would not let biologists survey their property, greatly hampering the collection of data needed to help the species. "So far, listing the Preble's under the ESA does not appear to have enhanced its survival prospects on private land," the researchers reported in *Conservation Biology*. "Our results suggest that landowners' detrimental actions cancelled out the efforts of landowners seeking to help the species. As more landowners become aware that their land contains Preble's habitat, it is likely that the impact on the species may be negative." In announcing the study, the Society for Conservation Biology, publisher of the journal and a staunch defender of the ESA, said, "New research confirms fears that Endangered Species Act listings do not necessarily help—and may even harm—rare species on private lands."

To learn how we might untie this Gordian knot, I visited members of the Malpai Borderlands Group, a nonprofit in southeastern Arizona and southwestern New Mexico that ranchers formed to preserve open space and return fire to an ecosystem with abundant endangered species. My guide was Peter Warren of The Nature Conservancy, who had spent years building trust with residents of the Malpai region. When we met at the Triple T truck stop for the drive out, Warren was wearing a cowboy hat, which I took as indicative of his group's acceptance of livestock grazing. That stance had generated friction between The Nature Conservancy and other environmental groups that held a dim view of ranching. At the moment, the Center and Defenders of Wildlife were trying to force the federal government to map critical habitat for the jaguar in the Malpai region, a move opposed by the local ranchers and even some jaguar biologists who feared it would increase the risk of poaching. "The guys that are suing for critical habitat aren't doing it for the jaguar, they're doing it to manipulate land use," Warren told me. "Their explicit goal is to get rid of grazing, so they're using the Endangered Species Act as leverage to attack grazing. They're not using it as an approach to actually benefit the species."

The Malpai Borderlands Group had formed a decade before to fight two threats moving across the high desert: shrubs and houses. Starting in the late 19th century, a combination of drought, overgrazing, and fire suppression caused mesquites and other shrubs to spread out from the drainages. Cattle accelerated the process by ingesting mesquite bean pods and depositing them back on the land in cow patties rich with natural fertilizers. The shrubs shaded the grasses, robbed them of water and nutrients, and dramatically reduced the amount of forage available for cattle. Researchers found that soil erosion from the wind increased nearly tenfold as native grasslands became mesquite-dominated savannahs.

Ranchers tried to knock back the shrub invasion with chain saws, herbicides, and heavy machinery; all too often, the plants would quickly sprout again unless fire was returned to the landscape. In July 1991, ranch manager Dale Cureton decided to do just that. As Nathan Sayre recounts in his book *Working Wilderness*, Cureton lit some dry grass near the border, along an unpaved road called Geronimo Trail, hoping that the flames would kill the creosote bushes that were growing back after his boss had spent $60,000 on chemicals to get rid of them. The winds were pushing the flames away from Warner and Wendy Glenn's Malpai Ranch, and the fire would eventually fizzle on its own due to a lack of fuel. But the Forest Service had other ideas and rushed to put out the blaze with helicopters, fire trucks, and firefighters, over the objections of the Glenns and other landowners who felt the burn, albeit an unauthorized one, would do some good.

A few months after the Geronimo Trail Fire, the Glenns hosted a meeting at their Malpai Ranch to discuss the government's problematic fire suppression, the increasing pressure from activists determined to boot cows off public land, and the prospect of development ruining the place they loved. Over the ensuing months and years, the group expanded in scope and ambition while drawing on the inspiration and expertise of an eclectic community of ranchers, scientists, and environmentalists. One leader was Drummond Hadley, a scion of the Anheuser-Busch family and fortune who came to Tucson to attend the University of Arizona, worked as a cowboy in Mexico for two years, then returned to the States to buy a ranch near the junction of Arizona, New Mexico, and Mexico. Hadley and his family tried to run cattle sustainably by protecting riparian corridors from grazing, aligning fences with the contours of the landscape, and restoring native habitat. Another guiding light for the Malpai group was Jim Corbett, a Quaker, philosopher, beekeeper, librarian, and cofounder of the Sanctuary Movement that aided Latin American political refugees. Ray Turner, an ecologist known best for his use of repeat photography to document ecological changes in the Southwest, grounded the discussions in hard science. By painstakingly re-creating photos taken over the past century and comparing them side by side, Turner could document major shifts in vegetation, especially the proliferation of shrubs in historic grasslands.

By the end of the 20th century, the 1-million-acre Malpai region was still home to fewer than 100 families, but there were abundant examples of such open space becoming populated. Ranching remained the predominant land use on nearly a half-billion acres in the West, but from 1954 to 1997, Arizona lost 300,000 acres of farms and rangeland to development each year, even more than Montana (nearly 200,000 acres) and Colorado (154,000 acres).

In the Malpai region, it looked like the 320,000-acre Gray Ranch—half the size of Rhode Island—would get folded into the statistics. Situated in the New Mexico boot heel, the Gray Ranch included nearly all of the Animas Mountains and held the Southwest's largest remnant of short-grass prairie. It had been grazed for more than a century, but it remained one of the continent's top areas for species richness, with 700 types of plants, 75 mammals, and 50 reptiles and amphibians. Throughout the 20th century, the Gray Ranch had traded hands among land and cattle companies, eventually winding up in the possession of a Mexican billionaire, Pablo Brener. In 1983, Brener put the ranch up for sale, and for the rest of the decade it sat there on the open market, ready to be carved up into smaller parcels or planted with fruit orchards. New Mexico's state lands commission expressed interest in extracting the oil and gas beneath the ground. Because the Gray provided habitat for so many imperiled species, the US Fish and Wildlife Service was a potential buyer, but rather than create the Animas National Wildlife Refuge, it opted to purchase another ranch that Brener owned in southern Arizona, the Buenos Aires. Although the Buenos Aires was a third the size of the Gray and not as biologically diverse, its proximity to Tucson made it even more vulnerable to development, and it looked to be the only place in the country where the federal government could reintroduce the endangered masked bobwhite quail.

Another entity with deep pockets, The Nature Conservancy, was also keenly interested in protecting the Gray Ranch. For the nation's wealthiest environmental group, the entire Malpai region offered some of the greatest biodiversity bang for its buck. Princeton University biologist David Wilcove wrote that the region has "the richest array of habitats in the nation." The diversity of plants and animals was matched by a varied set of landowners, a hodgepodge of private, state, and federal lands that were managed according to different laws and doctrines, and the type of fractured governance that could easily lead to the fragmentation of vital habitat.

The Nature Conservancy was no stranger to the Malpai area. It had already purchased the nearby San Bernardino Ranch, then sold it in 1982 to the federal government for conversion into a national wildlife refuge. An undisputed hot spot for biological diversity, the San Bernardino was also a sore spot for many local residents, who complained that The Nature Conservancy was doing the feds' bidding in a region where the government already owned more than enough land. The Gray Ranch was more than 100 times bigger than the San Bernardino Ranch—a landscape rather than a parcel—so if The Nature Conservancy went the same route and flipped the property to Fish and Wildlife, the political controversy was bound to be that much greater. Acquiring 502 square miles would also cost The Nature Conservancy a small fortune because Brener only wanted to sell the land outright. Toward the end of 1989, he gave The Nature Conservancy two weeks to accept a nonnegotiable offer: $18 million. The group's board gathered on a conference call and decided to take the plunge. It was the largest private-land conservation purchase in US history.

Soon after The Nature Conservancy acquired the Gray Ranch, it was looking to get rid of it. Besides the challenge of managing an entire mountain range and hundreds of thousands of acres, the group was burdened with interest payments of nearly $2 million per year, far more than the group could earn by grazing cattle sustainably on the property. At the urging of other environmental groups, The Nature Conservancy considered selling the Gray Ranch to the federal government, a course adamantly opposed by ranchers in the Malpai region, even more so when projections showed that up to 60,000 people a year might visit the little-known corner of the country. The refuge option, opposed by much of New Mexico's political establishment, went nowhere.

Discussions between The Nature Conservancy's lawyers and the Malpai area's residents finally yielded a solution: use ranching and philanthropy to permanently protect the Gray. The extended Hadley family pooled their resources and created the nonprofit Animas Foundation, which bought the ranch for $13.2 million. The sales price reflected a $4.8 million conservation easement held by The Nature Conservancy that would prevent the ranch from ever being subdivided but would still allow for some cattle grazing.

It was the beginning of a new approach for The Nature Conservancy. For many years, the group had purchased smaller biologically important parcels, like the San Bernardino Ranch and a series of properties on the nearby San Pedro River, then turned them into preserves that the group managed or sold to the government. But as experience mounted, the group saw that this strategy was having limited success around the world. To be sure, it was essential to protect sensitive areas like riparian habitat in a desert, but isolated preserves were buffeted by effects emanating far beyond their boundaries, such as invasive species, fire suppression, and severed migration corridors. Even more important, locking up land in refuges often neglected the real needs of humans who depended on those natural resources, causing people to disregard the protections, degrade valuable land elsewhere, and diminish the political will for conservation.

The Gray Ranch acquisition was the first under The Nature Conservancy's Last Great Places initiative, which sought to protect big chunks of habitat while still allowing for compatible economic activities. In and around the Gray Ranch, The Nature Conservancy would rigorously monitor plant composition and species populations so that science could inform future management decisions. The Nature Conservancy also seeded the Malpai Borderlands Group with a $1 million donation that was matched by the Animas Foundation. The funding allowed the Malpai group to incorporate as a 501(c)(3) nonprofit that was capable of holding conservation easements like the one that would safeguard the Gray Ranch in perpetuity.

Before visiting some of the Malpai ranchers, Warren and I went searching for the Chiricahua leopard frog in nearby Leslie Canyon National Wildlife Refuge, beside the Chiricahua Mountains. Leslie Creek, a verdant, shady oasis filled with ash, willow, walnut, and cottonwood trees, is surrounded by hundreds of square miles of bone dry desert where the spines of ocotillos and the stalks of century plants reach into the azure sky like antennas. We crept up on the stream with low expectations since leopard frogs typically dive underwater when approached, but the frogs sat motionless atop a mat of lime green algae, perfectly camouflaged from hawks, herons, raccoons, and other predators. Endangered Yaqui chub darted in the water below. One frog was nearly invisible, nestled in the pond scum like an alligator, with just its eyes peeking out. "The bugs will land and these guys are just perched there, waiting for something to eat," refuge biologist Nina King told us. Adult leopard frogs can grow to nearly six inches and are sizable enough to eat tiny birds. They mostly subsist on crickets, spiders, snails, water bugs, and occasionally other frogs. Normally, Leslie Creek flows continuously for a quarter mile. After nearly a decade of drought, the creek had been reduced to a few isolated pools.

Like all water holes in the desert, Leslie Creek feels fragile and fleeting. This is how it has been for millennia. In a region where many streams and wetlands are dependent on the caprice of rainfall, leopard frogs evolved in a dynamic system in which an area might be habitable one year and gone the next. The species persisted because the clusters of frogs were linked together in what biologists call a metapopulation. The frogs, able to hop several miles, could travel among the pools and ponds, seeking refuge in the more durable habitats during drought, then recolonizing abandoned locations when the water returned.

Our next stop was a visit with rancher Anna Magoffin, whose family had saved a population of Chiricahua leopard frogs on their 21,000-acre allotment. In 1994, dry weather began to shrink Rosewood Tank, a stock pond containing one of the only populations of leopard frogs in the area. For the next two years, the Magoffins hauled a thousand gallons of water per week to the pond in a truck with holes in its floorboard and no brakes. "If you practice," Anna told me, "you can roll it to a stop." Rosewood Tank was nothing special, only about 10 feet wide and coated with muck, but 10 years after the emergency water-hauling, it still held leopard frogs. The Magoffins had also voluntarily protected the endangered Cochise pincushion cactus by fencing off the plants from their livestock. "An endangered species isn't just a big minus," Anna said. "This family has always been real proud of the special, unique things found here, and it's important to keep them around."

To encourage other ranchers to follow the Magoffins' lead, the Malpai group, The Nature Conservancy, and government officials turned to a novel tool in the ESA that Interior Secretary Bruce Babbitt championed: the safe harbor agreement. These voluntary deals between the federal government and landowners, the brainchild of Michael Bean of the Environmental Defense Fund, inject some flexibility into an otherwise rigid law. If a landowner wants to improve habitat or attract a species, the government offers technical help and it promises it won't impose new regulations, what Babbitt's Interior Department termed the no surprises policy. The government also doesn't levy penalties if the federally protected animals subsequently die, so long as their population stays above the preexisting baseline, which is set at zero if the habitat is initially unoccupied. Elsewhere in Arizona, another safe harbor lets private citizens and local governments use endangered topminnows and pupfish for mosquito control in backyard ponds, storm-water basins, and wetlands fed by wastewater utilities. Previously, nonnative mosquito fish, which prey on the endangered natives, were the piscine weapon of choice.

Safe harbors are not a panacea, and they won't work for many endangered species. Still, the policy has been embraced by both Democratic and Republican administrations because it rewards conservation on private land and makes the ESA more proactive. The ESA's power stems from its ability to legally prohibit certain actions, such as killing a listed species or destroying its habitat, but this traditional command-and-control approach to regulation, with roots in the antipollution laws of the early 1970s, does little to actively promote habitat restoration or other positive measures. Michael Rosenzweig, founder of the University of Arizona's Department of Ecology and Evolutionary Biology, told me safe harbors epitomize win-win ecology, the title of his 2003 book. "I'd hate to be a private landowner facing the prospect of a rare or endangered species discovered on my property," he said. "It really does involve, in many cases, shutting down my livelihood with no compensation. Safe harbor agreements put an end to that." Along with a growing number of scientists, Rosenzweig believes that the nation must look beyond set-asides to protect and restore biodiversity, especially in light of global warming. Many, if not most, preserves are already too small and too isolated; now climate change threatens to make such refuges useless to the species they were designed to protect. "A degree or two of global warming and, behold, what was a habitat that could support its residents becomes one they can no longer use," Rosenzweig wrote. "In times past (say, when glaciers were retreating at the end of the last ice age), many species just drifted poleward or upslope. Today, that tactic may take them into a Wal-Mart parking lot, where they will die because they cannot digest asphalt."

After visiting the Magoffin ranch, Warren took me to see rancher Bill McDonald. As we swayed in rocking chairs on his porch and sipped ice tea, McDonald told me he was initially put off by The Nature Conservancy when it flipped the San Bernardino Ranch into a national wildlife refuge. But The Nature Conservancy earned McDonald's respect when it sold back the Gray Ranch to the local Animas Foundation. "A lot of other so-called environmental groups spend all their time in court or lobbying," he said. "Meanwhile, the battle is being lost while they're winning points in the newspaper." McDonald told me the safe harbor for the Chiricahua leopard frogs increased ranchers' comfort level in dealing with endangered species, but the Magoffins remain the only members of the Malpai group who have used the agreement to directly help the frogs. McDonald said the government needed to go further. "There still aren't the incentives we ought to have," he said. "People ought to actually be *paying* people to raise these frogs. You've got an endangered species in trouble, we've got places out here where they do well, and there should be out-and-out incentives, not just elimination of penalties."

By 2004, a decade after McDonald and other ranchers created the Malpai Borderlands Group, the community had accomplished a great deal. In a period when local real estate values doubled, two-thirds of the 468,000 acres of private land in the Malpai region were encumbered by conservation easements that would prevent the subdivision of the range. More than 300,000 acres had been burned in prescribed fires meant to knock back the spread of shrubs and trees. More than 2,000 erosion-control structures had been built. And more than 200 long-term vegetation plots had been established for regular monitoring by scientists, the most extensive network of its kind in the Southwest. Data from those plots help ranchers, ecologists, and land managers better understand arid lands grazing and adjust practices to minimize ecological impact. Through an instrument known as a grassbank, ranchers with allotments suffering from drought can move their cattle to plots that have more forage and are less vulnerable to damage from grazing.

Despite the Malpai group's successes, the region's future remains uncertain due to simple economics. Sold as a ranch, an acre might fetch $50 or $100, but marketed as a collection of smaller ranchettes, that acre could command $400 to $800, according to rangeland expert Nathan

Sayre. The result: a square mile that once provided enough grass to support 16 cows could host an equal number of 40-acre homesites. In the Southwest, ranchers typically own only a small fraction of the land where their cattle graze, but these private parcels are often located along watercourses or in pastures that harbor greater biodiversity than adjoining public lands.

Driving around the Malpai area, a development boom may seem unlikely. Houses are scarce. The FM dial spins aimlessly. Border Patrol SUVs are the most common vehicle on the road. But with signs advertising 40-acre parcels for as little as $25,000, a once-hidden corner of the Southwest is ripe for discovery.

Near Leslie Creek, where we saw the leopard frogs ensconced in slime, one ranch was divided into 90 lots and quickly gobbled up by buyers from Hawaii, Florida, and 15 other states, according to real estate records Warren examined. "The market out here for these rural parcels spans the continent," he said. Most of the parcels were 40 acres to begin with, but they could be subdivided five times, all the way down to four-acre lots, without permission from Cochise County. New residents would invariably fence their land, build roads that cause erosion, and import dogs, cats, and nonnative plants into the ecosystem. Additional homes would also make it harder to ignite prescribed burns. "We're barely in time," Warren said, "to protect this valley."

———————

Five valleys to the west, neighbors of the Buenos Aires refuge could only speculate why Shifflett, the sole manager the refuge ever had, was sacked. No one in the government was willing to talk about the matter. Some residents of the Altar Valley were more than happy to feed grist into the rumor mill and hardly heartbroken to see Shifflett go. He had made some enemies over the past 18 years; even within Fish and Wildlife, many considered him cavalier and a maverick. Crazy stories swirled around the Altar Valley about Shifflett being involved in a murder or the cross-border drug trafficking that was so prevalent in the area. A colleague tipped me off that Shifflett had been removed from his post, but Fish and Wildlife would only confirm that he was no longer the manager of the refuge and that he was the subject of an internal law enforcement investigation. Beyond that, however, the agency would say nothing more, on or off the record. Shifflett wouldn't return my calls on the advice of his lawyer, who also wouldn't comment.

Shifflett's alleged crime and his fate remained a mystery until I got my hands on a five-page, single-spaced typewritten letter that Shifflett had produced for his lawyer. In it, Shifflett described the chain of events leading up to his removal, and directly blamed Sue Chilton for Game and Fish's denial of his request to move the frogs from Schwalbe's backyard to the refuge. When I found out that Shifflett was dethroned because he transported some tadpoles, it was something of an anticlimax, given the scuttlebutt in the Altar Valley. But state and federal officials still weren't willing to talk about the case. Through her lawyer, Sue issued a statement calling Shifflett's allegations "disingenuous and a pack of misrepresentations." "It appears to me," she said, "that Mr. Shifflett has been accused of breaking the law, and is now trying to blame everyone but himself for his actions."

After Fish and Wildlife removed Shifflett from his post, he decided to retire from the agency after 38 years of service. The government's case against him was shopped around to federal prosecutors in Tucson and Phoenix, but none was interested, so the matter was referred to the environmental crimes unit at the Department of Justice. The Washington, DC, office opted to prosecute Shifflett and prepared to file federal felony charges that carried thousands of dollars in fines and even the possibility of jail time.

Eighteen months after he moved the tadpoles, Shifflett faced a decision. He could either pay a fine of $3,500 and end the matter, or cough up maybe seven times that in legal fees and try to clear his name in court. If Shifflett's case went to trial, he would blame Sue Chilton for stopping the Arizona Game and Fish Department from approving the tadpole transfer and perhaps shine a light into decision making at the highest levels of the Interior Department.

Shifflett, though certain of his innocence, chose to pay the penalty. He didn't want to bother with the hassle and said his court date would coincide with his daughter's wedding. A group that defends government workers, Public Employees for Environmental Responsibility, offered Shifflett legal assistance if he wanted to fight the charges. PEER also proffered help with fund-raising if Shifflett chose to pay the fine, but he opted to settle the tab on his own. After PEER publicized the case, Shifflett started getting $25 and $50 checks in the mail from fellow wildlife managers. "It was amazing all the letters I had from my peers all across the United States supporting what I'd done," Shifflett said. "People just couldn't believe you would fine a longtime professional for trying to save a frog. It's like ludicrous, and it was strictly politics."

The case appears to be the only prosecution of a wildlife refuge manager for a conservation-related offense. Jeff Ruch, PEER's executive director, told me it was appalling that Shifflett had been charged with anything. "He took the kind of decisive action managers are always encouraging their employees to take," he said. "Given the whole array of other things that are affecting wildlife, for scarce resources to be spent on this case shows that someone has their head lodged deep in their own posterior." Both Ruch and Shifflett's attorney, Jeff Buchella, acknowledged that Shifflett's actions may have strayed from procedures. At the time he moved the tadpoles, Shifflett's endangered species permit didn't include the Chiricahua leopard frog, but that's because the species had recently been listed. Ruch said Shifflett's actions were at most "a technical violation that would have been best handled by a letter of reprimand," while Buchella called it a "bookkeeping thing." "Some bureaucrat hadn't gotten around to going into the word processor to change the permit," Buchella said, adding that Fish and Wildlife employees regularly do what Shifflett did "without actually getting someone from Washington, DC, to hand them a specific piece of paper that says they can move this bumblebee today from location A to location B."

Ruch and Buchella argued that the case was motivated by a grudge against Shifflett and political pressure: the Chiltons said no to the tadpole transfer and senior officials with Fish and Wildlife weren't willing to back their man in the field. But, Buchella conceded, "You couldn't prove it unless you had a ton of people up on the stand under oath." When I finally interviewed Shifflett about the episode, he insisted that Sue Chilton had blocked the reintroduction of the frogs by pressuring Game and Fish's director, Duane Shroufe, from approving a safe harbor agreement. "I was sitting right across the desk from Duane," Shifflett said. "He definitely told me 'Sue will not let me sign it.'" Shroufe, the Chiltons, and others disputed Shifflett's account, saying the safe harbor wasn't finished and noting that the agreemant would only apply to private land, not the refuge. "There was nothing for anyone to sign," Sue said. In her view, Shifflett's prosecution was appropriate since he had acted unilaterally and sidestepped the safe harbor process, which the Chiltons supported. "He can't assume that because he had a noble goal, that excuses him from following the procedures," she said. "If the head of a refuge doesn't follow the law for wildlife, who can be expected to follow the law?" Shroufe, who also faulted Shifflett for breaking the rules, blamed the affair on "bad blood" and a "personality issue between the Chiltons and Shifflett." Other players in the drama emphasized antifederal sentiment at the Arizona Game and Fish; some said the Fish and Wildlife Service was looking for an excuse to get rid of Shifflett and turn the page at the Buenos Aires.

Ultimately, I saw the tadpole scandal and the hazy decision to depose Shifflett as symptomatic of an underlying problem that extended far beyond the Altar Valley and confronted hundreds of endangered species. Paradoxically, the strict protections of the ESA could inhibit recovery by turning a species into a liability that landowners were eager to eliminate. It could discourage wildlife managers with less gumption than Shifflett from taking bold actions. And it could stop researchers from collecting crucial data on a species' basic biology.

After Shifflett retired from Fish and Wildlife, he moved back to Virginia, where he had gone to school, and bought 30 acres along the Shenandoah River. He started helping Virginia's game and fish department with aquatic surveys and assisting researchers at the College of William and Mary who were studying the effects of mercury pollution on local bird populations. Shifflett also spent a couple of months a year leading safaris in Botswana. "In many ways," he said, "this has all been a blessing in disguise and I'm happier than you can ever believe." The decision to move the tadpoles ended his career with Fish and Wildlife, but Shifflett didn't have any regrets. "Ethically, biologically, it was the right thing to do," he said. "But Fish and Wildlife let me down. They didn't support me saving an endangered species."

11

Warming Up

When the 2004 wildfire season began, I figured Mt. Graham was due. Many of the surrounding sky islands had caught fire over the past few years, and the drought had only eased up a bit since its nadir in 2002. Foresters and firefighters described Graham as a powder keg and a tinderbox. Dark predictions from the Forest Service had become a rite of spring, and I sometimes brushed them off. The officials issuing the prophesies had a vested interest in hyping the threat, both to discourage human-caused fires and to attract more federal funding. It was like asking a barber if you needed a haircut. But with Graham, I didn't doubt the dire warnings. The spruce-fir forest atop the sky island had not burned since 1685 and was full of bug-killed trees. The forests lower on the mountain had been deprived of fire for decades and were choked with dry fuel.

In late May, with the wildfire season already under way, I headed up the mountain to take part in a squirrel survey, but not before sneaking in an overnight backpacking trip down the Ash Creek Trail. That hike helped me understand the mountain's layer cake of plant communities and how climate change could rearrange the configuration. The route, which begins 1,000 feet below Mt. Graham's summit and one mile west of the observatory, follows Ash Creek as it flows down the shady north face of the range, plummeting 6,300 feet in nine miles. It's the kind of trail where the ache in your knees while going down matches the burning in your lungs while hiking back up. As you head downhill on the Ash Creek Trail, you pass through a series of habitats that are defined by the wide variation in temperature and precipitation at various altitudes on the mountain (fig. 13). At the very top of Mt. Graham, annual precipitation averages three feet, much of it coming as snow in the winter. In the surrounding desert, just 10 inches of rain fall in a normal year.

At the Ash Creek trailhead, around 9,500 feet elevation, the forest is in a transition zone between the top two layers. Uphill, there are a couple thousand acres of Engelmann spruce and corkbark fir. This layer is the smallest, yet no other mountain in southern Arizona has such an extensive spruce-fir forest because no other range has so much terrain so high up. Initially, biologists believed that Mt. Graham's red squirrels relied almost exclusively on the top layer, the spruce-fir forest in which the telescopes were built. Subsequent surveys, however, found plenty of squirrels lower on the mountain, even at 7,800 feet.

As I started down Ash Creek Trail, the transition zone gave way to the mixed-conifer layer below: about 11,000 acres of forest dominated by Douglas fir, southwestern white pine, ponderosa pine, plus some aspen. Even in summer, as the desert below was baking in triple-digit heat, the trail was lined with ferns, mosses, and mushrooms. Every so often, I passed small strips of orange flagging that biologists had tied to branches to help them locate middens, the piles of debris where squirrels squirrel away pine, spruce, and fir cones.

About 1.5 miles down the Ash Creek Trail, I came to a historic mill site with a heavily rusted boiler, evidence of the logging that began on the mountain in the 1880s to supply lumber for the mines and farming towns below. Around the turn of the century, early settlers described the red squirrel as common atop Mt. Graham, but logging operations, including considerable clear-cutting, began to consume the squirrel's limited habitat.

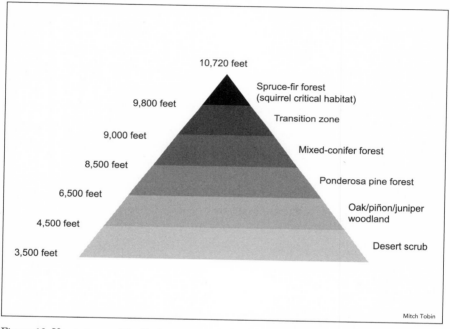

Figure 13: Vegetation on Mt. Graham.

Areas logged decades ago are still not suitable for the squirrel because the rodent, like its occasional predator, the threatened Mexican spotted owl, prefers old-growth forests. In these relatively undisturbed woods, squirrels find an abundance of nesting sites and hiding places in the downed logs and standing dead snags. The closed canopy above creates a cool, moist microclimate that supports mushrooms the squirrels eat and prevents the spoilage of cones stored in their middens. If it gets too dry or too hot, the cones open up, the nutritious seeds fall out, and they either sprout or end up in the bellies of other animals. In an old-growth forest the interlocking network of branches also provides the squirrels with cover from avian predators and convenient routes for retrieving cones.

After I hiked another mile or so downhill, the creek slid over a tilted slab of metamorphic rock; soon I could hear 200-foot Ash Creek Falls, the tallest perennial waterfall in southern Arizona. At this point, around 8,000 feet elevation, I started to leave the mixed conifers and enter the ponderosa pines, where the woods were noticeably less shady and lush. Because it's drier and warmer in this zone, cones stored in middens would open and spill their seeds, so the change in vegetation creates a downhill barrier for the squirrels as insurmountable as the ocean. Mt. Graham's red squirrels are essentially marooned atop the sky island.

The ponderosa pine layer is the lower limit for the red squirrels, but it is the preferred habitat for a nonnative competitor. In the early 1940s, the Arizona Game and Fish Department sought to bolster varmint hunting on the mountain by relocating some Abert's squirrels from the Flagstaff area. State game officials expected the Abert's squirrels would remain between 6,000 and 8,000 feet elevation because the animals eat the cambium layer beneath the bark of ponderosas. But the Abert's squirrel began migrating upslope into the mixed-conifer forest that lies above the ponderosa pines. It's likely that competition for food from the Abert's squirrels, plus continued logging on Mt. Graham, contributed to the sharp decline in red squirrels by the middle of the 20th century. By 1966, no red squirrels had been found on Mt. Graham for eight years, leading some biologists to mistakenly conclude the subspecies had blinked out.

Another two miles down the trail, I reached Oak Flat, an uncharacteristically level section that made for a choice camping spot. Now at about 6,000 feet elevation, roughly halfway between Graham's summit and its base, the ponderosa pines gave way to even drier, warmer woodlands with oaks, manzanitas, piñons, junipers, and other shrubby plants.

I retraced my steps after spending the night at Oak Flat, but if I had descended farther on the trail, the terrain would have become even drier and the vegetation would have become even sparser, ending in the Chihuahuan Desert with yuccas, prickly pears, and mesquite trees.

This ecological stratification on Mt. Graham has remained roughly the same for thousands of years, a product of the relatively stable climate that has prevailed since the last ice age. In that time, a very slight natural warming trend may have pushed the layers uphill a bit and reduced the amount of habitat available to the red squirrel. But those changes proceeded at a glacial, almost imperceptible pace. Human-caused climate change might accelerate the process from millennia to decades. As the planet warms and the Southwest's arid climate becomes even drier, the deserts, oak woodlands, and ponderosa pine forests could climb Mt. Graham's slopes and push the conifer forests, and the red squirrels that depend on them, right off the top of the mountain.

Throughout the Southwest, slight changes in temperature will have dramatic effects on other ecosystems because the region's deserts, grasslands, savannahs, woodlands, and coniferous forests lie so close together; in some cases, like Mt. Graham, all of the plant communities are found in a single range. In the nearby Santa Catalinas, scientists have recorded nearly 100 plant species blooming at a higher altitude than previously recorded. Numerous studies from around the world have documented similar shifts in the ranges of trees, birds, butterflies, and other species toward the tops of mountains, in what's known as the escalator effect. On a global scale, 400 to 550 bird species are expected to go extinct by 2100 due to the phenomenon, according to a study by Duke and Stanford scientists. The American pika, a small rabbitlike creature that lives in alpine boulder fields in western North America, faces an uncertain future because its montane habitat will shrink and it can die in a matter of hours if exposed to temperatures higher than 78 degrees.

In addition to moving uphill, red squirrels and other species are expected to move toward the poles as the planet heats up. Based on the popular Christmas bird count, National Audubon Society scientists found that 58 percent of the 305 most common species in North America had shifted an average of 35 miles northward in the past four decades. As my colleague Tony Davis reported, Audubon volunteers in southern

Arizona have been seeing more swallows, warblers, hummingbirds, and other species that winter in Mexico, including the first Arizona sightings of the flame-colored tanager, Sinaloa wren, rufous-capped warbler, and gray-collared becard. At the same time, finches, brown creepers, pygmy nuthatches, and other species are shifting north, out of the region.

Unfortunately, entire ecosystems will not move in unison. Each species will take its own course, and researchers are just beginning to understand how global warming will scramble seasonal patterns in blooming, breeding, migrating, and other events, what biologists call phenology. On a Wisconsin farm, for example, scientists took data on birds and flowers collected by Aldo Leopold from 1936 to 1947 and compared them with more recent observations to reveal that springtime activities for one-third of the species were happening earlier in the year. One meta-analysis of 99 species of birds, butterflies, and alpine herbs found that their ranges had shifted poleward by an average of 3.8 miles per decade and moved upslope by 20 feet per decade. Another study in same issue of the journal *Nature* in 2003 combed through 143 studies covering 1,468 species and found a "consistent temperature-related shift, or 'fingerprint', in species ranging from mollusks to mammals and from grasses to trees."

Insects and pathogens are especially sensitive to temperature and may dramatically expand their ranges in response to a degree or two of global warming. Many foresters believe the mountain pine beetle outbreak in Colorado, which will kill nearly all the mature lodgepole pines in the state, is at least partly attributable to rising temperatures and the lack of a severe cold snap, which can suppress the bugs. Warming and drought may be making aspen more vulnerable to disease and pests, contributing to a phenomenon known as Sudden Aspen Decline, or SAD.

On Mt. Graham, a cascade of infestations that started in 1992 showed how insects could remake a forest in short order. After an ice storm and subsequent winds knocked down a large number of trees, the resulting supply of dead timber provided a boost to the beetle population. Next, an obscure moth caterpillar defoliated the spruce and fir around the telescopes. Then scientists recorded a new insect on the mountain, the spruce aphid. Native to Europe, the spruce aphid had been confined in North America to the maritime forests of the Pacific Northwest, but toward the end of the 20th century, it began invading the Southwest. Because the insects are limited by cold temperatures, some scientists suspect their outbreaks will become more frequent and severe as the planet warms. On Mt. Graham, the aphid thrived in the relatively dry, warm winters of 1999 and 2000, defoliating the spruce by sucking sap from their needles. They also made the trees more vulnerable to the native spruce beetles, which kill their host by boring into the tree and laying eggs in the cambium layer beneath the bark. Spruce beetles would have eventually attacked the forest atop Mt. Graham—they are part of the natural cycle—but the drought and invasive spruce aphids probably accelerated the process. By the time I hiked the Ash Creek Trail, virtually all of the spruce-fir forest in Mt. Graham's top layer was dead. Tom Swetnam, director of the University of Arizona Laboratory of Tree-Ring Research and a former wildland firefighter in the Gila National Forest in New Mexico, told me that "Mt. Graham is a bit of a microcosm of what we're seeing elsewhere in the western US." "There's a synergism of disturbances going on up there with the drought, beetles, and fire hazards all combined in one place," he said.

Research by Swetnam and others has shown that climate change is already having profound effects on North American forests. Looking across the West, one team of scientists found that warming over the past half-century—just 1 degree Fahrenheit—caused the death rate among a wide variety of trees to double in 17 to 29 years. Writing in the journal *Science*, the researchers reported that their study of 76 plots in old-growth forests from British Columbia to northern Arizona revealed that the higher mortality could not be explained by other possible causes such as fire suppression, air pollution, the species of tree, its age, or the elevation. Combine higher temperatures with droughts, which are also expected to become more common and severe in the Southwest, and you have the recipe for massive changes in biotic communities, and not just atop mountains like Graham. Scientists believe the 3-million-acre die-off in piñon and ponderosa pines in 2002 and 2003, during a drought comparable to one in the 1950s, was much worse due to the warmer weather. Similarly, the cooler 1950s drought did not lead to the widespread loss of creosote and other bushes in the Sonoran Desert, while the one at the turn of the 21st century did.

The piñon pine mortality and its connection to climate prompted researchers to use the sealed-glass-dome Biosphere 2 facility outside Tucson to examine how higher temperatures would affect the trees. They trucked in 50 piñon pines from New Mexico, split them into two groups, and exposed one set to temperatures that were 7 degrees warmer than current conditions, well within projections for 2100. When exposed to drought, the trees in the hotter zone died 28 percent faster, and all perished before the first tree in the cooler zone died. The researchers projected that die-offs of piñon pines would occur five times as often; in essence, a 100-year event would become a 20-year event. The findings raised the prospect that the entire piñon-juniper ecosystem would become endangered by global warming, even without considering the increased likelihood of beetle outbreaks that many scientists expect.

Climate change can no longer be described in the future tense. In western forests, there is strong evidence that altered weather patterns are already increasing the frequency of wildfires. Megafires like Rodeo-Chediski, their size and ferocity unknown in modern times, appear to be the start of an ominous trend (figs. 14 and 15). In *Science*, Swetnam and other researchers reported that "large wildfire activity increased suddenly and markedly" starting in the mid-1980s, with most of the change due to a warming climate rather than fire suppression. Higher temperatures led to a thinner snowpack that melted earlier in spring, leading to more-flammable conditions in summer. The scientists looked at more than 1,100 large blazes that broke out from 1970 onward. Compared to the 1970–1986 period, wildfires in the 1987–2003 era were four times as frequent and burned more than six times the acreage. The length of the wildfire season increased an average of 78 days.

The consensus among ecologists and foresters is that further warming, much of it already in the pipeline due to the long life of carbon dioxide in the atmosphere, will make wildfires even more problematic in coming decades. The West's forests are already out of balance due to fire suppression, so any blazes that start today have the potential to grow into unnatural infernos. In a cruel twist, the greater fire activity could feed on itself: forests that remove carbon from the air will burn and release their carbon into the atmosphere, thereby forcing even more warming and more fires. On *60 Minutes*, Swetnam told Scott Pelley that half or more of the West's forests could become grasslands or other ecosystems by the end of the 21st century. Just in the Southwest, Swetnam calculates that nearly 2 million acres of forest might not come back for at least a century, in part because megafires often lead to disastrous erosion in a region where it may take millennia for an inch or two of topsoil to form.

Even without climate change, species like the spotted owl and the Mt. Graham red squirrel were facing an uphill climb in habitat prone to

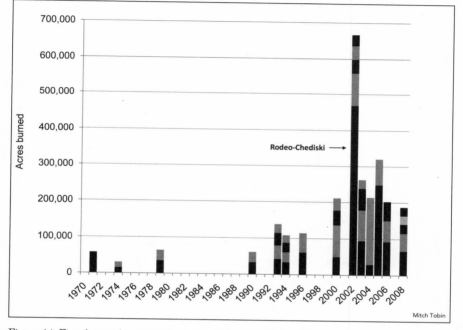

Figure 14: Fires larger then 20,000 acres in Arizona and New Mexico, 1970 to 2008.
Note: Each rectangle represents a fire larger than 20,000 acres.
Source: Southwest Coordination Center.

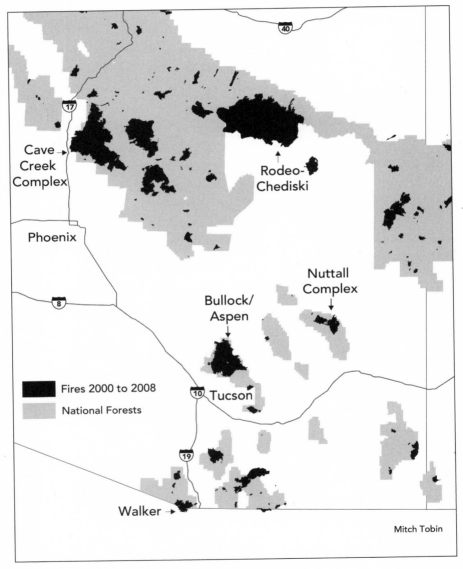

Figure 15: Wildfires on national forests, 2000 to 2008.
Source: US Forest Service, US Fish and Wildlife Service.

catastrophic wildfires and still suffering the effects of overlogging. Climate change could surpass all the other dangers by doing away with whatever habitat made it past those threats. There simply is no good solution for species like the Mt. Graham red squirrel if carbon emissions continue to rise as predicted. With enough warming, biologists may be forced to capture such mountaintop species and put them in zoos, transplant them to similar habitat elsewhere, or perform some other Noah-like rescue mission. Biologists are already planning a captive breeding program for the Mt. Graham red squirrel so that they can bolster the population in the wild. Some leading scientists, however, have written off the subspecies. Stanford biologist Terry Root, a promoter of using triage to save species threatened by climate change, told the Associated Press that some creatures atop the sky islands "don't have any place to move to." "Those species are functionally extinct right now," she said. "They're toast."

After I backpacked my way back up Ash Creek, I joined state, federal, and University of Arizona biologists for the semiannual red squirrel count. To estimate the population, researchers visit a random sample of the middens where the squirrels store their food. Each spring and fall, they monitor about one-quarter of the 1,300 known middens, most of them abandoned for years, then extrapolate the results. Those surveys have revealed a striking change in the squirrel's distribution due to the series of insect infestations that struck the top of Mt. Graham. In 1996, there were 184 squirrels recorded in the spruce-fir habitat that surrounds the telescopes; five years later, with the spruce-fir forest dead from bug damage, biologists found fewer than 10. The squirrels retreated down the mountain into the transition zone and mixed-conifer forest. Initially, they did just fine. By 1999, the total population was nearly 600, triple the estimate prior to the telescope construction and the highest level ever recorded (fig. 16). Astronomers weren't so bold as to claim their telescopes were responsible for the population increase, but a 10-year study of the observatory's impact conducted by University of Arizona biologists did conclude in 2000 that the project had no negative effect on the subspecies. As it had for thousands of years, the squirrel population was waxing and waning with the crop of pine, spruce, and fir cones. But that vital food supply took a major hit at the turn of the 21st century, when the drought reduced the cone crop across the Southwest's high-country forests. By May 2004, the overall red squirrel

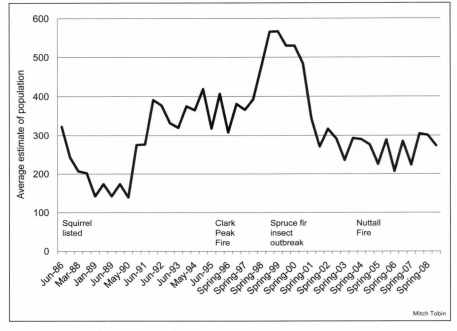

Figure 16: Mt. Graham red squirrel population.
Source: Arizona Game and Fish Department.

population was between 200 and 300, about the same level as when the subspecies was listed 16 years earlier.

My survey group was assigned the GPS coordinates of a dozen middens, but even with the assistance of satellites, it was tough to locate the sites. The thick canopy of the old-growth forest kept interfering with the GPS signals as we bushwhacked through the woods, so the biologists resorted to the old-fashioned technology of map and compass.

Once we arrived at the middens, we frequently saw and heard the resident squirrels since they fiercely defend their caches. As we approached the piles of debris, the squirrels bolted up the trees, then barked at us before leaping effortlessly from branch to branch. Even without an actual squirrel sighting, researchers can determine if a midden is active by looking for signs of digging or freshly peeled shells from cones. Tim Snow, an Arizona Game and Fish biologist, explained that the colder temperatures inside the middens prevent the cones from spilling their seeds. "If you reach in," Snow said, "it's like a refrigerator." Cut down too many trees in a forest, and the middens are exposed to more desiccating heat and sunlight. It's like unplugging the refrigerator. The food spoils.

Tree squirrels are constantly raiding the icebox and demand a continual supply of food because they have an internal motor that's stuck in high gear: their heart rate ranges from 150 to 450 beats per minute. The squirrels, which do not hibernate in winter, are in a perpetual struggle to turn food into energy because their small bodies lose heat rapidly. Cones and other nutrition are abundant in fall, but nearly absent in winter, so a squirrel must store energy as body fat and keep a backup supply of fuel in its cache. Finding and eating food therefore occupies the largest share of the squirrels' time, and food availability is usually the key determinant of their survival rate.

The spruce-fir forest appeared primeval as our survey team moved from midden to midden. The mud revealed bear and mountain lion tracks, the wind in the pines below sounded like surf on the shores of the sky island, and it was impossible to see the telescopes or any other human imprint. But long before the telescopes were built atop Mt. Graham, the range was hardly pristine. By the 1970s, about half the squirrels' habitat was already gone. The mountaintop was home to a state highway, plus a maze of dirt roads to support 12,000 acres of logging and development. There were campgrounds, parking lots, dozens of cabins, a Bible camp, a man-made lake, plus a forest of radio towers atop one of the tallest peaks. All the controversy swirled around the 8.6-acre observatory, but in the context of climate change, fire suppression, the insect outbreaks, and decades of development on the mountain, the project now seemed like a bit player in a much larger drama.

Even in late May, we found some snow on the shady north-facing slopes. All that moisture, however, would soon be gone as Arizona entered the parched season that precedes the arrival of monsoon thunderstorms, around July 4. As our survey crew dropped in elevation and searched for more middens, the fuel at our feet grew thicker and crunchier. After a few years of covering wildfires, I couldn't look at a forest without thinking about how it would burn. On Mt. Graham, it was easy to envision how the flames could capitalize on the funnel-like canyons that were jammed with trees wherever the soil could maintain its purchase. "Every time I drive up there, I wonder if this is the last time I'll see the mountain in this condition," biologist John Koprowski, head of the University of Arizona squirrel-monitoring program, told me a few days after I came down the mountain. "All kinds of gloom and doom scenarios keep me up at night."

On June 22, 2004, the first hint of monsoon moisture arrived in southern Arizona. As the sun cooked the desert and gave rise to convection currents, water vapor boiled up into the heavens, creating thunderheads resembling cauliflower florets above Mt. Graham and other sky islands. Inside the clouds, the drops grew fat enough to overcome the updrafts and fell to the earth; most evaporated before reaching the ground, creating wispy curtains of almost-rain known as virga. The rising heat and falling rain generated friction within the clouds, then produced forks of lightning that stabbed at Mt. Graham and the other ranges. One of the bolts sparked a fire on Graham's thickly forested north slope, about five miles east of where I had hiked in Ash Creek Canyon one month before and about six miles from the telescopes. The Gibson Fire, named for the canyon in which it began, smoldered for a few days as relatively light winds and elevated humidity kept the flames in check. Four days after the Gibson Fire began, another lightning strike started a fire in Nuttall Canyon, about five miles to the west of the Ash Creek Trail and also about six miles from the scopes. With drizzle occasionally falling, both the Nuttall and Gibson fires remained small for the next few days and sometimes didn't even give off much smoke. Observatory officials kept an eye on the fires, but business proceeded as usual atop the mountain.

Everything changed on July 2 with the resurgence of hot, dry, windy weather. Both the Nuttall and Gibson fires roared to life. As telescope workers fled the site that evening, they turned on outdoor sprinklers, hoping the artificial rain would temper the flames' inevitable charge toward the observatory. Apache activists claimed the lightning bolts were divinely inspired. "We believe that this fire was not accidental, but a warning that the mountain can defend itself," a former tribal council member said in a press release. "This mountain was quiet until they began disturbing it to build the telescopes."

Over the next few days, the Nuttall and Gibson fires doubled in size, were renamed the Nuttall Complex, and edged ever closer to the $200 million telescopes. Firefighters thinned trees beside the state highway that runs along the spine of the mountain, then set intentional burns to rob fuel from the wildfires so they wouldn't cross over the crest of the range and scorch Graham's southern face. There were hundreds of acres of critical habitat for the squirrel in between the highway and the blazes, but firefighters had no choice: it was either burn that acreage intentionally or risk losing even more to the wildfire.

At the telescope complex, fire crews braced for an inferno that was 319 years in the making. They cut down 1,000 to 1,500 trees around the congressionally designated footprint, completing in a few days a thinning proposal that many environmentalists vowed to fight for years. "If anything," an observatory official told me, "they've done a little bit more than we would have." Even on one of the nation's most heavily litigated patches of land, the ESA did not stand in the way of emergency firefighting. Photos from the evening of July 6 show the Nuttall Complex spreading from treetop to treetop, charging toward the telescope in a seemingly unstoppable crown fire. When the flames reached the area around the observatory that had been thinned, they dropped to the ground, according to fire officials on the scene. The telescopes were safe.

The flames marched on as the Nuttall and Gibson fires combined on the north face of Mt. Graham. Situated in the middle of the two blazes was Ash Creek Canyon, one of the red squirrel's sanctuaries and one of my cherished places. For several days, the maps released by the firefighting team showed the two fires creeping closer, their intensity tempered by the influx of monsoon moisture. Just as the flames were entering the upper reaches of Ash Creek Canyon, the rains arrived. When the final maps were drawn for the 29,400-acre Nuttall Complex, it looked like the hand of God had spared just that canyon.

Around Mt. Graham's summit, it was the first stand-replacing blaze in the spruce-fir forest since the 17th century. Koprowski and other researchers monitored squirrels they had radio-collared before the blaze and concluded that seven of the 20 animals that lived within the fire's perimeter had died. Besides the direct mortality, the fire jeopardized other squirrels by opening up the forest around their middens, making the rodents more vulnerable to predators, and causing the microclimate to become warmer and drier. But the fire's impact could have been even worse. Just 10 percent of the Nuttall Complex burned severely and reduced forests to blackened poles. Much of the intense burn covered the already dead spruce-fir forest. Where the fire burned lightly, it consumed the unnatural buildup of fuel and spurred the growth of grasses and forbs that would benefit deer, bears, and wild turkeys. For millennia, the squirrels had managed to muddle through major fires in the spruce-fir forest every few centuries, and the Nuttall Complex wouldn't ring their death knell.

Activists who had fought the telescopes for two decades argued that the emergency thinning and suppression tactics had further imperiled the squirrel. As my colleague Tom Beal reported, the Forest Service concluded that the observatory and other mountaintop developments had "precipitated aggressive firefighting techniques and inhibited the restoration of the natural ecosystem processes." But based on my review of the fire maps and discussions with both firefighters and biologists, I think the telescopes, the supposed nemesis of the Mt. Graham red squirrel, actually wound up helping the animal's cause. For starters, the observatory's construction was predicated on a number of conservation measures that protected the top of the mountain from further development. When the Nuttall Complex was burning, it was during the peak of the region's wildfire season and incident commanders were competing for helicopters, hotshot crews, and other firefighting resources. Yet for several days the Nuttall Complex was deemed one of the nation's top-priority fires. Federal officials allocated more than 1,000 personnel to the firefighting team and sent them the first air tankers to be recertified for flying after the nation's entire fleet was grounded over safety concerns. It was the telescopes atop Mt. Graham, plus dozens of cabins and a cluster of telecommunications equipment, that added urgency to the suppression effort, not the squirrels. By all accounts, the intentional fire that firefighters set to rob the blaze of fuels was extremely hot and torched most of the spruce-fir forest. But that area was already unsuitable for squirrels due to the insect outbreak. The suppression tactic worked, and the Nuttall Fire did not cross over onto Mt. Graham's south-facing slopes, which now support the highest density of squirrels.

Where the fires have already burned, it would ordinarily take more than a century for the spruce, fir, and pines to grow back and remake the squirrel's habitat. But global warming may make that recovery impossible. "The spruce-fir may never come back because it's so dry," said Thetis Gamberg, a wildlife biologist with the US Fish and Wildlife Service. "Nothing will ever be what it was before." Conditions may also deteriorate lower down on the mountain, in the transition zone and mixed-conifer forests where the squirrels live. Researchers have already documented that a couple of degrees of warming at a midden can cause the cones inside to spill their seeds. Enough warming could effectively burn out the refrigerators where the red squirrels store their food and wipe them off their namesake mountain.

12
Kangaroo Court

Two months after monsoon rains doused the Nuttall Fire, four Republican congressmen came to the base of Mt. Graham to hold a hearing on the ESA. Bomb-sniffing dogs and police officers from nine agencies scoured the grounds of Eastern Arizona College as hundreds of people filtered into the auditorium in Thatcher. Security forces searched bags and scanned for weapons, measures you wouldn't expect had the hearing dealt with Social Security or tax policy, but that were seemingly essential given the polarization over the ESA and the history of civil disobedience on Mt. Graham. From the parking lot in Thatcher, you could look up and see where the Nuttall Complex had turned the mountain from green to black.

The hearing in Thatcher was billed as a way for lawmakers to solicit the sage advice of expert witnesses who could help them craft reasonable reforms to the law. In reality, the meeting put the ESA on trial in a kangaroo court that doubled as a campaign rally for Rick Renzi, the first-term Republican who represented the area and faced an election in six weeks. The ostensible leader of the event was Richard Pombo, the Central Valley rancher turned California congressman who had tried nearly a dozen times to rewrite the law and failed. That elusive goal was drawing closer. In 2003, Republican leaders had named Pombo chairman of the House Resources Committee, bypassing nine committee members with seniority and making Pombo the youngest committee chairman in Congress, on his 42nd birthday. A few weeks before Pombo came to Thatcher, population 4,000, he was in New York City at the Republican National Convention, where the American Gas Association hosted a party for him—Pombo-Palooza— at a trendy night club with dance hall girls, a mechanical bull, and the fiddling of the Charlie Daniels Band. Pombo still had photos of cattle wrangling in his office, and President Bush had called him the Marlboro Man, but his public image, along with his home district, had morphed over the past decade. His white cowboy hat and mustache gave way to a goatee and slicked-back hair as his home of Tracy transformed itself from a farm town to a suburb. But his distaste for the ESA remained strong as ever.

This wasn't the first time Pombo and company had tried to use a wildfire to attack the ESA. The year before, Pombo had blamed the law for the deaths of four firefighters near Winthrop, Washington, during the Thirtymile Fire, claiming that protections for endangered salmon had prevented helicopters from scooping up water and dousing the flames in time to save the crew. The Forest Service's 13-member investigative team concluded that the helicopter was delayed for other reasons and that the deaths were attributable to poor decisions by commanders and the crew's disregard for safety rules.

Before the forum in Thatcher began, friend and foe of the ESA held rival demonstrations outside the auditorium. To my left, environmentalists held up hand-drawn signs: "Telescopes bad—Squirrels good," "Clearcut Renzi, not squirrels," and "Squirrels protect our sacred mountain." To my right, ranchers, farmers, and others held up their own declarations: "Worship the creator, not creation," "ESA is not about the environment, it's about control," "Regulation without representation is tyranny," and "Removing cows is larceny."

I ran the gauntlet, took a seat in the auditorium's orchestra pit, and began to transcribe the rhetoric. The Speaker of the Arizona House of Representatives, Jake Flake from Snowflake (a town named for his Mormon ancestors, the Flakes, and another family, the Snows), blamed the ESA for the demise of the Southwest's timber industry. Greg Walden, a congressman from Oregon, said the ESA had led farmers in his district to commit suicide after a water war broke out in the Klamath Basin in 2001. Pombo told the crowd the ESA had become "the preeminent law of our country." "There's not a single function of the federal government that takes precedence over the Endangered Species Act," he said, "not even national defense." The congressmen kept intimating that were it not for litigious environmentalists stalling and blocking forest-thinning projects, the recent wildfires wouldn't have been so bad. Over and over during the hearing, the lawmakers and their sympathetic witnesses bemoaned the litigation surrounding the ESA. Sure enough, on that very day, the Center for Biological Diversity had once again sued the US Fish and Wildlife Service, hoping to get the agency to protect two southwestern fish, the roundtail and headwater chubs.

There was a limit to the lawmakers' attacks, and judging by the ratio of cowboy boots to Birkenstocks in the audience, the congressmen probably didn't go far enough for many in the crowd. None of the legislators questioned evolution and promoted creationism, as many Americans do, and none said Congress was wrong to have passed the ESA. None hid their desire to shorten the act's reach and give landowners more wiggle room, but at least publicly they didn't argue that some species deserved to go extinct, as some of their constituents did. Taken at their word, it was all about boosting the act's effectiveness.

The policy decisions said otherwise. Even without modifying the language of the ESA, as Pombo hoped to do, the legislative and executive branches were already shaping how the law was applied, through policy making by the administration's political appointees and through the power of the purse entrusted to Congress. Throughout the ESA's history, during both Republican and Democratic administrations, political considerations have affected listing decisions, none more so than in George W. Bush's Interior Department, which protected fewer endangered species per year than any of its predecessors (figs. 17 and 18).

During the Bush administration, complaints from agency biologists about the politicization of their work prompted four environmental

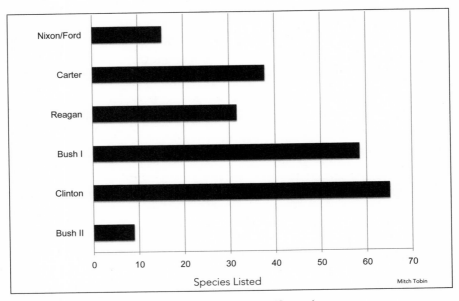

Figure 17: Average number of species listed per year by US presidents.
Note: Table does not include delistings or the 131 species listed before 1974.
Source: US Fish and Wildlife Service and Marris, Emma, "Endangered Species Chart a Fresh
Course," *Nature* online, March 10, 2009.

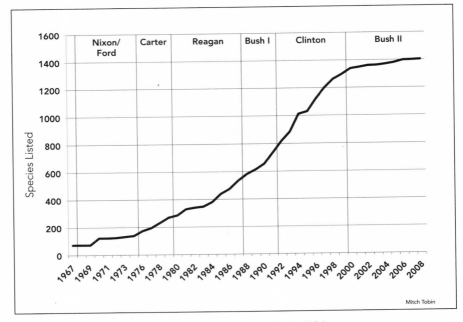

Figure 18: Cumulative number of US species protected by the ESA.
Source: US Fish and Wildlife Service.

groups to use the Freedom of Information Act to dig into the government's decision making. Their probe revealed that much of the undue
influence traced back to a single political appointee in the Interior
Department who had disregarded the advice of agency scientists at least
a half-dozen times. Deputy Assistant Secretary Julie MacDonald, an
engineer by training, mocked the biologists beneath her in the bureaucratic hierarchy and repeatedly did the bidding of industries that might
be affected by the listings, according to internal e-mails obtained by the
groups. As demands mounted to drill for oil and gas in the Four Corners region, MacDonald ordered a Fish and Wildlife regional office to
reverse its decision to list the Gunnison's prairie dog. "Per Julie please
made [*sic*] the pd [prairie dog] finding negative," one internal e-mail said.
Commenting on a proposal to protect the greater sage grouse, MacDonald wrote, "This paragraph completely ignores the comments received by
the Owyhee Cattlemen's Association and the Idaho Cattle Association."
In response to the criticism, MacDonald contended that she did nothing illegal and was merely exercising her discretionary authority. But an
Interior Department investigation concluded that MacDonald repeatedly violated federal regulations and said "her heavy-handedness has cast
doubt on nearly every ESA decision issued during her tenure."

Many federal biologists feared that speaking truth to power would
result in retaliation. When the Union of Concerned Scientists and Public
Employees for Environmental Responsibility sent out a survey to Fish and
Wildlife scientists, nearly half of the 1,400 respondents said they couldn't
honestly express concerns about the needs of species. One-fifth said they
had been forced to compromise their scientific integrity. In the survey,
several respondents singled out MacDonald for abusing her authority and
altering scientific findings. "I have never before seen the boldness of intim-
idation demonstrated by a single political appointee," one scientist said.
"She has modified the behavior of the entire agency." It got so bad that
some agency staffers began to refer her reviews as "getting MacDonalded."

To some extent, the survey was recording Bush-bashing among liberal biologists working for the Republican president, but the findings were
consistent with the numerous exposés of the administration's disregard for
the science of endangered species, climate change, stem cell research, and
other contentious issues. To combat political manipulation in listings and
other aspects of the ESA, environmentalists and others can always plead
their case in court. It's a tough fight, however, because the plaintiffs must

prove the action was "arbitrary and capricious." Courts will generally presume an agency's expertise has led it to act in a reasonable manner.

In Congress, legislators can do their share to stop or slow down ESA listings by not appropriating enough funding to complete the task. In the mid-1990s, when environmentalists began to flood Fish and Wildlife with petitions and lawsuits, the agency's modest budget for the listing program became entirely consumed by court-ordered actions. The Interior Department pleaded poverty before judges and estimated it would take about $150 million to process more than 250 candidate species, all of which had already been judged by biologists to be at risk of extinction and worthy of federal protection. The only reason those safeguards were withheld was the lack of money, manpower, and ultimately political will to complete the process.

With control of Congress and the White House, Republicans could keep a lid on the number of endangered species and limit the ESA's reach by exercising executive power and controlling federal funding. A more durable outcome would be to change the ESA itself and modify Fish and Wildlife's behavior no matter which party was in power. The event that Pombo and the others staged in Thatcher was a prelude to such lawmaking and was followed by a series of other hearings in which the set of witnesses was always heavily stacked with ESA critics. On Mt. Graham, and in the deserts, grasslands, and other habitats surrounding Thatcher, the past few decades had provided ample evidence that the ESA was an essential tool for preventing extinction. If anything, the experience in the Southwest and elsewhere showed that the government needed to think much bigger and create ambitious new policies to better manage natural resources, especially with climate change compounding traditional threats. The ESA, a safety net, was helpless to solve those problems. But now even that backstop was on shaky ground. After the November 2004 elections kept Republicans in control of the White House and Congress, the ESA itself became endangered.

In September 2005, a year after the Thatcher meeting, Pombo introduced his rewrite of the ESA. Disingenuously titled the Threatened and Endangered Species Recovery Act, the Pombo bill actually weakened the government's obligation to protect and recover species. One draft even included a sunset clause that would repeal ESA entirely in 2015. The bill attacked many parts of the statute, none more so than the language that explains how to decide the key question: to list or not to list? Pombo was essentially trying to legislate what MacDonald was doing administratively. The bill made it harder to get species into the endangered club by introducing an economic analysis into the process and by explicitly stating that listing of distinct populations of animals should be used sparingly. Rather than rely "solely on the best scientific and commercial data available," the government could consider any data that the interior secretary, a political appointee, determined was appropriate. Such information would be limited to empirical data and exclude the results from the sophisticated modeling that biologists regard as an essential tool of their trade. Pombo and other ESA critics had long demanded that Fish and Wildlife only use peer-reviewed studies in making decisions, which sounded reasonable enough. But for many endangered species, the only studies available haven't been published in a refereed journal. Restricting the agency's scientific knowledge to peer-reviewed studies, the gold standard for scientific research, would exclude graduate theses, government surveys, and other elements of the so-called gray literature that might be the only attempts to illuminate a species' behavior or threats.

The Pombo bill completely eliminated another major element of the ESA, and one of the law's most contentious topics: critical habitat. These maps, which delineate lands and waters that are "essential to the conservation of the species" can include areas that are currently occupied by a species and vacant habitat that is part of its historical range. Declaring an area as critical habitat doesn't turn it into a national park or wildlife refuge, and the designation doesn't necessarily stop people from going about their business. Projects that have no connection to the federal government, including most activities on private lands, aren't affected by critical habitat, but any work that requires a federal permit, funding, or loans could be curtailed by the designation. Unlike the listing decision, which is supposed to be made solely on the basis of biology, economics must be factored into critical habitat designations. Fish and Wildlife has considerable discretion in mapping critical habitat: it is to be done "to the maximum extent prudent and determinable." The agency can stall for up to a year if it doesn't think enough is known about the species, or the agency can avoid the matter entirely if it thinks a map would either not benefit the species or be counterproductive (for example, giving poachers or illegal collectors valuable information). The legislative history behind critical habitat suggests its creators expected the "not prudent" exemption to be applied sparingly. In practice, it has been used routinely. To this day, the government has only designated critical habitat for about one-third of listed species.

Critical habitat became a flash point for litigation starting in the early 1990s, with the first round emanating from environmental groups trying to force the government to draw the maps and the second wave coming from businesses trying to slash or overturn the designations. In their fight against critical habitat, business groups and property rights advocates found allies in the Bush Interior Department. Fish and Wildlife cut the size of 94 percent of the first 312 critical habitats it reviewed and decreased the acreage by an average of 79 percent. By comparison, the Clinton administration reduced 35 percent of critical habitat maps by an average of only 5 percent.

Habitat is obviously critical for any species, but ESA experts are split on whether the government always needs to map and protect critical habitat. Many environmental groups see the provision as essential because it can add a further layer of restrictions. A peer-reviewed paper by Martin Taylor and Kierán Suckling of the Center for Biological Diversity and Jeffrey Rachlinski of Cornell Law School found that species with critical habitat were more likely to be improving than those without. But some in the conservation community, not to mention industry, view the process as flawed, redundant to the prohibition against "take" of an endangered species, and an unnecessary drain on government resources. It takes an average of $85,000 to process a listing, but $515,000 to designate critical habitat for a species. In a 2001 op-ed piece in *The New York Times* titled "Bush Isn't All Wrong about the Endangered Species Act," Bruce Babbitt, Clinton's interior secretary, expressed his frustration with the critical habitat policy. In response to the avalanche of lawsuits seeking designations, Babbitt wrote, "Fish and Wildlife Service has diverted its best scientists and much of its budget for the Endangered Species Act away from more important tasks like evaluating candidates for listing and providing other protections for species on the brink of extinction." Babbitt and many biologists have argued that the nation's biodiversity would be better off if we had an endangered ecosystem act that focused on the integrity of entire ecological communities rather than a statute based on individual species, subspecies, and distinct population segments. But that approach has never made much headway, leaving the ESA to protect habitat in a somewhat oblique fashion with a vague policy that is a magnet for time-consuming lawsuits from both environmentalists and industry.

Pombo's bill also added several new elements to the ESA that were designed to highlight the economic impact of species protections and shift the financial burden from private parties onto the federal government. Western power and water interests would be required to include information on the costs of ESA compliance on customers' bills. Ranchers would be reimbursed for losses they sustained due to wolves and other reintroduced species, a measure that actually had some support among environmentalists and contained similarities to a compensation program run by Defenders of Wildlife. The federal government also would have to compensate landowners for conservation measures that reduced their property values.

This last provision was one of the most controversial and consequential in the Pombo bill. It tapped into a long-standing debate: did the government owe citizens or businesses any money if its regulations harmed their economic interests? In a 1992 case, *Lucas v. South Carolina Coastal Council*, the Supreme Court ruled that if a regulation deprived a property owner of *all* economic value of their land, it constituted a "taking." In Pombo's bill, landowners who believed ESA restrictions had cost them *any* money would be entitled to compensation from Fish and Wildlife or another agency without going to court. It remained to be seen if the bill's call for payments for "foregone uses" would withstand judicial scrutiny, but if so, the change could prove extremely expensive for the government. The measure might also entice developers to propose more projects in endangered species' habitat so they could receive government payments.

Pombo's bill, which had been in the works for years, was introduced on September 19, 2005, and put to the full House just 10 days later. The vote, 229 for and 193 against, was largely along party lines, though 36 Democrats (mostly from the South and West) supported the bill and 34 Republicans (mostly from the Northeast and Midwest) opposed the measure. After a dozen years in office, the rancher from the Central Valley had done all he could to achieve his ultimate political goal: a rewrite of the ESA. It was now up to the Senate to decide the fate of the nation's most important wildlife law.

13
No Bats, No Tequila?

One of Richard Pombo's biggest grudges against the ESA was the listing of species that weren't really endangered. To critics like Pombo, it was bad enough when obscure plants and animals were constraining landowners and dictating management of the nation's public lands. It was an absolute outrage if the species causing the trouble was actually doing just fine and in no need of humans' help.

The Southwest offered Pombo some examples of mistaken listings, which the congressman frequently publicized. The Mexican duck, a member of the 1967 inaugural class of endangered species, was delisted in 1978 when scientists concluded it had interbred with mallards so frequently that it was not a distinct species. The Tumamoc globeberry, a vine named for the hill next to A Mountain in Tucson, was listed as endangered in 1986 because there were only 2,300 plants known in 30 isolated populations in the United States. In 1988 and 1989, extensive surveys related to construction of the Central Arizona Project, the concrete river that transports the Colorado River to Phoenix and Tucson, concluded that scientists had vastly underestimated the plant's numbers and range. In 1993, the globeberry was delisted.

The lesser long-nosed bat, which roosts along the US-Mexico border for part of the year, looked like another case of an endangered species listing gone wrong. When the US Fish and Wildlife Service protected the bat in 1988, its prospects certainly did seem dismal. Three years before, the federal government had paid for a survey of every US site where the bat had ever been recorded. Just one location, a cave on private land in southern Arizona, yielded any bats, and biologists found only about 500 there. Based on sightings of bats visiting hummingbird feeders, experts thought there might be another colony or two in Cochise County, with one containing perhaps 300 individuals. At Colossal Cave, just southeast of Tucson, there was no trace of the thousands of bats recorded there through the 1950s.

The outlook was just as gloomy south of the border. Surveys were conducted at nearly every cave and mineshaft where the species had been seen, but only three sites were occupied, and two of those roosts harbored very few lesser long-nosed bats, often called leptos after their genus, *Leptonycteris*. At one site, a cave in the coastal state of Jalisco, a biologist estimated there were maybe 15,000 leptos roosting. The bats seemed to have suffered a "drastic decline," Fish and Wildlife said in 1988, noting "the near or total disappearance of most of their known large colonies." It wasn't clear why leptos were nowhere to be found. Some scientists suspected that unregulated harvesting of wild agaves by Mexican moonshiners was depriving the bats of an important food source. Because leptos pollinate other signature plants of the Sonoran Desert, including the giant saguaro cactus, their apparent disappearance was not only alarming for the species itself. The bat's decline also raised the specter of cascading damage to the region's web of life. As Fish and Wildlife granted ESA protection to leptos on September 30, 1988, it said the species' imperilment caused "concern for the future of entire southwest desert ecosystems." In the years that followed, the bat's endangered status provided fodder for a spate of antigrazing lawsuits that led to limits on public lands ranching in the Southwest, including Jim and Sue Chilton's Montana Allotment. The leptos' plight also earned them a glossy 11-page spread in the June 1991 issue of *National Geographic*.

But the doomsday scenario never became reality. Over the past decade, biologists have consistently counted tens of thousands of leptos in southern Arizona and southwestern New Mexico. Populations are not only stable; in many cases, they are growing. South of the border, hundreds of thousands of bats are known to occupy summertime roosts.

Leptos did not make a miraculous recovery. The bats were probably just as numerous in the mid-1980s, but back then scientists couldn't find them. Researchers went to the roosts at the wrong time, either before the bats had arrived or after they had left for the year, and they never visited some of the biggest colonies of all. "The bottom line is, they missed large numbers of these bats," said Ted Fleming, an expert on leptos at the University of Miami. "Go to a place at one time, and you won't see any bats. But go to that same place at the right time, and you'll find tens of thousands of them."

Fleming, who had studied bats for 40 years, was not some gadfly or scientific outlier. He wrote leptos' 1994 recovery plan and authored 15 papers or chapters on the species, including some for prestigious peer-reviewed publications like the *Journal of Mammalogy* and *Molecular Ecology*. Along with many other bat authorities, Fleming argued that Fish and Wildlife's claim about leptos' importance as a pollinator "was a gross and scientifically untenable exaggeration." "Leptos in most years are minor pollinators of saguaros," he told me. "The major pollinators are white-winged doves, and people have known that for decades." Lendell Cockrum, author of *Mammals of the Southwest* and a retired University of Arizona professor, minced no words when I asked him about leptos. "It was a mistake to have ever listed it," he said. "If we want to be truthful and scientific about it, which is what we're supposed to be as biologists, it's all a bunch of BS."

Many other bat experts told me that the government shouldn't have listed leptos as an endangered species in 1988. But decades later, the mistake appears to have been a fortuitous one because leptos now confront a problem that was largely overlooked at the time the species received federal protection: illegal border crossers. The caves where the bats roost provide perfect hiding spots for marijuana smugglers, putting the sites in more jeopardy than ever before. Had the bat not been listed in 1988, it would have saved ranchers some grief and saved the government millions of dollars, but biologists might not know that narco-traffickers are disrupting the handful of maternity roosts that leptos depend on for reproduction. If anything, the case of the lesser long-nosed bat reminds us that our knowledge of the natural world is inevitably imperfect. Even top experts may struggle to count creatures, let alone understand their behavior. In a matter of months or years, dangers that seemed remote at the time of listing or were unknown can become major threats.

———————

I visited two of the bats' most important roosts in consecutive summers and saw nearly as many leptos in those few hours as Fish and Wildlife had recorded across the entire region in the mid-1980s. On a balmy August evening, after swearing not to reveal the roost's exact location, I hiked a mile or so through a saguaro forest with two biologists and arrived at a mine tunnel in Organ Pipe Cactus National Monument, not far from where Ranger Kris Eggle was shot. Fish and Wildlife didn't check the site before the 1988 listing. Today it's the largest known roost in the United States.

After the sun set to unveil the Milky Way, up to 200 leptos bolted from the hole—every minute. The exodus continued for an hour as thousands of bats swirled around the mine's entrance, then darted out into the surrounding desert to gorge on nectar, pollen, and cactus fruit. Tim Tibbitts, a park biologist, and Karen Krebbs, a bat expert at the Arizona-Sonora Desert Museum, caught some of the exiting leptos by stringing out a mist net that looked like it belonged on a volleyball court. Most of the bats avoided the nylon threads, but some, especially unwary juveniles, were ensnared. I petted one of the bats while Krebbs held it in her leather gloves (leptos sometimes bite when handled). Its fur was surprisingly smooth, but also covered with mites. My headlamp's beam shone through its paper-thin, oversized wings, making the arm bones inside look like metal rods propping open an umbrella. The bat's tiny, squirming head resembled that of a fox or dog. During the day, there were about 15,000 bats hanging upside down, 10,000 below the peak population earlier in the summer.

The next August, I visited an even bigger roost in the Pinacates. This volcanic mountain range, part of a Mexican biosphere reserve, lies just south of the border and is home to one of the last remaining populations of Sonoran pronghorn. In the 1960s, NASA used the lava fields and craters to train astronauts bound for the moon, and with the temperature nearly 110 degrees the day of my visit, it certainly felt otherworldly. At the park's ramshackle visitor center, I met up with Eugenio Larios, the reserve biologist, and Lin Piest of the Arizona Game and Fish Department. I followed behind their pickup in my Subaru Forester, nearly destroying the car in the process. After we left the highway, it took an hour to go less than 10 miles over undulating lava flows interwoven with sandy washes and littered with basketball-sized boulders that were determined to slam into my car's undercarriage with sickening thuds. When our vehicles could go no farther, we hiked two miles across igneous rock that shredded leather boots like a cheese grater, taking care to weave between spiny ocotillos bearing brilliant green leaves as a result of recent monsoon rains.

Without a nose for the smell of bat droppings or GPS coordinates, you'd have a mighty tough time finding the hole in the ground that is home to leptos' largest known colony. It's a cavelike depression about 15 feet wide that's situated on a sienna-colored dome of solidified lava that sprawls over nearly 50,000 acres and was deposited only about 13,000 years ago. The Pinacate roost went unmentioned when Fish and Wildlife listed the bats. Since the mid-1990s, biologists have repeatedly counted around 200,000 leptos there, more than ten times Fish and Wildlife's 1988 estimate for the entire population in northern Mexico. At the roost's peak occupancy, up to 3,000 bats exit per minute and form a cloud above the hole. When I visited in mid-August, most of the bats had left for the season. Even so, about 600 leptos were flapping out of the lava tube each minute. The air traffic was crowded enough that the bats occasionally slapped into one another. Time and again, leptos swooped down toward me, then veered off at the last moment, just a few inches before hitting my face.

"We've been counting them since 1997, and they're pretty stable," Larios told me. North of the border, biologists were increasingly worried about illegal crossers disturbing roosts, but Larios said he had found no sign of visitation or disturbance around the Pinacates lava tube. "It's really hard to get to, and I don't think many people know about it," he said. "There's not a ranch or anything nearby, and it's all federal land." Once the sun went down, and before a full orange moon rose above sawtooth mountains to our east, I surveyed the hundreds of square miles around us. I could only see a couple of stationary lights and a few cars moving down Mexican Highway 8 toward the beach resort of Rocky Point.

Counting leptos, even if you're in the right place at the right time, is complicated because of the darkness and the sheer volume of biomass pouring out of the earth. Researchers like Larios and Piest turn to video to simplify the task. They use a digital camcorder and rig it with infrared lights that illuminate the bats on film. The camera is mounted on a tripod overlooking the opening, and the footage is later analyzed in slow motion. Luckily, biologists don't have to watch every second of the departure and count every single bat; they take a sample and extrapolate to get the overall population. Still, the job isn't easy because the bats sometimes hover around the opening and raise the risk of double counting. As a solution, biologists count the number of bats exiting and entering, then subtract. "It's really tough to count them when they do that: out and in, out and in," Piest said. "The juveniles are especially notorious for that because they're not very confident."

Young leptos need to acquire that confidence quickly because they don't have long before they must embark on one of the most impressive migrations of any bat species in the world. Leptos are kind of like reverse snowbirds. The bats spend fall and winter in the neotropical forests of central and southern Mexico. In spring, after female leptos have been impregnated, some of them begin a northward odyssey of more than 1,000 miles along Mexico's western coast and the Sierra Madre. On the ground, the sequential blooming of plants from south to north provides a trail of nectar that sustains the bats. Pregnant leptos arrive in the Sonoran Desert of Arizona and northern Mexico around April, then give birth to a single pup in May in the maternity roosts along the border. Initially, the pups feed off milk from their mothers' mammary glands. When they're one month old, the young ones learn how to fly. Mothers and their offspring can get all of their water from their food, and the bats eat so much on their nightly forays that they may appear pregnant upon returning to their home base. After the bats depart the maternity roosts for good in July and August, they switch to higher elevations, often in southeastern Arizona. There they can feed on a new food source, blooming agaves, before heading south in September or October.

As evidenced by their long-distance migration, leptos are phenomenal fliers. Weighing less than an ounce and with a body just three inches long, the bats boast a wingspan that extends more than a foot. Evolution has sculpted those wings into slender yet sturdy limbs that let leptos fly at more than 20 mph. Biologists have documented cases of the species flying more than 60 miles in one night while foraging. The bats' mobility lets them take advantage of food far from where they roost by day. In the Pinacates, for instance, there aren't many saguaro or organ pipe cacti near the lava tube, so many bats travel dozens of miles north to forage around Organ Pipe Cactus National Monument. Leptos' flying ability therefore makes them resilient to at least some natural and man-made shocks, ranging from crazy weather to disturbance of their roosts. At Organ Pipe, the bat population remained steady in 2004 at about 25,000, even when flowering of cacti in the preserve was just 10 percent of normal, a legacy perhaps of the terrible drought of 2002 that nearly finished off the area's Sonoran pronghorn. Leptos adapted and found alternate food sources, possibly by flying great distances and switching early to blooming agaves.

Once the bats arrive at a plant offering nectar, pollen, or fruit, they can gobble up the food and water thanks to a series of adaptations. Their slender muzzle fits inside the flower of a cactus like a key entering a lock, hence the *long-nosed* in leptos' common name. Their brush-tipped tongues swell with blood to become a third as long as their body, allowing the bats to soak up the nectar. As leptos fly between the flowers, a special leaf-shaped structure on their nose helps them navigate with echolocation that's similar to the sonar that submarines use to ply darkened seas. These special anatomical features are indicative of the tremendous specialization and diversity in the bat world. Some 50 million years of natural selection have produced nearly 1,000 varieties that range from bumblebee-sized creatures to the so-called flying foxes, which sport six-foot wingspans. There are only 45 types of bats in the United States, and leptos are among the seven listed as endangered.

Leptos' relationship with desert plants is a textbook example of both anatomical specialization and what biologists call mutualism. The bats feast on the pollen and nectar offered by the plants. Leptos then return the favor by flying around to other plants, spreading pollen, then excreting the seeds of the cactus fruit they eat. The bats have even altered the evolutionary path of the vegetation, so much that some plant species are called chiropterophilous, or bat-loving. Such plants will produce nectar at night, when bats are flying around. Their light-colored flowers—some practically glow in the dark—help attract the bats, as does a special odor the plants emit. And their funnel-shaped flowers tend to be at the top of the plant or on the tips of branches, far from the thorns and surrounding limbs that could make it tough for a bat to reach the pollen, nectar, and fruit.

For bat advocates, leptos' connection to agaves whose juice is fermented to produce tequila has been irresistible: it illustrates the usefulness of a creature that might otherwise suffer from an image problem. I certainly highlighted the point in a piece for the *Arizona Daily Star*. Anytime I wrote about endangered species, my editors would challenge me to make average readers care about exotic creatures they would never encounter. Finally, I thought, an example of ecological interconnections that even Joe Six-Pack will care about: no bats, no tequila. But some bat experts I spoke to felt that Fish and Wildlife's listing document and early press accounts had exaggerated the bat's role in pollinating agaves and saguaros.

When I visited Yar Petryszyn, a bat expert at the University of Arizona, he also downplayed Fish and Wildlife's claim that tequila production, either by legal means or bootleggers, was jeopardizing the agaves and bats in Mexico. In an office full of skulls, antlers, stuffed animals, and drawers filled with preserved mice, Petryszyn extolled leptos' abilities as pollinators and seed dispersers; he has personally counted bats visiting a single agave up to 5,000 times a night. But leptos' importance to saguaros and other plants was "tremendously overstated," he told me. "All you have to do is look at a map of the known range of the nectar-feeding bats and superimpose that on the known range of saguaros. Over half the saguaros have never seen a nectar-feeding bat in their life."

Within a few years of leptos' listing, Petryszyn and other scientists raised questions about the bat's endangered status. The critiques were met with silence from officialdom. Then, in 1991, Cockrum and Petryszyn voiced their concerns in a peer-reviewed article that concluded Fish and Wildlife's data on leptos were "a combination of over-optimistic estimates of past population sizes and overly pessimistic estimates of current numbers, both poorly documented." Cockrum and Petryszyn concluded that lepto populations were "little, if any, decreased from those of a quarter century ago." In fact, they wrote, there was a decent chance leptos' numbers had increased in the past century because mining had created so many more suitable roosts. With thousands of mineshafts, tunnels, adits, and natural caves sprinkled across millions of acres in the desert Southwest, it's possible that some roosts for leptos still haven't been discovered.

Cockrum and Petryszyn also leveled broadsides against biologist Donna Howell, nearly accusing her of fraud. Howell had written several peer-reviewed articles on leptos that Fish and Wildlife cited in 1988.

Her 1972 PhD dissertation reported that leptos and a close relative "are severely diminished or non-existent," and she coauthored a 1981 article in *Ecology* that said only 135 bats had turned up in all of Arizona during a 1974 survey. Howell quickly responded to Cockrum and Petryszyn's 1991 critique by saying more recent surveys had *overestimated* bat populations because biologists had mistakenly recorded other species and double-counted leptos swirling around roosts. Howell remains worried about leptos disappearing forever. "These bats have the formula for going extinct: they have a bad reputation and they have only one baby a year," she told me. Sure, more bats were found after the 1988 listing, but "this is always the case when a species gets to be a candidate or is listed," Howell said. "It gets more funding and research directed toward it, and you tend to find more of them because you're looking more."

The debate over leptos' listing wasn't just about science. It was also leavened by some animosity between Howell and Cockrum, who had declined to be Howell's PhD adviser at the University of Arizona. "She hates my guts and the ground I walk on," Cockrum said. For her part, Howell speaks of the "bitter personal politics that taint the leptos." "It's just a shame," she said, "that this kind of personal, political hurrah can threaten the continued existence of a very important animal." Ted Fleming, author of the 1994 recovery plan, believes that Howell won't accept challenges to leptos' listing because her "short-lived academic career had been built on ecological and behavioral studies of *Leptonycteris* and its interaction with agave flowers." "Having studied it for many years, Donna understandably had a deep emotional attachment to this bat," Fleming wrote in his memoir, *A Bat Man in the Tropics*. "Unfortunately, by the early 1990s, Donna's objectivity regarding the population status of *Leptonycteris* was highly suspect." It's important to correct the record on leptos, Fleming told me, because "enemies of the Endangered Species Act will take this as a case where us biologists were crying wolf." "If that's the case for this bat," he said, "people will ask, 'How many other times has this occurred?'" Fleming agreed with Howell that scientific knowledge of a species is bound to expand once it's declared endangered, but he had a slightly different take: "Once a species has been listed, a lot of attention is focused on it, and in many cases you find out your early ideas were wrong."

With a handful of other endangered species, time has also led to the discovery of new populations and removal of all federal protections for the plant or animal. In Appalachia, for instance, the snail darter that nearly scuttled Tellico Dam was subsequently found in five previously unknown locations. After limited success with transplants, the three-inch fish was upgraded from endangered to threatened. ESA critics like Pombo seize upon these isolated cases as evidence of "junk science" permeating the act, but such cases also show how the law improves our understanding of the natural world. "We view these sorts of discoveries as a strength of the ESA, not evidence of any problem," the nation's leading biological societies wrote in response to Pombo's bill.

The key point is that these scientific blunders are quite uncommon. Of the more than 1,300 US species ever listed as endangered, a grand total of five have been delisted because the species was found to be more abundant than originally thought, and seven have been delisted because scientists changed their classification scheme. In its study of the issue, the Government Accountability Office concluded that Fish and Wildlife "uses the best available science to make listing decisions" and said "little scientific disagreement surrounds listing decisions." The tiny error rate, which is probably unavoidable, also must be balanced against the converse situation: the many more cases in which declining species either haven't been listed or received federal protection too late.

I never found any proof that Fish and Wildlife deliberately understated leptos' population to inflate its power. Don Wilson, the biologist who was asked by the agency to conduct the crucial surveys in the mid-1980s, told me the Pinacate roost hadn't been recorded at the time and said that all the known sites were checked. "I certainly did not purposely miss any colonies or visit them at the wrong time of year," said Wilson, senior scientist and curator of mammals at the Smithsonian Institution's National Museum of Natural History. Wilson said the endangered label had raised the bat's profile and attracted funding, but the accompanying permit process had, paradoxically, made it harder for scientists to do research on leptos. "This is the catch-22 of the whole Endangered Species Act process," Wilson said. "By using the legal system to afford protection, we also greatly encumber the only way to really gather more knowledge about the species." It was a sentiment I heard over and over from scientists: cloaking animals with such strict protection could deter or forestall vital research needed to better understand species and help them recover. The Arizona-Sonora Desert Museum's Karen Krebbs wanted to inject tiny radio transmitters into leptos so she could determine where they fly after departing maternity roosts—a critical, unanswered question. The technology, a standard tool among wildlife biologists, has been implanted in millions of pets. But Krebbs's federal permit only let her attach the microchips with glue that lasted a few weeks. "My permitting stuff is a nightmare," she told me.

Leptos' regulatory bite has been modest since nearly all US roosts are either inaccessible, on protected federal lands, or both. But because leptos may forage on plants that lie dozens of miles from their roost, ranching across the Southwest was put under the microscope to gauge whether cows harm the agaves and cacti that the bats rely on for food. In 1998, the Center for Biological Diversity sued the Forest Service on behalf of leptos and four other species, seeking to limit cows on one-quarter of the 1.8-million-acre Coronado National Forest. Three years later, the Center and Forest Guardians sued the Forest Service over its management of 55 allotments covering 633,870 acres in the Southwest, citing leptos and five other species. Environmentalists then won a major victory in 2003 when a federal judge took the unusual step of booting 1,425 cows off 140,000 acres of national forest in Arizona and New Mexico in response to a lawsuit citing grazing's impacts on the bat and three other listed species. Doc Lane, lobbyist for the Arizona Cattle Growers' Association, told me all allotments in the southern half of the state had their permits altered so cows couldn't graze in places where agaves were flowering. "You can call any rancher that has a federal permit in southern Arizona," he said, "and they have all been affected, every single one of them." Others disputed that, and more recently Fish and Wildlife has focused on safeguarding bat roosts, rather than restricting grazing to protect agaves.

Leptos caused headaches for Jim and Sue Chilton. They were one of the species that prompted Fish and Wildlife to examine the Montana Allotment and one of the reasons why the agency limited the number of cattle allowed there. Without a doubt, there were agaves on the Montana Allotment that could feed leptos. As for the bats, the only evidence of them in the area was from 1959, when a dead one was found some 10 miles east of the allotment. Jim and Sue, already strong critics of the ESA, weren't about to warm up to the law when their ranching operation was being restricted by a species that shouldn't have been listed and wasn't even present on their grazing lease.

If cattle munch or crush agaves, they eliminate a potential food source for leptos. That is not in dispute. Most experts, however, think that cows' behavior in the bat's foraging habitat pales by comparison to a relatively new threat, one that exposes the Achilles' heel of an otherwise resilient species. Because pregnant and newborn leptos cluster in just a handful of colonies along the US-Mexico border, malicious or accidental damage to the roosts could have devastating consequences. As the leptos' recovery plan notes, "Loss of even one such site could eliminate a significant portion of the total population and contribute to the extinction of the species." In the Border Patrol's Tucson sector, home to most of leptos' US maternity roosts, agents were annually apprehending hundreds of thousands of illegal immigrants. Due to an unfortunate coincidence of biology and geography, leptos' maternity roosts provided ideal hiding places for smugglers and immigrants. This was especially true during the bat's summer occupancy because the mines and caves offered a dark, cool respite from triple-digit heat.

The border-crosser threat was highlighted when marijuana smugglers spooked leptos from a major roost at Cabeza Prieta National Wildlife Refuge. For years, refuge biologists had counted several thousand pregnant leptos and an equal number of juveniles roosting in the abandoned mine. But in 2001, refuge staff started to notice cans, clothing, and water bottles around the shaft; not really a surprise, since the roost was right along a well-known smuggling route. The next year started out promising, with about 6,000 bats counted in May. By mid-June, there were only 10 bats left. Refuge biologist Curtis McCasland looked inside the mine and found a telltale sign of drug runners: water jugs painted black to evade the Border Patrol's night-vision goggles. McCasland could also tell from the depth of the footprints that the visitors were carrying heavy packs. "When the ambient temperature is 108 degrees, it's about 80 degrees in there, so it's a choice site," McCasland said. "If you come across the border with 40 pounds of dope on your back, this is the right spot to hole up for a day." Refuge officials put up some minor barriers, but the colony of leptos was again rousted from its roost in 2003. The border crossers appeared to be building campfires nearby, and this was particularly worrisome. Smoke is one of the most common ways to drive bats from caves, especially in Mexico, where some residents fear all bats are of the so-called vampire variety or bearing disease. To protect other bat caves, land managers install metal grates that let bats in and keep people out. Unfortunately, leptos can have problems navigating such barriers, perhaps because they're not as adept at maneuvering as insect-eating bats.

As a solution, Cabeza Prieta spent nearly $10,000 in 2003 to build a 10-foot metal fence around the mine that also stops people from building campfires near the entrance. "It seems to have worked really well," McCasland said. By 2004, up to 5,000 bats were counted at the site.

At Organ Pipe, where the roost is flanked on either side by smuggling routes, monument officials held off on installing a new fence, fearing that it would attract too much attention to the roost. As it stands now, an aging sign warns visitors that the shaft is a radiation area. Although testing has shown that to be untrue, the park's staff isn't about to correct the record, because the sign just might scare off people about to disturb the nation's largest maternity roost for leptos. So even as the population of leptos at the monument's roost continues to grow, the bats there remain vulnerable. A few years after I visited the Organ Pipe roost, Tibbitts, Krebbs, and other scientists couldn't even survey the site because the number of border crossers in the area had created such safety concerns. "We've probably been on a honeymoon with this roost and all the illegal activity out here," Tibbitts told me. "Is this the most endangered species around? No. But it's certainly got its threats."

14
The Rancher's Revenge

For Jim and Sue Chilton, lesser long-nosed bats were less of a problem than another endangered species that hung around their Montana Allotment. The Sonora chub, a tiny minnow, had led the federal government to restrict grazing on the lease. It was one of the species tied up in a Center for Biological Diversity lawsuit against the Forest Service that covered the Montana, and it was featured in a 2002 press release from the Center that announced the group was appealing the Chiltons' grazing permit. The Center's two-page news advisory, written by Martin Taylor, an Australian-born entomologist, claimed the Chiltons "tried to suppress" Game and Fish's recommendations about the Montana Allotment and described the couple as having "an agenda hostile to wildlife and endangered species." Taylor, who received his PhD from the University of Arizona, argued that the grazing plan approved by the Forest Service would imperil Chiricahua leopard frogs and the Sonora chub, which was occasionally found in an ephemeral stream just north of the border that was supposed to be fenced off from cattle. "Whenever we go out there," Taylor quoted himself as saying, "much of it is grazed to bare dirt, and cattle are breaking into the Sonora Chub preserve." Taylor's release included a link to the Center's written appeal of the Chiltons' grazing permit and two appendices that were said to contain 21 photos of the Montana Allotment.

Taylor called me and a few other reporters to try to drum up coverage of the Center's campaign against the Chiltons. I passed. The appeal of a single grazing allotment on a 1.8-million-acre national forest had minimal news value. It also seemed like the Center was simply trying to embarrass the Chiltons after the failed bid to stop Sue from joining the Game and Fish Commission, a fight that centered on the Montana Allotment. I glanced at the four pages of photos. Most depicted bare ground devoid of forage and were accompanied by captions that blamed the range's poor condition on the Chiltons' cattle.

When Jim Chilton saw the photos and the press release, which were posted online, he cursed so loud that Sue could hear him in the other room. It was a hit piece from his antagonist, and it had crossed a line. In some of the photos, the barren landscape depicted wasn't even part of the Montana Allotment, nor were cows responsible for the damage.

The deception incensed Jim. The Center had been cursed by many a rancher, but few in the industry had invested more money in monitoring their grazing lease, and few had the wherewithal to fight back. Jim decided it was time to turn the tables on the Center. He hired one of Arizona's best First Amendment lawyers and sued the litigious group for libel.

The five-inch fish embroiled in this fight definitely was rare in the United States. It was, in fact, limited to two isolated populations just north of the international border. One was in California Gulch, a wash running through the Montana Allotment that had some isolated pools but was often dry for long stretches. Virtually all of the chub's 5,000-square-mile range was in Mexico. Curiously, the chub's 1992 recovery plan said the fish's current distribution was "little changed from its historic range," called it "locally abundant" in the United States, described it as "a tenacious, desert adapted species, adept at exploiting small marginal habitats," and lauded its ability to "survive under severe environmental conditions." The section titled Reason for Decline noted that "distribution of Sonora chub in the United States is intact and should remain secure, barring major environmental change," while in Mexico, the species was "reported secure." Not exactly a portrait of peril.

When the chub was listed in 1986, it was only known to inhabit Sycamore Canyon, part of a Forest Service lease next to the Montana Allotment. Fish and Wildlife was concerned about potential uranium mining in the area, plus the introduction of more nonnative aquatic predators. The agency didn't cite grazing as a threat. "Although the canyon is included in a livestock grazing allotment, there is little direct effect on the Sonora chub habitat," Fish and Wildlife said in its listing rule. "Indirect effects of grazing, such as erosion and siltation, are minor at present, but could have significant effects on the Sonora chumb [sic] habitat if grazing were increased." Listing the chub may have prevented its US habitat from being destroyed by tailings from a uranium mine or introduction of nonnative predators, but even if that did happen and the fish were extirpated from the country, the species wouldn't have gone extinct. A peer-reviewed study in 1990 concluded that in Mexico, the fish was "widely distributed" and "presently relatively secure." Nevertheless, federal officials wanted to curtail the Chiltons' ranching operations on behalf of the Sonora chub.

When I spent the day with Jim and Sue driving around the Montana Allotment, we chatted about the questionable listings of the lesser long-nosed bat and the Sonora chub. My own belief was that the vast majority of endangered species deserved federal protection, but having read the studies and talked to the scientists, I could see why the Chiltons felt that the bat and chub had become pawns in environmentalists' fight to end public lands grazing. We toured part of their 21,500-acre allotment in Jim's pickup, which had an AZ BEEF decorative front license plate and a small bumper sticker on the back: Bush: Yes. Saddam: No. The Ford F250 Lariat Super Duty Truck was a formidable vehicle, but it didn't have quite enough clearance to pass cleanly over all the rocks on the rugged dirt roads, evoking groans from Jim. A bit of his white hair peeked out from beneath a cream-colored cowboy hat. He was wearing a white button-down shirt, blue trousers, and black boots: dressed like a cowboy, but cleaner than most. We weren't about to round up cattle, though driving on the rough roads felt like being in the saddle and left me with a sore neck. The task for this day was to check on some rain gauges, a necessary obsession of arid lands ranchers.

From the backseat of the truck, Sue gave me a running botany lesson, sometimes annoying Jim when she interrupted his monologue to point out dozens of native species of grass, shrubs, legumes, and wildflowers. Sue, a foot shorter than Jim, wore glasses and had dark curly hair. The couple seemed fond of interrupting and correcting one another, but in an endearing way befitting four decades of marriage. When I looked out the window, I saw a bunch of grass and bushes, but Sue kept ticking off plant names: guajilla, sideoats grama, green sprangletop, cane beardgrass, curly mesquite, and fairy duster. "Different grasses green up at different times of the year," Sue explained. "They are more nutritious or less nutritious depending on the season, and the cattle and other wild animals know the difference."

Besides teaching me plant names, the Chiltons wanted to educate me about the two important cases that revolved around the Montana Allotment: Jim's libel suit against the Center and a tangle of litigation that eventually wound up before the Ninth Circuit Court of Appeals. The libel suit was much easier to grasp, and the crux of the case came down to a single meadow, Marijuana Flat, a private inholding in the Coronado National Forest that was unfenced and surrounded by the Montana Allotment, but not part of the grazing lease.

As we pulled up to the meadow, Jim recounted how hippies had purchased another 20-acre parcel nearby and taken up residence there. "They did everything hippies did back in the 1960s," Jim said. "They smoked dope, they made love, they ran around naked, and they just had a heck of a good time." In the years since, Marijuana Flat had hosted an annual May Day Festival. Photos of the 2002 event show bare-chested men sitting in camp chairs, holding cans of beer in insulated sleeves, and listening to a band play electric guitars. Pickup trucks and RVs are parked in the middle of the clearing. One of the Center's staff members, A. J. Schneller, attended the festival, then returned two weeks later and took photos of cattle sitting in the denuded clearing. The photo, part of the Center's formal appeal to the Forest Service, included a caption: "Ruby Pasture. California Gulch completely denuded of forage and severely compacted."

"He camped right over there, by that stump," Jim said. With the monsoon now under way, Marijuana Flat was covered with green grass and a sprinkling of wildflowers. "There were around 500 hippies having a great big festival here," Jim said. "They drove vehicles all over the place, and it was a dry year, so it looked bad. But to say Ruby Pasture? All of Ruby Pasture? All 5,000 acres had been 100 percent grazed by cows? It's just so far from the truth!"

After inspecting where Schneller had photographed the cows in Marijuana Flat, we walked a few hundred feet to the site of another photo included in the Center's appeal and press release. This one, looking back toward Marijuana Flat, showed a barren, pockmarked piece of land that had supposedly been damaged by cattle. "Stream banks and springs completely trampled," the Center's caption said. Jim pulled out his own photos, showing the same area. It was a seasonal lake, and under water. "It's not a spring. It's not a stream bank. It's the bottom of a dry lake bed on private land we don't own," he said. "I've been out there on a boat!"

Several of the images that accompanied the Center's press release were stamped with GPS coordinates, so it was easy for Jim, his surveyor, and his lawyer to find the spots where Schneller and Taylor had shot the photos. Prominent trees and other landmarks allowed them to identify the location of other images. "I knew they were lazy and they wouldn't get off the road," Jim said. "All we had to do is go down the road and find the spots."

We came to one such location, where the Center's photo showed a few scraggly mesquite trees surrounded by rocky red earth with not a blade of grass growing. "Upland sites are denuded," the caption read. "Rocks, soil compaction and bare dirt prevail. Cattle are eating and trampling young trees." In reality, the area depicted in the photo is a former mining site that the Chiltons believe was bladed a half century ago to make way for a house or shed. Hunters and other visitors to the national forest now use it as a tent site. I saw the charred remains of several campfires. "Now *that* is a bad spot. Anyone on earth would say that's a bad spot. But it's one-twentieth of one acre out of 5,000 acres. It wasn't cows! The implication and the whole message was that it's cattle!" Jim said. "These groups, the Center, Western Watersheds Project, Forest Guardians, have been using the same tactics for years. Misrepresentation, false charges, phony data, all for a theological mission of getting rid of cattle."

We passed by several pastures that hadn't been grazed for four or five months.

"Look at this range!" Sue said. "Look everywhere and you see native flowers, grasses, and bushes."

When ranchers use a rest-rotation system—on the Montana Allotment, cows are kept off pastures for a year and a half—they're attempting to use forage sustainably. It's the same principle that is supposed to guide professional forestry and game management: loggers cut down trees in one section, then move on to the next so the forest can regrow before the lumberjacks return, just as state agencies set bag limits for how many deer or elk can be harvested so that there are animals left for next year's hunt. Rest-rotation grazing, along with limits on the number of cattle allowed on an allotment and protection of watercourses, constitute the basics of modern rangeland management.

To a casual observer, much of the Montana Allotment appears to have escaped the hand of man, except for the occasional cluster of cows and the water bottles dumped by border crossers. The area is home to tropical species, including jaguars, Mexican vine snakes, and five-striped sparrows, and no other hunting unit in the state issues as many tags for white-tailed deer. Environmentalists, who have tried for years to get the area designated as a wilderness, call it one of Arizona's remaining true wildlands. They are not exaggerating when they describe the land in and around the Montana Allotment as one of the continent's treasures for biodiversity. For the Chiltons and neighboring ranchers, the lavish praise heaped on the area makes them wonder why a change in management is needed if the existing regime, complete with livestock grazing, has maintained the ecosystem's health for all this time.

As wild as it appears, the Montana Allotment has had cattle munching on its grasses for about 300 years. But like much of the rangeland in today's Southwest, it is less spoiled than it was a century ago. "One of the things I'd like to impress on you today is that this area was heavily populated in the 1880s, '90s, 1920s, 1930s," Jim told me. "These mountains back here are just honeycombed with tunnels and shafts." Ruby, now a mining ghost town overseen by Sundog, an eccentric caretaker with a long white beard and pet skunk, produced more lead and zinc than any other site in Arizona. At its peak, more than 1,000 people were living on the Montana Allotment. "Now it's totally depopulated," Jim said. "We used to have the towns of Ruby, Old Glory, Oro Blanco, Black Diamond, Warsaw, and Holden Canyon. There were 11 communities with little Wild West bars and general stores on the Montana Allotment. Now you've got Sundog back there, population of one."

Before it became a national forest, the Montana Allotment was open range and there was virtually no regulation of grazing on the commons. "That meant anyone could run cattle on it," Jim said. "If I decided the country was being too heavily grazed and said I was going to cut back 100 head, someone else was liable to say, 'I'm increasing my herd by 100.' There weren't fences, and so there was a real problem. It was very bad public policy. Congress wouldn't change it, and finally Teddy Roosevelt came along and helped establish the forest reserves." The Forest Service, under the leadership of Gifford Pinchot, systematized grazing on its land, allotting certain pastures to ranchers and, in principle, regulating how many head of cattle could be on the public's property at any time. The government would be the landlord, and the ranchers would rent the grass. For decades, however, the Forest Service often bowed to local political pressure and let ranchers have their way on public land. It wasn't until 1934, with the passage of the Taylor Grazing Act, that the federal government took a bold step toward managing grazing on the even larger acreage now overseen by the Bureau of Land Management. The Taylor Act ended the era of homesteading in the West, assigned grazing privileges for allotments delineated by barbed-wire fences, and more or less fixed the pattern of land ownership in the lower 48.

The Chiltons told me they didn't object to leasing land from the government and they didn't espouse the same antifederal attitudes you sometimes hear in the rural Southwest. They did, however, think Congress needed to significantly curb the ESA's reach and change the law's very nature. In testimony before a House subcommittee, Jim said it would be okay if the ESA outlawed "intentional killings and the economic trading of bald eagles." But he argued that the government shouldn't concern itself with "the development of a hospital in the fly space of an insect," a reference to the Delhi Sands flower-loving fly, which had stalled and altered construction of a $600 million medical center in California's San Bernardino County. "Such a premise would resonate with ordinary people because that is how truth and reason work," Chilton told Congress. "However, the Endangered Species Act is presently being employed to actively debase the Judeo-Christian respect for man and supplant it with a different religious viewpoint." Like most western ranchers, the Chiltons felt that environmentalists were conspiring with sympathetic federal biologists to attack public lands ranching, all the while using endangered species as proxies and turning reporters like me into shills. "In 1994 or 1995, we'd see an article in the *Star* saying that California Gulch was in horrible condition. Well, it wasn't. Some reporter was being told that it was in horrible condition," Jim said. "It's not the reporter. It's that they're being fed garbage."

Curious about why their grazing lease was receiving undue attention from the press and federal officials, the Chiltons obtained the Forest Service's file on the Montana Allotment by using the Freedom of Information Act, the same law that allows journalists and activists to expose the inner workings of government agencies. "It was just stuffed with information that wasn't true," Jim said, alluding to 30-year-old data that had never been verified. To balance out the negative information, the Chiltons decided to hire respected range scientists to conduct the studies they thought the Forest Service should have done in the first place. At a seminar in Tucson, Sue and Jim met Jerry Holechek, a scientist at New Mexico State University and coauthor of a leading textbook on range management. They asked Holechek to assess the condition of the Montana Allotment, and he made more than a dozen multiday trips over the succeeding years with his colleague Dee Galt. Twice they brought other specialists, including William Fleming, a riparian scientist from the University of New Mexico. "Yes, they were paid," Sue said of the consultants, "but it was either that or nothing." The scientists, all with doctorates in their fields, measured and catalogued the grass to determine if there was overgrazing and to compare the conditions to Forest Service records. They surveyed the trees along the watercourses. And they floated on the stock ponds in a boat so they could shove rods into the muddy bottoms to calculate the amount of soil eroding from the surrounding watershed.

The experts' conclusion: the Montana Allotment was in much better shape than when the Chiltons bought the grazing permit in 1991. In the December 2001 issue of *Rangelands*, a peer-reviewed, nontechnical counterpart to the prestigious *Journal of Range Management*, Fleming, Galt, and Holechek wrote an article titled "The Montana Allotment: A Grazing Success Story." The researchers described the grazing on the allotment as "light to conservative" and said that periodic censuses in California Gulch revealed dramatic increases in the number of riparian trees since the Chiltons acquired the lease. Compared to similar rangeland in the Southwest, the Montana Allotment "is a positive standout among all the sites we have evaluated that received livestock grazing," the scientists wrote. From 1998 to 2003, the Chiltons ran an average of 427 cows on the Montana Allotment, but according to Holechek's own widely used model, it could have safely supported 589 head without exceeding Forest Service guidelines.

The findings of Holechek and his colleagues stood in sharp contrast to the assessment of some Forest Service and Fish and Wildlife biologists who evaluated how grazing on the Montana Allotment would affect the lesser long-nosed bat and Sonora chub. The review, known as a biological opinion, was in response to a 1997 lawsuit from the Center and at the heart of the second legal case connected to the Montana Allotment. Fish and Wildlife ruled that continued grazing on the allotment could harm the chub, even though a fence already excluded cows from much of the ephemeral stream where the fish were sometimes found. That wash, located in California Gulch, is dry most of the year, but Fish and Wildlife said that some fish might swim upstream (when there was actually water) and exit the quarter-mile stretch that was fenced. The agency also feared that cattle grazing in the watershed above the 20-acre preserve could cause erosion that would wash downstream and hurt the fish within the preserve. Fish and Wildlife didn't present any evidence that this harm was actually happening, but it did note in its biological opinion that the Montana Allotment had "improved soil and riparian conditions" and concluded that "range condition is generally good with an upward trend."

The Chiltons said they felt obligated to challenge the biological opinion in court because Fish and Wildlife's mitigation measures would have forced them to spend about $25,000 a year on studies to keep tabs on range conditions and monitor the agaves that leptos feed on. Five scientists would need to assess the range two weeks before the Chiltons moved their cows into a pasture, then return again two weeks before the Chiltons moved the cattle out, then come back once more a month later to check for damage. Fish and Wildlife also wanted to exclude cows from the entire California Gulch watershed, where the chub were sometimes found, and sought to change the Chiltons' permit from a fixed limit of 500 cows to a range of 400 to 500.

Fish and Wildlife's requests seemed especially unreasonable to the Chiltons because the two species in question were rarely, if ever, present on the Montana Allotment. Leptos had never been documented on the grazing lease, and the habitat for the chub was dry most of the year. Jim and Sue wanted me to see that with my own eyes, so we drove down

California Gulch until we were almost at the border. Even though the summer rainy season was in full swing, we didn't see any water at all in the streambed. Jim produced photos taken in various other seasons that showed no water, and therefore no fish, in the sandy channel. Besides being totally devoid of water and chub, 20 acres around the ephemeral stream had been excluded from the Montana Allotment with a fence, the result of a partial settlement between the Center and Forest Service. "There is no Sonora chub habitat on the Montana Allotment. None. Zero. It also dries up in May or June every year, and every fish dies. You call that habitat?" Jim said. "According to a Forest Service hydrologist, there's no way you can create a perennial stream down there. It doesn't matter whether you graze it or don't graze it or napalm it or burn it or ignore it."

Out of 962 grazing leases reviewed by Fish and Wildlife, the Chiltons' Montana Allotment was one of only 22 where the agency concluded that cattle were likely to harm or kill endangered animals. Although California Gulch wasn't a perennial stream, government biologists considered it habitat for aquatic species that have always contracted to isolated pools when the weather dries up. The Arizona Cattle Growers' Association intervened in the suit on behalf of the Chiltons and several other ranchers, both to defend those operations and possibly challenge an important element of Fish and Wildlife's authority. On five allotments, including the Montana, the agency was imposing grazing restrictions even though the various endangered species weren't actually found on those leases. Jim told me his intervention in the lawsuit was what prompted environmentalists to target him as a troublemaker. "When you have a school yard bully and keep your nose clean and out of his way, you don't get picked on," he said. "When you've got a school yard bully and you challenge them, you become the enemy."

When the case, *Arizona Cattle Growers' Association v. U.S. Fish and Wildlife Service*, reached the US District Court in 1999, Judge Robert C. Broomfield, a Reagan appointee, decided against the agency, saying it couldn't impose restrictions to benefit creatures that only had potential habitat on an allotment, not an actual presence. Judge Broomfield's ruling, if applied elsewhere, could constrict Fish and Wildlife's power under the ESA by making it harder to protect habitat that was suitable for a species but currently unoccupied. Such areas are often crucial for recovering an endangered species. Unless the animals multiply, spread out from their current location, and recolonize their old haunts or suitable new habitat, they may always be at risk of extinction.

To defend Fish and Wildlife's authority, the Center united with an agency that it routinely sued and appealed Judge Broomfield's decision to the Ninth Circuit, which not only unanimously upheld Broomfield's ruling, but also expanded its reach. The 2001 decision held that Fish and Wildlife had been acting "beyond its authority" by regulating unoccupied habitat. The circuit court judges, two appointed by President Clinton, one by President Reagan, decided that Fish and Wildlife had the burden to prove there was an endangered species on an allotment. It wasn't the responsibility of a rancher to prove the species didn't live there. The agency also had to demonstrate some clear connection between the activity in question and the species' fate. Regarding the Montana Allotment, the Ninth Circuit Court threw out Fish and Wildlife's biological opinion, saying it "provides little factual support for its conclusion" that livestock grazing would harm the Sonora chub. The restrictions the agency sought to impose on the Chiltons were "based only on the very speculative 'potential' for these fish to move upstream and on the 'potential' downstream effects of grazing," the court said.

The decision set an important nationwide precedent because it was issued by a circuit court, only one rung below the US Supreme Court. The ruling, now highlighted in environmental law texts, is full of impenetrable legalese, but the judges' message is clear: Fish and Wildlife overreached, interpreted *take* too broadly, and let speculation rather than hard science drive its regulations. For all of the cases where economic interests trumped professional biologists at Fish and Wildlife, the Montana Allotment offered a pretty good example of the pressure being exerted in the opposite direction: environmentalists and agency scientists could impose unfair restrictions on private citizens, most of whom lacked the deep pockets needed to hire lawyers and push back in court.

Like the debate over which trees should be thinned, the science behind grazing and biodiversity isn't clear cut. Grazing takes many forms and rangeland varies widely from place to place. If there's one thing ranchers, biologists, and environmentalists do agree on, it's that grazing in the late 19th century was a disaster. With few, if any, constraints, livestock stripped watersheds of ground cover, caused long-lasting erosion problems, and upended the natural fire regime by removing fuel from grasslands and forests. There is also a consensus that stocking rates are lower and rangeland conditions are better today than they were decades ago. Even so, in many places the land's health is in worse shape than it was in presettlement days, and endangered species are continuing to pay the price.

Three-quarters of a century ago, Aldo Leopold recognized the potential damage caused by ranching in an arid region, though his writings display some ambivalence about cattle in the desert. Arizona's Blue River Valley, where Leopold had worked as a forest ranger on the Apache National Forest, also offered him a lesson in the dangers of overgrazing. In the early 20th century, livestock were largely unregulated in the valley and they left behind few plants to secure the soil when torrential rains struck. The dramatic increases in runoff destroyed homes along the Blue and carried off 90 percent of the arable land. Flooding also made it impossible to build a road in the valley, thereby isolating the community and forcing the government to spend a half-million dollars extra to construct a route on the adjoining highlands (today's US 191). "To 'replace' this smiling valley which Nature gave us for free," Leopold wrote, the government was simultaneously irrigating new farmland in the Salt River Valley, the site of modern-day Phoenix, with high-priced dams and canals. "But why is it that Nature is so quick to punish unintelligent 'development' in the Southwest?" Leopold asked in *Sunset Magazine* in 1924. The answer for Leopold was the region's climate. "In scantily watered country, to graze the range at all often means to overgraze the water-courses and the bottom lands," he wrote. "The situation does not call for a taboo upon grazing, but rather constitutes a challenge to the craftsmanship of our stockmen and the technical skill of grazing experts in devising controls that will work, and to the courage of our administrators in enforcing those controls in a manner fair both to the conflicting interests and to the community." Leopold advocated limiting the number of cows allowed on public lands, fencing off streams, and restoring willows along watercourses, practices still followed to this day.

Leopold would grow more pessimistic about arid lands ranching, especially after a 1936 deer-hunting trip to Mexico's Sierra Madre that exposed him to a more primitive version of the American Southwest. "A shocked Leopold realized that heretofore he had seen only sick land," wrote David Brown and Neil Carmony in their edited collection of

Leopold's essays. In a 1937 article in *American Forests*, Leopold noted a paradox: lands south of the border, where there was little deliberate conservation, "present so lovely a picture of ecological health, whereas our own states, plastered as they are with National Forests, National Parks and all the other trappings of conservation, are so badly damaged that only tourists and others ecologically color-blind, can look upon them without a feeling of sadness and regret." In the wilds of the Mexican state of Chihuahua, Leopold found teeming deer populations coexisting with lions, wolves, jaguars, and other predators, lush grasslands that had escaped overgrazing and erosion, and spacious pine forests that had flourished in the absence of fire suppression. "To my mind these live oak-dotted hills fat with side oats grama, these pine-clad mesas spangled with flowers, these lazy trout streams burbling along under great sycamores and cottonwoods, come near to being the cream of creation. But on our side of the line the grama is mostly gone, the mesas are spangled with snakeweed, the trout streams are now cobble-bars," Leopold wrote. "I sometimes wonder whether semi-arid mountains can be grazed at all without ultimate deterioration. I know of no arid region which has ever survived grazing through long periods of time, although I have seen individual ranches which seemed to hold out for shorter periods."

Many environmental groups have adopted Leopold's later view. WildEarth Guardians (formerly known as Forest Guardians) says on its website that it is "working to eliminate livestock grazing on federal public lands" because it is "the most widespread and destructive activity on arid and semi-arid western landscapes." The group argues that to make ranching economically viable in such areas, the government must subsidize the industry with below-market grazing fees and federally financed predator control. Western public lands only account for a few percent of the nation's livestock inventory, and arid lands ranchers typically send cows to massive feedlots for fattening before slaughter. When the General Accounting Office studied Bureau of Land Management allotments in the Sonoran, Chihauhuan, and Mojave deserts, it concluded that grazing in the hottest, driest parts of the West "risks long-term environmental damage while not generating enough revenues to provide for adequate management."

Some conservation groups, such as The Nature Conservancy and Environmental Defense Fund, have adopted an outlook closer to Leopold's earlier view, that ranching is not necessarily incompatible with the Southwest's ecology so long as it is properly regulated, monitored, and excluded from inappropriate locations. These greens see grazing as a potential check against subdivision of open space, and most ranchers now accept Forest Service and Bureau of Land Management regulations governing where their cows may graze. In 2003, a group of 20 ranchers, environmentalists, and scientists generated a considerable amount of press when they declared it was "time to cease hostilities" in the grazing fight. "We know that poor management has damaged land in the past and in some areas continues to do so, but we also believe appropriate ranching practices can restore land to health," read the invitation to the "radical center" produced by the Quivira Coalition, a Santa Fe–based group. "We believe that some lands should not be grazed by livestock; but also that much of the West can be grazed in an ecologically sound manner."

The idea that grazing could benefit biodiversity may seem counter-intuitive given the terrible damage done in the past and ongoing problems in many places. Jaguars, wolves, and other predators were extirpated largely due to the livestock industry, and a 1998 study concluded that 22 percent of endangered, threatened, and proposed species had been imperiled by livestock—nearly as many as had been harmed by logging, mining, and energy extraction combined. Still, some studies have found that it's possible to overrest the range and inhibit its species richness, just as it's possible to overgraze the land and eliminate biodiversity.

The Quivira Coalition, Malpai Borderlands Group, and other progressive ranching efforts have put great stock in the rest-rotation philosophy, arguing that it can heal the land. A bunch of cows stomping around and eating the grass can actually stimulate the growth of vegetation by breaking up soil and cropping plants that evolved with herbivorous animals that are now gone or greatly diminished, though the prehistoric Southwest never had as many grazers as the Great Plains. Yet very few scientific studies support the practice, and its applicability to arid regions is especially controversial. In a piece for *High Country News*, Tony Davis dug into the literature, interviewed dozens of experts, and reported that "the search unearthed plenty of anecdotal accounts, but only three examples of hard data, gathered independently of the ranching industry, to back up the claim at the heart of Quivira's philosophy: that extended use of 'rest-rotation' grazing results in ecological recovery." A review of 31 studies in arid to semiarid areas in the West published by the Society for Range Management concluded that light to moderate grazing could have positive impacts on forage compared to areas where livestock had been excluded. But the authors conceded that "research supporting this viewpoint is limited."

More studies are needed to clarify which cows should go where on the public's land and what areas should be put off-limits entirely. Much of the Southwest is simply too dry to support cattle, and protections for aquatic and riparian habitat will only become more critical as the planet warms. In the 21st century, agencies will also need to do a better job managing livestock during drought, when much of the damage occurs. At the global level, grazing's impacts in the West also must be balanced against the environmental harm caused by exporting livestock production to biodiversity hot spots like the rain forests of South America. It's tricky to calculate the environmental impact of any food, but it's clear that consuming beef leaves a larger ecological and carbon footprint than a vegetarian diet, especially if the meat is mass produced at factory farms.

––––––––––

The Chiltons' libel suit against the Center was a gamble. Even if they won, they were unlikely to cover their expenses, because state law prevented them from recouping their legal fees, which were already in the hundreds of thousands of dollars. "Our mission," Jim said, "was to win one dollar." The suit named the Center and three of its employees: Martin Taylor, who had left the Center and returned to Australia a year after writing the press release; A. J. Schneller, who had taken many of the photos and was no longer employed by the group; and Shane Jimerfield, the website designer who had posted the press release and still worked at the Center. The suit alleged that the Center's news advisory hurt Jim's ranching business and caused him "to suffer great mental anguish, humiliation, public hatred, contempt, ridicule," plus damage to his "integrity and reputation." Only the local paper in Arivaca ran a story based on the Center's press release, in some cases reprinting the Center's allegations verbatim, but that publication was not named in the suit.

Jim had strong evidence that the Center had lied in its press release. Still, it would be tough for him to prevail in a legal system that jealously guards the right to free speech. To prove the Center's material was libelous, Jim's attorneys not only had to show it was false, had defamed him, and had been published, they also had to demonstrate that the activists knew the material was false or showed reckless disregard for the truth. Such evidence of malice also had to be clear and convincing. The bar would have been lower had Jim not been ruled a public figure by Judge Richard Fields in pretrial hearings due to Jim's testimony before Congress and Sue's position on the Arizona Game and Fish Commission. An ordinary citizen would only have to show the Center was negligent through a preponderance of the evidence.

The easiest defense in a libel suit is to prove that the allegedly defamatory material is substantially true, or a matter of opinion. Failing that, defendants can argue that the First Amendment shields them. You can't, for instance, successfully sue someone for defamation if they criticize the government, say something derogatory in court, or submit a comment to a public agency that demeans a business. The Center sought to win the case by presenting all of those defenses: what they said about the Montana Allotment in the news release and accompanying photos was either factual or opinion, and it was all protected speech since it had rehashed the Center's legal appeal of the grazing permit. As the trial began, the Center described the libel suit as an attack on activists' ability to question public lands policies. "We're being harassed to chill our First Amendment rights," director Kierán Suckling told me. "You've got this wealthy, litigious banker who has filed suit and threats of suit against many people who've criticized his allotment."

The Center never failed to highlight Jim's net worth and his hiring of high-powered lawyers, referring to him as an "investment banker" (Jim preferred to call himself a "municipal financial consultant"). For prospective jurors, the label *rancher* would probably evoke more sympathy than *banker*, though some opinion surveys have shown that the public has negative (and false) views about livestock grazing. In one poll, a third of Americans said grazing should be banned on all federal lands. Less than one-fifth agreed with the statement that overgrazing on federal lands had declined over the past half century (in truth, public lands grazing peaked in the 1920s and fell 70 percent by the 1970s). Livestock grazing may not be popular, but for many Americans, the people behind the business still evoke positive images of rugged individualism and romantic notions about the Wild West. In reality, ranchers, like environmentalists, are anything but monolithic. The label *rancher* can be applied to everyone from limousine liberals like billionaire Ted Turner to dirt-poor hayseeds who belong to the John Birch Society.

One survey of the nearly 30,000 federal grazing leaseholders concluded there are no less than eight subspecies of *Rancherus americanus publica*. For starters, there is a divide between hobbyists, who receive less than a quarter of their income from ranching, and professionals, who depend on ranching for more than 70 percent of their income. For some, the ranch is a tax write-off; for others, it puts food on the table. Demographically, the subspecies also varies widely. Nearly 30 percent of "small hobbyists" and "trophy ranchers" have a graduate degree, while less than 10 percent of "dependent family ranchers" graduated from college. In every group, however, ranchers ranked the tradition and way of life ahead of making money. And with just cause: despite the government subsidies, economists have concluded that ranching in the West is usually economically irrational since the revenues are meager, unpredictable, and far less than can be obtained by selling land to developers. Typically, an arid lands rancher needs at least 300 cattle to be viable, and such a breeding herd requires an investment of at least $1 million. On average, investments in western ranching have yielded an annual return of 2 percent, so someone thinking about entering the business could expect to earn $20,000 a year while dealing with the vagaries of the weather, regulations, and commodity prices. Or they could sit back and earn double that or more with their money socked away in conservative investments. Jim Chilton, a banker and rancher, knew the numbers all too well. My sense from talking to him and Sue was that a love of the lifestyle and the desire to maintain a family tradition were why he was willing to stay in the ranching business, even as environmentalists sought to end his career.

The Center's focus on Jim's wealth was a bit hypocritical, given the group's own sizable assets. In the two years before the 2005 trial, the Center had pulled in a total of $5.2 million in revenues; by the end of 2004, its net assets were worth $2.2 million, according to its annual reports and filings with the IRS. Jim's attorney was, in fact, a prominent First Amendment lawyer and a partner at Jaburg and Wilk, a midsized firm in Phoenix whose clients included Bank of America and Allied Building. But the Center wasn't exactly relying on legal aid in its defense. Its lead attorney, appointed by the group's insurance company, worked for an even older and equally large Phoenix firm, Tiffany and Bosco, whose clients included Wells Fargo Bank and the China National Cereals, Oils and Foodstuff Import and Export Corporation.

The Center had grown from humble beginnings—Suckling and other Earth First! activists living in tepees—into a multimillion-dollar operation, thanks in part to donations from its growing membership.

But before the ranks soared, the Center sometimes made more money by recouping its legal fees in cases against the government. In 2003, for instance, the Center was reimbursed for $992,354 in expenses after winning in court, about double what its 10,000 members donated that year. This payment, known as legal return, is a well-established feature of environmental litigation. A brochure from the Vermont Law School, one of the nation's top institutions for training environmental attorneys, promises students that one of the courses "will teach you how to sue the government, win, and get paid." In the 1990s, environmental attorneys charging $150 to $350 an hour caused the US Treasury to pay out nearly $32 million in attorney fees for 434 environmental cases, with an average award of more than $70,000, according to an investigation by *The Sacramento Bee*'s Tom Knudson. ESA critics, especially Richard Pombo, latched onto such payments in their quest to weaken the law.

With George W. Bush in the White House, environmentalists were having a field day in the courts, and with Pombo attacking the ESA in Congress, the Center was attracting new members in droves. Historically, conservation groups have grown most rapidly during Republican administrations, when the environment is perceived to be in greater danger. Ray Ring of *High Country News* examined how the finances of environmental nonprofits changed during Bush's first six years and found that the administration had been a boon to many groups, and the Center in particular: its revenues more than tripled, its staff nearly doubled, and its membership shot up eightfold, from 5,000 to 40,000. As a result, membership donations soon dwarfed the legal fees that the Center recovered in court. Tax forms filed with the federal government showed that salaries for the Center's senior leadership rose steadily; Suckling's increased from about $35,000 in 2000 to $61,000 in 2006, although that still put him at less than half of what many leading conservation groups paid their top staff, to say nothing of the hundreds of thousands of dollars paid to the executive directors of the biggest environmental groups. You were as likely to get rich working at the Center as you were ranching in Arizona.

The Center, never shy about publicizing its litigation, didn't want the media to know about a case in which it was the defendant. I only found out about the Chiltons' libel suit after Joe Barrios, the *Arizona Daily Star*'s court reporter, noticed the case during his daily check of the docket. I couldn't attend the jury selection, but people who were there said the lawyers tried to weed out people who seemed sympathetic to environmentalism, especially vegetarians, and eliminate prospective jurors who seemed predisposed to support ranchers. The 10-person jury seated in Judge Richard Fields's courtroom may not have been a perfect representation of the community, but it was, more or less, a random sample of adults from a blue county in a red state.

Walking into the courtroom, I noticed a painting of a pronghorn above Judge Fields's bench. Supporters of the Chiltons and the Center had positioned themselves behind each side's lawyers; I grabbed a seat in the middle. Martin Taylor flew in for the trial from Australia, and early in the process he took the stand for nearly two hours of sharp questioning from Jim's lawyer, Kraig Marton. He asked Taylor if he was a vegetarian and pressed him on his knowledge of the Montana Allotment.

"You knew barely anything," Marton said. "How many times had you been there?"

"I would avoid the Montana Allotment because it was so heavily grazed," said Taylor, who estimated he'd passed through the allotment five times on recreational trips.

Since Taylor had a PhD, Marton wanted to know why he hadn't taken any measurements of the forage on the allotment. "You just wanted to make the Montana Allotment look bad," Marton said.

"No. I wanted to document the problem areas on the Montana Allotment," Taylor said. "I wasn't attempting or pretending to do good science."

Taylor told the jury he wrote the press release in an hour, faxed it to media outlets, then called me and other reporters in a bid to generate a story about the appeal, a practice known as chasing the media.

Why, Marton asked, hadn't Taylor called the Chiltons "to get their side of the story"?

"That's for journalists to do. Not us," Taylor said. "This was a news advisory, not a treatise."

To prove the Center's release had harmed Jim's business, Marton called James Webb, a rancher and real estate broker, to the stand. Webb, a paid witness, said if he were listing the ranch for sale, he'd be obligated to disclose the Center's published criticism to a prospective buyer. He estimated the negative publicity had cut $200,000 from the value of the permit that the Chiltons bought for about $750,000 in 1991.

To highlight the emotional impact of the Center's release, Marton called Sue Chilton and Jim's brother, Tom. Sue told the jury she was in the kitchen when her husband read the Center's press release online and heard him explode in rage. Since then, Sue said her husband had been withdrawn, "obsessed with clearing his name," and plagued by poor sleep and a pain in his side. Tom Chilton waxed about his life as a cowboy rounding up cattle by horseback and working 12-hour days on the range while wearing chaps and spurs.

As his last witness, Marton called Jim, who also played up the cowboy lifestyle. Marton projected 10 photos from the Center's release, many of them showing veritable wastelands that captions described as denuded by cows. Beside each of the Center's photos, Marton then displayed wide-angle shots taken from the same spot revealing the surrounding landscape as lush, even junglelike. "Pictures can lie," Jim said, "and liars can take pictures." Marton asked his client about the health problems he was experiencing. "Cowboys are tough," Jim said, "and I don't want to talk about that."

On cross-examination, the Center's attorney, Robert Royal, reminded Jim of his deposition, in which he said there was no evidence that the Center had doctored its photos. Royal then asked Jim a series of questions that actually seemed to help the rancher's cause.

"Do you consider yourself a conservationist?" Royal said.

"Yes, every day is Earth Day for cattlemen," Jim replied.

"Do you consider yourself an environmentalist?"

"Yes."

"Do you agree therefore that public lands should be protected from damage to their resources?"

"Of course. Every day we are in the field promoting wildlife, promoting resources, and by our very grazing, we're stimulating and healing the resource."

"You believe that endangered species protected under the law should be protected?"

"Definitely, if they're really there."

In closing arguments, Marton told jurors that the Center willfully ignored scientific studies praising the Chiltons' grazing practices. "They were out to do harm, out to stop grazing, and out to do whatever they can to prevent the Chiltons and others like them from letting cows on public land," Marton said. "We think this group will lie, defame, and do everything in its power for their own goal." The jury had heard from 21 witnesses and seen over 100 exhibits. That evidence, Marton said, had consistently refuted the Center's claim "that the cows did it." "How can these pictures *not* be false when at least four of them are not even pictures of the Montana Allotment?" he said. Taylor and Schneller had deliberately focused their cameras on small bald spots, Martin said, "when all you needed to do was look up and look around in any direction" to get an accurate view of the area's condition. And then there were Schneller's photos of Marijuana Flat. "Can you imagine someone camping out someplace—he said there were 300 to 500 people there—and then going back two weeks later, saying this is what the Montana Allotment is and the cows did it? That's the worst kind of lie. They knew their statements were false. This wasn't just careless."

Marton, a big guy with a booming voice, grew particularly impassioned as he spoke about the importance of reputation. He quoted from Shakespeare, Ben Franklin, and Warren Buffett. "They wanted to take this man out. They wanted this land for themselves so they could go backpacking there," Marton said. "They've been trying to hurt Jim Chilton for seven years. They need to be punished. If you're gonna lie, you have to pay the consequences." As he wound up his presentation, Marton reminded the jury that the Center had made more than $900,000 by suing the government in 2003 and suggested that they keep that figure in mind while deciding on damages. "What we're doing here is protecting a family, a culture, and a way of life," he said. "We leave the future of the Chiltons in your hands."

Royal stood up and told the jury to ignore the "pep talk" Marton had given about the Center's supposed goal of "ending all grazing on public lands." "They're blowing it out of proportion to motivate you, to excite you to award a large number of damages. The policy of the Center is to end abusive grazing, grazing that harms the resource, harms the land," Royal said. "We all have the same motivation here, and that motivation is to protect the public's lands and have them regenerate." Royal told the jurors they shouldn't even consider the photos since they hadn't been altered and they were all part of the Center's legal appeal of the Chiltons' grazing permit.

Royal sought to diminish the importance of the photos of Marijuana Flat, arguing that Schneller had no idea he was on private land. More generally, Royal said, the Center's photos were meant to depict "hot spots." "We never intended them to be representative of the whole allotment. It's 21,000 acres. How can we take a picture to show 21,000 acres?" he said. In closing, Royal focused on the protection of free speech, which seemed like the Center's strongest legal defense and a way for the group to align itself with other advocacy groups that the jury might find more sympathetic. "We must enforce the people's right to express their opinion and have public debate over issues," he said. "That is what makes this country great."

Marton had one more shot to give his rebuttal, and he began by disputing the notion that the Center wasn't against grazing on public lands. He cited the job description for Taylor's replacement, which listed "a strong antipathy toward public lands livestock grazing" as a requirement. The job announcement also said that if such animosity was not innate or based on previous experience, "it can be learned in a day." The Center may style itself as a watchdog, Marton told the jury, but it was an organization in need of some oversight itself. "It's you," he said, "who are the watchdogs of them."

When the jury left for deliberations in an adjoining room, they not only had to decide whether the Center's material was libelous. If they believed the Center defamed Jim, they would also have to choose how much money to award the rancher. In addition to actual damages, the jury had the option of awarding punitive damages meant to discourage similar conduct, but only if they thought the Center had acted with an "evil mind." Such an evil mind would be present if the Center or its employees intended to cause harm, were motivated by spite or ill will, or were acting to serve their own interest.

Two-and-a-half hours after the jury broke for deliberations, the bailiff summoned everyone to return to the courtroom. Jim sat between his two lawyers, and several of his supporters sat behind him in the gallery. About 10 backers of the Center were on the other side of the room. Schneller sat near me and held a crystal in his hand as the jury entered. The foreman passed the verdict to Judge Fields. As Fields read the paper to himself, it was so silent that I could hear the ventilation fan in the court reporter's computer.

The clerk announced the verdict: in a 9–1 vote, the jury decided that the Center had defamed Jim and his ranching business. It ordered the Center to pay Jim $100,000 in actual damages and $500,000 in punitive damages. Jim smiled. Jimerfield dropped his head to his lap. All 10 jurors agreed that the news advisory did not "accurately describe the condition of the Montana Allotment." Nine of 10 thought the Center had published misleading photographs. Nine of 10 said the group had made false statements.

After the trial, Suckling seemed shocked. Before TV cameras, he vowed to appeal the ruling. "We did things with the best of intentions. If there were some mistakes, they were honest mistakes," he said. "We really feel victimized by a wealthy banker who can afford to hire a large legal team to nitpick you to death." Although the $600,000 judgment amounted to about one-quarter of the Center's assets at the time, Suckling said the group wouldn't back down. "In our history we've lost some battles, which meant forests got cut down and endangered species got hurt. That's the darkest day," he said. "What happens to us as a group, as individuals, is nothing compared to the suffering of plants and animals." Jim, donning a white cowboy hat outside the courtroom, said he doubted he could collect all the money from the Center. "It does not matter if I ever collect a dime. We were in it because it's a righteous, just cause. People have taken too much abuse for too long in this community," he said. "I'm glad our system has a watchdog, and that's the jury system."

As expected, the Center appealed the jury's verdict. Its pleadings tried to get the judgment either overturned or reduced by raising a laundry list of objections: there was no malice, the material wasn't false, the press release was protected by the First Amendment, the punitive damages shouldn't have been allowed, the jury's award was excessive. The three-judge panel of the Arizona Court of Appeals unanimously rejected all of those arguments. The Arizona Supreme Court declined to hear the case, and the Center chose not to appeal to the US Supreme Court. Jim received $600,000, plus interest, with $500,000 coming from the Center directly and $100,000 paid by the group's insurer. In the end, though, Jim said he lost money on the case. He had financed the scientific studies by Holechek, Galt, and Fleming, and he said just his legal fees had already consumed more than $600,000. Still, he described the lawsuit as "one of the best things I've ever done, except for marry my wife." "I had been on the defensive for years," he said. "They'd been attacking me for years in various ways, and it was great to get on the offensive." *The Wall Street Journal* picked up on the story, and Jim was invited to speak to ranchers and others around the country who felt they had been abused by environmental groups. "Everybody is so pleased," Jim said. "It was the same kind of response you get when there's a big school yard bully pushing everyone around and someone steps up and knocks him out. Everyone who's been pushed around by the bully pats you on the back and says 'great job.'"

15

El Tigre

We saw neither hide nor hair of him, but his personality pervaded the wilderness; no living beast forgot his potential presence, for the price of unwariness was death. No deer rounded a bush, or stopped to nibble pods under a mesquite, without a premonitory sniff for el tigre. No campfire died without talk of him.

—Aldo Leopold, "The Green Lagoons," in *A Sand County Almanac*

Nearly a decade before Jim Chilton won his libel suit, another southern Arizona rancher who ran cattle in a biodiversity hot spot mounted his mule and rode into the Peloncillo Mountains in search of a mountain lion. It was March 7, 1996, just after sunrise, and Warner Glenn was beginning the fourth day of a 10-day hunt that a paying client had booked with his family, which supplemented its income by providing outfitting services. Glenn was 60, six foot six, a fourth-generation rancher, and a second-generation lion hunter. His skin told of many days in the saddle in the Malpai region of southeastern Arizona and southwestern New Mexico.

The Peloncillo Range, rising to about 7,000 feet, is short compared to its neighbors, Mt. Graham and the Chiricahuas. But what the Peloncillos lack in height they make up for in length. For nearly 100 miles, the string of mountains runs along the Arizona–New Mexico border, serving as a sort of elevated bridge between the high country of the American Southwest and the even more rugged terrain of Mexico's Sierra Madre Occidental.

It was clear and windy as the hunting party ascended Hog Canyon on the east side of the Peloncillos. Glenn and the others followed the lead of a half-dozen white hounds with brown, floppy ears, their wet noses glued to the trail, searching for the scent of a cat. After the group split up, one of the hounds picked up a strong track and took off. In pursuit on his mule, Snowy River, Glenn could smell skunk, and he figured the lion he was chasing had picked up the scent after killing one. For 45 minutes, he followed the dogs, amazed by the cat's stamina. The prints looked especially big to Glenn, and not unlike those he'd seen a few months back in these parts. *Dang that booger!* Glenn thought to himself. *He must be a wild son-of-a-gun!* This was tough country, where Geronimo had eluded more than 5,000 soldiers under the command of General Nelson Miles, until he finally surrendered in nearby Skeleton Canyon on September 4, 1886.

Glenn could tell by the dogs' barking that they had finally cornered the cat on a bluff. Alone on Snowy River, he approached the rock outcropping and tied the mule to a strong limb. At first, it looked like the dogs had bayed a big, buff-colored lion. As Glenn got closer and rounded some brush, he saw the unmistakable spotted coat of *el tigre*. "God Almighty!" he said aloud. "That's a jaguar!" The cat was crouched and quietly watching the barking hounds circling below. Years ago, a lion hunter would have reflexively fired on the ultimate trophy animal. Glenn started shooting photos. He wished his dad, Marvin, were there. They'd talked about seeing a jaguar, dreamed of the day, but in 50 years of hunting together they'd never been so lucky.

Hounded by Glenn's dogs, the trapped jaguar made a break for it and the dogs took up the chase, despite Glenn's calls for them to stop. He mounted Snowy River and followed the barking, thinking back to the large tom lion he'd caught a few months back, its face and shoulder clawed, its tail and hindquarters bitten by another cat, perhaps the one he was now following. He remembered how Dale Lee, a famous big-cat hunter, told him about losing seven dogs to a jaguar in a single day.

After a half-mile chase, the dogs caught up to the jaguar in a steep canyon and backed the cat into a rocky chute. Approaching, Glenn could hear the jaguar roaring, the dogs barking. He reached the hounds, looked under a ledge, and discovered the jaguar's face 10 feet from his. "He exploded out of that hole toward me, with fire in his eyes," Glenn recalls in his book, *Eyes of Fire*. "I was amazed at his speed. Maple and Cheyenne met him head-on as I jumped backwards. Right there, they saved me from having my lap full of biting, clawing jaguar." Glenn hollered and kicked small rocks at the jaguar, which bit, clawed, and grabbed three of the dogs, breaking a small bone in one hound's leg and slashing two in the throat. Sensing an opening, the jaguar bolted toward freedom, causing the dogs to give chase yet again. Glenn whistled and hollered, trying to call them off, afraid they'd end up like Dale Lee's dogs. Finally, after a quarter mile, the dogs gave up and the jaguar headed toward Mexico and the even wilder country from which it had come.

No one had ever photographed a live jaguar in the United States outside of captivity, though plenty of dead cats had shown up on film, strung up by their hind legs next to grinning hunters. Associated with tropical jungles, jaguars also roamed across North America until ranchers and predator-control agents wiped them out. The jaguar's ancestors colonized the Western Hemisphere about 2 million years ago via the Bering Land Bridge, along with lions, cheetahs, and saber-toothed cats that went extinct at the end of the last ice age. The jaguars endured and lived throughout the southern tier of the United States, but by the mid-20th century, unregulated hunting had confined jaguars to Arizona and New Mexico. The last known take of a US jaguar was in 1986, when a rancher shot a cat about 50 miles north of Glenn's sighting. The one before that was in 1971, just north of the border along the Santa Cruz River. By the time Glenn stumbled across the jaguar in 1996, many biologists and hunters in the Southwest figured the jaguars were confined to the Sierra Madre, just like another persecuted predator, the Mexican gray wolf.

Glenn's discovery made it clear that at least one jaguar was on American soil, but many scientists felt it was a stretch to call the species a resident of the United States. Evidence of jaguars breeding north of the border in modern times was limited to three reports around the turn of the 20th century: in the late 1880s, a female and two kittens were shot near the Grand Canyon; in 1906, a female was killed and her two kittens were captured in the Chiricahua Mountains, close to where Glenn spotted the jaguar; and in 1910, a female jaguar and her young were taken in the White Mountains, where the last female jaguar recorded in the United States was shot in 1963. Many biologists preferred to describe Glenn's cat as a transient that had dispersed from a known population 130 miles south of the border. Like its human counterparts, the jaguar had apparently come north seeking a better life. In Latin America, jaguars are still found in 16 countries, from Mexico all the way down to Argentina, but overhunting and habitat loss has extirpated the cat from half its range. By one estimate, hunters were killing 15,000 jaguars annually in the Brazilian Amazon in the late 1960s. In Mexico and Central America, the decline was especially steep, with jaguars eliminated from about two-thirds of their historic habitat.

Evolution in both the Old and New Worlds honed jaguars into agile, muscle-bound killers that could instantly dispatch prey many times their weight. The jaguar that Glenn photographed was probably no more than 150 pounds, but in South America, the species may weigh more than 300 pounds. In the family of roaring cats, only the lions of Africa and tigers of Asia are larger. Opportunistic and adaptive, the jaguar subsists on a diet as diverse as the habitats in which it lives. The menu of more than 85 species includes monkeys, caimans, sea turtles, iguanas, armadillos, and, to the jaguar's detriment, livestock. In tropical environments, jaguars have been known to swim across mile-wide rivers. From the shoreline, they may hit the water with their tail to lure fish to the surface so they can swipe them with their paws. In the arid borderlands, where jaguars have been recorded at elevations ranging from 2,000 to 9,000 feet, they subsist primarily on deer and javelina, though they also eat raccoonlike coatis, cottontail rabbits, and even desert tortoises. Unlike mountain lions, jaguars will eat carrion from animals that died of natural causes, so ranchers have sometimes falsely blamed them for killing cows.

Glenn rightly feared for his life as the jaguar surged toward him. According to one translation, the word *jaguar* means "killer of us." Yet jaguar attacks on humans have always been exceedingly rare. Ditto for any face-to-face encounters with *el tigre*. Like mountain lions, jaguars in the borderlands lay low during the day and rely on their mottled coat to blend into the dense, thorny brush. Typically, a solitary jaguar will stalk its quarry from the side or behind. With a sudden rush it pounces, snaps its prey's neck, and in a coup de grâce, sinks its teeth into the animal's skull. "Beast that kills with one leap" is how the indigenous people of Amazonia described the *yaguara*. After killing its prey, a jaguar frequently drags its meal to a concealed spot and begins feeding on its face, neck, and chest. It may leave nothing behind but some hair and bones.

Fiercely territorial, jaguars maul mountain lions and even kill other jaguars in order to defend turf they mark with their urine. If a jaguar can't displace another cat, it must find its own space and may travel hundreds of miles in search of food or a mate. The jaguar Glenn photographed may have been on such an expedition. Earlier in the century, hunters shot the cats several times in the Peloncillos, a range that has always been a topographical link between the jaguar's sanctuaries to the south and its old stomping grounds in the American Southwest.

At dawn on August 31, 1996, nearly six months after Glenn's encounter and 150 miles to the west, another longtime lion hunter rode on horseback into the mountains, this time the Baboquivaris, near where Wayne Shifflett had rescued the Chiricahua leopard frogs. Jack Childs, his wife Anna Mary, and two friends were on a recreational trip meant to exercise the hounds and keep their feet from getting too soft. It had been a wet monsoon, so the jagged range seemed almost tropical, with vines scaling trees and mosquitoes buzzing in the humid air. The dogs picked up a strong scent. Like Glenn, Childs thought the hounds were tracking a big lion. When he caught up to them, he found a jaguar lying on the branch of an alligator juniper. With a full belly, the adult male dozed off as Childs and the others shot video and photos from below. "We felt like we'd been blessed," Childs told me.

Childs's chance encounter inspired him to learn more about jaguars. After visiting their habitat in Brazil, he wrote a booklet explaining how to identify their paw prints. He also set out to capture the cats on film once again. With help from the Arizona Game and Fish Department, Childs installed a series of automatic cameras along suspected travel corridors near the border. Years went by without any jaguars turning up. Finally, on December 9, 2001, one of Childs's cameras photographed an adult male jaguar about four miles north of the border, further proof that *el tigre* was at least visiting the United States. Nearly two years later, the same adult male jaguar was photographed at another station about four miles farther north, just a day after Childs had changed the film.

Although Childs knew where to find big cats, he was trained as a land surveyor, not as a wildlife biologist. Serendipitously, he connected with Emil McCain, a graduate student who had worked with jaguars in Latin America and wanted to research them for his master's degree at Humboldt State University. McCain took over the detection project and, with the help of Childs and volunteers, he increased the number of camera stations to 50. In the first few months that McCain was involved, the cameras recorded four more pictures of jaguars. McCain and Childs have only surveyed about 12 percent of the potential habitat in the borderlands, but they have captured 70 images of jaguars, including one 50 miles north of the border. The cameras, which are activated by heat and motion, have also recorded revealing snapshots of the area's nightlife: bobcats courting, mountain lions engaging in foreplay, and foxes carrying dead squirrels and wood rats in their mouths. Illegal immigrants, smugglers hauling burlap sacks of marijuana, and Border Patrol agents also had their photos taken, as did two male hikers wearing only tennis shoes.

I set out from Tucson to meet McCain and Jack and Anna Mary Childs in the adobe ranch house where McCain lived while doing his fieldwork. As I neared the ranch house just after sunrise, a bobcat scampered across the dirt road, right in front of a Forest Service sign warning visitors about the smuggling and illegal immigration that was prevalent in the region. In McCain's 300-square-mile study area, the illegal traffic was weighted toward human mules carrying loads of marijuana. On the Mexican side, access to the border was challenging, so there weren't a huge number of job seekers crossing through the area. The trail cameras regularly photographed the drug smugglers, and McCain occasionally ran into them while hiking alone. "I speak enough Spanish," he said, "to tell them in straight Sonoran slang, 'Hey, man, don't worry. I don't want any trouble. I don't care what you're doing. I'm just passing through, so I'll go my way and you'll go yours.'" McCain said he didn't snitch to the Border Patrol, and he tacked up signs next to his cameras explaining, in English and Spanish, that they were just used for scientific research. But many of the $500 devices were destroyed anyway. Twice, McCain found the remains of border crossers, once bleached bones, the other time a woman who had died the day before.

The mountains west of the border city of Nogales are not very tall. They top out around 6,000 feet, and much of the intervening terrain consists of rolling hills dotted with oaks and mesquites. In the steep, shady canyons there are thick riparian forests and some perennial streams. Otherwise the area is arid, rocky, and seemingly too dry for a jaguar. In this environment, McCain described jaguars' behavior as "completely unstudied and completely unknown." "Everywhere else they've been studied is in the tropics," he said. "The prey base here is completely different, the land cover is completely different, and the land use is completely different." Biologists do know that jaguars' eclectic diet is matched by an ability to thrive in a broad spectrum of ecosystems, ranging from deserts to rain forests and from coastal swamps to forested mountains nearly two miles above sea level. Generally, the cats stick to places with enough vegetation to provide cover. A quest for food or a mate may prompt them to travel hundreds of miles, but if a jaguar's needs are being met locally, it may be satisfied with a home range of less than 10 square miles.

Before visiting the cameras, McCain wanted to show us his big find from the day before: fresh jaguar tracks in a hot, waterless canyon surrounded by saguaro cacti, a habitat type where biologists had never recorded the cats. It was only the 10th time jaguar tracks had been documented in the United States. McCain had also discovered scrapes on the ground where a mountain lion had dragged its meal a half mile into the brush. After following the path, McCain found a freshly killed javelina that the lion hadn't opened yet.

As we walked along the canyon bottom, McCain or Childs would occasionally point to the ground and say, "There he is." When I looked down, I saw a bunch of uneven sand and dirt. But McCain and Childs could somehow trace the jaguar's toes and determine his direction of travel, even if the cat's back foot had stepped on the print made by its front paw. The depressions had the circumference of a softball, and that gave me pause.

Tracks age, but unlike wine they do not improve. Rain will erase them and wind will collapse their walls. Prints made in sand or loose soil may disintegrate in a day. Wildlife trackers find it's easiest to spot prints when the impressions lie between their eyes and the sun—that way the shadows stand out. This was why McCain and Childs kept looking behind them as they walked down the dry wash, part of the Chiltons' Montana Allotment. We avoided lots of cow patties and saw plenty of calves running around—"lion bait," according to Childs.

We had lunch beneath the shade of an Arizona ash. Jack and Anna Mary Childs pointed out vermilion flycatchers, summer tanagers, and cardinals, all bright red and in high contrast to the greenery around us. Jack Childs was wearing a silver belt buckle embossed with the image of a mountain lion. Tentatively, I asked him about what seemed like a contradiction: he and Glenn shot mountain lions out of trees, yet both men had become some of the jaguar's biggest advocates. Why kill one type of cat while working to save another?

Childs's answer pointed to another seeming contradiction: over the past half century of exponential population growth, mountain lions, also known as pumas or cougars, had become *more* numerous in the Southwest. When Childs began lion hunting in 1963, the state still paid a $75 bounty. "You could kill all the lions you wanted and make money off it," he said. In 1971, Arizona became the last state to repeal bounties for mountain lions, but by then the hunting pressure had made it impossible to locate the cats in several ranges around Tucson where they're found today. Lions, and perhaps some jaguars, also died after eating the poisons that federal officials indiscriminately applied to the landscape to kill predators. The pressures drove lions into the most inaccessible terrain, but after Arizona enacted a bag limit of one cat per year, the animals began to spread out again. California went so far as to outlaw trophy hunting of lions in 1990. Across the West, the cats' numbers have rebounded due to stricter controls on hunting and the dramatic revival in deer, elk, and other prey species that had dwindled by the early 20th century. Lions also face less competition than they did centuries ago, thanks to humans nearly wiping out grizzlies, jaguars, and wolves. Today, mountain lions in the Southwest are anything but endangered. Licensed hunters in Arizona take about 300 lions per year, and the cats are found virtually everywhere there's a healthy deer population. At the same time, Americans have been moving into lion habitat, leading to an increasing number of attacks on humans and pets, though the risk to most people remains miniscule.

After lunch, we checked one of McCain's cameras near an old ghost town. Stepping out of the car we noticed flames racing up a peak a few miles behind us. Border crossers hoping to attract rescuers had started a come-get-me fire. It was a gusty day, but helicopters and air tankers flew past us and confined the blaze to about 200 acres.

To reach the camera we needed to walk around a stock pond that was infested with nonnative bullfrogs and therefore devoid of Chiricahua leopard frogs. Along the shore, a bull watched us. I turned my back on him so I could take a photo of McCain, and the beast charged. I escaped being gored only because the animal sank into the mud 12 inches before hitting me.

McCain's trail camera was attached to a tree, and its lens gazed across a path onto which all sorts of mammals were funneled by the surrounding landscape. The Border Patrol was using a similar strategy, concentrating its efforts on the crossroads and choke points that undocumented workers had to pass through to reach civilization. McCain, strapped for research funds, was forced to use regular old film in some of his cameras, delaying the results until he visited the one-hour photo shop in the Nogales Wal-Mart. But the camera we were checking afforded instant gratification because it recorded images digitally. McCain popped the compact flash card into his point-and-shoot camera and began describing the 14 images taken over the past six weeks: "Illegal, kitty, more illegals, kitty food, another kitty." The camera had picked up a couple of border crossers, three lions, some deer and javelina, but no sign of a jaguar. Before we left, McCain reloaded the camera, then crawled before it on his hands and knees to make sure the motion sensor registered his presence. On a rock in the center of the camera's field of view, he poured a noxious liquid that he said was made from the fermented anal glands of a skunk and other animal parts. The smell, which made me nauseous, was meant to entice jaguars and other wildlife to stop and sniff right in front of the camera.

Each jaguar has a unique pattern of spots, known as rosettes, so careful examination of the photos can reveal the identity of individual cats. Childs's and McCain's cameras had already identified two male jaguars, known as Macho A and Macho B, the latter distinguished by a spot on his right rib cage that resembled Pinocchio and another rosette on his left side that looked like Betty Boop. In 2006, McCain reexamined Childs's film from 1996 and realized the jaguar in the Baboquivaris was Macho B. "He's been around here for a decade...it blew us away," McCain said. "That really solidified the fact he's a resident. He's not just passing through and going back to Mexico to live. He's staying here." Macho B may have killed or driven off Macho A, who has not been photographed since 2004.

The next morning, McCain and I began what was advertised as a 10-mile loop down to the border to check more cameras. Weaving through patches of poison oak and thickets of thorn-covered branches, we headed south on trails blazed by border crossers heading north. Interspersed with the sneaker prints of the migrants and smugglers were more jaguar and lion tracks. The canyon attracts bird-watchers from across the nation because it's the northernmost extent of some avian species. On this morning, McCain picked out the *brr brr brr brr* of an elegant trogon, a handsome red-bellied, green-backed flycatcher that was sitting in a sycamore. "It's kind of like the jaguar," he said. "It's tropical but only comes this far north." In the cloudless sky, we saw more than a dozen turkey vultures circling above, floating on the currents rising from the sweltering desert. At our feet, the stream would disappear into the sand then reappear as an ephemeral pool with tiny Sonora chub darting beneath the surface. This canyon and the one we had visited the day before were the only places where the minnows were found in the United States.

Walking down the streambed, just north of the border, we were hit by the stench of death. To our right, wedged between two giant slabs of rock, a dead white cow stared at us. It was a trespasser from Mexico, and its tail sat on a nearby rock. The side of the cow's head was rotting and swarming with flies. It looked like it had died within the past few days. McCain's eyes darted around. "I bet you there's a jaguar right around here. Let's get out of here," he said. It wasn't that McCain was afraid the cat would pounce on us, he explained. He was worried that leaving our scents at the kill site could drive away the jaguar. "It's not fair for us to be nosing around and blow that much food for them," he said. "I just had a really strong presence of him there."

A few miles away, after seeing more jaguar tracks, we checked a digital camera in a boulder-filled canyon flanked by ocotillos, shin daggers, and desert brome. McCain popped the card into his camera and a smile slid across his face. "There's the boy—that's Macho B!" he said. The most recent image was recorded just five days before, at 4:55 AM, and we were sitting on the exact spot where the jaguar had walked. "He's got a full belly," McCain said. "Look at how fat he is!" The same camera also captured the butt of a lion and a perfect shot of a big black bear, which seemed incongruous in such a dry, sparsely vegetated environment. We had already covered 10 miles and it was getting dark; five miles later, we reached the ranch house by the light of our headlamps. I was fried, and my forearms looked like a cat had scratched them. "I've never had a day like this, seeing so much sign over such a long distance," McCain said. "I've seen more tracks today than I've seen in two years of doing this."

A few weeks later, McCain e-mailed me some photos from a camera he had set up near the dead cow. A closer inspection of the carcass led McCain to conclude that a jaguar hadn't killed the cow, but his photos show Macho B standing atop the carcass and yanking out a fetus.

While McCain, Childs, and I were hiking, we came to the border twice, and in both cases there was nothing more than a few strands of barbed wire separating the United States and Mexico. Any jaguar—or human—could easily crawl under or jump over that barrier. In one spot, we found a makeshift gate in the fence. In some stretches, there was simply nothing at all, as cattle from Mexico have discovered.

But this was in the summer of 2006, while Congress and the nation were still debating the wisdom of erecting nearly 700 miles of stout fencing along the US-Mexico border. The year before, the House had passed a bill ordering the construction of tall steel barriers that would stretch continuously for 361 miles, from Calexico, California, to just east of Douglas, Arizona, thereby slicing through the mountains where McCain, Childs, and others were tracking jaguars. Workers would erect two layers of 10- to 15-foot fencing about 50 yards apart and put a road in between that Border Patrol agents could drive up and down. There were already some fences and walls along the border, many of them made from metal landing mats cast off by the military. It would be relatively easy to extend those barriers across neighboring valleys because there was often an existing border road or a highway nearby. But in the mountainous boonies, like McCain and Childs's study area, there were only a few spots where an unimproved dirt road reached the border. To build a fence in the intervening areas, the government would either have to blade hundreds of miles of new roads or airlift manpower and material with helicopters.

Even without new barriers at the border, many scientists were confident that as the Border Patrol added more agents, lights, roads, and overflights, jaguars and other animals would shy away from the area. "They're sensitive to human presence," said University of Arizona biologist Lisa Haynes, a board member of the nonprofit Northern Jaguar Project. "All the lights, the ATVs, the driving up and down, plus the migrant traffic itself, is not something that wildlife adapts to very well. It's a significant impact."

Environmentalists opposed to the fence and mounting Border Patrol operations were quick to invoke the jaguar, and they couldn't have asked for a better poster child: the symbol of a sports car, NFL team, and Macintosh operating system. Yet even the nexus of the most charismatic of megafauna and the nation's toughest environmental law wouldn't necessarily give environmentalists any power to control what the federal government was doing at the doorstep to Mexico. Right along the border, a 1907 proclamation signed by President Theodore Roosevelt reserved a 60-foot-wide strip of land for patrols and protective measures, regardless of how the adjoining land was managed. Farther inland, the Department of Homeland Security was allowed to bypass any laws it wanted, including those protecting wilderness, endangered species, and human health, while constructing border infrastructure. When Congress passed the Real ID Act in 2005, it not only tightened standards for driver's licenses but also gave Homeland Security "authority to waive all legal requirements" after a 14-mile fence near San Diego was stalled for years over ecological concerns. As he wielded that power in September 2005, Homeland Security Secretary Michael Chertoff reserved the authority "to make further waivers from time to time." If Congress approved the border fence, some environmentalists would surely use the jaguar and other endangered species to fight the construction. But with the Real ID waiver in hand, Homeland Security would have absolute power.

If a continuous, impenetrable fence were constructed across the southwestern border, it would undoubtedly prevent jaguars from naturally reoccupying their historic range in the United States. But no one could say that would jeopardize the species, which was still found throughout Latin America. Unable to wave the banner of extinction, jaguar advocates were forced to call upon other justifications: The animal was part of the nation's natural heritage. The US population helped sustain the jaguars living in northern Mexico. The cats deserved full protection under the ESA. "This animal is part of the American landscape and other animals evolved alongside it," Michael Robinson of the Center for Biological Diversity told me. "It's one of the reasons that deer had their alertness, that bighorn sheep can climb across sheer cliffs...it influenced all the other animals that it shared the landscape with, and it probably even influenced the plants." Some biologists argued that US habitat was acting like a holding pattern for jaguars that could recolonize areas in Mexico when cats there died and territories opened up. "This may be the relief valve that allows the population in Mexico to continually maintain itself," said Bill Van Pelt, an Arizona Game and Fish Department biologist. In light of global warming, some scientists argued that populations on the edge of a species' range were even more important to conserve. These plants and animals would be at the vanguard as species shifted toward the poles, and their ability to survive in habitat at the margins might allow them to adapt to the new climate with more ease than core populations. The American Society of Mammalogists, for example, argued that the jaguar's US habitat was "vital to the long-term resilience and survival of the species, especially in response to ongoing climate change."

But other jaguar experts downplayed the importance of US habitat. Alan Rabinowitz, director for science and exploration for the Bronx Zoo–based Wildlife Conservation Society, was brought in to evaluate the habitat after Glenn's sighting. He concluded that "the southwest has, at least in recent times, never been more than marginal habitat at the extreme northern limit of the jaguar's range." Rabinowitz, author of several books on the jaguar, applauded the cat's 1997 listing under the ESA—and Fish and Wildlife's decision not to map critical habitat in Arizona and New Mexico. "Scientifically, there was no justification to protect critical habitat for jaguars," he said. "In fact, any steps taken which would adversely affect the lives of people who have been long-time residents of the area, or anger people unnecessarily, might actually work against the survival of the few jaguars that still move through the area." To David Brown, an adjunct professor of biology at Arizona State University and coauthor of *Borderland Jaguars*, the cats roaming north of the border offered "entertainment value" and were just a sideshow to the main drama playing out in the wilderness of Sonora, where poaching remained a serious threat. "If they have a healthy population down there and it can sustain itself, that's probably as good as it's going to get," Brown told me.

Our knowledge of the jaguar's range and behavior in Sonora remains hazy, but many biologists point to a breeding population that's about 130 miles south of the US border. Despite the area's remoteness, its jaguar population is anything but secure. Killing jaguars is technically illegal in Mexico, but people who've visited the area say cowboys earning $13 a day can make up to $700 by killing a jaguar for a rancher, then get some extra cash by selling the pelt on the black market. More than 50 jaguars have been shot in northern Sonora over the past decade, including four lactating females, two of them with cubs. There's also long been talk of building more roads, damming the rivers, and opening up new mines in the area.

Seeking to safeguard the population in Sonora, the Mexican environmental group Naturalia purchased a 10,000-acre ranch in the heart of the jaguar colony in 2003. Just in the preceding three years, biologists documented that poachers and ranchers had killed 25 jaguars, including females with kittens. American environmental groups pitched in to support on-site researchers and fence the preserve to keep out cows. This Northern Jaguar Reserve, which now encompasses 45,000 acres, is a classic example of the umbrella effect: motivated by a charismatic cat, the preserve is also home to more than 150 bird species and more than 100 types of butterflies. And in Mexico, buying or otherwise protecting land is dirt cheap: most of the jaguar preserve cost about $50 an acre. Mexican ranchers can do their part to reduce livestock predation, such as confining calves, but this won't happen overnight, or maybe ever, given the weak enforcement of environmental laws south of the border and the centuries of tradition that have cast jaguars as enemies.

———————

US environmentalists could only do so much for jaguars in Mexico. North of the border, American activists' power was also limited, despite the cat's status as an endangered species. In 1972, Fish and Wildlife labeled jaguars endangered due to their persecution in Latin America, but the listing only applied to animals that lived south of the border. Fish and Wildlife later termed this an oversight, and in 1979 it vowed to rectify the mistake as soon as possible. In an exemplary case of bureaucratic foot-dragging, it would take another 18 years for US jaguars to gain federal protection. In 1992, a college biology instructor and his students asked Fish and Wildlife to list jaguars in the United States. The agency ignored the petition until a lawsuit by the Center for Biological Diversity prompted Fish and Wildlife to propose listing in 1994. Ranchers and hunters in Arizona and New Mexico, already fighting the Mexican gray wolf's reintroduction, pressured their game and fish departments to develop a state-based voluntary agreement in lieu of federal involvement. A year after Glenn and Childs filmed jaguars on American soil in 1996, Fish and Wildlife listed the US cats.

In response to the antifederal sentiment in rural Arizona and New Mexico, federal authorities ceded power to a state-led voluntary effort known as the Jaguar Conservation Team. State governments are not necessarily enemies of strong environmental policy. California, for instance, has been a pioneer in energy regulation and coastal preservation. But until recently, when the federal government handed over authority to the states in the environmental arena, it has usually meant less protection for natural resources, especially in the interior West. The surrogate for federal involvement, the Jaguar Conservation Team, has no regulatory power and can't force any changes in policy or land management practices. The team was made toothless by design to appease ranchers and state politicians, and to reduce the risk that wild jaguars would be shot by opponents, a problem crippling the effort to reintroduce Mexican gray wolves to the Southwest.

Critics of the jaguar's listing feared environmentalists would use the ESA to restrict ranching and hunting of prey species such as deer. When Fish and Wildlife did take action in 1997, the Center's Peter Galvin told a reporter that the jaguar would help limit public lands grazing, Border Patrol operations, and water use along the San Pedro River, particularly by the army's Fort Huachuca. At the time, Fish and Wildlife declined to map critical habitat for the jaguar, saying there was no evidence of the cats breeding in the United States. Federal officials also predicted such a map could do more harm than good by encouraging poaching. Defenders of Wildlife and the Center grew frustrated with the lack of action. In 2003, they went to court yet again with hopes that a judge would force Fish and Wildlife to write a recovery plan and designate critical habitat. But in July 2006, Fish and Wildlife again declined to draw a critical habitat map, saying US land was marginal and covered less than 1 percent of the jaguar's current range. "Preservation and recovery of the jaguar depends almost entirely on conservation efforts in Mexico and Central and South America," the agency said.

The handful of jaguars in the United States weren't posing any problems for ranchers, even though their lands were apparently managed well enough to attract the cats. The specter of critical habitat, however, drew howls of protest. Glenn told me fellow ranchers saw critical habitat as a threat to their livelihoods, and he predicted the map would take food and water out of the jaguar's mouth. Predator control might cease or be curtailed, he said, leading more mountain lions to eat more deer and javelina. With a greater number of predators out in the wild, "the prey base would take two or three years to get wiped out, and the jaguar would no longer have anything to eat," he said.

I was chatting to Glenn during a break at a Jaguar Conservation Team meeting in Lordsburg, New Mexico, after he had put on a slide show. A couple months before, while lion hunting in the boot heel of New Mexico with his daughter, Kelly, and five others, Glenn had seen and photographed yet another jaguar on a large, privately owned ranch. The cat, which bit three of Glenn's dogs, was neither Macho A nor Macho B. Glenn estimated the adult male weighed nearly 200 pounds and told me he believed the animal was depending on stock ponds in the area, just like Chiricahua leopard frogs. "Right now, you can ride through those mountains and the natural springs are just about dry," he said. "The only water the wildlife has is water being maintained by livestock operators." Some biologists, however, disputed Glenn's claims about the importance of stock ponds to the jaguar and the potential impact of new predator control rules.

It was my first time at a meeting of the Jaguar Conservation Team, and it didn't take long to see why environmentalists were so disenchanted with the process. When the meeting began in Lordsburg's civic center, a bare-bones conference room with plastic folding chairs and no lights in the bathroom, the only parties able to vote were six government agencies. By day's end, voting power had been granted to 21 soil and water conservation districts from New Mexico, some of them located hundreds of miles from the jaguar sightings. The districts, which do some good conservation work but were clearly proxies for ranchers, were able to join the team so easily because they too were government agencies and had letters of support from their boards. According to the Jaguar Conservation Team's rules, the existing members had no choice but to approve the expansion. A couple of the conservation district officials made the mistake of asking questions during the meeting and revealed their ignorance of jaguar biology and regulatory issues. Within minutes, the newly constituted team voted to limit jaguar conservation efforts in New Mexico to just one border county and leave out other areas that had both suitable habitat and plenty of ranchers suspicious of the ESA.

The other big item at the meeting was a discussion about the plan to capture a jaguar along the border and attach a satellite-tracking collar. Images from the remote cameras only revealed what happened in one spot, at one moment. "Right now," McCain told the group, "we're literally dealing with a shot in the dark." McCain was trying to locate jaguar scat so its DNA could be analyzed, but he and some other jaguar researchers thought the only way to truly understand a jaguar's behavior in the borderlands was to analyze detailed data on its wanderings. "Let him tell us exactly what habitat he likes to use," Childs said. With a radio collar, the cat's precise location would be periodically bounced off satellites and downloaded to biologists' computers, where GIS mapping technology could determine the cat's home range and patterns of movement. Soon after a jaguar track or photograph was recorded, a team of scientists would use hounds to corner a cat, dart it with a tranquilizer, and take measurements, vital signs, and DNA samples. They would slap on the collar and let the animal go on its way when the drugs wore off. "If you're going to manage the jaguar," Childs said, "you've got to learn something about it."

Jaguars have been repeatedly captured in Latin America and fitted with collars, but sometimes with disastrous results. In 2003, with backing from the Northern Jaguar Project and Defenders of Wildlife, McCain and another biologist, Sergio Avila, tried to collar jaguars in Sonora using a cable snare that was supposed to latch on to a front leg. The cable was 10 feet long "so when you stepped into that 10-foot radius, you were live bait," McCain recalled. One biologist would distract the cat while the other snuck up and tried to blow a tranquilizer dart through a tube and into the cat's hide. The procedure worked with the first jaguar they caught. But they had more trouble with the second one. "He'd hear me blow, flinch, and dart out of the way," McCain said. On a day of record-breaking heat, the second jaguar became increasingly agitated. "It was a very open place," Avila recalled, "the animal could move 360 degrees, and so could we, so it was a lot more infuriating for the jaguar." The trap had also snagged the cat's back leg and blown out the tendons of one of its joints. Finally, using a stick, the biologists jabbed the jaguar with the dart and knocked him out. The cat, an older male, was in bad shape and may have been given too much sedative, but McCain said he and Avila had to check 15 other traps to make sure another cat wasn't ensnared for too long in the heat. The next day, they homed in on the beeping of the collar on the second cat, only to hear it emit the mortality signal, triggered when the device hadn't moved for 12 hours. "My heart just dropped," McCain said. "I've seen the risk of this. I've lived through it and still have nightmares. But I think it's worth it to gain that knowledge." Avila said he was also crushed by the cat's death, but the episode led him to become a vocal opponent of capturing jaguars in the borderlands for research. "Having a dead jaguar, for any reason, was in complete contrast to the conservation goals that we had," Avila said, "so from that moment on, even if we were working together, Emil and I took very different perspectives on jaguar conservation and research in their northern range."

When McCain and Childs presented the capture plan to the conservation team in Lordsburg, ranchers and government officials in the room rallied around the proposal. But Michael Robinson of the Center and Craig Miller of Defenders of Wildlife weren't buying any of it. "The risks are too great," Robinson told the crowd. "Jaguars, as Emil can attest to, are much more liable to fight back. The risks to them are greater than to mountain lions, black bears, and other animals that are commonly immobilized." Miller said proponents of the capture were still missing the point: just collecting data wouldn't mean much because the team had done nothing to translate its knowledge of the jaguar into on-the-ground conservation measures. "Our focus," he said, "has been more on conversation than conservation." Environmentalists argued that the conservation team had given McCain, Childs, and the Arizona Game and Fish Department too much control over the research agenda and excluded scientists; McCain countered that the plan was developed collaboratively, but green groups chose not to participate, only criticize. In the end, the team, now dominated by the conservation districts, took a vote and supported the capture plan unanimously. Further approvals from state and federal officials would be necessary, but the day was nearing when biologists could figure out exactly where Macho B or another jaguar was prowling.

During much of 2006, illegal immigration and the proposed fence dominated political discourse inside the Beltway and along the border. In nationwide surveys, public opinion on the fence bounced up and down, but supporters flooded Congress with e-mails, faxes, and calls. The measure gained momentum, and when it came time for a vote in September, the Secure Fence Act passed easily: 283 to 138 in the House and 80 to 19 in the Senate. The law authorized construction of nearly 700 miles of fences and vehicle barriers along the border, much of it in Arizona.

With a midterm election coming up and Iraq imploding, reforming the ESA wasn't exactly at the top of Congress's agenda. Richard Pombo's bill, which had passed the House in September 2005, stalled in the Senate, where even many Republicans argued it was too extreme.

Senator Lincoln Chafee, a moderate Republican from Rhode Island whose father, John, was an ESA supporter as a US senator, played a critical role in blocking Pombo's offensive, offering a reminder that American environmental policy often hinges on the behavior of moderate legislators rather than the most vocal partisans. As Republicans hemorrhaged political capital along with the bloodshed in Iraq, the Pombo bill died a slow death and its author became embroiled in a series of scandals that endangered his own political career. Pombo had built a war chest, partly by collecting more than $1 million in his congressional career from the industries his committee regulated. But the allegations against Pombo fit squarely into the narrative of GOP lawmakers as cocky and corrupted by power. *Rolling Stone* called him an "enemy of the earth." *High Country News* called him "the Jerry Falwell of the property rights movement." The Sierra Club branded him an "eco-thug" and "the most frightening man in Congress," then sent 300 volunteers to work for his opponent in the final weeks of the election. Pombo's standard retort to reporters: "They need a bogeyman to help raise money." And raise money they did. Defenders of Wildlife spent more than $1 million to oust him. When the votes came in on November 7, 2006, Pombo lost by six points and Democrats gained control of the House.

The ESA dodged a bullet in November 2006, but for species like the jaguar, policy decisions made before the election would cast a long shadow. Along the US-Mexico border, workers began to erect hundreds of miles of fencing, and with each mile completed in jaguar habitat, the odds diminished that the Western Hemisphere's largest cat would reoccupy its historic territory in the American Southwest. Even with the Bush presidency weakened and Democrats back in control of the House, the Department of Homeland Security still had the ability to waive the ESA and plenty of other laws in order to finish the fence.

16
Living with El Lobo

Biologically, restoring wolves is easy. Just drop off a few in an area with enough food—deer, elk, moose, sheep, goats, caribous, muskoxen, bison—and they will thrive. The problem comes when people enter the picture, and they always do.

—David Mech, wolf biologist

Loretta Rabenau was on horseback just before noon, rounding up her calves for branding, when she discovered one of her young cows was dead. The calf, about three months old and 200 pounds, had been bitten on its rear end, probably that May morning or the night before. Ravens and vultures had already gone to work and disturbed the dirt around the carcass, so Rabenau couldn't spot any tracks that might identify the culprit. She did see what looked like two coyotes trotting along a ridge in the distance and figured they were the responsible parties.

The next evening, Rabenau's husband, William, staked out the remains so he could take care of the problem when the coyotes returned to finish their meal. Coyotes are abundant in the Southwest, and people in New Mexico are generally allowed to shoot them on sight. "With ranchers, it's just sort of a general practice that you keep them thinned out," Loretta told me. As the sun began to set on the Black Range, a chain of pine-clad mountains strung along the Continental Divide, William surveyed the area around the dead calf with the scope of his rifle. The animal that appeared was not a coyote, but a wolf. For most of the 20th century, a rancher like William would not have hesitated to fire on the predator hated most by the livestock industry. "Now it would have meant going to prison," Loretta said. "It was just a helpless feeling knowing there was nothing that could be done until they killed enough of our cattle."

A pair of endangered Mexican gray wolves, the sole members of the Nantac Pack, had killed the Rabenaus' calf and committed their first strike. Two more strikes and they would likely be incarcerated for life or shot and killed, according to rules enacted at the behest of ranchers. Since 1998, when wolf reintroduction began in Arizona and New Mexico, the government has killed 12 wolves and placed 23 in permanent captivity. The program in the Southwest also subjects wolves to aggressive management if they exit the 7,000-square-mile recovery zone, which includes the Apache National Forest, Gila National Forest, and White Mountain Apache Reservation. In all, more than 93 animals have been translocated since 1998, and as many as 18 Mexican gray wolves—one of the most endangered mammals in North America— have died as a result of captures.

For most cattle growers in the Southwest, the wolf remains a bête noire and an added financial burden in an already marginal business. Conservationists have compensated ranchers for cows killed by wolves, and economic studies have downplayed the livestock industry's financial losses, but opposition to the reintroduction program remains strong as ever. Like many ranchers, Loretta Rabenau was against reintroduction from its outset, though she held out some hope that the wolves would be no more of a menace than coyotes. But when the Nantac Pack took down her calves and full-grown, half-ton cows, the old-time stories of wolves killing for kicks, not just sustenance, no longer seemed like exaggerations to her. "It's worse than what I could have imagined," she said. "You start to believe the only good wolf is a dead wolf because of what they can do. If there were a couple in the area and they weren't causing trouble, I don't think we'd shoot them just to shoot them. But there might be people who would."

Some opponents of the program have apparently jumped at the chance to fire on reintroduced wolves. From 1998 through 2008, people illegally shot 30 lobos in the Southwest; in all but two cases, the killers were never caught. The shootings are the population's top source of mortality and account for nearly half the deaths, more than double the next greatest threat: vehicle collisions (fig. 19). If you add the number of wolves lost to poaching to the number of animals the government has killed, incarcerated, or harmed, the sum is a recovery effort treading water, if not slowly sinking. Initially, the wolf population rose in line with expectations thanks to continual releases; by 2003, it was up to 55, exactly what had been projected by federal officials prior to the start of the program (fig. 20). But for the next five years, the wolf population never got above 60 and even dipped to 42. There wasn't much debate about why the program was falling short of expectations: people were shooting more wolves than expected and the government was frequently rounding up or destroying wolves that preyed on cattle or lived too close to houses.

Part of the problem was the nature of the beast being reintroduced. Unlike the program in the Northern Rockies, which imported wild wolves from Canada, the Southwest program had to rely on wolves bred in zoos because the subspecies was nearly extinct in the wild by the time the federal government got around to recovering them. "Captive-raised wolves just don't have the basic fear of humans that strikes terror in the hearts of wild wolves and makes them avoid any fresh sign of humans," the distinguished wolf biologist David Mech wrote. "Thus captive wolves released into the wilds where their ancestors long ago roamed tend to spend too much time in the open, to frequent roads, and to haunt the local livestock grazing areas. This, of course, renders them vulnerable to any handy wolf-hater with a gun."

The poaching in the Southwest (and Northern Rockies) was only the latest manifestation of an age-old contempt for wolves. It's tough to find an animal that has been persecuted with such zeal or to name a creature

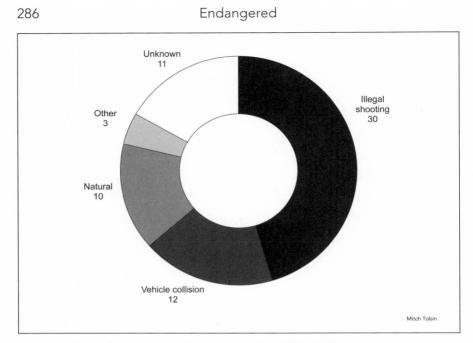

Figure 19: Cause of mortality for Mexican gray wolves, 1998 to 2008.
Source: US Fish and Wildlife Service.

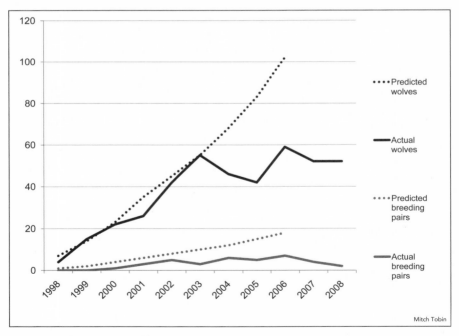

Figure 20: Mexican gray wolf population versus estimates, 1998 to 2008.
Note: Final environmental impact statement made no predictions beyond 2006; mean of range used in 2004 and 2005.
Source: US Fish and Wildlife Service.

upon which more human sins and foibles have been projected. At times in human history, individuals and entire cultures have lionized wolves, viewed them as brothers, invested them with benevolent spiritual powers, even credited them with nurturing Romulus and Remus, the legendary twin founders of Rome. More often, people have maintained a reservoir of venom for wolves far deeper than those reserved for other predators.

The lupine style of attack only amplifies the antagonism. A solitary mountain lion pounces, bites a cow's neck or head, and thereby delivers an execution with the swiftness of a guillotine. Packs of wolves run down their quarry, rip chunks of flesh from the still-live prey, and deliver a death sentence akin to a slow stoning. As the livestock industry took hold in the Southwest in the late 19th century, stoic ranchers were aghast to find pregnant cows with their fetuses ripped out, genitalia consumed, and left for dead by wolves that had moved on. In his 1951 memoirs, *Slash Ranch Hounds*, New Mexico rancher and hunter G. W. "Dub" Evans recalled seeing cows that had been eaten alive by wolves. "I remember one night hearing an animal moaning as if in great distress," Evans wrote. "We could not get to her in the darkness but, next morning, found a fine heifer, hamstrung still alive and suffering in spite of the fact that a wolf had eaten at least twenty pounds of flesh off her body. A few incidents like this will teach anyone to hate wolves."

There was no shortage of wolf haters in both the Southwest and Northern Rockies. But in the latter program, which has received far more attention, the wolf population was able to grow enough to become one of the great conservation stories of our time. Since wolves were reintroduced to Yellowstone in 1995, scientists have documented a so-called trophic cascade in the park that has had a ripple effect on the landscape, a change Aldo Leopold had accurately predicted a half century before. Reinstating the predator to the top of the food chain thinned out the elk population and caused herds to shy away from thickly vegetated riparian areas where the risk of wolf attacks was higher, in what two Oregon State University scientists, Robert Beschta and William Ripple, call "the ecology of fear." As a result, willows and other plants along streams and rivers rebounded, altering the entire hydrology of some watercourses, in part by attracting more beavers. In Yellowstone, at least nine other species feed on wolf kills, including eagles and bears. "We are confident," scientists reported in the journal *Bioscience*, "that form and function of the Yellowstone ecosystem will change because of wolf recovery."

If the Yellowstone reintroduction demonstrates the capacity for humans to atone for past sins and restore the health of ecosystems, the sputtering recovery in the Southwest reminds us that deep-seated hatred and entrenched interests are often immune to federal mandates. State and federal law enforcement personnel continue to investigate the shootings in the Southwest, which have taken place every year except 1999. There's now a $52,000 reward for turning in a wolf killer, courtesy of the government and conservation groups. Illegal wolf killings are also punishable by criminal penalties of up to $50,000 and a year in jail, or a civil penalty of up to $25,000. The authorities reportedly use undercover agents, but they've always declined to describe suspects or leads. "Wildlife poachings, in general, are very hard crimes to solve," Doug McKenna, a Fish and Wildlife agent, told me. When a wolf is found shot to death, authorities turn the area into a crime scene, collect evidence, and ship the animal's remains to Fish and Wildlife's lab in Ashland, Oregon, for forensic analysis. "You're dealing with a gunshot, maybe vehicle tracks, and not much beyond that," said Jon Cooley, head of the local office of the Arizona Game and Fish Department. Witnesses are the key to solving the crimes, which are taking place in one of the least populated areas of the country.

The Blue Range Primitive Area is the last of its kind. In 1933, the Forest Service labeled the 174,000 acres in eastern Arizona as primitive in an attempt to preserve its roadless, wild nature. By the start of World War II, the agency had created a total of 76 primitive areas, all of which were converted into federal wilderness, except for the Blue. An anachronism, the Blue is situated in one of the Southwest's blank spots. Surrounding Greenlee County covers 1,848 square miles, nearly the size of Delaware, but the government owns more than 90 percent of the land and it remains the least populous of Arizona's 15 counties. From 1990 to 2005, Arizona's population rose 62 percent, to nearly 6 million; in Greenlee County it fell from 8,008 to 7,521. The area still shows up as a dark splotch on nighttime satellite imagery. Tucson, Phoenix, Flagstaff, Albuquerque, and El Paso are all more than 150 miles away as the crow flies, and much farther as the vehicle drives.

A couple dozen ranchers and others live on private parcels in and around the Blue Range Primitive Area. I met many of them one chilly November morning.

Neighbors had gathered at Bill and Barbara Marks's ranch house, set amid a broad meadow along the Blue and flanked by copper-colored cliffs, the sort of rimrock Leopold might have been sitting on in 1909 when he shot the wolf with a fierce green fire in her eyes. It had snowed the day before, and a wood-burning stove warmed the Markses' living room, where two dozen people, half local residents, half government officials, were snacking on items from the potluck. On the wall, a Forest Service official projected his PowerPoint presentation on an empty spot where there weren't old rifles, spurs, horseshoes, or photos of prize-winning cows.

I had met some of the same ranchers six months before, in an overly air-conditioned banquet hall in the mining town of Morenci. They had driven an hour or two to voice their opposition to the pending release of wolves near their homes. The hall was decorated for a wedding reception later that night, with congratulatory signs taped to the wall and white crepe paper spread across tables, but the meeting felt more like divorce court. Folks from the Blue pleaded with federal and state officials not to release the pack. Their county supervisor read aloud from a half-dozen letters of opposition: "a serious and cruel injustice is being done"…"this is already a predator-infested area"…"the wolf people are using the animals as pawns to further their selfish agenda"…"my home is being turned into a zoo." Officials with the multiagency state-federal team that oversees the wolf project—"a six-headed serpent," according to one rancher—tried to assuage fears while also standing firm: the releases were essential for boosting the population's genetic diversity and necessary to compensate for the illegal shooting of six alpha wolves the year before.

Three months after the Morenci meeting, biologists gathered two adult wolves and three pups from Ted Turner's Ladder Ranch in New Mexico. The wolves were packed in by mule to a mesh pen in the Blue Range Primitive Area, about 10 miles from houses along the Blue. After four days of acclimation in the pen, the wolves, dubbed the Aspen Pack, were set free.

These wolves were especially valuable because they had a mix of all three lineages that account for the population's genetic diversity. Every Mexican gray wolf traces its DNA to just seven founding animals. Most of the animals in the wild derived from a single lineage that had become somewhat inbred and was apt to produce two pups, rather than five, in a litter.

The five-member Aspen Pack initially hung around the release site, but on September 11, the wolves were at the Blue post office. Local residents then reported continuous encounters with the wolves and no success in scaring them off. After the pack reportedly harassed a calf in a corral, the wolf team installed boxes with bullhorns that would blare the sound of gunfire, sirens, and helicopters when activated by wolves' radio collars. Biologists set off firecrackers in an attempt to haze the animals. But the wolves kept coming back. In early November, the pack scuffled with some dogs near the river, prompting a resident to fire a shotgun to scare them off.

I arrived in the Markses' living room a few weeks after that incident, and all of the ranchers in attendance were eager to vent their frustrations. Barbara Marks, whose husband's family arrived in the area in 1891, told me settlers and current-day residents along the Blue recognized that predators were part of the bargain of living in the area, but the grizzlies and wolves had to go. "They're kind of like criminals in society," she said. "You remove them because they don't play well with others." The idea of wolves howling at the moon may give urban residents a warm and fuzzy feeling, but in these parts it left many people in a cold sweat. "When the wolves come down, I don't sleep the rest of the night," rancher Jean Hutchison told me. Besides causing insomnia, the wolves were increasing Hutchison's labor and costs. She felt obligated to put her livestock indoors at night and buy feed for them; it was just too risky to let them graze in the open. "They impact our economy, our lifestyle, and our very basic right to feel safe and secure in our homes," she said. "Don't we have a God-given right to be top dog? The government has taken that away from us. The wolf is now the top dog."

Hutchison and others in the room were well aware that polls have consistently shown that residents of the Southwest favor the reintroduction. This, the ranchers told me, was precisely the problem: the five counties encompassed by the wolf recovery area made up less than 2 percent of the population of Arizona and New Mexico, so a tiny minority was suffering under the weight of the distant majority's desire to have wolves back in the region. "My rights have been destroyed," Hutchison said, "because some guy sitting on concrete, at a desk in Phoenix, thinks it's romantic that they howl. What if I decided it would be so cool to have rattlesnakes in downtown Phoenix? Maybe I should gather some and put them in their backyards!"

Left unsaid was the fact that most of the land within the city limits of Phoenix is private property. About 95 percent of the wolf recovery area is managed by the federal government and owned by the nation as a whole. That joint custody of national forests is reflected in their management under the multiple-use philosophy, which charges the agency with an often impossible task. The Forest Service is supposed to simultaneously satisfy the needs of ranchers, loggers, miners, ATV riders, wilderness lovers, and a suite of species that sometimes prey on one another, all in habitat hurting from decades of misguided fire, grazing, and logging policies. The ESA is what put wolves on the ground in the Southwest, but the subspecies' ability to thrive would hinge on the government's attitude toward public lands and the ranchers who ran cattle on them. If the government tilted toward the endangered species and its advocates, ranchers would lose either sleep, money, or both, some to the point of abandoning the business. If the government tilted toward the ranchers and continued to constrain the program on their behalf, the wolves would have a hard time ever becoming more than a token presence in the region.

Along the Blue, and in the mountains above the Markses' home, the high tension produced a conflict zone where biologists served as go-betweens. After leaving the Markses' place, I spent some time with one of the peacekeepers as he tracked the Aspen Pack's radio collars with an antenna, much like his counterparts with the Peregrine Fund who were searching for condors. Because the Aspen Pack hadn't killed any livestock, the state-federal wolf team decided a capture was unwarranted, but it couldn't let the wolves keep hanging around people and houses. To avoid a confrontation or stressful relocation, biologists were positioned along the river virtually 24/7, ready to scare off wolves with shouting, noisemakers, and other forms of aversive conditioning. Shawn Farry, the Arizona Game and Fish biologist stationed on the Blue, told me the wolves appeared to be naive about humans and were mostly staying away from of the houses. "When push comes to shove," Farry said, "the animals will lose, so it's in their interest to learn to give people a wide berth."

A month later, the wolves were still too close for comfort for residents along the Blue. The wolf team decided the pack's time was up and captured the animals using leg snares and traps with padded jaws. The wolves were taken back to Ted Turner's Ladder Ranch, then rereleased into the Gila Wilderness of New Mexico. By the summer of 2006, the alpha male and female of the pack had moved their territory and established a den in the nearby Aldo Leopold Wilderness.

––––––

The conflict along the Blue could have been averted altogether if the wolves had been initially released into either the Aldo Leopold or Gila wildernesses, both of which are unpopulated, largely cow-free zones in the Gila National Forest. Accounting for about three-quarters of the recovery area, the Gila National Forest provides some of the best wolf habitat in the region because it has few roads and lots of elk. It makes perfect biological sense to do initial releases in the Gila National Forest, but that is verboten. The federal government can't do any initial releases anywhere in New Mexico, another concession made to ranchers in order to launch the reintroduction. Captive-bred wolves released in Arizona are allowed to wander into New Mexico, and wild wolves that are causing problems are sometimes relocated to that state's Gila National Forest, but as soon as a wolf crosses out of the recovery zone in either state, it can be apprehended and taken into custody.

The perils of the intrusive management style were tragically illustrated when the project's poster wolf, and one of the first 11 released into the wild, died from stress after she was captured. In 1998, wolf number 511, nicknamed Brunhilda, was photographed trotting across a snow-covered forest and wound up on thousands of maps, books, pamphlets, and promotional materials. A yearling when released, Brunhilda became the alpha female of the Francisco Pack, but tragedy followed her as she roamed across the high country. Her first mate died in a vehicle collision near Silver City after the pack was relocated from Arizona to New Mexico. Then Brunhilda's litter of five pups died after being brought back into captivity, possibly because construction near their pen induced stress. A month before Brunhilda died, her second mate was injured during trapping and had to have one of his legs amputated. During her nearly seven years in the wild, Brunhilda was captured three times for violating the boundary rule and once for preying on cattle.

Scientists inside and outside the government who evaluated the reintroduction concluded that the boundary rule ignores basic wolf biology and may actually increase human-wolf conflict. Because wolves are not allowed to disperse naturally across the landscape, they may saturate certain areas that are also home to humans and cows. Since only recaptured wolves can be released into New Mexico, that state winds up being the dumping ground for problem wolves that get too close to people or are charged with strikes, so the prohibition against initial releases in New Mexico may actually make things worse for its residents. As early as 1999, officials with the US Fish and Wildlife Service raised concerns about their own rules and began to draft language to soften the restrictions; the changes were never made. In 2001, a three-member panel of independent scientists led by Paul Paquet, a prominent wolf biologist at the University of Calgary, urged Fish and Wildlife to immediately do away with the prohibition against initial releases into the Gila National Forest. "This is by far the most important and simplest change the Service can make to the existing reintroduction project," the Paquet report said.

Past and current leaders of the wolf team have openly expressed frustration with the restrictions. Dave Parsons, coordinator of the project from 1990 to 1999, told me that when he and other Fish and Wildlife officials initially wrote the rules for wolf removals, they never intended them to be used so frequently to kill and capture animals. Such actions are sanctioned by a part of the ESA that gives officials more flexibility in dealing with reintroduced populations, but any policies based on that provision must further the conservation of the species in question. It took some tortured logic to argue that shooting and incarcerating the wolves was furthering their cause. The rules allowed for the management to be modified as the reintroduction matured. Changes were made, but not in the direction Parsons and others wanted or expected. In 2005, the government made enforcing the three-strikes rule mandatory after local ranchers and Congressman Steve Pearce, a New Mexico Republican, enjoyed a private audience with top Fish and Wildlife officials. "This process is ignoring the science," Parsons said. "It's putting all the emphasis on concerns of livestock interests by issuing decisions that more wolves be taken out, even in the face of a declining population, which violates the ESA's mandate to recover listed species."

In their own five-year review, which was released on the last day of 2005, nearly eight years after the program began, the reintroduction team acknowledged that the self-imposed restrictions were inhibiting the wolf's recovery. The review set in motion a process for possibly changing the rules governing initial releases and boundary violations, but the particulars won't be worked out for years because the government must go through another laborious round of public comment and environmental studies. Judging from the tone of the 14 hearings and 10,000 comments received during the five-year review—suggestions ranged from repealing the ESA and exterminating the wolves to abolishing all hunting and grazing on public lands—the federal government will continue to outrage partisans of all stripes no matter what it does.

The three-strikes policy upset not only environmentalists and other wolf advocates. Ranchers like Loretta Rabenau felt the rule had gaping loopholes. For starters, if a wolf or a pack killed more than one cow in a 24-hour period, it still counted as just one strike. As in a criminal case, the government needed solid proof of a wolf kill to charge the animal with another strike, but such evidence was often impossible to obtain. When the Rabenaus realized the Nantac Pack was killing their cattle, they reported the incident to government investigators who went out to the site and searched for the culprit. In *Rangeland CSI*, experts examine the dirt near a carcass for paw prints, fur, or scat. They measure the bite marks on the remains, look for subsurface hemorrhaging, and try to rule out other possible causes of death, such as accidents, illness, starvation, lightning strikes, or other predators. These investigators, however, don't use fancy software or run DNA tests like their counterparts on television. It's an inexact science at best, and frequently a cow's death can only be qualified as a probable wolf kill. Sometimes ranchers in the Southwest don't even find remains of livestock because their allotments are typically measured in the tens of thousands of acres. For every confirmed kill there may be as many as seven or eight other cows lost to wolves.

Hoping to charge the Nantac Pack with two more strikes, Loretta and William Rabenau crisscrossed their Forest Service allotment in search of dead cows so they could report them immediately. "Six or seven weeks of our summer were just consumed with being on the watch," Loretta said. William, a flight attendant based in Phoenix, took several weeks of unpaid leave (like most ranching families in the Southwest, the Rabenaus must rely on a second source of income to get by). After the third confirmed kill, there were still more delays as the federal government sought to trap the wolves alive rather than shoot them. At the time, environmentalists were hammering Fish and Wildlife because in the preceding two months, five adult wolves and six four-week-old pups had been killed due to trapping and lethal control orders. The half-dozen pups died after they were put in captivity with a pair of "foster parents" and were then eaten by their surrogate father, perhaps because he was agitated by the new surroundings.

The Nantac Pack refused to be captured, so Fish and Wildlife issued a death sentence. A little more than a month after Loretta Rabenau found the first dead calf, a government hunter shot the male wolf to death.

The female wolf, a particularly valuable animal since she contained genes from all three lineages, eluded predator-control agents for nearly three more weeks before she was found and killed. In the end, Loretta believes the pair of lobos claimed eight full-grown cows and five calves, a loss of about $15,000. "That was just two wolves," she said. "If they had been a full pack, they could have wiped us out in one summer during calving season, enough to where we couldn't get back on our feet for years, if at all." Defenders of Wildlife reimbursed the Rabenaus for about three-quarters of their loss, a process Loretta described as fair.

The three-strikes rule also caught up with the Aspen Pack. After being relocated from the Blue River in Arizona to the Gila National Forest in New Mexico, the pack grew to as many as a half-dozen wolves, including four pups. But like so many other families of Mexican gray wolves, the Aspen Pack would soon collide with the constraints imposed upon the recovery program. The Aspen and Durango packs started hanging around the 275,000-acre Adobe-Slash Ranch. The wolves attracted the attention of Mike Miller, a ranch employee who was able to determine their location with a radio antenna that the government had supplied him and other ranchers to help them keep track of the predators. In an interview with John Dougherty of *High Country News*, Miller said he branded a cow that was about to give birth less than a half mile from a wolf den with hopes that the smell of seared flesh would entice the wolves to kill another cow and force the government to remove them, dead or alive. "We would sacrifice a calf to get a third strike," Miller told the paper, though he later recanted his account after federal authorities began to investigate the incident. The Durango Pack took the bait, killed the calf, and led the government to shoot the alpha female. The aroma of seared beef may have also enticed the Aspen Pack, which started to kill cattle on the Adobe-Slash Ranch. Even though the wolves may have been baited by Miller and federal officials knew of the ploy, they still removed the entire Aspen Pack from the wild, consigning the adults to permanent captivity.

There's always lively discussion whenever the wolf reintroduction project holds a public meeting in the Southwest, but nowhere do the tempers flare hotter than in Reserve, a town of about 400 residents that is located in New Mexico's Catron County and surrounded by the Gila National

Forest. Reserve has no stoplights and no love for the federal government. In the early 1990s, as the ESA and other environmental regulations began to tighten restrictions on grazing and logging, Catron County spearheaded a county independence movement that sought to reject dictates about land use emanating from far-off officials in Albuquerque and Washington, DC. This echo of the Reagan-era Sagebrush Rebellion, which sought to put federal lands under state control, was not unlike the assertion of states' rights heard in the 1950s and 1960s as southerners tried to supress educational opportunities and civil rights for blacks. In Catron County, bigger than three eastern states but with about 3,400 residents, the revolt appeared motivated by prejudice against forest rangers, spotted owls, and gray wolves. To intimidate federal workers, the county commission passed a resolution in 1994 urging every household to own a gun, pulling back from an initial proposal to mandate gun ownership since that, after all, would have violated the libertarian ethos. "We want the Forest Service to know we're prepared," a county commissioner said at the time, "even though violence would be a last resort."

On a muggy afternoon in July, with thunderheads beginning to build over the surrounding mountaintops, the opposing sides in the wolf program gathered at Reserve's civic center, which looks like a small airplane hangar. A big exhaust fan at the end of the building provided the only climate control. No one could hear anything with the fan on, so the switch was flipped shortly after the meeting began. As the temperature inside rose, so did the level of rancor.

The first order of business was a report from Eva Sargent of Defenders of Wildlife about the group's compensation program for ranchers who lose livestock to wolves. Sargent told the crowd of three dozen that other environmentalists lampooned her group as Defenders of Livestock when it supported a special designation for wolves under the ESA that would allow for more intensive management. "We did that for two reasons. One, we hoped that would build tolerance. Two, we thought it would be the only way we'd ever get wolves on the ground," she said. "We were right about the second thing, but I'm not so sure about the first." Sargent explained that Defenders of Wildlife had liberalized its payments and was now paying the higher, autumn value of cattle, up to $3,000 a head, for confirmed wolf kills rather than paying for a cow's lower value at the time of the attack. It also now paid 50 percent in cases of probable wolf kills and was trying to head off conflicts by sharing costs with ranchers who erected fences, hired extra cowboys, and took other steps to scare off wolves. In the Southwest, Defenders of Wildlife has made about 40 payments to ranchers totaling more than $106,000; in the Northern Rockies, it has paid out more than $1 million. "Despite all these efforts," Sargent said, "I've never seen a program where trying to give away money is generating more ill will."

That spite surfaced before Sargent was done talking as ranchers in the audience interrupted her and complained about how hard it was to prove a wolf killed a cow. Sargent acknowledged that the program had its shortcomings, then suggested ideas for turning wolves in Catron County from liabilities into assets. In Sweden, for example, reindeer herders get paid money based on the density of the local predator population. "That encourages the ranchers to be more tolerant of the predators, because the higher the count goes, the more compensation they get," she said. In the Northern Rockies, Defenders had tried paying landowners a bonus of $5,000 if they had a wolf den on their property. But this created new conflicts because neighboring ranchers got no money but lots of hungry new wolf pups roaming their land. The problem might be solved if the money were distributed to a community board that could try to allocate the bonus fairly. There was also the prospect of ecotourism. "When ranchers tell me, 'Hell, I see those wolves on my allotment every day,' all I can say is put up a guesthouse," Sargent said. "You'll be rolling in the dough because people will come from across the state." That proposal prompted snickers among the ranchers, then complaints that money from ecotourists wouldn't necessarily benefit the ranchers who were feeding the wolves with their cows. "I don't think the wolf is the issue here. You're all trying to destroy us!" local resident Tom Macnab said to a chorus of amens. "We don't live in Sweden. We live in the United States of America. We're entitled to life, liberty, and the pursuit of happiness. In my opinion, your activities are treasonous!" Just a half hour after it started, the meeting was descending into ad hominem attacks, until an Arizona state official threatened to close the proceedings unless everyone behaved.

The overall financial bite of the Southwest reintroduction program is difficult to gauge because not all wolf kills are documented and it's unknown how many extra hours ranchers spend in the saddle keeping an eye on their cows. As part of the five-year review, an economic consulting firm hired by Fish and Wildlife concluded that ranchers as a whole lost somewhere between $38,650 and $206,290 worth of cows to wolves from

1998 through 2004. The wide range reflects the varying estimates of wolf attacks. At the low end, government officials reported an annual average of five confirmed cases of wolves killing cattle. At the high end, ranchers claimed that 33 cows were lost each year. Even if wolves had killed 33 cows annually, that loss amounted to 0.01 percent of the 34,800 cattle grazing in the recovery area and 2.5 percent of the 1,310 cows and calves that died each year on the range due to illness and other causes.

Ranchers at the Reserve meeting and elsewhere said the economic study lowballed their losses. They did have some valid criticisms: the study was done when the wolf population was less than halfway to the goal of getting 100 animals in the Blue Range recovery area. And in many cases, the costs were borne by a small subset of ranchers like the Rabenaus. Three out of four ranchers in the area run fewer than 100 cattle, so even the loss of a few cows could be significant to an operation of that size. Still, the economic study showed that fears of the wolf bankrupting ranchers were overblown. Even if you accepted the most generous estimate of cattle lost to wolves and accounted for its cascading effects on the regional economy—for example, poorer ranchers buying fewer supplies in local stores—the wolf's annual economic impact was never more than $99,000. Prior to reintroduction, hunting outfitters and state game agencies worried that wolves would kill so many elk and deer that the region's $18 million sporting industry would suffer. An analysis of wolf scat did find that elk made up 73 percent of their prey (cattle accounted for 4 percent), but the review team found no evidence that wolves were depressing game populations. In fact, the state sold more elk permits in the area in 2004 than it did in 1998.

No economic analysis would be complete without also looking at the financial benefits of wolf reintroduction. On that side of the ledger, the review team found that wolf lovers had organized at least 15 tours in the area. The participants surely bought gas, food, and lodging, though the increased revenue wasn't calculated. The project's biggest financial impact was the government spending that filtered through the local economy, boosted output by $1.5 million annually, and generated the equivalent of 31 jobs.

Much of the wrath directed toward the wolves was rooted in hatred of the animal and the predator's ability to impose economic pain on ranchers. But tiny fish and secretive birds had also spurred similar indignation around Reserve. As the meeting progressed, I was reminded that much of the bile flowed from a pool of hatred of a political animal: the big bad federal government. It was a curious complaint in Catron County. The feds had worked for decades to facilitate settlement of the region by exterminating the Apaches, wolves, grizzlies, and jaguars. The despised Forest Service and Bureau of Land Management, which jointly controlled more than two-thirds of the county, had also promoted economic development across the West by subsidizing grazing, mining, and logging on public lands, often with devastating environmental consequences. Even economists from the right end of the political spectrum argued that the government was giving grazing permits to ranchers at below-market rates, letting mining companies extract billions of dollars of precious metals without paying royalties, and selling timber at a loss while building roads for lumberjacks. But all that government aid sure had bred plenty of animus. "Get out and give us more money" is how historian Bernard DeVoto summed up the western philosophy.

Antifederal rhetoric and livestock losses provided more than enough raw meat for attacks on the wolf program. But it was the wolf's purported threat to people's lives, not just their livelihoods, that generated the most hostility in Reserve. Standing before the crowd, Jess Carey, a former sheriff now serving as Catron County's official wolf interaction investigator, said that local children had been traumatized after watching their pets get killed. (The five-year review of the program found that wolves had only killed five dogs across the region.) "A rancher losing a cow is one thing, but having your child with mental problems is something else again," Carey said. "Yes, we live in an area where there are wild animals. But if a lion comes in and guts a dog that the child was just playing with, the mother or father can shoot that lion." Carey told me later that a psychologist he consulted had determined that local children were suffering from post-traumatic stress disorder. The anxiety extended to the parents. "People are having nightmares of a wolf carrying off their one-year-old child," he said. "If and when a wolf attacks one of our children, this program will be over."

A wolf *could* attack a child in Catron County or elsewhere in the recovery zone. Over the millennia, wolves are believed to have killed hundreds of children in Europe and Asia. In Alaska and Canada, as both the human population and protections for wolves have increased, biologists have documented a rise in unprovoked wolf aggression toward humans: from zero cases between 1900 and 1969 to 18 cases between

1969 and 2000, including three instances since 1996 in which children were seriously injured. In 2005, wolves in northern Saskatchewan may have killed a 22-year-old member of a survey crew for an energy exploration company. Some experts believe a black bear was responsible, but if wolves did kill the man, it was the first fatal attack in North America in more than a half century.

Despite these incidents, scientists agree that the risk of being injured or killed by the fang of a wolf is vanishingly small. None of the reintroduced Mexican wolves has made physical contact with a member of the public, let alone injured anyone. The most comprehensive study of wolf attacks, published in 2002 by John Linnell and colleagues, looked across the globe and concluded that most of the incidents over the past four centuries were perpetrated by rabid wolves. Prior to treatment methods pioneered by Louis Pasteur in 1885, such bites were usually fatal. In the 20th century, as rabies waned in the developed world with the spread of vaccines, the number and severity of attacks by rabid wolves declined dramatically. The researchers also found that a large share of attacks were by wolf-dog hybrids. Wolves were most likely to attack if they were cornered, habituated to humans, or living in highly modified environments. Children were the most likely victims. Still, Linnell and his colleagues argued that "wolves are among the least dangerous species for their size and predatory potential." Even though there were about 15,000 wolves in Europe, 40,000 in Russia, and 60,000 in North America (nearly all in Canada and Alaska), the Linnell report concluded that over the past half century, nonrabid wolves had only killed four people in Europe, four in Russia, and none in North America (not including the 2005 attack in northern Saskatchewan).

The Linnell report also noted that other wildlife are involved in far more fatal attacks. Grizzly bears killed 71 people in North America during the 20th century, and mountain lions fatally attacked 17 from 1890 to 2001. On average, nearly five dozen Americans die annually due to bites from snakes, spiders, scorpions, bees, wasps, and hornets. Deer-vehicle collisions injure 29,000 people and kill more than 200. And each year, dogs bite an estimated 4.7 million Americans, injure 800,000, send 386,000 to the emergency room, and kill about a dozen, according to the Centers for Disease Control and Prevention. To be sure, many of these other animals are far more numerous than wolves, so people have much more exposure to the attendant dangers. Even so, it's fair to say that someone has a better chance of dying while driving to wolf country than ending up mauled by the animals.

––––––––––

Driving to my campsite after the Reserve meeting, I turned on the satellite radio to hear what was happening with the war between Israel and Lebanon. The age-old conflict between ranchers and wolves seemed about as tractable as peacemaking in the Middle East. Many ranchers would go to their graves cursing wolves, and the illegal shootings would no doubt continue. Wherever wolves are reintroduced, humans are the number one source of mortality. Despite these challenges, the wolf is in a better situation than most endangered species. The animal's prolific breeding makes it relatively easy to boost its population, and unlike some endangered species, wolves can make a living in a wide variety of habitats, provided there are enough deer, elk, and other prey species. Outside of ranching communities, few species are as popular or have more constituents. In the century since Aldo Leopold shot the wolf in the Apache National Forest, much of the public has become captivated by wolves, and no species better exemplifies the turnaround in our attitudes toward wildlife. The quintessential charismatic megafauna, the wolf will always have interest groups in its corner and far more friends than endangered snakes or bushes.

If there were no ranchers and no cattle in the wolf's habitat, lobos would have little trouble recovering, so the elimination of grazing on these public lands may seem like an obvious solution. Similarly, if the government banned all hunting in California condor country, far fewer birds would eat lead bullet fragments and the species' prospects would be that much brighter. Realistically, neither traditional use of public lands will be ending anytime soon. Easing, if not solving, the rancher-wolf conflict means figuring out a way to get the two species to coexist in reasonable peace, just as protecting condors will hinge on changing hunters' choice of ammo, not hoping the activity will go away. For the foreseeable future, the best hope for *el lobo* is a sort of two-state solution that recognizes both ranchers and wolves as legitimate users of the Southwest's high country.

Some needed reforms are obvious and may be on the way. The boundary rule and the ban on initial releases in New Mexico should be eliminated, as numerous scientists have argued for years. That change, however, could lead to more wolf kills and greater animosity among ranchers, so the government should do its share to reimburse people who lose livestock to reintroduced wolves rather than rely on a conservation group to make the compensation payments. This wouldn't cost much money, especially compared to the more than $1 million the federal government spends each year on the Mexican wolf reintroduction. In the long run, compensation could even *save* tax dollars by staving off expensive litigation to defend the program and accelerating the wolf's recovery to the point where federal involvement is no longer needed. Polls show the compensation idea earns the support of about three-quarters of Arizona and New Mexico residents.

Another strategy backed by some ranchers and environmentalists involves buying out grazing privileges from willing sellers and permanently retiring their allotments. This approach, already applied to some state and federal grazing leases in the West, also has the support of free-market economists who see it as a way to monetize, but not mandate, the public's preference for wolves over cows. As it stands now, the federal government's grazing program expends $115 million more than it receives in revenues from ranchers, according to a 2005 report from the nonpartisan Government Accountability Office. Voluntary buyouts, funded by environmentalists, philanthropists, or the government, could help ranchers retire comfortably, rest the land, reduce conflict with wolves, hasten the animal's recovery, and allow the government to focus on more imperiled species. But Congress has never funded such a program or adopted regulations to facilitate the process. Industry groups for cattle growers have strongly opposed buyout bills, seeing them as the first step toward booting livestock off public land and killing off the ranching culture. They also argue that a rancher holding a permit today shouldn't be allowed to forestall grazing on that government allotment forever. You would think the Bush administration, known for its embrace of markets, would have supported buyouts, but when the Grand Canyon Trust tried to retire leasing on nearly 1 million acres in the Grand Staircase–Escalante National Monument, Bush's Interior Department sought to block the move. The administration received a C– for its efforts in this area from the Property and Environment Research Center, a conservative environmental think tank that favors market-based solutions.

Other innovative approaches make large predators more valuable to local communities if they're kept alive. In northern Mexico, biologists and environmentalists have set up a program, Fotos Felinos, that rewards local residents if jaguars or other cats are found on their land. Using a motion-activated trail camera, the Northern Jaguar Project pays residents for each photo of a wild cat on their property, ranging from $100 for a bobcat to $500 for a jaguar. The idea is to create a self-policing system in which residents view poachers as taking pesos out of their pockets.

Ranchers can do their share to reduce conflicts with the wolf. Proper disposal of dead livestock can prevent depredation since wolves that first scavenge on cattle that have died for other reasons may be more inclined to prey on live cows nearby. The Paquet report recommended that Arizona and New Mexico ranchers either remove livestock carcasses or apply non-toxic chemicals to make them inedible. Federal land agencies, however, argue that they don't have the legal authority to mandate such practices, and even well-meaning ranchers are unlikely to find the remains of all dead cows before wolves do since their allotments are typically so large.

Ranchers can also change how they manage live cows. As a model of progressive husbandry, wolf supporters point to Will and Jan Holder's Anchor Ranch, located about 25 miles to the southwest of the Blue. Will's grandfather used to kill wolves—he's credited with killing the last lobo in the area, around 1932—so Will grew up with plenty of horror stories about the animals. "It was bogeyman kind of stuff," he said. When Will and his wife, Jan, moved back to the family ranch in Greenlee County, they decided to produce organic, grass-fed, "predator-friendly" beef. Just like organic tomatoes, dolphin-safe tuna, and free-range chicken, the Holders' product would use its environmental credentials as a selling point. "We used to ranch like pretty much everyone else and just throw our cattle out there," Will said. "The wolf changed everything for us." To live in peace with *el lobo*, the Holders kept a close eye on their cows, rotated them frequently, and made them herd together so they looked more formidable to predators.

Like other ranchers, the Holders blamed the government for a botched implementation of an inherently controversial program. "We have spent millions reintroducing the wolf to our modern environment," Jan told lawmakers at the 2004 ESA hearing near Mt. Graham, "but we haven't spent one cent reintroducing the ranching community to the wolf." Officials were so bad about communicating with ranchers that Jan had to contact her sister in San Francisco with an old-fashioned radio-phone and ask her to search the Internet for information about where

wolves were being released (the Anchor Ranch is so remote it had neither phone nor Internet service). "There was never one bit of information
passed out to anyone saying how a wolf behaves, what the people out
there should expect, what's normal wolf behavior, what they tend to do,
how they hunt, what to watch out for, that sort of thing," Jan said.

The Holder's predator-friendly beef earned a good deal of press, even
a nationally distributed radio piece by Charles Osgood. But the business
model wouldn't fly. Jan said she had plenty of customers, even though
her product was double the cost of regular beef, but getting the steaks
into their shopping carts was a hurdle too high. A handful of companies
process the vast majority of the nation's beef, so in that supply chain it
would be impossible to differentiate the Holders' cows from those raised
on predator-unfriendly ranches. Independent processors were few and far
between. Jan wrote a book, *How to Direct Market Your Beef*, and travelled
across the country to promote the concept. She and Will threw themselves into the operation, but ultimately they abandoned the business,
pulled most of their cows off the allotment, and moved back to Tucson so
Will could get his nursing degree.

The idea of predator-friendly beef still holds promise, given the
expanding public interest in green products and many consumers' willing-
ness to pay a premium for food that is local, organic, and sustainably produced. In this approach, markets can benefit a species and steer millions of
dollars, voluntarily doled out by consumers, toward less harmful practices.
The larger challenge seems to be changing ranchers' attitudes and their
husbandry. When the Holders started breaking with tradition, Will said
the response from neighbors was "abject hatred." "We've been real fearful
of people doing harm to us or burning down our house," he said. "Part of
me wants to be quiet and stay friends with everyone. Part of me wants to
tell people that if ranching is going to survive it's got to do this. It can't
remain status quo. It's got to evolve and become something new."

17
Battling the Blob

In March 1902, an eight-year-old girl named Caroline Brown posed for the camera while sitting on top of a dead jaguar in downtown Tucson. The male cat, stretched out before a saloon owned by Caroline's father, had forearms measuring 19 inches around. Nearly 10 feet separated the tip of his nose from the end of his tail. William Brown was showing off his recent purchase from two Mexican bounty hunters who had killed the jaguar in the Rincon Mountains, a sky island range rising just east of Tucson that was also once home to wolves and grizzlies. During the hunt atop the Rincons, the cornered jaguar lashed out and killed two hounds before he was forced into a cave, smoked out, and shot. The cat's arrival in Tucson must have generated a buzz in the hardscrabble outpost, and it excited Herbert Brown, a naturalist and owner of the *Arizona Citizen* newspaper who named and advocated for the masked bobwhite quail. "I do not think the habitat of this jaguar (*Felis onca*) has ever been credited to Arizona," Brown told a colleague in a letter accompanying the photo, "but you will I think, agree with me that it is fairly well established."

In 1902, there was little but empty desert in the 25 miles between William Brown's saloon and the cave where the jaguar met his end. Tucson's population was about 7,500, and most of the city's residents lived along the Santa Cruz River, a marshy stream that supported fish, turtles, and enough malarial mosquitoes to force the US Army to relocate its Fort Lowell seven miles to the northeast in 1873. Early settlers or soldiers who continued east from Fort Lowell would have found no roads leading up the 8,664-foot Rincons or the neighboring 9,157-foot Santa Catalinas. The latter range, managed by the Forest Service, was eventually developed and subject to intense fire suppression, setting it up for the catastrophic wildfire seasons of 2002 and 2003. Near the Rincons' summit, little has changed since 1905, when former Tucson mayor and newspaper reporter Levi Manning built a log cabin in the pines where he could escape the summer heat. Manning Camp remains the only place in the Rincons with buildings, and the annual visitation there is measured in the dozens. Protected as part of Saguaro National Park, the forests atop the range are among the healthiest in the Southwest—open, spacious, and carpeted with wildflowers in spring and summer. Why? The National Park Service let wildfires burn, initially by necessity, recently by choice. There is still no private property to defend in the Rincons, and there is still no easy way to get crews to the fire line, short of a helicopter ride.

I made it to the top of the Rincons only once because getting there requires backpacking at least 10 miles one-way and climbing 4,000 feet. The views from that trip have stayed with me. By day, I could see mountains in New Mexico and Old Mexico. After sunset, I climbed a rock outcropping and looked west, down on the Tucson valley. The city lights below twinkled like the Milky Way above, and I felt equidistant between the two. I could see Speedway Boulevard and the city's main thoroughfares, laid out in a checkerboard aligned with the compass points. To the north, the lights grew dimmer and more spread out as denser neighborhoods within the Tucson city limits gave way to the custom-built homes and gated communities that ascend the foothills of the Santa Catalinas. In other directions, the city lights eventually dissipated into the inky darkness of the desert as trailer parks in unincorporated Pima County gave way to state and federal lands that were home only to cattle. The surrounding mountains, protected as a national forest or park, were totally black except for a few red antenna lights blinking.

Tucson's sprawl is staggering when viewed from nearby peaks or through the window of an airliner, even during the daytime. The sharp geometry of development, rooted in parcel maps and aligned with rectilinear roadways, refuses to blend into a landscape with little vegetation to cover up the scars. Seen from above, the hard corners of newly built subdivisions knife into the desert like an arrowhead.

The landscape is the product of the laissez-faire attitude toward development that reigned across the Sunbelt for decades (fig. 21). Local politicians and civic boosters were invariably pro-growth. There always seemed to be another patch of desert available for blading and grading just a few minutes down the road. Such undeveloped parcels on the outskirts were not only cheaper, but also more scenic and "closer to nature"—at least until the next subdivision leapfrogged beyond the last. When I climbed up to Manning Camp in 2002, Pima County's population was growing by about 20,000 annually, heading toward 2 million in 2050, and posing a direct threat to scores of species in one of the nation's pinnacles of biodiversity.

From the top of the Rincons that night, I could follow I-10 as it left Tucson and headed northwest toward Phoenix, a dull orange glow on the horizon. The line of headlamps and taillights on I-10 made it look as if the interstate was an umbilical cord between the parent city and its offspring. Edward Abbey, a Tucson-area resident for many years, likened Phoenix to a tumor and the monstrous amoeba in the movie *The Blob*. "Pink, palpitating and running amok, egged on by the Chamber of Commerce and growing growing ever-GROWING, this thing threatened to devour the planet," Abbey wrote in *The Journey Home*, which included a self-portrait of the author: half man, half vulture.

Phoenix's metastasizing style of growth offered one model for Pima County officials as they grappled with an influx of retiring baby boomers seeking sunshine and with immigrants from Mexico looking for work. Through a steady stream of annexations, the city of Tucson had already mushroomed from 10 square miles in 1953 to 100 square miles in 1981

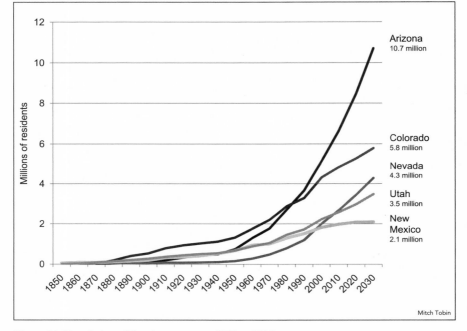

Figure 21: Population of Southwest states, 1850 to 2030.
Source: US Census Bureau.

to nearly 300 square miles today. Paradoxically, Tucson actually got less crowded over time because the city was expanding in size faster than it was growing in numbers: its density fell from about 5,000 people per square mile in the early 1950s to less than half that at the start of the 21st century. If the Pima County Board of Supervisors preserved existing land-use regulations that governed development on the city's periphery, Tucson would be emulating Phoenix. Ten square miles of desert would be bladed each year, and what little streamside habitat was left in the county would be further imperiled. Taking growth as it came would outrage environmentalists and others, but strictly restricting development with a moratorium on permits would enrage builders, prompt lawsuits, scare off potential campaign contributors, and alienate plenty of constituents whose paychecks depended on the growth industry.

Most everyone was unsatisfied with the status quo. "Not another Phoenix" had become a mantra among politicians and the public alike, even conservative Republicans. Liberal Tucsonans gazed longingly at cities like Portland, Oregon, where local governments had drawn urban growth boundaries to corral sprawl, protect open space, and promote denser cities that were less auto dependent. Tucson's business community was also demanding change. For many builders and developers, the regulatory environment was maddening because two diminutive species, the cactus ferruginous pygmy owl and the Pima pineapple cactus, happened to live in the two parts of town that were growing fastest. On the northwest side of Tucson, a handful of pygmy owls had stalled construction of a high school and made it harder for some landowners to develop their property. Toward the end of the 1990s, owl-related restrictions and rising land prices on the northwest side pushed the growth to Tucson's south and southeast sides. But in the flat spots perfect for building, developers found yet another endangered species: the Pima pineapple cactus. Many more battles were looming. Pima County had habitat for 22 listed species, putting it in the 95th percentile of US counties. Local politicians could foresee a succession of developer versus environmentalist train wrecks that would pit new housing against seldom seen plants and animals.

The pygmy owl was in particularly dire straits. Biologists could only count about 40 in all of Arizona, though the birds were more numerous in Mexico. Northwestern Tucson was the owl's stronghold, with a dozen birds recorded there in 1996. There were a handful of owls in the Altar Valley and the Buenos Aires National Wildlife Refuge, where Wayne

Shifflett struggled to recover Chiricahua leopard frogs and masked bob-white quail. There were also a few nests in Organ Pipe Cactus National Monument, where Sonoran pronghorn and lesser long-nosed bats were contending with illegal border crossers. Scientists believed at least some pygmy owls lived in the 100 miles between the Buenos Aires and Organ Pipe, but those 6 million acres were part of the Tohono O'odham Nation, where surveys were precluded without tribal approval.

While biologists had many unanswered questions about the pygmy owl, there was no doubt the birds were far less abundant in Arizona than they were a century ago. Early naturalists routinely found the pygmy owls in the thickets along rivers, nesting in the cavities of cottonwoods. It's unclear whether the birds were also living nearby in upland areas, which ornithologists were less apt to travel and survey. During the 20th century, the pygmy owl's range in Arizona contracted as riparian forests were destroyed, either cut down for firewood, trampled by cattle, killed by nearby groundwater pumping, or starved of water by upstream diversions and dams. Phoenix lost its pygmy owl population by midcentury. In Tucson, the Santa Cruz and Rillito became ghost rivers, their woodlands dying along with the disappearance of their surface flows and the declining water table. But even in riparian habitat that held on, along the San Pedro River and downstream from sewage plants on the Santa Cruz River, the pygmy owls disappeared. Some of the remaining birds found refuge in northwestern Tucson, where irrigated landscaping provided new habitat for the owls and their prey. But by the start of the 21st century, it appeared that the northwest side was a death trap, not a source of new birds for the population. With the new houses came vehicles, pets, and other lethal threats.

The Pima pineapple cactus's prospects weren't much brighter. In 1993, the government listed the species based on a recommendation that the Smithsonian Institution had made 18 years earlier. In the interim, an untold number of Pima pineapple cacti were lost, and the size of the remaining population remains unknown. Surveying for the cacti is notoriously difficult. Because the immature plants are so small, biologists must sometimes crawl on their hands and knees, and it's rare to find more than one cactus per acre. Scientists aren't sure why the cactus is scattered so widely across the desert. Some suspect it keeps its distance from other pineapple cacti because of parasites. Others say it's an adaptation to fire, with the cacti found only where the ground isn't full of flammable grasses. A state-run database includes about 5,500 records of the plants, but just between 1997 and 2003, at least 1,168 of the cacti were destroyed or transplanted because of development.

The pygmy owl and pineapple cactus stood right in the path of the bulldozers and posed the same quandary for Pima County that other cities in the greater Southwest had faced. San Diego, Riverside, and Orange counties; Las Vegas; and Austin, Texas, had all tried to resolve their conflicts by turning to a controversial element of the ESA: the habitat conservation plan, or HCP. The results in those cities weren't necessarily encouraging, but an HCP at least offered Pima County the promise of having it all: a more rational pattern of growth, less conflict over development, and an intact ecosystem that could preserve dozens of sensitive species, some already listed under the ESA, others heading that way. When I surveyed Tucson from the top of the Rincons, Pima County's HCP was beginning to gel. It seemed like the only hope for containing the blob before it totally wrapped around the protected darkness of the Rincons and other mountains nearby.

HCPs trace their roots to a small mountain just south of San Francisco, near the airport. In the early 1980s, endangered butterflies on 1,314-foot San Bruno Mountain thwarted plans for a residential community, leading a group of developers, biologists, environmentalists, and government officials to craft a compromise meant to protect the butterflies while still allowing homes to be built. The 3,500-acre deal, which protected 90 percent of the butterfly habitat and obligated the developers to pay about $60,000 a year on conservation measures, served as a model for Congress as it formally created HCPs in the 1982 amendments to the ESA.

Rather than stop economic activity, HCPs are meant to shape it and strike a balance, however awkward, between development and conservation. These legal deals between Fish and Wildlife and a private party or local government allow a permit holder to kill endangered wildlife and destroy their habitat, provided that the fate of the species isn't jeopardized. In essence, federal regulators say they'll accept "take" of individual animals if it's incidental to otherwise legal activity and if the HCP promotes the overall species' recovery. To improve the species' chances, an HCP often requires that landowners pay a set fee for each acre they disturb or house they build. The proceeds from this fee are then devoted to conservation measures elsewhere, such as protection of valuable habitat. In this way, participating in an HCP is similar to buying a carbon credit to offset emissions. An individual, business, or municipal agency that participates in an HCP doesn't necessarily have to buy land outright and turn it into a preserve or wildlife refuge. That approach is not only expensive on the front end but also saddles the buyer with maintenance costs in perpetuity, not to mention the potential for political fights over how the habitat is managed. Instead, a developer or local government can safeguard important areas by purchasing the development rights to a parcel and retiring them or by paying for a conservation easement that restricts land or water use on the property. HCPs also include a no-surprises guarantee assuring permit holders that if unforeseen circumstances require additional conservation measures, the government will have to provide compensation. The deals can last 30 or 50 years, even longer.

It took a decade for HCPs to take off. Initially, developers and businesses found that creating a plan could be too costly, time consuming, complicated, and contentious. The whole point of creating an HCP was to avoid those problems, so by the time Bill Clinton entered the White House in 1992, Fish and Wildlife had only approved 14 HCPs in 10 years. Several high-profile ESA fights prompted Interior Secretary Bruce Babbitt to dramatically expand the use of the tool. In 1993, listing of the California gnatcatcher, a small migratory songbird, halted home building in the coastal sage scrub between San Diego and Los Angeles, one of the fastest-growing areas of the state. Stories about stalled subdivisions and out-of-work contractors began to attract the attention of Babbitt's boss. "The inquiries from the White House political staff started flowing in," Babbitt would later recall. "Was I aware that the president had carried California's fifty-four electoral votes on the way to victory in 1992 and that he would be needing them again for reelection in 1996?"

Recovering the gnatcatcher could put thousands of acres of high-priced private real estate permanently off-limits to development. And it might only be the first in a daisy chain of clashes between the ESA and Southern California's sprawl. Any number of declining species in the region, which boasted an exceptional combination of habitats, could be the next to stand in the way of the graders and excavators.

California was more environmentally minded and ready to work with the feds than most other western states, but like local governments across the nation, San Diego and Orange counties were hesitant about using their zoning powers to restrict new developments. The ESA, by effectively imposing a moratorium on building, brought the parties to the table with a strong motivation to work out a deal. It was the ESA that served as the crucial catalyst for the kind of urban and regional planning that had been sorely lacking in Southern California for decades. In Orange County, a single landowner, Donald Bren and his Irvine Company, owned much of the valuable habitat. Babbitt met personally with Bren, choosing a Phoenix hotel so as not to attract media attention, and in 1996 Orange County signed on to an HCP that preserved more than 30,000 acres. In San Diego, there were far more players. After several years of public input and scientific studies, Fish and Wildlife blessed HCPs for the city and county of San Diego. These plans, while motivated by the gnatcatcher, were designed according to the needs of more than 100 species, some already listed as endangered, others headed that way without intervention. Developers had to either set aside a portion of their land or purchase habitat elsewhere.

There aren't many developers who are anxious to pay more fees to the government. Yet many around the nation have embraced the HCP process because it provides regulatory certainty and lets them complete their projects. In many communities, builders already fork over impact fees to local governments in order to make growth pay its own way. Such levies fund construction of the new roads, sewers, libraries, and schools that new homes and residents demand. With HCPs, the per-acre or per-home payments are akin to a biodiversity impact fee. For businesses, paying into such a fund is usually less costly and uncertain than negotiating directly with Fish and Wildlife, especially if the HCP covers a variety of species. Such a multispecies HCP can therefore offer developers one-stop shopping for their regulatory approvals and an umbrella protection against species-related restrictions. Rather than deal with the Fish and Wildlife Service on a project-by-project and species-by-species basis, property owners can simply go to the planning department, get their permit, and get to work if the entire county is covered by the HCP.

HCPs can employ a variety of other tools, with considerable discretion left up to the entity submitting the plan for approval. A local government can put a ceiling on the amount of development in an area through the issuance of building permits, then allow private parties to buy and sell those permits in a market. This is similar to the cap-and-trade program that reduced acid rain in the United States and the system that could limit greenhouse gas emissions. HCPs can also restrict how landowners develop their property by forcing them to set aside some portion of the parcel.

Pima County's decision to pursue an HCP was part of a gradual greening of its board of supervisors. In 1996, a Democratic neighborhood activist was elected to the board, and a year later an environmentally minded Republican was appointed after another supervisor died, giving greens a majority that was sympathetic to their concerns. County officials began to work on the HCP in 1998, and a year later the supervisors shot down a proposed 6,000-home subdivision near the retirement community of Green Valley, the first defeat of a major rezoning in a quarter century. Two years later, the board approved a scaled-back plan for the development that allowed for 2,200 homes but left 81 percent of the former ranch preserved as open space.

In 2000, the Sierra Club and others succeeded in getting an antisprawl initiative on the ballot that was modeled after the Oregon urban growth boundary. Surveys showed that most Arizona voters wanted something done about sprawl, but the measure was trounced at the polls as developers and home builders spent millions of dollars in opposition and flooded the airwaves with negative ads. Babbitt thought much of the problem was the messenger: voters didn't consider the Sierra Club a reliable guide on growth issues, and the initiative's backers couldn't effectively counter charges that the measure would cripple the state's economy. "Uncomprehending as a mule being whacked with a two-by-four," Babbitt wrote, "those on the environmental side seemed unable to absorb the lesson: open space proposals that can be stigmatized as limiting growth are not likely to succeed."

As Pima County officials, their consultants, and the various interest groups were grappling with how to structure their HCP, the *Arizona Daily Star* sent me to Austin and Las Vegas, and my colleague Tony Davis to San Diego. Our assignment: bring back lessons from those cities' experiences using HCPs to manage sprawl.

In no cases did Davis or I find that an HCP had wrecked or even dented the local economy, nor had any of the plans impeded steady population growth. Developers, home builders, and others in the business community appeared to be the winners: the HCPs created regulations that were predictable and costs that were easy to calculate. There was better coordination among different levels of government, and landowners could finally get maps showing them where it was okay to turn dirt. To be sure, some landowners in all three cities saw their property values decline as speculative purchases didn't pan out, but plenty of others enjoyed huge windfalls when neighboring parcels were preserved as open space. For city and county officials, the HCPs allowed the community to develop a bottom-up plan that covered a multitude of species, rather than suffer under the weight of the federal bureaucracy while fighting one single-species battle after another. For environmentalists, HCPs offered some benefits: they went beyond single-species management, they gave conservation groups a seat at the table, and they included a way to pay for habitat preservation, typically through impact fees or open-space bonds. Still, many environmentalists viewed the process with suspicion, then remorse, because the plans seemed to do more to facilitate growth than to slow it.

For the endangered species they were meant to protect, the HCPs offered some help, but not necessarily enough. Preserves were made too small. Financing for land purchases was shaky. Little monitoring was done to see if the HCPs were working. When the *Seattle Post-Intelligencer's* Robert McClure and Lisa Stiffler examined nearly 100 HCPs across the nation in a series titled License to Kill, they found the same problems Davis and I discovered. While no species covered by an HCP has gone extinct, McClure and Stiffler concluded that many plans were plagued by incomplete science, inadequate public involvement, and insufficient funding. Even on San Bruno Mountain near San Francisco, the very first HCP had failed to create as much butterfly habitat as promised, and its $37 per year levy on homeowners had not generated enough money to tackle an invasive weed problem. In the Southern California desert, a three-month investigation by the Riverside *Press-Enterprise* found serious problems with that community's 240-square-mile 146-species conservation plan. "In case after case," the paper concluded, "city and county officials have approved homes, stores and industry on land they had identified as essential habitat."

The main argument against HCPs is that the quid pro quo they establish invariably favors developers over critters. In San Diego, for instance, Davis found that areas identified for protection by biologists were lost after developers exerted pressure on local officials. In many ways, the HCP had come too late in the region's evolution. Highways were already built and subdivisions were already approved. Scientists were also forced to perform triage because some valuable habitat cost more than $750,000 an acre and was simply too expensive to protect.

The San Diego HCP also exposed a fundamental drawback in the process after the 2003 wildfires destroyed hundreds of homes, killed 14 people, and gave a critical push to the Bush administration's Healthy Forests Initiative. When Fish and Wildlife approves an HCP, it promises the permit holder that no new regulations will be imposed to benefit a listed species, the no surprises policy. But nature is all about surprises and shocks to the system, what scientists call stochastic events. Ideally, an HCP will be developed with such dynamism in mind. Water holes will dry up. Rivers will flood. Forests will burn. In October 2003, a series of wind-whipped wildfires in Southern California scorched nearly 27,000 acres of Californian gnatcatcher habitat, plus thousands more acres critical to the recovery of the endangered mountain yellow-legged frog and least Bell's vireo. Even though those areas were no longer suitable for the various endangered species, the developers and local governments that paid for the parcels weren't forced to protect additional habitat to make up for the loss.

In Austin, fifth in the nation for population growth in the 1990s, wildfires also threatened to destroy some of the open-space preserves that were created through the Balcones Canyonlands Conservation Plan. After laboring to raise money to buy habitat for the golden-cheeked warbler and the black-capped vireo, two migratory songbirds, Austin officials struggled to manage the forested hill country and protect the birds from fires, pets, mountain bikers, nonnative hogs, an excess of deer, and other threats. As the digital economy in Austin and surrounding Travis County boomed in the 1990s, homes and businesses quickly surrounded many of the islandlike preserves created by the HCP. Most biologists I interviewed thought the preserve system was made far too small as ecological concerns were pushed aside by economic interests. Scientists originally recommended a preserve of 60,000 to 120,000 acres, but that got whittled down to 30,428 acres. The fragmentation of habitat also created so-called edge effects that diminished the value of what little bird habitat remained. Fence off a wildlife preserve, and the land just inside the perimeter is vulnerable to incursions by invasive plants and bird-hungry cats, just as the outer edge of a protected old-growth forest is subject to more damage from winds sweeping across the surrounding clear-cut.

Many Austin residents cheered the preservation of green spaces. Still, humans and the preserves didn't always make for good neighbors. As he showed me around one rainy afternoon, Don Koehler, manager of the city's portion of the preserves, told me that residents loved the open spaces so much that they dug barbecue pits, erected tree houses, and extended their patios within the habitat. Real-estate ads promoted nearby preserves, "so the inference is it's open for you to play in," Koehler said. In an example of the conflict, local mountain bikers were outraged when a prized riding area was put off-limits by city officials, who said cyclists were blazing new trails, chopping down trees, and cutting metal fences with power saws.

Setting aside tracts of land for wildlife in a city or suburb costs something up front, but it can also generate plenty of economic value in return, as I learned in Austin. Protecting open spaces for species creates local amenities and almost always boosts property values for neighbors of a preserve. During my visit to the Texas Hill Country, I found concrete evidence of that as I walked through the aptly named Grandview Hills subdivision. While standing on his deck, media executive Hugh LeVrier pointed to hundreds of acres of rolling forests behind him and told me, "What made us choose this house was that—period." LeVrier had paid about $420,000 for his 3,000-square-foot home. He could have bought nearly the same house across the street for $75,000 less, but the view wasn't as impressive. Economists have measured this positive effect by comparing similar houses at varying distances from a park using a technique called hedonic regression, which sounds like fun but is actually a run-of-the-mill tool in real estate appraisals. In Boulder, Colorado, researchers concluded that homes adjacent to a greenbelt were one-third more expensive than comparable houses 3,200 feet away. In Tucson, University of Arizona economists surveyed more than 25,000 homes near a desert wash and found that houses within a half mile of the thickly forested riparian area sold for 3 to 6 percent more and generated an extra $103 million in value.

Elsewhere in the Southwest, I found little evidence of habitat protections bankrupting local economies. In Las Vegas, an HCP inspired by the desert tortoise did nothing to stop America's fastest-growing metropolitan area from continuing to boom. Bulldozers in Sin City can steamroll the tortoises thanks to an HCP that covers 78 other species and 5.5 million acres in Clark County. The plan basically casts off the Las Vegas valley in exchange for protecting the tortoise in outlying areas with the proceeds from a $565-per-acre development fee. The revenues also fund a tortoise-relocation program that depends on a telephone hotline to scoop city-dwelling tortoises out of harm's way.

Las Vegas once faced a conundrum similar to Tucson's. The tortoise's emergency listing in 1989, largely due to the spread of a serious respiratory illness, raised fears of an economic implosion. Developers and activists squared off in court and in person. After an unsuccessful legal battle to kill the listing, Las Vegas builders agreed to spend several million dollars on a tortoise relocation facility and became a driving force behind the HCP. The Las Vegas plan freed up 418,200 acres for development and appears to have done more to promote growth than constrain it. Because nearly 90 percent of Clark County is federal land, the Las Vegas HCP depends on getting federal officials to manage their property with the tortoise in mind. Limits have been placed on off-road vehicle use, and money from developers' $565-per-acre fee has purchased grazing leases on federal lands, funded additional law enforcement, and purchased fencing to keep tortoises from getting squashed on roads. Some environmentalists I spoke to had stuck with the process for more than 15 years, but many thought the per-acre fee was a pittance and argued that federal land managers still weren't doing enough to protect tortoises. "Compromise isn't the answer," said Betty Burge, a biologist who founded Tortoise Group. "We're trying to catch up from what's happened for years, so you have to overcompensate."

Many of the plan's other participants also had misgivings, but the HCP did forge some unlikely alliances. When Clark County began to draft its HCP, the situation was so contentious that a metal detector was installed at the entrance to the meetings. "Each side believed the other was out to get 'em," recalled Ann Schreiber, who started out representing mining interests. Thirteen years after the process began, I found Schreiber running a grassroots program to protect endangered fish in the Moapa Valley, population 1,200 and seemingly much farther than 60 miles northeast of the Las Vegas Strip. Money for the stream restoration was coming from the fee that builders pay to blade desert. Full of nonnative tamarisk, the Muddy River was on the road to being declared critical habitat for the Moapa dace and the Virgin River chub. In a land where the country store sold bobcat pelts beside the beef jerky, residents feared the fish would disrupt the rural economy. Unwilling to see the federal government control their destiny, Schreiber and others went to work removing tamarisk and restoring the stream's habitat to ward off added regulation. Schreiber still faulted the HCP for harming the interests of miners like her ex-husband, but she now counted an environmentalist as a friend. "I don't consider I've turned a real dark shade of green," she told me, "or that she's lightened up a whole lot. We just understand each other a lot better."

———

The experiences in San Diego, Austin, Las Vegas, and elsewhere guided Tucson-area environmentalists, landowners, and government officials as they began crafting an HCP for Pima County. Early on, county supervisors endorsed an expansive vision for the Sonoran Desert Conservation Plan, or SDCP, that would not only immunize the community against further ESA conflicts but also preserve its ecological integrity, cultural artifacts, historic ranches, and scenic vistas. Chuck Huckelberry, the county administrator who had once laid out new roads to support growth while serving as public works director, became a strong backer of the SDCP, both for its promise of an environmental détente and its potential to keep the county budget from exploding. Pima County estimated that each new home in an unregulated "wildcat" subdivision on the outskirts would sock taxpayers with $23,000 in additional costs as the county provided services to those residents. By steering growth toward Tucson's urban core and making it harder to develop outlying parcels, the SDCP could reduce the need for the county to build more roads, libraries, sheriff's substations, and health clinics.

One of Huckelberry's critical first moves was to erect a "firewall" around the SDCP's science team and insulate it from political pressure as the group determined which species to focus on. The team, which included academic, government, and private sector scientists, cast a wide net and picked 200 species of concern out of more than 12,000 possibilities. Then they filtered out all the animals that lived in habitat outside the county's control. For example, the Mexican spotted owl was dropped since the bird was only found in the Rincons, Santa Catalinas, and other sky islands that were managed by the US Forest Service and the National Park Service. Also excluded were species that were declining in Pima County but not at risk overall, and species for which conservation was best done elsewhere.

Including more species in the SDCP would seem to guarantee more headaches for developers, and many in the business community were early critics of the process, feeling it was too dominated by environmentalists. But other southwestern conservation plans had included dozens of species that weren't threatened or endangered, often at the behest of developers seeking more regulatory certainty. Austin covered 9 listed and 26 nonlisted species; San Diego dealt with 26 listed and 59 nonlisted species; Las Vegas's Clark County had 2 listed and 77 nonlisted species. After several years of work, Pima County's science team recommended protecting 55 species, including the pygmy owl, Pima pineapple cactus, and several other animals described in this book: the jaguar, Sonoran pronghorn, lesser long-nosed bat, masked bobwhite quail, Chiricahua leopard frog, and southwestern willow flycatcher.

The list of 55 species guided scientists as they determined which parts of the county should be preserved and which should be developed. Using GIS mapmaking technology, scientists plugged in the species' requirements and plotted suitable habitat, then layered the maps on top of one another. If a piece of land had suitable habitat for three or more species, though didn't necessarily contain the creatures themselves, it became a target for protection. Some hot spots, particularly riparian areas, provided habitat for more than a dozen species and would be the top priorities for protection.

The county also emphasized preservation of the wildlife corridors that connect the Rincons, Santa Catalinas, and other mountains, a strategy that will prove even more critical as climate change causes species to shift their ranges. One such corridor, just south of where I climbed the Rincons, became known as the Missing Link. Serving as a bridge to another sky island, the 9,453-foot Santa Ritas, the Missing Link helped connect the high country of the American Southwest with Mexico's Sierra Madre, much like the Peloncillo Range, where Warner Glenn photographed the jaguar. The Missing Link's thousands of acres of high desert and grasslands were both an ecological choke point and prime real estate on the edge of Tucson. With enough protection, the Missing Link could serve as a pathway for bears, mountain lions, and other animals. It could even provide a route for a wild jaguar traveling north or a reintroduced Mexican gray wolf heading south, should those endangered species ever reach the area. When I looked down on the Missing Link from the top of the Rincons in 2002, the landscape was still black, dark enough, it seemed, for a lobo or *el tigre* to make it through. But it was all too easy to envision the lights from nearby Tucson bleeding into the empty space, guided there by the thin vein of headlamps on I-10.

The Missing Link was just one of many worthy candidates for protection. The county might also devote its resources to safeguarding rare wetlands jeopardized by overpumping of groundwater, craggy volcanic ranges with desert bighorn sheep, or ironwood forests with a cornucopia of birds. How to decide? Huckelberry and the supervisors wanted to let science be their guide, but they also had to temper biologists' wish lists with a respect for property rights and the plan's price tag. To build consensus behind the SDCP, the supervisors appointed about 80 stakeholders to a steering committee, roughly one-third builders and developers, one-third environmentalists and neighborhood activists, and one-third ranchers and private property advocates. To give the group something to talk about, the county paid millions of dollars to consultants and called upon the good graces of hundreds of experts to produce more than 16,000 maps and 250 technical reports. Simply assembling this mass of data on the county's biological resources was a major, lasting achievement that garnered several awards.

Over a period of years, and after a dizzying number of meetings, the county created an HCP that focused on some 600,000 acres, mostly on the periphery of Tucson. The number of vulnerable species was narrowed to 36, but rivers and streams continued to receive the most protection since they were crucial to the fate of so many plants and animals. In all, the county would protect about 242,000 acres over a 30-year period through land purchases and acquisition of grazing leases and development rights. Nearly 67,000 acres would likely be developed.

Rather than create a per-acre or per-home fee, Pima County relied on its zoning power to restrict how ecologically valuable land could be used. In general, the plan didn't affect a parcel's existing zoning, but it did make it much harder, if not impossible, for landowners to rezone their property to a more intensive use. Landowners within the biological reserve could still build on their property, but they might only be allowed to use a fraction of their land. Long before Pima County submitted its HCP to federal officials, it reduced housing density on 46,000 acres by amending its comprehensive land-use plan. It also spent millions to either buy ranchland on the city's outskirts or pay for conservation easements that would prevent the open space from being broken up.

By the time the SDCP was drafted, pygmy owls were already on the brink of disappearing from northwestern Tucson. Rather than sink scarce resources into a losing battle and a neighborhood where land prices were steep, the county wrote off patches of owl habitat there, over the objections of some environmentalists, and chose to protect even more land farther from town, where land prices were cheaper. Each acre of potential owl habitat in northwestern Tucson might cost $50,000, 10 times what the county would pay for equally valuable parcels in the Altar Valley or elsewhere.

The SDCP also wound up forsaking Pima pineapple cactus habitat on the city's southern fringes and instead focused on protecting the plants elsewhere. In some cases, an undeveloped parcel on Tucson's southeast side contained habitat for none of the target species, except the pineapple cactus. It therefore made sense to sacrifice those properties, which were typically close to existing developments, and use the money instead to preserve other parts of the county that were less expensive to protect and held a greater number of sensitive species.

Around Tucson, some developers could avoid the pineapple cactus entirely by taking care with the alignment of roads and homesites, especially if it was a high-end project featuring large lots. With more-modest developments, home builders could purchase credits in a conservation bank to offset their impact. I went to one of those projects with photographer David Sanders so we could photograph the cacti before they were moved. The 19-acre subdivision, located across the street from a golf course, would have 72 homes. Unfortunately for the developer, the land also contained 64 pineapple cacti. It was one of the densest concentrations ever recorded, but if the plants hadn't been flagged with fluorescent tape, Sanders and I would have never found them on the desert floor, which was littered with crushed beer cans and broken bottles. The cacti were so small and inconspicuous that Sanders had to lie on his belly right next to them in order to shoot photos. To get the project built, Canoa Homes spent $35,000 to buy seven acres of cactus habitat from a conservation bank located in the Altar Valley, near the Buenos Aires National Wildlife Refuge. Canoa Homes president John Shorbe Sr., head of the Southern Arizona Homebuilders Association at the time, told me the conservation bank could be a useful tool, but he still bemoaned his snail's pace dealings with the government. Protecting the cactus on-site forced Canoa Homes to scale back the project by five lots and incur another

$50,000 in costs for surveys and consultants. Divide the total cost of dealing with the cactus, $85,000, by 72 lots and the cost per home comes to $1,181. "These costs will be pushed on straight to the homeowners," Shorbe told me. "For that, a homeowner would much rather put in an upgraded carpet or sound system."

In exchange for the payment from Canoa Homes, the Palo Alto Ranch conservation bank agreed not to develop the seven acres and put some of the money toward monitoring and erosion control. Conservation easements prevented the land from ever being developed, even if the ranch was sold. Ross Humphreys, a Tucson publisher who paid $2 million for the ranch, said that without the conservation bank in place, homes could be built on much of the 1,400 acres, and probably without the federal nexus needed to trigger an ESA consultation. Humphreys and his wife, Susan Lowell, didn't apologize for trying to make money from the bank, though they doubted it would ever be very profitable. "No margin, no mission," Lowell told me. She and Humphreys said that novel approaches like conservation banks were essential for saving biodiversity. "There's not enough money in the world to protect all of the open space in public and private hands today," Humphreys said. "We believe—to our toes—that private citizens can be a cost-effective solution to open-space protection."

One advantage of a conservation bank is that it can give landowners a financial incentive to create habitat for an endangered species and bolster its numbers. By doing so, a conservation banker can sell more credits and make more money. In the Southeast, where economists have found that ESA restrictions induce timber companies to preemptively harvest forests suitable for the red-cockaded woodpecker, conservation banks have turned the birds into a moneymaker for timber companies. Fish and Wildlife and the landowner agree on a target number for breeding pairs and if the business meets that target, it's free to use the land as it sees fit. If biologists find additional nests on the property, the company is allowed to sell credits to other landowners for about $100,000 per pair. The land that's most valuable to the woodpeckers can therefore make more money for the timber company if it's preserved rather than reduced to pulp or two-by-fours.

Conservation banks offer other potential benefits. First, they can capture economies of scale by conserving large blocks of contiguous habitat. With the Pima pineapple cactus, that approach is essential because the plant is so widely distributed. Second, conservation banks can spur owners of the land to improve habitat so they can sell more credits, the kind of proactive conservation that the ESA has done little to encourage. The law generally doesn't compel landowners to help species; it merely commands them to avoid harm. Third, conservation banks, and HCPs in general, can protect habitat that is currently unoccupied by a species but suitable for its eventual return or establishment. This is crucial because an endangered species generally won't recover unless it's spreading into unoccupied habitat.

Conservation banks have their limits and downsides. They're only feasible if development pressure creates a base of potential customers for the credits. And there won't be much demand for those credits if Fish and Wildlife doesn't aggressively enforce the ESA. Fish and Wildlife also must ensure that developers don't get off too easy when they buy into a conservation bank. It's one thing if developers are paying a handsome fee in exchange for destroying a small, relatively unimportant population of a listed species, and quite another if they pay peanuts to wreck habitat that is crucial to the species' survival.

On their own, Pima County officials were able to promote conservation banks and other measures, but to fulfill the SDCP's promise, they would need to enlist the general public's support. Money, perhaps a half-billion dollars over the next half century, would be required to purchase some parcels and place conservation easements on others. Raising taxes directly was off the table, and the county budget was already overcommitted. In need of a new, dedicated funding source, the county turned to open-space bonds and backers of the SDCP were politically savvy in marketing the package. Rarely was the phrase *endangered species* used in promoting the ballot measure, which was paired with five other bond questions. In all, voters would be deciding on $732 million worth of public works, including popular projects like widening roads and buying better radios for first responders. To give the SDCP's open-space bonds an even greater chance of passing, the county linked them on the ballot with bonds to support land acquisition around Davis-Monthan Air Force Base that were meant to reduce residential encroachment and insulate the facility during the next round of base closures.

A bond election in May doesn't attract many Pima County voters, but the 22 percent who turned out were convinced that the new debt was worth assuming. On May 18, 2004, they supported the $174 million open-space package by a margin of nearly 2 to 1. After decades of doing little to control growth or insulate rare species from Tucson's outward expansion, local voters finally decided it was time for a new way forward. Before the HCP was developed, planners assumed Pima County would absorb 100,000 new residents by 2020 in outlying, unincorporated areas. With the SDCP in place, that figure would drop to 17,250. Most of the other new residents are expected to live inside the city limits of Tucson, Oro Valley, Sahuarita, and other urbanized areas where the ecological impacts of development won't be as great. Maeveen Behan, the county official in charge of the SDCP, summed it up this way: "Pima County is out of the growth business."

———————

The SDCP put Pima County on a more sustainable path, but just up I-10, neighboring Pinal County seemed to be embracing sprawl. Before Arizona's real estate market imploded, Pinal was the nation's second fastest-growing county (fig. 22). Eventually, planners project that Phoenix and Tucson will connect in Pinal County and form a "Sun Corridor" with 10 million residents along I-10.

The prospect of Tucson and Phoenix merging may seem like an environmental nightmare, but if I had to pick a place to put 10 million people in Arizona, the desert along I-10 from Tucson to Phoenix would be my first choice. Much of the landscape has already been converted into agricultural fields that may guzzle more water than the homes that will replace them. And there's already an aqueduct between Tucson and Phoenix, the Central Arizona Project, that will allow much of the new growth to be served by the Colorado River, a renewable if not secure supply.

The merging of Tucson and Phoenix will carry its own ecological costs and will probably give birth to a new generation of ESA conflicts. Pinal County's pygmy owl may be the Tucson shovel-nosed snake, which is heading toward listing due to work by herpetologist Phil Rosen and others. Employing its spadelike nose, this nocturnal snake moves by "swimming" under or on top of loose desert soil. Its favored habitat, sandy flatlands, is exactly the type of land that home builders prize. Once reasonably abundant around Tucson (hence the name), the subspecies was last sighted in Pima County in 1979. Most of its remaining habitat lies right between Tucson and Phoenix, including many parcels slated for large-scale subdivisions. The snake is covered by the proposed HCPs in both Pima County and the town of Marana, so the listing's impact may be

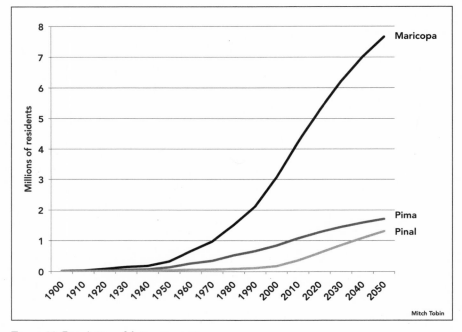

Figure 22: Population of Arizona counties.
Source: Arizona Department of Economic Security.

slight around Tucson. But in Pinal County, where the Phoenix and Tucson blobs will meet, time-consuming surveys for the snake and habitat protections could slow and stop plenty of projects. "Legally," Rosen told the *Tucson Citizen*, "it's right in the path of where every environmentally unfriendly developer would hope to build seas of tile roofs." Perhaps that conflict will inspire Pinal County, which has historically had its head in the sand when it comes to growth, to develop an HCP that sets aside the land for the shovel-nosed snake and other species.

Growth in Arizona and the rest of the Southwest is inevitable. Each year, a new cohort of baby boomers will retire, and many will seek out a warm, sunny place to live out their days. Immigration, legal and otherwise, will further swell the region's population. The challenge for Tucson, Phoenix, and other cities in the Southwest is not to stop growth but to direct development away from ecologically sensitive areas where imperiled species live. Ultimately, HCPs like the one pursued by Pima County are probably the best we can hope for in a world where human desires invariably outweigh the needs of rare plants and animals. If you use the loss of individual animals or acres of habitat as a metric, HCPs will always measure up short. With the Pima pineapple cactus, for instance, the SDCP identified about 141,000 acres of valuable habitat and predicts that nearly 40 percent will be lost to development in the next 30 years. To some that may sound like a raw deal for the cactus, but given the expected population growth in southern Arizona and the ESA's weak protections for plants, the county's ability to keep bulldozers off 60 percent of the cactus habitat is no small feat.

The prospects for Arizona's pygmy owls appear increasingly grim. When the species was listed in 1997, there were only a couple dozen birds in the entire metropolitan area, so any effort to save the species was star-crossed from the start. By the time county voters approved the $174 million in open-space bonds in 2004, there were just a handful of the birds left in northwestern Tucson. A few years later, there were none. The SDCP could have done more to preserve those owls by purchasing more habitat in the neighborhood. But every dollar spent in northwestern Tucson could have bought even more habitat on the outskirts of the city.

Once the SDCP is approved by Fish and Wildlife, it will last for 30 years, a period in which several hundred thousand more people will make Pima County their home. Were I to climb atop the Rincons three decades from now, assuming I can still walk, I have no doubt that the city lights will have spread even farther into the desert and consumed more darkness. It's unavoidable unless we do away with our system of private property rights or have the Arizona Highway Patrol blockade the entrances to the state. With the SDCP in place, at least the growth will be smarter and tempered by concern for the jaguar, pygmy owl, Pima pineapple cactus, Tucson shovel-nosed snake, and dozens of other species that make southern Arizona unique. Will it be enough to prevent those plants and animals from blinking out? As long as there are still places like the Rincons where species can take refuge, and as long as science continues to guide our decision making, we'll at least have a fighting chance at keeping the blob in check.

18
Damn the Dam?

We survived the Ice Age floods and droughts when the river was low
But the trouble really started when the Bureau built the dam, 36 years ago…
The only way the barons of water and power in the Colorado Basin states
Want to see us is filleted on a sesame bun with tartar sauce on their plates.

"Songs of the Humpback Chub,"
Words and music by Larry E. Stevens

For millions of years, the flow of the Colorado River was as uneven as the topography of its 240,000-square-mile watershed. Every spring, snow and ice would begin to thaw in the forested high country of the Colorado Rockies and Wyoming's Wind River Range, giving birth to countless nameless rivulets of water that would merge into brooks, creeks, streams, and rivers. Coursing through Utah's burnt orange canyonlands, the torrent would scour sandstone and turn the water a chestnut color. To describe a river they saw as reddish, Spanish explorers used the word *colorado*. In northern Arizona, flows occasionally topped 100,000 cubic feet per second, meaning that every minute, more than 45 million gallons of wild water were whisked through the bottom of the Grand Canyon, helping carve the depths of the chasm down to 1.7 billion-year-old bedrock.

By the time the Colorado reached the Virgin River, near modern-day Las Vegas, the snowmelt had dropped more than two miles in elevation from the glaciers and snowfields at its headwaters to a desert where three inches of rain fell in an average year. Hooking to the south, the river searched for the sea along the border of Arizona and California, worming its way through craggy chocolate-colored mountains, spilling over its banks when it wanted to, and navigating through sand dunes made of silt the river had deposited over the eons. In Mexico, the Colorado splayed out into a fan-shaped, swampy delta that covered hundreds of thousands of acres. As the river emptied into the Gulf of California, it created a tidal bore, a wavelike mass of water that would swell a dozen feet high then flow south and ebb north in synchronicity with the rhythms of the tides and lunar cycle.

In 1922, Aldo Leopold and his brother explored the Colorado's delta by canoe. It was a decade before construction of Hoover Dam began an era of civil engineering that would rival Egypt's pyramid building. In the delta, the Leopolds roasted quail over mesquite campfires and climbed cottonwoods to scout the river's path to the sea. "On the map," Leopold wrote, "the Delta was bisected by the river, but in fact the river was nowhere and everywhere, for he could not decide which of a hundred green lagoons offered the most pleasant and least speedy path to the Gulf. So he traveled them all, and so did we." The river was too muddy to drink, the lagoons too brackish, so the Leopold brothers dug shallow wells. To see if they had hit sweet water, they would lower their dog into a hole by his hind legs and wait to see if he drank freely. Leopold recorded clouds of waterfowl, bobcats fishing for mullet, and families of raccoons munching on water beetles.

The Colorado, blasting through the Grand Canyon in spring like a freight train, was typically tame by fall. It might be trickling at a few thousand cubic feet per second in places where it had been a ferocious flood just a few months before. The snowmelt was long gone, rains from the summer monsoon had played out, and week after week of sunny skies had come to dominate the Colorado Plateau. The river water, once near freezing, was now a lukewarm 80 degrees. Winter storms would periodically inject some life into the river, but it would not be until the spring thaw that the Colorado would once again turn into a muddy monster. The cycle repeated, year after year, millennium after millennium.

The Colorado's native fish evolved strange, almost prehistoric looking forms to cope with the river's sediment and its Jekyll and Hyde swings in flow and temperature. Three-quarters of the basin's 32 native fish species were found nowhere else in the world, a higher rate of endemism than all other river basins in North America. One of the most bizarre creatures came to be known as the humpback chub. The Quasimodo of the Colorado had an unmistakable protrusion behind its flattened head that may have acted like a ship's keel while helping push the fish toward the less-turbulent bottom of the river. The chub's tiny eyes reflected a cloudy submarine world where sight was a challenge, but the fish was able to stay safe and fed thanks to its acute sense of smell and its ability to sense the vibrations of a nearby insect or freshwater shrimp. Flaps on its nostrils excluded sediment, and a fleshy snout overhung its mouth to keep water from rushing in.

During the Great Depression, people along the Colorado had no choice but to eat the humpback chub and other native species. They reported limited success in dissolving the bones by canning the fish or putting them in pressure cookers. Because the Colorado's native fish were so unpleasant to eat, locals were thrilled when the government decided to poison the river's tributaries and stock them with trout. In September 1962, state and federal officials applied 21,500 gallons of rotenone, a fish poison, to 445 miles of the Green River, a tributary of the Colorado. The toxic chemical began flowing downstream in west-central Wyoming and eventually reached the Utah-Colorado border, killing thousands of fish, including humpback chub and other species now listed as endangered. Just east of the Utah border, potassium permanganate was added to the Green River with hopes of neutralizing the poison and protecting fish in Colorado's Dinosaur National Monument. But the rotenone concentration was too high, and there wasn't enough potassium permanganate on hand, so the fish kill extended into the monument, wiping out thousands more fish. As had happened with the California condor, Mexican gray wolf, and so many other endangered species, the chub was intentionally killed in an era before Americans and the government paid attention to protecting biodiversity.

Other efforts to promote exotic fish in the Colorado, often carried out by the same agencies now struggling to recover the chub, had a more indirect but no less lethal effect. The invasive species either swallowed the natives or outcompeted them for food. It wasn't until 1964 that the National Park Service finally ended a four-decade program of planting rainbow and brown trout in the Grand Canyon. Upstream, in the shadow of Glen Canyon Dam, state and federal agencies created a blue-ribbon rainbow trout fishery in the frigid tailwaters; into the mid-1990s, government officials were still stocking 20,000 trout there. Today, 23 nonnative species—trout, carp, shiner, bullhead, catfish, bass, and others—live in the Grand Canyon. The Colorado River has a total of 60 exotic species, nearly double the number of native ones. Nationwide, the introduction and spread of nonnative plants and animals remains the number two cause of species endangerment, behind habitat loss.

The stocking of nonnative competitors and predators would have been enough to jeopardize the humpback chub and other Colorado River fish. But humans multiplied the threat by building colossal dams to generate hydropower, irrigate farms, and quench the growing thirst of southwestern cities. With predictable, and perhaps irreversible, ecological consequences, the federal government commandeered the river to supply drinking water for more than 25 million people and irrigate 4 million acres of crops, mostly cattle feed. As more than 20 major dams leveled out the Colorado's peaks and troughs, and as exotic fish continued to be stocked in its waters, native species like the humpback chub, razorback sucker, and Colorado pikeminnow were reduced to less than 10 percent of their historic populations. A river that was once murky and mercurial had become clean and calculated, its silt backed up by hydroelectric dams that doled out water in accordance with the Southwest's demand for air-conditioning, not the caprice of nature.

Saddled with new responsibilities, the Colorado has been relieved of the laws of hydrology and gravity. In one of its sources, Colorado's Rocky Mountain National Park, a 13-mile pipeline drilled through the Continental Divide siphons off up to 101 billion gallons a year, removes it from the basin, and sends it toward the Denver area. Behind Hoover Dam, Las Vegas dips its straw into Lake Mead and uses the Colorado to run fountains on the Strip. California takes about 30 percent of Lake Havasu's flow, transporting some water all the way to the Pacific Coast. On the opposing shoreline, Arizona grabs another 20 percent of the river and pumps much of it uphill via the Central Arizona Project to Phoenix and Tucson. A 1944 treaty entitles Mexico to about 10 percent of the Colorado's flow, but as soon as the depleted river crosses the border, it's diverted into canals to irrigate low-value crops like alfalfa. In most years, the river doesn't even reach the Gulf of California and simply dies in the desert. A delta that was once swampy is now dominated by hundreds of square miles of sterile salt flats cracked by the Sonoran sun. "The vast flat bowl of wilderness rimmed by jagged peaks" that Leopold wrote of is no more. "The despot of the Delta," as Leopold called the jaguar, was deposed long ago. Knowing what Hoover Dam had done, Leopold never returned to the delta. "It is the part of wisdom never to revisit a wilderness, for the more golden the lily, the more certain that someone has gilded it," he wrote. "To return not only spoils a trip, but tarnishes a memory. It is only in the mind that shining adventure remains forever bright."

About 75 years after Leopold's visit to the Colorado River delta, Interior Secretary Bruce Babbitt returned to his home state to start a fake flood. On March 26, 1996, before a large gathering of reporters, photographers, and television cameras, Babbitt stood atop the 710-foot Glen Canyon Dam, pushed a button, cranked a lever, turned a wheel, and opened the first of four outlet tubes to begin the imitation inundation. Millions of gallons of water shot out of the eight-foot-wide tubes, arced 150 feet, and collided, turning the normally calm river into a white-water maelstrom. The sound of roaring water echoed off the canyon's sheer sandstone walls, and great clouds of mist rose before the dam's concrete face.

The experimental flood on the Colorado was the culmination of more than a decade of planning. It was one of several tactics the federal government was pursuing to restore the downstream ecosystem and bring back the Grand Canyon's native wildlife, especially the humpback chub. Four of the canyon's eight native fish species had already been extirpated, and the chub was heading toward the same fate. Scientists hoped that if they replicated the historic floods that once rushed through the canyon during the spring snowmelt, they could re-create the beaches, sandbars, and calmer backwaters that disappeared after Glen Canyon Dam started impounding the river in 1963. The larger strategy was to tweak the dam's releases throughout the year to improve conditions for native species in one of the world's premier national parks.

The 1996 flood, which released nearly 337,000 gallons per second, enough to fill the Empire State Building or Sears Tower in 20 minutes, continued for a week, drained 117 billion gallons from Lake Powell, and dropped the reservoir level by more than three feet. It made for one helluva trip for the river rats allowed to ride it downstream, yet it was only a third or a fourth as big as some floods in the pre-dam days. Atop Glen Canyon Dam, Babbitt heralded the experiment, the first of its kind, as "a new era for ecosystems, a new era for dam management, not only for the Colorado but for every river system and every watershed in the United States."

By the time Babbitt took office, only 2 percent of American rivers were free flowing. Since the signing of the Declaration of Independence, the United States had added the equivalent of nearly one dam *a day*. The dams, many of them smaller earthen structures, often provided beneficial flood control, irrigation, hydropower, and potable water supplies. But some had outlived their usefulness or imposed environmental costs that far exceeded the economic benefits, which often had been exaggerated when the projects were proposed. For decades, interior secretaries had traveled to dams to christen them and extol their virtues; Babbitt, however, toured the nation to "undedicate" and decommission a few of the worst offenders.

Downstream effects of Glen Canyon Dam were an afterthought when the project was planned in the 1950s. By the early 1980s, with the ESA in place and the public's environmental consciousness blooming, the dam's ecological fallout could no longer be ignored. In 1982, the federal government launched a series of studies, but it took a lawsuit from environmental groups and river guides to force the federal government to prepare a colossal environmental impact statement that would choose how to adjust the dam's operations. Over a period of seven years, researchers conducted more that 150 river trips and federal officials gathered 55,000 public comments in scores of public hearings. Languishing in the federal bureaucracy, the effort got a kick start in 1992 when Congress passed the Grand Canyon Protection Act, which compelled the interior secretary to operate Glen Canyon Dam in order to "protect, mitigate adverse impacts to, and improve the values for which Grand Canyon National Park and Glen Canyon National Recreation Area were established."

For some environmentalists and scientists, mitigating the downstream impacts with the dam still in place was a fool's errand. While Babbitt was unleashing a man-made flood, Sierra Club leader David Brower was pushing hard to drain Lake Powell completely and begin restoring Glen Canyon to its former splendor. "The dam itself would be left as a tourist attraction, like the Pyramids, with passers-by wondering how humanity ever built it, and why," Brower wrote shortly after the Sierra Club board unanimously approved his motion to drain the reservoir, a reservoir the group had accepted in order to save Dinosaur National Monument from being drowned in the 1950s. Even with a Democrat in the White House and an environmentally minded interior secretary, the Sierra Club's strategy remained a fantasy.

The federal government focused instead on how to modify the dam's releases so the river downstream would approximate the natural system. In the pre-dam days, the Colorado's flow varied greatly across the year, but on any given day the volume of water in the channel was fairly constant, only changing by an average of 500 cubic feet per second over 24 hours. From 1963 to 1991, however, when the dam was managed to maximize power generation, releases in a single day could vary by 25,000 cubic feet per second, causing the river below the dam to rise and fall up to 13 feet. The volume of water that passed through the dam's turbines changed by the hour to meet the rising and falling demand for electricity. Unlike reservoirs, which can hold water and release it in dry times, an electrical grid can only transport electrons, not store them. When power use spiked on a summer afternoon, Glen Canyon's hydropower was in especially high demand. Compared to a power plant using fossil fuels, it was easier to dial up or down the dam's electrical output simply by adjusting how much water flowed through the turbines. Before 1963, the Colorado on a June afternoon would have been slow and steady, but that's when power was needed most to run air conditioners in Phoenix and the rest of the Southwest. Maintaining the naturally low, flat flows would put a major damper on the dam's hydropower potential. If the operators of Glen Canyon Dam were unable to adjust its power output to match the demand on the grid, utilities would be forced to go out on the open market and buy expensive electricity. That supplemental power could come from burning coal and would carry its own environmental consequences.

Consumers benefited from Glen Canyon Dam's flexibility and its provision of subsidized emissions-free power. The downstream environment paid the price. Not only were the flows too variable on a daily basis and too strong in both summer and winter, they were also the wrong temperature. Once Glen Canyon Dam was in place, its outlet pipes continually released frigid water from the dark abyss of Lake Powell—perfect conditions for nonnative trout in the tailwaters, but a shock to native species like the humpback chub, which needed warmer water to reproduce.

And then there was the problem of sediment, which carried nutrients that supported the base of the aquatic food chain and created the sandbars and tranquil backwaters that fish used as spawning grounds. The Colorado once carried an average of 29 million tons of sediment into the Grand Canyon each year, leading some to describe the river as "too thick to drink, too thin to plow," but now Glen Canyon Dam trapped nearly all of that behind its face.

To mitigate the harm caused by Glen Canyon Dam, the Bureau of Reclamation settled on a new regime that remains in place to this day. The upshot of all the studies and public hearings, a process that cost $105 million, was a new rule book for the timing and quantity of releases. Awkwardly labeled the modified low-fluctuating flow alternative, the system put a ceiling on releases, limited daily fluctuations, and restricted how fast the dam could increase and decrease its output. These changes cut generating capacity by up to one-third and slashed hydropower revenues by up to $50 million a year, yet the Colorado was still out of whack. Before the dam, for example, flows averaged 542 cubic feet per second; after Glen Canyon Dam was built, they increased to 8,580 cubic feet per second.

For all the controversy surrounding Glen Canyon Dam's operations, the artificial flood in 1996 garnered broad support. When Babbitt unleashed the torrent, which cut hydropower revenues by $2.5 million and cost another $1.5 million to study, biologists, river guides, environmentalists, even the Western Area Power Administration lavished praise on the effort. Two weeks later, at a Washington, DC, briefing, Babbitt concluded the flooding "worked brilliantly." "The flood is over, the waters have receded," he told reporters. "What we have found is really quite extraordinary." Down in the Grand Canyon, atop newly formed sandbars, reporters interviewed researchers who also proclaimed the flood a success. The experiment had, in fact, exceeded scientists' expectations in its ability to move sediment up onto the banks. It even buried $70,000 worth of equipment at one monitoring site. The gains, however, were fleeting. As the flood subsided and the dam's operations returned to normal, the unnaturally high flows ate away at the new beaches and sandbars. In the end, some areas were even worse off than they were before the flood.

————————

"You've got to be freakin' kidding me." At least that's the G-rated version of what came out of David Sanders's mouth as he peered into the canyon, two cameras dangling around his neck. Thousands of feet below us, we could see the turquoise thread of the Little Colorado River, but there was no sign of a trail leading into the plunging, boulder-strewn drainage that lay between my car and the river.

We had come to this dusty spot on the Navajo Reservation, not far from Grand Canyon National Park, to join a survey for humpback chub in their inner sanctum. The biologists had warned me that the hike in would be no cakewalk, and like Sanders, I felt weak in the knees survey-ing the descent. The three researchers would be flying into the canyon the next morning in a helicopter, but Sanders and I couldn't join them on the flight because of permitting issues that I never fully grasped. In any event, the scientists planned to be in the canyon for nearly two weeks, and we could only stay for two days, so the hike out was unavoidable. "Don't worry, it won't be so bad," I told Sanders, lying through my teeth.

The Little Colorado River, home to the largest of six chub popula-tions, is critical to the species' survival because water released from the depths of Lake Powell is usually in the 40s year-round. Below the dam, rafters who flip overboard may flirt with hypothermia in July, when the ambient temperature is in the triple digits. For the chub, the numbing water acts like birth control. Biologists have found that the fish have trou-ble spawning if the water temperature is less than 61 degrees, but even in summer and dozens of miles downstream from the dam, the Colorado is usually between 45 and 54 degrees. The chub's response has been to use the last nine miles of a tributary, the Little Colorado, as their maternity ward. In the Little Colorado, life for the chub proceeds swimmingly. The flow is more or less natural, and nonnative trout tend to avoid its warmer waters. But when the young chub enter the main stem of the Colorado River, they are stunned by the cold water, making them even more suscep-tible to attacks by nonnative fish that thrive in the unnatural conditions. In one experiment, chub swimming in 68-degree water were fatigued after 85 minutes, but those put in 57-degree water were exhausted after 2 minutes. Historically, a sight-based predator like a trout would have had a tough time eyeing prey in the muddy Colorado; in today's clear water, it's easy pickings on chub that evolved in a cloudy world.

Carrying backpacks and serious doubts we could make it to the bottom, Sanders and I set off. We found the first pile of rocks marking the Hopi Salt Trail, named for deposits below that indigenous people once mined, but the cairns marking the route were scarce. The upper reaches of the canyon were so steep that we had to scoot down boulders on our butts, or lower our backpacks before us so we could rock climb in reverse. Losing the trail, we found ourselves at an impassable cliff and had to retrace our steps. After five hours of painfully slow progress, we finally reached the Little Colorado, only to look back up at the ascent awaiting us in two days. We camped on a sand terrace above the river, stared silently at the 1,500-foot sandstone cliff rising from the opposing shore, then slept for 10 hours.

The Little Colorado begins 200 miles to the southeast, in the subalpine meadows and pine-covered slopes of 11,403-foot Mt. Baldy, in eastern Arizona's White Mountains. It then snakes to the northwest, often as a trickle, sometimes with no surface flows at all, before reaching the Painted Desert and Navajo Reservation, where mineral-laden springs generate the river's base flow. Near the confluence with the Colorado, the Little Colorado glistens like one of the turquoise necklaces fashioned by the Navajo thousands of feet above, on windswept plateaus peppered with hogans and sagebrush. I found the Little Colorado enchanting—once I was resting on its shores—but when explorer John Wesley Powell's party came to the tributary in 1869, one member described it as "a loathsome little stream, so filthy and muddy it fairly stinks," while another said it was "as disgusting a stream as there is on the continent." The first explorers to float the Grand Canyon were having a tough time. "Thank God the trip is nearly over," one member of the party wrote, not knowing that the most treacherous part of the journey lay ahead.

The Little Colorado's stunning color, which fades in times of heavy runoff, is due to its turbidity; up close, it looks more like watered-down skim milk. The river's sandy banks are encrusted with a white ring, and in a few spots, the dissolved minerals have emerged from solution to form a series of travertine dams made of calcium carbonate. River rats say you could drink the water in an emergency, but soon you'd be losing as much fluid in diarrhea. Accordingly, the teams of researchers who came by helicopter to study the chub brought in their own water, along with a half ton of other supplies, to support their 12-day survey.

After breakfast, Sanders and I watched the skies for that helicopter. Hours passed without sight or sound of an aircraft, and we grew nervous. We were down to our last Nalgene bottle and not anxious to drink from the Little Colorado. Finally, at 11 AM, a chopper appeared, slinging a net stuffed with supplies. It began to ease down into a canyon that looked only a bit wider than the rotor blades. The first of two loads was dumped, then the helicopter returned to land on a makeshift clearing encircled by rocks. It seemed like a gust of wind could send the helicopter into the canyon walls, so it made sense that the three biologists emerged wearing flame-retardant jumpsuits.

The scientists' mission was to set nets along the Little Colorado, then return the following morning to see what was caught. The trio measured the fish and used syringes to inject PIT tags, passive integrated transponders that are a half-inch long, enclosed in glass, and similar to the microchips used to reunite pets with their owners. When the fish is passed through an O-shaped wand, each of these PIT tags emits a unique alphanumeric code, sort of like a Social Security number for each animal. By continually recapturing the fish, jotting down their dimensions, and recording the PIT tag's codes, scientists can get a handle on population trends and growth rates. The chub in the Little Colorado have become one of the world's most intensively studied fish populations. Most of the adults now carry PIT tags. Nevertheless, key aspects of their biology are not well understood. Scientists, for example, have never witnessed the fish spawning. Once the chub descend into the Little Colorado's dark, turbid depths, their habits are a mystery.

Hiking along the shore of the Little Colorado River, the smell was almost marine, the mud sometimes became quicksand, and the cordon of plants—mesquite, acacia, cattail—lashed our shins. After the biologists pulled the hoop nets to shore, they dumped the captured chub into plastic buckets from Ace Hardware that wobbled from the fish thrashing inside. Classified as minnows, the chub can grow to 18 inches and are so muscle-bound that it's a struggle to hold them down for measurements. "This is a fish made to run the rapids," explained Bill Pine, a scientist at the Mote Marine Laboratory at the Center for Fisheries Enhancement. "It's a body shape built for speed, and it's highly evolved for this river." Embedded scales make the chub feel leathery and reduce drag in the river. The big sickle-shaped tail is like a tuna's and helps propel the chub through swift currents. Young chub, however, appear to prefer the more placid backwaters, habitat that has been lost as Glen Canyon Dam has trapped sediment and prevented sandbars from forming downstream.

We worked our way up to Lower Atomizer Falls. Below calcium carbonate dams coated in algae and overtopped by waterfalls glinting in the sunlight, Fish and Wildlife biologist Dennis Stone swam halfway across the turquoise river, only his bespectacled head visible, to check on the nets. I took a liking to Stone because he cursed as much as he giggled. He has surveyed for Little Colorado chub over the past dozen years and has spent up to 120 days a year in the canyon. At night, as we sipped from Nalgene bottles containing a cocktail of water and Black Velvet whiskey, both flown in by helicopter, Stone recounted the exploits of other river rats, including one who was bitten on the testicles by a scorpion while he was drunk. But Stone was deadly serious about the chub's plight.

The perennial water we were seeing in the Little Colorado comes mostly from Blue Spring, 13 miles upstream from the confluence, and is supplemented by more than two dozen smaller springs downriver. These springs, which reliably discharge about 54 billion gallons a year into the Little Colorado, are outlets for a series of aquifers covering more than 26,000 square miles in northeastern Arizona and northwestern New Mexico, most notably the Coconino aquifer. No one knows how climate change will affect the groundwater, the springs, or the Little Colorado. The Coconino aquifer is largely replenished by water seeping into the ground in the Flagstaff area and along the Mogollon Rim, where the population is rising fast. "If Blue Springs ever dries up," Stone said, "these fish are toast."

Chub researchers also worry about water quality. About 50 miles upstream from our position, a US highway passes over the Little Colorado, so if a truck carrying fuel or other hazardous material were to crash on the narrow bridge, its payload could fall into the river and harm, if not totally destroy, the chub's prime spawning grounds. Pollution from the plateau above can also cascade down during flash floods. During our hikes along the Little Colorado's shores, seemingly in the middle of nowhere, I noticed a toddler's flip-flop, an empty motor oil bottle, and a plethora of other trash that had been washed into the canyon. This last stretch of the Little Colorado was damn tough to get to, but it wasn't immune to the world around it.

I was reminded of the area's isolation on our hike out, which didn't live up to the nightmare that Sanders and I conjured. Back at the trail-head, I took one last look at the turquoise thread below. Surrounded by thousands of square miles of arid canyonlands, the Little Colorado looked like a fish out of water, and as fragile as any place I knew.

The humpback chub's fate is intertwined with the Little Colorado's because of Glen Canyon Dam. Can the fish survive with the dam still in place? Some scientists and activists think not. David Haskell, who ended his 33 years with the federal government as science director of Grand Canyon National Park, told me the conditions facing the chub down-stream of Glen Canyon Dam are so unnatural that "it's as if you took a rhino or an elephant out of the African heat and tried to raise them in Alaska." "There's really nothing that can be done with this dam in place to allow this species to survive," he said. "It's doomed to extinction in the Grand Canyon unless the dam is decommissioned and warm, silty water once again flows through the Grand Canyon."

Decades after Earth First! staged its inaugural protest at Glen Can-yon Dam, a new generation of activists wielding hydrographs and tree-ring studies continue to carry the banner of draining Lake Powell, if not destroying the dam. The vanquished foe might remain in place as a symbol of human hubris, with the Colorado allowed to bypass it. The gist of the argument for decommissioning the dam is this: Lake Mead and reservoirs upstream could compensate for the reduction in storage (all told, impoundments on the Colorado can hold six times the river's annual flow). No more Lake Powell means several billion gallons saved every year from evaporation losses. Other river water might be stored in under-ground aquifers in the deserts of Arizona and California, something already done to a limited extent. Hydropower losses could be compen-sated by improved energy conservation. And the lakeside tourist town of Page could still eke out a living with the help of hikers and bird-watchers coming to see the unveiled Glen Canyon.

In a technical sense, the dam's foes make strong arguments that are backed up with serious study of the basin's hydrology rather than the neo-Luddite chest-beating of Earth First! There's no doubt that the waterworks on the Colorado River are highly inefficient. The Bureau of Reclamation estimates that annual evaporation losses just from Lake Powell amount to nearly 600,000 acre-feet, with another 400,000 acre-feet of water seeping into the banks of the reservoir, some of which returns to the lake, some of which drains into the bowels of the earth. The difference between the volume of water flowing into Lake Powell and exiting Glen Canyon Dam, about 1 million acre-feet, or nearly 326 billion gallons, could meet the needs of about 2 million households.

Low-cost electricity was a major reason for building Glen Canyon Dam, leading some to call it a cash-register dam. Hydropower from Glen Canyon Dam serves about 4 million customers in seven western states. Without that electricity, 250 utilities, cities, towns, tribes, and irrigation districts would be forced to buy more expensive power. The substitute electricity would likely come from the combustion of coal or natural gas. Just six miles away from the dam, the Salt River Project's coal-fired Navajo Generating Station emits nearly 20 million tons of carbon dioxide into the atmosphere each year and contributes to poor air quality in the Grand Canyon. Coal stripped from Black Mesa, on nearby Hopi and Navajo land, also winds up at the Four Corners power plant, the nation's second largest emitter of smog-causing nitrogen oxides. From an emissions standpoint, Glen Canyon Dam is tough to beat. If, however, lost hydropower from Glen Canyon Dam could be backfilled with electricity generated by solar or wind, there would be one less benefit to keeping the dam in place.

Whatever the merits of decommissioning the dam, the campaign hasn't had any legs. Both Democratic and Republican administrations have rejected even studying the idea. There simply isn't the political will to do away with a dam that has the backing of well-heeled water and power interests, plus the support of many voters. The system, after all, has worked so far and allowed water managers to guide the nation's fastest-growing region between the Scylla and Charybdis of flood and drought. At the dawn of the 21st century, reservoirs like Lake Powell provided enough storage to blunt the impact of one of the driest spells in centuries, forcing hardly any sacrifice among urban residents of the Southwest. Hydrologists concluded that without Lake Powell, the 2002 drought would have caused shortages across the region and deprived Las Vegas of 90 percent of its water because Lake Mead would have been so depleted. Even if the government agreed to pursue the idea of decommissioning Glen Canyon Dam, it could take decades to carry out. It took no less than 13 years to decide how to alter the dam releases to benefit the downstream ecosystem. For the foreseeable future, Glen Canyon Dam will continue to plug the Colorado, and its importance to the region may actually increase in the 21st century. If global warming causes droughts and wet spells to become more intense and more frequent, as climate scientists predict, reservoirs may become more valuable for evening out the Colorado's inherently irregular flow. Then again, enough drying could turn Lake Powell into a persistent puddle and make the dam expendable.

Rather than do away with Glen Canyon Dam, the federal government has focused its efforts on modifying the releases and engineering floods. Since Babbitt's inaugural inundation in 1996, the experiments have been repeated several times and modified somewhat. Scientists realized that spring might not be the best time to try the floods if there was a lack of sediment in the river that could be deposited up on the shores, so in November 2004, releases from the dam were synchronized with the input of sediment from tributaries to the Colorado, most critically the Paria River, 15 miles below the dam. The timed release piled six feet of sediment atop sandbars, yet once again the abnormally high flows in the river washed away many of the gains over the ensuing months.

After a decade of tinkering with the dam's daily releases and trying several experimental floods, the US Geological Survey evaluated what progress had been made and found little. Beaches and sandbars continued to disappear due to ongoing erosion, a net loss of fine sediment in the river, and an expansion of nonnative tamarisk, leading to a 55 percent decline in summer camping areas along the river in the Grand Canyon. The humpback chub's adult population had plummeted by more than half, from about 11,000 in 1989, to around 5,000 in 2001. During the same period, however, densities of nonnative rainbow trout had quintupled, while brown trout had expanded their range and numbers. For the chub, the modified dam releases "had either a negative effect or no effect at all," the scientists concluded. "It is clear that the restrictions on dam operations since 1991 have not produced the hoped for restoration and maintenance of this endangered species." The federal government had spent some $100 million on a program that had shrunk the dam's power generation by up to a third. Scientists had used lasers, underwater cameras, century-old photos, satellite imagery, and experimental flumes in a lab. They had even developed new instruments, including the flying eyeball, a digital microscope embedded in a steel wrecking ball that could withstand the turbulent river while rolling along its bottom and capturing video of sediment grains. But nothing seemed to be working.

The experiments and high-tech gadgets were all part of a $10-million-a-year adaptive management program that could, in theory, adjust the dam operations to benefit the chub and other species. At the heart of adaptive management is the belief in the dynamic nature of ecosystems and the need to repeatedly modify tactics and strategies in light of changing conditions, new evidence, and improved scientific understanding. It's essentially learning by doing, which seems like common sense, but that flexibility can collide with the strictness of the ESA and other laws. In the extreme, researchers would be in Glen Canyon Dam's control room adjusting dials and calibrating releases while their colleagues measured the response downstream to find the formula most beneficial for the ecosystem. In reality, the adaptive management program is a contentious decision-making process in which scientists are just one of many stakeholders on a 25-person panel. Naturally, hydropower interests argue that environmentalists have too much sway, while advocates for the humpback chub insist it's the other way around. The new paradigm of adaptive management is still subject to old-school power politics. In this case, it has produced a stalemate: little has changed in the operation of Glen Canyon Dam since 1995, aside from a few experimental floods and releases.

Adaptive management is likely to become even more important in the years to come because climate change will be continually modifying habitats and posing new threats. More immediately, the approach is essential for explaining the recent turnaround in the humpback chub's fortunes. The adult population, in free fall from 1989 to 2001, has since risen to about 7,500. There are at least three possible reasons. First, the experimental releases might actually be working. Second, the drought had so depleted Lake Powell that water released from the depths of the reservoir was warmer than at any time since Powell was first filled. At the confluence of the Little Colorado and Colorado rivers, the water temperature exceeded 61 degrees, the warmest observation since 1980 and about the minimum needed for chub to successfully reproduce. Third, thousands of nonnative fish that prey on and compete with the chub were removed from the confluence between 2003 and 2006. Biologists used electricity to stun the fish, separated out the natives, euthanized the trout, and gave the remains to the local Hualapai tribe for use as organic fertilizer. The net result: an 80 percent reduction in the abundance of rainbow trout. Scientists do not know which of these factors is responsible for the rebound, or whether there is a synergy among them, but further experimentation with releases from the dam and removal of nonnative fish could yield an answer that boosts the chub's prospects.

Instead of relying on a drought to warm releases from Lake Powell, humans could dial up the thermostat if Glen Canyon Dam were retrofitted with something called a temperature control device. The Bureau of Reclamation has already evaluated the merits and risks of this technological fix, which would draw water from near Lake Powell's sunny surface, instead of from the reservoir's chilly depths, before sending it through the turbines and downstream. At a cost of around $100 million, the bureau could modify two of the eight penstocks that feed the turbines, testing that partial fix before touching the other six inlets. Similar technology is already in place at Flaming Gorge Dam in Wyoming, Shasta Dam in California, and some five dozen other sites the bureau has studied. Dennis Kubly, the agency's point man for the project, told me that "in almost every example, the outcome has been positive." At Glen Canyon Dam, the temperature control device would cut the generation of electricity by less than 1 percent, so hydropower interests have not been strong opponents. But there hasn't been much movement on the proposal in recent years, and the technology, derided as an expensive Band-Aid, carries its own risks. Warming the water below the dam could also make the river more hospitable for some nonnative fish and parasites, thereby putting the chub in even more danger. It will also be difficult to convince Congress to spend $100 million or more on the temperature control device if drought, and perhaps climate change, warm the releases from Lake Powell for free.

The temperature control device will only do so much to mitigate the effects of a 710-foot-tall dam. In the long run, yet another technology may come to the chub's rescue. Advances in water treatment could turn the sea and sewage into potable supplies that replace the Colorado River and make dams like Glen Canyon unnecessary. The price of river water will continue to rise in coming decades as the demand increases and supply shrinks due to climate change. At the same time, it will become comparatively less expensive for Southern California cities to desalinate the Pacific Ocean and for communities throughout the Southwest to recycle treated wastewater.

Desalination has grown exponentially since the 1960s, and its cost has plummeted in the past few decades. Regulated appropriately, desalination could be a boon to species that depend on rivers, streams, and wetlands. The pivotal question: will harm to marine and coastal life, plus the technology's high demand for energy, outweigh the benefits? Billions of fish larvae and other creatures may be harmed when pumps suck in water from the ocean, though screens and buried intakes might mitigate the damage. On the other end of the process, supersalty brine released into the ocean can create toxic plumes. In between, lots of power is needed to push seawater through membranes that filter out the salt, raising serious questions about the associated greenhouse gas emissions, not to mention the power needed to pump the water inland and uphill. In California, moving and treating water already consumes 19 percent of the state's electricity.

Inland states like Arizona may seem unlikely customers for desalinated water, but the Gulf of California is less than 200 miles from both Phoenix and Tucson. Other inland states could also benefit if California embraces the technology. Colorado, Utah, New Mexico, or Nevada could pay for the desalination plants along the coast, then take the Colorado River water that California would no longer need. We may be decades away from the sea supplying a significant chunk of the Southwest's water supply, but it's hardly science fiction to envision a fleet of desalination plants, powered by renewable energy, making at least some dams and reservoirs obsolete.

Whether desalination will eventually make Lake Powell unnecessary hinges on climate change. Putting aside the prognosis for precipitation, warmer temperatures and higher evaporation rates will thin the snowpack that supplies about 85 percent of the river's volume. Thawing of the snowpack earlier in the season could also force water managers to spill from reservoirs like Lake Powell to prevent spring floods, leaving less water behind to meet the peak summertime demands.

Even without climate change, the Colorado River is arguably the most contested, litigated, and overburdened river in the world. Water managers have known for decades that the 1922 compact that divided the Colorado River's water among western states was based on an overly generous estimate of the annual flow. The instrumental record from 1905 to 1920 suggested the average was 16.4 million acre-feet, but those 15 years were exceptionally wet. As river gauge readings were complemented by tree-ring studies and scientists' view of the river expanded from years to centuries and millennia, the long-term average looked closer to 14.6 million acre-feet. Just as troubling was the recognition that the 240,000-square-mile basin would sometimes descend into decades-long droughts that would keep the Colorado's flow below the long-term average for many years at a time. In 2002, when flows into Lake Powell were 25 percent of normal and Arizona's forests were going up in flames, it may have seemed like a freak event; in reality, the drought was hardly unprecedented and is a harbinger of the more extreme weather that climate scientists expect in the 21st century and beyond.

As early as 1993, federal officials acknowledged that global warming might affect the flow of the Colorado. In 2004, a half-dozen researchers said that under conservative estimates of climate change, the Colorado wouldn't even satisfy the Southwest's current demand for water. "Basically," the researchers wrote, "we found the fully allocated Colorado system to be at the brink of failure." Then, in one of the scariest predictions, researchers reported in *Science* that global warming would make the deep droughts of the Dust Bowl, 1950s, and early 21st century the new norm in the Southwest. In all but one of the 19 climate models, the region got drier, leading the researchers to predict that annual precipitation would drop by 10 to 20 percent by 2100. Several studies have estimated the odds of Lake Mead and Lake Powell going dry and come up with a wide range of results, from a 50 percent chance by 2021 to a 30 percent chance by midcentury. The findings are sensitive to assumptions about future emissions of greenhouse gases, warming rates, and water managers' behavior, but the consensus among hydrologists is that the Colorado's flow will decline significantly in the 21st century.

There is evidence that climate change is already shrinking streams and rivers throughout the West. Researchers reported in *Science* that the region's entire hydrological cycle shifted in the last half of the 20th century. Up to 60 percent of the changes—warmer winter temperatures, thinner snowpacks, earlier snowmelt, and altered stream flows—were due to humans heating up the planet. The findings, the scientists wrote, portend a "coming crisis in water supply for the western United States" and mean that modifications to the region's water infrastructure will be "a virtual necessity."

Dire forecasts about the Colorado's flow and mounting demands have even reawakened interest in schemes such as seeding clouds to generate more rain and clear-cutting forests in the Rockies to increase run-off. As outlandish as they seem, these ideas are hardly the most extreme proposals that engineers have floated to let an arid region exceed its native water supply. Decades ago, studies looked at pumping the Mississippi River west across Texas using a series of nuclear plants to power the waterworks. In Arizona, researchers evaluated the feasibility of detonating atomic bombs to excavate craters where water from the Gila, Salt, and Little Colorado rivers could be stored. Others thought about converting the Yukon and Columbia from rivers of the Pacific Northwest into reservoirs for the Southwest. Not even the Great Lakes were off-limits to the most creative of planners.

Whatever happens to the climate, time will eventually catch up with Glen Canyon Dam. Every year, millions of tons of sediment get washed into Lake Powell and virtually none of it leaves. Downstream, the lack of silt and sand has transformed the river corridor and eliminated crucial beach and backwater habitat. Upstream, the trapped sediment is slowly reducing Glen Canyon Dam's life expectancy. In 1986, the Bureau of Reclamation found that sediment had already reduced Lake Powell's capacity by 3 percent. One of the many reasons for building Glen Canyon Dam was to extend the life of Lake Mead by trapping the sediment upstream, so the Bureau of Reclamation robbed Peter to pay Paul. Taking sediment from Lake Powell and dumping it below Glen Canyon Dam could extend the life of the reservoir and possibly benefit the Grand Canyon ecosystem, but some of that material would start accumulating downstream in Lake Mead. Over the years, proposals have called for adding sand, silt, and clay below Glen Canyon Dam by using trucks, barges, or a slurry pipeline. An underwater slurry pipeline is the favored option, but recent ballpark estimates from the Bureau of Reclamation put the construction cost in the hundreds of millions of dollars and annual operating costs at around $10 million. The bureau maintains that Powell's life span is hundreds of years, but some environmentalists predict that within the century the sediment will become so thick it will clog the dam's intakes for power generation and so severely reduce capacity in Lake Powell that a flood could overtop, then topple, the dam. Such a megaflood may seem a remote possibility, given that the Southwest is expected to get drier, but one of the underappreciated risks of climate change is the greater likelihood of extreme weather events. Areas that become wetter, for instance, may simultaneously confront droughts that are more severe and frequent.

It wasn't until 1998 that the Bureau of Reclamation formally examined the consequences of Glen Canyon Dam failing. That was 15 years after a near-disaster in 1983, when Lake Powell rose so fast that it nearly flowed over the dam. Engineers had planned for such a contingency by routing tubes through the adjoining cliffs that could dispense with the high water. But in one of the tunnels, the 1983 flood ripped out a huge section of concrete, 35 feet deep by 50 feet wide by 134 feet long, and raised questions about the dam's structural integrity. In the 1998 inundation study, the bureau looked at two scenarios: a sunny-day failure, in which the foundation would suddenly give way, and the failure of Flaming Gorge Dam upstream, causing Glen Canyon Dam to be overtopped and destroyed. "Anyone still on the river at the time of this flooding," the report warned, "would have to climb the equivalent of a 40-story building, at a minimum, to have any hope of surviving."

This would be a deluge of biblical proportions, not unlike the one that creationists believe carved the Grand Canyon and carried Noah's ark. The wall of water would reach Lake Mead within a day, burying all the settlements and recreational facilities along its shores. Hoover Dam could be overtopped as well, possibly leading to its failure and the destruction of other dams downstream in a deadly domino effect. Either way, the wave would wash over Laughlin, Needles, Blythe, Bullhead City, Lake Havasu City, and Yuma before reaching Mexico, the delta, and the Gulf of California. With the water supply for more than 25 million people jeopardized in an instant, the Southwest's society, economy, and psyche would be thrown into disarray. Were Glen Canyon Dam to fail because of a flood, or a fanatic, the fate of humpback chub would hardly be among the nation's top concerns. But given that the species evolved with epic floods for millions of years, the fish might have a better shot of surviving the aftermath than many of the human creations now dependent on the Colorado River.

Plenty of other disaster scenarios, ranging from a toxic spill on the Cameron Bridge to Blue Springs drying up from overpumping, seem even more likely to lead to the chub's demise. By the end of the 20th century, any aquatic species in the Southwest was already facing long odds; with climate change thrown into the equation, these animals will be swimming against the current of the 21st century just to survive.

19

Effluence

As the 2006 monsoon approached, I resigned myself to yet another late start to the storms and disappointing rainfall totals, but Mother Nature finally delivered the goods. The moisture arrived a week early, built up over southern Arizona, and climaxed on July Fourth in what meteorologists call a mesoscale convective system. It was better than any fireworks display. Clusters of anvil-shaped thunderheads pooled their resources into a superstorm that spawned squall lines. I watched the beast develop on National Weather Service radar as a giant blob of orange, red, and purple pixels swept from east to west across the southern half of the state. At my house, I stood atop patio furniture so I could watch pitchforks of lightning stab at the desert as the storm approached from the southeast. The thunder that followed the flashes sounded like volleys of artillery on a nearby battlefield. Sultry breezes arrived, along with the earthy, almost acrid smell of rain in the desert. The gutters along my roof's edge turned into waterfalls, and the temperature plummeted 20 degrees in 20 minutes.

With the ground saturated, the next day's storms caused normally dry washes to fill with runoff. I left for the San Pedro River to join a survey for southwestern willow flycatchers just as the black clouds were moving north up the Santa Cruz River Valley. When I crossed over the Santa Cruz at the base of A Mountain, the channel was filled bank to bank with muddy water. To see the Santa Cruz flowing is such a rare occurrence that several motorists had pulled off to the side of the road so they could stare with slack jaws and take pictures with their cell phones. The sight of water in the river worried me. In order to meet up with the biologists, I would soon have to cross the San Pedro, and without the aid of a bridge. Lightning flickered in my rearview mirror as I tried to outpace the storm.

I drove around the western and northern flanks of the Santa Catalina Mountains, where the Bullock, Aspen, and other wildfires had burned nearly 200 square miles over the past few years. Runoff from the Catalinas, which is naturally subject to extreme spikes, grew exponentially after the fires. The flames incinerated plants that held soil in place and their heat made the ground impervious in some spots. Close to where I was driving, a local publisher was killed in 2002 after a monsoon thunderstorm dropped 1.5 inches of rain in 25 minutes on the blackened slopes, sending an 8- to 12-foot wall of water into his home. That summer, the San Pedro looked like an oil slick and smelled like an ashtray once rainfall washed soot and debris down from the mountains. A forest could grow back in a matter of decades or centuries, but replacing topsoil in an arid land would take thousands of years, if it were to come back at all.

As I crested over the Santa Catalinas' northern foothills, near Oracle, I was rewarded with an expansive view of the San Pedro River Valley. The river's course was unmistakable: an emerald ribbon set against muted brown desert and overseen by a slate gray sky. I arrived in Dudleyville, a humble town of 1,300 populated largely by workers from the nearby Asarco copper mine. Many of the homes in Mammoth and Dudleyville are trailers, so the area doesn't seem primed for a growth spurt, but what was once considered a rural outpost may well become a bustling suburb in the next half century as Arizona's population doubles.

I approached the old farmhouse along the San Pedro where the biologists were staying—part of a preserve managed by The Nature Conservancy—and my vehicle had no trouble splashing through a stream only
a few inches deep and a few feet wide. It hadn't rained as much here in
the past few days, and runoff from the storms around Tucson still hadn't
flowed far enough downstream. The dark clouds that were following me
still looked menacing, but as I ate barbecue with the biologists at sunset,
I watched the puffy cumulonimbus clouds rise over the Catalinas, dump
their moisture, and vanish.

Like many birds, the flycatchers are most active around sunrise, so
we set our alarms for 4:30 AM. A coyote did laps around my campsite
as I struggled to fall asleep, half naked atop my sleeping bag, drenched
in sweat, but thankfully protected from the swarms of insects that had
enticed the flycatchers to migrate more than 1,000 miles, from Latin
America to southern Arizona. I was on the road at 5 AM with Allen
Graber and Lisa Ellis, biologists with the Arizona Game and Fish
Department who were surveying for flycatchers around the confluence of
the San Pedro and Gila rivers, one of the species' havens. As we left the
farmhouse and drove over the San Pedro to get on the state highway, the
clear river was still so low that I could have hopped over it. But after we
drove upstream for about 15 minutes, we came to the San Pedro's edge
and found a 200-foot-wide flash flood the color of chocolate milk. Flotil-
las of dead leaves and fallen branches were shooting by us. Runoff from
the storms to the south had finally arrived and converted the San Pedro
from a trickle into a torrent. "Usually there's this much water," Graber
said, holding his hands about six inches apart. Such radical swings are
perfectly normal along the San Pedro and other rivers in the Southwest.
Once, a stream gauge along the San Pedro recorded its flow rising from
40 cubic feet per second to more than 100,000 in a single day.

Suddenly looking like a real river, the San Pedro prevented us from
accessing the flycatcher nests, so Graber and Ellis took me to another
site along the nearby Gila River. From its headwaters in southwest New
Mexico, the Gila crosses into Arizona, passes by Mt. Graham, and pools
behind Coolidge Dam, on Apache land. About 30 miles downstream
from the reservoir, the Gila meets the San Pedro, then begins its winding
journey toward Phoenix. Today, there is almost never water in the Gila
when you drive over it on I-10, southeast of Phoenix. One of the city's
sewage plants dumps some water into the channel, but the flow peters

out as the river departs the city and heads west, toward the Colorado River, in line with I-8, and across some of the most forbidding desert on the continent. California-bound argonauts and Sonoran pronghorn once found salvation at the Gila's shady shores; today, a man or beast looking for lifesaving water in the river would die of thirst along its banks.

The confluence of the Gila and San Pedro rivers has been dramatically altered by Coolidge Dam, upstream diversions for agriculture, and nearby groundwater pumping. Yet its riparian forests persist, and they support one of the highest known concentrations of flycatcher territories in the nation: nearly a fifth of the total. To access some of the remote nests, biologists kayak down the Gila, which sounds like a glorious assignment, but the nesting site that Graber and Ellis brought me to was next to the sewage plant in the town of Kearny. Four pairs of flycatchers were building and tending nests in a wetland dependent on the treated wastewater. As you would expect, it smelled pretty rank as we entered a forest sustained by effluent. There were a bunch of cows moping around and abundant cow patties to avoid, but the shade was a welcome relief from the sun, which was broiling, even at 7 AM.

Cows and flycatchers are routinely found in the same habitat. One of the densest concentrations of nests is on a working cattle ranch along the Gila in New Mexico. But livestock can also cause major problems for the birds. Cows are often accompanied by brown-headed cowbirds, a parasite that doesn't bother to build its own nests or even incubate its own eggs. Instead, the cowbirds commandeer the nests of flycatchers and more than 100 other avian species throughout their range, then lay their eggs there, sometimes removing or eating whatever eggs were deposited by the nest's creator. Flycatchers and other birds often abandon nests that cowbirds have parasitized, but some will incubate a cowbird's egg and even feed the chick that hatches, which can greatly reduce the survival odds of their own offspring. Cattle can also harm riparian habitat by destroying plants and increasing soil erosion. As a result, land managers have been forced to fence off hundreds of miles of streams and rivers in the Southwest on behalf of the flycatcher and other species, thanks in large part to lawsuits from the Center for Biological Diversity and Forest Guardians. While cows treat young cottonwoods and willow saplings like candy, they don't find nonnative tamarisk palatable, so that can give a leg up to that exotic plant.

Tamarisk, also known as salt cedar, was imported to the United States from Africa and the Middle East starting in the 19th century for windbreaks, erosion control, and ornamental use. Even Aldo Leopold planted one in front of his home in Albuquerque around 1920. The shrub has since come to dominate 1.5 million acres of the West's precious riparian habitat. Tamarisk's extensive root system can swipe water from other vegetation. Its leaf litter is salty and can discourage other plants from growing nearby. And it will readily burn when conditions are right. The plant's spread has inspired multimillion-dollar eradication campaigns that employ chain saws, prescribed fires, natural insect enemies, and airborne spraying of herbicides.

For all the problems associated with tamarisk, southwestern willow flycatchers and other native birds readily nest in the nonnative thickets that have replaced cottonwood, willow, and mesquite. In the 1990s, 90 percent of the flycatcher nests found in Arizona were built in tamarisk, including the ones I was searching for with Graber and Ellis. When the flycatcher was listed in 1995, Fish and Wildlife cited tamarisk as one of the causes of the species' decline; today, about a quarter of all flycatcher territories in the United States are dominated by the plant. On the lower Colorado River, one study found that many bird species were most abundant when tamarisk covered 40 to 60 percent of an area, leading the authors to caution that complete removal of tamarisk—an expensive proposition—might not always be the best strategy. Some researchers have begun rehabilitating tamarisk's reputation by exposing how scientists and the popular press have often overstated the shrub's water use and soil salination. Citing a "reflexive antiexotic bias" and describing themselves as "reformed xenophobes," one group of leading riparian scientists argued that "generation by generation, citation by inappropriate citation, a mythology has been created about [tamarisk]."

One thing about tamarisk is clear: moving through dense stands of the plant is a bitch. I kept tripping over downed trunks, slipping on the black muck at our feet, sinking up to my knees in algae-coated puddles, and running into the tamarisk branches with my face. "That's how you know you're in flycatcher habitat; you can't walk around," Graber said.

For many endangered species, protecting habitat means preserving its current condition; banning logging, for instance, to maintain the integrity of an old-growth forest where spotted owls or red squirrels live. Flycatchers, however, build their nests in a highly dynamic system that can be remade by a single storm. The birds favor an intermediate stage in the succession of riparian habitat. Right after a major flood, the birds may not find any trees where they can build their nests if the stream channel has been scoured. Flycatchers also avoid building nests in the later stages of the vegetative progression, when a so-called gallery forest of large cottonwood and willow trees shades and inhibits the smaller plants beneath the canopy. Such spacious forests, while charming for hikers and campers, can expose flycatchers to predators like the Cooper's hawk, one of which we heard as we struggled through the tamarisk. What flycatchers want is the middle ground in the succession: dense stands of young to middle-aged willow, cottonwood, mesquite, and tamarisk that are all vying for the same water, sunlight, and soil nutrients.

The water sloshing beneath our feet was the key ingredient attracting the flycatchers because it generated a healthy population of insects for the birds to eat. Some biologists also suspected that the birds favored nesting and raising their chicks in the cooler microclimate along the river. Flycatchers aren't finicky eaters and will grab pretty much any type of flying or crawling bug. Whiskers around the flycatcher's face aid the bird in funneling insects into its mouth, and their wings' shape makes them nimble fliers able to snag bugs in midair. "The birds are definitely tied into that surface water," Graber said. "There are areas where the water goes back underground and you don't see flycatchers, but then the water comes back up and there are flycatchers right there. That happens especially along the San Pedro."

As I stumbled around the wetland, wondering about the effectiveness of the Kearny wastewater plant, Graber and Ellis listened closely for flycatchers and scanned the lattice of branches above. "There!" Ellis exclaimed. The small, inconspicuous bird had twigs in her mouth and was ferrying the material to a nest she was building above us, where two tamarisk branches forked. We heard the flycatcher's telltale song, *FITZ-bew*, and then she was gone. The other half of the pair, which probably emitted the call, was somewhere in the forest, watching as his mate carried the load and maybe even trying to get some action on the side. The female does almost all of the work building the nest, a tiny cup about two inches deep that's typically 10 to 15 feet above the ground and usually made from fibers, bark, and grass. The female also takes the lead on incubating the egg for about 12 days, though male birds will help defend the nest and feed the newborn chicks.

Before we left the forest, Graber tied a piece of blue flagging around a tamarisk limb. He scribbled down a description of where the nest was, sketched a picture of its location, and marked a code with the letter *D*, signifying that this nest was the flycatcher's fourth attempt. Three times before, her eggs had disappeared, probably into the belly of a king snake or avian predator. Because the nests are often 10 feet or more aboveground, biologists sometimes use mirrors or video cameras attached to tall poles in order to peek inside and see if there's an egg there. Only about half of the flycatcher's nesting attempts are successful, and plenty of the chicks that fledge succumb to predators before they can begin the migration back south, a journey of more than 1,000 miles. Biologists know precious little about the flycatchers' status and threats in their wintering grounds in Latin America, and even less about their journeys each spring and fall.

Like many species in the Southwest, the flycatcher's conservation straddles the US-Mexico border, so the ESA is only relevant to part of the bird's life cycle. Flycatchers and other migratory animals also face special challenges because they use a variety of habitats, any one of which may disappear, thereby jeopardizing the species. Like the lesser long-nosed bat, another reverse snowbird, the flycatcher is particularly vulnerable due to its dependence on a small number of sites for breeding. For the bats, the caves and mine shafts they use as roosts are also attractive to smugglers; for the flycatchers, the riparian forests that serve as nesting grounds are nourished by water humans covet.

The surveys that Graber and Ellis were conducting were being bankrolled by the Bureau of Reclamation to make up for the impact of raising Roosevelt Dam, on the Salt River. In 1996, crews completed a retrofit of the federal government's first big reclamation project and increased the dam's height by 77 feet. The taller dam would create a larger reservoir and submerge vegetation that flycatchers and other species were using at the lake's edge. To mitigate the damage, the Bureau of Reclamation and Salt River Project had to not only pay for flycatcher surveys, but also buy or protect substitute flycatcher habitat elsewhere. The confluence of the San Pedro and Gila rivers, where Graber, Ellis, and I were searching for flycatchers, was an obvious choice for the offset purchase since it was only 50 miles away and a likely destination for some of the birds displaced by the rising reservoir.

It also made sense for the water agencies to partner with The Nature Conservancy, which was apolitical, nonconfrontational, and had a long-standing interest in protecting the San Pedro. Since naming the river one of the world's last great places in 1991, The Nature Conservancy has spent tens of millions of dollars to protect the San Pedro. Initially, the group focused on purchasing valuable habitat along the river and its tributaries, many of them world-renowned birding spots. But turning private land into a preserve was expensive and came with management responsibilities. Selling the property to the federal government created its own set of problems because many rural residents opposed such deals, as The Nature Conservancy learned in the 1980s when it helped create the San Bernardino National Wildlife Refuge in the Malpai region. To avoid controversy and get a better return on its conservation investment, The Nature Conservancy shifted its strategy. In the Malpai region, the group worked to keep environmentally minded ranchers in business and helped them create conservation easements. Along the San Pedro, The Nature Conservancy bought farms that guzzled millions of gallons of groundwater every day and sold them off as large residential parcels with tight restrictions on their water use. Since 1990, the group has retired enough water rights along the lower half of the San Pedro to keep nearly 3 billion gallons of groundwater in the ground each year.

I first learned of the approach in 2001, when The Nature Conservancy bought a 528-acre farm on the San Pedro that accounted for two-fifths of the groundwater pumped along the river's final 18 miles. On the farm, which mostly grew alfalfa for cattle feed, a young forest of cottonwood and willow trees would occasionally sprout on the mineral-rich sandbars that formed in the streambed after floods. But the trees would eventually die because well pumping lowered the water table below their roots. When I went to the farm in 2001, the San Pedro was a hot, dry, sandy channel. As if to illustrate the river's poor health, a guy on an ATV zoomed up the streambed with a kid on his lap and a cooler strapped to the rear rack while I interviewed The Nature Conservancy's Dave Harris. "Five to 10 years from now, if we come back out here, we'll have a flowing river," Harris told me. Sure enough, when I returned to the farm in 2006, Harris's prediction had come true. The Nature Conservancy eventually sold the land to a Scottsdale wildlife rehabilitation facility that was looking to expand its facilities, in part because Phoenix's sprawl was increasing the number of wild animals captured in urban areas.

The Nature Conservancy spent several million dollars to buy an even larger farm, 2,150 acres, that was pumping about 1 billion gallons of water from underneath the San Pedro every year. The Three Links Farm only lined about 6 miles of the river, but hydrologic models predicted that slashing its groundwater pumping would restore year-round flows to 14 miles, while another 6 miles of the San Pedro would see enhanced flows. The Nature Conservancy subdivided the farm into five parcels ranging from 284 to 601 acres, then put them up for sale. Easements restricted new construction to one single-family residence per parcel, limited well pumping to about one-tenth of what the farm used, and forbade buyers from splitting their lot more than once. The Nature Conservancy said it didn't expect to profit on the deal, because the conservation easements reduced the land's value; it just wanted to break even.

Elsewhere, similar deals have drawn criticism from environmentalists who feel The Nature Conservancy permits too much development and activity on its land, including home building, logging, grazing, even oil and gas drilling. In 2003, *Washington Post* investigative reporters David B. Ottaway and Joe Stephens published a scathing multiday critique that uncovered cases in which The Nature Conservancy sold raw land at a loss to its supporters, then let the buyers adorn the property with such environmentally insensitive features as swimming pools. The *Post* series, a finalist for the Pulitzer Prize, led to significant changes in The Nature Conservancy's policies and disclosure of its land dealings. At least along the San Pedro, the flipping of alfalfa farms into very low-density housing seems to be a noncontroversial and effective means for keeping more water in the river.

The Nature Conservancy's avoidance of political fights contrasts with the aggressive litigation of environmental groups like the Center for Biological Diversity. But these differing advocacy styles can actually complement one another. By strictly enforcing the ESA, the Center has pushed agencies like the Bureau of Reclamation into spending millions on habitat protections and motivated landowners to work out a deal with The Nature Conservancy or a land trust. "Some years," the Center's Kierán Suckling told me, "I've succeeded in raising more money for The Nature Conservancy than I did for the Center."

The Nature Conservancy's biggest holding along the San Pedro is a 6,600-acre farm that was purchased with funds from the Bureau of Reclamation to mitigate its impact at Roosevelt Lake. The preserve is also home base for Graber, Ellis, and the other biologists who monitor flycatcher nests. When we returned there from our survey, the San Pedro was no longer a few inches deep and a few feet wide. It was now swollen with enough water to give me the willies as we forded the river in the biologists' SUV. I had read and written enough stories in the *Arizona Daily Star* about motorists being swept away in normally dry washes to develop a healthy fear of flash floods.

When we got back to the preserve, manager Rob Burton showed me around the property. "This used to be all pecans and acres and acres of ponds where they grew catfish," he said. "That was all taken out of production and then this (the San Pedro) started running again. People are always like, we're not using the river water, we're using the groundwater. But it's obviously the same thing. The river is where it's expressing on the surface. So you pump the water out of the ground here, most of it evaporates into the air, you drop the water table, the cottonwoods die, and you lose the whole system." Instead of growing catfish, The Nature Conservancy was now rearing thousands of endangered pupfish and razorback suckers in the ponds. The fish were then transplanted throughout the state, sometimes with the aid of helicopters.

Government biologists have also reintroduced a keystone species, beavers, to the San Pedro, hoping that "nature's engineer" can bring back the dams and ponds that helped define the river's flow. "This used to be known as the Beaver River," Burton said. "They took about 100,000 out of here in about 20 years in the early 1900s. Do the math, and 100,000 beavers is about 20,000 dams because there are four to six beavers per dam. Take 20,000 dams and spread that out over 150 miles, and this whole river would have had beaver ponds. Those ponds expanded the width of the riparian area. They slowed down all that water, and it recharged much better." Early settlers threw bass and trout into the beaver ponds so they could fish, but those nonnative species ate the pupfish and topminnows that helped control the growth of mosquitoes in the warm standing water. Back then, mosquitoes meant malaria, dengue, and yellow fever. So many settlers and soldiers fell ill that the San Pedro watershed was described as "the valley of the shadow of death" in an 1879 article in the *Arizona Daily Star*. "So then they got mad at the beavers," Burton continued, "and they yanked out all the beaver dams to get rid of the mosquitoes." Fewer beaver ponds meant less pooling of the San Pedro and fewer opportunities for the water to seep into the ground or stream bank for later discharge into the river. Now, the reintroduction of beavers on the upper San Pedro was beginning to restore the natural order, as was The Nature Conservancy's rearing of native pupfish and suckers. "You can come down here on a muggy summer evening," Burton said, "and there really aren't mosquitoes."

In the brief time Burton and I spoke beside the pond, we saw an amazing array of birds: coots, phoebes, purple martins, tropical kingbirds, vermilion flycatchers, northern rough-winged swallows, a great blue heron, a peregrine falcon, and several types of blackbirds. "If you look in your bird book at all those tropical birds from Mexico," Burton said, "all those maps have a little bump coming up into Arizona—that's this river." The San Pedro corridor also provides a critical pit stop for birds traveling along the Pacific Flyway. The southwestern willow flycatchers are just one of more than 250 migratory species that are part-year residents of the San Pedro. In all, the river provides habitat for about 400 avian species—nearly half of the birds found in North America—and more than 100 types of butterflies. As a result, The Nature Conservancy properties that are open to the public have become magnets for ecotourism. A 2001 Fish and Wildlife survey concluded that bird-watching in the area had a bigger impact on tourism and the economy than golf did.

The San Pedro's tremendous biodiversity isn't limited to species that fly. Scientists estimate the watershed is home to between 61 and 87 types of mammals, an unusually high number for a nontropical location. Burton said he regularly finds bear and mountain lion tracks in the mud along the river. "If you have things like that in the system," Burton said, "it's a pretty good indicator that most everything down below them is still there and that the system is still intact and functioning." Curious about the San Pedro's species diversity, Burton researched how many birds, mammals, reptiles, and amphibians were in each of our national parks. Big Bend National Park in Texas came out on top with nearly 600 species; the San Pedro (which isn't a national park) came in a close second with about 530. By comparison, the Arctic National Wildlife Refuge, site of the contested oil-drilling proposal, had fewer than 200 species. Big Bend covers 801,000 acres; the San Pedro's riparian corridor covers less than 8,000.

The San Pedro's flycatchers and thousands of other species live in an ecosystem where change and disturbance, especially in the form of floods, are natural and essential. But that doesn't mean places like the San Pedro are easy to put back together once they've been dismantled by humans. Before he came to southern Arizona, Burton learned that lesson well while working on restoration of the Salinas River in central California, which he described as "another overpumped, overfarmed, overpopulated river." "To try and bring back a system like that manually is really hard to do. You've got all these invasive species, you've modified the hydrology.

We really don't know how to do it," he said. "It makes a lot more sense to protect the systems that are still functioning as they are now than try to go back and fix them later."

It's also a lot cheaper to prevent destruction of riparian habitat than it is to repair the damage. To rejuvenate the lower Colorado River for the flycatcher and dozens of other species, the federal government, Arizona, California, and Nevada signed a $626 million habitat conservation plan in 2004 meant to restore riparian and fish habitat from Las Vegas down to Mexico. The 50-year deal gives urban and agricultural interests immunity from ESA restrictions that might otherwise kick in as they consumed the Colorado. In exchange, the states and federal government support rehabilitation projects on the river and set-asides elsewhere. All that money will only net 8,132 acres of new or improved habitat for the flycatcher and other species.

When The Nature Conservancy, Bureau of Reclamation, and Salt River Project buy farms and retire their water wells, the San Pedro clearly benefits. But it may be too little, too late. Whatever victories the group has achieved may be overshadowed by new home building and well drilling along the river that The Nature Conservancy and other groups are powerless to control. Just upstream of the group's San Pedro preserve and the Three Links Farm, the mining company BHP has closed down the San Manuel copper mine and begun to sell off the riverside land to developers. "If the BHP development goes in as they'd like it to be," Burton said, "there will be 100,000 people living here." "Here" is Pinal County, where local officials have embraced growth, in contrast to the pains taken by Pima County to protect riparian habitat through its Sonoran Desert Conservation Plan. "It's dumb," Burton said. "We've already done that experiment, and we know what will happen. You put 100,000 people or more next to the river, and it'll go dry." There was no better example than Tucson's assault on the Santa Cruz River one valley to the west.

The San Pedro's prospects are even grimmer farther upstream, where the burgeoning city of Sierra Vista has been overpumping the aquifer that feeds the river for decades. Not even incorporated until 1956, Sierra Vista now has 44,000 residents. The area's population is expected to double in the next two or three decades, with much of the growth connected to the US Army's Fort Huachuca, the largest employer in southern Arizona. The upper San Pedro is such an ecological treasure that Congress created a 47,688-acre national conservation area along the river in 1988. The federal government has fenced off the streambed from cows and banned new wells within the conservation area's boundaries, but the protections only go so far because someone drilling a well on nearby private property can snatch groundwater before it reaches the river.

In rural Arizona, as in much of the West, new wells are subject to minimal regulation. Sometimes they're not regulated at all if they just serve a house or two and are not part of a formal subdivision. As a result, water managers don't really know how many straws have been dipped into a local aquifer. These wells, which can legally pump more than 1 million gallons a year, typically extract far less water than allowed, but taken together they can have a devastating impact. Arizona's landmark Groundwater Management Act restricted well pumping in Tucson, Phoenix, and elsewhere. But Fort Huachuca, Sierra Vista, and the rest of Cochise County aren't covered by the same regulations.

The ESA is what ultimately forced the military to be more judicious with its water use on Fort Huachuca. In 1992, Defense Department officials proposed relocating the Defense Language Institute from Monterey to Fort Huachuca, a move that would have increased the base's population by 5,000 and further stoked the Sierra Vista economy. Environmentalists led by Robin Silver of the Center for Biological Diversity, ensured that the expansion was reviewed for its potential impacts on endangered species, including the flycatcher; Mexican spotted owl; lesser long-nosed bat; Sonora tiger salamander; two fishes, the spikedace and loach minnow; and two plants, the Canelo Hills ladies' tresses and Huachuca water umbel. The military and its backers fought Fish and Wildlife's attempts to limit pumping at Fort Huachuca, but ESA lawsuits ultimately forced the army to rethink its use of water. Since 1989, the fort has slashed its consumption by more than 500 million gallons a year, a drop of more than 50 percent, even though the number of jobs on post has increased by 3,000 since 1995. Instead of irrigating its parade grounds, golf course, and athletic fields with groundwater destined for the San Pedro River, the fort spent $6 million on a reclaimed wastewater system that uses treated effluent for irrigation. On the other end of the sewage supply, the army installed nearly 700 waterless urinals in its bathrooms, a simple move that saves tens of thousands of gallons per stall. And along the San Pedro itself, the military spent several million dollars in partnership with The Nature Conservancy to buy conservation easements that limit well pumping on former farms. Like the monitoring program for Sonoran pronghorn on the Barry M. Goldwater Range, the conservation measures cost millions of dollars but did nothing to impede the mission of Fort Huachuca, which trains many of the intelligence officers who work in Iraq, Afghanistan, and elsewhere.

If Fort Huachuca's halving of its water use could be replicated elsewhere along the San Pedro, the river and its wildlife would have a much brighter prognosis. But it will take more than the ESA to make that so. The biological opinion that spurred the aggressive water conservation came about because the military's activities at Fort Huachuca had a clear connection to the federal government and therefore triggered a formal consultation with Fish and Wildlife. There is no federal nexus, however, if someone moves to southern Arizona to work at Fort Huachuca and sinks a well on his private property. About 70 percent of Fort Huachuca's personnel live off-base, where their water consumption isn't subject to the same strict controls that exist on post, thanks in part to an exemption tacked on to the 2003 defense spending bill.

Along the San Pedro and other watercourses, the ESA alone cannot save riparian wildlife. Individuals, utilities, businesses, and governments need to do a much better job of conserving the groundwater that nurtures rivers and streams. Public education campaigns that emphasize conservation are certainly valuable in this regard, but relying solely on altruism guarantees disappointing results. New policies that create the right incentives are also needed to escape the tragedy of the commons and prevent people from depleting the West's most precious resource.

For starters, we must evolve from guzzlers into misers. In much of the West, the majority of water consumed by homeowners is used for outdoor irrigation, much of which is incredibly wasteful. Phoenix, in the heart of the Sonoran Desert, is full of grass. Plenty of Tucsonans also plant lawns, but more often you'll see drought-tolerant xeriscaping and front yards covered with pebbles. In Phoenix, outdoor irrigation accounts for more than 60 percent of water use; in Tucson, it's about 40 percent. The conservation ethic has always been stronger in Tucson, where citizens tend to be more environmentally minded and where the city is more dependent on local groundwater. Per capita water use in Tucson's single-family houses averages 107 gallons a day, while in Phoenix it's 144 (the hotter temperatures in Phoenix only explain a fraction of the difference). Tucson Water, the city-owned utility that botched initial delivery of Colorado River water, has become a national leader in promoting water-saving policies and practices, including harvesting rainwater and reusing gray water from sinks and showers for irrigation. Tucson Water does this for both ecological and economic reasons. Reducing peak summertime demand saves the utility, and ratepayers, from having to buy new sources of water. As with electricity, conservation and efficiency are almost always cheaper than acquiring new supplies. Recognizing this, the city offers free water audits to its customers, bans ornamental turf in new commercial developments, requires desert landscaping in large-scale subdivisions, and even tickets residents who let water run down the street.

Faced with limited water resources, other southwestern cities have begun to step up and improve their conservation efforts, including Las Vegas, where residents use around 230 gallons per day in a desert that averages four inches of rain a year. Even as the Southern Nevada Water Authority promotes a plan to tap groundwater aquifers hundreds of miles to the north with a $2 billion pipeline, the utility pays local residents if they rip up the grass in their yard and replace it with xeriscaping. The net result is that Clark County's overall water use has been falling, even as Las Vegas's population has been soaring. If Las Vegas can cut its per capita water use, any city can.

Utilities could shrink their customers' water consumption with a single, bold stroke: charge more for the product. To this day, many Americans have little financial interest in conserving water because their monthly bills are so low. In some communities, residents don't even pay for water, or they're charged a set fee regardless of how much they use. For many renters, the water bill is the landlord's responsibility, creating a classic principal-agent problem of misaligned incentives. Even in Tucson, which has a tiered rate structure that charges homeowners more per gallon the more water they use, monthly water bills are still the cheapest utility for most residents. Nationwide, monthly water bills average about $20 and customers get about four gallons for every penny they spend. Utilities typically only charge their customers the cost of pumping and delivering water, not for the resource itself or its replacement cost. Americans' love affair with SUVs didn't sour until gas prices topped $3 and $4 a gallon. Similarly, many Americans don't give energy conservation a second thought until their gas and electric bills skyrocket. There's no reason to expect that people will rethink their water use unless it hits them in the wallet.

Raising the price of water to account for the associated ecological damage and the cost of securing new supplies, however sensible from an environmental standpoint, can be fraught with political risks. In 1976, for example, after several slow-growth advocates gained seats on the Tucson City Council, Tucson Water hiked water rates and imposed new fees to recover the costs of pumping groundwater up to the ritzy Catalina Foothills. In what would become the first of many fumbles, the city enacted the rate changes in summer and caused some residents' water bills to suddenly quadruple. The resulting political firestorm led to the recall of three city council members, with another stepping down before he could be removed. For the next few decades, the phrase *remember the recall* would dog any high-minded official in city hall who sought to boost water rates in order to promote conservation. But the aversion to raising water bills didn't last forever, and Tucson now has one of the most progressive rate structures in the nation. Other communities will follow suit, whether they like it on not. As demand for water goes up due to population growth and the supply of water goes down due to climate change, it will be economics rather than politics that forces the appropriate pricing of water.

Becoming more efficient in our use of water, electricity, and gasoline is good for the pocketbook and the planet. But it won't completely solve our problems if our population keeps growing. In Tucson, for instance, per capita water use fell 14 percent from 1997 to 2007, but Tucson Water's customer base increased 21 percent. In effect, the city took two steps up and three steps back. Further gains in water conservation will be even harder to achieve because much of the low-hanging fruit, like offering low-flow toilet rebates and banning outdoor fountains, has been plucked. "Conservation is great, and it needs to be done," Tucson environmentalist Randy Serraglio told me, "but at a certain point, no matter how small the human footprint becomes, there will be too many feet." I had met Serraglio in 1995, while he and I were canvassers with the League of Conservation Voters, and he always cut to the heart of the matter. "People just don't want to talk about the carrying capacity of the Sonoran Desert," said Serraglio, now a conservation advocate at the Center for Biological Diversity. "How many people should really live in Tucson or Phoenix?"

Because the human population is growing so quickly in such dry places, it's all the more important to modernize our antiquated water laws. At the start of the 21st century, many western states still manage their water according to a 19th-century misunderstanding of hydrology that ignores the connection between groundwater and surface flows. The doctrine of prior appropriation, which encourages people who hold water rights to pull as much out of a river as they're allowed, is also a vestige of the imperative to settle the West in the late 1800s. These outmoded policies are examples of what University of Colorado law professor Charles Wilkinson calls the lords of yesterday: "A battery of nineteenth-century laws, policies, and ideas that arose under wholly different social and economic conditions but that remain in effect due to inertia, powerful lobbying forces, and lack of public awareness." At the start of the 21st century, mining in the West is still guided by an 1872 statute that gives away public land to mining companies for as little as $5 an acre and generates zero royalties on the billions of dollars worth of metal that's extracted. Arid-lands agriculture persists thanks to the philosophy enshrined by the 1902 Reclamation Act.

These policies and subsidies are not written in stone. In the 21st century, they can be amended, discarded, or replaced with new laws and approaches that at least incorporate the knowledge we gained in the 20th century. With water, the federal government could stop propping up farmers who grow low-value, water-intensive crops in the desert, often by pumping groundwater with artificially cheap electricity, or at least require the use of more efficient technology, such as drip irrigation. In California, for instance, researchers believe that farms could reduce their water use 17 percent by shifting away from flood irrigation, improving scheduling of irrigation, and applying less water during drought-tolerant stages of plant growth. On the federal level, former interior secretary Bruce Babbitt has suggested amending the Clean Water Act to prohibit the depletion of streams and rivers below a certain baseline. On the state level, legislators could impose stricter limits on wells near important riparian areas, or tax the withdrawals and devote the revenues to protections elsewhere. In Oregon, well pumping is restricted within a mile of critical groundwater aquifers. Washington state has established minimum levels for streams and rivers to benefit wildlife and recreational users, then denied applications to drill new wells nearby. Throughout the West, conservation groups are acquiring instream flow rights that keep a set amount of water in a river for environmental purposes, a strategy similar to acquiring a grazing lease and not running any cattle on the allotment. On the local level, communities like Pima County have adopted policies that restrict suburban and rural development on the basis of water supply, and prevented property owners from developing land near riparian areas.

Any attempt to better manage the West's water must eventually grapple with what to do with farms, which still consume about three-quarters of the region's supply. To grow an acre of alfalfa in the California desert, farmers may need to pour on more than 2 million gallons in a year, enough to pile the water eight feet high. All the while, cities and industries in the region are desperate to acquire new water supplies and willing to pay top dollar. The obvious solution is a market in which urban utilities buy or rent water from farms. "In California, one acre-foot used to grow alfalfa generates approximately $60 in revenue," wrote University of Arizona law professor Robert Glennon, "but the same amount of water used in the semiconductor industry generates almost $1 million." Water rights are already being sold and leased across the West; there were more than 3,000 transactions from 1987 to 2005, covering 31 million acre-feet, about double the Colorado River's annual flow. "The United States is entering an era of water reallocation, when water for new uses will come from existing users who have incentives to use less," Glennon wrote in his 2009 book, *Unquenchable.*

It makes clear economic sense to transfer water from low-value to high-value uses, but there are environmental risks to such exchanges, plus major political hurdles. In some places, irrigated cropland or runoff provides important habitat for birds and other wildlife. Shifting water from farms to cities may enrich farmers and allow them to raise martinis in La Jolla, as the saying goes, but businesses dependent on those farms would wither and receive no compensation. Concerns over local economic impacts nearly scotched a multibillion-dollar deal to transfer about 300,000 acre-feet a year from the Imperial Irrigation District, along the Colorado River, to Los Angeles and San Diego.

Improved conservation, more enlightened laws, and effective water markets can buy the Southwest's remaining riparian areas more time. Ultimately, however, the region's booming population will butt up against its limited water supply. Where will the next bucket come from? Desalination of seawater is likely to become an important part of the West's water portfolio. So is another promising, if not appetizing, source: our toilet bowls.

Turning sewage into drinking water is no longer the stuff of dreams (or nightmares). It is becoming increasingly common, especially in arid regions, due to improvements in treatment technology and the imperative to find new supplies. Unlike other water sources, effluent is controlled locally, and it's the only supply that grows as a city does. Effluent already supplies 3 percent of Arizona's water; in Tucson, it accounts for nearly 10 percent and irrigates more than 900 parks, golf courses, and other sites. In Orange County, a half-billion-dollar effluent project will serve the needs of 144,000 families. Using microfiltration, reverse osmosis, ultraviolet light, and hydrogen peroxide, the process is expected to produce potable water that costs 1.5 cents per 100 gallons. That's a bit less than the district would pay to import water from the Colorado River or Northern California, and two to five times less expensive than desalinating ocean water. Like many other communities, Orange County already makes its sewage clean enough to use for irrigation, which is where much of the Southwest's potable water winds up. Of the 130 gallons that Arizonans use per person, per day, only 1.5 gallons is for drinking and cooking.

Along the Santa Cruz River, Tucson Water has been pursuing the idea of recycling effluent into potable water, even though the toilet-to-tap idea riles many residents. It's a strategy born of necessity. Tucson is only entitled to a limited share of Arizona's CAP water, a supply that will face the first cuts if the Colorado's flow dwindles, and it can only pump so much groundwater without running afoul of the state's groundwater act. When I interviewed Tucsonans about the toilet-to-tap idea, many turned up their noses, as did I when I toured the local sewage plant and saw what is filtered out of the effluent stream. When it arrives, the sewage is more than 99 percent water, but workers have discovered a dead body, aborted fetuses, tires, and two-by-fours. "Anything anyone can stuff down a manhole," the plant's superintendent told me. "You'd be surprised what people flush down their toilets or put down their drains." The debris is fed onto a conveyor belt for disposal in a landfill; on my visit, I watched a procession of condoms, cockroaches, cigarette butts, sanitary napkins, and, as always, a steady supply of undigested corn kernels.

Making wastewater potable would not be cheap. In Tucson, it would cost $278 million in today's dollars to retrofit the city's main sewage plant. Nearly half the construction cost would be for evaporation ponds to hold the reject stream coming out of the reverse-osmosis step, when water molecules are forced through membranes and minerals are trapped behind. The ponds could claim hundreds of acres, and the dregs left over would have to be disposed of, possibly in a special landfill. Using today's engineering, some 15 percent of the water passing through a reverse-osmosis plant would be lost to the reject stream, though gains in water technology treatment are expected to reduce that level.

The nature of effluent will continue to pose technical challenges for engineers and political challenges for policy makers. Even the most rigorous treatment technologies may not block the trace quantities of prescription drugs, insect repellents, and fragrances that go down the drain. However, those chemicals, often measured in parts per billion or trillion, are already found in today's water supply because sewage plants that aren't along the coast typically dump their effluent into streams and rivers that feed groundwater aquifers. People in New Orleans are already drinking water that was previously flushed down a toilet in St. Louis and other communities up the Mississippi. Four out of five streams sampled by the US Geological Survey had traces of prescription drugs, including antidepressants and birth control medication, and several studies have found male fish living downstream from wastewater plants either developing female sexual organs or bearing eggs, apparently due to their exposure to hormones.

In Tucson, sewage is now treated to meet Clean Water Act standards and then released into the Santa Cruz River. As it seeps into the earth on its way toward the Gila River, the effluent supports a narrow strip of riparian vegetation that extends many miles downstream from the sewage plant. These forests hint at what Father Kino saw when he entered the Santa Cruz River Valley in 1692. With enough time, the forests might once again host southwestern willow flycatchers. But if Tucson starts to treat its sewage for delivery to customers, the discharges into the river will dwindle and the vegetation downstream will wither. Even recycling our own wastewater isn't necessarily a good thing for the environment, and even the supply of effluent has its limits. Unless a major desalination project brings the sea to Tucson or freshwater is transported overland from hundreds or thousands of miles away, the city will eventually wring every possible drop out of its water supply. If traffic, air pollution, or even hotter weather in the 21st century haven't already stopped Tucson from growing, the lack of water will.

I must confess that I reserve a special place in my heart for treated sewage because it helped me find a bride. Tucson was not an ideal place to be a single guy in his 30s, and I resorted to placing a personal ad online. Hoping to stand apart from the competition, I used a photo of me holding up a desert tortoise that I had adopted. A few responses trickled in, and then the traffic dried up altogether. I gave up. Months later, I checked my inbox on the site and discovered a message that had been sitting there unread for many weeks. She seemed perfect: an attractive, aspiring environmental attorney who loved the outdoors. I responded but heard nothing back, until about six months later, when I came within a nanosecond of deleting a message titled "Hello again" from some stranger named Ginette. She had noticed my name and e-mail address at the bottom of a story I had written about Tucson Water irrigating more ball fields with effluent. Ginette, a student of Glennon's, was writing a law review article on the legal issues surrounding treated wastewater, so it gave her a pretext to contact me.

For our second date, I suggested one of my favorite places in Arizona: Aravaipa Canyon, a gash in the Galiuro Mountains north of Tucson that has a rare perennial stream flanked by saguaro cacti and lined with a riparian forest. It was an unusually gloomy January day, but we had the canyon practically to ourselves and talked for hours while trudging up the streambed. We crept up on a great blue heron perched in a cottonwood tree and flushed a troop of coatis out of the brush, the first Ginette had ever seen in the wild.

We were married the next year and prepared to leave Tucson after Ginette accepted a fellowship at the EPA's San Francisco office. I had reservations about departing Arizona, but after seven years in the desert, much of it during a deep drought, a wetter, greener place did seem appealing. Shortly before we left, the skies opened up during the summer monsoon and pounded southern Arizona with strong thunderstorms. On July 28 and August 1, floods barreled through Aravaipa Canyon and reset its ecological clock. Tom Beal, one of my colleagues at the *Arizona Daily Star*, interviewed residents who scrambled up a hillside to escape floodwaters that rose five feet in five minutes. The US Geological Survey stream gauge didn't last long, so the severity of the flood was unclear, but scientists estimated that the creek shot up from a couple hundred cubic feet per second to at least 20,000. Canyon residents, seven of whom were airlifted to safety, said the water rose several feet higher than during the 1983 flood, which peaked at 70,000 cubic feet per second. The deluge yanked out willows as if they were weeds and tossed 50-foot cottonwood trees like toothpicks. As destructive as it was, the flood was part of Aravaipa's natural cycle and the means for the riparian habitat to regenerate. Cottonwood and willow saplings quickly sprouted in the sediment and would become a spacious gallery forest within a few decades.

20
Get the Lead Out

When I visited condor 134 at the Phoenix Zoo in March 2006, one of the veterinarians treating the bird, Dean Rice, made an offhand comment that I didn't fully grasp until years later. "We're like a M*A*S*H hospital here," he said after the blood transplant was over and 134 had pulled out of the anesthesia. Back then, I saw Rice, Kathy Orr, and the others treating the condor for lead poisoning as akin to emergency room physicians in an urban hospital. But as time went by and the threats to species seemed to multiply by the day, I realized that the M*A*S*H unit that Rice mentioned was quite a different place than an ER, and an even more appropriate metaphor for the ESA. In the age of climate change, the law's work is actually closer to what transpires in a surgical tent on a battlefield, where the brutality of war is never far, lifesaving resources are always lacking, and the cold calculus of triage forces uncomfortable decisions. In M*A*S*H units and urban ERs, and with the ESA, we struggle to "do no harm" while still taking the calculated risks needed to save lives or entire species.

Like most M*A*S*H patients, 134 arrived for treatment at the Phoenix Zoo via helicopter. One month after Thom Lord descended into the

Grand Canyon and the nearly dead condor was airlifted from the shores of the Colorado River, the staff at the Phoenix Zoo had managed to reverse the bird's fortunes. Now able to stand on his own and nourished by a feeding tube, the bird gradually gained weight. Once the lead was purged from his system, 134 started to eat again. On June 9, 2006, after more than three months of treatment, Orr determined that condor 134 was well enough to be transported up to northern Arizona—this time on the highway—and readied for release. For three weeks, 134 was kept inside a barnlike enclosure near the Vermilion Cliffs and fed stillborn calves. Biologists then drove 134 up the sandy road that snakes up the back side of the Vermilion Cliffs and placed him inside a more spacious flight pen. Able to fly around with other birds, 134 exercised muscles that had atrophied after months in captivity.

On the morning of July 21, about six months after being rescued, 134 left the pen and took to the sky. He eventually reunited with 210, his potential mate. Lord, the biologist who had hiked into the Grand Canyon and saved 134, later saw the bird in the wild, picking up where he left off after ingesting the lead. "This is a great example," he said, "of a bird that would have no problem doing just fine in the wild—with the exception of this lead issue."

The next spring, 134 and 210 built a nest in a cave high on a wall in a remote part of Grand Canyon National Park. The Peregrine Fund monitored the site regularly and observed the two condors traveling great distances to forage for food. But it wasn't until September that a biologist caught the first glimpse of the five-month-old chick, designated as bird 441. Six weeks later, 441 fledged, only the sixth condor chick to do so in Arizona. From the rim of the Grand Canyon, biologists watched 441 soar over the chasm, evade a golden eagle, and eventually leave his parents' watch to strike out on his own.

———————

As 441 was learning to make a living off carrion around the Grand Canyon, I was struggling to find a paycheck in the Bay Area. Our rent in Berkeley was triple the mortgage in Tucson for less than half the space. In other ways, Berkeley seemed like the inverse of Tucson. Cowboy hats gave way to berets. Pickups with Support the Troops magnets morphed into Priuses with Subvert the Dominant Paradigm stickers. One morning, I stepped outside for the paper and into a fog bank so thick that

I could barely see across the street. In the evening, I could no longer find the stars and constellations; the abundant city lights illuminated the marine layer from below and turned the night sky silver. It was as if the film of my life was suddenly being shot in the negative.

My fellowship ended and newsrooms weren't hiring. In fact, newspapers were shrinking both their staff and the printed product to cut costs as readers and the classifieds migrated to the Internet. The *San Francisco Chronicle* and San Jose *Mercury News* announced plans to lay off a quarter of their newsrooms. When I called an Associated Press editor, he chuckled and gently suggested I start looking into other careers. Soon enough, the *Tucson Citizen* would go extinct after 138 years of publication, and the entire profession of environmental journalism would become an endangered species.

I stumbled into a job at a small consulting firm, California Environmental Associates, that was looking for someone to write the final report for a big project on climate change known as Design to Win. During the hiring process, the principals at CEA asked me to write a hypothetical memo that offered advice to a philanthropist ready to spend $10 million on climate change. Once I got in the door, I realized the assignment was missing a few zeros. CEA had been hired by a half dozen of the world's largest environmental foundations to come up with a road map for reducing greenhouse gas emissions. The recommendation was $600 million a year. Six months later, the Hewlett, Packard, and McKnight foundations had committed more than a billion dollars to start a new foundation, ClimateWorks, to carry out the plan.

It was interesting, important work, animated by great colleagues, but I still pined for my days as a reporter. The CEA office was down the block from a busy fire station literally in the shadows of the Transamerica Pyramid and inauspiciously designated as Station 13. Hearing the doleful sirens echo in the concrete canyons, I yearned to be aboard one of the engines heading to a wildfire or some other life-or-death crisis. But the more I learned about climate change, the more I saw it as the ultimate emergency.

In retrospect, the 2006 flood that blasted through Aravaipa Canyon, the 2002 drought that strangled the entire Southwest, and the other crazy weather I reported on were omens and the beginning of a wave of natural disasters that climate change was cooking up in the 21st century. Like Hurricane Katrina in 2005 and the deadly European heat wave in 2003, these individual storms and extreme events cannot be directly attributed to climate change. But scientists are quite sure that epic storms, floods, fires, droughts, and heat waves will become more common as the planet warms.

Solutions to global warming will create their own problems. The imperative to leave our 20th-century energy system behind us has led to a deluge of applications to build solar farms in the Southwest. California is trying to generate one-third of its power from solar, wind, and other clean sources by 2020, and more than half of the US states now have similar renewable portfolio standards. These much-needed policies, which will slash emissions and stimulate billions of dollars in clean-tech investments, have ushered in a mad dash for sunny, flat places in California, Arizona, and Nevada. Developers have filed more than 200 proposals covering 2 million acres overseen by the Bureau of Land Management, which tends to own the desert basins that are perfect for solar facilities. Those lands, however, also host endangered species like the desert tortoise, so an otherwise green project may wind up blading habitat for rare plants and animals. It sounds simple enough to pick up some desert tortoises and move them out of harm's way, but such actions are inherently risky. In 2008, when the US Army expanded Fort Irwin in the Mojave Desert, it committed to spend some $9 million to move nearly 2,000 tortoises to nearby public lands. But the helicopter translocation was halted after at least 90 of the first 556 animals died, most eaten by coyotes that were apparently extra hungry because drought had diminished other food sources.

In Arizona, biologists are drawing up plans to move some Sonoran pronghorn to new habitat that is part of the animal's historic range, farther from border traffic, and simply inaccessible due to roads and other barriers. But those same areas are choice spots for generating solar power. In the plains and interior West, wind power could be restricted by two candidates for ESA listing: the lesser prairie chicken and greater sage grouse. The birds avoid tall vertical objects like turbines and transmission towers, perhaps because they associate these structures with trees that offer perches to predatory raptors. Wind turbines can also kill bats and birds directly, though proper siting of towers greatly reduces the hazard.

The environmental impacts of renewable power are not limited to the number of acres claimed by solar panels and wind farms. The cheapest form of solar power, which uses mirrors to generate steam and run turbines, can fry any animal that flies too close to towers where the sunlight is concentrated. This type of solar technology can also consume gobs of water, sometimes even more than power plants that use coal, natural gas, or nuclear fuel. In southern Nevada, the National Park Service raised alarms about such projects taking water from Devils Hole, an isolated spring holding an endangered species of pupfish that was down to just 38 individuals in 2006. The park service calculated that if all the proposals were built, more than 16 billion gallons could be removed each year from the Amargosa Valley. Concerns over one project's water use led developers to switch to a "dry-cooling" technology that uses fans and heat exchanges. The alternative will cut water consumption by 90 percent, but the tradeoff is higher costs and lower efficiency.

Throughout the country, another major challenge for renewables is the need for old-school transmission lines that can bring the electricity to market. It took San Diego Gas and Electric three years to win approval for a $1.9-billion 120-mile power line that was originally proposed to go through Anza-Borrego Desert State Park. Environmentalists' challenges to that project and others provoked a strong rebuke from politicians on the left and right. "If we cannot put solar power plants in the Mojave Desert," California governor Arnold Schwarzenegger said at a Yale climate change conference, "I don't know where the hell we can put it."

We certainly should be using our rooftops, warehouses, industrial sites, unproductive farmland, and other degraded areas to generate emissions-free energy, but if we ever hope to scale up solar and wind, we will invariably harm some habitat. A comprehensive approach that encourages clustering of projects and puts the most ecologically valuable sites off-limits will minimize some of the impact. A mitigation fund could offset some of the damage by paying for protections elsewhere. Still, when it comes to making and moving energy, there is no free lunch, which is why it's so critical to reduce our appetite for power, both through lifestyle choices and the adoption of energy efficiency policies such as appliance standards and building codes.

Biomass energy offers another example of how alternatives to fossil fuels offer tremendous opportunities but can also carry significant threats to endangered species and entire ecosystems. Biomass, mostly in the form of power plants that burn wood pellets, has already surpassed hydropower as the nation's leading renewable energy source, and according to some projections, it will produce more electricity than both wind and solar power by 2030. In the Southwest, a few biomass power plants are already keeping the lights on using the scrawny trees that are clogging the region's forests. In the eastern Arizona towns of Eagar and Snowflake, where many evacuees from the Rodeo-Chediski Fire fled, power providers built two facilities that burn hundreds of tons of wood each day, most from forest thinning projects. While biomass energy is often more expensive than power from fossil fuels, it emits less greenhouse gases and typically counts toward state-mandated goals for renewable power. But the facilities still emit air pollution, and many environmentalists are suspicious of the approach. Some fear that rising demand for the feedstock could increase pressure to log forests, not just thin around vulnerable communities.

Plant matter is also a potential fuel for vehicles. The first generation of biofuels promoted in the United States, namely the boom in corn-based ethanol, turned out to be a bust for the environment because the production process uses so much energy, water, and fertilizer. More than 20 pounds of corn, about four gallons of water, and a half-gallon of fossil fuels are needed to produce just one gallon of ethanol. Likewise, clearing tropical rain forests to plant oil palms, another ethanol crop, eliminates vital "sinks" that soak up carbon dioxide from the atmosphere and destroys some of the most biologically diverse places in the world. But biofuel technology is maturing rapidly, stoked by the prospect of billion-dollar payoffs. The next generation of biofuels—cellulosic ethanol—at least promises the holy grail: a 90 percent reduction in emissions compared to petroleum-based gasoline. The federal government and venture capital firms are pouring hundreds of millions of dollars into research on making ethanol from nontraditional sources, including wood chips. The Forest Service has even proposed using woody biomass to replace 15 percent of the nation's gasoline.

It remains to be seen whether excess fuel from the West's forests can be converted into vehicle fuel at a reasonable cost or become a significant part of utilities' power portfolios. Transportation costs remain a major hurdle, and most research focuses on crops that are easier to grow and harvest, such as switchgrass. Nevertheless, there are advantages to using fuel from overgrown forests: there is no need for water, fertilizer, or additional land, and removing the kindling reduces the risk of unnaturally intense wildfires that are a threat to so many species. The key benefit is that biofuel crops—be they trees, grass, or algae—remove carbon dioxide from the air before being turned into energy, thereby erasing much of their carbon footprint. There is, however, a balancing act. Once a tree is chopped down and hauled away from a forest, it can no longer pull carbon out of the atmosphere, so that loss—plus the energy needed to extract the wood—must be factored into the equation. At least in the Southwest, research suggests that thinning could be carbon neutral or provide a net benefit to the climate by preventing crown fires that emit copious amounts of greenhouse gases.

These are the tough choices awaiting us: biofuels versus biodiversity; solar panels versus desert tortoises; wind turbines versus birds and bats; treated effluent plants versus riparian forests; desalination versus marine life. Unfortunately, we will have to swallow some irreparable harm, perhaps even extinctions, to mitigate emissions and avoid the far greater threat of catastrophic climate change. As one biologist put it to me: "Not frying the planet may be a little more important than some ultra rare orchid or some narrowly endemic frog."

———————

For all the challenges facing the California condor, global warming posed a relatively minor threat to a bird that could eat all sorts of dead animals and fly hundreds of miles to its next meal. Bird 134's return to the Grand Canyon and the successful fledging of his chick, 441, were big wins in the ongoing struggle to stave off the condor's extinction. Heroic interventions were also playing out in California, where a rapidly spreading wildfire in 2007 forced the San Diego Zoo's Wild Animal Park to evacuate its condors, just hours before the breeding facility was destroyed. The next June, a wildfire on the central California coast caused the Ventana Wildlife Society to evacuate its sanctuary. With the flames approaching, US Coast Guard helicopters flew through thick smoke to airlift seven condor chicks and an adult that had been left behind in a flight pen. The 188-square-mile fire displaced 43 condors, more than half the population in California and a quarter of the total number of free-flying birds. Without access to the rugged country, biologists feared for the condors, but they managed on their own by picking apart a dead whale and sea lion along the Big Sur Coast. After the fire, only 2 of the 43 condors were missing.

The condor recovery program, mostly financed by private groups like the Peregrine Fund and Ventana Wildlife Society, was fighting daily battles to save the birds and winning most of them. But the war might still be lost. When a blue-ribbon panel of independent biologists evaluated the condor program at the request of the American Ornithologists' Union, the six scientists concluded that the bird would remain endangered until the lead threat was eliminated. "Recovery of the California Condor, once almost inconceivable, has become imaginable, and the public believes the condor program to be a success," the scientists wrote. "But enormous obstacles to recovery still exist, so much so that the possibility that California Condors could once again be extirpated in the wild is as conceivable as recovery." The risk of lead poisoning hung over the species like a Sword of Damocles and stopped the condors from becoming truly wild. They had to be monitored intensively, captured frequently, subjected to stressful chelation therapy, and fed subsidies of lead-free carrion, all of which could acclimate the birds to humans and inhibit their journey toward self-sufficiency. "Condors almost certainly would not survive in the wild were they not regularly trapped, tested and treated for lead," the panel concluded. So much effort was devoted to protecting the birds from lead that "one might argue that they constitute little more than outdoor zoo populations," the scientists said.

If there were no hunting in condor country, the birds wouldn't keep getting sick from lead. But such a ban was as likely to happen as decommissioning Glen Canyon Dam to save humpback chub or eliminating public lands ranching to recover the gray wolf. Besides being a political nonstarter, limiting hunting could actually harm the condor because it would remove a key source of food for the birds: gut piles and dead animals left behind after the hunt. The trick, according to many condor experts, was to get the lead out of ammunition while simultaneously encouraging hunting of big game and feral pigs so the condors had enough nontoxic food to eat. But how to effect that change divided condor advocates, just as the launch of the captive breeding program had split the community decades ago. Many supported a legal ban on the use of lead ammo in condor country, maybe even throughout the nation, since so many other species were falling ill to lead poisoning. Others believed that educational campaigns, rebates for non-lead ammo, and voluntary measures would be more effective than punitive regulations, which could prompt a lethal backlash against the bird.

Most hunters in Arizona and California opposed the mandatory approach, arguing that unleaded ammo, typically made from copper, tungsten, tin, bismuth, steel, or alloys, was hard to find or too expensive. When I started reporting on the issue in 2004, I called around to Arizona sporting goods stores and found that few carried unleaded ammunition, so these complaints had some merit. But there were plenty of options on the Internet, and with each passing year, unleaded ammo was becoming more widely available in stores. Anthony Prieto, a condor advocate and avid hunter from Santa Barbara, told me it was ridiculous that hunters were griping about the higher cost of lead-free bullets—the premium was 10 to 20 percent in his experience—because the price of a box of ammo, maybe $30 or $40, paled in comparison to the sport's other costs. A hunter could easily spend $1,000 on a rifle and $500 on a scope, plus hundreds to thousands of dollars for gas, food, and lodging on a hunting trip. Prieto told me psychology, not economics, was what made hunters resist the change to lead-free bullets. "I always use the analogy of a baseball player with a certain bat or a certain glove," he said. "They're superstitious, and they don't want to give it up." Sociology and politics were also at play: many hunters didn't trust messages coming from environmental groups and thought the condor-lead connection would be used as a pretext for banning hunting altogether.

After Prieto spent time volunteering with the condor program, he and other hunters brainstormed with biologists about ways to accelerate the switchover to unleaded ammo. The product was Project Gutpile, a nonprofit group that served as a clearinghouse for information on alternatives to lead bullets. Besides highlighting the risk to wildlife, Project Gutpile tells hunters they're also risking their own lives by shooting with lead: "Hunters eating game killed with lead ammunition are unavoidably ingesting small quantities of lead. Period." Studies have found elevated lead levels in the blood of subsistence hunters in Canada and similar results among North Dakota residents who ate wild game. When researchers analyzed venison from 30 Wyoming deer killed with lead bullets, they found metal fragments, nearly all of them lead, in 80 percent of the deer and 32 percent of the meat packages processed from the animals' carcasses. The increasing awareness of the health threat associated with lead ammo stems in large part from the plight of the California condor, a true canary in the mine.

Seeking to ban lead ammo in condor country, Prieto and another hunter joined with environmentalists and a Native American group in 2005 to petition the California Fish and Game Commission. A month after the request was filed, the commission shot down the proposal 3–1. "We certainly care about the California condor," commission president Jim Kellogg said. "But there was not a lot of science that proved that lead bullets are where the birds are getting their lead from." The dissenting vote, Bob Hattoy, said the science was there and suggested his colleagues lacked the courage to approve the ban. "It just seems ridiculous," he said, "that on the one hand we're recovering them, and on the other, we're allowing them to be poisoned."

Environmentalists then filed suit against the Fish and Game Commission and made a failed bid to pass a state law prohibiting lead ammo in the bird's 2,385-square-mile range. Taking a cue from firearms and hunting groups, Governor Arnold Schwarzenegger's office downplayed the lead threat. "Data collected in California during the past 10 years does not suggest that bullets used only in hunting are the main source of lead exposure," a form letter from Sacramento said. "In fact, there is no firm evidence of the source of any of the lead ingested by wild condors."

There were, in fact, heaps of data linking spent ammunition and condor mortality. A 2003 report commissioned by the California Department of Fish and Game and conducted by University of California at Davis scientist Michael Fry had concluded that the other possible sources of lead in the environment were very unlikely to be making condors sick. The amount of lead in the air had fallen by 97 percent since the switch to unleaded gasoline in the 1970s, and industrial emissions in California were both small and not upwind from condor country. There was also no evidence that ingestion of lead from trash dumps or other sources was making the condors sick. "When all potential sources of lead in the environment are compared," Fry concluded, the carcasses and gut piles of hunted animals "appear to be the most likely sources of lead exposure to condors."

No fewer than five scientific papers published in 2006 solidified the link between lead ammo and condor deaths. Lead poisoning was found to be the most frequently diagnosed cause of death among free-ranging condors from 1996 to 2005. A study on deer carcasses proved that lead bullets explode inside big game. X-rays also showed shotgun pellets in the stomachs of seven condors and fragments that were likely from spent bullets in another seven. Researchers who tracked condor movements found that the birds frequently visited deer remains, and they recorded spikes in lead poisoning tied to the hunting season.

The smoking gun was published in the journal *Environmental Science and Technology*. Researchers at the University of California at Santa Cruz drew blood from 18 condors in central California, one-fifth of the world's wild population at the time. As expected, the scientists found that wild condors had far more lead in their systems than captive condors that had yet to be released—10 times as much. The scientists then went a step further to determine the metal's source. Lead in bullets has a distinct fingerprint that is revealed by measuring the relative abundance of four naturally occurring isotopes. When the researchers examined the lead fingerprint in the blood of wild condors, it closely tracked the fingerprint of lead in bullets. In the most severely poisoned condors, the lead fingerprints matched exactly. The study's title said it all: "Ammunition Is the Principal Source of Lead Accumulated by California Condors Re-Introduced to the Wild." Even so, two months after the slam-dunk study was published, the president of the Wildlife Management Institute, a hunting group, told *USA Today* it still wasn't clear that lead ammo was poisoning condors. "There are other potential pathways for the lead," said Steve Williams, President George W. Bush's first director of the US Fish and Wildlife Service. "I wouldn't want to speculate on what those might be."

The lead ban faced an uncertain future with the California Fish and Game Commission, especially after Hattoy, the lone vote in favor of the measure, died in early 2007. A poll of California hunters showed that two-thirds opposed the plan, but other players were making moves. In February 2007, the 270,000-acre Tejon Ranch, the state's largest private landholding and game preserve, announced that it was prohibiting lead bullets on its property in the Tehachapi Mountains, 60 miles north of Los Angeles. In the California state legislature, the ban on lead bullets started gaining momentum, fueled by a sizable grassroots lobbying effort that produced more than 40,000 e-mails and faxes. Confronted with overwhelming scientific evidence, the California Fish and Game Department reversed its position and recommended that the commission ban lead bullets in condor country. But the NRA and other hunting groups remained adamantly opposed, calling the proposal draconian and saying that it "reflects a hidden agenda by some to ban all hunting in California." There were some valid concerns about the availability of ammunition in a few calibers and the cost differential. But for many firearms advocates, the opposition focused on questioning the science connecting lead bullets to dead condors.

The conflict came to a head in the fall of 2007. The California legislature, in a party-line vote, approved the ban and sent the bill to Governor Schwarzenegger. The California Fish and Game Commission was nearing a vote on the same matter. In preparation for the decision, one of the commissioners, R. Judd Hanna, compiled and annotated 167 pages of research on lead and condors, including many of the peer-reviewed studies, and sent the packet to his fellow commissioners. The NRA saw its target. The group mobilized its own grassroots attack against Hanna, triggering hundreds of calls to the State Capitol and leading 34 Republican lawmakers to call for Hanna's ouster in a letter to Schwarzenegger that accused the commissioner of not being impartial. Hanna resigned at the administration's request. After Hanna was sacked, he openly accused the NRA of hijacking the system. Hanna, who called the evidence of lead poisoning from ammunition overwhelming and irrefutable, wasn't some hippie: he was a lifelong Republican, ex-navy pilot, Stanford MBA, and former real estate developer who had once belonged to the NRA himself. Hanna's purge became an embarrassment for Schwarzenegger, who portrayed himself as a green Republican and supported California's ambitious global warming law. Somewhere, somehow, Schwarzenegger saw the light. On October 13, 2007, he signed the bill and banned the use of lead bullets for hunting in California's condor country. In the ensuing months, the Fish and Game Commission approved the regulations and expanded them to cover the hunting of more types of animals.

California's lead ammo ban was no silver bullet. Plenty of game was taken without a hunting license, and there were only 200 game wardens to patrol a state spread over 155,000 square miles. Eight months after the ban went into effect, the Fish and Game Department reported it had made 6,500 contacts in the field and had only been forced to issue 63 warnings and 9 citations, which could carry a $500 fine. But some hunters continued to use lead ammo. In the months and years after the ban took effect, condors were still being poisoned and killed by swallowing lead bullet fragments.

In Arizona, condor reintroduction was established under a special provision of the ESA that prevented the federal government from forcing any regulatory changes, a concession made to ranchers, hunters, and others who worried the bird's endangered status would be used against them. On its own, the Arizona Game and Fish Commission could follow California's lead and ban lead bullets in condor country, but it chose to pursue a voluntary approach. Starting in 2005, Arizona spent $105,000 of its lottery proceeds to give hunters coupons for free nontoxic ammo if they were selected for permits to shoot game on the Kaibab Plateau, a prime foraging area for bird 134 and other condors just north of the Grand Canyon. About two-thirds of the 2,393 hunters redeemed their coupons, and 81 percent said they used the bullets in the field. Judging by the survey, hunters gave high marks to the unleaded rounds: only 7 percent said the ammo didn't perform as well as lead; about three-quarters said they would recommend it to a friend.

There are signs that Arizona's voluntary program is having an impact. Hunters continue to report that they are using nontoxic ammo, with compliance rates estimated between 70 and 90 percent. For three years, there were no lead-related deaths in Arizona or Utah, but in January 2010, three birds died in northern Arizona after swallowing toxic ammo. Many backers of the voluntary effort concede that if the lead threat isn't greatly diminished within a few years, it will be time to abandon the carrot for the stick. The American Ornithologists' Union's review also cast doubt on the voluntary approach, which is also starting up in Utah, arguing that "virtually a 100% compliance with the voluntary lead-free ammunition program will be needed to avoid severe lead poisoning incidents."

The varying approaches in California and Arizona, the former mandatory, the latter voluntary, created a sort of public policy experiment. It will take years to determine which strategy works better, in part because the small number of birds confounds the statistical analyses needed to tease out causes and effects. Unintended consequences will also be hard to detect. In March 2009, for example, a condor captured in Monterey County was not only suffering from lead poisoning, it had also been hit with a lead-filled shotgun blast. A few weeks later, another condor was found nearby with lead shot in its body and lead fragments in its digestive tract. A case of backlash? Without catching the shooter or shooters, we'll never know.

That spring, Peregrine Fund biologists in Arizona were trying to trap all of the free-flying birds so they could administer blood tests and head off lead poisoning. They managed to capture the entire population, except for 134 and one other condor. Unable to locate 134, technicians attached a GPS transmitter to his mate, 210, and were able to track her movements. But there was still no sign of 134. Three years before, the bird had also disappeared for more than a month, but as time went on without a sighting, the odds diminished that 134 was still alive. With her mate gone, 210 partnered with another bird, convincing Peregrine Fund biologists that 134 had died just short of his 14th birthday. By early 2010, 134's remains still hadn't been found, so the cause of his death will probably never be known, but the presumption was lead poisoning, the population's top source of mortality. Condors can live long past 40, so 134 died in the prime of his life.

In the grand panoply of threats facing endangered species—climate change, habitat loss, invasive predators, and exotic diseases, to name a few—eliminating lead from ammunition seems like a relatively easy problem to knock off. It's also common sense. We've known that lead is poisonous for more than 2,000 years, and alternatives to leaded ammo are readily available. Virtually all of the major manufacturers—Winchester, Federal, Remington—now make unleaded bullets for a wide range of calibers. As demand grows for unleaded ammo, the price premium will continue to fall and may disappear entirely. Decades ago, we started removing lead from paint, pipes, pencils, gas—products that are used far more widely than bullets—so extending the policy to ammunition would hardly be revolutionary. It might also save lives and prevent debilitating illnesses among the millions of Americans who eat game shot with lead bullets.

Now that California has banned lead ammunition, other states may follow suit, and support may build for action on the federal level. Two decades ago, the government endured withering criticism from hunters when it banned lead shotgun shells for waterfowl hunting, and it will no doubt run into a similar buzz saw if it tries to mandate the use of nontoxic bullets. In 2009, when the National Park Service announced it wanted to eliminate lead bullets in the handful of parks where hunting is allowed, the proposal was dismissed by the National Shooting Sports Foundation as "arbitrary, over-reactive and not based on science."

Without hunters and anglers, American conservation would be a shadow of itself. Sporting groups helped create refuges and funding streams for wildlife that remain critical. In the Southwest, hunters played a leading role in restoring deer, elk, pronghorn, bighorn sheep, and other game species that were nearly wiped out by the first wave of settlement. Without countless hours of labor donated by anglers, the endangered Gila trout would not have been upgraded to threatened and made numerous enough to support limited catch-and-release fishing. But on the issue of lead and condors, a fear of slippery slopes and a knee-jerk reaction to any regulation of firearms is causing many hunters to snub the storied tradition of conservation that Aldo Leopold, Theodore Roosevelt, and other sportsmen established. The question hanging over the condor's head is whether hunters will step up, switch their ammunition, and help pioneer a 21st-century ethic that extends beyond the animals we hunt and fish to encompass all species.

Epilogue
Triage

*One of the penalties of an ecological education is that one lives alone
in a world of wounds. Much of the damage inflicted on land
is quite invisible to laymen. An ecologist must either harden his shell
and make believe that the consequences of science are none of his business,
or he must be the doctor who sees the marks of death in a community that
believes itself well and does not want to be told otherwise.*

—Aldo Leopold

Looking back, I learned a lot about the West by looking down on it
from planes. Being strapped into the backseat of a Cessna and circling
an expanding wildfire taught me more about how blazes burn than any
book I read or expert I interviewed. The bulk of my aerial education took
place in the window seat of a commercial airliner, flying around 500 mph

and seven miles above the ground. I'm one of those people who will coax, wheedle, and cajole ticket agents at the counter and in call centers in India so they'll give me a seat with a view, even for night flights. Granted, you can't see much when it's overcast, but in the southwest corner of the continent, the jet stream often ridges north and forms a dome of high pressure over the region that suppresses cloud formations and creates a dry, clean lens through which to examine the land below.

My memory is anything but photographic, yet I retain sharp images from many flights: From Tucson to Salt Lake City on a blue June day, passing over the red earth of the Grand Canyon and seeing a slender column of smoke rising from the green Kaibab Plateau. From Phoenix to Denver during the monsoon, watching puffy cumulonimbus clouds gather over the Mogollon Rim and pulse with lightning, like brains deep in thought. From Los Angeles to Tucson on a starry night, until the Phoenix grid appeared and kept on going, even at eight miles per minute. Beyond the region's mega metro areas, the almost ethereal perspective from an airliner suggests humanity's imprint is slight across much of the interior West. When you head east from San Francisco to Denver, nearly 1,000 miles, the only sizable nuclei of lights you can see after leaving California's Central Valley are Reno and Salt Lake City, way off to the north.

It's a route I got to know well after Ginette and I moved to Colorado. The Bay Area was too crowded, too expensive, and too far from big mountains, so we relocated to Denver and began settling down. Ginette started clerking for Greg Hobbs, a Colorado Supreme Court justice and expert on western water issues, and I kept working for CEA and Climate-Works. I made a lot of trips back to San Francisco and burned plenty of jet fuel along the way. I always sat beside a south-facing window to get a better view of the Rockies on the departure from Denver. On clear mornings, when the low angle of the sun casts deep shadows on the rumpled topography along the Continental Divide, you can see millions of acres of rust-colored forest where the beetle outbreak has killed the lodgepole pines. In fall, there are striking yellow patches of aspen, but like the lodgepoles, those trees are suffering, possibly because of climate change. Over the Roan Plateau, in northwest Colorado, you can see the lattice of roads and pads for drilling natural gas, then trace the squiggly thread of the Green River as it snakes through Desolation Canyon on its way to meet the Colorado River near Moab. The next hour, flying over Utah's Sevier Desert and Nevada's basin-and-range country, gets a little redundant, but then you come to 13,147-foot Boundary Peak, the high point in a hulking range along the border with California that's even more impressive than Mt. Graham and topped with snow most of the year, at least for now. Soon after passing the upper reaches of the Owens River Valley, dewatered by the Los Angeles Aqueduct a century ago, you're above Half Dome in Yosemite, a national park that we once thought was big enough and sufficiently isolated from its surroundings to protect its natural inhabitants. But now, with the namesake snow of the Sierra Nevada endangered by global warming, even one of our grandest national parks seems tiny compared to the landscape-level changes that are already transpiring. Gazing down on the West, vast expanses may appear to have escaped the human hand, but if you look carefully enough, you can see the signs of sickness everywhere.

When I tried to put this book to bed, I also saw disease in the people I knew. I sent e-mails to biologists and government officials I'd lost touch with for a few years only to find out they were gone. John Morgart, head of the Sonoran pronghorn and Mexican gray wolf recovery teams, was dead of cancer at 58. Maeveen Behan, the architect of Pima County's Sonoran Desert Conservation Plan, was dead of cancer at 48.

My own mom was diagnosed with advanced ovarian cancer, so I spent a lot of time in airplanes between Denver and New York, looking out at the clouds. They did a double hysterectomy and surgically removed as many of the tumors as possible, but some tiny particles of cancer were impossible to extract. For chemo, the doctors prescribed Taxol, the world's best-selling anticancer drug—and one of most compelling examples of why preventing extinctions is in our self-interest. Taxol was derived from the Pacific yew, long considered junk wood by foresters because it couldn't be made into lumber. For decades, the yew was chopped down and burned in slash piles so loggers could harvest the commercially valuable Douglas firs in the coastal ranges of the Pacific Northwest. But hiding within the bark of this discarded tree was an exceptional chemical. In 1993, 31 years after a federal botanist collected the bark of a single yew in Washington state, drug maker Bristol-Myers Squibb started selling Taxol, and the company was soon making more than $1.5 billion a year on the medicine. A trash tree to some, the Pacific yew had been generating value for centuries as a snowshoe, harpoon, hunting bow, canoe paddle, fence post, and cooking utensil. Indigenous people turned the plant into a contraceptive for women, salve for wounds, cure for stomach pains, and remedy for colds, presaging its use as an anticancer drug.

For all its wonders, Taxol was pure hell on my mom. After surgical ports were inserted into her torso, an IV bag with Taxol and other drugs dripped into her abdominal cavity twice a month. The treatments made her hair fall out, caused her to lose 30 pounds, and sometimes forced her to lie in bed the whole day. After her six months of chemo, she was emaciated and drained, but the medicine worked, at least for a while. The cancer came back, and she only lived another 18 months, so I can't say that Taxol and the seemingly useless Pacific yew had saved my mom, but for every extra day it gave me, I was grateful. At an intellectual level, I'd known for many years that protecting biodiversity could lead to a cure for cancer and other diseases. But it wasn't until after I looked my mother's death in the eyes that I could see and feel what it means to lose a life, or understand why protecting species is more than just a lofty ideal and moral obligation. It's also a matter of self-preservation.

Since I arrived in Tucson in 1995 and started canvassing for the Arizona League of Conservation Voters, my view of the ESA and other environmental laws has evolved. I used to believe that we simply needed legal sticks to prod landowners, businesses, and the government into doing the right thing. I used to think that technology, markets, and hands-on management of wildlife would only cause problems. But with climate change under way, I see things differently. The command-and-control style of regulation that produced the ESA and other laws in the early 1970s can be effective at cleaning up rivers or reducing local air pollution, but it doesn't always work when we try to address threats that are more ubiquitous and less tractable than a drainpipe or smokestack. I now recognize the need to supplement punitive measures with incentives that encourage good behavior and make endangered species into assets for property owners, not just liabilities they're determined to erase. I now see technological innovation and intensive human management as the only hope for rescuing many of our endangered species.

Desperate times demand aggressive measures. When the 2002 drought reduced the US population of Sonoran pronghorn to 21, wildlife officials had no choice but to build artificial water holes, plant forage plots, and import animals from Mexico, even after the first five pronghorn died from the stress of the translocation. Those hands-on strategies, plus some wetter weather, boosted the wild population to 76 by 2008 and bought the species a little more time.

But the Southwest also offered plenty of examples of how our interventions can sometimes lead to disaster. One such episode began on a cold night in February 2009, when the jaguar nicknamed Macho B was prowling in a canyon southwest of Tucson, close to where biologist Emil McCain and I had checked trail cameras a few years before. Unlike condor 134, who died entering middle age, Macho B was geriatric. But the jaguar was still making a living along the US-Mexico border, stalking deer and javelina under the cover of darkness and steering clear of the growing number of border crossers and law enforcement officers in his territory. As Macho B passed by a stout oak tree that night, a snare suddenly grabbed his leg. Macho B struggled to free himself, leaving scratches seven feet high in the tree and digging at roots in an eight-foot radius around the trap. The temperature dropped below freezing.

The Arizona Game and Fish Department said it had set the trap so it could capture black bears and mountain lions, fit them with GPS collars, and track their movements, in part to learn where the animals crossed the border. On a check of the traps the following morning, February 18, researchers discovered Macho B, sedated him, fitted him with a GPS collar, and then set him free.

The transmitter around Macho B's neck offered McCain and Jack Childs a trove of data. By satellite, they received Macho B's exact coordinates and elevation every three hours. It was the continuous stream of observations needed to learn which habitats Macho B was using and how he was navigating the increasingly busy borderlands. McCain, Childs, and others had wanted to deliberately capture Macho B or another jaguar to conduct such research, but the plan had yet to receive government approval.

Right after the capture, the telemetry was unremarkable. "He behaved exactly as you would expect: he fled the capture site to a secluded area to recover," McCain said. "However, in the following days it became clear that his movements were not normal, and that he was spending a huge portion of the time not moving." By February 26, a team from the Arizona Game and Fish Department was looking for Macho B. They recaptured him shortly before noon on March 2, about five miles from where he was initially caught, and transported him to the Phoenix Zoo by helicopter.

In the two weeks since his capture, Macho B's weight had plummeted from 118 to 99.5 pounds. Three veterinarians on the scene, including Dean Rice, who had treated a starving condor 134 for lead poisoning three years before, concluded that the jaguar was dying of irreversible kidney failure. Macho B was put down at 5:13 PM. Based on a quick necropsy, Rice concluded that the jaguar had been suffering from kidney problems long before the capture, but the stress of the incident and the tranquilizers used in the process had probably aggravated his condition. Rice predicted the cat would have been dead within the next two months due to the kidney disease. Macho B was two or three years old in 1996, when Childs and his party discovered him lying on an alligator juniper in the Baboquivari Mountains, so Macho B had lived to 15 or 16, making him the oldest jaguar ever documented in the wild.

Macho B's story didn't end there. Dogged reporting by Tony Davis and Tim Steller, two of my former colleagues at the *Arizona Daily Star*, raised serious questions about how the capture had been handled, whether Macho B had been put down too soon, and whether he had been intentionally baited rather than accidentally ensnared. Some veterinarians suspected that Macho B had suffered capture myopathy, the same condition that had killed the Sonoran pronghorn transplanted from Mexico. Macho B had definitely struggled while in the trap—the tip of his claw was embedded in the bark of the tree that held him and one of his canine teeth was broken. When the results of tissue samples came back from a University of Arizona lab, they showed no sign of kidney disease. "For a supposed 15-year-old cat, he had damned good looking kidneys," pathologist Sharon Dial told the *Star*. She and other experts argued that intravenous fluids and anti-inflammatory drugs might have saved Macho B. Rice, however, maintained that kidney failure was to blame, telling *The Arizona Republic* that the "readings weren't high, they were off the scale." The full truth about Macho B's condition in his final days will remain unknown, because a Fish and Wildlife official only ordered a "cosmetic" necropsy so that the jaguar's hide could be used in a display or for public education.

Days later, the *Star* reported a stunning accusation. Right before Macho B was captured, McCain had checked the trap with a Game and Fish employee and one of his technicians, Janay Brun. After Macho B died, Brun told the *Star* that McCain had asked her to bait the trap with jaguar scat. McCain denied that allegation and said he was unaware that Brun had used the scat. E-mails the *Star* obtained through public records requests showed that McCain and others were preparing to capture a jaguar in the weeks before Macho B was snared. But McCain told me that he was simply taking precautions in case a jaguar was caught inadvertently by one of the traps meant for lions and bears.

The accusations prompted a criminal investigation by the US Fish and Wildlife Service, which concluded in January 2010 that Macho B had been intentionally captured in violation of the ESA. The report from the Interior Department's inspector general concluded that the Arizona Game and Fish Department lacked the necessary permits for the capture and said that an unnamed subcontractor (read: McCain) was facing potential prosecution. As of March 1, 2010, the US attorney's office still hadn't filed charges and wasn't commenting on the case. Was Macho B euthanized prematurely? The inspector general's report said that studies by the US Geological Survey and University of California at Davis concluded that the jaguar had, in fact, been suffering from kidney failure.

The story was still evolving as this book went to press, but for many environmentalists, the verdict was already in. Critics of the state-led jaguar conservation team saw the dead cat as proof positive that the federal government had wrongly ceded management of an endangered species to an unaccountable entity. "Just the existence of the conservation team is a case study in the application, or lack thereof, of the ESA," said Sergio Avila, a biologist with the Sky Island Alliance who had worked with McCain in Mexico trapping jaguars for research. "At the meetings, every time I opposed the trapping of jaguars, I got yelled at by ranchers, not by other scientists."

Emil McCain, like Wayne Shifflett, was facing the prospect of federal charges for meddling with an endangered species he was trying to help. He continued to do research on jaguars in Mexico and told me he felt persecuted by environmental groups. "I found that these 'green' groups were ready and willing to sacrifice me, my hard work, and my scientific integrity for a good sound bite in the local paper," McCain wrote me. "And they would sacrifice the jaguar's well-being to please their donors or recruit more members. I began to see they were not in this game for the jaguar, but for political power to push larger agendas. They wanted to use the jaguar to push bigger issues like eliminating cattle from public lands and hunting. I felt those were different issues that had nothing to do with jaguar conservation and only turned the local people against the cat."

While Macho B's death was being investigated, environmentalists were in court over jaguars, arguing that Fish and Wildlife needed to map critical habitat and write a recovery plan. In 2006, the agency had declined to designate critical habitat, saying that the United States accounted for less than 1 percent of the jaguar's current range and was "not essential to the conservation of the species." Likewise, Fish and Wildlife said a recovery plan would only benefit "a small number of individual jaguars peripheral to the species, with little potential to effect recovery of the species as a whole." But on January 12, 2010, in response to a lawsuit from Defenders of Wildlife and the Center for Biological Diversity, Fish and Wildlife agreed to create a recovery plan and map critical habitat. The agency's about-face was met with complaints of political meddling from ranchers who felt threatened by the habitat map and recovery plan. One of the world's leading jaguar biologists, Alan Rabinowitz, slammed the decision in a *New York Times* op-ed, writing that Fish and Wildlife had "bent to the tiresome litigation" and would be wasting resources trying to recover an animal in marginal habitat. "As someone who has studied jaguar for nearly three decades," he wrote, "I can tell you it is nothing less than a slap in the face to good science." While recovery plans are not enforceable, one for the jaguar might outline a strategy for reintroducing the cats to the United States and recommend significant changes to land use in the borderlands, including limits on predator control, lion hunting, and livestock grazing. Critical habitat carries the weight of law, so the map could affect those policies and the building of additional infrastructure along the border, provided that the federal government does not exempt such projects from environmental review.

At least during the Bush administration, that assumption was a big if. In May 2005, Congress had given the Department of Homeland Security the power to waive laws ranging from the ESA to the National Historic Preservation Act in order to build fences and other barriers along the border. The first exemption, for 14 miles of fencing near San Diego, came in September 2005 and was followed in January 2007 by another waiver that would accelerate construction of 37 miles of fencing, roads, and surveillance towers on the Barry M. Goldwater bombing range. Nine months later, Homeland Security Secretary Michael Chertoff invoked the power yet again after environmentalists sued to block construction of two miles of fencing and barriers in the San Pedro Riparian National Conservation Area, a potential corridor for jaguars where 19,000 border crossers had been arrested and 14 had died in the previous year. The first three exemptions under the Real ID Act drew the ire of environmentalists, but those waivers were nothing compared to what happened on April 1, 2008. Chertoff laid down the trump card and applied the exemption to 470 miles of border so that crews could finish building the last 267 miles of barriers called for in the Secure Fence Act without paying heed to the ESA and 34 other laws.

In just a few years, the border had undergone a transformation that skeptics predicted would take decades. In September 2006, there were about 25 miles of formidable fencing and 45 miles of vehicle barriers along Arizona's 378-mile border with Mexico. By March 2009, there were 124 miles of fences and 183 miles of vehicle barriers. More than four-fifths of Arizona's border now had something stronger than a few strands of barbed wire as an obstacle, up from less than one-fifth 30 months before. Just as important, the number of Border Patrol agents had soared to 18,000 in 2008, double the level seven years before. The new fences were taller, tougher to climb, and more resistant to cutting. Where deployed, the vehicle barriers cut down on drive-through smuggling. By early 2009, the Border Patrol's Tucson Sector, the nation's top spot for illegal immigration and drug smuggling, was reporting steep declines in apprehensions. From Texas to California, the number of arrests along the border dropped to levels not seen since the mid-1970s. The new fences, barriers, and agents surely played some role, but the countermeasures were deployed just as the American job market started tanking. So economics, not just the infrastructure, was also stopping migrants from crossing the border. A 2008 Congressional Research Service study concluded that much of the illegal border traffic had simply shifted elsewhere, just as it had during past crackdowns.

Scientists couldn't say for sure how the border buildup was affecting the movements of Macho B, mountain lions, and other large predators. The fences, most erected in valleys, may not have directly blocked the jaguar's path. Although Macho B had once traveled 37 miles between mountain ranges, apparently by crossing through intervening lowlands, he and other jaguars appeared to favor the higher country. The problem with the fence was its indirect effect: the foot traffic was being funneled into the more-mountainous terrain, which in turn drew the Border Patrol into those areas. The situation was especially troubling because many of the smugglers and migrants traveled at night, the time when jaguars are most active. And yet another charismatic predator was entering the border debate: in early 2010, Mexican officials were preparing to release a handful of wolves in northeastern Sonora, raising the prospect of lobos moving into the United States and reconnecting with the population reintroduced to the Blue Range.

The Obama administration has not been enthusiastic about building new fences and other obstacles along the border, but neither is Congress rushing to revoke Homeland Security's power to exempt border projects from environmental reviews. Chertoff's successor, former Arizona governor Janet Napolitano, once quipped, "You build a 50-foot wall, somebody will find a 51-foot ladder." But faced with strong public support for beefing up the border, she and other early critics came to support the Secure Fence Act. President Obama, who voted for the fence while a senator, later expressed doubts about the approach. "There may be areas where it makes sense to have some fencing," Obama said. "But for the most part, having [the] border patrolled, surveillance, deploying effective technology, that's going to be the better approach."

To reduce illegal immigration from Mexico in the years ahead, the federal government will likely rely on both physical barriers and a virtual fence that uses video cameras, motion sensors, ground radar, unmanned drones, and other technology. The first 28 miles of virtual fencing were installed in the Altar Valley, including part of the Buenos Aires National Wildlife Refuge, but the experiment delivered disappointing results. The radar had trouble picking out people, the system didn't work well in the rain, and the various pieces weren't well integrated. Project 28 was just a "proof of concept" that used off-the-shelf technology, so in early 2009, Homeland Security announced a new plan: 17 towers along 23 miles in the Altar Valley and 12 towers along 30 miles in Organ Pipe Cactus National Monument. In each location, about 200 ground sensors would supplement towers topped with cameras able to zoom, pan, and see objects six miles away. By 2016, at a cost of nearly $7 billion, Homeland Security hopes to have such technology along the entire US-Mexico border, except for 200 miles of rugged terrain around Big Bend National Park, which would be covered later.

The virtual fence will carry its own environmental consequences. It was never meant to stand in isolation, and it will be accompanied by road construction so that agents can quickly respond to the entrants picked out by the cameras, radars, and sensors. Use of stadium-style lighting or aircraft to supplement the vehicle barriers and virtual fence will invariably harm some sensitive species. But the virtual fence, unlike the physical one right along the border, cannot be exempted from environmental laws under the Real ID Act.

The federal government will gauge the virtual fence's effectiveness on two wildlife preserves with abundant endangered species. How the cat-and-mouse game of law enforcement will shift in response is anyone's guess. At Organ Pipe Cactus National Monument, the high-tech approach could decrease human intrusion into habitat for the Sonoran pronghorn and lesser long-nosed bat, or it could lead to even more Border

Patrol agents, vehicles, and helicopters in the area. On the Buenos Aires National Wildlife Refuge, the virtual and physical fences could push border crossers into nearby mountains, where there are fewer manmade barriers but plenty of prime habitat for jaguars. At the same time, the heightened enforcement in the Altar Valley could do the area some good by reducing the illegal traffic on the Buenos Aires.

The refuge had begun a new era after the tadpole scandal deposed manager Wayne Shifflett. Quietly, officials convened a team of more than a dozen outside scientists to evaluate the quail program. Attendees later told me that no one in the room thought it was smart to keep throwing the birds out into the refuge and have them die soon thereafter, so the reintroduction was halted. "It's been many, many years of releases, and you really can't say we're fully succeeding here, to be honest," said Sally Gall, Shifflett's former deputy. "I think everyone is aware of that." Gall told me that Shifflett's overly optimistic portraits of the quail's recovery had been counterproductive because they discouraged Fish and Wildlife's regional office from devoting more resources to the program. Gall also didn't agree with Shifflett's decision to move the tadpoles. "Yes, he cared about the frogs and the resources, and yes he had good intentions, but it was very sneaky the way he did it," she said. "Our staff didn't even know."

By 2008, four years after the federal government stopped the failed releases of masked bobwhite quail, only two were heard on the refuge. "I wouldn't be surprised if there's just a couple of small coveys out there, at the most," Gall told me. In northern Mexico, a survey of the only other wild population of masked bobwhites turned up just a handful of birds. When the Interior Department released its State of the Birds report in 2009, it put the number of masked bobwhite quail in the United States at 10. Refuge officials were preparing to experiment with new techniques for restoring the Buenos Aires, including ripping out mesquite trees, aerating the soil, and building woodpiles. Bringing cows back on the range was not high on the list, but also not ruled out as a means for controlling Lehmann lovegrass, an invasive species that some scientists regarded as a lost cause. "There's a reason it was selected for distribution after a worldwide search 70 years ago," Guy McPherson, then a University of Arizona professor of natural resources, had told me years before. "It may be something we're just stuck with."

The struggle to control lovegrass on the refuge was emblematic of a much larger problem confronting the deserts of the Southwest, and one that was likely to expand as the planet warmed. Buffelgrass, red brome, and other invasive plants were once a minor nuisance, but by the end of the 20th century, they had expanded across the region and into protected areas. The biggest problem with these plants is their flammability in an environment where fire is foreign. The high-desert grasslands of the Altar Valley and Malpai region have burned for thousands of years, which is why restoring fire to these areas is so important, but the lower-elevation deserts around Tucson and Phoenix are supposed to be fire free. Not so in landscapes dominated by buffelgrass, which grows so thick it can carry superhot fires that kill cacti, desert tortoises, and other native species that never evolved with fire. Climate change could give a leg up to such weedy invaders, promote unnatural fires, and allow the nonnative plants to gain even more ground. "In arid regions where ecosystems have not coevolved with a fire cycle," the federal government warned in 2008, "the probability of loss of iconic, charismatic megaflora such as saguaro cacti and Joshua trees will be greatly increased."

The fight against nonnative grasses in the Altar Valley was not going well, but biologists were making headway against another pest: the bullfrog. Threatened Chiricahua leopard frogs had flourished on the Buenos Aires in the years since Shifflett surreptitiously moved them there. Shortly after word got out that he had put the frogs in three ponds, someone dumped predatory green sunfish into two of them, which would have killed the frogs had the introduction not been botched. But all of the sunfish died, and subsequent wet years helped the frogs spread to 11 locations by 2009. "Wayne Shifflett's legacy, in spite of his problem and the fine he had to pay, was that he saved that species in the valley for a decade," herpetologist Cecil Schwalbe told me. "If he hadn't acted right then, the story would have been over, and it would have been another case of extinction by inertia, which is one of the great threats in Arizona or anywhere."

With funding from the federal stimulus package and other sources, Schwalbe, Phil Rosen, their students, and volunteers ramped up efforts to control the bullfrogs by draining water sources, snagging the frogs by hand, gigging them with spears, and shooting them with pistols and .22 rifles. "There's been this incredible positive surge in the past year," Schwalbe told me in early 2010. "If you pick your battles, you can handle the bullfrog as long as you take care of the source ponds. We've kept them from breeding on the Buenos Aires refuge for 10 years." Schwalbe and Rosen were now speaking to grazing groups and helping ranchers in the Altar Valley eliminate bullfrogs from their land. "The fact we're a hot item on the ranching circuit says a lot," Schwalbe said. Although climate change threatens to cause more droughts like the one in 2002 and could dry up the leopard frogs' water holes, the bullfrogs, which evolved in wetter environs, would be even more vulnerable to the drier weather. "That's the silver lining," Schwalbe said. "We can take advantage of the drought and really pound the invasive species."

The Chiricahua leopard frog was also getting help from some unexpected allies: Jim and Sue Chilton. The species that had ended Shifflett's career and been tied up in the litigation surrounding the Montana Allotment was now covered by a safe harbor agreement that would immunize the Chiltons from added regulations if they voluntarily helped the amphibian. "I wanted to do something positive for a species rather than defending myself," Jim told me. The Chiltons signed the safe harbor agreement, part of a statewide program inspired by the work of the Malpai Borderlands Group, and they spent $5,000 to construct a predator-proof refuge on their private land. Jim had worried that leopard frogs would colonize stock ponds on his Forest Service allotment and restrict cattle grazing. Now he had legal assurances that his good deed would not be punished. In August 2009, biologists moved 60 frogs from the Buenos Aires National Wildlife Refuge to the Chiltons' facility. The frogs were the offspring of Shifflett's clandestine tadpole translocation. Since winning the libel suit against the Center for Biological Diversity, Jim said he hadn't been bothered by the group. "They've gone on to other issues," he said. "They've grown, and they've prospered."

The Center's size and power certainly had increased since Jim had won his $600,000 lawsuit. Its membership soared past 60,000 and its annual revenues topped $9 million by the end of 2008 as it campaigned to list species imperiled by global warming. The best-known case was the polar bear, but the Center also filed petitions and follow-up lawsuits to protect corals, penguins, walruses, seabirds, and other species that lived thousands of miles from its desert headquarters in Tucson.

Scientists were issuing grim forecasts for polar bears and the sea ice they depend on, but listing the species was complicated by their dramatic rebound in the late 20th century due to antihunting restrictions and habitat protections. The current population, 20,000 to 25,000, was more than double the number in the 1960s and quadruple the level in the 1950s. Minus climate change, many scientists considered the population stable, but the Arctic was already warming far faster than the rest of the world. Listing the polar bear could further restrict hunting and oil and gas drilling in its habitat, but an even bigger prize for the Center was the possible use of the ESA to restrict greenhouse gas emissions. The logic was straightforward, even if the cause and effect were not proximate: a coal-fired power plant in Kansas emits carbon dioxide that warms the planet, melts sea ice, and pushes the polar bear toward extinction. If the polar bear were protected by the ESA, Fish and Wildlife could theoretically block the power plant's construction if the agency determined the project jeopardized the species.

As a practical matter, using the ESA to regulate carbon emissions was out in left field and dismissed by many attorneys and environmentalists as impractical. But as a communications tool, listing the polar bear, the quintessential charismatic megafauna, was a total coup for the Center. On April 3, 2006, *Time* produced an iconic cover with a polar bear and the headline "Be worried. Be **very** worried." I think the plight of the polar bear did as much to raise consciousness about climate change as Hurricane Katrina, *An Inconvenient Truth*, and the Nobel Prize awarded to Al Gore and the Intergovernmental Panel on Climate Change. The Center's Kierán Suckling told me the campaign to list the polar bear had raised consciousness of global warming just as Earth First! had popularized the protection of old-growth forests.

As usual, Fish and Wildlife stalled on its decision to list the polar bear. But just before Christmas 2006, the Bush administration's Interior Department acknowledged the dire threat from climate change and proposed labeling the bear as threatened. Fish and Wildlife concluded that two-thirds of polar bears could be gone by 2050 and 97 percent of the ice they rely on could vanish by 2100 if current trends in emissions continued. Sixteen months later, Interior Secretary Dirk Kempthorne made the listing official, but there was a catch. As part of the decision, Fish and Wildlife prevented the animal's ESA protections from addressing the root cause of the polar bear's endangerment: greenhouse gas emissions. The listing also excluded critical habitat for the polar bear, a move that could have restricted drilling in the Arctic. It felt like a hollow victory for many activists, but they held out hope that a new administration might view the issue differently.

Plenty of ESA experts and environmentalists also thought it unwise to use the law to regulate SUVs, electric utilities, cement plants, and other sources of carbon dioxide. For starters, the ESA couldn't do anything to affect coal-fired power plants in China, slash-and-burn agriculture in the Amazon, or other foreign sources that would cumulatively have a much bigger impact on the climate than domestic emissions. Even in the United States, the ESA was never envisioned as a means for governing the energy economy. The agencies that administered the law, the US Fish and Wildlife Service and National Marine Fisheries Service, were totally unequipped for that job. And legally, the arguments for blocking power plants in Arizona to protect polar bears in Alaska were on grounds as shaky as 21st-century sea ice. An important 1995 Supreme Court ruling, *Babbitt v. Sweet Home*, required proof of a direct link between an activity and harm to endangered species.

Barack Obama's win in November 2008 raised environmentalists' expectations, but the president's choice for interior secretary, Ken Salazar, a rancher and conservative Democratic senator from Colorado, provoked howls from the Center and other hard-line groups, many of whom wanted to see President Obama select Raúl Grijalva, a Tucson-area congressman who had been a strong proponent of the Sonoran Desert Conservation Plan.

Salazar, a former Colorado attorney general like Gale Norton, upset many greens shortly after he took office when he allowed wolves in the Northern Rockies to be delisted and shot by hunters. Since 1995, the population had increased by about 25 percent per year, to more than 1,600 in 2009, even though hundreds of wolves were being killed each year for preying on livestock. Salazar did, however, win praise for reversing the 11th-hour decision by the Bush administration to eliminate the process of consultation that causes projects to be reviewed by Fish and Wildlife biologists, a core element of the ESA's regulatory authority. In the courts, judges started to overturn the listing and critical habitat decisions that were tainted by the political influence of Julie MacDonald, who resigned after the Interior Department's inspector general concluded that "her heavy-handedness has cast doubt on nearly every ESA decision issued during her tenure."

After eight years of heading backward under the Bush administration, there were glimmers of hope for endangered species once Obama took office. In the Southwest, the Mexican gray wolf's recovery was given a boost when Fish and Wildlife agreed to scrap the three-strikes rule that forced the government to execute or incarcerate wolves for life if they killed too many cattle. Salazar's Interior Department also broke with the Bush administration in announcing plans to engineer more artificial floods in the Grand Canyon to benefit the humpback chub. The new protocol will synchronize the releases from Glen Canyon Dam with the input of sediment from tributaries and place less importance on the loss of hydropower revenues.

Salazar seemed determined to clean up at least some of the mess created by his predecessors. But based on Obama's first year in office, it was clear the administration was using its political capital in the environmental arena to push for climate legislation and promote renewable power, not focus on the ESA. Given the overwhelming importance of global warming, it was tough to argue with that strategy. Salazar's Interior Department only listed two plants in 2009, leading the Center to give the Obama administration a C for its handling of endangered species. But Fish and Wildlife pledged it would start tackling the backlog of some 250 candidate species by focusing on ecosystem-based listings that would cover numerous species at once.

The fate of the polar bear listing rule, put off for months, was finally announced on May 8, 2009: the Obama administration would not revoke the Bush-era decision that stopped the ESA from being used to regulate emissions. "To see the polar bear's habitat melting and an iconic species threatened is an environmental tragedy of the modern age," Salazar said. But the ESA wasn't the solution to that overarching problem, Interior ruled, nor was it possible for biologists at the Fish and Wildlife Service to evaluate how emissions sources were affecting a bear thousands of miles away. "We have to have the smoking gun and the dead animal," explained Valerie Fellows, a Fish and Wildlife Service spokeswoman. "You can't link the power plant in Florida with a dead bear in Alaska."

I thought it was the right call. Having Fish and Wildlife make energy policy was impractical and would do little to address a global phenomenon. It would also give enemies of the ESA more ammunition in their quest to undermine or abolish the law. To be sure, Fish and Wildlife should be doing all it can to determine which species are most endangered by rising temperatures. Climate change should suffuse all of our thinking and decision making around biodiversity. But the essential battle against the fundamental problem, greenhouse gas emissions, was better fought elsewhere and with other weapons.

———————

Our climate has always been in flux, and species have always been moving, adapting, and dying out in response to the changes. But what transpired eons ago is only a rough guide for what's coming. Over the next century, we may heat up 10 times as fast as we have since the last ice age, putting even greater pressure on species. And unlike warming events of the past, this one will play out on a planet where 83 percent of the land has been partially or totally altered by humans. Some natural systems are inherently brittle and will simply break. Just 3.6 degrees of warming will cause mass mortality of coral reefs. Other species, such as wolves and jaguars, are remarkably resilient and can thrive in a wide range of habitats, provided that we stop shooting them.

In the Southwest and beyond, climate change is bound to create more and more thorny dilemmas for the biologists and resource managers who tend to our endangered species. Rather than be content with documenting the decline, as one frustrated researcher described her work to me, some scientists are beginning to advocate for aggressive measures to save species, including moving plants and animals to new locations. Variously referred to as assisted migration and assisted colonization, the strategy is generally regarded as a last resort for species facing imminent extinction, but such efforts are already under way. In the Florida Panhandle, one group has deliberately spread a conifer, the Florida torreya, more than 300 miles northward because the plant is threatened by global warming and not reproducing; it is now down to fewer than 1,000 individuals. The government of British Columbia is allowing logging companies to plant tree seeds up to 1,600 feet higher than their current location and has distributed thousands of seedlings across the Pacific Northwest to test how 15 tree species will respond to new climate conditions. In England, biologists have successfully translocated two species of butterflies, marbled whites and small skippers, 22 to 40 miles north of their current range, to habitat that has become more suitable in the warmer climate. As radical as this approach seems, the ESA is already forcing federal and state officials to be increasingly hands-on when it comes to managing wildlife. Trapping, breeding, and releasing gray wolves and California condors into their historic habitat is only a small leap from rescuing other species from a death trap and moving them to a new home.

The prospect of shifting species around has sparked a rich debate among conservation biologists, one that will continue for decades to come. In 2008, researchers writing in the journal *Science* laid out a decision framework for assisted colonization that included the following questions: What's the extinction risk? Is it technically possible? Could you create new habitats? Do the benefits outweigh the costs? The authors acknowledged that the idea of moving species beyond their current range "flies in the face of conventional conservation approaches," and they noted that "the world is littered with examples where moving species beyond their current range into natural and agricultural landscapes has had negative impacts." "We are not recommending placing rhino herds in Arizona or polar bears in Antarctica," the authors wrote. But enough warming, changes to precipitation, and acidification of the oceans could mean that "the future for many species and ecosystems is so bleak that assisted colonization might be their best chance."

That paper and others provoked a backlash from other biologists, who argued that our knowledge of the natural world is too poor and the risk of unintended consequences is too high. Likening assisted colonization to ecological roulette, Daniel Simberloff, editor of the journal *Biological Invasions*, and Anthony Ricciardi of McGill University argued that "even if preceded by careful risk assessment, such action is likely to produce myriad unintended and unpredictable consequences." To Simberloff and Ricciardi, the approach would be better described as planned invasions, and would continue a long line of disastrous introductions of nonnative species. Just in the Southwest, invasive grasses were burning up the Sonoran Desert, bullfrogs were gobbling Chiricahua leopard frogs, rainbow trout were preying on juvenile humpback chub, and Abert's squirrels were competing with Mt. Graham red squirrels. On the world stage, there were even stronger cautionary tales. In Africa's Lake Victoria, introduction of the Nile perch helped wipe out 200 endemic fish species, the largest mass extinction of vertebrates in modern times. In Australia, introducing cane toads to attack the beetles eating the sugar crop turned the amphibian into a feral menace that kills native species after they swallow the toads' poisonous glands. Even efforts to help declining species have sometimes backfired. Red squirrels not unlike those atop Mt. Graham were introduced to Newfoundland to provide food for pine martens, but the squirrels' appetite for spruce cones nearly caused the extinction of a bird, the Newfoundland red crossbill.

The potential for doing more harm than good is sobering, and the choices will be among lesser evils: Which species should we write off? Which should we move first? The politics may be just as challenging. A provision in the ESA already allows the federal government to move, breed, and reintroduce listed species. But would a rural county or conservative statehouse take kindly to the Fish and Wildlife Service unloading a critically endangered animal on their land if it wasn't historically found there? Get ready for another round of litigation in the fight between states and the federal government over who controls America's wildlife.

For plants and animals that are only found in certain locations, assisted colonization may be pointless. In Florida, scientists would surely evacuate the last key deer before the sea swallowed their island habitat, and atop Mt. Graham, biologists would surely swoop in and capture the last red squirrels before warming pushed their habitat off the mountain. But where would scientists put these animals? Have we really saved the key deer if it's only found in a zoo or on the mainland? Would relocating the red squirrels off their namesake mountain be tantamount to extinction of the subspecies? It would be small consolation, but in captivity these animals at least would be aboard an ark of sorts and available to seed the repopulation of their home islands should the waters ever recede or the forests ever return.

Climate change and traditional threats may become so overwhelming and insoluble that we have no choice but to create such arks, if for no other reason than to store species' DNA before it's lost forever. I wasn't a big fan of the movie *Jurassic Park*, but I can't help but think that we'll someday figure out how to resurrect species that are extinct in the wild but locked away in some subzero freezer. We are, in fact, already taking such steps in response to worst-case scenarios that no longer seem so hypothetical. In 2007, scientists announced plans to create an amphibian ark to protect nearly 2,000 species of frogs, toads, and salamanders, largely due to the threat of the chytrid fungus. Scattered at zoos and other facilities around the world, these secure biobanks are designed to store frog sperm and amphibian colonies so that biologists can reintroduce species and re-create populations that have vanished in the wild. Scientists at the National Zoo in Washington, DC, have used frozen semen from endangered black-footed ferrets to breed new animals, a decade after the sperm was collected from the males. In the Sacramento–San Joaquin Delta near San Francisco, the state of California has spent more than $2 million on a special hatchery for producing delta smelt in case the fish is driven extinct by pumping, pollution, and invasive species in the ecosystem that supplies drinking water to some 25 million people.

The most ambitious attempt to build an ark for biodiversity—at least for seeds—is the so-called doomsday vault that is burrowed 400 feet into a frozen mountainside on the Norwegian island of Spitsbergen. Located 700 miles from the North Pole, the Svalbard Global Seed Vault can store up to 4.5 million varieties and billions of individual seeds at about zero degrees. It is high enough on the mountain to escape rising seas should the polar ice caps melt, and it would keep the seeds cold even if the freezers failed thanks to the surrounding permafrost, though that might not last either. Built at a cost of nearly $10 million, the vault already has samples of one-third of the planet's most important food crops. As he dedicated the facility, European Commission president Jose Manuel Barroso summed up the strategy: "We hope and work for the best but have to plan for the worst."

This is where we're heading, unless we get a handle on greenhouse gases and avoid the worst effects of climate change: An Arctic without sea ice. The San Pedro River and Lake Powell without water. The Sonoran Desert without Sonoran pronghorn. Mt. Graham without red squirrels. Joshua Tree National Park without Joshua trees, and Glacier National Park without glaciers. If there is any cause for optimism, it is our own species' ability to adapt to changing circumstances and use our oversized brains to solve problems. We need to use the same ingenuity and capacity for innovation that brought us to this precipice in order to find a way back to safety and sustainability.

The ESA may be our most powerful environmental law, but it can't do it all. In case after case, the act has been helpless to close the loopholes and gaping voids in federal, state, and local policies that contribute to species endangerment. When a pronghorn perishes after being spooked by a smuggler or Homeland Security helicopter, the fault lies in our failed drug and border policies, not the ESA. The fact that so many riparian species in the Southwest are increasingly imperiled isn't due to the ESA's shortcomings. It's because many states retain a legal system for governing water use that disregards the needs of nonhuman creatures and ignores the obvious connection between groundwater pumping and surface flows.

If our nation is ever to make significant progress in protecting biodiversity, we need to transcend the ESA, ditch the 19th-century philosophies that still govern our use of natural resources, and adopt a set of 21st-century policies to manage our land, water, and air. Endangered species will always need a strong ESA. But their ultimate fate will depend even more on our ability to reduce greenhouse gas emissions, curb urban sprawl, prevent invasions of nonnative species, adopt progressive water laws, create guest-worker programs to solve the border problem, clear fuel from overgrown forests, promote voluntary buyouts of grazing leases, and use unleaded ammunition while hunting. We must stop dumping all of our unresolved environmental problems onto the ESA and hoping it will clean up the ecological mess. Unless we think beyond the ESA and take action in all of these other realms, we'll never fulfill the law's bold promise.

12-Step Plan for Recovery

*Angry as one may be at what careless people have done and
still do to a noble habitat, it is hard to be pessimistic about the West.
This is the native home of hope. When it finally learns that cooperation,
not rugged individualism, is the pattern that most characterizes and
preserves it, then it will have achieved itself and outlived its origins.
Then it has a chance to create a society to match the scenery.*

—Wallace Stegner

The underlying threats to our nation's biodiversity—global warming, population growth, introduced species, toxic chemicals—are often intractable and beyond the ESA's reach. By comparison, changing how the ESA is applied and funded is firmly within our control. We don't need to open up the statute's language in Congress, where ESA foes could do more harm than good. Simply spending more money on existing programs, expanding innovative approaches, and adopting new internal regulations to account for climate change will go a long way toward improving the ESA's effectiveness.

Nasty fights over the ESA, including the heated rhetoric surrounding Richard Pombo's bill, actually mask considerable agreement about how to improve the law's performance. In honor of the ESA's 30th anniversary, lawyers and scientists convened nearly 30 leading experts whose affiliations ran the gamut from the Center for Biological Diversity to the National Cattlemen's Beef Association. "The discussions produced a remarkable degree of consensus on potential avenues for increasing the act's effectiveness," the project's organizers wrote in 2006. There was considerable support for expanding many of the initiatives promoted by former interior secretary Bruce Babbitt, including safe harbors, candidate conservation agreements, and habitat conservation plans that encourage species protection on private lands. The chronic problem of insufficient funding for science and for uncharismatic species could be erased by a renewed commitment to protecting our wildlife.

My reporting and experiences in the Southwest and beyond have led me to these 12 recommendations for making our biodiversity policy more responsive to 21st-century challenges:

1. Reframe our thinking around climate

Even without global warming, big questions remain about the behavior of many species, the character of their habitats, and the nature of their imperilment. Add in one of the most abrupt and severe shifts the earth has experienced in millions of years, and it becomes all the more daunting to predict where species will move, how ecosystems will come apart, and what new ecological communities will emerge. Nevertheless, most biologists believe we know enough *now* to take concrete actions to help wildlife adapt. Scientists already work with a variety of climate models that project shifts in species' ranges. The challenge is getting those tools and assessments into the hands of land and water managers. It's not necessarily expensive: one study of climate change impacts in Yosemite National Park only cost about $40,000.

Unfortunately, our environmental agencies are woefully unprepared for climate change. The Forest Service, National Park Service, Fish and Wildlife Service, and Bureau of Land Management are only now receiving guidance from Washington on how to incorporate climate change into their planning and day-to-day management. Reframing these agencies' priorities so they emphasize climate change would not require Congress to rewrite their founding legislation, which could open a Pandora's box. Executive orders and regulations would be enough, but without resources to back them up, these unfunded mandates would accomplish little.

There is broad agreement among biologists on the need for core protected areas, surrounding buffer zones, and a network of connectivity among various habitats that will allow at least some species to adapt to the novel climate by moving to new locations. If Congress doesn't create such arks, the executive branch could use the Antiquities Act. Since the law was signed in 1906 by President Theodore Roosevelt, it has been used by all but two presidents to protect vulnerable lands and waters. Follow-up funding for monitoring and management, which has often been lacking, is even more important in light of global warming because many ecosystems will be changing more rapidly.

2. Don't neglect nonclimate stressors

For many species, traditional threats will be far more important in the near term than global warming. Any strategy for climate adaptation will be worthless if a plant or animal is driven extinct or to the brink by pollution, habitat destruction, and other immediate dangers. In many cases, addressing these issues now and bolstering populations is our best defense against climate change's future impacts. Minimizing the destruction and fragmentation of habitat will give animals like the Sonoran pronghorn more room to roam. Maintaining genetic diversity by preserving numerous populations will help species like the Chiricahua leopard frog adapt to the changing weather. There are abundant "no regrets" strategies that are wise to pursue regardless of the future scenario for emissions and warming.

3. Act earlier

Most of the species described in this book received protection far too late. Hunting and other threats had virtually wiped out California condors and Mexican gray wolves. Overgrazing eliminated masked bobwhite quail from the United States, overlogging took much of the habitat for Mexican spotted owls, and overpumping dried up the riparian habitat where southwestern willow flycatchers breed. In general, the longer the government waits to protect an endangered plant or animal, the more imperiled the species becomes. Earlier intervention may initially increase costs for the government and private sector, but in the long run, this dose of preventive care can wind up saving money for taxpayers and businesses. To use the emergency room analogy, it's far better to inoculate children or detect breast cancer with mammograms than to wait until medical problems become so acute that they demand a visit to the hospital or become terminal. Climate change makes it all the more imperative that we not wait until the very last minute to apply ESA protections.

4. Spend more on science

Scientists trying to save endangered species not only confront stubborn biological threats and formidable economic powers; they also must cope with their own ignorance of the creatures they're trying to save. How can we recover an endangered species if we don't know how many individuals are left, where they live, or how they reproduce? With some high-profile animals, biologists have a solid understanding of the species' behavior and its role in the larger ecosystem. With less charismatic creatures, however, scientists and land managers often must make recommendations and take action despite yawning gaps in their knowledge of the species. As with earlier intervention, a more generous commitment to biological research will increase costs now, but such investments could ultimately save the government money and reduce the ESA's economic impact. When Fish and Wildlife knows little about the basic biology of a listed species, it's often forced to use a broad brush as it maps critical habitat and creates protections. Armed with more precise information about a species' needs, regulators can zero in on the land and water that's most important. Funding for science in government agencies, universities, and other settings can also serve as an economic stimulus.

5. Protect more habitat

There will never be enough money to buy or otherwise protect all the valuable habitat that plants and animals need. But if we're smart, we can get more biodiversity bang for our buck by using science to select the most vital areas and by using alternatives to outright purchases, such as leases and easements. We already know where these hot spots, choke points, and missing links are located and we have a rough sense of the price tag for protecting them. In the United States, one analysis estimated it would cost $5 to $8 billion per year over the next 40 years to secure a strategic network of top-priority habitat. Another study found that the government spent an average of $3.2 billion annually on such programs between 1992 and 2001, so this suggests a funding gap of $2 to $5 billion per year. Defenders of Wildlife concluded it would cost $219 billion over the next 30 years to implement comprehensive state wildlife action plans (discussed below) by using rentals and leases, but nearly $1 trillion if such areas were protected through fee-simple purchases. These are big numbers, but protecting such habitat also delivers a variety of economic benefits, including ecotourism, carbon sequestration, and clean water.

6. Embrace some hands-on research and management

The history of wildlife management certainly abounds with examples of well-meaning experiments creating new pests and other problems. We've also killed plenty of endangered species while trying to move or study them. But we can't let those failures stop us from trying to do better. I'm not suggesting that we ignore the dangers of capturing jaguars, moving Mexican gray wolves, transporting Sonoran pronghorn, or relocating desert tortoises. In these cases and others, endangered animals have suffered and died due to our interventions. Every proposal needs some kind of review to ensure that wildlife are not being subjected to unnecessary risks. But these threats must be balanced against the costs of inaction and the vacuum in knowledge that may persist if we're too wary of handling listed species.

There's also a growing need for thoughtful habitat manipulation and restoration, such as thinning overgrown forests to help Mexican spotted owls, eliminating bullfrogs from water holes to aid Chiricahua leopard frogs, adjusting releases from Glen Canyon Dam to help humpback chub, and erecting barriers around mine shafts where lesser long-nosed bats roost. We'll never have a complete understanding of the natural world, nor will we be able to guarantee our actions won't cause harm, but satellite tracking, microchip implants, GIS mapping, remote sensing, and other technologies offer 21st-century scientists powerful tools as they try to monitor and manage species and their habitats. The key will be a flexible, adaptive approach that's rooted in the best science, untainted by politics, and designed to learn from the inevitable mistakes.

7. Clear the candidate backlog

If the nation is truly committed to protecting our native biodiversity, we can't let some 250 candidate species languish in regulatory purgatory. Biologists have deemed all of these plants and animals at risk of extinction, but 73 of them have been waiting for federal protection for more than a quarter century. They aren't being protected simply because the federal government has not allocated enough money or summoned enough political will to process their listing. As with listed species, the roster of candidates includes a few charismatic creatures, such as trout, turtles, rabbits, and prairie dogs, but also plenty of snails and cave beetles. It would take about $150 million over five years to clear the backlog of candidate species stuck in the listing pipeline. That's real money, but a pittance in comparison to the overall federal budget. Fish and Wildlife's entire budget for endangered species programs, $150 million in 2008, only consumed about 1 percent of the money allocated to the Interior Department (fig. 23). The longer a species sits in the candidate category, the harder and more expensive the recovery will be once it does receive federal protection.

In some cases, a candidate species may not need to be listed if landowners and public agencies anticipate and address threats. Candidate conservation agreements encourage private property owners to take proactive measures. If the species is listed, the landowner doesn't have to go beyond the conservation measures outlined in the agreement. In the Southwest, this tool has helped protect a talus snail found in a single canyon on Mt. Graham, a half-dozen desert fish species, and close relatives of

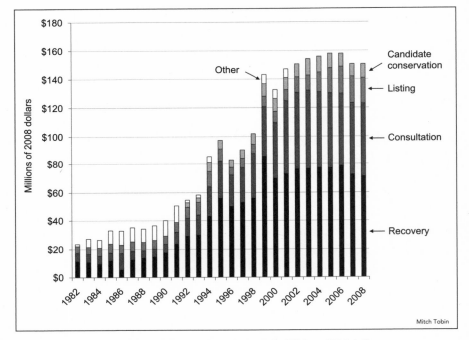

Figure 23: US Fish and Wildlife Service Spending on the ESA in 2008 dollars.
Source: US Fish and Wildlife Service.

the Chiricahua leopard frog. Over the past few years, Fish and Wildlife has spent less than $10 million on its entire candidate conservation program. Congress should increase funding for this program to help keep even more species off the endangered list while also ensuring that the agreements aren't used to water down protections or deprive species of the help they need.

8. Insulate science from politics

Biologists shouldn't be kings, but their studies and recommendations should be better shielded from meddling politicians determined to bury, ignore, or warp their findings. High-stakes decisions about endangered species will invariably bubble up to the level of political appointees at Fish and Wildlife, and sometimes even higher, to the interior secretary or president. This is how our democracy works. What's essential is transparency in the decision-making process so that people can be held accountable. If Fish and Wildlife favors economic interests or discards biologists' conclusions, the public and policy makers need to know. That will require strict protection for whistle-blowers and continued access to public records through the Freedom of Information Act.

Listing decisions are often the most contentious part of the ESA, so rather than have the God Squad—the cabinet-level panel empowered to sanction extinction—we ought to create a new team, the Gatekeepers, to help us decide which species to allow aboard the legislative ark. This expert panel of independent biologists, perhaps convened by the National Academy of Sciences, could review the most critical and controversial listing proposals. If protection under the ESA is supposed to be apolitical and strictly scientific, why let a political agency like Fish and Wildlife handle the entire process? The federal government has already used the National Academy of Sciences to evaluate biological opinions along rivers with a history of endangered species conflicts, including the Colorado in the Southwest, the Platte and Missouri in the Midwest, and the Klamath in the Pacific Northwest.

9. Offer landowners more carrots

Only about 5 percent of the United States lies within a nature preserve, and more than half of the nation's plant communities have less than 10 percent of their range protected. Now climate change is forcing plants and animals to move outside the political boundaries that mark our national parks and wildlife refuges. Even without global warming, it would be essential to protect biodiversity on private property because the survival of many endangered species depends on nongovernment land. In recent years, Congress has considered offering hundreds of millions of dollars in tax credits to landowners who put easements on their property or promote the recovery of a listed species, but only a piece of this worthwhile program was incorporated into the 2008 Farm Bill. Safe harbor agreements, the legal instruments that stop people from being punished for improving habitat, offer landowners another way to help species without hurting pocketbooks, as do candidate conservation agreements.

10. Capitalize on the power of markets

We can harness the power of markets to produce environmentally friendly outcomes, such as the dramatic reduction in acid rain due to a cap-and-trade policy. When landowners create conservation banks and sell their credits, the profit motive will entice them to help the species in question, but only if vigorous enforcement of the ESA creates a demand for their product. After The Nature Conservancy or another group buys farms along the San Pedro River, turns off their water wells, and flips the properties into residential parcels with conservation easements, the surface flows, riparian forests, and flycatchers will return. If conservation groups are allowed to bid on grazing leases in the Southwest and pay for their desire to rid public lands of cattle grazing, both the US Treasury and Mexican gray wolves will benefit. Markets for water, pollution, development rights, and endangered species' habitat have the potential to efficiently allocate conservation dollars and deliver environmental benefits, but only if they're set up with great care.

11. Partner with states

The ESA is a federal law, so the US Fish and Wildlife Service and National Marine Fisheries Service will always dominate the discussion. But our success in recovering many species will hinge on federal officials' ability to partner with their counterparts in other levels of government. States retain significant jurisdiction over wildlife within their borders and will forever be key players in addressing many threats to biodiversity, including urban sprawl, water use, and transportation. In exchange for more say on management issues, states are sometimes willing to foot the bill for surveys and conservation measures. In 2000, Congress mandated that every state and territory create a comprehensive conservation strategy for its wildlife, and it approved all 56 plans in 2007. These state wildlife action plans have no teeth, vary widely in their quality, and need funding to become more than documents, but in many states they offer a solid framework for keeping common species common and avoiding new ESA listings.

Until recently, handing off environmental regulations to states was bound to lead to weaker protections. But in the Bush era, many states took the lead on issues like climate change and vehicle mileage standards, so devolution isn't necessarily a bad thing. The fight over banning lead bullets in California and Arizona reminds us that game and fish departments still see hunters and anglers as their primary clients. This is understandable since the agencies' budgets are so dependent on hunting and fishing licenses. By diversifying these organizations' funding, perhaps through federal matching programs focused on climate change, the agencies could become more responsive to nongame species and their advocates. We also shouldn't forget the state and local level when it comes to funding for wildlife and habitat. Since 1988, American voters have approved three-quarters of 2,228 proposed conservation measures on their state and local ballots, generating $54 billion for wildlife and open space (figs. 24 and 25).

12. Broaden the base

Only about 15 percent of Americans identify themselves as members of environmental groups. If wildlife advocates want to strengthen political support for the ESA, they need to start finding more common ground with new allies, be they hunters and anglers who are working to improve habitat, farmers and ranchers who are trying to preserve a lifestyle based on open space, or religious leaders who are preaching stewardship of creation. You don't need to subscribe to Darwinian evolution or be a Sierra Club member to support the moral imperative underlying the ESA. Plenty of conservative Christians feel that humans have an obligation to take care of other species and follow Noah's lead.

Especially in the West, where historically red states like Arizona, Nevada, and Colorado are now considered purple on political maps, largely due to migration and changing demographics, there has always been a strong independent streak in thinking and living that defies the simple Democrat versus Republican story line. That dichotomy is about

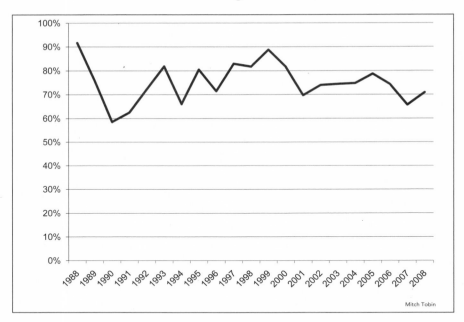

Figure 24: Passage rate of state and local conservation ballot measures.
Note: Ballot measures are less common in odd years because they are off-year elections.
Source: Trust for Public Land.

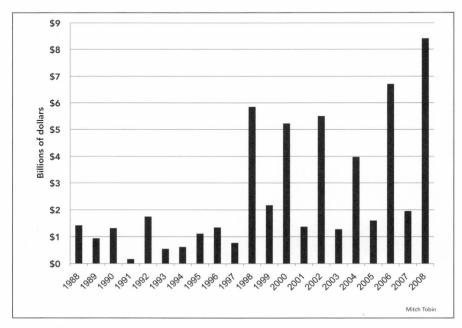

Figure 25: Approved conservation funding from state and local ballot measures.
Source: Trust for Public Land.

as useful today as the false choice between jobs and the environment that often characterized ESA fights in the late 20th century.

One issue that can unite everyone who cares about the natural world is fighting the so-called nature deficit disorder that afflicts an increasing number of children. Kids today spend way more time staring into a screen than watching wildlife or even being outdoors. There's little chance that Americans will care about protecting wild places or endangered species if they never take a hike in the woods, camp out under the stars, or follow the footprints of a wild animal.

Above all, efforts to protect endangered species must be reframed so that rare plants and animals are no longer viewed as rivals or even enemies of people. The ESA doesn't necessarily set up a zero-sum game between humans and critters. Improving forest health and reducing the risk of infernos helps both homeowners and spotted owls. Restoring natural buffers along the Gulf Coast protects both New Orleans and coastal species. Getting lead out of ammunition benefits condors and people who eat wild game. Healthy human communities depend on healthy ecosystems, so we drive species extinct at our own peril.

Acknowledgments

I couldn't have written this book without the help of hundreds of people who granted me interviews, let me tag along on surveys, welcomed me into their homes, and provided me with a wealth of knowledge and perspectives about endangered species. Reviewers who read all or parts of the manuscript sharpened my thinking and saved me from some blunders. All errors and omissions, of course, are my own. My sincere thanks to: Marit Alanen, Eileen Ashton, Sergio Avila, Sandy Bahr, Rick Brusca, Rob Burton, Carolyn Campbell, Ginette Chapman, Jack Childs, Jim and Sue Chilton, Amy Dickie, Sam Drake, Matthew Elliott, Lisa Ellis, Mitch Ellis, Sally Gall, Thetis Gamberg, Joe Ganey, Warner and Wendy Glenn, Allen Graber, Jan Hamber, John Hervert, Jan and Will Holder, Chuck Huckelberry, Ross Humphreys, Bob Irvin, John Koprowski, Karen Krebbs, Dennis Kubly, Jim Malusa, Emil McCain, Guy McPherson, Sam Negri, Ernie Niemi, Sophie Osborn, Chris Parish, Dave Parsons, Jim Paxon, Yar Petryszyn, Jim Rorabaugh, Phil Rosen, Michael Rosenzweig, Eva Sargent, Nathan Sayre, Cecil Schwalbe, Wayne Shifflett, Duane Shroufe, Tim Snow, Dennis Stone, Julie Stromberg, Kierán Suckling, Phyllis Tobin, Laura Viggiano, Ranger Ward, and Peter Warren.

The genesis of this book was a 10-part, yearlong series I wrote for the *Arizona Daily Star* in 2004. Were it not for the support of many people in the newsroom, that series, and this book, would have remained in my mind's eye. My editors at the *Star*—Norma Coile, B. J. Bartlett, Dennis Joyce, Tim Konski, and Bobbie Jo Buel—challenged me to crystallize a complex, contentious issue into stories that would engage average newspaper readers. Thanks to Tony Davis for teaching me so much about the Southwest and its environment. Thomas Stauffer, Chris Richards, Aaron Latham, A. E. Araiza, Tom Beal, and Anne Minard were great companions during wildfire coverage and other assignments.

The *Star*'s photographers produced stunning images that lured in readers who might otherwise skip to the sports pages. David Sanders stood with me atop a freezing hilltop at dawn to photograph Sonoran pronghorn and risked puncture wounds to get down and dirty with Pima pineapple cacti. He also joined me on a treacherous hike down the Hopi Salt Trail to reach humpback chub in the Little Colorado River and spent several hours filming California condors from within a cramped blind atop the Vermilion Cliffs, unable to either sit or stand up because of the awkward configuration. Max Becherer lay on his belly for nearly an hour to capture Chiricahua leopard frogs before he went off to cover the wars in Iraq and Afghanistan. Kelly Presnell accompanied me on surveys for Mt. Graham red squirrels two miles above sea level and helped me track masked bobwhite quail on a steamy August morning at the Buenos Aires National Wildlife Refuge. Mamta Popat hiked with me during the summer heat to reach a bat cave in Organ Pipe Cactus National Monument. Thanks to Rick Wiley and Teri Hayt for helping me get some of those photos into the book.

Graphics accompanied many of my species stories, and I'm indebted to artist Dave Castelan for producing such informative and beautifully illustrated maps, figures, and drawings. A tip of the hat to all the reporters, editors, designers, and photographers at the *Star*, *Tucson Citizen*, and *Napa Valley Register* who taught me how to be a better journalist and made the work so much fun.

I was fortunate to receive several fellowships for journalists that allowed me to take a breath, escape deadlines for a while, and learn about the natural world from some brilliant scientists, scholars, and experts. Many thanks to the Alicia Patterson Foundation, National Tropical Botanical Garden, Center for Environmental Journalism at the University of Colorado, and Property and Environment Research Center. I learned about the legal issues surrounding the ESA through a media fellowship at the Vermont Law School, where I audited Bob Irvin's fascinating course on biodiversity protection.

A special thanks to the entire staff at Fulcrum Publishing, and particularly to Faith Marcovecchio for her expert editing and invaluable insights. I'm grateful to my agent, Elizabeth Wales, for inspiring me to think big and sticking with me during the long, winding journey from proposal to publication.

My friends and family provided much-needed moral support during my Sisyphean struggle writing this book. My parents never stopped believing in me or the project. My wife, Ginette Chapman, put up with a lot while I was immersed in the book and threw me countless life preservers with her optimism, laughs, and love. To everyone who contributed to this book, in large ways and small, thank you.

Sources

Listed below, by chapter, subject, and species, are many of the sources I consulted while researching and writing this book. Not listed is the voluminous paper trail produced by the government as it administers the ESA. Readers interested in petitions, listing rules, critical habitat designations, and recovery plans can find them on the US Fish and Wildlife Service's website (www.fws.gov/endangered). More information on ESA resources and issues is at www.endangeredbook.com.

Introduction
The Endangered Species Act and Wildlife Law

Baden, John A., and Pete Geddes. *Saving a Place: Endangered Species in the 21st Century*. Burlington, VT: Ashgate, 2001.

Barker, Rocky. *Saving All the Parts: Reconciling Economics and the Endangered Species Act*. Washington, DC: Island Press, 1993.

Baur, Donald C., and William Robert Irvin. *Endangered Species Act: Law, Policy and Perspectives*. Chicago: American Bar Association, 2002.

Bean, Michael J., and Melanie J. Rowland. *The Evolution of National Wildlife Law*, 3rd ed. Westport, CT: Praeger, 1997.

Burgess, Bonnie B. *Fate of the Wild: The Endangered Species Act and the Future of Biodiversity*. Athens: Univ. of Georgia Press, 2001.

Czech, Brian, and Paul R. Krausman. *The Endangered Species Act: History, Conservation Biology, and Public Policy*. Baltimore: Johns Hopkins Univ. Press, 2001.

Freyfogle, Eric T., and Dale D. Goble. *Federal Wildlife Statutes*. New York: Foundation Press, 2002.

Glicksman, Robert L., and George C. Coggins. *Modern Public Land Law in a Nutshell*. St. Paul, MN: West, 2006.

Goble, Dale D., J. Michael Scott, and Frank W. Davis. *The Endangered Species Act at Thirty*. Vol. I, *Renewing the Conservation Promise*. Washington, DC: Island Press, 2006.

Kohm, Kathryn. *Balancing on the Brink of Extinction: The Endangered Species Act and Lessons for the Future*. Washington, DC: Island Press, 1991.

Mann, Charles C., and Mark L. Plummer. *Noah's Choice: The Future of Endangered Species*. New York: Alfred A. Knopf, 1995.

Scott, J. Michael, Dale D. Goble, and Frank W. Davis. *The Endangered Species Act at Thirty*. Vol. II, *Conserving Biodiversity in Human-Dominated Landscapes*. Washington, DC: Island Press, 2006.

Stanford Environmental Law Society. *The Endangered Species Act*. Stanford, CA: Stanford Univ. Press, 2001.

Tobin, Richard. *The Expendable Future: U.S. Politics and the Protection of Biological Diversity*. Durham, NC: Duke Univ. Press, 1990.

Yaffee, Steven L. *Prohibitive Policy: Implementing the Federal Endangered Species Act*. Cambridge, MA: MIT Press, 1982.

———. *The Wisdom of the Spotted Owl: Policy Lessons for a New Century*. Washington, DC: Island Press, 1994.

Biodiversity and Extinction Crisis

Adams, Douglas, and Mark Carwardine. *Last Chance to See*. New York: Ballantine Books, 1990.

Angier, Natalie. "New Creatures in an Age of Extinctions." *The New York Times*, July 26, 2009.

Chivian, Eric, and Aaron Bernstein. *Sustaining Life: How Human Health Depends on Biodiversity*. Oxford: Oxford Univ. Press, 2008.

Kolbert, Elizabeth. "The Sixth Extinction?" *The New Yorker*, May 25, 2009.

Lovejoy, Thomas. "The Earth Is Crying Out for Help." *The New York Times*, December 9, 2009.

Meffe, Gary K., and C. Ronald Carroll. *Principles of Conservation Biology*, 3rd ed. Sunderland, MA: Sinauer Associates, 2006.

Stein, Bruce A., Lynn S. Kutner, and Jonathan S. Adams. *Precious Heritage: The Status of Biodiversity in the United States*. Oxford: Oxford Univ. Press, 2000.

Wilcove, David S. *The Condor's Shadow: The Loss and Recovery of Wildlife in America*. New York: W. H. Freeman, 1999.

Wilcove, David S., Margaret McMillan, and Keith C. Winston. "What Exactly Is an Endangered Species? An Analysis of the U.S. Endangered Species List: 1985–1991." *Conservation Biology* 7 (2002): 87–93.

Wilson, E. O. *The Diversity of Life*. New York: W. W. Norton, 1992.

———. *The Future of Life*. New York: Knopf, 2002.

———. *The Creation: An Appeal to Save Life on Earth*. New York: W. W. Norton, 2006.

Challenges to Extinction Crisis

Lomborg, Bjorn. *The Skeptical Environmentalist: Measuring the Real State of the World*. Cambridge: Cambridge Univ. Press, 2001.

Lovejoy, Thomas. "Biodiversity: Dismissing Scientific Process." *Scientific American*, January 2, 2002.

Wilson, E. O., et al. *Biodiversity Distortions in Lomborg's The Skeptical Environmentalist*. Cambridge, MA: Union of Concerned Scientists, 2001.

———. "Vanishing Point: On Bjorn Lomborg and Extinction." *Grist*, December 12, 2001, www.grist.org/article/point (accessed February 1, 2010).

Noah's Flood

Clarke, Garry, et al. "Superlakes, Megafloods, and Abrupt Climate Change." *Science* 301 (August 2003): 922–923.

Hostetler, S. W., et al. "Simulated Influences of Lake Agassiz on the Climate of Central North America 11,000 Years Ago." *Nature* 405 (2000): 334–337.

Ryan, William, and Walter Pitman. *Noah's Flood*. New York: Simon and Schuster, 1998.

Turney, Chris S. M., and Heidi Brown. "Catastrophic Early Holocene Sea Level Rise, Human Migration and the Neolithic Transition in Europe." *Quaternary Science Reviews* 26 (2007): 2036–2041.

Economic Benefits of Protecting Biodiversity

Balmford, Andrew, et al. "Economic Reasons for Conserving Wild Nature." *Science* 297 (August 2002): 950–953.

Costanza, Robert, et al. "The Value of the World's Ecosystem Services and Natural Capital." *Nature* 387 (May 1997): 253–260.

Farnsworth, N. R., et al. "Medicinal Plants in Therapy." *Bulletin of the World Health Organization* 63 (1985): 965–981.

Farnsworth, N. R., and D. D. Soejarto. "Potential Consequence of Plant Extinction in the United States on the Current and Future Availability of Prescription Drugs." *Economic Botany* 39 (1985): 231–240.

Newman, David J., Gordon M. Cragg, and Kenneth M. Snader. "Natural Products as Sources of New Drugs over the Period 1981–2002." *Journal of Natural Products* 66, no. 7 (2003): 1022–1037.

US Department of the Interior, Fish and Wildlife Service, and US Department of Commerce, US Census Bureau. 2006 National Survey of Fishing, Hunting, and Wildlife-Associated Recreation (2006).

Southwest (Natural) History

Abbey, Edward. *Desert Solitaire: A Season in the Wilderness.* New York: Simon and Schuster, 1968.

Arizona-Sonora Desert Museum. *A Natural History of the Sonoran Desert.* Tucson: Arizona-Sonora Desert Museum Press, 2000.

Bowden, Charles. *Blue Desert.* Tucson: Univ. of Arizona Press, 1986.

Brown, David E., ed. *Arizona Wildlife: The Territorial Years, 1863–1912.* Phoenix: Arizona Game and Fish Department, 2009.

Krutch, Joseph Wood. *The Desert Year.* New York: Viking, 1963.

Lowe, Charles H. *Arizona's Natural Environment.* Tucson: Univ. of Arizona Press, 1964.

Lumholtz, Carl. *New Trails in Mexico.* Tucson: Univ. of Arizona Press, 1990.

McNamee, Gregory. *Named in Stone and Sky: An Arizona Anthology.* Tucson: Univ. of Arizona Press, 1993.

McPhee, John. *Basin and Range.* New York: Noonday Press, 1981.

Nabhan, Gary Paul. *The Desert Smells Like Rain.* New York: North Point Press, 1982.

Sheridan, Thomas E. *Arizona: A History.* Tucson: Univ. of Arizona Press, 1995.

Wilkinson, Charles F. *Crossing the Next Meridian.* Washington, DC: Island Press, 1992.

———. *Fire on the Plateau.* Washington, DC: Island Press, 1999.

Wilshire, Howard G., Jane E. Nielson, and Richard W. Hazlett. *The American West at Risk: Science, Myths, and Politics of Land Abuse and Recovery.* New York: Oxford Univ. Press, 2008.

1: Saving 134

Condors and Recovery Program

Finley, William L. "Life History of the California Condor: Part II: Historical Data and Range of the Condor." *The Condor: A Magazine of Western Ornithology* 10 (1908): 5–10.

Meretsky, V. J., et al. "Demography of the California Condor: Implications for Reestablishment." *Conservation Biology* 14 (2000): 957–967.

Nielsen, John. *Condor: To the Brink and Back—The Life and Times of One Giant Bird.* New York: Harper Collins, 2006.

Ogburn, Stephanie Paige. "Bred for Success." *High Country News*, November 13, 2006.

Osborn, Sophie A. H. *Condors in Canyon Country.* Grand Canyon: Grand Canyon Association, 2007.

Snyder, Noel F. R., and Helen Snyder. *The California Condor: A Saga of Natural History and Conservation.* New York: Academic Press, 2000.

Tobin, Mitch. "There's Hope for Giant Bird." *Arizona Daily Star*, March 21, 2004.

Zakin, Susan. "Fight of the Condors." *LA Weekly*, February 16, 2005.

Anthropocene

Crutzen, P. J., and E. F. Stoermer. "The 'Anthropocene.'" *Global Change Newsletter* 41 (2000): 17–18.

deBuys, William. "Welcome to the Anthropocene." *Rangelands* (October 2008): 31–35.

Ruddiman, William F. "The Anthropogenic Greenhouse Era Began Thousands of Years Ago." *Climatic Change* 61 (2003): 261–293.

Zalasiewicz, Jan, et al. "Are We Now Living in the Anthropocene?" *GSA Today* 18, no. 2 (2008): 4–8.

Pleistocene Extinctions

Barnosky, Anthony D., et al. "Assessing the Causes of Late Pleistocene Extinctions on the Continents." *Science* 306 (2004): 70–75.

Gill, Jacquelyn L. "Pleistocene Megafaunal Collapse, Novel Plant Communities, and Enhanced Fire Regimes in North America." *Science* 326 (November 20, 2009): 1100.

Martin, Paul S., and R. G. Klein. *Quaternary Extinctions: A Prehistoric Revolution*. Tucson: Univ. of Arizona Press, 1984.

Martin, Paul S., and H. E. Wright Jr. *Pleistocene Extinctions: The Search for a Cause*. New Haven, CT: Yale, 1967.

Lead Poisoning

See chapter 20 sources.

2: A Fierce Green Fire

Aldo Leopold

Brown, David E., and Neil B. Carmony. *Aldo Leopold's Southwest*. Albuquerque: Univ. of New Mexico Press, 1995.

Gibson, James William. "Lessons from Aldo Leopold's Historic Wolf Hunt." *Los Angeles Times*, December 13, 2009.

Leopold, Aldo. "Forestry and Game Conservation." *Journal of Forestry* 16 (April 1918): 404–411.

———. "Piute Forestry vs. Forest Fire Prevention." *Southwestern* 2 (March 1920): 12–13.

———. "Grass, Brush, Timber, and Fire in Southern Arizona." *Journal of Forestry* 22 (1924): 1–10.

———. "Pioneers and Gullies." *Sunset Magazine*, May 1924.

———. *Game Management*. New York: Charles Scribner's Sons, 1933.

———. "Threatened Species: A Proposal to the Wildlife Conference for an Inventory of the Needs of Near-Extinct Birds and Animals." *American Forests* 42 (March 1936): 116–119.

———. "Conservationist in Mexico." *American Forests* 43 (March 1937): 118–120, 146.

———. *A Sand County Almanac, with Essays on Conservation from Round River*. New York: Ballantine, 1991.

Meine, Curt. *Aldo Leopold: His Life and Work*. Madison: Univ. of Wisconsin Press, 1988.

Newton, Julianne Lutz. *Aldo Leopold's Odyssey*. Washington, DC: Island Press, 2006.

Environmental Philosophy

Cronon, William. *Uncommon Ground: Rethinking the Human Place in Nature*. New York: W. W. Norton, 1996.

Miller, Char. *Gifford Pinchot and the Making of Modern Environmentalism*. Washington, DC: Island Press, 2001.

Worster, Donald. *Nature's Economy: A History of Ecological Ideas*, 2nd ed. New York: Cambridge Univ. Press, 1994.

Wolves

Bass, Rick. *The New Wolves*. New York: Lyons Press, 1998.

Brown, David E. *The Wolf in the Southwest: The Making of an Endangered Species*. Silver City, NM: High-Lonesome Books, 2002.

Leonard, J. A., C. Vilá, and R. K. Wayne. "Legacy Lost: Genetic Variability and Population Size of Extirpated US Grey Wolves (*Canis lupus*)." *Molecular Ecology* 14 (2005): 9–17.

Lopez, Barry Holstun. *Of Wolves and Men*. New York: Charles Scribner's Sons, 1978.

Lynch, Tom. *El Lobo: Readings on the Mexican Gray Wolf*. Salt Lake City: Univ. of Utah Press, 2005.

Mech, L. David. *The Wolf: The Ecology and Behavior of an Endangered Species*. Garden City, NY: Natural History Press, 1970.

Mech, L. David, and Luigi Boitani. *Wolves: Behavior, Ecology, and Conservation*. Chicago: Univ. of Chicago Press, 2003.

Robinson, Michael J. *Predatory Bureaucracy: The Extermination of Wolves and the Transformation of the West*. Boulder: Univ. Press of Colorado, 2005.

Important Legal Cases

Babbitt v. Sweet Home Chapter of Communities for a Great Oregon, 515 U.S. 687 (1995).

Cape Hatteras Access Preservation Alliance v. U.S. Department of the Interior, 344 F. Supp. 2d 108 (D.D.C. 2004).

Defenders of Wildlife v. Babbitt, 958 F. Supp. 670 (D.D.C. 1997).

Geer v. Connecticut, 161 U.S. 519 (1896).

Gifford Pinchot Task Force v. U.S. Fish and Wildlife Service, 378 F.3d 1059 (9th Cir. 2004).

Hughes v. Oklahoma, 441 U.S. 322 (1979).

Hunt v. United States, 278 U.S. 96 (1928).

Kleppe v. New Mexico, 426 U.S. 529 (1976).

Missouri v. Holland, 252 U.S. 416 (1920).

National Association of Home Builders v. Babbitt, 130 F.3d 1041 (D.C. Cir. 1997).

National Wildlife Federation v. Coleman, 529 F.2d 359 (5th Cir. 1976).

Oregon Natural Resources Council v. Daley, 6 F. Supp. 2d 1139 (D. Or. 1998).

Pyramid Lake Paiute Tribe v. Department of the Navy, 898 F.2d 1410 (9th Cir. 1990).

Spirit of the Sage Council v. Norton, 294 F. Supp. 2d 67 (D.D.C. 2003).

TVA v. Hill, 437 U.S. 153 (1978).

Wyoming Farm Bureau Federation v. Babbitt, 199 F.3d 1224 (10th Cir. 2000).

Colorado River and Glen Canyon Dam

Boxall, Bettina. "A River Losing Its Soul." *Los Angeles Times*, May 10, 2004.

Brower, David. *The Place No One Knew: Glen Canyon on the Colorado*. Layton, UT: Gibbs Smith, 2000.

Collier, Michael, Robert H. Webb, and John C. Schmidt. *Dams and Rivers: A Primer on the Downstream Effects of Dams*. Denver, CO: US Geological Survey, 2000.

deBuys, William. *Seeing Things Whole: The Essential John Wesley Powell*. Washington, DC: Island Press, 2001.

Gross, Matthew Barrett. *The Glen Canyon Reader*. Tucson: Univ. of Arizona Press, 2003.

Hartman, Todd. "Fish Story." *Rocky Mountain News*, December 3, 2000, special section.

McKinnon Shaun. "Journey Down a Troubled River." *The Arizona Republic*, July 25, 2004, special section.

McPhee, John. *Encounters with the Archdruid*. New York: Noonday Press, 1971.

Pearson, Byron E. *Still the Wild River Runs: Congress, the Sierra Club, and the Fight to Save Grand Canyon*. Tucson: Univ. of Arizona Press, 2002.

Reisner, Marc. *Cadillac Desert: The American West and Its Disappearing Water*. New York: Penguin, 1986.

Stegner, Wallace. *Beyond the Hundredth Meridian: John Wesley Powell and the Second Opening of the West*. New York: Penguin, 1992.

Tobin, Mitch. "Unending Water Fight." *Arizona Daily Star*, April 30, 2001.

———. "Barely a River." *Arizona Daily Star*, June 3, 2001.

Worster, Donald. *Rivers of Empire: Water, Aridity, and the Growth of the American West*. New York: Oxford Univ. Press, 1985.

Edward Abbey and Earth First!

Abbey, Edward. *The Monkey Wrench Gang*. New York: Avon, 1975.

———. *The Journey Home*. New York: E. P. Dutton, 1977.

Calahan, James M. *Edward Abbey: A Life*. Tucson: Univ. of Arizona Press, 2001.

Zakin, Susan. *Coyotes and Town Dogs*. Tucson: Univ. of Arizona Press, 1993.

Tellico Dam

Kinkead, Eugene. "Tennessee Small Fry." *The New Yorker*, January 8, 1979.

Neely, Jack. "Tellico Dam Revisited." *Metro Pulse Online*, December 9, 2004.

US Department of the Interior. Endangered Species Committee. Statement of Charles Schultze, Chairman of the President's Council of Economic Advisors. Hearing 26, January 23, 1979, 25–26.

Wheeler, William Bruce, and Michael J. McDonald. *TVA and the Tellico Dam: 1936–1979*. Knoxville: Univ. of Tennessee Press, 1986.

3: Scopes versus Squirrels

Mt. Graham History

Associated Press. "Group Opposed to Observatory Starts Camp-In on Mt. Graham." *Arizona Daily Star*, June 12, 1994.

———. "$20,000 Damage Caused to Mt. Graham Machinery." *Arizona Daily Star*, January 11, 1994.

Dougherty, John. "Making a Mountain into a Starbase: The Long, Bitter Battle over Mount Graham." *High Country News*, July 24, 1995.

Erickson, Jim. "Group Says Scopes Will Be Destroyed." *Arizona Daily Star*, August 31, 1988.

———. "Telescope Foe Says Cop Tried to Incite Sabotage." *Arizona Daily Star*, November 12, 1992.

———. "DPS Spent $208,304 to Defend Mt. Graham during Protest." *Arizona Daily Star*, September 3, 1993.

———. "Telescope Foes Take Protest to Posh Celebration." *Arizona Daily Star*, September 18, 1993.

———. "10 Arrested in Protest of Mt. Graham Telescopes." *Arizona Daily Star*, September 19, 1993.

———. "Squirrels Unharmed, UA Study Concludes." *Arizona Daily Star*, May 13, 2000.

———. "A Forest No More." *Arizona Daily Star*, October 1, 2000.

Grissino-Mayer, H. D., C. H. Baisan, and T. W. Swetnam. "Fire History and Age Structure Analyses in the Mixed-Conifer and Spruce-Fir Forests of the Pinaleno Mountains, Southeastern Arizona." Final Report, Mt. Graham Red Squirrel Study Committee. Phoenix, AZ: US Fish and Wildlife Service and US Forest Service, 1994.

Istock, Conrad A., and Robert S. Hoffmann. *Storm over a Mountain Island: Conservation Biology and the Mt. Graham Affair*. Tucson: Univ. of Arizona Press, 1995.

Jones, Lisa. "The University Aimed for the Stars and Hit Mount Graham." *High Country News*, July 24, 1995.

Kornblum, Janet. "Telescope Foes, Police Scuffle at UA." *Arizona Daily Star*, July 7, 1993.

Leary, Warren E. "Interior Secretary Lujan Questioning Species Act." *The New York Times*, May 11, 1990.

Mydans, Seth. "Stars or Squirrels: University's Choice." *The New York Times*, May 21, 1990.

The New York Times. "The Real Red Squirrel Peril." May 29, 1990.

Steele, Michael A., and John L. Koprowski. *North American Tree Squirrels*. Washington, DC: Smithsonian, 2001.

Tobin, Mitch. "Disputes Dog Astronomy's Star." *Arizona Daily Star*, October 15, 2004.

US General Accounting Office. "Views on Fish and Wildlife Service's Biological Opinion Addressing Mt. Graham Astrophysical Facility." GAO Report T-RCED-90-92, June 26, 1990.

———. "Spotted Owl Petition Evaluation Beset by Problems." GAO Report RCED-89-79, February 1989.

Waldrop, M. Mitchell. "The Long, Sad Saga of Mount Graham." *Science* 248 (June 1990): 1478–1481.

The Wall Street Journal. "A Species of Extremism." May 23, 1990.

Warshall, Peter. "The Biopolitics of the Mt. Graham Red Squirrel (*Tamiasciuris hudsonicus grahamensis*)." *Conservation Biology* 8, no. 4 (December 1994): 977–988.

4: Take Me to the River

Santa Cruz River

Bowden, Charles. *Killing the Hidden Waters: The Slow Destruction of Water Resources in the American Southwest*. Austin: Univ. of Texas Press, 1977.

Logan, Michael F. *The Lessening Stream*. Tucson: Univ. of Arizona Press, 2002.

Tellman, Barbara, Richard Yarde, and Mary G. Wallace. *Arizona's Changing Rivers*. Tucson: Univ. of Arizona Water Resources Research Center, 1997.

Other Arizona Rivers

McKinnon, Shaun. "Rivers Pushed to the Brink." *Arizona Republic*, August 6, 2006.

———. "Thirsty Cities Press the Search for Water." *The Arizona Republic*, August 7, 2006.

———. "Upstream Damage Dooms River System." *The Arizona Republic*, August 8, 2006.

———. "Mines, Farms Put Gila River on Life Support." *The Arizona Republic*, August 9, 2006.

———. "Efforts to Resuscitate Rivers Having Limited Success." *The Arizona Republic*, August 10, 2006.

———. "Saving Rivers Will Also Save Us." *The Arizona Republic*, August 11, 2006.

———. "Animals Disappear When Rivers Die." *The Arizona Republic*, August 12, 2006.

Central Arizona Project and Groundwater

See chapter 19 sources.

Riparian and Aquatic Habitat

Jelks, H. L., et al. "Conservation Status of Imperiled North American Freshwater and Diadromous Fishes." *Fisheries* 33 (2008): 372–407.

Tobin, Mitch. "Study: Native Fish Being Allowed to Die Off." *Arizona Daily Star*, October 30, 2003.

———. "Warm-Water Native Fish Are Left Out in the Cold." *High Country News*, January 19, 2004.

5: A Movement

Center for Biological Diversity

Aleshire, Peter. "A Bare-Knuckled Trio Goes after the Forest Service." *High Country News*, March 30, 1998.

Bagwell, Kieth. "Pygmy Owl Champions Crusade for Humanity." *Arizona Daily Star*, December 7, 1997.

Bevington, Douglas. *The Rebirth of Environmentalism: Grassroots Activism from the Spotted Owl to the Polar Bear*. Washington, DC: Island Press, 2009.

Davis, Tony. "Healing the Gila." *High Country News*, October 22, 2001.

Dowie, Mark. *Losing Ground: American Environmentalism at the Close of the Twentieth Century*. Cambridge: MIT Press, 1995.

Humes, Edward. *Eco Barons*. New York: Ecco, 2009.

Kiefer, Michael. "Owl See You in Court." *Phoenix New Times*, August 1, 1996.

Lemann, Nicholas. "No People Allowed." *The New Yorker*, November 22, 1999.

Poole, B. "Group a Force of Nature for Endangered Species." *Tucson Citizen*, January 29, 2008.

Ring, Ray. "Bush Brings More Green into the Green Movement." *High Country News*, March 17, 2008.

Stone, Daniel. "List Limbo." *Newsweek*, April 30, 2009.

Zakin, Susan. "The Gods of Small Things." *LA Weekly*, November 22, 2002.

Mexican Spotted Owl

Ganey J. L., and R. P. Balda. "Habitat Selection by Mexican Spotted Owls in Northern Arizona." *Auk* 111 (1994): 162–169.

Ganey, J. L., et al. "Mexican Spotted Owl Home Range and Habitat Use in Pine-Oak Forest: Implications for Forest Management." *Forest Science* 45 (1999): 127–135.

Industrial Economics. "Final Draft Economic Analysis of Critical Habitat Designation for the Mexican Spotted Owl." Arlington, VA: US Fish and Wildlife Service Division of Economics, March 22, 2004.

Jenness, J. S. "The Effects of Fire on Mexican Spotted Owls in Arizona and New Mexico." Master's thesis, Northern Arizona Univ., 2000.

Jenness, J. S., P. Beier, and J. L. Ganey. "Associations between Forest Fire and Mexican Spotted Owls." *Forest Science* 50 (2004): 765–772.

Johnson, George. "In New Mexico, an Order on Elusive Owl Leaves Residents Angry, and Cold." *The New York Times*, November 26, 1995.

Schneider, Keith. "US Would End Cutting of Trees in Many Forests." *The New York Times*, April 30, 1993.

6: Political Science

Nelson Polsby

London Times. "Professor Nelson Polsby: American Political Scientist Who Became Director of Institute of Government Studies at Berkeley." February 8, 2007.

Martin, Douglas. "Nelson W. Polsby, 72, Author and a Scholar of Politics, Dies." *The New York Times*, February 9, 2007.

Shafer, Byron E. "Nelson W. Polsby: A Scholarly Appreciation." *The Forum* 5 (2007).

Wildermuth, John. "Nelson Polsby: Noted UC Political Scientist." *San Francisco Chronicle*, February 10, 2007.

Forest Service

Kaufman, Herbert. *The Forest Ranger: A Study in Administrative Behavior.* Washington, DC: RFF Press, 2006.

Simon, Herbert A. *Administrative Behavior: A Study of Decision-Making Processes in Administrative Organizations.* New York: Free Press, 1976.

Spending on Endangered Species

My analysis of species-by-species spending is based on a database I constructed using information from the US Fish and Wildlife Service. By law, the agency must estimate how much money is spent on each listed species, and it compiles spreadsheets showing the amount of state and federal funding dedicated to the conservation of each plant and animal. Looking at a single year can be misleading because of one-time expenditures, so I merged data from fiscal years 2000 through 2004, the most recent data available when I conducted the analysis in 2006.

Fish and Wildlife's spending figures should only be regarded as a minimum estimate of how much money the government devotes to endangered species. The agency makes no effort to tally spending by city and county governments to protect endangered species. Even with state and federal agencies, the database doesn't capture every single dollar spent. While state and federal officials are supposed to make a good faith effort to break out spending by species, that's not always feasible. For example, some wildlife refuges protect habitat for many species, so dividing up costs by species is difficult, if not impossible. Agencies also aren't expected to take "extensive or extraordinary measures," like prorating workers' salaries by species.

Spending on Biodiversity

Associated Press. "Plenty Spent on Endangered Species List's Tortoise." *(Salt Lake City, UT) Deseret News*, January 20, 2009.

Barnard, Jeff. "Salmon Gets One Out of Four Endangered Species Dollars." *The Olympian*, February 25, 2006.

Coursey, Don L. "The Revealed Demand for a Public Good: Evidence from Endangered and Threatened Species." *NYU Environmental Law Journal* 6 (1998): 411–449.

Doyle, Alister. "Amid Extinctions, Parrots, Panthers Get Costly Aid." ABC News.com, May 11, 2006.

Duffield, Jon W., D. A. Patterson, and C. J. Neher. "Wolf Recovery in Yellowstone Park Visitor Attitudes, Expenditures, and Economic Impacts." *Yellowstone Science* 16 (2008): 20–25.

Fahrenthold, David A. "Saving Species No Longer a Beauty Contest." *The Washington Post*, June 29, 2009.

Lerner, Jeff, Janet Mackey, and Frank Casey. "What's in Noah's Wallet? Land Conservation Spending in the United States." *BioScience* 57, no. 5 (2007): 419–423.

Loomis, John B., and Douglas S. White. "Economic Benefits of Rare and Endangered Species: Summary and Meta-Analysis." *Ecological Economics* 18 (1996): 197–206.

Miller, Julie K., J. Michael Scott, Craig R. Miller, and Lisette P. Waits. "The Endangered Species Act: Dollars and Sense?" *BioScience* 52, no. 2 (February 2002): 163–168.

Platt, John. "How Much Did the U.S. Spend in 2007 to Protect Endangered Species?" *Scientific American*, October 13, 2009.

Shaffer, Mark L., J. Michael Scott, and Frank Casey. "Noah's Options: Initial Cost Estimates of a National System of Habitat Conservation Areas in the United States." *BioScience* 52, no. 5 (May 2002): 439–443.

Simmons, Randy T., and Kimberly Frost. *Accounting for Species: The True Costs of the Endangered Species Act.* Bozeman, MT: Property and Environment Research Center, April 2004.

Tobin, Mitch. "Charisma Counts If You Want to Be Saved." *Arizona Daily Star*, December 19, 2004.

US General Accounting Office. "Endangered Species Program: Information on How Funds Are Allocated and What Activities Are Emphasized." GAO Report 02-581, June 2002.

US Government Accountability Office. "Endangered Species: Fish and Wildlife Service Generally Focuses Recovery Funding on High-Priority Species, but Needs to Periodically Assess Its Funding Decisions." GAO Report 5-211, April 6, 2005.

Wilcove, David S., and Linus Y. Chen. "Management Costs for Endangered Species." *Conservation Biology* 12, no. 6 (December 1998): 1405–1407.

Bruce Babbitt

Babbitt, Bruce. "Bush Isn't All Wrong about the Endangered Species Act." *The New York Times*, April 15, 2001.

———. *Cities in the Wilderness: A New Vision of Land Use in America*. Washington, DC: Island Press, 2005.

Davis, Tony. "Babbitt Development Role Draws Flak." *Arizona Daily Star*, June 22, 2008.

Kenworthy, Tom. "Pragmatic Critic Is Set to Be Interior's Next Landlord." *The Washington Post*, January 19, 1993.

Larmer, Paul, ed. *Give and Take: How the Clinton Administration's Public Lands Offensive Transformed the American West*. Paonia, CO: High Country News Books, 2004.

Leshy, John D. "The Babbitt Legacy at the Department of the Interior: A Preliminary View." *Environmental Law* 31 (2001): 199–227.

———. "Shaping the Modern West: The Role of the Executive Branch." *University of Colorado Law Review* 72, no. 287 (Spring 2001): 287–310.

Ruhl, J. B. "Endangered Species Act Innovations in the Post-Babbittonian Era: Are There Any?" *Duke Environmental Law & Policy Forum* 14, no. 2 (2004): 419–439.

Wagner, Dennis. "Environment a Contradiction for Babbitt." *The Arizona Republic*, May 25, 2008.

Richard Pombo

Boxall, Bettina. "Foe of Endangered Species Act on Defensive over Abramoff." *Los Angeles Times*, February 14, 2006.

Carlton, Jim. "Conservationists' 'Bogeyman.'" *The Wall Street Journal*, January 21, 2006.

Coile, Zachary. "Lawmaker's Agenda Just Part of His Nature." *San Francisco Chronicle*, May 3, 2004.

Gammon, Robert. "'Welcome to Pombo Country.'" *East Bay Express*, August 24, 2005.

Lee, Mike. "Spurred to Action." *The San Diego Union-Tribune*, February 19, 2006.

Pombo, Richard. "Old ESA Not Saving Anything." *Tracy Press*, July 9, 2006.

Pombo, Richard, and Joseph Farah. *This Land Is Our Land*. New York: St. Martin's Press, 1996.

Weiser, Matt. "The Many Faces of Richard Pombo." *High Country News*, July 25, 2005.

Whitney, David. "Pombo Lays Out Case against Species Act." *The Sacramento Bee*, July 16, 2006.

Mexican Gray Wolf

Babbitt, Bruce. "The Mexican Gray Wolf Has Senior Rights in the Arizona Wilderness." *Arizona Daily Star*, January 25, 1998.

Bodfield, Rhonda. "Wolf Killings Upset U.S., but Alpine Growls Back." *Arizona Daily Star*, November 15, 1998.

Brooke, James. "A Predator Returned to the Wild Discovers It Is Now Prey." *The New York Times*, December 22, 1998.

Holaday, Bobbie. *The Return of the Mexican Gray Wolf.* Tucson: Univ. of Arizona Press, 2003.

O'Connell, Maureen. "U.S. Will Apologize for Its 'In-Your-Face' Wolf Questionnaire." *Arizona Daily Star*, December 19, 1998.

Paquet, P. C., et al. *Mexican Wolf Recovery: Three Year Program Review and Assessment.* Apple Valley, MN: Prepared by the Conservation Breeding Specialist Group (IUCN) for the US Fish and Wildlife Service, 2001.

Steller, Tim. "Mexico to Place 5 Wolves Near AZ." *Arizona Daily Star*, February 7, 2010.

Taugher, Mike. "Wolf Questionnaire Angers Recipients: Hunters Close to Shooting Queried by Investigators." *Albuquerque Journal*, December 17, 1998.

7: Cub

Buenos Aires National Wildlife Refuge

Bagwell, Keith. "A Wild Land: Cattlemen Want to Tame Quail Preserve." *Arizona Daily Star*, December 10, 1995.

Sayre, Nathan. *Ranching, Endangered Species, and Urbanization in the Southwest.* Tucson: Univ. of Arizona Press, 2002.

Tobin, Mitch. "Range of Controversy." *Tucson Citizen*, September 5, 2000.

————. "Will a Watched Refuge Ever Revive?" *High Country News*, November 6, 2000.

————. "Quail Releases Halted as Success Eludes 2-decade Program." *Arizona Daily Star*, October 17, 2004.

Jim and Sue Chilton

Alaimo, Carol Ann. "Controversial Pick." *Arizona Daily Star*, January 27, 2001.

Fischer, Howard. "Panel Backs Controversial Rancher for G&F Post, 7-1." *Arizona Daily Star*, January 19, 2001.

O'Connell, Maureen. "Ranching Life: The Work's Just the Half of It." *Arizona Daily Star*, February 18, 2001.

Parham, Maria. "Southern Arizona Rancher Was a Victim of One-Sided Coverage." *Arizona Daily Star*, February 11, 2001.

Bush Administration

Bowman, Chris. "Analysis: Bush Team Battered by Courts on Environment." *The Sacramento Bee*, May 19, 2008.

Clarren, Rebecca. "Inside the Secretive Plan to Gut the Endangered Species Act." *Salon* http://www.salon.com/news/feature/2007/03/27/endangered_species/ (accessed February 1, 2010).

Eilperin, Juliet. "Since '01, Guarding Species Is Harder." *The Washington Post*, March 23, 2008.

Jehl, Douglas. "Norton Record Often at Odds with Laws She Would Enforce." *The New York Times*, January 13, 2001.

Leshy, John D. "Natural Resources Policy in the Bush (II) Administration: An Outsider's Somewhat Jaundiced Assessment." *Duke Environmental Law & Policy Forum* 14, no. 2 (2004): 347–362.

Snape, William III, et al. *Sabotaging the Endangered Species Act.* Washington, DC: Defenders of Wildlife Judicial Accountability Project, Fall 2003.

Tobin, Mitch. "Species Act May Be in for Changes." *Arizona Daily Star*, November 10, 2001.

————. "Enviros Outnumbered at Hearing on Act." *Arizona Daily Star*, September 21, 2004.

Environmental Journalism

Institutes for Journalism and Natural Resources. "Matching the Scenery: Journalism's Duty to the North American West." Missoula, MT, 2003.

Nieman Foundation for Journalism. *Special Issue of Nieman Reports on Science, Environment, Health, and Medicine Reporting.* Cambridge, MA: Nieman Foundation, 2004.

Tucson Water

See chapter 20 sources.

8: Ghost of the Desert

Sonoran Pronghorn

Byers, John A. *American Pronghorn: Adaptations and the Ghosts of Predators Past.* Chicago: Univ. of Chicago Press, 1998.

Cohn, Jeffrey P. "Return of the Pronghorn." *BioScience* 57, no. 5 (April 2007): 317–319.

Lindstedt, S. L., et al. "Running Energetics in the Pronghorn Antelope." *Nature* 353 (October 1991): 748–750.

Tobin, Mitch. "Pronghorn Protection Prompts Vast Desert Closure." *Arizona Daily Star*, March 4, 2002.

———. "2 Sonoran Pronghorn Survive Trek." *Arizona Daily Star*, January 22, 2004.

———. "A Run along the Abyss." *Arizona Daily Star*, March 7, 2004.

———. "World's Greatest Endurance Athlete." *Arizona Daily Star*, March 7, 2004.

Turbak, Gary. *Pronghorn: Portrait of the American Antelope.* Flagstaff, AZ: Northland, 1995.

Water Holes

Davis, Tony. "Groups: Kofa Refuge Bighorns aren't Helped by Water Tanks." *Arizona Daily Star*, September 17, 2009.

Tobin, Mitch. "Artificial Water Holes Awash in Controversy." *Arizona Daily Star*, January 18, 2004.

———. "Water Holes Awash in Controversy." *High Country News*, April 26, 2004.

50/500 Rule

Traill, Lochran W., et al. "Pragmatic Population Viability Targets in a Rapidly Changing World." *Biological Conservation* 143 (January 2010): 28–34.

Organ Pipe and Cabeza Prieta

Bassett, Carol Ann. *Organ Pipe: Life on the Edge.* Tucson: Univ. of Arizona Press, 2004.

Tobin, Mitch. "S. Arizona Park on List of Most Dangerous." *Arizona Daily Star*, May 31, 2001.

———. "Dangerous Parks." *High Country News*, August 27, 2001.

———. "Devil's Highway Has Long History of Deadliness." *Arizona Daily Star*, March 4, 2002.

———. "Wheels Still Spin after Desert Lockdown." *High Country News*, April 1, 2002.

———. "Organ Pipe 'Under Siege' Due to Crime." *Arizona Daily Star*, January 14, 2004.

———. "Cabeza Prieta Refuge on List of 10 in Danger." *Arizona Daily Star*, October 8, 2004.

Goldwater Bombing Range

Faherty, John. "A Modern Bombing Range, An Ancient Way of Life." *The Arizona Republic*, November 22, 2009.

Kaufman, Leslie. "A Base for War Training, and Species Preservation." *The New York Times*, February 22, 2010.

Krausman, Paul R., Lisa K. Harris, and Jennifer S. Ashbeck. "The Effects of Aircraft Noise on Pronghorn and Other Species: An Annotated Bibliography." Special Report no. 14, US Geological Survey, Cooperative Park Studies Unit. Tucson: Univ. of Arizona, 1998.

Landon, Deborah M., et al. "Pronghorn Use of Areas with Varying Sound Pressure Levels." *Southwestern Naturalist* 48 (December 2003): 725–728.

Malkin, Michelle. "Hostile Fire from Eco-Extremists." *Jewish World Review*, December 7, 2001.

Muir, John. "A Plan to Save the Forests: Forest Preservation by Military Control." *Century Magazine* 49 (February 1895): 630–631.

Pianin, Eric. "Environmental Exemptions Sought." *Washington Post*, March 6, 2003.

Shogren, Elizabeth. "Pentagon Asks Easing of Rules." *Los Angeles Times*, April 20, 2002.

Tobin, Mitch. "Where War, Nature Coexist Warily." *Arizona Daily Star*, June 22, 2003.

The Wall Street Journal. "Oh Deer!" April 10, 2003.

Border Crisis

Cart, Julie. "In Border Battle, Land and Wildlife Are Casualties." *Los Angeles Times*, March 3, 2006.

Segee, Brian P., and Jenny L. Neeley. *On the Line: The Impacts of Immigration Policy on Wildlife and Habitat in the Arizona Borderlands*. Washington, DC: Defenders of Wildlife, 2006.

Tobin, Mitch. "Danger Funnels Northward." *Arizona Daily Star*, September 8, 2002.

———. "Understaffing Tolerated—Until Disaster Strikes." *Arizona Daily Star*, September 8, 2002.

———. "Border's Sensitive Areas Are Trampled." *Arizona Daily Star*, September 9, 2002.

———. "Entrants Tied to Costly Wildfires." *Arizona Daily Star*, September 9, 2002.

———. "Fortifying Border Would Hurt Wildlife." *Arizona Daily Star*, February 5, 2003.

———. "Fences Go up along the Mexican Border." *High Country News*, March 3, 2003.

9: Blame Game

Forests and Wildfires

Barker, Rocky. *Scorched Earth: How the Fires of Yellowstone Changed America*. Washington, DC: Island Press, 2005.

Beal, Tom. "Burning Our Forests is the Best Way to Save Them." *Arizona Daily Star*, December 6, 2009.

Bowden, Charles. *Frog Mountain Blues*. Tucson: Univ. of Arizona Press, 1987.

Boxall, Bettina. "A Santa Barbara Area Canyon's Residents Are among Many Californians Living in Harm's Way in Fire-Prone Areas." *Los Angeles Times*, July 31, 2008.

Boxall, Bettina, and Julie Cart. "As Wildfires Get Wilder, the Costs of Fighting Them Are Untamed." *Los Angeles Times*, July 27, 2008.

Covington W. W., and M. M. Moore. "Postsettlement Changes in Natural Fire Regimes and Forest Structure: Ecological Restoration of Old-Growth Ponderosa Pine Forests." *Journal of Sustainable Forestry* 2 (1994): 153–181.

———. "Southwestern Ponderosa Forest Structure." *Journal of Forestry* 92 (1994): 39–47.

Durbin, Kathie. "The War on Wildfire." *High Country News*, April 17, 2006.

Hammer, R. B., et al. "Wildland-Urban Interface Housing Growth during the 1990s in California, Oregon, and Washington." *International Journal of Wildland Fire* 16 (2007): 255–265.

Maclean, Norma. *Young Men and Fire*. Chicago: Univ. of Chicago Press, 1993.

McPhee, John. "Balloons of War." *New Yorker*, January 29, 1996.

Nijhuis, Michelle. "Written in the Rings." *High Country News*, January 24, 2005.

Pyne, Stephen J. *Year of the Fires: The Story of the Great Fires of 1910*. New York: Penguin, 2001.

————. "Meeting Fire on Its Terms." *The New York Times*, June 25, 2002.

Ring, Ray. "A Losing Battle." *High Country News*, May 26, 2003.

Rodeo-Chediski and 2002 Fires

Center for Biological Diversity, Sierra Club, and Southwest Forest Alliance. "Prelude to Catastrophe: Recent and Historic Land Management within the Rodeo-Chediski Fire Area." July 2002.

Finney, Mark A., Charles W. McHugh, and Isaac C. Greenfell. "Stand- and Landscape-Level Effects of Prescribed Burning on Two Arizona Wildfires." *Canadian Journal of Forest Research* 35 (2005): 1714–1722

Holdcroft, Gary P. *Walking through the Ashes: A Volunteer Firefighter's Perspective on the Rodeo-Chediski Fire*. Bloomington, IN: Trafford Publishing, 2006.

Pacific Biodiversity Institute. *Analysis of Land Ownership and Prior Land Management Activities within the Rodeo and Chediski Fires, Arizona*. Winthrop, WA, July 2002.

Paxon, Jim. *The Monster Reared His Ugly Head*. Snowflake, AZ: Cedar Hill Publishing, 2007.

Strom, Barbara A. "Pre-Fire Treatment Effects and Post-Fire Forest Dynamics on the Rodeo-Chediski Burn Area, Arizona." Master's thesis, Northern Arizona Univ., 2005.

Tobin, Mitch. "A Moving, Fuming, Irate force of Nature." *Arizona Daily Star*, May 30, 2002.

————. "The Danger, the Adrenaline." *Arizona Daily Star*, June 16, 2002.

————. "Observatory Sits atop Tinderbox." *Arizona Daily Star*, June 21, 2002.

————. "Aerial View Shows Fire's Destruction." *Arizona Daily Star*, June 22, 2002.

————. "A Surreal World of Ash and Embers." *Arizona Daily Star*, June 24, 2002.

————. "From Its Start, Rodeo Was 'Totally Nuts.'" *Arizona Daily Star*, June 28, 2002.

————. "Lack of Chediski Fire Arrest Is Seen as Unequal Justice." *Arizona Daily Star*, July 2, 2002.

Aspen Fire

Baisan, Christopher H., et al. *Fire History in Ponderosa Pine and Mixed-Conifer Forests of the Catalina Mountains*. Tucson: Univ. of Arizona Laboratory of Tree-Ring Research, 1998.

Beal, Tom, Thomas Stauffer, and Mitch Tobin. "Smoke, Flames, and Ash." *Arizona Daily Star*, August 17, 2003, special section.

Tobin, Mitch. "An Odd Mix of Ruin and Salvation." *Arizona Daily Star*, June 21, 2003.

————. "How Rincons and Catalinas Went Their Own Ways in Wildfire Management." *Arizona Daily Star*, October 5, 2003.

————. "Experts: Aspen Fire Spread on Ground." *Arizona Daily Star*, October 17, 2003.

Thinning and Healthy Forests Initiative

Associated Press. "Forest Service Defends Record on Thinning Forests to Prevent Wildfire." *The Oregonian*, June 27, 2009.

Daly, Matthew. "Law Speeds Tree-Cutting." *Arizona Daily Star*, May 21, 2004.

Dombeck, Mike, and Jack Ward Thomas. "Declare Harvest of Old-Growth Forests Off-Limits and Move On." *Seattle Post-Intelligencer*, April 24, 2003.

Flatten, Mark. "Lawsuits Stall Forest Thinning." *East Valley Tribune*, April 27, 2003.

Flatten, Mark, and Dan Nowicki. "Green Group Lawsuit Blocked Forest Thinning." *East Valley Tribune*, July 8, 2002.

Jehl, Douglas. "The West Is Culling Forests That Fueled Fires of the Past." *The New York Times*, May 12, 2001.

Knudson, Tom. "Spin on Science Puts National Treasure at Risk." *The Sacramento Bee*, April 25, 2001.

McKinnon, Shaun. "Study: Western Fire-Prevention Efforts Leave Homes At Risk." *The Arizona Republic*, June 9, 2009.

Noss, R. F., et al. "Managing Fire-Prone Forests in the Western United States." *Frontiers in Ecology* 4 (2006): 481–487.

Schoennagel, Tania. "Implementation of National Fire Plan Treatments near the Wildland–Urban Interface in the Western United States." *Proceedings of the National Academy of Sciences* 106 (June 2009): 10706–10711

Teich, G. M. R., J. Vaughn, and H. J. Cortner. "National Trends in the Use of Forest Service Administrative Appeals." *Journal of Forestry* 102, no. 2 (March 2004): 14–19.

Tobin, Mitch. "In Wildfire Risk Control, 1 'Size' May Fit None." *Arizona Daily Star*, August 7, 2002.

———. "Bush to Promote Forests Plan." *Arizona Daily Star*, August 10, 2003.

———. "Bush Calls for Fast Action to Fix 'Failed' Forest Policies." *Arizona Daily Star*, August 12, 2003.

———. "Feds: Owl Suit Raises Fire Risk." *Arizona Daily Star*, October 3, 2003.

———. "Government, Business Unite to Thin Forest." *Arizona Daily Star*, August 11, 2004.

US Forest Service. "The Process Predicament: How Statutory, Regulatory, and Administrative Factors Affect National Forest Management." Washington, DC, June 2002.

US General Accounting Office. "Forest Service: Information on Appeals and Litigation Involving Fuels Reduction Activities." GAO Report 04-52, October 2003.

Vaughn, J., and Cortner, H. J. *George W. Bush's Healthy Forests: Reframing the Environmental Debate*. Boulder, CO: Univ. Press of Colorado, 2005.

Wildfire Solutions

Allen, Craig D., et al. "Ecological Restoration of Southwestern Ponderosa Pine Ecosystems: A Broad Perspective." *Ecological Applications* 12, no. 5 (2002): 1418–1433.

Associated Press. "Years of Planning, Quick Response Help Stop Flagstaff Fire." *Arizona Daily Star*, June 15, 2006.

Aumack, Ethan, and Molly Pitts. "Forests in Arizona Facing Historic Moment, Change." *The Arizona Republic*, January 10, 2009.

Beal, Tom. "When Fire Is a Benefit." *Arizona Daily Star*, July 27, 2009.

Cole, Cyndy. "Snuffed Out?" *Arizona Daily Sun*, June 22, 2008.

Fonseca, Felicia. "Agreement Could Yield Fewer Lawsuits Over Forest." *Arizona Daily Star*, August 12, 2009.

Friederici, Peter. *Ecological Restoration of Southwestern Ponderosa Pine Forests*. Washington, DC: Island Press, 2003.

Pyne, Stephen J. *Tending Fire: Coping with America's Wildland Fires*. Washington, DC: Island Press, 2004.

Reese, April. "Industry, Enviro Groups Jointly Pursue Ariz. Ponderosa Restoration." *Land Letter*, April 30, 2009.

Ring, Ray. "Even Hard-Liners Want to Experiment in Arizona." *High Country News*, July 13, 2009.

Villa, Judi, and Mark Shaffer. "Flagstaff Beats Flames." *The Arizona Republic*, June 16, 2006.

10: Friends of the Frogs
Chiricahua Leopard Frogs

Erickson, Jim. "Foreign Fungus Linked to Leopard Frog Deaths." *Arizona Daily Star*, July 11, 1998.

————. "In Arizona, a Skin Fungus is Making the Native Amphibians Die Off." *Arizona Daily Star*, April 30, 1999.

Muro, Mark. "Exotic Predators Swallow the Southwest's Native Frogs." *High Country News*, May 25, 1998.

Tobin, Mitch. "Leopard Frog Gets Protection." *Arizona Daily Star*, June 14, 2002.

————. "Orgy in a Desert Water Hole." *Arizona Daily Star*, July 27, 2002.

————. "Ranchers Helping Leopard Frog—A Species on the Spot." *Arizona Daily Star*, April 18, 2004.

————. "Frogs' Friend Could Face Federal Rap." *Arizona Daily Star*, May 16, 2004.

————. "Wildlife Manager Moved Tadpoles, Will Pay $3,500." *Arizona Daily Star*, February 22, 2005.

Invasive Species

Baskin, Yvonne. *A Plague of Rats and Rubbervines: The Growing Threat of Species Invasions*. Washington, DC: Island Press, 2002.

McNamee, Gregory. "The Grass That Ate Sonora." *Tucson Weekly*, April 18, 1996.

Tellman, Barbara, ed. *Invasive Exotic Species in the Sonoran Region*. Tucson: Univ. of Arizona Press, 2002.

Tobin, Mitch. "Buffelgrass Unwelcome Here." *Arizona Daily Star*, March 4, 2005.

Amphibian Decline

Conlon, J. M. "The Therapeutic Potential of Antimicrobial Peptides from Frog Skin." *Reviews in Medical Microbiology* 15, no. 1 (January 2004): 17–25.

Daly, John William. "Thirty Years of Discovering Arthropod Alkaloids in Amphibian Skin." *Journal of Natural Products* 61 (1998): 61, 162.

Duhigg, Charles. "Debating How Much Weed Killer Is Safe in Your Water Glass." *The New York Times*, August 23, 2009.

Hayes, Tyrone, Atif Collins, Melissa Lee, Magdelena Mendoza, Nigel Noriega, A. Ali Stuart, and Aaron Vonk. "Hermaphroditic, Demasculinized Frogs after Exposure to the Herbicide Atrazine at Low Ecologically Relevant Doses." *Proceedings of the National Academy of Sciences* 99 (2002): 5476–5480.

Hayes, Tyrone, Kelly Haston, Mable Tsui, Anhthu Hoang, Cathryn Haeffele, and Aaron Vonk. "Atrazine-Induced Hermaphroditism at 0.1 ppb in American Leopard Frogs (*Rana pipiens*): Laboratory and Field Evidence." *Environmental Health Perspectives* 111, no. 4 (April 2003): 568–575.

Kerby, Jacob L., et al. "An Examination of Amphibian Sensitivity to Environmental Contaminants: Are Amphibians Poor Canaries?" *Ecology Letters* 13 (2009): 60–67.

Lips, Karen R., Jay Diffendorfer, Joseph R. Mendelson, and Michael W. Sears. "Riding the Wave: Reconciling the Roles of Disease and Climate Change in Amphibian Declines." *PLoS ONE* 6 (March 2008): 441–454.

Mendelson, Joseph R. III, et al. "Confronting Amphibian Declines and Extinctions." *Science* 313 (2006): 48.

Pounds, J. Alan. "Widespread Amphibian Extinctions from Epidemic Disease Driven by Global Warming." *Nature* 439 (2006): 161–167.

Relyea, Rick A. "The Lethal Impact of Roundup on Aquatic and Terrestrial Amphibians." *Ecological Applications* 15 (2005): 1118–1124.

Stuart, Simon N., et al. "Status and Trends of Amphibian Declines and Extinctions Worldwide." *Science* 306 (2004): 1783–1786.

Conservation on Private Land

Bean, Michael J. "The Endangered Species Act and Private Land: Four Lessons Learned from the Past Quarter Century." *Environmental Law Reporter News and Analysis* 28 (1998): 10701–10710.

Brook, A., M. Zint, and R. De Young. "Landowners' Responses to an Endangered Species Act Listing and Implications for Encouraging Conservation." *Conservation Biology* 17 (2003): 1638–1649.

Dubner, Stephen J., and Steven D. Levitt. "Unintended Consequences." *The New York Times Magazine*, January 20, 2008.

List, John A., Michael Margolis, and Daniel E. Osgood. "Is the Endangered Species Act Endangering Species?" Working paper 12777, Cambridge, MA: National Bureau of Economic Research, 2006.

Lueck, Dean, and Jeffrey A. Michael. "Preemptive Habitat Destruction under the Endangered Species Act." *Journal of Law and Economics* 46, no. 1 (2003): 27–60.

Rosenzweig, Michael L. *Win-Win Ecology: How the Earth's Species Can Survive in the Midst of Human Enterprise.* Oxford: Oxford Univ. Press, 2003.

Scott, J. Michael, et. al. "Nature Reserves: Do They Capture the Full Range of America's Biological Diversity?" *Ecological Issues in Conservation* 11 (2001): 999–1007.

Stroup, Richard. *The Endangered Species Act: Making Innocent Species the Enemy.* Bozeman, MT: Property and Environment Research Center, 1995.

Tobin, Mitch. "Fish May Join Mosquito Fight." *Arizona Daily Star*, November 28, 2003.

———. "'Safe Harbors' Cut Gordian Knot of Species Conflict." *Arizona Daily Star*, April 18, 2004.

———. "New Land Rush Gives Ranchers a Tough Choice." *Arizona Daily Star*, September 18, 2005.

———. "Save a Species, Save on Taxes." *PERC Reports* 25, no. 3 (September 2007): 12–14, 25.

US Government Accounting Office. *Species Protection on Nonfederal Lands.* Washington, DC, 1995.

Malpai Borderlands Group

Enquist, Carolyn A. F., and David F. Gori. "An Assessment of the Spatial Extent and Condition of Grasslands in the Apache Highlands Ecoregion." In *Connecting Mountain Islands and Desert Seas: Biodiversity and Management of the Madrean Archipelago II*, edited by G. J. Gottfried et al. Proceedings RMRS-P-36. Fort Collins, CO: US Department of Agriculture, 2005.

Feiger, Richard S., and Michael F. Wilson. "Northern Sierra Madre Occidental and Its Apachian Outliers: A Neglected Center of Biodiversity." In *Biodiversity and Management of the Madrean Archipelago: The Sky Islands of Southwestern United States and Northwestern Mexico*, edited by Leonard F. DeBano et al. General Technical Report RM-GTR-264. Fort Collins, CO: US Department of Agriculture, 1995.

Martin, Douglas. "James A. Corbett, 67, Is Dead: A Champion of Movement to Safeguard Illegal Refugees." *The New York Times*, August 12, 2001.

Sayre, Nathan. *Working Wilderness: The Malpai Borderlands Group and the Future of the Western Range.* Tucson, AZ: Rio Nuevo Press, 2005.

Turner, Raymond M., et al. *The Changing Mile Revisited.* Tucson: Univ. of Arizona Press, 2003.

Weisman, A. "Paradise Ranch." *Los Angeles Times Magazine*, March 21, 1993.

11: Warming Up

Nuttall Fire

Beal, Tom. "UA-run observatory harms Pinaleños' forest, enviros and Forest Service say." *Arizona Daily Star*, December 8, 2009.

Koprowski, J. L., M. I. Alanen, and A. M. Lynch. "Nowhere to Run and Nowhere to Hide: Response of Endemic Mt. Graham Red Squirrels to Catastrophic Forest Damage." *Biological Conservation* 126 (2005): 491–498.

Koprowski, J. L., et al. "Direct Effects of Fire on Endangered Mt. Graham Red Squirrels." *Southwestern Naturalist* 51 (March 2006): 59–63.

Tobin, Mitch. "Feds Cleaning, Pruning near UA Scopes." *Arizona Daily Star*, July 3, 2002.

———. "Squirrels, Scopes Share Wildfire Threat." *Arizona Daily Star*, June 6, 2004.

———. "Fire May Devastate Imperiled Squirrels." *Arizona Daily Star*, July 5, 2004.

———. "Red Squirrels' Beautiful Canyon Home Threatened." *Arizona Daily Star*, July 8, 2004.

———. "Trees near Telescopes Thinned Despite Enviros." *Arizona Daily Star*, July 9, 2004.

———. "Fire Hurts Squirrels' Cause." *Arizona Daily Star*, July 22, 2004.

———. "Squirrels and Scopes in the Line of Fire." *High Country News*, August 30, 2004.

Climate Change and Biodiversity

Barnosky, Anthony D. *Heatstroke: Nature in an Age of Global Warming*. Washington, DC: Island Press, 2009.

———. "Megafauna Biomass Tradeoff as a Driver of Quaternary and Future Extinctions." *Proceedings of the National Academy of Sciences* 105 (August 2008): 11543–11548.

Brown, James H., et al. "Reorganization of an Arid Ecosystem in Response to Recent Climate Change." *Proceedings of the National Academy of Sciences* 94 (September 1997): 9729–9733.

Botkin, Daniel B., et al. "Forecasting the Effects of Global Warming on Biodiversity." *BioScience* 57 (2007): 227–236.

Fischlin, A., et al. "Ecosystems, Their Properties, Goods, and Services." In *Climate Change 2007: Impacts, Adaptation and Vulnerability. Contribution of Working Group II to the Fourth Assessment Report of the Intergovernmental Panel on Climate Change*, edited by M. L. Parry et al. Cambridge: Cambridge Univ. Press, 211–272.

Hannah, Lee, and Thomas E. Lovejoy. *Climate Change and Biodiversity*. New Haven, CT: Yale Univ. Press, 2005.

Parmesan, Camille, and Gary Yohe. "A Globally Coherent Fingerprint of Climate Change Impacts across Natural Systems." *Nature* 421 (2003): 37–42.

Root, Terry L., et al. "Fingerprints of Global Warming on Wild Animals and Plants." *Nature* 421 (2003): 57–60.

Rosenzweig, Cynthia. "Attributing Physical and Biological Impacts to Anthropogenic Climate Change." *Nature* 453 (May 2008): 353–357.

Saunders, Stephen, et al. *Hotter and Drier: The West's Changed Climate*. New York: Rocky Mountain Climate Organization and Natural Resources Defense Council, March 2008.

Thomas, C. D., et al. "Extinction Risk from Climate Change." *Nature* 427 (2004): 145–148.

US Climate Change Science Program. "The Effects of Climate Change on Agriculture, Land Resources, Water Resources, and Biodiversity in the United States." Final Report, Synthesis and Assessment Product 4.3. Washington, DC: US Environmental Protection Agency, 2008.

Walther, Gian-Reto, et al. "Ecological Responses to Recent Climate Change." *Nature* 416 (2002): 389–395.

Weiss, J. L., and J. T. Overpeck. "Is the Sonoran Desert Losing Its Cool?" *Global Change Biology* 11 (2005): 2065–2077.

Williams, John W., Stephen T. Jackson, and John E. Kutzbach. "Projected Distributions of Novel and Disappearing Climates by 2100 AD." *Proceedings of the National Academy of Sciences* 104 (2007): 5738-5742.

Zimmer, Carl. "Previous Eras of Warming Hold Warnings for Our Age." *Yale Environment 360* http://e360.yale.edu/content/feature.msp?id=2154 (accessed February 1, 2010).

Escalator Effect, Range Shifts, and Other Climate Effects

Bradley, Nina L., et al. "Phenological Changes Reflect Climate Change in Wisconsin." *Proceedings of the National Academy of Sciences* 96 (1999): 9701-9704.

Crimmins, Theresa M., Michael A. Crimmins, and C. David Bertelsen. "Flowering Range Changes across an Elevation Gradient in Response to Warming Summer Temperatures." *Global Change Biology* 15 (2008): 1141-1152.

Davis, Tony. "Persistent Hiker Discovers Plants Blooming at Higher Elevations Than Ever Before." *Arizona Daily Star,* February 15, 2009.

———. "Audubon: Climate Change Is Shifting Bird Migration." *Arizona Daily Star,* June 10, 2009.

Monahan, William B., and Gary Langham. *Mapping Avian Responses to Climate Change in California.* Emeryville, CA: Audubon California, 2008.

National Audubon Society. "Birds and Climate Change Ecological Disruption in Motion." www.audubon.org/news/pressroom/bacc/pdfs/Birds%20and%20Climate%20Report.pdf (accessed February 1, 2010).

Sekercioglu, C. H., et al. "Climate Change, Elevational Range Shifts, and Bird Extinctions." *Conservation Biology* 22 (2008): 140-150.

Schmid, Randolph. "Should We Move Species to Save Them?" *USA Today,* July 17, 2008.

Climate, Wildfires, and Vegetation

Adams, Henry D., et al. "Temperature Sensitivity of Drought-Induced Tree Mortality Portends Increased Regional Die-Off under Global Change-Type Drought." *Proceedings of the National Academy of Sciences Early Edition,* April 2009.

Archer, Steven R., and Katharine I. Predick. "Climate Change and Ecosystems of the Southwestern United States." *Rangelands* 30, no. 3 (June 2008): 23-28.

Beal, Tom. "State in 'Bull's-Eye' for Change." *Arizona Daily Star,* June 17, 2009.

Bowers, Janice E. "Effects of Drought on Shrub Survival and Longevity in the Northern Sonoran Desert." *Journal of the Torrey Botanical Society* 132 (2005): 421-431.

Breshears, David D., et al. "Regional Vegetation Die-Off in Response to Global-Change-Type Drought." *Proceedings of the National Academy of Sciences* 102, no. 42 (October 2005): 15144-15148.

McKenzie, D., et al. "Climatic Change, Wildfire, and Conservation." *Conservation Biology* 18 (2004): 890-902.

Nijhuis, Michelle. "What's Killing the Aspen?" *Smithsonian,* December 2008.

Riccardi, Nicholas. "Global Warming Blamed for Aspen Die-Off across the West." *Los Angeles Times,* October 18, 2009.

Robbins, Jim. "Some See Beetle Attacks on Western Forests as a Natural Event." *The New York Times,* July 7, 2009.

Shogren, Elizabeth. "Outlook Bleak for Joshua Trees." *National Public Radio,* February 4, 2008.

Simon, Stephanie. "Aspen Trees Die across the West." *The Wall Street Journal,* October 14, 2009.

Tobin, Mitch. "A Warmer Arizona and Southwest Chill Scientists to the Bone." *Arizona Daily Star,* February 16, 2005.

Van Mantgem, Phillip J., et al. "Widespread Increase of Tree Mortality Rates in the Western United States." *Science* 323 (January 2009): 521–524.

Westerling, A. L., et al. "Warming and Earlier Spring Increase Western U.S. Forest Wildfire Activity." *Science* 313 (August 2006): 940–943.

Zimmerman, Janet. "Desert Icon Joshua Trees Are Vanishing, Scientists Say." *The (Riverside, CA) Press-Enterprise*, June 21, 2009.

12: Kangaroo Court

Politicization of Science

Becker, Jo, and Barton Gellman. "Leaving No Tracks." *The Washington Post*, June 27, 2007.

Lee, Christopher. "Scientists Report Political Interference." *The Washington Post*, April 24, 2008.

Mooney, Chris. *The Republican War on Science.* New York: Basic Books, 2005.

Pasternak, Judy. "Hundreds of EPA Scientists Report Political Interference." *Los Angeles Times*, April 24, 2008.

Wilkinson, Todd. *Science Under Siege: The Politicians' War on Nature and Truth.* Boulder, CO: Johnson Books, 1998.

Pombo Bill

American Fisheries Society, Ecological Society of America, Entomological Society of America, Society for Conservation Biology-North America, Society for Range Management, and The Wildlife Society. "Scientific Societies Statement on the Endangered Species Act." February 27, 2006.

Irvin, William Robert. "Opinion: Silk Purse of Sow's Ear? The Pombo Bill and the Endangered Species Act." *Endangered Species Update* 22 (2005): 125–127.

Taugher, Mike. "'Pombo-ized' Bills Worry Lawmakers." *Contra Costa Times*, March 30, 2006.

Critical Habitat

Davis, Tony. "Critical Habitat: The Inside Story." *High Country News*, February 20, 2006.

———. "High Noon for Habitat." *High Country News*, February 20, 2006.

———. "ESA Talks End in Stalemate." *High Country News*, March 20, 2006.

Davis, Tony, and Greg Hanscom. "Reality Check." *High Country News*, March 20, 2006.

Keystone Center. "Final Report of Working Group on Endangered Species Act Habitat Issues." Keystone, CO: The Keystone Center, April 2006.

Parenteau, Patrick. *An Empirical Assessment of the Impact of Critical Habitat Litigation on the Administration of the Endangered Species Act.* Faculty Papers, Vermont Law School, 2005.

Taylor, M. F. J., K. F. Suckling, and J. J. Rachlinksi. "The Effectiveness of the Endangered Species Act: A Quantitative Analysis." *BioScience* 55 (2005): 360–367.

Winter, Greg. "U.S. Acts to Shrink Endangered Species Habitats." *The New York Times*, March 20 2002.

Julie MacDonald

Clayton, Mark. "Politics Undercut Species Act, Suit Says." *The Christian Science Monitor*, November 20, 2007.

Colorado Springs Gazette. "More to Julie MacDonald Case Than Meets the Eye." September 6, 2007.

Eilperin, Juliet. "Bush Appointee Said to Reject Advice on Endangered Species." *The Washington Post*, October 30, 2006.

———. "Report Faults Interior Appointee." *The Washington Post*, March 30, 2007.

————. "7 Decisions on Species Reversed." *The Washington Post*, November 28, 2007.

Knickerbocker, Brad. "Controversy Erupts over Endangered Species Act." *The Christian Science Monitor*, July 25, 2007.

US Department of Interior. "Investigative Report: The Endangered Species Act and the Conflict between Science and Policy." Office of the Inspector General, December 10, 2008.

US Government Accountability Office. "Endangered Species Act Decision Making." GAO Report 08-688T, May 2008.

Wilson, Janet. "7 Federal Wildlife Decisions to Be Revised." *Los Angeles Times*, November 28, 2007.

13: No Bats, No Tequila?

Lesser Long-Nosed Bats

Arita, Hector T., and Don E. Wilson. "Long-Nosed Bats and Agaves: The Tequila Connection." *BATS Magazine* 5, no. 4 (December 1987): 3–5.

Bagwell, Keith. "Lawsuit Seeks Grazing Cuts on Coronado Forest Land." *Arizona Daily Star*, August 7, 1998.

Chilton, Jim. "Statement by the National Cattlemen's Beef Association and the Public Lands Council on the Endangered Species Act." Submitted to the Fisheries, Wildlife and Water Subcommittee of Senate Environment and Public Works Committee, June 25, 2003.

Cockrum, E. Lendell, and Yar Petryszyn. "The Long-Nosed Bat, *Leptonycteris*: An Endangered Species in the Southwest?" *Occasional Papers of the Museum of Texas Tech University*, no. 142 (July 1991): 1–32.

Fleming, Theodore H. *A Bat Man in the Tropics: Chasing El Duende*. Berkeley: Univ. of California Press, 2003.

————. "Following the Nectar Trail." *BATS Magazine* 9, no. 4 (Winter 1991): 4–7.

————. "Pollination of Sonoran Desert Cacti." *American Scientist* 88 (2000): 432–400.

Fleming, Theodore H., and Alfonso Valiente-Banuet. *Columnar Cacti and Their Mutualists*. Tucson: Univ. of Arizona Press, 2002.

Hawley, Chris. "Scientists Fleeing Border, Smugglers." *The Arizona Republic*, December 27, 2007.

Nabhan, Gary Paul, and Richard C. Brusca. "Migratory Pollinators and Their Nectar Corridors in the Southwestern U.S. and Northwestern Mexico." Final Report to the Turner Foundation and Endangered Species Fund. Tucson: Arizona-Sonora Desert Museum, December 2002.

Tobin, Mitch. "Suit Charges Cattle Overgrazing in Coronado." *Arizona Daily Star*, October 23, 2001.

————. "Bat's 'Endangered' Listing a Blunder, Many Experts Say." *Arizona Daily Star*, September 19, 2004.

Tuttle, Merlin D. "Bats: The Cactus Connection." *National Geographic*, June 1991.

ESA Listing Decisions

General Accounting Office. "Endangered Species: Fish and Wildlife Service Uses Best Available Science to Make Listing Decisions, but Additional Guidance Needed for Critical Habitat Designations." GAO Report 03-803, August 29, 2003.

Tobin, Mitch. "Agave Hybrid Is Losing Status as Endangered." *Arizona Daily Star*, December 14, 2003.

14: The Rancher's Revenge

Chilton Libel Suit and Montana Allotment

Arizona Cattle Growers Association v. U.S. Fish and Wildlife Service, 273 F.3d 1229 (9th Cir. 2001).

Carlton, Jim. "Rancher Turns the Table: Environmental Group Loses Lawsuit Filed by Cattleman." *The Wall Street Journal*, August 19, 2005.

Carpenter, J., and O. E. Maughan. "Macrohabitat of Sonora Chub (*Gila ditaenia*) in Sycamore Creek, Santa Cruz County, Arizona." *Journal of Freshwater Ecology* 8, no. 4 (1993): 265–278.

Fenske, Sarah. "The Rancher's Revenge." *Phoenix New Times*, May 26, 2005.

Fischer, Howard. "Environmental Grop Appeals $600K Jury Verdict." *Arizona Daily Star*, September 7, 2007.

———. "Environmental Group Still Owes Rancher $600,000." *Arizona Daily Sun*, December 7, 2006.

Fleming, William, Dee Galt, and Jerry Holechek. "The Montana Allotment: A Grazing Success Story." *Rangelands* 23, no. 6 (December 2001): 24–26.

Hendrickson, D. A., and L. Juarez-Romero. "Los Peces de la Cuenca Del Rio de la Concepction, Sonora, Mexico y el Estatus del Charalito Sonorense, *Gila ditaenia*, una Especie en Amenaza de Extincion." *The Southwestern Naturalist* 35, no. 2 (June 1990): 177–187.

Stinson, Paul. "*Arizona Cattle Growers Association v. U.S. Fish & Wildlife Service*: Has the Ninth Circuit Weakened the 'Take' Provisions of the Endangered Species Act?" *Ecology Law Quarterly* 30 (2003): 497.

Tobin, Mitch. "Rancher's Suit Puts Enviros on Defensive." *Arizona Daily Star*, January 12, 2005.

———. "Rancher's Suit May Go to Jury Today." *Arizona Daily Star*, January 20, 2005.

———. "Enviro Center That Lives by the Suit Gets Burned by the Suit." *Arizona Daily Star*, January 22, 2005.

———. "Rancher Wins $600K in Suit against Enviros." *Arizona Daily Star*, January 22, 2005.

———. "Rancher Wins Big in Libel Suit Against Enviros." *High Country News*, February 21, 2005.

Vanderpool, Tim. "Ranching with Lawyers." *Tucson Weekly*, February 24, 2005.

Environmental Litigation

Knudson, Tom. "Litigation Central." *The Sacramento Bee*, April 24, 2001.

Taylor, Phil. "Lawsuit Abuse Charge by Western Lawmakers Enrages Enviro Groups." *The New York Times*, November 19, 2009.

Grazing

Dagget, Dan. *Gardeners of Eden: Rediscovering Our Importance to Nature*. Santa Barbara: Thatcher Charitable Trust, 2005.

Davis, Tony. "Rangeland Revival." *High Country News*, September 5, 2005.

———. "Science: The Chink in Quivira's Armor." *High Country News*, September 5, 2005.

Gentner, Bradley J., and John A. Tanaka. "Classifying Federal Public Land Grazing Permittees." *Journal of Range Management* 55 (2002): 2–11.

Holechek, Jerry. L., Rex D. Pieper, and Carlton H. Herbel. *Range Management: Principles and Practices*. London: Prentice-Hall, 2003.

Holechek, Jerry L., Terrel T. Baker, Jon C. Boren, and Dee Galt. "Grazing Impacts on Rangeland Vegetation: What We Have Learned." *Rangelands* 28, no. 1 (2006): 7–13.

Knight, Richard L., Wendell C. Gilgert, and Ed Marston. *Ranching West of the 100th Meridian*. Washington, DC: Island Press, 2002.

Maestas, J. D., et al. "Biodiversity across a Rural Land-Use Gradient." *Conservation Biology* 17 (2003): 1425–1434.

Milchunas, Daniel G. "Responses of Plant Communities to Grazing in the Southwestern United States." General Technical Report RMRS-GTR-169. Fort Collins, CO: US Forest Service Rocky Mountain Research Station, April 2006.

Quivira Coalition. *Forging a West That Works: An Invitation to the Radical Center.* Santa Fe: Quivira Coalition, 2003.

Stauder, Jack. "Aldo Leopold and the Blue: Grazing, Erosion and Wilderness." Dartmouth: Univ. of Massachusetts, n.d.

Tobin, Mitch. "Suit Charges Overgrazing in Coronado." *Arizona Daily Star*, October 23, 2001.

———. "Grazing Foes Win Key Case." *Arizona Daily Star*, November 5, 2003.

US General Accounting Office. "Rangeland Management: BLM's Hot Desert Grazing Program Merits Reconsideration." GAO Report RCED-92-12, November 26, 1991.

US Government Accountability Office. "Livestock Grazing: Federal Expenditures and Receipts Vary, Depending on the Agency and the Purpose of the Fee Charged." GAO Report 05-869, September 2005.

Wilcove, David S., et al. "Quantifying Threats to Imperiled Species in the United States: Assessing the Relative Importance of Habitat Destruction, Alien Species, Pollution, Overexploitation, and Disease." *Bioscience* 48 (1998): 607–615.

Intermediate Disturbance Hypothesis

Connell, J. H. "Diversity in Tropical Rain Forests and Coral Reefs." *Science* 199 (March 1978): 1302–1310.

Grime, J. P. "Competitive Exclusion in Herbaceous Vegetation." *Nature* 242 (March 1973): 344–347.

Horn, H. S. "Markovian Properties of Forest Succession." In *Ecology and Evolution of Communities*, edited by M. L. Cody and J. M. Diamond. Cambridge, MA: Belknap Press, 1975.

Wilkinson, David M. "The Disturbing History of Intermediate Disturbance." *Oikos* 84 (1999): 145–147.

Ecological Footprint of Food

Niman, Nicolette Hahn. "The Carnivore's Dilemma." *The New York Times*, October 31, 2009.

Pollan, Michael. *The Omnivore's Dilemma.* New York: Penguin Press, 2006.

15: El Tigre

Jaguars

Arizona-Sonora Desert Museum. *Sonorensis* 28, no. 1 (Winter 2008), special issue.

Bagwell, Keith. "Jaguars in Arizona, Texas, New Mexico 'Endangered.'" *Arizona Daily Star*, July 17, 1997.

Brown, David E., and Carlos A. Lopez Gonzalez. *Borderland Jaguars.* Salt Lake City: Univ. of Utah Press, 2001.

Chadwick, Douglas H. "Phantom of the Night." *National Geographic*, May 2001.

Childs, Jack L. *Tracking the Felids of the Borderlands.* El Paso, TX: Printing Corner Press, 1998.

Childs, Jack L., and Anna Mary Childs. *Ambushed on the Jaguar Trail: Hidden Cameras on the Mexican Border.* Tucson, AZ: Rio Nuevo, 2008.

Davis, Tony. "Experts to Collar Jaguar." *Arizona Daily Star*, May 1, 2006.

Glenn, Warner. *Eyes of Fire: Encounter with a Borderlands Jaguar.* El Paso, TX.: Printing Corner Press, 1996.

McCain, Emil B., and Jack L. Childs. "Evidence of Resident Jaguars (*Panthera onca*) in the Southwestern United States and the Implications for Conservation." *Journal of Mammalogy* 89 (2008): 1–10.

Nistler, Carolyn. "Seeing Spots: The Return of the Jaguar." *PERC Reports* (Winter 2007): 10–12.

Robinson, Michael. "Jaguar and Wolf Recovery in the American Southwest." *Wild Earth* (Winter 1999): 60–67.

Tobin, Mitch. "Wandering Jaguar Shakes Things Up." *Arizona Daily Star*, February 24, 2002.

———. "Sonora Ranch Becomes Jaguar Preserve." *Arizona Daily Star*, July 31, 2003.

———. "Future Wilderness? Tumacacori Highlands Dispute." *Arizona Daily Star*, March 13, 2004.

Voas, Jeremy. "Cat Fight." *High Country News*, October 15, 2007.

Mountain Lions
Baron, David. *The Beast in the Garden*. New York: W. W. Norton, 2004.

Border Fence
Flesch, A. D., et al. "Potential Effects of the United States-Mexico Border Fence on Wildlife." *Conservation Biology*, June 23, 2009. http://avianscience.dbs.umt.edu/documents/Flesch_ConBio_borderfences_2009.pdf (accessed February 1, 2010).

Grigione, Melissa M., and Robert Mrykalo. "Effects of Artificial Night Lighting on Endangered Ocelots (*Leopardus paradalis*) and Noctual Prey along the United States–Mexico Border: A Literature Review and Hypothesis of Potential Impacts." *Urban Ecosystems* 7 (2004): 65–77.

Hurowitz, Glenn. *Prairie Chicken: Why Environmental Groups Have Been Slow to Fight the Border Wall*. October 17, 2007. www.grist.org/article/hurowitz/ (accessed February 1, 2010).

Matlock, Staci. "Mexico, United States Join Forces to Protect Jaguar." *Santa Fe New Mexican*, October 17, 2007.

McCombs, Brady. "River Treasure vs. U.S. Security." *Arizona Daily Star*, October 21, 2007.

———. "New 'Virtual Fence' on Verge of Going Up." *Arizona Daily Star*, February 8, 2009.

———. "Border Fences Grow, as Does Debate That Rages over Them." *Arizona Daily Star*, March 15, 2009.

16: Living with El Lobo
Reintroduction Program
Adaptive Management Oversight Committee. *Mexican Wolf Blue Range Reintroduction Project 5-year Review*. Phoenix: Arizona Game and Fish Department, 2005.

Associated Press. "Ranch Hand Disputes Claim That He Lured Endangered Wolf." *Arizona Daily Star*, December 21, 2007.

Associated Press. "Poll: Most in N.M., Ariz. Back Wolf Recovery." *Tucson Citizen*, June 16, 2008.

Cart, Julie. "Recovery of Mexican Gray Wolves Remains Elusive." *Los Angeles Times*, July 26, 2009.

Dougherty, John. "Last Chance for the Lobo." *High Country News*, December 24, 2007.

Industrial Economics Incorporated. *Mexican Wolf Blue Range Reintroduction Project 5-Year Review: Socioeconomic Component*. Cambridge, MA: Prepared for Division of Economics, US Fish and Wildlife Service, 2005.

Paskus, Laura. "Who's Afraid of…" *Santa Fe Reporter*, July 16, 2009.

Povilitis, A., et al. "The Bureaucratically Imperiled Mexican Wolf." *Conservation Biology* 20 (2006): 942–945.

Soussan, Tania. "U.S. Proposes New Restrictions on Wolf Releases." *Albuquerque Journal*, May 1, 2005.

Steller, Tim. "U.S. to Step up Control of Wolf Recovery Program." *Arizona Daily Star*, November 15, 2009.

Tobin, Mitch. "Arizona Waffles on Wolves." *High Country News*, June 18, 2001.

———. "Reintroduced Gray Wolves Fighting Tooth and Nail." *Arizona Daily Star*, November 28, 2004.

———. "Blue River Wolf Pack Soon to Be Released." *Arizona Daily Star*, December 11, 2004.

Trophic Cascade

Beschta, Robert L., and W. J. Ripple. "River Channel Dynamics Following Extirpation of Wolves in Northwestern Yellowstone National Park, USA." *Earth Surface Processes and Landforms* 31, no. 12 (2006): 1525–1539.

———. "Recovering Riparian Plant Communities with Wolves in Northern Yellowstone, USA." *Restoration Ecology*, published online, October 6, 2008. www.cof.orst.edu/cof/fs/PDFs/Beschta/RestorEcol2008.pdf (accessed February 1, 2010).

Binkley, D., et al. "Was Aldo Leopold Right about the Kaibab Deer Herd?" *Ecosystems* 9 (2006): 227–241.

Morell, Virginia. "Aspens Return to Yellowstone, with Help from Some Wolves." *Science* 317 (July 2007): 438–439.

Ripple, W. J., and R. L. Beschta. "Wolf Reintroduction, Predation Risk, and Cottonwood Recovery in Yellowstone National Park." *Forest Ecology and Management* 184 (2003): 299–313.

———. "Wolves and the Ecology of Fear: Can Predation Risk Structure Ecosystems?" *Bioscience* 54 (2004): 755–766.

———. "Linking Wolves and Plants: Aldo Leopold on Trophic Cascades." *BioScience* 55 (2005): 613–621.

———. "Linking Wolves to Willows Via Risk-Sensitive Foraging by Ungulates in the Northern Yellowstone Ecosystem." *Forest Ecology and Management* 230 (2006): 96-106.

Smith, Douglas W., R. O. Peterson, and D. B. Houston. "Yellowstone after Wolves." *BioScience* 53 (2003): 330–340.

Attacks by Wolves and Other Wildlife

Conover, M. R. "Monetary and Intangible Valuation of Deer in the United States." *Wildlife Society Bulletin* 25 (1997): 298–305.

Conover, M. R., et al. "Review of Human Injuries, Illnesses, and Economic Losses Caused by Wildlife in the United States." *Wildlife Society Bulletin* 23 (1995): 407–414.

Linnell, J. D. C., et al. *The Fear of Wolves: A Review of Wolf Attacks on Humans.* Trondheim, Norway: NINA: Norsk Institutt for Naturforskning, 2002.

McNay, Mark E. "Wolf-Human Interactions in Alaska and Canada: A Review of the Case History." *Wildlife Society Bulletin* 30 (2002): 831–843.

Reserve and Catron County

"Catron County Readies for Battle." *High Country News*, September 19, 1994.

Daly, Matthew, and Shannon Dininny. "Timber Law Becomes Vast Entitlement." *The Washington Post*, December 7, 2009.

Davis, Tony. "Catron County's Politics Heat up as Its Land Goes Bankrupt." *High Country News*, June 24, 1996.

Romo, Rene. "Catron Gets Tough on Wolves." *Albuquerque Journal*, February 8, 2007.

Predator Conservation

Bohrer, Becky. "Ranchers Hope 'Predator Friendly' Gets Sales." *(Salt Lake City, UT) Deseret News*, July 19, 2004.

Bryan, Susan Montoya. "Fund Will Help Ranchers Deal with Mexican Wolves." *Las Cruces Sun-News*, October 7, 2009.

Holder, Jan. "Better Beef by Far: Raised Predator-Friendly." *Sky Island Alliance Newsletter*, Winter 2004.

———. *How to Direct Market Your Beef.* Beltsville, MD: Sustainable Agriculture Network, 2005.

Osgood, Charles. "Wolf Friendly Beef." *The Osgood File.* CBS Radio Network. January 2, 2004.

Yozwiak, Steve. "Greener Brand of Beef: Ranchers' Methods Embrace Ecosystem, but Still Threaten Riparian Areas." *The Arizona Republic*, April 12, 1998.

Grazing Buyouts

Reese, April. "The Big Buyout." *High Country News*, April 4, 2005.

Tobin, Mitch. "Giving Cattle the Boot." *Arizona Daily Star*, December 4, 2001.

———. "Plan Would Have U.S. Buy Up Grazing Permits." *Arizona Daily Star*, January 24, 2003.

———. "Ranchers, Enviros May Be Able to Live Together." *Arizona Daily Star*, April 5, 2003.

———. "State Land No Longer Just for the Cows." *High Country News*, September 1, 2003.

17: Battling the Blob

Habitat Conservation Plans

Beatley, Timothy. *Habitat Conservation Planning: Endangered Species and Urban Growth*. Austin: Univ. of Texas Press, 1994.

Gang, Duane W., David Danelski, and Devona Wells. "Losing Ground: Ambitious Conservation Plan Applied Unevenly." *The (Riverside, CA) Press-Enterprise*, December 8, 2006.

McClure, Robert, and Lisa Stiffler. "Flaws in Habitat Conservation Plans Threaten Scores of Species." *Seattle Post-Intelligencer*, May 3, 2005.

Sonoran Desert Conservation Plan

Davis, Tony. "US Review of Snake's Status Could Stall Growth in Pinal." *Arizona Daily Star*, July 31, 2008.

———. "Desert Protection Plan Takes Key Step." *Arizona Daily Star*, January 6, 2009.

———. "Desert Plan Shifts Focus to Habitat to Cut Costs." *Arizona Daily Star*, January 7, 2009.

———. "Desert Protector Maeveen Behan Dies." *Arizona Daily Star*, November 4, 2009.

———. "Maeveen Behan Dies." *Arizona Daily Star*, November 13, 2009.

Davis, Tony, and Mitch Tobin. "Saving the Desert." *Arizona Daily Star*, December 15, 2002, special section.

———. "U.S. Seeks to Delist Arizona's Pygmy Owl." *Arizona Daily Star*, August 2, 2005.

———. "Behind the Debate: Pygmy Owl Facts." *Arizona Daily Star*, August 6, 2005.

ECONorthwest. "Economic Benefits of Protecting Natural Resources in the Sonoran Desert." Tucson, AZ: Coalition for Sonoran Desert Protection, August 2002.

Jehl, Douglas. "Rare Arizona Owl (All 7 Inches of It) Is in Habitat Furor." *The New York Times*, March 17, 2003.

Johnson, R. J., et al. "Cactus Ferruginous Pygmy-Owl in Arizona: 1872–1971." *Southwestern Naturalist* 48 (September 2003): 389–401.

Poole, B. "Expert: Decline in Snake's Numbers 'Stunning.'" *Tucson Citizen*, July 30, 2008.

———. "Rare Snake May Cause Battle over Development." *Tucson Citizen*, July 30, 2008.

Snape, William III, et al. "Protecting Ecosystems under The Endangered Species Act: The Sonoran Desert Example." *Washburn Law Journal* 41 (2001): 14–49.

Tobin, Mitch. "Our Shangri-La." *Arizona Daily Star*, August 26, 2001.

———. "Endangered Species—Or Land Grab?" *Arizona Daily Star*, March 24, 2002.

————. "Native Birds Being Pushed to Outskirts." *Arizona Daily Star*, April 1, 2002.

————. "Conservation Bank for Pineapple Cactus." *Arizona Daily Star*, December 27, 2002.

————. "'Endangered' Cactus May Really Be Prolific." *Arizona Daily Star*, May 9, 2004.

————. "Farms: Subdivisions Waiting to Sprout." *Arizona Daily Star*, February 23, 2005.

Sprawl and Open Space

Brabec, Elizabeth. "On the Value of Open Space." Scenic America Technical Information Series. Washington, DC: Scenic America, 1992.

Brookings Institution. *Mountain Megas: America's Newest Metropolitan Places and a Federal Partnership to Help Them Prosper*. Washington, DC: Metropolitan Policy Program, 2008.

Colby, B., and S. Wishart. "Quantifying the Influence of Desert Riparian Areas on Residential Property Values." *The Appraisal Journal* 70 (2002): 304–308.

Correll, M. R., J. H. Lillydahl, and L. D. Singell. "The Effects of Greenbelts on Residential Property Values: Some Findings on the Political Economy of Open Space." *Land Economics* 54 (1978): 207–217.

Gillham, Oliver. *The Limitless City: A Primer on the Urban Sprawl Debate*. Washington, DC: Island Press, 2002.

Roach, John. "'BioBlitz' Finds 800-Plus Species in New York Park." *National Geographic News*, July 8, 2003.

18: Damn the Dam?

Humpback Chub

Bulkley, R. V., et al. "Tolerance and Preferences of Colorado River Endangered Fishes to Selected Habitat Parameters." Colorado River Fishery Project Final Report, part 3. Salt Lake City: US Bureau of Reclamation, 1981.

Coggins, Lewis G., Jr., and Carl J. Walters. "Abundance Trends and Status of the Little Colorado River Population of Humpback Chub: An Update Considering Data From 1989–2008." US Geological Survey Open-File Report 2009-1075, 2009.

Gloss, Steven P., Jeffrey E. Lovich, and Theodore S. Melis. "The State of the Colorado River Ecosystem in Grand Canyon." Reston, VA.: US Geological Survey Circular 1282, 2005

McKinnon, Shaun. "Endangered Fish Rebound at Grand Canyon." *The Arizona Republic*, April 28, 2009.

Minckley, W. L. *Fishes of Arizona*. Phoenix: Arizona Game and Fish Department, 1973.

Mueller, Gordon A., and Paul C. Marsh. *Lost, A Desert River and Its Native Fishes: A Historical Perspective of the Lower Colorado River*. Denver: US Geological Survey, 2002.

Quartarone, Fred. *Historical Accounts of Upper Colorado River Basin Endangered Fish*. Recovery Program for Endangered Fish of the Upper Colorado River Basin. Washington, DC: US Government Printing Office, 1995.

Stevens, Larry E. "Songs of the Humpback Chub." *Boatman's Quarterly Review*, Winter 1998/1999. www.gcrg.org/bqr/12-1/chub.html (accessed February 1, 2010).

Stone, Dennis. "Fifteen Years in the Grand Canyon." *Eddies* 1 (Summer 2008): 16–19.

Stone, Dennis M., and Owen T. Gorman. "Ontogenesis of Endangered Humpback Chub (*Gila cypha*) in the Little Colorado River, Arizona." *The American Midland Naturalist* 155 (2006): 123–135.

Valdez, Rich. *A Fish with Finesse*. www.gcrg.org/bqr/6-1/fishfinesse.htm (accessed February 1, 2010).

————. "Of Humpbacks and Bonytails: Fascinating Ancient Survivors." *Swimming Upstream*. US Fish and Wildlife Service, Upper Colorado River Endangered Fish Recovery Program (Winter 2004): 2.

"What's in a Song: 'Songs of the Humpback Chub.'"*Weekend Edition*, NPR, Sunday May 15, 2005.

Glen Canyon Dam Experimental Floods

Associated Press. "Thundering Water Begins Turning Back Canyon Clock." *Arizona Daily Star*, March 27, 1996.

———. "Rafters Get Ride of Lifetime Down Colorado during Eco-Flood." *Arizona Daily Star*, April 8, 1996.

———. "Flood Is Called Right Tonic for Grand Canyon." *The New York Times*, April 14, 1996.

Babbitt, Bruce. "A River Runs against It : America's Evolving View of Dams." *Open Spaces* 1, no. 4. www.open-spaces.com/article-v1n4-babbitt.php (accessed February 1, 2010).

Davis, Tony. "Efforts Fail to Fix Canyon Erosion, Threat to Fish." *Arizona Daily Star*, October 29, 2005.

Eilperin, Juliet. "Interior Ignored Science When Limiting Water to Grand Canyon." *The Washington Post*, January 28, 2009.

George, Doug. "An Artificial Flood Does Good in the Grand Canyon." *The Christian Science Monitor*, July 10, 2008.

Henetz, Patty. "Scientists Want to Flush Water Past Glen Canyon Dam Again." *The Salt Lake Tribune*, December 13, 2007.

McKinnon, Shaun. "Nature Demands Her Share." *The Arizona Republic*, July 25, 2004.

———. "River Study Yields Few Positives." *The Arizona Republic*, October 28, 2005.

———. "Water Battle Rages at Grand Canyon." *The Arizona Republic*, February 22, 2009.

———. "Federal Plan Could Mean More Floods in Grand Canyon." *The Arizona Republic*, December 12, 2009.

Minard, Anne. "Re-opening Glen Canyon's Floodgates." *High Country News*, July 8, 2002.

Myers, Amanda Lee. "Artificial Flood in Canyon is a Grand Spectacle." *Arizona Daily Star*, March 6, 2008.

———. "Grand Canyon Replenished." *The (San Jose) Mercury News*, March 14, 2008.

O'Driscoll, Patrick. "Colorado River Gets Soaked in Name of Science." *USA Today*, November 21, 2004.

Reese, April. "Colorado River Adaptive Management Program Needs Overhaul, Critics Say." *Greenwire*, May 7, 2009.

Smith, Luke. "Grand Canyon Renaissance: Flood Recedes, Natural Patterns Begin Anew." *Arizona Daily Star*, May 26, 1996.

Tobin, Mitch. "Interior Department Favors More Canyon Flooding." *Arizona Daily Star*, October 29, 2003.

———. "Odds Seem Long, Time Short For Canyon Chub." *Arizona Daily Star*, August 1, 2004.

Wilson, Janet. "Plan to 'Flush' Grand Canyon Stirs Concerns." *Los Angeles Times*, March 4, 2008.

Decommissioning Glen Canyon Dam

Boorstein, Michelle. "Lake Powell Foes Want It Drained." *Arizona Daily Star*, May 27, 1997.

Brower, David. "Let the River Run through It." *Sierra*, March/April 1997.

Latham, Stephen E. *Glen Canyon Dam, Arizona: Dam Failure Indundation Study*. Denver: US Bureau of Reclamation, 1998.

Living Rivers. *The One-Dam Solution*. Moab, UT: Living Rivers, 2005.

Randle, Timothy J., et al. "Colorado River Ecosystem Sediment Augmentation Appraisal Engineering Report." Denver: US Bureau of Reclamation, 2007.

Desalination

Cooley, Heather, Peter H. Gleick, and Gary Wolff. "Desalination, with a Grain of Salt: A California Perspective." Oakland, CA: Pacific Institute for Studies in Development, Environment, and Security, June 2006.

Davis, Tony. "State's Desalination Prospects Downplayed." *Arizona Daily Star*, April 25, 2008.

———. "Ultimate Solution?" *High Country News*, November 24, 2008.

———. "Salt Water Foreseen as Vital to Southwest." *Arizona Daily Star*, June 25, 2008.

Ferguson, Kevin. "Water Needs Electricity Needs Water...." *The New York Times/Green Inc.*, May 21, 2009.

McKinnon, Shaun. "Arizona Mulls New Water Source: Ocean." *The Arizona Republic*, August 31, 2008.

National Research Council. *Desalination: A National Perspective.* Washington, DC: The National Academies Press, 2008.

Tobin, Mitch. "Desalination May Be on the Way." *Arizona Daily Star*, July 6, 2003.

Climate Change and Water

Associated Press. "West's 2 Major Reservoirs Imperiled, Scientists Warn." *Arizona Daily Star*, February 14, 2008.

Barnett Tim P., et al. "Human-Induced Changes in the Hydrology of the Western United States." *Science* 319 (February 2008): 1080–1083.

Barnett, Tim P., and David W. Pierce. "When Will Lake Mead Go Dry?" *Water Resources Research* 44 (March 2008): 29.

———. "Sustainable Water Deliveries from the Colorado River in a Changing Climate." *Proceedings of the National Academy of Sciences* 106 (May 2009): 7334–7338.

Cook E. R., et al. "Long-term Aridity Changes in the Western United States. *Science* 306 (2004): 1015–1018.

Davis, Tony. "Study Warns of Less Colorado River Water." *Arizona Daily Star*, February 22, 2007.

———. "Is Our Drought a Sign of Longterm Climate Change." *Arizona Daily Star*, April 21, 2008.

———. "Expert: AZ in Climate-Change Bull's-Eye." *Arizona Daily Star*, March 18, 2009.

———. "Severe AZ Water Shortage Possible." *Arizona Daily Star*, April 26, 2009.

Dean, Cornelia. "That 'Drought' in Southwest May Be Normal, Report Says." *The New York Times*, February 22, 2007.

Kundzewicz, Z. W., et al. "Freshwater Resources and Their Management. Climate Change 2007: Impacts, Adaptation and Vulnerability." In *Contribution of Working Group II to the Fourth Assessment Report of the Intergovernmental Panel on Climate Change*, edited by M. L. Parry, O. F. Canziani, J. P. Palutikof, P. J. van der Linden, and C. E. Hanson. Cambridge: Cambridge Univ. Press, 173–210.

McKinnon, Shaun. "Source of Water for West at Risk." *The Arizona Republic*, November 25, 2007.

———. "Warming Could Spur Water Crisis." *The Arizona Republic*, April 21, 2009.

Meko, D. M., et al. "Medieval Drought in the Upper Colorado River Basin." *Geophysical Research Letters* 34 (2007).

National Research Council. *Colorado River Basin Water Management: Evaluating and Adjusting to Hydroclimatic Variability.* Washington, DC: The National Academies Press, 2007.

Powell, James Lawrence. *Dead Pool: Lake Powell, Global Warming, and the Future of Water in the West.* Berkeley: Univ. of California Press, 2008.

Rajagopalan, B., et al. "Water Supply Risk on the Colorado River: Can Management Mitigate?" *Water Resources Research* 45 (2009): 1–7.

Seager, R., et al. "Model Projections of an Imminent Transition to a More Arid Climate in Southwestern North America." *Science* 316 (May 2007`): 1181–1184.

Tobin, Mitch. "Dwindling Snowmelt Trouble for Thirsty SW." *Arizona Daily Star*, March 25, 2003.

———. "Thinning Snowpack May Hurt West's Water Supply." *Arizona Daily Star*, September 29, 2005.

Woodhouse, C. A., et al. "Updated Streamflow Reconstructions for the Upper Colorado River Basin." *Water Resources Research* 42 (2006).

19: Effluence

Water Policy

Cooley, Heather, Juliet Christian-Smith, and Peter Gleick. "Sustaining California Agriculture in an Uncertain Future." Oakland, CA: Pacific Institute for Studies in Development, Environment, and Security, July 2009.

Devine, Dave. "Down the Drain…" *Tucson Weekly*, January 16, 1997.

Glennon, Robert. *Water Follies: Groundwater Pumping and the Fate of America's Fresh Waters*. Washington, DC: Island Press, 2002.

———. "The Quest for More Water: Why Markets Are Inevitable." *PERC Reports* 24, no. 3 (September 2006): 7–9.

———. *Unquenchable: America's Water Crisis and What to Do about It*. Washington, DC: Island Press, 2009.

McClurg, Sue, ed. "Layperson's Guide to Arizona Water." Sacramento: Water Education Foundation, 2007.

McKinnon, Shaun. "Rural Water: Growth Taxing Water Supplies." *The Arizona Republic*, June 26, 2005.

———. "Pima Gets Tough about Turf." *The Arizona Republic*, December 5, 2005.

———. "Climate Shift May Cut Flow." *The Arizona Republic*, February 22, 2007.

———. "Water Shortage Possible." *The Arizona Republic*, March 1, 2007.

———. "Unabated Use of Groundwater Threatens Arizona's Future." *The Arizona Republic*, August 2, 2009.

———. "Farms Looked at as Water Resources Vanish." *The Arizona Republic*, October 25, 2009.

———. "Cleaning Dirty Air Risks Costlier Arizona Water." *The Arizona Republic*, November 1, 2009.

Minard, Anne, and Mitch Tobin. "Water Solvable." *Arizona Daily Star*, June 21, 2005.

Sax, Joseph L., Jr., Barton H. Thompson, John D. Leshy, and Robert H. Abrams. *Legal Control of Water Resources*. 3rd. ed. St. Paul, MN: West Group, 2000.

Tobin, Mitch. "Lack of Water Might Stunt Tucson's Growth." *Arizona Daily Star*, May 1, 2001.

———. "Keeping Arivaca's Wetlands Wet." *Arizona Daily Star*, October 3, 2001.

———. "More Effluent, CAP Called Vital for City." *Arizona Daily Star*, October 31, 2001.

———. "Planning for 2050." *Arizona Daily Star*, November 19, 2004.

———. "Despite Soaring Growth, Southwest Uses Less Water." *Arizona Daily Star*, January 27, 2005.

———. "We Have to Drink That?" *Arizona Daily Star*, June 19, 2005.

Wagner, Dennis. "Tribe's Environmental Fight." *The Arizona Republic*, November 2, 2009.

Migratory Species

Wilcove, David S. *No Way Home: The Decline of the World's Great Animal Migrations*. Washington, DC: Island Press, 2008.

San Pedro River

Cart, Julie. "Lush River Struggles to Survive." *Los Angeles Times*, August 17, 2005.

Christensen, Jon. "In Arizona Desert, a Bird Oasis in Peril." *The New York Times*, May 4, 1999.

Davis, Tony. "A Thirst for Growth." *High Country News*, August 30, 2004.

———. "San Pedro River Is Running Dry." *Arizona Daily Star*, July 13, 2005.

———. "SV Not Blamed for Dry San Pedro." *Arizona Daily Star*, September 23, 2005.

———. "Huachuca Jobs Won't Harm River, Study Says." *Arizona Daily Star*, June 16, 2007.

———. "San Pedro River in Danger, BLM Says." *Arizona Daily Star*, May 25, 2008.

Pederson, Brian J. "Tiny Mammoth Has Some Big Growth Plans." *Arizona Daily Star*, April 10, 2008.

Stromberg, Juliet C., and Barbara Tellman, eds. *Ecology and Conservation of the San Pedro River*. Tucson: Univ. of Arizona Press, 2009.

Tobin, Mitch. "Trying to Revive San Pedro." *Arizona Daily Star*, April 19, 2001.

———. "Clear San Pedro Now Black with Runoff." *Arizona Daily Star*, July 21, 2002.

———. "Nature Lovers Buy the Farm." *Arizona Daily Star*, September 6, 2002.

Southwestern Willow Flycatcher

Davis, Tony. "Agencies Dunk Endangered Songbird." *High Country News*, September 15, 1997.

Durst, S. D., et al. *Southwestern Willow Flycatcher Breeding Site and Territory Summary—2005*. Flagstaff, AZ: USGS Southwest Biological Science Center, October 2006.

Fenske, Sarah. "For the Birds." *Phoenix New Times*, May 19, 2005.

Finch, Deborah M., and Scott H. Stoleson, eds. "Status, Ecology, and Conservation of the Southwestern Willow Flycatcher." Gen. Tech. Report RMRS-GTR-60, Ogden, UT: US Forest Service Rocky Mountain Research Station, 2000.

Markley, Jennifer. "Bye Bye Birdie." *Phoenix New Times*, July 19, 2001.

Paradzick, C. E., and A. A. Woodward. "Distribution, Abundance and Habitat Characteristics of Southwestern Willow Flycatchers (*Empidonax traillii extimus*) in Arizona, 1993–2000." *Studies in Avian Biology* 26 (2003): 22–29.

Tamarisk

Chew, Matthew K. "The Monstering of Tamarisk: How Scientists Made a Plant into a Problem." *Journal of the History of Biology* 42 (2009): 231–266.

Krza, Paul. "It's 'Bombs Away' on New Mexico Saltcedar." *High Country News*, November 10, 2003.

Stromberg, Juliet C., et al. "Changing Perceptions of Change: The Role of Scientists in *Tamarix* and River Management." *Restoration Ecology* 17 (2009): 177–186.

Van Riper, Charles, III, et al. "Rethinking Avian Response to *Tamarix* on the Lower Colorado River: A Threshold Hypothesis." *Restoration Ecology* 16 (2008): 155–167.

Aravaipa Canyon Flood

Beal, Tom. "Aravaipa Canyon Scoured by Summer Floods." *Arizona Daily Star*, October 16, 2006.

Effluent

Fahrenthold, David A. "Male Bass in Potomac Producing Eggs." *The Washington Post*, October 15, 2004.

Kolpin, Dana W., et al. "Pharmaceuticals, Hormones, and Other Organic Wastewater Contaminants in US Streams, 1999-2000: A National Reconnaissance." *Environmental Science & Technology* 36, no. 6 (2002): 1202–1211.

Tobin, Mitch. "Reusing 'Gray Water' Is Often a Fine Idea, but Dangers Lurk." *Arizona Daily Star*, June 8, 2001.
Woodling, John D., et al. "Intersex and Other Reproductive Disruption of Fish in Wastewater Effluent Dominated Colorado Streams." *Environmental Science and Technology* 42 (2008): 3407–3414.

20: Get the Lead Out
Condors and Lead Poisoning

Anderson, W. L., S. P. Havera, and B. W. Zercher. "Ingestion of Lead and Nontoxic Shotgun Pellets by Ducks in the Mississippi Flyway." *Journal of Wildlife Management* 64 (2000): 848–857.
Barker, Rocky. "Study: Lead Bullets Taint Game Meat." *Idaho Statesman*, May 14, 2008.
Cade, Tom J. "Exposure of California Condors to Lead from Spent Ammunition." *Journal of Wildlife Management* 71 (2007): 2125–2133.
Church, M. E., et al. "Ammunition Is the Principal Source of Lead Accumulated by California Condors Re-introduced to the Wild." *Environmental Science and Technology* 40 (2006): 6143–6150.
Cone, Tracie. "California Condors' Animal Instinct Takes Over in Fire." *Lodi News-Sentinel*, July 18, 2008.
Fisher, Ian J., Deborah J. Paina, and Vernon G. Thomas. "A Review of Lead Poisoning from Ammunition Sources in Terrestrial Birds." *Biological Conservation* 131 (2006): 421–432.
Fonseca, Felicia. "Condor Protectors Target Lead Ammo." *Arizona Daily Star*, December 31, 2008.
Fry, D. Michael, and Jeffrey R. Maurer. *Assessment of Lead Contamination Sources Exposing California Condors*. Sacramento: California Department of Fish and Game, 2003.
Halper, Evan, and Nancy Vogel. "Fish and Game Official, Criticized for Stance on Bullets, Resigns." *Los Angeles Times*, September 14, 2007.
Hunt, W. Grainger, et al. "Lead Bullet Fragments in Venison from Rifle-Killed Deer: Potential for Human Dietary Exposure." *PLoS ONE* 4 (April 2009): 1–5.
Hunt, W. Grainger, et al. "Bullet Fragments in Deer Remains: Implications for Lead Exposure in Avian Scavengers." *Wildlife Society Bulletin* 34 (2006): 167–170.
Kettmann, Matt. "Taking Aim at Hunters' Ammo." *Time*, April 4, 2007.
Morgante, Michelle. "Effort to Ban Lead Ammo in Condor Habitat Rejected." *Orange County Register*, February 6, 2005.
Platt, John. "Fight to Protect California Condors from Lead Ammunition Moves to Arizona." *Scientific American*, November 20, 2009.
Ritter, John. "Lead Poisoning Eyed as Threat to California Condor." *USA Today*, October 23, 2006.
Samuel, M. D., and E. F. Bowers. "Lead Exposure in American Black Ducks after Implementation of Non-Toxic Shot." *Journal of Wildlife Management* 64 (2000): 947-953.
Schoch, Deborah. "Wildlife Commissioner Blames NRA for His Ouster." *Los Angeles Times*, September 25, 2007.
Tobin, Mitch. "Getting the Lead Out." *High Country News*, March 2007.
Walters, Jeffrey R., et al. "Status of the California Condor and Efforts to Achieve Its Recovery." Emeryville, CA: American Ornithologists' Union and Audubon California, 2008.
Weiser, Matt. "Another Shot in Ammo Battle." *The Sacramento Bee*, September 14, 2007.
Wharton, Tom. "Condor Advocates Ask Hunters to Ditch Lead Bullets." *The Salt Lake Tribune*, October 5, 2009.

Renewable Energy and Biodiversity

Alexander, Lamar. "Energy 'Sprawl' and the Green Economy." *The Wall Street Journal*, September 17, 2009.

Archibold, Randal C. "Devils Hole Pupfish, Saved by Court in '76, Is at Brink in '08." *The New York Times*, August 23, 2008.

Barringer, Felicity. "Environmentalists in a Clash of Goals." *The New York Times*, March 24, 2009.

Dickerson, Marla. "Solar Thermal Projects Gather Steam—and Opposition." *Los Angeles Times*, December 3, 2008.

Eilperin, Juliet, and Steven Mufson. "Renewable Energy's Environmental Paradox." *The Washington Post*, April 16, 2009.

Fletcher, Ed. "Rooftop Solar Just a Small Part of Energy Solution, Experts Say." *The Sacrameto Bee*, June 2, 2009.

Fry, Michael. "Wind Power Might Blow a Hole in Bird Populations." *Los Angeles Times*, November 2, 2009.

Glod, Maria. "Tiny Bat Pits Green against Green." *The Washington Post*, October 22, 2009.

Jarman, Max. "Skyrocketing Solar Projects Creates Demand for Desert Land." *The Arizona Republic*, June 4, 2009.

Lewis, Judith. "High Noon." *High Country News*, May 11, 2009.

McDonald, R. I., et al. "Energy Sprawl or Energy Efficiency: Climate Policy Impacts on Natural Habitat for the United States of America." *PLoS ONE* 4 (August 2009): 1–11.

McKinnon, Shaun. "Amid State's Push for Solar Power, Water-Supply Worries Arise." *The Arizona Republic*, January 17, 2010.

Pavlik, Bruce. "Could Green Kill the Desert?" *Los Angeles Times*, February 15, 2009.

———. "My View: Solar Gold Rush Puts Public Lands at Risk." *The Sacramento Bee*, April 28, 2009.

Power, Stephen. "In a Small Fish, a Large Lesson in Renewable Energy's Obstacles." *The Wall Street Journal*, June 16, 2009.

Riley, Michael. "Greens, New-Energy Backers at Odds over Use of Desert." *The Denver Post*, September 3, 2009.

Sahagun, Louis. "Renewable Energy Sparks a Probe of a Modern-Day Land Rush." *Los Angeles Times*, June 1, 2009.

———. "Environmental Concerns Delay Solar Projects in California Desert." *Los Angeles Times*, October 18, 2009.

Stoddard, Ed. "Sage Grouse Unlikely Focus of Wyoming Wind Wars." *Reuters*, August 3, 2009.

Streater, Scott. "Fast-Tracked Solar Project Could Speed Mojave Desert's Demise." *The New York Times/Greenwire*, November 12, 2009.

Wasson, Matt. "Misleading 'Energy Sprawl' Study Pollutes Climate Debate." Huffington Post, October 1, 2009. www.huffingtonpost.com/matt-wasson/misleading-energy-sprawl_b_306051.html (accessed February 1, 2010).

Woody, Todd. "Alternative Energy Projects Stumble on a Need for Water." *The New York Times*, September 30, 2009.

———. "Solar Developer Abandons Water Plans." *The New York Times*, November 16, 2009.

Zimmerman, Janet. "Rush to Tap Mojave Desert Resources Raises Botanist's Concern." *The (Riverside, CA) Press-Enterprise*, November 16, 2009.

Desert Tortoise

Danelski, David. "Army Suspends Fort Irwin Tortoise Relocation Plans after Deaths of 90 Animals." *The (Riverside, CA) Press-Enterprise*, October 9, 2008.

————. "The Mojave Desert Tortoise Population Is Losing Ground and Facing Increasing Threats." *The (Riverside, CA) Press-Enterprise*, November 16, 2009.

Davis, Tony. "Endangered Status Sought for Sonoran Desert Tortoise." *Arizona Daily Star*, October 9, 2008.

Sahagun, Louis. "Army Suspends Relocation of Ft. Irwin Tortoises." *Los Angeles Times*, October 11, 2008.

Tobin, Mitch. "Top Tortoise Experts Ask: To List or Not to List?" *Arizona Daily Star*, February 20, 2005.

Van Devender, Thomas R. *The Sonoran Desert Tortoise: Natural History, Biology, and Conservation.* Tucson: Univ. of Arizona Press, 2002.

Epilogue: Triage

Macho B

Davis, Tony. "Jaguar's Capture Hailed as Info Boon." *Arizona Daily Star*, February 21, 2009.

————. "Officials Euthanize AZ Jaguar; He was Ill." *Arizona Daily Star*, March 3, 2009.

————. "Jaguar Ill Before 1st Capture." *Arizona Daily Star*, March 5, 2009.

————. "Death Won't Stop Jaguar Captures." *Arizona Daily Star*, March 6, 2009.

————. "Did Jaguar Macho B Have to Die?" *Arizona Daily Star*, March 29, 2009.

————. "Signs of Infection Seen in Jaguar." *Arizona Daily Star*, July 7, 2009.

————. "2 Jaguars Released in Mexico, but 1 Dies." *Arizona Daily Star*, July 19, 2009.

————. "UA Vet Lab Employees Under 'Gag Rule.'" *Arizona Daily Star*, September 19, 2009.

————. "Enviros Sue in Jaguar's Death." *Arizona Daily Star*, September 25, 2009.

————. "Jaguar-Tracking Data Hard to Come by from Game and Fish." *Arizona Daily Star*, October 18, 2009.

————. "Inquiry into Jaguar Death Focusing on Anesthetic." *Arizona Daily Star*, November 3, 2009.

————. "In Reversal, Feds Support Jaguar's Habitat, Recovery." *Arizona Daily Star*, January 13, 2010.

Davis, Tony, and Brady McCombs. "Captured Jaguar 1st in US to Get Collar for Tracking." *Arizona Daily Star*, February 20, 2009.

Davis, Tony, and Tim Steller. "I Baited Jaguar Trap, Research Worker Says." *Arizona Daily Star*, April 2, 2009.

————. "New Details Trigger Call for Federal Investigation Into Jaguar Capture." *Arizona Daily Star*, April 2, 2009.

————. "Feds Agree to Look at Jaguar's Capture." *Arizona Daily Star*, April 3, 2009.

————. "Jaguar's Capture Flawed, Some Say." *Arizona Daily Star*, April 12, 2009.

————. "Permit for Jaguar's Capture Questioned." *Arizona Daily Star*, May 24, 2009.

————. "AZ Wanted a Jaguar Collared Despite 2 Deaths in Sonora." *Arizona Daily Star*, June 14, 2009.

————. "Jaguar's Capture Broke Law, Feds Say." *Arizona Daily Star*, January 22, 2010.

Dougherty, John. "U.S. Opens Inquiry into Death of Rare Jaguar." *The New York Times*, April 5, 2009.

Faherty, John. "Feds Launch Criminal Probe of Jaguar's Death." *The Arizona Republic*, April 3, 2009.

Hoch, Heather. "Ailing Collared Jaguar Put Down." *The Arizona Republic*, March 3, 2009.

Steller, Tim. "Jaguar May Have Experienced 'Capture Myopathy.'" *Arizona Daily Star*, March 29, 2009.

————. "Other Jaguars Wear Study Collars." *Arizona Daily Star*, March 29, 2009.

————. "Worker in Jaguar Capture Cited Earlier." *Arizona Daily Star*, April 26, 2009.

————. "Jaguar Team Ceases Work Amid Disputes, Big Cat's Death." *Arizona Daily Star*, October 18, 2009.

Turner, Channing. "Vet: Drugs, Stress Affected Jaguar's Kidneys." *The Arizona Republic*, March 4, 2009.

Biomass Energy

Brown, Rick. *The Implications of Climate Change for Conservation, Restoration, and Management of National Forest Lands*. Eugene: Univ. of Oregon Press, 2008.

Campbell, J. E., D. B. Lobell, and C. B. Field. "Greater Transportation Energy and GHG Offsets from Bioelectricity Than Ethanol." *Science Express*, May 2009: 1–3.

Finkral, A., and A. Evans. "The Effects of a Thinning Treatment on Carbon Stocks in a Northern Arizona Ponderosa Pine Forest." *Forest Ecology and Management* 255, no. 7 (April 2008): 2743–2750.

Gable, Eryn. "Can Dead Wood Fuel the Future?" *Land Letter*, February 28, 2008.

Gold, Russell. "Biomass Power Generates Traction." *The Wall Street Journal*, June 1, 2009.

————. "Wood Pellets Catch Fire as Renewable Energy Source." *The Wall Street Journal*, July 7, 2009.

Hampton, H. M., et al. *Analysis of Small-Diameter Wood Supply in Northern Arizona. Flagstaff: Forest Ecosystem Restoration Analysis Project*. Flagstaff, AZ: Center for Environmental Sciences and Education, Northern Arizona Univ., 2008.

Leber, Jessica. "If You Hug the Trees, Can You Have More Renewable Energy and Protect the Forest?" *The New York Times*, June 16, 2009.

LeVan-Green, Susan L., and Jean M. Livingston. "Uses for Small-Diameter and Low-Value Forest Thinnings." *Ecological Restoration* 21 (March 2003): 34–38.

Malakoff, David. "Arizona Ecologist Puts Stamp on Forest Restoration Debate." *Science* 297 (September 2002): 2194–2196.

Mitchell, Stephen R., Mark E. Harmon, and Kari E. B. O'Connell. "Forest Fuel Reduction Alters Fire Severity and Long-Term Carbon Storage in Three Pacific Northwest Ecosystems." *Ecological Applications* 19 (2009): 643–655.

Myers, Amanda Lee. "Wood-Fired Power Plant for E. Arizona." *Arizona Daily Star*, January 14, 2007.

Tobin, Mitch. "New Uses for Little Trees." *Arizona Daily Star*, December 20, 2003.

US Government Accountability Office. "Federal Agencies Are Engaged in Various Efforts to Promote the Utilization of Woody Biomass, but Significant Obstacles to Its Use Remain." GAO Report 05-373, May 2005.

Watson, Traci. "More States Turning to Wood Power." *USA Today*, October 14, 2009.

Doomsday Seed Bank and Other Arks

Choi, Charles Q. "Can the 'Amphibian Ark' Save Frogs from Pollution/Extinction?" *Scientific American*, June 19, 2008.

Jarvie, Jenny. "'Amphibian Ark' Seen as Species' Last Best Hope." *Los Angeles Times*, February 16, 2007.

Montenegro, Maywa, and Nikki Greenwood. "In Seeds We Trust." *Seed Magazine*, June 15, 2009.

Roach, John. "'Doomsday' Vault Will End Crop Extinction, Expert Says." *National Geographic News*, December 27, 2007.

Steenhuysen, Julie. "Massive Effort Underway to Save Endangered Seeds." Reuters, February 15, 2009. www.reuters.com/article/idUSTRE51E19I20090215.

Weiser, Matt. "Scientists Breed Smelt in Case Species Becomes Extinct in Delta." *The Sacramento Bee*, March 31, 2008.

Assisted Migration

Appell, David. "Can 'Assisted Migration' Save Species from Global Warming?" *Scientific American*, March 3, 2009.

Biello, David. "Deporting Plants and Animals to Protect Them from Climate Change." *Scientific American*, July 17, 2008.

Chang, Alicia. "Hot Issue: Should We Deliberately Move Species?" *The Seattle Times*, July 20, 2009.

Hoegh-Guldberg, O., et al. "Assisted Colonization and Rapid Climate Change." *Science* 321 (July 2008): 345–346.

McLachlan, J. S., J. J. Hellmann, and M. W. Schwartz. "A Framework for Debate of Assisted Migration in an Era of Climate Change." *Conservation Biology* 21 (2007): 297–302.

Ricciardi, A., and D. Simberloff. "Assisted Colonization Is Not a Viable Conservation Strategy." *Trends in Ecology & Evolution* 24 (2009): 248–253.

Richardson, David M. "Multidimensional Evaluation of Managed Relocation." *Proceedings of the National Academy of Sciences* 106 (2009): 9721–9724.

Willis, Stephen G., et al. "Assisted Colonization in a Changing Climate: A Test-Study Using Two U.K. Butterflies." *Conservation Letters* 2 (2009): 46–52.

Polar Bear

Bowles, Jennifer. "Environment Lawyer Loves Joshua Tree Home." *The (Riverside, CA) Press-Enterprise*, September 4, 2008.

Davis, Tony. "Obama Retains Bush Policy Limiting Protections for Polar Bears." *Arizona Daily Star*, May 9, 2009.

Doremus, Holly. "Polar Bear Politics." *Slate*, January 17, 2008. www.slate.com/id/2182307/ (accessed February 1, 2010).

Fahrenthold, David A. "Species Act Won't Be Used to Force Lower Emissions." *The Washington Post*, May 9, 2009.

Green, Kenneth P. "Is the Polar Bear Endangered, or Just Conveniently Charismatic?" *Environmental Policy Outlook*. Washington, DC: American Enterprise Institute, May 2008.

Revkin, Andrew C. "U.S. Curbs Use of Species Act in Protecting Polar Bear." *The New York Times*, May 9, 2009.

Ruhl, J. B. "Climate Change and the Endangered Species Act: Building Bridges to the No-Analog Future." *Boston University Law Review* 88 (2008): 1–61.

Stone, Daniel. "List Limbo." *Newsweek*, April 30, 2009.

Obama Administration

Broder, John M., and Ben Werschkul. "Salazar Plots Cautious Course at Interior." *The New York Times*, December 1, 2009.

Winter, Allison, and Patrick Reis. "Endangered Species: Obama Admin Confronts 'Candidate Species' Backlog." *The New York Times/Greenwire*, September 8, 2009.

Winter, Allison. "New Endangered Species Listings Wait as Obama Admin Charts New Course." *The New York Times/Greenwire*, November 24, 2009.

A 12-Step Plan for Recovery

Casey, Frank, et al. *The Cost of a Comprehensive National Wildlife Conservation System: A Project Completion Report for the Wildlife Habitat Policy Research Program.* Washington, DC: Defenders of Wildlife Conservation Economics Program, 2008.

Davison, R. P., et al. "Practical Solutions to Improve the Effectiveness of the Endangered Species Act for Wildlife Conservation." Bethesda, MD: Wildlife Society Technical Review 05-1, 2005.

Environmental Law Institute. *Mitigation of Impacts to Fish and Wildlife Habitat: Estimating Costs and Identifying Opportunities.* Washington, DC: Environmental Law Institute, October 2007.

Lawler, Joshua J., et al. "Resource Management in a Changing and Uncertain Climate." *Frontiers in Ecology and the Environment* 7 (2009).

Reese, April. "Conservation or Cop-Out?" *High Country News*, April 13, 2009.

Ruhl, J. B. "Endangered Species Act Innovations in the Post-Babbittonian Era—Are There Any?" *Duke Environmental Law & Policy Forum* 14, no. 2 (2004): 419.

Speth, James Gustave. *The Bridge at the Edge of the World.* New Haven, CT: Yale Univ. Press, 2008.

Shellenberger, Michael, and Ted Nordhaus. Break Through: From the Death of Environmentalism to the Politics of Possibility. New York: Houghton Mifflin, 2007.

Index